INTRODUCTION TO
SOCIOLOGY
THIRD EDITION

INTRODUCTION TO
SOCIOLOGY
THIRD EDITION

Lewis A. Coser
State University of New York, *Emeritus*

Steven L. Nock
University of Virginia

Patricia A. Steffan

Daphne Spain
University of Virginia

Under the General Editorship of
Robert K. Merton
Columbia University

Harcourt Brace Jovanovich College Publishers
Fort Worth   Philadelphia   San Diego
New York   Orlando   Austin   San Antonio
Toronto   Montreal   London   Sydney   Tokyo

PREFACE

Sociology, the study of human beings in society, is a relatively young discipline — only about two-hundred years old. The first sociologists sought to explain abrupt changes in the human condition that accompanied the industrial revolution, the growth of large organizations, and the decline of rural life. Today, with vast social changes again taking place, sociologists offer valuable insights into the upheavals of our own time — the shift to a service economy, the rapid changes in relationships between men and women, and the startling demands for political and economic freedom in the long-stagnant societies of Central Europe. This textbook is based on the belief that sociological understanding of our society is as critical now as an understanding of the industrial society was at the dawn of the modern era.

Despite its short history, sociology can boast a body of knowledge comparable to that of much older disciplines. Sociology claims such seminal scholars as Karl Marx, Max Weber, and Émile Durkheim, whose works have had a profound impact on the way we think about social phenomena. Contemporary sociology utilizes an impressive collection of data accumulated over more than a century of systematic inquiry into the social world. This book introduces beginning students to the rich heritage of sociology — both its theoretical perspectives and its body of scientific knowledge.

To its fortunate authors, each new edition offers a chance to improve and update their work. Happily, sociology never lacks either fascinating research or controversial issues to draw upon for inspiration. Some new topics discussed in this third edition are homelessness (Chapter 2), Carol Gilligan's latest research on moral development (Chapter 5), workfare (Chapter 7), Gorbachev's reforms and economic changes in Central Europe (Chapter 12), terrorism (Chapter 17), workplace democracy (Chapter 19), and the social side effects of a slower population growth in the developed world (Chapter 20). New boxed inserts provide original analyses of current issues, including entrepreneurship versus bureaucracy (Chapter 6), identifying the poor (Chapter 7), abortion and politics (Chapter 10), the moral questions raised by test-tube babies and the new technologies of conception (Chapter 11), the AIDS epidemic (Chapter 14), and why Americans don't vote (Chapter 16).

Like its predecessors, this third edition stresses four aspects of sociological study:

1. **The interdependence of theory and research.** Many students find it hard to move from the grand conceptualizations of the theorists to what may at first appear to be the rather humdrum findings of empirical investigators. This book builds bridges between the two. We have provided a clear explanation of sociology's theoretical foundations, but we are also intent on showing beginning students the importance of empirically validated knowledge. In Chapter 17, for example, a whole section is devoted to applying Charles Tilly and Anthony Obershall's theory of resource management to the black civil rights movement. Other chapters show how Robert K. Merton's theory of anomie and opportunity structures is borne out by Richard A. Cloward and Lloyd E. Ohlin's research on delinquent gangs and how C. Wright Mills's concept of a power elite has been modified by subsequent research.

2. **Historical context.** Throughout this book we have emphasized the historical context in which specific events occur. Whole sections of chapters are devoted to explaining the backgrounds of contemporary American race and ethnic relations, family life, economic developments, and educational institutions. The contrast between the rural community *(Gemeinschaft)* and the urban society *(Gesellschaft)* is a pervasive theme in sociology, and we have often had occasions to note how rapidly and profoundly the industrial revolution changed the way human beings live and work. Many photographs in the book illustrate this theme by contrasting preindustrial and industrial life.

3. **Private troubles and public issues.** We have tried to help students enlarge what Mills called their "sociological imagination" so that they can make the connection between their own experiences as individuals and the larger world of public events. For example, Chapters 5, 10, and 12 show that the private troubles of the elderly widow, the working mother, and the laid-off steelworker can best be explained not by the characteristics of individuals but by the characteristics of the society in which they happen to live.

4. **Familiar facts and strange discoveries.** We hope that students will find some materials in this book familiar enough to strike a responsive chord. Hardly anyone will disagree with the sociological finding that poverty is associated with high crime rates and that the poor are more likely to be charged with crimes than the middle or upper classes. We also hope, however, that the student reading this book will often be struck by the novel and unfamiliar conclusions it reaches. In Chapter 8 the student will discover that poverty is not the only explanation for crime, or even its leading cause. In fact, if every crime were detected and every criminal caught, some sociologists believe that the well to do would show a higher crime rate than the poor.

The organization of this book follows the usual course sequence. Part I, The Science of Society, and Part II, Basic Concepts, should probably be covered first, but the chapters in Part III, Inequalities, Part IV, Social Institutions, and Part V, Challenges of Contemporary Society, can be read in any order. Part IV departs from the typical textbook treatment by including a separate chapter on health. The origins and development of social movements and the relationship between social change and social conflict are covered in more detail in Chapters 17 and 18 than they are in other introductory books.

Instead of stressing any single theoretical approach, we have used the three major sociological perspecitives — functional analysis, conflict theory, and symbolic interactionism — as a tool kit of concepts to be applied as complementary rather than contradictory explanations. We have emphasized not only how the sociological perspectives put the events of everyday life in a new light, but also how they broaden our understanding of larger historical processes — the success or failure of revolutionary movements, the persistence of racial inequality, the rise of special interest politics, the world population explosion, and the effects of bureaucratic organizations on individuals and on society as a whole. The last section of each chapter brings the points home by offering an analysis of contemporary issues from a sociological perspective. In every discussion we have made a major effort to avoid unnecessary jargon. Sociology, like any other discipline, cannot do without a certain number of technical terms, but we use them only when they are essential to explain important concepts.

Each chapter contains a variety of aids for the student. Boxed inserts illustrate and elaborate the text discussion by providing excerpts from such writers as Kurt Vonnegut, Clifford Geertz, E. B. White, Robert Coles, Robert Heilbroner, Gloria Steinem, Frances FitzGerald, and Jonathan Schell. Some new boxes in this edition include: "The Social Sciences as a Moral Philosophy," "Wanted — A Wife," "The Triumph of Capitalism," and "How Culturally Literate Are You?" Chapter outlines, end-of-chapter summaries, a list of key terms, and suggested readings are provided for each chapter. A Study Guide offers students useful aids and review exercises for every chapter of the textbook. As well, Terry Arendell at Hunter College of The City University of New York has written an Instructor's Manual and the Testbook for this edition.

For their sympathetic interest and expert advice, we are grateful indeed to our colleagues who reviewed the third edition: William R. Kelly, The University of Texas at Austin; C. Paul Marsh, North Carolina State University; Robert P. Snow, Arizona State University; and Steven Stack, Wayne State University.

Our special thanks go to Helen Beckstrom at the University of Virginia for her invaluable help in revising the chapters on Deviance, Education, Health Care, and Religion. We also wish to thank other friends and colleagues at the University of Virginia for their generosity in sharing their ideas with us, especially Mark Lupher, Gianfranco Poggi, Paul Kingston, Jeff Hadden, and Marian Borg.

We are indebted to the many people at Harcourt Brace Jovanovich who contributed their talents to the publication of the third edition. It was a pleasure to work with Cynthia Sheridan, Associate Acquisitions Editor; David Watt, Manuscript Editor; Avery Hallowell, Art Editor; Dee Salisbury, Production Editor; Linda Wooton Miller, Designer; Lynne Bush, Production Manager; and Marc Boggs, Executive Editor.

Once again, we wish to express our gratitude to Robert K. Merton, our indispensable General Editor. Every page of this book has benefited from his legendary scholarship, urbane wisdom, and patient insistence upon clarity of thought and expression.

It is often argued that a science that claims to help us understand the public scene is useless if it does not give us specific guides to action. Until we develop a reliable knowledge of what motivates human beings, however, we must be hesitant in proclaiming the way to a better world. We hope that this book will take its readers at least one small step toward a greater knowledge of themselves and a better understanding of the challenges that confront the social world in which we all must live.

Lewis A. Coser
Steven L. Nock
Patricia A. Steffan
Daphne Spain

CONTENTS

ix

PART FIVE   CHALLENGES OF CONTEMPORARY SOCIETY   527

PART 1

THE SCIENCE
OF SOCIETY

The saying
"Know thyself"
is not well said.
It were more
practical to say
"Know other
people."

Menander
(343–292 B.C.)

CHAPTER 1

THE SOCIOLOGICAL PERSPECTIVE

H ell is other people!" cries the hero of Jean-Paul Sartre's *No Exit* when he realizes that he must spend eternity in fiendishly incompatible company. The play is about three people, locked up forever in a French drawing room, who torment each other just by being together. Sartre's ingenious conception is sociological: since other people largely define our world, they can make it absolute hell for us.

Even if we are not to share the next life with others, we are certain to live most of this one surrounded by our fellow human beings. We are born into a family, we grow up with our schoolmates, we work with a group of colleagues and play with a group of friends, we may marry and start a family of our own. Throughout our lives, most of our thoughts and hopes revolve around other people. Very few of us become hermits or lonely lighthouse keepers; nearly everyone would find life without companionship unbearable.

Equally unbearable, perhaps, would be a life in which the behavior of others was completely unpredictable. Every day, each of us engages in dozens — even hundreds — of acts involving other people, yet the result is not total chaos but more or less orderly routines. When we leave home on a weekday morning, we can expect the world to be pretty much as it was yesterday — traffic will be moving in the streets, schools and offices will be open, storekeepers will sell us the goods we need, newspapers will be written in a language we understand, and so on through the myriad kinds of ordinary behavior we take for granted. We rarely stop to think about the miracles of coordination that must take place to make so many separate individual actions into the orderly patterns of daily life.

In its larger sense, a **society** is a cluster, or system, of patterned interactions among organized groups of human beings. Western society, for instance, is the name we give to the distinct patterns of social life that first developed in Western Europe. Industrial capitalism, parliamentary democracy, public education, and monogamous marriage are some characteristically Western social arrangements.

More specifically, a society is organized groups of people who have distinctive social patterns, occupy a defined territory, and share a sense of common identity. Thus we speak of American society as being different from French or Dutch society, although each can be called "Western."

A social experience always involves a relationship, a give-and-take between two or more people. A social situation is one in which people **interact**, or direct their behavior toward one another. Parents and children interact, and so do employees and managers, blacks and whites, politicians and voters. The term **social structure** refers to the relatively predictable and continuing patterns of these relationships and interactions. A family has a social structure; so does a college class, a church, a city, or a corporation. The term *society* usually refers to people, and the term *social structure* to the orderly pattern of their relationships.

Social behavior is also guided by **culture**, or the beliefs, rules, and ideas that characterize a society's way of life. Western culture, for example, encompasses an advanced industrial technology, a faith in scientific progress, and religious and political traditions that stress individual striving and accomplishment. Culture and social structures regulate individual behavior so that people can act together to achieve a common goal, whether it is raising a family, running a large university, or exploring outer space.

Reliable social structures and a shared culture are essential to human survival. None of us would last long if parents didn't believe in caring for their children, if farmers grew only enough food for their own use, or if we had to fear and distrust everyone we met. **Sociology** is the scientific study of these patterns of social interaction. Sociologists are interested in how society affects the way men and women think and feel and act, not only individually in their everyday lives, but collectively at critical moments in history. In studying society, sociologists seek to answer this question: *Why do people behave the way they do?* Obviously, the question of human behavior is vast in both scope and significance. It is one that has fascinated not only sociologists but also generations of philosophers and poets, psychologists and economists, historians and political scientists.

The sociologist's answer can be put like this: *To a large extent people behave the way they do because of the social situation in which they find themselves.* Of course, the sociological answer cannot provide the entire explanation for all the varieties and intricacies of human behavior. No single science can claim to do that. But, as we shall find in the course of this book, the extent of social influence is very large indeed and it can shape our behavior in unexpected ways.

Sociology seeks the answer to another question that is asked only by the social sciences: *Granted that people's behavior is partly affected by their social situations, why are their social situations the way they are?* This question is so complex that

Gift giving is a common social ritual. From the sociological perspective, this couple is receiving presents not because their friends feel generous but because guests at a wedding shower are expected to bring gifts.

much of the sociological work described in this book is concerned with finding the answer to it.

This chapter introduces the sociological perspective on human behavior and the new insights it provides into ourselves and our everyday experiences. First it discusses the ways society affects individual lives. Then it shows that "the social" is a real and identifiable dimension of behavior. Following that, in the section titled "The Sociological Perspective," the three major types of sociological theory — functional and structural analysis, conflict theory, and symbolic interactionism — are introduced, and the perspectives of other social sciences are briefly noted. The next section summarizes the contributions of three theorists who are usually considered the founders of sociology. The final section, "The Promise of Sociology," suggests that the study of social behavior offers the hope of improving the societies in which we live.

THE SOCIAL SIDE OF EVERYDAY LIFE

HOW SOCIAL SETTINGS INFLUENCE OUR BEHAVIOR

The key insight of sociology is that *all human behavior is social in some respect*; in other words, it is influenced by other people. Consider, for example, your own reactions when you are alone in a room and another person appears. The other person may do something that calls for a response (ask for the time, say hello, stare at you, smile), but even if he or she does nothing, the situation will be changed from a solitary into a social one. And, almost always, your behavior will change along with it.

A change of social setting also brings a change in behavior. People act differently at home than they do in church or at a ball game or on a factory assembly line. George Orwell, writing of his experiences as a dishwasher in a French restaurant, has vividly described how a waiter's behavior changes as he leaves the filthy scullery for the elegant dining room:

> As he passes the door a sudden change comes over him. The set of his shoulders alters; all the dirt and hurry and irritation have dropped off in an instant. He glides over the carpet, with a solemn priest-like air. I remember our assistant *maître d'hôtel,* a fiery Italian, pausing at the dining-room door to address an apprentice who had broken a bottle of wine. Shaking his fist above his head he yelled (luckily the door was more or less soundproof):
>
> *"Tu me fais*—do you call yourself a waiter, you young bastard? You a waiter! You're not fit to scrub floors in the brothel your mother came from. *Maquereau!"*
>
> . . . Then he entered the dining-room and sailed across it dish in hand, graceful as a swan. Ten seconds later he was bowing reverently to a customer. And you could not help thinking, as you saw him bow and smile, with that benign smile of the trained waiter, that the customer was put to shame by having such an aristocrat serve him.[1]

Although the influence of social situations is particularly apparent when people go from one setting to another, it can also be seen—when you look for it—in any gathering. Suppose, for example, that you get on an elevator with several strangers. More often than not, all of you will go through an elaborate ritual of glancing at each other and then looking quickly away. Then everyone will stare at the elevator buttons, at the floor, or into space until the elevator stops. Erving Goffman, an American sociologist, has called this polite ignoring of strangers "civil inattention."

> In performing this courtesy the eyes of the looker may pass over the eyes of the other, but no "recognition" is typically allowed. When the courtesy is performed between two persons passing on the street, civil inattention may take the special form of eyeing the other up to approximately eight feet, during which time sides of the street are apportioned by gesture, and then casting the eyes down as the other person passes—a kind of dimming of lights. In any case, we have here what is perhaps the slightest of interpersonal rituals, yet one that constantly regulates the social intercourse of persons in our society.[2]

In this case, the physical setting is the same but the social one has been changed by the appearance of a stranger. People suddenly behave differently because new rules are now in force.

One task of sociology is to make us aware of how much our daily behavior is shaped by just such mundane situations as these examples describe. An equally important task is to find the reasons why some of these familiar, ordinary settings are the way they are. This question leads sociologists beyond the immediate situation to the distant historical and social factors that created it. Take, for example, this rather typical worker's reaction to her job as a bank teller:

---

[1] George Orwell, *Down and Out in Paris and London* (New York: Harcourt Brace Jovanovich, 1961), pp. 68–69.

[2] Erving Goffman, *Behavior in Public Places* (New York: Free Press, 1963), p. 84.

Strangers in an airport departure lounge are expected to ignore each other. Erving Goffman called this peculiar behavior "civil inattention."

We have a time clock. It's really terrible. You have a card that you put in the machine and it punches the time that you've arrived. If you get there after eight-forty-five, they yell and they scream a lot and say, "Late!" Which I don't quite understand because I've never felt you should be tied to something like a clock. It's not that important. If you're there to start doing business with the people when the bank opens, fine.

■ ■ ■

We work right now with the IBM. It's connected with the main computer bank which has all the information about all the savings accounts. To get any information, we just punch the proper buttons. There are two tellers to a cage and the machine is in between our windows. I don't like the way the bank is set up. It separates people. . . . They object to your going into somebody else's cage, which is understandable. . . . Cages? I've wondered about that. It's not quite like being in prison, but I still feel very locked in.[3]

This kind of highly controlled work is familiar enough. Many jobs in factories and offices involve machines and time clocks, and many other people feel "caged up" away from their fellow employees. But why does so much modern work have to be this way? At the beginning of the twentieth century, more than one out of three American workers was a farmer; today barely one out of thirty works on the land. Clerical jobs are

---

[3] Studs Terkel, *Working* (New York: Random House, 1974), pp. 257–58.

now the largest single occupational category, and most of them are as mechanical and dehumanizing as the bank teller's. Obviously, this particular worker's situation was created by the social and economic developments that revolutionized the nature of work. The emergence of a service economy, in which more workers produce services (such as banking) than goods (such as food), is one reason for her plight; another is the domination of the workplace by large bureaucracies, which tend to dehumanize work by making it a highly regulated and specialized activity. By taking the control of the work process away from the worker, modern machine technology has also contributed to the teller's feeling that she is locked into a meaningless job. Chapter 6, "Organizations," Chapter 12, "The Economy," and Chapter 19, "Work and Leisure," explore these sweeping social changes that have made work into what Max Weber called an "iron cage" for so many people.

The way we feel about ourselves is also affected by larger social structures. A house painter gave the sociologist interviewing him this explanation of why he felt nervous and ill at ease:

> It's not you, you're all right — but you see . . . whenever I'm with educated people, you know, or people who aren't my own kind . . . I feel like I'm making a fool of myself if I just act natural, you know? See, it's not so much how people treat you, it's feeling like you don't know what to do. Like — see, I remember, for instance, going to a Knights of Columbus social, and there were all these people in suits and I had on a jacket, you know, a windbreaker, and somehow people were introducing themselves to each other all over the place, but nobody was introducing themselves to me. So that's how it is.[4]

It wasn't the interviewer himself who made this man uncomfortable; it was the entire system of social ranking that made him feel lonely and out of place. Attitudes toward the relatively uneducated derive from a class system that relegates some people to the lower rungs of the social ladder. Once again, the sociologist is interested not only in how this ranking affects people, but also in the reasons why such a system developed in the first place. Chapter 7, "Social Inequality," describes the theories explaining the origins of the American class structure, as well as its effect on our individual values.

An article in *The Wall Street Journal* provides a final example of the impact of large-scale social developments on individual lives. Under the headline "Husband's Hazard," the article describes the difficulties of middle-aged husbands whose wives return to full-time jobs:

> "I really didn't anticipate how it would affect our attitudes toward each other," Herb Gleason says of his wife's return to her career eight years ago. "I thought she'd always be there just like before — supportive, adjusting to my needs."
>
> For middle-aged men like Mr. Gleason, trying to accommodate to a wife's new career can be a confusing, bruising experience. These men are of a generation in which marriage was typically a one-provider, one-homemaker effort, not a professional joint venture.
>
> ■ ■ ■
>
> Suddenly, the intrusive evening and weekend phone calls from the office are for her. Vacation plans are postponed because of her job pressures. Responsibility for household chores shifts. . . .

---

[4] Richard Sennett and Jonathan Cobb, *The Hidden Injuries of Class* (New York: Vintage, 1973), pp. 115 – 16.

Most disconcerting of all, many husbands are no longer sure they know the women they married. New facets of their wives' personalities emerge. Meticulous housekeepers become more tolerant of sloppiness. Easygoing mothers flare up over the children's balkiness or dawdling. . . . "She is no longer the never-judging homemaker," says Dr. Dorosin, a psychiatrist. "She is a forceful, critical intelligence." [5]

As this account makes clear, the strange behavior of many wives today is related to their social situation. The first sociological question —"Why do people behave the way they do?"— is answered like this: Millions of working wives behave the way they do because they are trying to cope with the conflicting demands of being both conscientious homemakers and responsible employees. Chapter 4, "Social Structure," discusses the concept of role conflict, or the incompatible demands of our various social roles. In this case, the second sociological question is "Why did so many full-time homemakers get into this situation by returning to work?" The answer lies in recent social and economic changes that can be listed only briefly here: the creation of tens of millions of new jobs in service occupations which are usually considered "women's work," the trend toward smaller families, the need and desire for higher family income, technological improvements that make housework and food preparation less time-consuming, and the feminist attack on traditional femininity. Chapter 10, "The Sexes," offers a more detailed analysis of the social developments that have so quickly changed the way men and women behave toward each other.

THE SOCIOLOGICAL IMAGINATION

As the preceding examples clearly show, most people never realize just how deeply their feelings and behavior are affected by social forces beyond their personal control. It requires a sociological imagination, as the American sociologist C. Wright Mills called that "quality of mind essential to grasp the interplay of man and society, of biography and history, of self and world." [6] Many of the personal troubles of individuals, he argued, can be understood — and solved — only on a broader, society-wide level. When only one man is unemployed, for example, that is his personal trouble. His problem can be explained by his own lack of skills, opportunities, or willingness to work. When 40 percent of black youths are unemployed, however, that is a social problem which goes beyond the failings of individuals. The economy is not producing enough job opportunities or the educational system is not turning out enough qualified workers or some other impersonal social force is at work. A couple may be unhappily married, but when one out of three American marriages ends in divorce, it is time to look beyond the particular couple's personal troubles to the social developments that have made married life less satisfactory. As Mills put it,

Insofar as the economy is so arranged that slumps occur, the problem of unemployment becomes incapable of personal solution. . . . Insofar as the family as an institution turns women into darling little slaves and men into their chief providers and unweaned dependents, the problem of a satisfactory marriage remains incapable of purely private solution. [7]

---

[5] Mary Bralove, "Husband's Hazard," *The Wall Street Journal,* November 9, 1981, pp. 1, 24.

[6] C. Wright Mills, *The Sociological Imagination* (New York: Oxford University Press, 1959), p. 10.

[7] Ibid.

The same is true of other social phenomena in which the fates of individuals are woven into the fabric of their society — racial discrimination, urban decline, religious movements, crime, population growth.

The purpose of this book is to analyze these patterns of social life so that you can better understand yourself and the world in which you live. What is human nature? How are people trained to behave in certain ways in certain situations? Why do you feel the way you do about a college education, the kind of job you desire, the sort of family life you want to have? How much chance do you have of achieving these goals? What causes poverty, revolutions, riots, terrorism? What will the society of the future be like? By giving you new answers to these questions, your study of sociology will probably change the way you think about your life. As you find new ways of understanding human behavior, you will see your society and the people you meet in a different light. From the sociological perspective, even the events reported in the daily newspaper will not look the same.

THE NATURE OF SOCIAL REALITY

All of us have close personal knowledge of society. We find the patterns of interaction in the restaurant and the bank immediately familiar, even though we have never met the particular waiter or teller involved. Society, then, is a reality with special characteristics all its own.

SOCIETY: A WHOLE GREATER THAN THE SUM OF ITS PARTS

The first characteristic of society is that it exists independently of the individuals who belong to it. Social structures such as General Motors remain fairly constant, even though auto workers and chairmen of the board come and go rather frequently. That is because the *relationship* among its individual parts, not the parts themselves, makes the structure what it is. The corporation is an **emergent social reality**: it appears in the arrangement of parts, or the patterns of interaction among workers, supervisors, engineers, executives, and so on. Furthermore, the behavior of the people who make up a corporation could not be predicted from knowing them only as individuals. If you know what a corporation is like, you can predict how a dozen strangers will behave in it; however, if you know the dozen individuals well but know nothing about corporations, you will not be able to account for their behavior at work. A social structure, in other words, is a whole that is greater than the sum of its parts.

SUICIDE AND SOCIETY.   Émile Durkheim, one of the founders of modern sociology, provided scientific proof that society has a reality beyond the individuals who belong to it. In *Suicide* (1897),[8] he showed that suicide — apparently a most personal and private act — is influenced by social conditions and that society is a peculiar phenomenon that cannot be understood by studying only the personal characteristics of its members. Before Durkheim, most investigators explained suicide by referring to the motives

---

[8] Émile Durkheim, *Suicide* (New York: Free Press, 1951).

of the people who had taken their own lives. Some, they found, had committed suicide after a doctor had diagnosed an incurable illness, others had failed in business, and still others had had unhappy love affairs. These researchers concerned themselves with the *incidence* of suicide and the individual reasons for it.

Durkheim followed an entirely different strategy of research. He was struck by the fact that the *rate* of suicide — the number of suicides per 100,000 people — was considerably different in various groups and categories of the population. He found, for example, that in several countries the suicide rate for Catholics was lower than that for Protestants. He reasoned that the differences could not be explained in terms of motive; Catholics were as likely as Protestants to have unhappy love affairs, bankruptcies, or incurable diseases. He concluded that the differences in the rate of suicide among various groups were not due to the psychological characteristics of their members but to the characteristics of the groups to which they belonged.

Men and women were more prone to take their own lives, Durkheim reasoned, when the bonds that attach them to other people have loosened. When the father in a close family comes home with some bad news, for example, the members of the family rally around him, "hold his hand," and assure him of their love and support. Someone who lives alone in a rooming house, on the other hand, will not usually have such support. And, in fact, Durkheim found that the suicide rate was generally higher for single men than for married men. Catholics, who were strongly integrated into their church, were likely to receive compassionate advice from their parish priest and find consolation in participating in its rituals. Protestants, however, more often lacked priestly guidance, were less bound by ritual, and were taught to rely on their own conscience when they were in trouble. Durkheim concluded that Protestants had a higher suicide rate than Catholics because they were not as closely integrated into their religious group and thus were less securely cushioned against the impact of personal crises. The strength or looseness of the social network, according to Durkheim, accounted for differences in the suicide rate.

Durkheim distinguished types of suicides not in terms of motives, but according to the relationship of the actor to society. When people become "detached from society," when the bonds that once held them to others are loosened and they must fall back on their own resources, they are prone to *egoistic suicide.* People who commit egoistic suicides are isolated and lonely: the divorced or widowed, the chronically unemployed, the youthful drifter. Men and women can also be victims of **anomie,** Durkheim's famous term for a condition of social and moral disorder. *Anomic suicides* take place during periods of social instability, when a group cannot maintain the usual constraints over its members' behavior. A wave of anomic suicides occurred, for example, during the early 1930s, when the Great Depression caused many more people to conclude that life was not worth living.

Durkheim's *Suicide* marked the emancipation of sociology from the previously dominant psychological explanations of human events. By showing that social life has a reality beyond its individual members, Durkheim proved that society must be investigated on its own terms and not reduced to the study of individual psychology. "A whole is not identical with the sum of its parts," he wrote. Furthermore,

> society is not a mere sum of individuals. Rather, the system formed by their association represents a specific reality which has its own characteristics. . . . The group thinks,

Would you ask someone to give you a seat in this subway car? The results of Stanley Milgram's experiment indicated that few people are able to break even this minor rule of appropriate behavior.

feels and acts quite differently from the way in which its members would were they isolated. If, then, we begin with the individual, we shall be able to understand nothing of what takes place in the group.[9]

SOCIAL PRESSURE WITHIN AND WITHOUT

Since sociologists are mainly concerned with society, their view of human behavior stresses the fact that most people, most of the time, follow the social patterns already set for them. In contrast to the biologist's conception of a humanity driven by genetic programming or the psychologist's emphasis on the makeup of individual personalities, the sociologist shows us "social man"—a creature who has learned to direct biological drives into socially acceptable channels, and who has made the values and goals of a particular time and place part of his or her personality.[10] What Durkheim called "society living in us" gives men and women a sense of moral obligation to obey the rules and accept the mutual responsibilities required of human relationships.

An experiment on social conformity provided an example of how strongly the "society living in us" can affect individual emotions and behavior. Stanley Milgram, a social psychologist, asked each member of the graduate school class he taught to go up to someone on a crowded New York subway train and ask for the individual's seat. His students objected. No one would give up a seat just because a stranger asked for it. Finally, one brave student volunteered to ask twenty strangers, politely and without excuses, to get up so that he could sit down on the subway. Within the week, a rumor

[9] Émile Durkheim, *The Rules of Sociological Method* (New York: Free Press, 1938), pp. 102–104.
[10] Alex Inkeles, *What Is Sociology?* (New York: Prentice-Hall, 1964), pp. 49–50.

began to circulate through the graduate center: "They're getting up!" The students were delighted but astonished to hear that half the people who were asked for their seats got up without demanding a reason. But Milgram noticed in the student's report that he had approached only fourteen people instead of twenty. "I just couldn't go on," the student said. "It was one of the most difficult things I ever did in my life." When Milgram tried to carry out the assignment himself, he too was overwhelmed by the idea of breaking this unwritten rule. When he finally got up the nerve to ask for another man's seat, he collapsed into it, feeling faint and sick. "We are all fragile creatures entwined in a cobweb of social constraints," Milgram concluded. He added: "If you think it is easy to violate [them], get onto a bus and sing out loud. Full-throated song, now, no humming. Many people will say it is easy to carry out this act, but not one in a hundred will be able to do it."[11]

Experiments like Milgram's support the sociological argument that people are to some extent products of society, moved by social forces within and without. The conception of a social man leads to the first lesson of sociology: *Much human behavior is best explained not in terms of the innate characteristics of individuals, but as an outcome of social arrangements that affect particular individuals because of their positions in the social structure.* Durkheim's explanation of suicide is an example of this kind of reasoning.

The sociologist's view of human nature leads to a second conclusion: *Human behavior will change when social conditions change, and not the other way around.* In other words, the rate of suicide, violent crime, or any other undesirable behavior can be reduced only by altering the social situations in which it is likely to occur.[12]

A related message of sociology is that societies and people *can* be changed through deliberate social action. "If we grow up in a racist society," one sociologist has written,

> we will be racists, unless we learn what racism is and how it works and then choose to refuse its impact. In order to do so, however, we must recognize that it is there in the first place. People often are puppets, blindly danced by strings of which they are unaware and over which they are not free to exercise control. A major function of sociology is that it permits us to recognize the forces operative on us and to untie the puppet strings which bind us, thereby giving us the option to be free.[13]

THE SOCIOLOGICAL PERSPECTIVE

A perspective is an angle of vision, a way of looking at things. It is also a way of not looking, since in order to attend closely to one perception others have to be screened out. Note, for example, what happens when you are asked, "How many red things do you see?" A moment before you weren't paying attention to red things, but as you start to think about them, you stop paying attention to everything else. Suddenly, the amount of red in your surroundings becomes much more apparent. Similarly, the

---

[11] Carol Tavris, "The Frozen World of the Familiar Stranger: A Conversation with Stanley Milgram," *Psychology Today* 8 (June 1974): 70–80.

[12] Inkeles, *What Is Sociology?* p. 51.

[13] Reece McGee, *Points of Departure: Basic Concepts in Sociology* (Hinsdale, Ill.: Dryden Press, 1972), p. *x*.

sociological perspective requires us to pay particular attention to certain aspects of social reality while deliberately neglecting others.

A famous research report shows the sociological perspective in action. During the 1940s the sociologist William F. Whyte was asked to make a study of restaurants and their personnel problems.[14] Whyte observed that there was a great deal of friction between employees. In particular, cooks and bartenders were not getting along with the waitresses, who were calling out the customers' orders for food and drinks. Whyte noticed that the cooks and bartenders, all men, were high-status personnel (some of the cooks were also owners). The waitresses, in contrast, were women with a lower standing in this occupational system. From his sociological perspective, Whyte identified the source of the problem: waitresses were giving orders to the cooks and bartenders. The higher-status men resented taking orders from lower-status women because the procedure reversed the sort of behavior considered appropriate in their society.

Whyte's solution was to have the waitresses write out the orders and pass them through some sort of barrier (a physical barrier, such as a pantry separating them from

---

[14] William F. Whyte, "The Social Structure of the Restaurant," *American Journal of Sociology* **54** (January 1949): 302–308.

the kitchen, or a human barrier, such as a kitchen supervisor who directed the food preparation). This device made face-to-face confrontations impossible. The cooks and bartenders were then free to prepare the food and drinks in whatever order they considered most efficient. Many restaurants, you will notice, are organized according to Whyte's "principle of social insulation": orders are written out on checks and physical partitions reaffirm the social divisions between cooks and waitresses. Although personnel problems of this sort are usually blamed on individual personalities, the solution in this case turned out to be a change in the structure of the work situation. By focusing on the patterns of interaction, Whyte simply noticed what was under everybody's nose all along.

The sociological perspective provides a view of human behavior that enables us to see situations — and ourselves — in a special light. As a result, the familiar looks new to us, as if we were outsiders. Much of the humor in the film *Back to the Future* comes from seeing our everyday customs from a stranger's point of view. From the perspective of the 1950s, the latest fads in music, clothes, and gadgets seem peculiar indeed.

Seeing ourselves as others might see us is useful, and it can be very important. One of the tragic and enduring problems of American history, the unequal and unjust treatment of blacks, was seen in a new light when an outsider was assigned to study the situation. The Swedish economist Gunnar Myrdal, who did the study, saw what had always been the case: that there was a vast discrepancy between American beliefs in "liberty and justice for all" and white Americans' actions toward blacks. By bringing what he called the "American dilemma" out into the open, Myrdal helped make Americans aware of the moral implications of racial discrimination. His new look at the familiar paved the way for the social reforms that followed World War II (see Chapter 9, "Race and Ethnicity").

In addition to giving us a new view of familiar situations, the sociological perspective helps us understand strange behaviors and unfamiliar situations. Lewis A. Coser, for example, was able to explain the surprising fact that many of the high-ranking positions in the classical Eastern empires were held by eunuchs.[15] In Ming China, whole departments of eunuchs conducted the emperor's business; in Byzantium, parents castrated their sons to ensure them successful careers as statesmen, diplomats, or generals; in Persia, eunuchs filled virtually all the chief offices of the state. The eunuch system, Coser argued, was so widespread because it satisfied the Oriental despot's demand for absolute loyalty from political officials. Since eunuchs cannot have descendants and typically had little connection to their families, they made ideal instruments for the emperor's will. Without close ties to the community, without roots or kin, eunuchs owed allegiance only to their rulers. By showing us how a physical mutilation served important social purposes, Coser made sense of a behavior that would otherwise be incomprehensible.

Viewing events from a new perspective is essentially an act of imagination. All sciences develop aids to the imagination, or concepts, which allow us to see reality from a certain perspective. We have already encountered some sociological concepts:

---

[15] Lewis A. Coser, "The Political Eunuch," in *The Pleasures of Sociology*, ed. Lewis A. Coser (New York: New American Library/Mentor, 1980), pp. 304–12.

society, interaction, social structure, culture, role, status. Although scientific terms are sometimes popularly dismissed as "jargon," they are not simply obscure words substituting for common ones. Concepts are the means of replacing one viewpoint with another. It makes a great deal of difference, for example, whether a certain type of behavior is seen as an expression of personality or of social role. The personnel problems in Whyte's restaurants came about not because the waitresses had bossy personalities, but because they were playing a role in which they had to tell other people what to do. Moreover, what policymakers do about social problems such as unemployment, for example, depends on whether they see the situation as the result of individual incompetence or of a society's failure to provide enough jobs. What we see as the "facts" of the matter usually depends on what kind of perspective, or theoretical concepts, we are using (see "How the Rosewater Foundation Saves Lives").

Sociologists themselves take different approaches to the social order. There are three major sociological perspectives, each based on somewhat different concepts of society and different views of the social "facts."

FUNCTIONAL AND STRUCTURAL ANALYSIS

The phrase **functional and structural analysis** covers a variety of theoretical approaches that share a common interest: the relating of one part of a society to another part or to the social system as a whole.

From the perspective of functional and structural analysis, society is a system of coordinated and interdependent parts. Like the tissues of a living organism, the various parts are interrelated and are affected by the system to which they belong. Functional theorists are less interested in discovering the causes of a social phenomenon than in pinpointing its consequences for the society. In many cases the phenomenon has *functional* consequences: it contributes to the maintenance of the system or some of its parts. In some cases, however, the phenomenon has a *dysfunctional,* or negative, impact on the system or some parts of it.

In emphasizing the actual consequences of certain kinds of social behavior, functional theorists take care to point out that people are often unaware of these consequences. After World War II, for example, a large number of married couples decided to have several children within a relatively short time. The result was the postwar "baby boom," an important social consequence that was certainly not intended by the individual couples themselves.

Robert K. Merton, one of the founders of functional and structural analysis, analyzed the unintended consequences of another kind of social behavior: the big-city political machine.[16] Around the turn of the century, urban politicians won votes by providing food baskets, jobs, legal advice, and other services for the newly arrived immigrants in their districts. The politicians' goal was to ensure themselves a dependable vote, but their actions also helped men and women from the rural areas of Europe adjust to the ways of the American city. Intended consequences of social actions (the rise of urban political machines) are called **manifest functions**, and unintended consequences (the assimilation of the immigrants) are called **latent functions**

---

[16] Robert K. Merton, *Social Theory and Social Structure* (New York: Free Press, 1968), p. 128.

HOW THE ROSEWATER FOUNDATION SAVES LIVES

Eliot Rosewater, the hero of Kurt Vonnegut's satiric novel God Bless You, Mr. Rosewater, *uses his sociological imagination (and his inherited wealth) to prevent a suicide.*

The telephone rang three times.
"This is the Rosewater Foundation. How can we help you?"
"Mr. Rosewater—" said a fretful man, "you don't know me."
"Did someone tell you that mattered?"
"I'm nothing, Mr. Rosewater. I'm worse than nothing."

■ ■ ■

How did you happen to hear of us?"
"There's this big black and yellow sticker in the phone booth. Says, *'Don't Kill Yourself. Call the Rosewater Foundation,'* and it's got your number . . . Maybe you think it's funny to put up signs about people who want to commit suicide."
"Are *you* about to?"
"And what if I was?"
"I wouldn't tell you the gorgeous reasons I have discovered for going on living."
"What *would* you do?"
"I'd ask you to name the rock-bottom price you'd charge to go on living for just one more week."
There was a silence.
"Did you hear me?" said Eliot.

"I heard you."
"If you're not going to kill yourself, would you please hang up. There are other people who'd like to use the line."
"You sound so crazy."
"You're the one who wants to kill himself."
"What if I said I wouldn't live through the next week for a million dollars?"
"I'd say, 'Go ahead and die.' Try a thousand."
"A thousand."
"Go ahead and die. Try a hundred."
"A hundred."
"Now you're making sense. Come on over and talk."

■ ■ ■

. . . Eliot wrote in a cumbersome ledger he kept under his cot. . . . [He wrote] the name of the suicidal man who had called him, who had come to see him, who had just departed.. . . .
"Sherman Wesley Little," wrote Eliot. *"Indy, Su-TDM-LO-V2-W1K3-K2CP-RF $300."* Decoded, this meant that Little was from Indianapolis, was a suicidal tool-and-die maker who had been laid off, a veteran of the Second World War with a wife and three children, the second child suffering from cerebral palsy. Eliot had awarded him a Rosewater Fellowship of $300.

SOURCE: Kurt Vonnegut, Jr., *God Bless You, Mr. Rosewater, or Pearls Before Swine* (New York: Dell, 1965), pp. 74–78.

The functional perspective, as used by Merton and his followers, focuses on the motives and behavior of people whose choices are limited or facilitated by their position in the social structure. Although individuals always have a choice of how to behave in specific situations, the choices are structurally patterned, or laid out, by society. The jobs available to an unskilled laborer, for example, are very different from those available to a business school graduate. Until very recently, the patterns of choice for women were much more restricted than those for men, and in many cases still are. Given the different opportunities for the upper class and lower class, or for men and women, it is clear why people are motivated to choose different ways of earning a living. Their behavior, and the motives behind it, also contribute to a larger social process: the maintenance of a system in which wealth and power are very unequally distributed.

Functional and structural analysis, in all its versions, explains specific events by showing how they are embedded in a social web of opportunities and constraints. Using the functional perspective, Andrew Cherlin argues that the American divorce rate more than doubled between 1960 and 1980 because record numbers of women entered the paid labor force during the same period. Having a job outside the home does not in itself make women want a divorce, nor does a wife's new job necessarily cause marital problems. Cherlin explains instead that a paying job created new opportunities for millions of married women. In his view, the rising divorce rate simply reflected the fact that many unhappily married wives could now afford to leave their husbands.[17]

Some early functional analysts, especially A. R. Radcliffe-Brown and other British anthropologists, viewed society as a wholly integrated system in which each part contributes functionally to the whole. Modern functional theorists maintain that integration is never complete, noting, however, that society is a coordinated system in which change in one part brings about adaptive change in another. In the late nineteenth century, for example, the American educational system expanded enormously

---

[17] Andrew Cherlin, *Marriage, Divorce, and Remarriage* (Cambridge, Mass.: Harvard University Press, 1981).

This farm couple's personal loss is partly the result of the broad economic trend toward the concentration of farming in huge "agribusinesses."

in response to the industrial economy's need for literate, technically skilled employees; for the first time, children were legally required to attend school, and thousands of new public schools were opened (see Chapter 13, "Education"). Change in one part of the social system — the economy — also produced changes in the family (as wives took jobs in offices and factories), in population (the growth of cities, the arrival of millions of immigrant workers), and in social values (the growth of democratic liberalism).

Conservatives have sometimes used functional theory to justify the existing social order and to deplore disruptive changes. Functional explanations, however, do not imply that the existing way of fulfilling social functions is the best or the only way. For example, one of the functions of the family in pre-industrial societies was the care of the aged. But in the Israeli kibbutz (a kind of commune), old people are cared for by the community, and in most industrial societies Social Security provides for the aged. The fact that the family served particular functions in the past does not mean that other arrangements cannot serve the same functions in other times and settings.

Merton, in particular, has questioned the conservative assumption that every social arrangement is necessarily functional. Patterns of racial discrimination, for example, are clearly dysfunctional for the society as a whole, since they prevent the best use of the potential labor force. Racial discrimination is highly functional, however, for those members of the society who benefit from being considered racially superior. The increasingly large number of working mothers in recent decades is functional for increasing the productivity of American society, but it has been dysfunctional for the maintenance of traditional sex roles and family arrangements.

Societies made up of diverse groups and social classes will always have conflicting interests and values as well as shared ones. While a certain amount of consensus is necessary to keep a society from falling apart, functional theorists recognize that the balance between consensus and conflict is bound to be a shifting one.

CONFLICT THEORY

While functional and structural analysis acknowledges the existence of conflict in society, **conflict theory** focuses analytical attention on it. This approach studies the social processes that arise from the struggle to attain whatever social actors consider desirable — wealth, high social position, power, or prestige.

Modern conflict theory was largely inspired by the works of Karl Marx, Georg Simmel, and Max Weber. Its guiding assumptions come from Marx's theory of class conflict:[18]

1. All social systems distribute scarce and valuable resources unequally.

2. The resulting inequalities and inequities create conflicts of interest among the various strata and classes in the system.

3. These conflicts of interest eventually generate overt conflicts between those who control valuable resources and those who do not.

---

[18] Jonathan Turner and Leonard Beeghley, *The Emergence of Sociological Theory* (Homewood, Ill.: Dorsey Press, 1981), p. 545.

4. In the long run, these conflicts result in the reorganization of social systems. In the past, new patterns of inequality always brought about further conflict and change. (Marx maintained, however, that the victory of the modern industrial working class over its capitalist oppressors would initiate a final classless — and hence conflictless — society.)

Most modern conflict theorists share some of Marx's assumptions, but they often combine his approach with those of Simmel and Weber. Even those who follow Marx's analytical model fairly closely, however, do not necessarily accept his vision of an ultimately classless society.

Simmel, who was of course familiar with Marx's thought, believed conflict could bring about social integration as well as dissension. He thought that by providing a safety valve for hostility, conflict could actually increase, rather than undermine, social solidarity. In fact, Simmel wrote, "There probably exists no social unit in which convergent and divergent currents among its members are not inseparably interwoven. An absolutely centripetal and harmonious group . . . not only is empirically unreal, it could show no real life process." [19] In contrast to Marx, who dealt mainly with class conflicts, Simmel analyzed a variety of conflicts — among men and women, among members of different generations, between labor and management, and among ethnic groups.

Building on the work of Simmel and E. A. Ross, Lewis A. Coser contributed an analysis of conflict as a social process. He found that flexible, complex social structures are more likely to absorb conflicts than simple, tightly integrated societies.[20] When there are many different group affiliations, multiple conflicts crisscross each other and prevent the formation of deep cleavages (see Chapter 18, "Social Change and Social Conflict"). In large, modern, democratic societies like the United States, the many cross-conflicts among a variety of ethnic, economic political, and regional groups tend to weave society together by preventing basic, irreparable divisions. The Republican and Democratic parties are well-known examples of the way diversity can lead to compromise among competing groups. In smaller, more traditional societies, according to Coser, group affiliations are more likely to overlap, so that religious, ethnic, and political allegiances do not crisscross but run together on one axis. The history of Northern Ireland has been a tragic example of how a society split into opposing camps fails to find a working consensus: on one side are Protestant, pro-British, largely middle-class Conservatives and on the other Catholic, anti-British, largely working-class supporters of union with Ireland.

In analyzing a social structure, conflict theorists typically ask, Who benefits from this arrangement? *Schooling in Capitalist America* (1976), by Samuel Bowles and Herbert Gintis, analyzes the American educational system from this perspective.[21] The authors argue that U.S. public schools are supposed to provide every child with an equal opportunity to succeed, but they also benefit capitalist employers and reinforce the economic inequalities of the larger society.

---

[19] Georg Simmel, *Conflict and the Web of Group Affiliations* (New York: Free Press, 1955), p. 15.

[20] Lewis A. Coser, *The Functions of Social Conflict* (Glencoe, Ill.: Free Press, 1956).

[21] Samuel Bowles and Herbert Gintis, *Schooling in Capitalist America* (New York: Basic Books, 1976).

According to Lewis Coser, the conflict in Northern Ireland is so difficult to resolve because religious, ethnic, and political allegiances do not overlap.

Education in the United States, according to Bowles and Gintis, meets economic needs by motivating young people to work hard and to obey their superiors. It also teaches them the kinds of technical and social skills which will make them more productive workers. Since the educational system produces more skilled employees than the number of jobs available, schools enhance the employer's chief advantage — the power to hire and fire. Moreover, schools create economic inequality by tracking students toward different occupational levels, and thus tend to reinforce existing patterns of discrimination on the basis of class, sex, and race. Finally, Bowles and Gintis maintain that schools help legitimize inequality by fostering the illusion that most people succeed or fail because of differences in intelligence, ability, or other purely personal characteristics.

SYMBOLIC INTERACTIONISM

Social life depends on human interaction, or mutual communication and response. This social interaction takes place through language and other symbolic communications (music, art, body language). In order to communicate, men and women must interpret the meaning of these symbolic messages and respond to them in a way that will be understood. In sociology, **symbolic interactionism** emphasizes that these shared meanings are the basis of social life. From the symbolic interactionist's perspective, social reality is a fluid, interpretive process, in which the social actor is continuously involved in negotiations with other people about how to behave. By concentrating on the momentary, routine communications of everyday life, symbolic interactionism uncovers the web of shared meanings that creates social life.

Body language is an example of symbolic communication. Every member of the same culture should have no difficulty understanding the meaning of this track team's behavior.

The most fascinating writer in this field is undoubtedly Erving Goffman.[22] Most of his work provides an intriguing analysis of the kinds of symbolic games people play. Impression management, for instance, is a game in which the players try to influence what others think of them by manipulating visual and verbal symbols. A college student at a job interview will wear special clothes (usually a sober business suit) and change his or her appearance (with a fresh shave, a haircut, or makeup) to convey the impression of a serious, able young person. The interviewers also stage manage a different impression of themselves in the office than they convey with their children and close friends. When talking to a job applicant, their script (conversation) will be more formal, and their offices as carefully decorated as a stage set, complete with props (telephone, dictating machine) and scenery (framed photographs of dignitaries and prestigious diplomas).

Television is a very powerful communicator of symbolic meanings. During the 1984 presidential campaign, Ronald Reagan's advisors proved to be brilliant at stage managing the impressions the public received from the television news. Reagan's campaign stops were meticulously planned to suggest upbeat, patriotic themes. The

---

[22] Erving Goffman, *The Presentation of Self in Everyday Life* (New York: Doubleday/Anchor, 1959); *Asylums: Essays on the Social Situation of Mental Patients and Other Inmates* (Chicago: Aldine, 1961); *Stigma: Notes on the Management of Spoiled Identity* (Englewood Cliffs, N.J.: Prentice-Hall, 1963).

usual news coverage showed enthusiastic crowds cheering and waving flags while a vigorous, confident leader delivered a few lines celebrating the nation's strength, prosperity, and optimistic future. These skillfully arranged visual images appealed to voters who longed for strong leadership and who felt nostalgia for the traditional values of smalltown America.

The use of pleasing symbolic messages for political purposes fits well with Goffman's view of society, which the anthropologist Clifford Geertz described as "an unbroken stream of gambits, ploys, artifices, bluffs, disguises, conspiracies, and outright impostures." [23]

If you see society as a collection of games, Geertz points out, you are also likely to notice the conventions and rules by which the games are played. Related to symbolic interactionism is **ethnomethodology**, the study of how people invent and convey shared meanings as they go about (or play by the rules of) their everyday routines. Its founder, Harold Garfinkel, attempted to bring the unspoken rules of social life out into the open by breaking them. In one experiment, Garfinkel instructed his students to address their parents as Mr. and Mrs. and to treat them as if they were strangers. Family social life was so disrupted that the students had to end their performance after only a few minutes.[24] Some of Garfinkel's other experiments involved bargaining over prices for goods in a supermarket and moving closer and closer to the other person in a conversation. Breaking the unspoken rules of everyday life always produced anger, confusion, and embarrassment in others. These apparently insignificant rules are considered so important because they represent the consistent social patterns that make it possible for people to live and work together. By questioning the unquestioned assumptions of daily existence, ethnomethodologists show how strong the social order actually is.

Each major sociological theory focuses on a different aspect of human society. Although each perspective seems quite incompatible with the others at first, together they make up a tool kit of concepts and explanations that can be applied to particular social events. The social world is so complex, and each situation so full of variables, that no one theory can account for its every aspect. This book will often use more than one sociological perspective to explain how society operates. The discussion will also occasionally draw upon the viewpoints of other social sciences.

OTHER SOCIAL SCIENCES

The **social sciences** encompass a number of academic disciplines that are devoted to the study of human behavior. Besides sociology, the major disciplines in this area are economics, political science, history, anthropology, and psychology. The social sciences tend to study the same phenomena and to use each other's insights whenever they are useful. Nevertheless, each field has a unique approach and a separate theoretical basis.

Economics is the study of the production, distribution, and consumption of goods and services in society. Economists have developed sophisticated mathematical

---

[23] Clifford Geertz, *Local Knowledge: Further Essays in Interpretive Anthropology* (New York: Basic Books, 1983). p. 25.

[24] Harold Garfinkel, *Studies in Ethnomethodology* (Englewood Cliffs, N.J.: Prentice-Hall, 1967), p. 47.

methods of analyzing and forecasting the effects of such variables as taxes, government economic policy, and industrial output on the way people earn and spend money. Many problems (inflation, unemployment, low productivity) that are usually called "economic" involve sociological issues as well.

Political science is the study of government and of the distribution of power. Political scientists and sociologists both are interested in who votes and why, how political attitudes are formed, and how interest groups affect public policy. In fact, research on the political process of voting and governing and their influence is known as *political sociology*.

Not everyone agrees that *history* is a science, since it usually stresses unique or distinctive circumstances rather than the repetitive patterns underlying specific events. Another distinction between history and sociology is that historians usually study social behavior as it occurred in the past, while sociologists base their study on past behavior but are typically more concerned with the present and the future.

Anthropology is closest to sociology in theory and research. Literally translated as the "study of man," anthropology has traditionally concentrated on the cultures of nonliterate societies. These societies are rapidly disappearing, and *cultural anthropologists* have lately branched out into studies of modern ways of life.

Psychology looks for the causes of behavior in the emotions, motivations, perceptions, and personalities of individuals. Since most behavior is the behavior of individuals in social situations, psychology and sociology are complementary disciplines. They are merged in *social psychology*, the study of how individual personality is changed by the social situation.

THE ORIGINS OF SOCIOLOGY

Although the study of social influences on human behavior is at least as old as the ancient Greeks, sociology began to be considered a science little more than a century ago. Society became a subject of keen interest during the late nineteenth century, when Western civilization was undergoing the vast social upheavals that accompanied the Industrial Revolution. This "Great Transformation" [25] turned Western Europe from a rural, integrated, stable society into an urban, diverse, rapidly changing one. The first kinds of sociological analysis attempted to explain what was happening and why.

The founder of sociology is usually said to be Auguste Comte (1798–1857), a French philosopher who argued that the social world should be studied in the same scientific manner as the natural world. He invented the term "sociology"—an untidy combination of a Latin word, *socius* (the social), and a Greek word, *logos* (reasoning) —for the discipline of "reasoning about the social." According to his famous motto, Comte believed the purpose of science was "to know in order to predict and to predict in order to control." For Comte, the purpose of sociology was to discover the laws of social order so that stability could be maintained. He divided the subject matter of sociology into *statics* and *dynamics*. Statics covered the stable structures of society which endured over time, and dynamics dealt with the forces of change and conflict

---

[25] See Karl Polanyi, *The Great Transformation* (Boston: Beacon Press, 1944).

that disrupted the social order. To this day, sociology retains Comte's concern with extending scientific knowledge of social behavior, his interest in continuity and change, and his faith that sociology can make significant contributions to human progress and well-being. Comte's own pet theories, however, have been overshadowed by those of later writers, especially the great theorists of the so-called classical period (1890–1920), when the foundations of modern sociology were laid.[26]

In little more than half a century the United States was transformed into a complex modern society. Sociology began as an attempt to explain the vast social changes that accompanied industrialization.

ÉMILE DURKHEIM

Émile Durkheim (1858–1917) was one of the several founders of sociology as an academic discipline. As a professor of social science at the Sorbonne, he deeply influenced the development of sociological thought; he was also a leading spokesman for the republican, progressive Left during the intellectual and political crises of the French Third Republic. Both his life and his work were devoted to the search for a harmonious social order. All his life Durkheim sought to answer the question, What makes mutually hostile and self-seeking individuals work together in a society?

Society, Durkheim concluded, is held together by its members' common bonds. Integration comes from participation in shared activities — praying together in religious ceremonies, for example, or working together on a common task. It also comes from shared beliefs, or what Durkheim called a "collective consciousness." He distinguished between two kinds of social unity: **mechanical solidarity**, based on a moral consensus among people who have many social similarities, and **organic solidarity**, based on mutual dependence among people of different backgrounds and beliefs. A rural village, for example, typically has mechanical solidarity: its inhabitants share many traditional customs and mutual loyalties. Organic solidarity, in contrast, characterizes the contractual ties among the residents of a modern city, where disparate peoples have few emotional bonds but are held together by an interdependent division

[26] Robert A. Nisbet, *The Social Bond* (New York: Knopf, 1970), pp. 21–23.

of labor. The shift from one type of social order to the other was, of course, a significant aspect of the Great Transformation.

The search for the sources of social unity led Durkheim to study moral values.[27] He concluded that religion gave people the sense of moral obligation that led them to give up their own selfish purposes for the sake of the community. Since traditional religion was declining in Durkheim's day, he saw the possibility that the sense of religious solidarity could break down into a state of anomie. "We must discover," he argued, "the rational substitutes for these religious notions that for a long time have served as the vehicle for the most essential moral ideas." [28] In modern sociological terms he looked for a *functional equivalent* to religious faith in a strong secular morality. Durkheim's concern with the functional relationships between systems of belief and social structure has greatly influenced the development of sociology. "We use the word 'function,'" Durkheim wrote,

> in preference to "end" or "purpose," precisely because social phenomena do not generally exist for the useful results they produce. We must determine whether there is a correspondence between the fact under consideration and the general needs of the social organism . . . without occupying ourselves with whether it has been intentional or not.[29]

KARL MARX

Although Karl Marx (1818–1883) is best known as an economist or historian, he has been called the most famous of sociologists. For Marx, society is and always has been fundamentally divided between two classes—the one that controls the means of production (land, factories) and the one that does not. The guiding principle of the social and historical process is not functional collaboration but conflict between the exploiters and the exploited.

All history, Marx declared, is the history of class struggles. In the ancient world the struggle was between master and slave; in the medieval world, between lord and peasant; and in the modern era, between capitalist and worker. Marx believed, however, that the contenders and the historical situation were different in every case and that the situation of the factory worker was unique. Unlike other exploited classes, the industrial proletariat were forced to sell their labor to the capitalists who controlled the means of production. According to Marxist theory, historical change comes about as each society collapses from its own internal conflicts and is replaced by another. Marx predicted that the contradictions of capitalism would destroy it from within and that a classless society would finally be created.

In every era, Marx claimed, the dominant means of production determines a society's organization and even its beliefs and ideas—its science, art, and religious values. "The mode of production of material life," Marx said, "determines the general character of the social, political and spiritual processes of life. It is not the consciousness of men that determines their being, but, on the contrary, their social being

---

[27] Émile Durkheim, *The Elementary Forms of the Religious Life* (New York: Free Press, 1954).

[28] Émile Durkheim, *Moral Education* (New York: Free Press, 1961), p. 9.

[29] Durkheim, *The Rules of Sociological Method*, p. 95.

determines their consciousness." [30] Every scholar since Marx—historian, economist, or sociologist—has had to reckon with this concept of class and class struggle. As we noted above, the Marxist influence in sociology is seen primarily in various theories of social conflict.

MAX WEBER

Max Weber (1864–1920) defined sociology as "the science which aims at interpretive understanding (in German, *Verstehen*) of social behavior in order to gain an explanation of its causes, its course, and its effects." [31] To Weber, this **Verstehen** can be achieved only by discovering the subjective meanings that individuals give to their own behavior and to the behavior of others.

Weber's work is often said to be a running debate with the ghost of Karl Marx. In the Marxist view all social life, including what people think and believe, ultimately depends on the conditions of economic production. In order to refute Marx, Weber tried to prove that cultural ideas and social structures influence each other and that social life, including economic processes, ultimately depends on what people think and believe. In his most famous work, *The Protestant Ethic and the Spirit of Capitalism* (1905),[32] Weber argued that the Calvinist emphasis on hard work and self-denial influenced the development of attitudes and practices favorable to a capitalist economy (see Chapter 12, "The Economy").

Whether Weber was right or wrong about capitalism is less important than his view that culture affects social structure. Weber maintained that human behavior could not be fully understood without taking into account what people believe, feel, and want.

Weber found that his own culture was becoming increasingly dominated by purposive rational behavior. In earlier times tradition or religion had been a great motivating force, but modern societies more often tried to find the most efficient application of rational means to rational ends. Weber believed that the demands of rational efficiency were outweighing the claims of custom and personal feelings, not only in the economic sphere of capitalist enterprise, but also in politics, the law, and even personal relationships.

In Weber's view this distinctively modern rationality could be seen dramatically in the growth of bureaucracy. Rational decision making is

> the more fully realized the more bureaucracy "depersonalizes" itself, i.e., the more completely it succeeds in achieving the exclusion of love, hatred, and every purely personal, especially irrational and incalculable, feeling from the execution of official tasks. In the place of the old-type ruler who is moved by sympathy, favor, grace, and gratitude, modern culture requires for its sustaining external apparatus the emotionally detached, and hence rigorously "professional," expert.[33]

[30] Karl Marx, *Selected Writings in Sociology and Social Philosophy,* (London: McGraw–Hill, 1964), p. 51.

[31] Max Weber, *Basic Concepts in Sociology* (New York: Citadel Press, 1964), p. 29.

[32] Max Weber, *The Protestant Ethic and the Spirit of Capitalism* (New York: Scribner's, 1930).

[33] Quoted in Reinhard Bendix, *Max Weber: An Intellectual Portrait* (Garden City, N. Y.: Doubleday, 1960), pp. 421–22.

THE SOCIAL SCIENCES AS A MORAL PHILOSOPHY

In a 1985 study, Habits of the Heart, *Robert Bellah and his associates found that many Americans are torn between individual goals—their desire to win, to make it on their own—and their yearning for love and attachment to others. Like the nineteenth-century French social scientist, Alexis de Tocqueville, the authors believe that the politics of a society are shaped by the characters of its individual citizens. In this selection they conclude that Americans need a revival of moral philosophy to change their definition of the good life and the good society.*

Although Tocqueville's contemporary and fellow countryman Auguste Comte was one of the most ardent disseminators of what we might call the myth of social science—the idea that social science is soon to become like natural science—there is no reason to believe that Tocqueville shared that idea. Indeed, Tocqueville's argument for a new science rested specifically on the notion that the object of study—namely, society in a new world—was new and therefore required a new approach . . .

If we, too, have had to find a new way to deal with new realities, we have done so not by imagining that with us a truly scientific social science has at last arrived but by consciously trying to renew an older conception of social science, one in which the boundary between social science and philosophy was still open. During the century and a half since

Tocqueville wrote *Democracy in America,* a "hard" social science has not emerged, but certainly a "professional" social science with significant achievements has . . . [It] is also true that we understand many particular social processes better than anyone did in the 1830s. Yet Tocqueville's sense of American society as a whole, of how its major components—family, religion, politics, the economy—fit together, and of how the character of Americans is affected by their society, and vice versa, has never been equaled. Nor has anyone ever better pointed out the moral and political meaning of the American experiment. It is that synoptic view, at once philosophical, historical, and sociological, that narrowly professional social science seems not so much incapable of as uninterested in. It is in order to reappropriate that larger view that we must try to restore the idea of social science as public philosophy.

■ ■ ■

Let us consider how such a social science differs from much current work. It is of the nature of a narrowly professional social science that it is specialized and that each specialized discipline disavows knowledge of the whole or of any part of the whole that lies beyond its strictly defined domain. It is the governing ideal of much specialized social science to abstract out single variables and, on the natural science model, try to figure out what their

THE PROMISE OF SOCIOLOGY

Human beings are the only animals able to reflect upon their behavior. While other creatures are imprisoned in the immediate present, men and women alone have the capacity to think about the past, to judge their own conduct, and to plan for the future. This capacity for reflection has made human beings into what philosophers have called "dissatisfied animals." When they find their own behavior wanting, people think about self-improvement. When they are dissatisfied with the world as it is, they try to change it.

Human beings not only can think back and plan ahead but are uniquely able to change themselves and the world in which they live. Nature controls nearly all the behavior of other animals, but people have generally been able to dominate nature and overcome many of its constraints. Besides being able to change their own behavior and transform their natural environment, human beings are also capable of changing their human environment—that is, the society in which they live. Without the sting of effects would be if everything else were held constant. Yet in the social world, single variables are seldom independent enough to be consistently predictive. It is only in the context of society as a whole, with its possibilities, its limitations, and its aspirations, that particular variables can be understood. Narrowly professional social science, particularly in its most reductionist form, may indeed deny that there is any whole. It may push a radical nominalism to the point of seeing society as a heap of disparate individuals and groups lacking either a common culture or a coherent social organization. A philosophical social science involves not only a different focus of attention but a different understanding of society, one grounded, as we will see, in commitments to substantive traditions.

■ ■ ■

The most important boundary that must be transcended is the recent and quite arbitrary boundary between the social sciences and the humanities. The humanities, we are told, have to do with the transmission and interpretation of cultural traditions in the realms of philosophy, religion, literature, language, and the arts, whereas the social sciences involve the scientific study of human action. The assumption is that the social sciences are not cultural traditions but rather occupy a privileged position of pure observation. The assumption is also that discussions of human action in the humanities are "impressionistic" and "anecdotal" and do not really become knowledge until "tested" by the methods of science, from which alone comes valid knowledge.

It is precisely that boundary between the social sciences and the humanities that social science as public philosophy most wants to open up. Social science is not a disembodied cognitive enterprise. It is a tradition, or set of traditions, deeply rooted in the philosophical and humanistic (and, to more than a small extent, the religious) history of the West. Social science makes assumptions about the nature of persons, the nature of society, and the relation between persons and society. It also, whether it admits it or not, makes assumptions about good persons and a good society and considers how far these conceptions are embodied in our actual society. Becoming conscious of the cultural roots of these assumptions would remind the social scientist that these assumptions are contestable and that the choice of assumptions involves controversies that lie deep in the history of Western thought. Social science as public philosophy would make the philosophical conversation concerning these matters its own.

SOURCE: Robert N. Bellah et al., *Habits of the Heart: Individualism and Commitment in American Life* (Berkeley, CA: University of California Press, 1985), pp. 297–8; 300–301.

reflection and the urge to make new social arrangements, men and women would still be living in caves.

The urge toward self-knowledge is at least as old as Socrates' statement that "the unexamined life is not worth living." Sociology has a much shorter history than philosophical reflection, but it is part of the same human quest for self-understanding and self-improvement (see "The Social Sciences as a Moral Philosophy"). Modern sociologists are aware of the human capacity to transform the world, but they also recognize the constraints, both natural and human, that stand in the way of deliberate social change. Twentieth-century men and women know that there are limits to the earth's natural resources, and they are constantly reminded of the restraints on human action imposed by other human beings. The Chinese government's suppression of dissident students is only one example of how easily powerful groups can thwart even small efforts at social reform. Sociologists are interested not only in the willful controls placed on human behavior, but also in the impersonal limits imposed by culture and social structure.

Although human actors usually have a choice of actions to take, the decision is always between structured alternatives, and not a choice of any conceivable alternative. Our social bonds literally bind us in a culture, or to the web of customs and beliefs in which we have been raised. Other bonds enmesh us in a social structure of groups and organizations extending from our closest friends and family to distant institutions that affect us in ways we barely notice. When we choose to act, we are knowingly or unknowingly guided by the patterns of behavior already laid down for us.

Two contemporary sociologists summed up the human dilemma of freedom and constraint this way:

> The English word *bonds* expresses very eloquently what is at issue here: one cannot have the solidarity of other human beings, the bonds that tie one together with them, without the bondage of social controls over one's life. Put differently, there is no bonding between human beings without the effect of boundedness.[34]

The promise of sociology lies in its continuation of the age-old effort to understand the human species. Comte's motto — "to know in order to predict and to predict in order to control" — is still the task of the sociological enterprise. If the message of sociology is that human beings are to a great extent products of their social environment, the promise of sociology is that we can change that environment and thus free ourselves to create a better world.

---

[34] Peter L. Berger and Hansfried Kellner, *Sociology Reinterpreted* (Garden City, N.Y.: Doubleday/Anchor, 1981), pp. 91–92.

SUMMARY

1. Sociology is the study of society — of the patterned interactions among organized groups of people.

2. Human behavior is guided by socially structured relationships and by culture, the beliefs and ideas that characterize a society's way of life. The sociological perspective shows us that people behave the way they do largely because of the social situations in which they find themselves. Sociologists also try to find the reasons why social situations are the way they are.

3. The sociological imagination enables us to see the personal troubles of individuals as the results of impersonal social forces.

4. A social structure is an emergent reality: the relationship among its members, not the nature of individual members, makes the structure what it is.

5. In *Suicide* (1897), Émile Durkheim concluded that social life has a reality beyond the characteristics of individuals. Specifically, he showed that the rate of suicide is affected by the strength or looseness of the social networks to which people belong. The motives of the individuals who commit suicide determine the incidence of suicide in a society, he found, but not its rate. Egoistic suicides are likely to occur when people become detached from the bonds that tie them to others; anomic suicides are likely to occur during periods of anomie, Durkheim's term for a condition of social and moral disorder.

6. Since human behavior is affected by social structures, much of it is best explained not in terms of individual personality but as products of social arrangements. Two conclusions follow from this sociological argument: human behavior will change when social conditions change, and social conditions can be changed through deliberate action.

7. There are three major theoretical perspectives in sociology. Functional and structural analysis emphasizes the relationships of one part of society to

other parts and to the social system as a whole. Robert K. Merton and other functional theorists are mainly interested in the consequences of a social phenomenon, which may be functional or dysfunctional (positive or negative) for the system or some of its parts. Much social behavior has unintended consequences, or latent functions, as well as intended consequences, or manifest functions.

8. Conflict theorists study the processes arising from the struggle of social actors to attain whatever they consider desirable. The assumptions of conflict theory are based largely on Karl Marx's theory of class conflict.

9. Symbolic interactionism emphasizes how the meaning that individuals give to social events affects the way they behave. Erving Goffman's work analyzes how people communicate meanings by "stage managing the impressions" others have of them. A related approach is ethnomethodology, the study of how people invent and convey shared meanings in everyday routines.

10. The founder of sociology is usually assumed to be Auguste Comte, the nineteenth-century French philosopher, but the foundations of modern sociology were laid in the nineteenth and early twentieth centuries by Durkheim, Marx, and Max Weber.

11. Durkheim's life and work were devoted to the search for a harmonious social order. He described two kinds of social unity: mechanical solidarity based on a moral consensus among people who have many social similarities, and organic solidarity based on a mutual dependence among people of different backgrounds and beliefs.

12. Marx declared that all history is the history of class struggle. In the modern era he saw a society divided between capitalists, who control the means of economic production, and the proletariat, or wage laborers.

13. Weber aimed at interpretive understanding (*Verstehen*) of social behavior. He believed that cultural ideas and social structures influence each other, and that social life ultimately depends on what people think and believe.

14. The message of sociology is that human beings are to a large extent products of their social environment; the promise of sociology is that human beings can change that environment for the better.

KEY TERMS

society 4
interaction 4
social structure 4
culture 4
sociology 4
emergent social reality 10

anomie 11
functional and
  structural analysis 16
manifest functions 16
latent functions 16
conflict theory 19

symbolic interactionism 21
ethnomethodology 23
social sciences 23
mechanical solidarity 25
organic solidarity 25
Verstehen 27

SUGGESTED READING

* Peter L. Berger. *Invitation to Sociology*. Garden City, NY: Doubleday/Anchor, 1963.

Peter L. Berger and Hansfried Kellner. *Sociology Reinterpreted*. Garden City, NY: Doubleday/Anchor, 1981.

* Lewis A. Coser, ed. *The Pleasures of Sociology*. New York: New American Library/Mentor, 1980.

* Erving Goffman. *The Presentation of Self in Everyday Life*. Garden City, NY: Doubleday/Anchor, 1959.

* Alex Inkeles. *What Is Sociology?* Englewood Cliffs, NJ: Prentice-Hall, 1964.

National Academy of Sciences. *Behavioral and Social Science Research: A National Resource*. Washington, DC: National Academy Press, 1982.

* Alexis de Tocqueville, *Democracy in America*, trans. George Lawrence, ed. J. P. Mayer. New York: Doubleday/Anchor Books, 1969.

* Available in paperback.

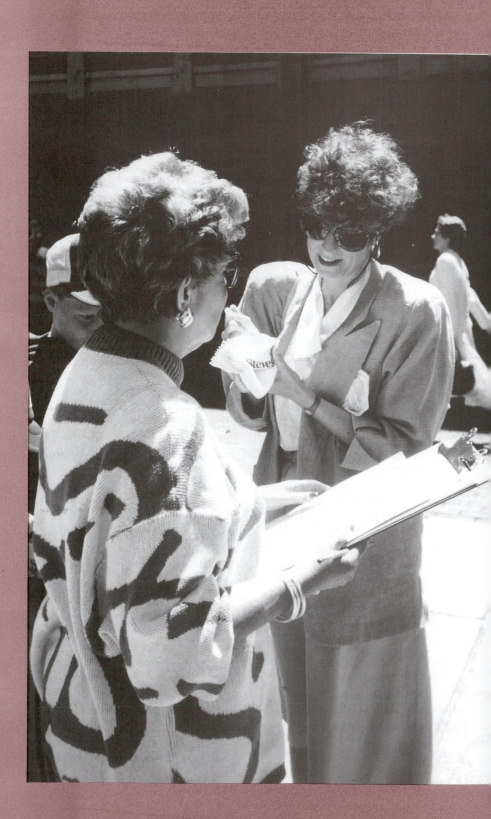

It ain't so much
the things we
don't know that
get us in
trouble. It's the
things we know
that ain't so.

Artemus Ward

CHAPTER 2

SOCIOLOGICAL RESEARCH

When Galileo (1564–1642) was a very young and very irreverent professor of mathematics at the University of Pisa, he shocked his dignified colleagues with a famous experiment. For nearly 2,000 years, mathematicians had never questioned Aristotle's statement that an object weighing ten pounds would fall a given distance ten times as fast as an object weighing one pound. To show they were wrong, Galileo climbed to the top story of the Leaning Tower with two cannonballs, one weighing ten pounds and the other weighing one pound. As his fellow professors and their students were crossing the campus to their lecture halls, he dropped the two balls from the tower. They landed almost simultaneously, but the scholars were not convinced; they insisted their eyes had deceived them because Aristotle could not be wrong.

According to this legend, the Leaning Tower of Pisa experiment was a practical demonstration of Galileo's law of falling bodies, which states that, in a vacuum, all objects fall at the same rate. Until that moment no one had ever bothered to find out if what Aristotle said was true, including Aristotle. The very idea of disputing the wisdom of the ancients was practically unheard of in the sixteenth century, and Galileo's discoveries were bitterly rejected by the university. It was not the last time that Galileo was to get into trouble for challenging authority. At the end of his life, the judges of the Inquisition forced him to retract the "absurd, philosophically false, and . . . heretical" proposition that the earth moves around the sun.[1]

---

[1] Bertrand Russell, *The Scientific Outlook* (1931) (New York: Norton, 1962), pp. 20–25.

Most people do not submit their beliefs to the test of science. The Biblical story of the Garden of Eden is widely accepted as true. Advertising claims are sometimes believed because they appear to be based on a reliable authority.

Modern science has traditionally traced its origins to Galileo's experiments, which were an early use of the scientific method of inquiry. Simply put, the **scientific method** consists of (1) observing significant facts and (2) finding the general laws that govern those facts. In his experiments on falling objects, Galileo was not only trying to find out whether particular weights fell at the same rate, he was also trying to test a general truth about all falling objects. Until the seventeenth century, human knowledge was largely unscientific in this sense: much of it was based upon authoritative sources (like Aristotle or the Catholic church) or upon myths (the story of creation, the legends of the Greek gods). Even now, in societies supposedly dominated by a rational and scientific outlook, most people do not bother to test and verify most of the opinions they hold. Many beliefs are still based upon authority (the Bible, the Constitution, the Communist Manifesto) and popular myths (the myth of female inferiority, the myth that hard work inevitably brings success). One of the great intellectual revolutions of history, the rise of modern science, rested squarely upon a new willingness to submit such beliefs to the test of fact.

As a science sociology has essentially the same aim as Galileo: to discover and verify generalizations about the world, especially the human beings who live in it. In analyzing the statistics on suicide, for example, Durkheim was not solely interested in finding out why Protestants took their own lives more often than Catholics (see Chapter 1). He wanted to use this knowledge to develop a general understanding of suicide that would apply to everyone. He was also trying to generalize from a specific behavior, suicide, to the nature of human societies. Although social scientists have discovered

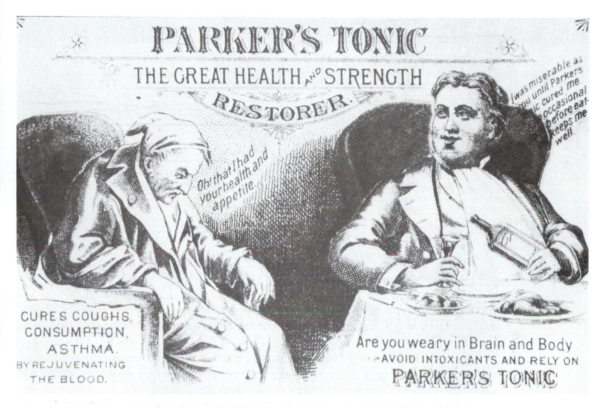

few, if any, reliable laws of human behavior, the spirit of all scientific inquiry is the same. As Robert Nisbet put it,

> The fundamental objectives of sociology are the same as those of science generally — discovery and explanation. To *discover* the essential data of social behavior and the connections among the data is the first objective of sociology. To *explain* the data and the connections is the second and larger objective. Science makes its advances in terms of both of these objectives.[2]

This chapter discusses how sociologists go about discovering and explaining the patterns of human behavior. The first part describes science as a special kind of inquiry into the facts of human life. The next section shows how these facts are collected and how they lead to explanations, or theories of social behavior. After considering some of the ethical problems involved in studying people, the chapter closes with an assessment of the value of sociological research.

THE SPIRIT OF SCIENCE

Science may be broadly defined as a system of rational inquiry disciplined by empirical test. **Empirical facts** are observed through the senses: only the phenomena we can

---

[2] Robert A. Nisbet, *The Social Bond* (New York: Knopf, 1970), p. 5.

TRUE OR FALSE?

Using only your personal experience and common sense as a guide, mark the following "obvious" statements true or false:

1. You can't change human nature.

2. Money can't buy happiness.

3. Most working women don't really have to work.

4. Love is blind.

5. The amount of money a community spends on its schools strongly affects its students' achievements.

6. The stress of modern city life is psychologically unhealthy.

7. The leaders of revolutionary movements usually come from the lower classes.

8. Revolutions are less likely to occur during periods of economic growth and social progress.

9. Blue-collar (manual) workers are more likely to dislike their jobs than white-collar (office) workers.

10. The population explosion is caused by high birth rates in the developing countries.

For answers see p. 40

see, hear, smell, taste, or touch are considered scientific evidence. Scientific knowledge, in other words, ultimately depends on the facts revealed through observation and experiment.

Most of what we know about society is distinctly non-scientific: our understanding of social life is largely a result of our own observations and common sense, not scientific research. This knowledge is acquired through ordinary personal experience, and it is, on the whole, accurate and reliable. In some cases, however, the "obvious" is not a dependable guide to the truth. Some widely held beliefs turn out to be untrue, and some social facts just don't make common sense (see "True or False"). Knowledge based only on personal observation, moreover, is seldom accompanied by explanations of why things are as they appear to be. The desire for explanations, whether in physics, economics, or sociology, lies at the heart of the scientific enterprise.[3]

Sociology is thus primarily an attempt to understand the intricacies of human behavior. This understanding is often what the sociologist Peter Berger called "an act of pure perception,"[4] and it links sociology to history, philosophy, and the other humanistic disciplines. Max Weber's *The Protestant Ethic and the Spirit of Capitalism* (1905), one of the most famous of all sociological works, was based on just such a perception: that the Protestant Reformation had provided cultural conditions which promoted the growth of the capitalist economy.

Like other social sciences, sociology also depends on the basic architecture of the scientific method. The division between its twin goals of discovery and explanation — between the quantitative and qualitative aspects of the field — has sparked a good deal of debate (see "Defining the Discipline"). Most sociologists agree, however, that the

---

[3] T. S. Kuhn, *The Structure of Scientific Revolutions*, 2d rev. ed. enl. (Chicago: University of Chicago Press, 1970); Karl Popper, *Objective Knowledge* (New York: Oxford University Press, 1972), especially Chapter 2; Norman W. Storer, *The Social System of Science* (New York: Holt, Rinehart & Winston, 1966).
[4] Peter L. Berger, *Invitation to Sociology: A Humanistic Perspective* (Garden City, N.Y.: Doubleday/Anchor, 1963), p. 5.

thrust of their discipline remains theoretical and interpretive. Statistical data are not properly called "sociology," for example. Émile Durkheim's careful compilation of suicide rates was not "sociological" until he made them part of a theory about the effect of social structure on behavior — in other words, until discovery led to explanation.

"The fascination of sociology," Berger once wrote,

> lies in the fact that its perspective makes us see in a new light the very world in which we have lived all our lives. . . . As a result, there is a deceptive simplicity and obvious- ness about some sociological investigations . . .— until one is suddenly brought up against an insight that radically questions everything one had previously assumed about this familiar scene. This is the point at which one begins to sense the excitement of sociology.[5]

For an example of how sociologists go about their work, let us take a scientific study of a growing social problem — the urban homeless.

THE CHICAGO HOMELESS STUDY: AN EXAMPLE OF SOCIOLOGICAL RESEARCH

During the 1980s, hundreds of ragged derelicts and "bag ladies" appeared in the streets of virtually every American city. When this homeless population began to overwhelm the public shelters, more and more began to sleep in doorways, on park benches, in bus and train stations, or in makeshift shelters in empty parking lots. On winter nights some of them froze to death.

Despite rising public concern for their plight, very little was actually known about the homeless. There was no reliable information about who they were, why they were homeless, or even how many of them there were. Answers to these questions had to be found before any effective policy for relieving the misery of the homeless could be implemented.

Two sociologists, Peter H. Rossi and James D. Wright, decided to tackle the prob- lem by studying the urban homeless. First they reviewed the existing literature to see what others knew — or thought they knew — about the causes of homelessness. Sociol- ogists, editorial writers, and politicians had offered several explanations. According to one theory, most of the new homeless were former mental hospital patients who had been released into the community as a result of improved drugs and outpatient treat- ments. Another cause of homelessness was said to be the Reagan administration's cuts in social welfare benefits, which had caused the average family income for the poorest fifth of the population to decline by 6 percent between 1979 and 1987.[6] Others blamed the national low-income housing shortage, which had affected the inner city in particu- lar. Not only had no new government-subsidized housing projects been built during the 1980s, but arson, urban renewal, and gentrification had removed many low-cost dwellings from the market.

Wright himself believed that the new homelessness resulted from a combination of more poor families on the one hand and fewer low-cost housing units on the other.

---

[5] Ibid., pp. 21–22.

[6] House Ways and Means Committee, "Background Material and Data on Programs Within the Jurisdiction of the Committee on Ways and Means" (Washington, D.C.: U.S. Government Printing Office, 1989).

DEFINING THE DISCIPLINE

Is sociology a discipline of statisticians and poll-takers or of scholars and intellectuals? To use its own terms, is it quantitative or qualitative? **The New York Times** *asked several sociologists to discuss their discipline and where it is — or should be — going. Here are some of their answers.*

Sociology came on the field somewhat later than economics and psychology, and it has a problem legitimizing itself as a science. There still is a very, very strong impulse to present itself as a legitimate science, encouraged by many of the research agencies that fund us, particularly the National Science Foundation, but others as well. So that impulse toward being a science is rewarded by those who, in many respects, are responsible for our sustenance.

But there's still a large portion of the field that is basically sympathetic to human problems and human suffering, and in that sense it is more humanistic in character. There are sociologists who are committed to a more human understanding of a subject than you can get by experimentation or the application of standardized survey questions. You get a more qualitative understanding of the human condition by doing field work and participant observation, getting in and mixing with people and understanding their situations, which the more scientific mode obviously does not do.

■ ■ ■

Rather than talk about the divisions, I would talk about the diversity and catholicity of sociology. There's a general understanding that there are a variety of research styles, a variety of kinds of topics to be pursued, and that in most departments and the profession as a whole these are regarded as valuable. There has to be a representation and diversity of approaches, just from the standpoint of

the discipline's intellectual health and quality of research as well as the capacity to train and direct graduate students. If you look at practically any other social science, you will find them as internally divided as you find us. Economics has experienced it, political science, history, and in the life sciences I'm sure you find competition among approaches. That's healthy.

Neil Smelser
University Professor of Sociology,
University of California at Berkeley

Sociology tends to be divided among the interpretive sociologists, who are interested in exploring general laws of society; the positivists, who do largely quantitative work, and the neo-Marxists, who are beginning to fade because they can find no basis for their theories. But there's a wide variety of work going on in the field that cuts across lines, all sorts of reportage about all sorts of things.

■ ■ ■

I believe that a return to interpretation is going on — in other fields as well as in sociology. People get disappointed with what you can do with numbers. They are showing more interest in looking at the meaning of things.

Daniel Bell
Henry Ford 2d Professor of Social Sciences,
Harvard University

The mainstream of sociology is empirical and quantitative. And I would guess about 85 percent of sociologists are of that persuasion. But that doesn't mean they have no use for theoretical issues. The divisions aren't all that clear, and they've existed

During the early 1980s, the time finally came when there were more poor people than housing for them.[7]

To go beyond these speculations and "get the facts," Rossi and Wright conducted a survey of the homeless in a typical large city, Chicago.[8] They searched out both the

---

[7] James D. Wright and Julie A. Lam, "Homelessness and the Low-Income Housing Supply," *Social Policy* 17 (Spring 1987), pp. 48–53.

[8] P. H. Rossi, J. D. Wright, G. A. Fisher, and G. Willis, "The Urban Homeless: Estimating Composition and Size," *Science* 235 (March 13, 1987): 1336–41.

ever since I've been a sociologist, for about 50 years.

The big movement in the last 15 years or so has been the rise of "complex multivariate" styles of research. All it means is that there are many variables that help to explain social behavior, and that they must be taken into account. And to take them into account requires big samples, large data bases.

Say that you're trying to develop a social policy for increasing equality of educational opportunity. Well, you have to know why some people receive less education than others. So you have to investigate such things as an individual's social origins, the occupation and education of his or her family, how rich or poor they were. You'd want to know what effect race and sex have on educational opportunity. How much does intelligence matter?

To put all these factors together you need statistical techniques that tell you which make the most difference and which handicaps are amenable to policy changes. Then the policy-makers can target their programs.

■ ■ ■

We've always had that style of research, but with the coming of large-scale computers and large sample surveys, it's been possible to do many more of those kinds of studies. And as our younger scholars have learned those techniques, it has taken away from the more purely theoretical kinds of operations.

William H. Sewell
Vilas Professor of Sociology Emeritus,
University of Wisconsin

I think it is incorrect to say that there is a division in sociology at this point. It is true that mainstream journals tend to include more quantitative than nonquantitative articles, but all the leading journals welcome nonquantitative articles, too, because they tend to be more widely read and discussed.

There are different styles of research. Some sociologists are largely quantitative. Some focus on substantive materials but interpret the data with quantitative techniques. Some use qualitative techniques like historical research. Some are not involved in actual data collection but write interpretative essays on broad, theoretical arguments.

■ ■ ■

If there is a problem in sociology, it is not the so-called split between quantitative and nonquantitative but the fact that there are no leading schools of thought that excite both the quantitative and the nonquantitative sociologist. I get the impression that sociology is not unique in this regard.

I feel we desperately need intellectual leadership. We need highly imaginative and original scholars regardless of their styles of research, scholars who are likely to raise new questions, creatively challenge existing interpretations and stimulate research.

And I think that departments whose decisions are organized around this view will more likely become, or remain, leaders of disciplines than those who squabble over styles of research.

William Julius Wilson
Chairman of the Sociology Department,
University of Chicago

SOURCE: *The New York Times Week in Review*, April 28, 1985, p. E7.

residents of emergency shelters and the people who were sleeping in alleys, hallways, roofs, and basements, abandoned buildings, and parked cars. Interviewers (accompanied by off-duty policemen) made their street surveys between midnight and 6 a.m., waking up their subjects, if necessary. All in all, over 700 homeless people were questioned about their income, employment, former places of residence, and personal histories.

As expected, these homeless men and women were very different in some respects from the general adult population of Chicago. They were predominantly male (76 percent vs. 46 percent in the general population), and disproportionately black and

ANSWERS TO TRUE OR FALSE:

1. False. Much of the behavior we call "human nature" is learned from others, and can therefore be changed (see Chapter 3).

2. False. A 1977 study reported that 46 percent of people with incomes over $20,000 said they were "very happy," compared to only 29 percent of people whose income was below $10,000 (see Chapter 7).

3. False. The majority of working women are either single women who have to support themselves or women whose husbands earn too little to support their families (see Chapter 10).

4. False. Although Cupid's arrow is supposed to strike at random, most marriages take place between people of the same age, race, religion, and social class (see Chapter 11).

5. False. A famous research report concluded that the amount of money spent on schools has little effect on achievement scores. Family background has a far greater effect on how well students do in school (see Chapter 13).

6. False. Urban living does not appear to have any effect on mental health (see Chapter 14).

7. False. It is a curious fact that revolutionary movements are often led by members of classes with the most to lose from social change. Two-thirds of the founders of the Chinese Communist party, for example, came from the landlord-gentry class (see Chapter 17).

8. False. Revolutions are most likely to occur when social conditions are generally improving (see Chapter 18).

9. True. When asked whether they would choose the same kind of work if they could start over again, 43 percent of white-collar workers, but only 24 percent of blue-collar workers, said they would (see Chapter 19).

10. False. The world's population has grown because of a drop in the death rate, not a rise in the birth rate. While birth rates are actually declining, population momentum and longer life expectancies are causing population growth (see Chapter 20).

native American (as opposed to white and Hispanic). But the most striking characteristics of the homeless were their extreme poverty and the extent of their disabilities.

According to Rossi and Wright, the homeless they studied subsisted on an average monthly income of $168. Housing for them was virtually unavailable, since the cheapest single rooms in Chicago at the time had an average monthly rent of $195. Rather surprisingly, almost two out of five people surveyed had worked during the previous month, mainly at poorly paid part-time jobs. Even more of a surprise was the finding that only a quarter of the homeless received any welfare payments at all, and only about one-fifth received pension or disability benefits.

The homeless were found to suffer from severe disabilities that made ordinary social life impossible. One in four said they were physically unable to work, and one in three were drug addicts or alcoholics. More than four out of five (82 percent) of the homeless were disabled by poor health, mental illness, or alcohol or drug abuse. Furthermore, most of the homeless were unwilling or unable to rely on friends or relatives for help. Very few of the women surveyed wanted to return to their families; many of the men would have liked to live with relatives but felt they were unwelcome. This rejection of the homeless is possibly related to recent social trends that have loosened family ties and created new economic roles for women, the traditional care-

Like other social problems, homelessness has complex social causes. These men are members of a homeless population that is characterized by extreme poverty, severe disabilities, and lack of social ties to friends and family.

takers for the family's weaker members. (See Chapter 11, "The Family," and Chapter 10, "The Sexes.")

Noting that very few (only 3 percent) of the Chicago poor are without housing, Rossi and Wright concluded that the most important causes of homelessness are: the extreme poverty of the homeless, which, in the 1980s, was accentuated by reduced welfare benefits; severe disability, largely due to alcoholism, drug use, or mental illness; and the absence of social ties to family and friends.

Like most social scientists, Rossi and Wright were not trying to find a single cause of the problem, but to identify the most important reasons for it. Their research indicates that homelessness, like other social problems to which it is related (poverty, unemployment), results from the interplay of individual character and complex political, social, and economic processes.

DISCOVERING THE FACTS

The first aim of sociologists is to "get the facts." When told that "more people are homeless than ever before," the sociologist asks, "Is it really so? And if so, why?" To answer these questions, researchers use special procedures which make sociology, like all science, a systematic pursuit of factual knowledge.

DEFINING THE QUESTION.   The first step in a scientific study is a clearly formulated idea of what is to be investigated. Most often it is a **causal relationship**, which is an association between events, behaviors, persons, or things in which one leads to the occurrence of another. As we saw in Chapter 1, Durkheim was able to pinpoint a causal relationship between the rate of suicide and certain social variables. The term **variable** refers to any measurable characteristic or property that is subject to change. Age and income are variables because they vary from one person to the next. Some characteristics are called *constants* because they do not vary. For residents of California, "state of residence" is a constant which does not vary from one person to the next. Research deals with variables, but takes constants into account. In testing the relationship between homelessness and poverty, a scientist might design a research study in which poverty is the **independent variable** and homelessness is the **dependent variable**. That is, poverty would be taken as a given, as the starting point in the relationship, as a cause of homelessness. As the dependent variable, homelessness would be the outcome, the effect of poverty. Clearly, few social processes or events are that simple, and there are usually several independent variables involved. Rossi and Wright discovered that drug and alcohol abuse, mental illness, and social isolation are also causes of homelessness. Scientists try to measure as precisely as possible the influence of each variable in a relationship.

A **correlation** is a measure of the empirical relationship of two or more variables. If variable A and variable B tend to go together, as extreme poverty and homelessness do, they are said to have a positive correlation. If a rise in one variable is accompanied by a decrease in the other, the correlation is negative. The closer to $+1.0$ (a positive correlation) or -1.0 (a negative correlation), the stronger the relationship between variables. Researchers generally interpret weak correlations ($+.10$ to $-.10$) to mean that the variables have no significant relationship.

Positive correlations, however, should never be taken as proof of cause and effect. A study done in the coastal towns of the Federal Republic of Germany (West Germany), for example, uncovered a significant positive correlation between the number of storks and the number of babies born over a 20-year period.[9] Before jumping to the obvious conclusion, a conscientious researcher will look for other variables in the relationship. It turns out that the size of the local harvest affected the size of the frog population, which in turn affected the number of storks nesting in the neighborhood. Since the people in these German towns tended to have more babies in prosperous times when the harvest was abundant, the cause-and-effect relationship between variable A (number of storks) and variable B (number of babies) breaks down completely when variable C (size of harvest) is introduced. Sociologists have to be aware of such pitfalls, especially when the results of their research appear to make "common sense."

Human behavior is so complex that it is always difficult to pinpoint cause and effect precisely. We know, for example, that two out of three high school students who smoke cigarettes regularly also smoke marijuana regularly.[10] In contrast, only one in 10 high school students who have never smoked cigarettes regularly are marijuana users. We also know that most of the students began smoking cigarettes *before* they smoked marijuana. Can we conclude that smoking cigarettes leads to (causes) marijuana use? Only if three conditions are met:

[9] Morton Hunt, *Profiles of Social Research: The Scientific Study of Human Interactions.* New York: Russell Sage Foundation, 1985.

[10] National Institute on Drug Abuse, "National Trends in Drug Use and Related Factors Among High School Students and Young Adults: 1975–1986." Washington, D.C.: U. S. Department of Health and Human Services (Publication No. ADM 87-1535), 1987.

1. If one factor (variable A) is causing some event (variable B), the two must be empirically related (correlated). If A is present, the probability that B is also present is greater than the probability that B is present when A is absent. In this case, the probability that students who use marijuana regularly is 66 percent if they are cigarette smokers, but only 10 percent if they aren't. Since this difference is significant — or unlikely to be due to chance — smoking cigarettes and smoking marijuana are correlated.

2. The suspected cause must precede the effect: A must come before B. Since the students report that they smoked cigarettes before they smoked marijuana, this condition is met.

3. The correlation between A and B must not be the result of some third factor (variable C again!) As in the case of babies and storks, something else entirely may be causing both cigarette smoking and marijuana use. Smoking cigarettes might be an emotional response to the distress caused by divorce or other family problems among younger students, while smoking marijuana might be a response to the same problems among older students. Or the students might belong to groups that encourage smoking cigarettes in junior high school and smoking marijuana in high school. Researchers can sometimes rule out such variables in further studies. For example, students from intact families could be compared with students with divorced parents to see if the cigarette-marijuana correlation held for both. Because some relevant information is always unavailable or even unknowable, social scientists are usually cautious about claiming cause-and-effect relationships.

THE HYPOTHESIS.   The second stage in scientific work is the formation and testing of hypotheses. A **hypothesis** is a hunch about a possible or probable relationship existing between variables. The original proposition is usually "refined," or stated in concrete terms. For example, the relationship between poverty and homelessness would be elaborated in more detail. A researcher might argue that poverty causes homelessness only when the poor do not get help from friends or relatives. This raises the question of why the homeless are not taken in by their families. The data collected in the Chicago homeless study provided one answer: most of the homeless have never been married and are so disabled (by mental illness, alcohol or drug abuse, physical ailments) that they are unable to maintain relationships with other people.

THE POPULATION.   An important aspect of scientific research is the **population**, or group of people being studied. In the Chicago study the "homeless" were defined as clients in shelters for the homeless as well as people who were found sleeping outdoors at night. Other populations used in the research cited in this chapter are high school students, black and white schoolchildren, readers of the *Literary Digest,* voters in the 1936 presidential election, the staff and patients in a mental hospital, Stanford University students, and workers in a Western Electric plant.

Practically, researchers cannot interview or observe all poor people or all college students, so they must draw a sample from the population under investigation. A **sample** is a portion of a particular population (poor people in towns of a certain size, college students registered in sociology classes at major universities). Most sociological and social scientific research deals with samples rather than total populations. A sample in which everyone in the population has an equal chance of being picked is known as a **simple random sample**, from which it is possible to make generalizations about the population as a whole. If the population of interest is "working people," every working person must have an equal chance of being selected. A random sample is *not* a haphazard one. In the Chicago homeless study, for example, virtually every homeless person had the same chance of being studied. Interviewing the homeless between midnight and 6 a.m. was designed to exclude a very small number of homeless individuals.

EXPLAINING THE FACTS

Collecting and organizing information about social or physical phenomena help us to develop concepts. **Concepts** are ideas that enable us to organize and interpret our experiences. They refer to what is common in a phenomenon — what special attributes single out a group or a social behavior, for example. When sociologists or other theorists "conceptualize," they are specifying more narrowly what they mean. In the case of "poverty" all of us have some notion of what it is, but if we wish to communicate at all on the subject, we must narrow the definition and use it consistently to organize observations and analysis of data. The United States government defines poverty as an annual income below the official poverty line, which in 1987 was $11,611 for a family of four. By agreeing on this concept of poverty, government statisticians can begin to answer such questions as, How many Americans are poor? Is the rate of poverty rising? Where do most poor people live? Which groups have the highest rates of poverty?

Gathering data and reasoning about it culminates in the formation of a theory. A **theory** is a general statement that explains the relationship among facts. Some theories about the relationship of poverty to the homeless are discussed in Chapter 8, "Deviance and Social Control." Robert K. Merton's theory of anomie and opportunity structures, for example, states that American society gives members of the lower class less hope than other people for achieving success in legitimate ways. Not only are the poor unable to enjoy the material comforts and self-esteem that come from a substantial income, but they are also likely to be blamed for being "lazy" or "stupid." When success of any kind seems impossible, some people give up the struggle entirely. Many of the homeless are social "dropouts" who are classified in this category. Merton's theory has stimulated new hypotheses and research strategies by offering us a fresh look at a piece of social reality we thought we had fully understood.

BASIC RESEARCH PROCEDURES

"Doing sociology" means applying scientific methods to the study of society. Like all scientific researchers, sociologists follow certain step-by-step procedures.

1. *Selecting a topic.* Since curiosity is the motivating force in most research, a scientific study typically begins with a question. The previously mentioned survey of student drug use, for example, provided an answer to the question, Is smoking marijuana related to smoking cigarettes?

2. *Reviewing the literature.* A second step in a scientific study is to find out whether the researcher's question has been asked or answered before. Many libraries now

"Good evening, Mr. Belknap. As you may know, there are three women to every man in New York. Here are your other two."

Drawing by Lorenz; © 1983 The New Yorker Magazine, Inc.

have computerized systems for retrieving the titles of every book and article published on specific subjects. Assembling the available information on the topic enables the researcher to focus attention on questions that have not yet been adequately answered or perhaps even asked before.

3. *Defining terms.* Concepts relevant to the study — such as poverty or homelessness — are defined in operational terms, or in terms that can be measured. The Chicago study distinguished between the literal homeless, who had no conventional dwelling, and the marginally housed, who had temporary, marginally adequate housing. Only the former were studied.

4. *Forming a hypothesis.* A next step is to develop testable hypotheses about the relationship among different variables. The group of researchers who designed the drug use survey hypothesized that there was a relationship between drug use and such variables as year in school, academic performance, use of alcohol, and smoking cigarettes.

5. *Choosing a research method.* The following section, "Methods of Research," describes the methods that sociologists use to test their hypotheses. The researchers who designed the study of drug use, for instance, used the survey method. They distributed questionnaires to thousands of students and recent high school graduates. The sample was selected at random from American public high schools. Since the high schools were chosen to ensure that each region of the country was represented in proportion to its population, the survey was based on a **stratified sample** of all public high school students.

6. *Collecting the data.* After a method has been chosen, the next step is to put it into operation. Sociologists make on-the-spot observations, conduct face-to-face and

telephone interviews, design experiments, and analyze various kinds of documentary evidence.

Since these methods of data collection are often very expensive, researchers often rely on *secondary data,* or data that has already been collected. Large national surveys taken by public agencies (Census Bureau, Department of Labor) or private polling organizations (the National Opinion Research Center) provide reliable information at minimal cost.

7. *Interpreting the data.* Finding the facts is not always easy. The results of a research project can confirm a hypothesis, but they can also falsify it, or they can do a little of both. As the following example shows, the most interesting results are sometimes those the researcher never expected to find.

   In 1964, the sociologist James Coleman was put in charge of a massive government study of the American school system.[11] After ten years of desegregation efforts, many black children were still in predominantly black schools, and black children still tended to have lower scores on achievement tests than white children. The sponsors of the project expected to find huge disparities between the physical facilities and educational resources of predominantly black and predominantly white schools, and they were prepared to use these inequalities to argue for more federal aid to education. After the data were collected, Coleman and everyone else was surprised to discover that there was generally little difference between the quality of education offered by predominantly white and predominantly black schools. Even more astonishing, perhaps, was the finding that the gap between black and white achievement scores which appeared at an early age became larger the longer the children were in school. Coleman was forced to reject his original hypothesis that the amount of money a community spent on schooling had a major effect on students' achievement. He concluded instead that family background was a far more important factor in determining how well students — black or white — do in school. (For a more detailed discussion of educational differences, see Chapter 13, "Education.")

8. *Publishing the findings.* The final research procedure is to make the findings public so that new information is available to others. For example, the results of Coleman's study of the schools was published by the Office of Education under the title *Equality of Educational Opportunity.* Sociologists report both their methods and their findings so that their research may be criticized and evaluated. Other sociologists might draw different conclusions from the same data, or they might get different results from repeating the study with other subjects.

METHODS OF RESEARCH

Sociologists use five basic research methods. These are surveys, interviews and case histories, observation, experiments, and analysis of historical documents. The choice of

---

[11] James S. Coleman et al., *Equality of Educational Opportunity,* Report of the Office of Education to the Congress and the President (Washington, D.C.: U.S. Government Printing Office, 1966).

method depends on many factors: the nature of the problem, the restrictions of time and space, the degree of cooperation from the people being studied, the resources available, and considerations of privacy and the rights of the subjects.

SURVEYS

A **survey** is a poll of a sample of people whose responses are likely to be representative of the opinions, attitudes, and values of the population under study. This is sometimes accomplished by using a random sample. If researchers want to know how the residents of a small town feel about a new highway, they might take every twentieth name from a city directory for the sample. In contrast, a stratified sample would include a representative number of townspeople of various "types"—males and females, whites and blacks, working- and middle-class, Catholics, Jews, and Protestants, college-educated and those with high school or grade school education, and the like. Like a random sample, a stratified sample can be **extrapolated**—that is, the researcher can estimate the opinions and values of larger groups using known data about a sample.

   Since it is not possible to question an entire population on a number of questions and issues, survey researchers attempt to construct a representative sample, or group of respondents who represent a cross section of the population at large. A common source of error in survey research is to assume that the larger the sample the more

In the presidential election of 1948, the Chicago Daily Tribune printed this premature headline on the basis of early opinion polls. Improved sampling methods have made political polling far more accurate; the predicted results of elections usually deviate less than 2 percent from the actual outcomes.

representative it is likely to be. As the following story indicates, large samples are not necessarily more representative than smaller ones.

During the presidential campaign of 1936, the *Literary Digest,* a mass circulation magazine of the period, conducted a political poll in which 2 million readers indicated how they intended to vote. The magazine reported that Alf Landon would win in a landslide. At the same time, George Gallup, who was then an unknown young pollster, predicted President Franklin Roosevelt's reelection from a sample of just over 300,000. With such a large sample, how could the *Literary Digest* have been so wrong?

The answer is that Gallup had drawn a stratified sample of the voters in the 1936 election, and the *Literary Digest* had not. The *Digest* took its sample from its own subscribers and from people who had home telephones, a majority of whom at that time were middle- and upper-class voters inclined to support Landon and the Republican party. Gallup was less concerned with how many *people* answered his questions about the coming election than about how many different *kinds* of people responded. Gallup made certain that he sampled opinions from the right proportions of the well-off, the poor, the employed, the unemployed, city dwellers, and farmers. Since the adoption of modern statistical methods, predictions based on political polls have usually deviated less than 2 percent from the actual outcomes of elections.[12]

Today surveys are widely used outside of social scientific research. Politicians, according to many observers, could not begin to develop campaigns without them; TV shows live or die depending upon their "ratings," which are based on sample surveys of the viewing audience. Advertising firms use surveys (called "marketing research" in the trade) to determine what products and what types of packaging appeal to consumers. In yet another use of survey research techniques, public officials constantly refer to survey data (the population census) to decide where public facilities such as schools, roads, libraries, and parks should be located.

THE USES AND LIMITATIONS OF SURVEYS.   Survey results are especially useful because they can be quantified, or translated into numerical data. The questions are standardized: all respondents are asked the same questions, and in most questionnaires they are given the same choice of answers. These techniques enable the researcher to make fairly precise measurements and comparisons among respondents.

A survey is the best method to use in research work (1) when other methods such as observation are neither suitable nor possible as, for example, in a study of American attitudes toward divorce; or (2) when researchers wish to learn the frequency of a particular behavior — for instance, the number of people who attend church regularly. Survey questionnaires, however, have some drawbacks. One problem is their high cost. Almost any effective sampling method requires the researcher to question people in many different locations, whether across town or across the country. When the cost of time and travel are added to the expenses involved in selecting a sample and training interviewers, an accurate survey may cost several hundred dollars for each respondent. For this reason researchers resort more and more to telephone interviews or mailed, self-administered surveys.[13]

[12] *Gallup Poll: Public Opinion,* vol. 2, 1972–1977, ed. George H. Gallup (Wilmington, Del.: Scholarly Resources, 1978).

[13] Seymore Sudman and Norman M. Bradburn, *Asking Questions* (San Francisco: Jossey-Bass, 1983).

Another problem with the survey method is the attitude of the respondents. Many people are not disposed to discuss their lives with strangers, others are reluctant to answer even when the questionnaire is anonymous, and still others may make responses that are not entirely truthful.

INTERVIEWS AND CASE HISTORIES

An **interview** is a guided conversation between the investigator and the research subject or subjects. Like surveys, interviews are based on particular sets of questions but the procedures are more flexible. For one thing, if a respondent does not understand a question, an interviewer may restate it or explain it in more familiar language. In research of this sort, the skill of the interviewer is often the key factor in success or failure. Interviewers, however, can have unintended effects on their respondents. Subjects may answer in ways they think will please the interviewer rather than reveal their real attitudes and opinions.

Case histories, or biographies of individuals, give the investigator an opportunity to study closely the behaviors, feelings, and minds of particular individuals. Of course, relying exclusively on individual life histories to indicate the views of a group is scientifically questionable. Nevertheless, skillful researchers have achieved some remarkable results using a combination of in-depth interviews and case histories. Thomas Cottle, for example, has made some extraordinarily perceptive investigations of adolescents. By winning the confidence of his subjects, he was able to find out that

The chances are that this mugging will never be reported to the police. One survey found that most people who have been victimized do not notify the authorities either because they do not believe the crime was serious enough or because they do not believe the police can do anything about it.

Face-to-face interviews are one method of collecting data for sociological research.

some were suffering from the burden of keeping family secrets — the sexual irregularities of a mother or father, for example, or a relative's criminal record, or some other shameful secret.[14] Similarly, Jean Evans followed the lives of three deeply troubled men in great detail. Her account provided a record of her subjects' social environment, how they negotiated it, coped with it, or succumbed to it.[15] Both studies suggest that the problems their subjects experienced were not unique but occurred frequently in the society as a whole. Perhaps the most important contribution of such case histories is that they humanize sociology by putting its tools to use in studying one or two individuals carefully.

The difficulties of studying people pervade all social research. At any point during an investigation, individuals may decide that they no longer wish to endure the scrutiny of the researcher, that they want the sociologist, in short, to "get lost." Sabotaging research is also fairly easy; many people do not bother to answer questionnaires; others misrepresent their feelings and opinions or act out of character to "please" the interviewer. Sociologists are usually satisfied when they obtain a response rate of 60 or 65 percent to their questionnaires. Even then, the inevitable question arises: Are those who cooperate answering truthfully and reliably?

Sociologists have devised numerous methods to cope with this dilemma. Proper research designs, reliable measuring procedures, and **replication** (repeating the same

---

[14] Thomas Cottle, *Children's Secrets* (Garden City, N.Y.: Doubleday, 1980).
[15] Jean Evans, *Three Men* (New York: Knopf, 1954).

THE RESEARCHER AS PART OF THE RESEARCH

Elliot Liebow's study of streetcorner men is a classic example of participant observation, since the writer was actively involved with those he was studying. The following passage illustrates Liebow's participation and analysis.

In many instances, it is precisely the streetcorner man's orientation to the future—but to a future loaded with "trouble"—which not only leads to a greater emphasis on present concerns ("I want mine right now") but also contributes importantly to the instability of employment, family and friend relationships, and to the general transient quality of daily life.

Let me give some concrete examples. One day, after Tally had gotten paid, he gave me four twenty-dollar bills and asked me to keep them for him. Three days later he asked me for the money. I returned it and asked why he did not put his money in a bank. He said that the banks close at two o'clock. I argued that there were four or more banks within a two-block radius of where he was working at the time and that he could easily get to any of them on his lunch hour. "No, man," he said, "you don't understand. They close at two o'clock and they closed Saturday and Sunday. Suppose I get into trouble and I got to make it [leave]. Me get out of town, and everything I got in the world layin' up in that bank? No good! No good!"

In another instance, Leroy and his girl friend were discussing "trouble." Leroy was trying to decide how best to go about getting his hands on some "long green" (a lot of money), and his girl friend cautioned him about "trouble." Leroy sneered at this, saying he had had "trouble" all his life and wasn't afraid of a little more. Anyway," he said, "I'm famous for leaving town."

Thus, the constant awareness of a future loaded with "trouble" results in a constant readiness to leave, to "make it," to "get out of town," and discourages the man from sinking roots into the world he lives in. Just as it discourages him from putting money in the bank, so it discourages him from committing himself to a job, especially one whose payoff lies in the promise of future rewards rather than in the present. In the same way, it discourages him from deep and lasting commitments to family and friends or to any other persons, places or things, since such commitments could hold him hostage, limiting his freedom of movement and thereby compromising his security which lies in that freedom.

SOURCE: Elliot Liebow, *Tally's Corner: A Study of Negro Streetcorner Men* (Boston: Little, Brown, 1967), pp. 68–71.

study with different researchers and different subjects) are techniques that minimize errors of the types just mentioned. But even these provide no absolute guarantee against error and distortion. As a result, researchers tend to use multiple methods in their work, where possible, in order to *cross-validate* their findings—that is, in order to check the consistency and reliability of their data.

Despite the limitations of survey and interview techniques, resourceful and imaginative researchers have produced some striking results using them. Alfred Kinsey and his associates, sex research pioneers, used a mixture of these methods to study American male and female sexual behaviors and values. The Kinsey reports are still admired today, many years after their appearance, for having unearthed significant truths, although some of the findings have been questioned.[16]

OBSERVATION

Observation is one of the cornerstones of scientific research. Field studies are based on the researcher's own observations of social behavior in its natural setting. Field work is

---

[16] Alfred C. Kinsey, Wardell B. Pomeroy, and Clyde E. Martin, *Sexual Behavior in the Human Male* (Philadelphia: Saunders, 1948).

obviously the best method for studying certain kinds of behavior—the interaction between police officers and the suspects they arrest,[17] for example, or the actions of "token" black or female managers in a large corporation.[18]

Participant observation is a type of field study in which the researcher becomes a member of the group being studied. Sometimes the sociologist is a secret observer, reporting on the group; in other cases the researcher is out in the open. The main virtue of this method is its directness. Social behavior can be studied in its natural settings, as it occurs, largely uncontaminated by the presence of strangers and interviewers. Some of the most perceptive and powerful portrayals of society have emerged out of participant observation, including studies of ghetto street life (see "The Researcher as Part of the Research"),[19] the wards of mental hospitals,[20] and the life-styles of pool hustlers,[21] to mention just a few. Let us take a look at one of those studies.

ASYLUMS: PARTICIPANT OBSERVATION IN A MENTAL HOSPITAL.   Erving Goffman's study of life in mental hospitals has been justly hailed as a landmark in social scientific research. Goffman employed participant observation methods to gather data, snoop around the wards, and watch the ebb and flow of life among staff and patients in what he aptly called a "total institution."

---

[17] See Piliavin and Briar, "Police Encounters with Juveniles," in Chapter 8, "Deviance and Social Control."

[18] See Kanter, *Men and Women of the Corporation,* in Chapter 6, "Organizations."

[19] Elliot Liebow, *Tally's Corner: A Study of Negro Streetcorner Men* (Boston: Little, Brown, 1967).

[20] Erving Goffman, *Asylums: Essays on the Social Situation of Mental Patients and Other Inmates* (New York: Doubleday/Anchor, 1961).

[21] Ned Polsky, *Hustlers, Beats, and Others* (Chicago: Aldine, 1967).

Which one is the sociologist? Participant observation would be an appropriate method of studying motorcycle gangs.

Since most of the literature about mental patients is written from the perspective of the medical professional, Goffman reasoned that it had a built-in bias. He hypothesized that the hospital setting was an important dimension in the understanding of the mental patient. He predicted further that, in any group of persons living in such a controlled, enclosed environment, an "underlife" would naturally develop.

Goffman wanted to explore this underlife, which he described as the patients' way of achieving personal control over their lives by bargaining, manipulating, and deceiving the hospital staff. His study attempted to show that the conventional doctor-patient relationship could not survive the demands and realities of hospitalization.

In order to carry out his research, Goffman joined the staff of a mental hospital as an assistant athletic director. In this job he could mingle easily and unobtrusively with patients and staff. He wandered throughout the hospital and made contact with patients — especially those permanently hospitalized in the "back wards." Goffman did not divulge his real identity or reveal his real purpose except to a few administrators. From his year of field work, Goffman produced a study of mental hospitalization that has profoundly changed our understanding of how social relationships in these institutions affect the self-image and treatment of mental patients.

PROBLEMS IN PARTICIPANT OBSERVATION.   The value of studies like Goffman's is that they give us an opportunity to take a close look at the life-styles of fairly small groups. Fresh and startling facts, impressions, and pieces of knowledge are often uncovered only because the observer is on the scene. The insight and sympathetic understanding of such studies are often difficult to achieve, however.

Gaining access, cultivating informants, winning the trust and confidence of subjects — all require interpersonal skills and rapport; without them, the research is doomed to failure. There is also the danger of identifying with the points of view of the study population. The researcher-observer risks becoming an advocate of the group rather than a student of it. In order to overcome these handicaps, field workers seek out as many different informants and sources of data as possible. Cross-checking and corroborating responses by different informants are needed to cope with the problems described above.

EXPERIMENTS

The **experiment**, a test of cause and effect under controlled conditions, is not as unusual in sociology as one might imagine. The main limitations on investigations of this type have to do with the many moral and ethical concerns about experimentation with human beings. In 1974 the U.S. Department of Health, Education, and Welfare published its code of ethics for research involving human subjects. The code required that all experimental subjects be informed in advance of the nature of the research, and that they give their consent before participating.[22] The boundaries defining the limits of research are clearly important, but they also place restraints on the kinds and amounts of knowledge social scientists can hope to acquire.

---

[22] Paul Reynolds, "The Protection of Human Subjects: An Open Letter to NIH," *American Sociologist* 9:4 (November 1974): 221–25.

The most familiar form of experimental research consists of three basic steps. First, two comparable groups are set up. The *experimental group* is composed of subjects who will be exposed to a stimulus or a test factor; the *control group* is made up of subjects who are as similar as possible to those in the experimental group. Second, the experimental group is exposed to some influence, stimulus, or conditioning, while the control group is not. Third, both groups are carefully measured and compared to determine what effects and influence, if any, the stimulus has had on the experimental group.

The purpose of experimentation is to study the cause-effect relationship between two variables. We might, for example, wish to determine the effect, if any, of television violence on children — whether it makes them more likely to accept violence as normal, or whether they tend to imitate the violent behavior that they see on TV. In this case TV violence is the experimental stimulus. The question to be answered in our experiment is this: Does watching violent television programs (the independent variable) increase aggressive behavior among children (the dependent variable)? The next step in the research is to set up an experimental group (children who will be exposed to TV violence) and a control group (children who will not watch TV violence). Both groups of children must be the same in terms of age, school grade, social class, and other physical and psychological measures such as health and IQ. Every effort must be made to control the influence of extraneous factors, such as reading materials that emphasize violence and aggressive behavior. Needless to say, many problems face the researcher who attempts to limit the effects of these factors.[23]

Having set up the test groups, we first conduct a pretest to measure the levels of violent and aggressive tendencies in each group so that the effects of TV violence (the test variable) may be determined. If members of the two groups are similar to each other, the average amount of aggressiveness and violence in the two groups should be about the same. Then we expose only the experimental group to TV violence. Afterward, we again measure the aggressiveness and violence of both groups. If TV violence increases aggressive tendencies, we should expect to find an increase in the level of aggressiveness and violence in the experimental group but not in the control group. The experiment thus satisfies the criteria for demonstrating causation.

PRISONERS AND JAILERS: AN EXPERIMENT. One of the most attractive aspects of experimental work is that researchers can control relationships. They can tamper with factors and measure with a high degree of reliability the effects of such manipulations of behavior. In this regard the work of the social psychologist Philip Zimbardo on the effects of imprisonment is an ingenious piece of experimental work.[24] Briefly, Zimbardo designed a study in which he created a mock jail and randomly selected volunteer students to play the roles of inmates and guards. He wanted to determine to what extent the respective roles of inmate and guard, played out in accordance with prison regulations, affected attitudes and behavior. The results were alarming. The volunteers, all of whom came from similar social backgrounds, virtually recreated the

---

[23] Many experiments on the effects of TV violence have been conducted. Some of their findings are cited in Chapter 5, "Socialization."

[24] Philip Zimbardo, "Pathology by Imprisonment," *Society* 9 (April 1972): 4–8; and "The Mind Is a Formidable Jailer: A Pirandellian Prison," *The New York Times,* April 18, 1973, pp. 38–60.

hostility displayed by real guards and the apathy or rebelliousness of real prisoners. Their behavior changed to such a frightening extent that the experiment had to be ended prematurely. Zimbardo was able to conclude, contrary to the opinion of prison authorities, that personality factors were less important than the social structure of the prison in determining the behavior of guards and inmates.

THE HAWTHORNE EFFECT.   Sometimes experimental social research can succeed by "failing"; in other words, it can change the investigator's own assumptions about the behavior being studied. This was the case in the famous Hawthorne study.[25] In the 1930s, the Western Electric Company invited Elton Mayo and a research team to study the ways employees' morale and productivity were affected by the working environments in its Hawthorne plant. Mayo decided to look at the activities of five women who assembled telephone relays. The research team isolated this small work force in a special room in order to control their working conditions.

After making initial observations to determine normal levels of work output, the Mayo team systematically changed the working environment. By varying conditions (a test variable), they tried to discover which conditions either contributed to or interfered with morale and productivity (the dependent variable). First, the method of paying the workers was changed. Instead of weekly salaries, based mainly on seniority and the number of relays each woman assembled, the researchers substituted a scheme of piecework pay. The workers' earnings were now determined by how many relays the group as a whole put together. Production went up. Next, three "work breaks" were introduced. Again, production climbed. The lighting was changed; longer hours were added, then a shortened work week; production goals were increased, then decreased. Still, production continued to rise. No matter what conditions in the work environment were varied, production rose.

At this point the research team concluded that their effort was a failure. They had hypothesized that certain working conditions would either stimulate worker morale and productivity or hinder it. But all the variations they introduced had had the same effect.

Nevertheless, a great deal was eventually learned from this experiment. By isolating some members of the Hawthorne work force, the researchers encouraged the formation of common bonds, which developed into friendships. Although they did not realize it at the time, the Mayo researchers created a group identity that strengthened the workers' capacity to work in spite of adverse conditions. Second, and more important, the very presence of the research team influenced the pace and quality of work. Knowing that they were being studied, the workers apparently became determined to overcome all obstacles in order to show how resourceful and capable they were.

The most important and unexpected finding of the Western Electric study was that individuals who are aware of being studied may change their behavior to fulfill what they believe are the researchers' expectations. Sociologists have labeled this phenomenon the "Hawthorne effect."

---

[25] Elton Mayo, *Human Problems of an Industrial Civilization* (New York: Viking Press, 1966); Fritz J. Roethlisberger and William J. Dickson, *Management and the Worker* (Cambridge: Harvard University Press [1939], 1961).

During the 1930s experimental attempts to improve efficiency at the Hawthorne plant of the Western Electric Company near Chicago had some surprising results: no matter how the experimenters changed the working conditions of the women who assembled telephone relays, the morale and productivity of the workers increased. This sort of phenomenon is now known as the Hawthorne effect.

DRAWBACKS OF EXPERIMENTATION.   Sociological experimenters face some serious dilemmas. Experiments are necessarily limited in scope, and there is the danger that what is learned under laboratory-like conditions will not apply in the world outside. Experimental studies of how couples make decisions, for example, are sometimes cited as "proof" in statements about married life. Since this research typically used college students for subjects, and since the experiments were conducted under artificial laboratory conditions, the findings tell us very little about how men and women actually behave when they are married to each other. Although sociological experiments can be very productive, they can also be easily abused. To inform a subject in advance of an experiment may destroy its validity; to fail to inform the subject opens the researcher to charges of being deceptive and inflicting harm upon others. Careful planning can avoid both disadvantages.

CONTENT ANALYSIS

The research methods examined so far have involved direct observation of behavior or the questioning of individuals about what they think and do.

Studies based on **content analysis** use documents as a data base. Researchers who use this method study records (birth and death certificates, licenses, public deeds) as well as the archeological evidence from which inferences about social behavior may be drawn. By analyzing the content of newspapers, literature, art, and personal documents, the researcher gains insight into cultural values and social concerns of a particular society. Content analysis techniques have been employed in propaganda studies and in the study of sex-role stereotyping in children's books.

CONTENT ANALYSIS IN ADVERTISING.   According to popular belief, advertising was originally only a source of factual, rather dull information about available products. Modern advertising, which dates from the 1920s, is thought to have introduced the openly sexual appeals and emotional persuasions we associate with television commercials and magazine ads. Jackson Lears' study of early national advertising, however, found this belief to be wholly untrue. In turn-of-the-century ads "the fun of living" and sexual titillation were already a well-established means of getting attention. "By 1910," he discovered, "an electric sign advertising corsets showed a young woman dressing and undressing atop Times Square." [26] Content analysis often provides fresh insights into popular culture, showing in this case that Americans of the Victorian era were not so straitlaced after all.

SOCIOLOGICAL RESEARCH: AN ASSESSMENT

In an influential book first published in 1966, Eugene Webb and his associates criticized many conventional research strategies. They proposed additional procedures to improve the reliability and validity of data so that findings could be confidently generalized to populations beyond those immediately studied. In particular they recommended using such *unobtrusive measures* as public records and government documents.

The researcher, however, cannot be sure of the authenticity and reliability of memoirs, autobiographies, and even official documents. Forgeries and misrepresentations are common. Webb and his associates insist, therefore, that these data sources not be used in place of other current procedures, but as supplements to them. Additional proofs and tests, either for or against a hypothesis, make the conclusions surer and firmer. Regarding the reliability of archival sources, they quote a Chinese proverb: "The palest ink is clearer than the best memory." [27]

Given the inherent limitations of the methods we have reviewed, it is often desirable to combine research methods (a process known as *triangulation*). William B. Sanders, noting the similarities between criminal investigations carried on by detectives and the procedures employed by social science investigators, makes the point concisely: "By using more than one method and source of data in a single study, as detectives do, sociologists can discover and compensate for the weaknesses of the various methods and will multiply their strengths." [28]

THE ETHICS OF RESEARCH

There are many ethical issues in sociological research. Perhaps the most controversial concerns the scientist's right to research and the subjects' rights to dignity, self-determination, and privacy. Only when all the conditions of informed consent — full information, a fair explanation and description of the methods, goals, benefits, and possible

---

[26] T. J. Jackson Lears, "Some Versions of Fantasy: Toward a Cultural History of American Advertising: 1880–1930," *Prospects*, vol. 8 (New York: Cambridge University Press, 1984). Cited in Michael Schudson, *Advertising, The Uneasy Persuasion* (New York: Basic Books, 1984), p. 59.

[27] Eugene J. Webb et al., *Nonreactive Measures in the Social Sciences*, 2nd ed. (Boston: Houghton Mifflin Company, 1981).

[28] William Sanders, *The Sociologist as Detective: An Introduction to Research Methods* (New York: Praeger, 1974), pp. 2–3.

What method would you use to study this social group? Little research has been done on transvestites, partly because they are secretive and partly because of the ethical issues involved.

risks to subjects—have been fulfilled, may researchers feel confident that the well-being of their subjects has been given satisfactory consideration.[29]

But there are other questions not covered by the recommendations just listed. When research is sponsored by government agencies, for example, what are the investigators' responsibilities concerning its use? Must researchers worry about how special interests use or distort their findings? Or, if sociologists uncover illegal practices when they study an organization, do they have a social duty to report the matter? Sociologists must also be wary of cooptation when they work for the government as well as private organizations; it is difficult to resist assuming, over time, the viewpoint of their employers and grantors, or to deny permission for their research to be used to provide a scientific "gloss" for whatever policies an organization wishes to implement. Too often sociologists as well as other researchers have been manipulated into endorsing the policy of an organization that employs them.[30]

Researchers must assume the responsibility for deciding when they have crossed beyond the bounds of ethics. To illustrate the issues sociologists must confront, let us consider the question of deception. In his observation of homosexual activities in a public restroom, researcher Laud Humphries kept the identity of the participants secret but did not make clear to them at the time that they were subjects in a sociological study.[31] Obviously, had he done so, it is doubtful that any assurances of anonymity could have persuaded them to cooperate. The real ethical issue in that research is not so

---

[29] Paul Reynolds, *Ethical Dilemmas and Social Science Research* (San Francisco: Jossey-Bass, 1979).

[30] Irving Horowitz, ed., *The Rise and Fall of Project Camelot* (Cambridge, Mass.: MIT Press, 1967).

[31] Laud Humphries, *Tearoom Trade: Impersonal Sex in Public Places* (Chicago: Aldine, 1970).

much whether the researcher was justified in not disclosing his purpose but whether this deliberate deception was itself morally proper.

In order to gain entry into the scene, Humphries posed as a "watchqueen"—a voyeur and lookout. He misled his unwitting subjects into thinking that his sole purpose was the pleasure he derived from observing homosexual acts. Further, the researcher infringed upon their right to privacy. Most of the subjects did not want their sexual activities known and probably would have refused to participate in a research study. One commentator on such research ploys has observed that had the researcher been unable to keep secret the identities of his subjects, their careers could have been ruined, their families disrupted, and their mental health impaired.[32] Quite apart from giving sociology a bad name, the use of deception in field work poisons the atmosphere of all social science research.

THE USES OF SOCIOLOGY

The aim of sociological research is to enlarge our understanding of human behavior by uncovering and explaining the facts of social life. Many of the concepts of sociology have become part of our everyday vocabulary. Such terms as "in-group," "status symbol," "bureaucracy," "middle class," "white-collar crime," "minority group," and the "self-fulfilling prophecy" were all coined by sociologists. The findings of social science research have shaped government policies in education, social work, health care, and urban planning. Sociological facts and theories are part of the public discourse on such issues as poverty, industrial productivity, voting behavior, crime and delinquency, feminism, racial discrimination, and the origins of riots and revolutions.

Yet some people still wonder whether sociology is of any practical use. In their search for social truth, researchers are often caught in what Robert K. Merton has described as a quadruple bind. If they succeed in proving that the "obvious" is true, sociologists are called bores for telling us what we already know. If they find that what appears unlikely is in fact untrue, they are called fools for wasting their time proving what is only common sense. If researchers find, as Galileo did, that widely held beliefs are incorrect, they are denounced as heretics for daring to question eternal truths. And if in their investigations they turn up some facts that seem unbelievable, they are considered charlatans who are trying to make us believe the impossible. Merton concludes, "The point is, of course, that we don't know in advance of systematic research which widely held beliefs are untrue and which widely rejected beliefs are, in fact, true.[33] Sociological research serves the practical purpose of telling us not only some of the things we don't know, but also that some of the things we think we know just "ain't so."

---

[32] Donald P. Warwick. "Tearoom Trade: Means and Ends in Social Research," *The Hastings Center Studies* 1: 1 (1973): 27–38.
[33] Robert K. Merton, "Notes on Problem-Finding in Sociology," in *Sociology Today: Problems and Prospects,* eds. Robert K. Merton, Leonard Broom, and Leonard S. Cottrell, Jr. (New York: Basic Books, 1959), pp. xv–xvi, n. 5.

SUMMARY

1. The aim of sociological research is to enlarge our understanding of human behavior by discovering and explaining the facts of social life. Common-sense approaches to problems are often inadequate because they are based on limited knowledge or on tradition.

2. Science is a system of rational inquiry disciplined by empirical test. The scientific method consists of observing significant facts and finding the general laws that govern those facts. There are few, if any, laws of social behavior, so sociological knowledge is based on generalizations made from the facts of observation and experiment.

3. Scientific research follows certain procedures: selecting a topic, reviewing the literature, forming a hypothesis, choosing a research method, collecting the necessary data, interpreting the data, and publishing the findings.

4. In survey research individuals are asked questions through self-administered questionnaires. Surveys are widely used when the sociologist wants to gather data on certain behaviors, opinions, or attitudes in a large population.

5. Interviews and case histories offer researchers methods of studying particular subjects more closely. In many cases, the experiences of individuals offer insights into the behavior of a group.

6. Field studies, especially participant observation, entail the researcher's getting into the natural setting of subjects and carefully observing and recording their behavior.

7. The experiment is a less frequently used method of research. By limiting the factors affecting the behavior being studied, experimenters are able to test the cause-effect relationship between two variables.

8. The content analysis method uses documents as a data base. Sociologists apply this method to study the cultural values and social concerns of a particular group or society.

9. Sociological research on human subjects presents problems in data gathering and observation. The study of human behavior requires scientists to be vigilant in protecting individual rights and privacy.

10. Sociological knowledge has many applications in government, business, and private life. The practical value of much social research lies in finding that some widely held beliefs about society and social behavior are untrue, while some widely rejected beliefs are in fact true.

KEY TERMS

scientific method 34
science 35
empirical facts 35
causal relationship 41
variable 42
independent variable 42
dependent variable 42
correlation 42

hypothesis 43
population 43
sample 43
simple random sample 44
concepts 44
theory 44
stratified sample 45
survey 47

extrapolate 47
interview 49
case history 49
replication 50
participant observation 52
experiment 53
content analysis 56

SUGGESTED READING

Hubert M. Blalock, Jr. "The Real and Unrealized Contributions of Quantitative Sociology." *American Sociological Review* 54 (June, 1989), pp. 447–60.

* Kai T. Erikson. *Everything in Its Path.* New York: Simon and Schuster, 1978.

* Available in paperback.

* Stanley Lieberson. *Making It Count: The Improvement of Social Research and Theory.* Berkeley, CA.: University of California Press, 1985.

* Robert Lynd. *Knowledge for What? The Place of Social Science in American Culture.* Princeton, NJ: University Press, 1969.

PART 2

BASIC CONCEPTS

In Boston they ask, How much does he know? In New York, How much is he worth? In Philadelphia, Who were his parents?

Mark Twain

CHAPTER 3

CULTURE

On Salisbury Plain in southern England, a huge prehistoric monument stands outlined against the peaceful landscape of green fields and grazing sheep. Thousands of years ago, great slabs of stone, some weighing thirty tons, were dragged from quarries twenty miles away and carefully arranged in a pattern of concentric circles. But what do they form?

The mystery of Stonehenge, as this structure is called, has tantalized generations of scientists. About thirty years ago, an astronomer named Gerald Hawkins discovered that the stones were almost perfectly aligned with the positions of the sun and the moon at different seasons.[1] Stonehenge, he decided, is an incredibly accurate solar and lunar calendar. No one, however, knows exactly what this arrangement of stones meant to the Stone Age people who designed it. Was it a guide to the planting of crops? Was it a temple for the worship of the sun and moon? Or was it simply a magnificent work of abstract art? Without written records or other clues, scientists can only speculate on what could have been worth all that trouble.

Stonehenge remains a mystery because we have no way of knowing the idea behind it. We find these peculiar stones puzzling because, as human beings, we do not

---

[1] Gerald S. Hawkins and John B. White, *Stonehenge Decoded* (Garden City, N.Y.: Doubleday, 1965).

Stonehenge is primarily a cultural mystery. Without written records there is no way of knowing for certain why or how a Stone Age people built this remarkable structure.

react directly to our environment but to our interpretations of it. The sheep grazing around Stonehenge react to it as they would any other pile of rocks, but men and women behave differently according to what those rocks mean to them. If people have the idea that Stonehenge is a holy place, for example, they will speak in reverential tones and perhaps conduct religious rites on that spot. If other people have the idea that Stonehenge is a popular tourist attraction, they will take photographs of it or try to scratch their initials into the stones.

In Chapter 1, "The Sociological Perspective," we said that the sociological answer to the question "Why do people behave the way they do?" is "Because of the situations in which they find themselves." The answer could be more accurately stated like this: *People behave the way they do because of the ideas they have about the situations in which they find themselves.* Most of their ideas are learned from other people and passed on from generation to generation. These shared ideas are called **culture**. Americans, for example, share ideas about success. Being successful in American culture means winning some competition, whether it is getting a college scholarship or having more money than other people.

Stonehenge is above all a cultural mystery. Its unknown creators left no information about it for us to share, and therefore we have "no idea" how to interpret it.

This chapter begins with a discussion of the way human beings communicate their shared ideas through symbols, especially language. The second section, "The Content of Culture," covers the kinds of ideas that have the greatest influence on behavior — ideas about reality, ideas about what is "right," ideas about how to behave, and ideas about the self. The third section discusses some implications of the enormous diversity of human cultures. The fourth section shows that societies, including American society, often have contradictory beliefs and behavior. The chapter ends with an explanation of how culture can both change and remain essentially the same.

CULTURE AS SHARED IDEAS

Pierre de Beaumarchais, the nineteenth-century French dramatist, remarked that the only difference between animals and human beings is that people drink when they are not thirsty and make love in any season. The sociologist's definition of the difference is less fanciful and more scientific: only human beings have the capacity for creating and

St. Patrick's Cathedral in New York was modeled after the Gothic cathedrals of medieval Europe. The process of cultural transmission has given Americans a rich artistic heritage from many different cultures.

transmitting culture. More than any other species, human animals are able to surpass their biological limitations by sharing ideas and passing on what they learn to future generations.

All animals, including human beings, have certain problems in common. In order to survive as a species, they must find a home, acquire food, and provide for their young. Animals are guided by instincts, or innate biological mechanisms that enable them to cope with these problems of existence. They respond to their environment in a fixed, predictable manner: beavers build dams as homes, lions hunt antelopes for food, and birds build nests to protect their fledglings. Should these solutions turn out to be inadequate, animals for the most part will still go on making the same responses to the same problems. It is true that much of the behavior of higher animals, especially chimpanzees and other primates, is learned through direct experience. As everyone knows, dogs can be taught to overcome their instinctive dislike of cats, and parrots often learn new calls through imitation of other voices. In some cases animals have also been known to teach their offspring what they themselves have learned. Nevertheless, human beings are unique in their far greater ability to learn from experience, to create new solutions to old problems, and — most important — to use language to transmit what they have learned to future generations. Without the benefit of the learning passed down from our ancestors, each new generation would have had to reinvent the wheel, not to mention such other cultural innovations as agriculture, religion, and the family. Even when a civilization dies out, its knowledge can survive by being handed on orally or in writing. Contemporary American culture, for example, has incorporated elements of cultures long since vanished from the earth — the monotheism of the ancient Hebrews, the democracy of the ancient Greeks, the alphabet of the Romans, and the numerical system of the medieval Arabs. Our almost complete reliance on shared ideas, as opposed to instincts, is what makes human beings different from other animals.

SYMBOLISM: THE WEB OF SIGNIFICANCE

Human beings are the "culture-bearing animals" because they have the unique capacity to create and use symbols. When two or more people agree that something — an object, a gesture, a word, a drawing — stands for something else, then it becomes a **symbol** conveying a shared idea. The word "statue" is not a statue; it is a symbol which represents that object. Just as a person from a statue-less country would not share an American's understanding of the word "statue," so most Americans do not fully share the meaning conveyed by a Japanese scroll or a Russian icon.

The anthropologist Clifford Geertz calls these shared meanings the essence of culture. "Believing, with Max Weber, that man is an animal suspended in webs of significance he himself has spun," he writes, "I take culture to be those webs."[2] This web of meaning is what makes Americans "Americans." What does it mean in American culture to be a success, to wear a hairpiece, to go to Harvard, to gain 20 pounds, to drive a BMW, to go on welfare, to be over 65, to be a good mother, to smoke pot, to live in Miami, to be a housewife, or a lawyer or a homosexual? When you know what shared

---

[2] Clifford Geertz, *The Interpretation of Cultures* (New York: Basic Books, 1973), p. 5.

ideas are attached to these phenomena — what they symbolize — then you know something about American culture.

LANGUAGE

Men and women communicate shared meanings through such sets of symbols as art, myth, music, ritual, and especially language. Compared to human beings, other animals can communicate only in crude and limited ways. Dogs bark and growl in warning, birds sing to attract prospective mates, and horses whinny to their foals if they stray too far away. More intelligent animals can also learn to respond to verbal signals, including human words like "sit," "whoa," and "suppertime!" but humankind has the unique ability to assign meanings to those sounds. Only people can invent words like "rain," "God," and "next week," and agree that they are symbols for certain thoughts.

Until very recently, there was no evidence that even the most intelligent animals had the brain capacity for language. Attempts to teach primates to speak had always failed; after three years of intensive training by two psychologists, one bright chimpanzee could pronounce only three words recognizably.[3] During the 1970s, however, other investigators obtained better results teaching chimpanzees to communicate through hand signs instead of spoken words. Their success has led some people to question whether the human capacity for language is indeed unique.

In one well-known study, a female chimpanzee named Washoe was taught a 140-word vocabulary in the American Sign Language for the deaf. After a few years of practice, the animal could put together sentences such as "Listen dog" (at the sound of barking) and "Come hug-love sorry sorry" (to apologize for some wrongdoing). But Washoe did not use syntax, or rules for organizing words systematically, and her signaling capacity — and hence her capacity for culture — was still far less advanced than that of a two-year-old child.[4] Washoe has also been unable to teach the signs she knows to other chimpanzees, and without a common language she has no culture of accumulated learning to leave to her posterity. Without a socially inherited culture, each generation of apes goes through the same learning experience and acquires the same knowledge all over again.

Human culture could not exist without a means of symbolic communication. Language gives human beings access to what was thought and experienced in the past, as well as a way of passing new information on to future generations. When this language link is broken, as it was at Stonehenge, then a culture is lost to us forever.

THE SAPIR-WHORF HYPOTHESIS. Since language is part of culture, it also shapes and colors our experiences of the world around us. Some years ago, the linguist Edward Sapir went so far as to say that people "construct" reality through their particular choice of terms and the grammar of their language.[5] Sapir's student, Benjamin L. Whorf, claimed that speaking different languages caused people to *think* differently.

[3] C. Hayes, *The Ape in Our House* (New York: Harper & Row, 1951).
[4] B. T. Gardner and R. A. Gardner, "Two-way Communication with an Infant Chimpanzee," in *Behavior of Nonhuman Primates,* eds. Allan M. Schrier et al. (New York: Academic Press, 1972), vol. 4.
[5] Edward A. Sapir, *Selected Writing in Language, Culture, and Personality,* ed. David G. Mandelbaum (Berkeley: University of California Press, 1949), p. 162.

Human beings are the "culture-bearing animals" because they have the unique capacity to communicate through symbols, especially language.

Some languages, for example, have more words for certain colors or tastes than others; people equipped with a greater number of finely differentiated words are actually aware of gradations of color and taste that people without such words fail to notice. To an American, for example, rice is only rice, but a Filipino can use ninety-two different words to talk about it. Many languages, including English, have the concepts of past, present, and future built into their verb forms, but some, like the language of the Trobriand Islanders, do not. English-speaking people accordingly see events as following each other in a linear sequence, while the Trobrianders see events as coming in clusters. The belief that words determine thoughts is called *linguistic relativism,* or the Sapir-Whorf hypothesis.

Although few sociologists fully accept the notion that people's view of reality is entirely constructed by the language they speak, they do generally agree with the Sapir-Whorf hypothesis to this extent: there are differences in the way languages represent experience, and these differences influence how people perceive the world and therefore how they behave.

THE CONTENT OF CULTURE

Human beings obviously share some of the same ideas, from the way to hold a fork to the way to get the most out of life. Although culture includes everything people have ideas about, some kinds of shared ideas influence human behavior more than others. For sociologists, the most important cultural ideas fall into four categories: ideas about reality, ideas about what is desirable, ideas about how to behave, and ideas about ourselves.

FACTS: IDEAS ABOUT REALITY

What is "reality"? Most of us would say simply that reality is what is "out there" for everyone to see, feel, hear, and otherwise experience. The answer, however, is far from being this simple. What is real to us is actually what we *think* is real, and different peoples with different cultures do not give the same meanings to their experiences.

When we look out at the ocean, for example, and see the straight line of the horizon, we interpret it as the limit of our vision; in the fifteenth century, people thought that the horizon marked the limit of a world that they could "see" was flat. We "know" that bubonic plague is caused by a bacillus and carried by rats and fleas; in the Middle Ages, people were just as sure that plague was the punishment of an angry God. We even believe in the reality of some things we have never directly experienced, like schizophrenia and black holes in the universe. In short, people can experience only in terms of their culture; it is the lens through which they see the world. W. I. Thomas, the American sociologist, put it memorably: "If men define situations as real, they are real in their consequences." [6] If people believe the world is flat, they will not attempt to cross the ocean; if they define bubonic plague as retribution for their sins, then they will attempt to cure it with prayer instead of better sanitary conditions. Future scientists may find that black holes and schizophrenia don't "really" exist after all, but in the meantime astronomers and psychiatrists will go on behaving as if they do. Culture thus affects *subjective reality*, the reality of our sense experiences, changing how we perceive the world around us and therefore how we behave.

The Vietnam War provides an illustration of how our experience of reality is culturally defined. From the beginning, most of the American press reported the war as a conflict between the United States and a Communist enemy; to the journalists, this was the "reality." Other interpretations of the same events were possible, however. The struggle between North and South Vietnam could have been perceived as the latest

---

[6] W. I. Thomas and Dorothy Swaine (Thomas) Thomas, *The Child in America* (New York: Knopf, 1928), p. 572.

"Am I to understand that my proposal is greeted with some skepticism?"
Drawing by Stevenson; © 1984 The New Yorker Magazine, Inc.

outbreak in a civil war that had been going on for more than a generation. American reporters did not interpret what they saw in this way because the Vietnam War did not fit the idea Americans shared about what a civil war was like. In the early 1960s, civil wars in developing countries were not yet part of American experience, and the American Civil War was too distinctive to provide a model for Vietnam. Americans are still more likely to see foreign wars in which Communists are involved as episodes in the Cold War than as primarily local conflicts.[7]

VALUES: IDEAS ABOUT WHAT IS DESIRABLE

Cultural ideas not only define what our experiences are, but also identify them as "good" or "bad." A **value** is a shared idea about what is morally right and desirable, or what "ought to be." Cultural values are the standards by which we judge our behavior and choose our goals in life. If our definition of the good life is a house in the suburbs and a professional career, then we have certain ideas about personal success and family life that motivate us toward these goals. Needless to say, the values people hold greatly influence how they will behave.

VALUES AND THE AMERICAN CHARACTER. Cultural values are also the basis of national character. When we refer to the "typical American" or the "American way of life," we are noting that certain personality traits and certain customs reflect the established, dominant values of the American society. The sociologist Robin Williams identified fifteen characteristic American values, including achievement and success, activity and work, and equality.[8]

ACHIEVEMENT AND SUCCESS. American culture has always stressed the importance of individual achievement, especially if it leads to financial rewards. Success is thought to depend on individual effort, and failure is likely to be blamed on personal inadequacies rather than on such impersonal forces as blind fate or God's will. People who are poor or out of work, for example, will often blame themselves for their troubles, and not the social and economic conditions that lead to poverty and unemployment.

A cultural emphasis on achievement means that accomplishments are respected in many walks of life—as a scientist, soldier, athlete, politician, actress, writer. American culture, however, puts an equal—or perhaps even greater—emphasis on their economic rewards. Wealth in America indicates success and therefore personal worth and accomplishment. And wealth in the American psyche has traditionally been linked to work.

ACTIVITY AND WORK. Many foreign visitors have described America as a land of "get up and go," of strenuous competition, of constant hustle and bustle. As a rule, Americans feel uncomfortable "doing nothing." When they are not working, many spend their leisure time in useful activity—exercising, making household repairs, starting new hobbies and projects.

---

[7] Herbert J. Gans, *Deciding What's News* (New York: Random House/Vintage Books, 1980), p. 202.
[8] Robin M. Williams, Jr., *American Society: A Sociological Interpretation,* 3d ed. (New York: Knopf, 1970), pp. 452–502.

Work is a highly valued activity in American culture.

This inclination toward activity can be explained historically by the ceaseless change and vast opportunities that Americans have always experienced. In addition, the taming of the American wilderness demanded tremendous physical effort that often paid off handsomely in land and other resources. Added to this lesson was the American Protestant tradition that hard work is virtuous and will be rewarded by success. Finally, most of the original American settlers came from the European working classes. Except in a few parts of the South and New England, there was no aristocracy to shun trade or manual labor and lend prestige to a life of leisure.

EQUALITY.   Almost 160 years ago Alexis de Tocqueville, a perceptive French observer of the young United States, wrote that the great master key to American society was the desire for equality. European social inequalities had little effect on America, where the majority of settlers came chiefly from lower- and middle-class origins, and where abundant resources helped to dissolve old distinctions based on land ownership and other wealth. Generation after generation in America asserted the value of equality by abolishing primogeniture (the right of the eldest son to inherit all his parents' property), imprisonment for debt, slavery and indentured servitude, and the requirement that a person own property in order to vote and hold public office. According to long American tradition, the power and privileges that once belonged only to the few can legitimately be claimed as the rights of the many. In our own day, discrimination against women and other minorities is being attacked in the name of equality.

The belief in democracy, patriotism, and humanitarianism; a distrust of authority; and a faith in freedom, independence, and scientific progress are all American values that grow out of a moral commitment to equal opportunity. Although most Americans hold most of these values, they obviously do not always practice what they preach. American racism, the belief in the inherent inferiority of nonwhites, has long been a conspicuous exception to the principle of equality.

NORMS: IDEAS ABOUT HOW TO BEHAVE

Values are ideas about what goals are desirable, and **norms** are ideas about how to achieve them. Values identify what we are expected to be; norms govern what we are expected to do. A culture that values individual achievement, for instance, is likely to have norms that emphasize studying hard in school (to be a good student), winning football games (to be a good team), and working hard for a promotion to a better-paying job (to be a good breadwinner).

William Graham Sumner, one of the founders of American sociology, distinguished between enacted norms and crescive norms. *Enacted norms* are all the official rules and laws which are intentionally designed to guide behavior. These range from the petty regulations of daily life ("Fasten seatbelts," "Residents only," "No bare feet") to state laws against such crimes as theft and murder. *Crescive norms*, which Sumner called **folkways**, develop spontaneously, as if by common consent. In the United States these customs include eating three meals a day and being polite to one's elders. In small, tightly knit communities most norms are crescive: they arise from unspoken agreement on the proper ways to behave. Complex, modern societies, which are made up of people from many different cultural backgrounds, rely more often on enacted norms to govern the behavior of their members.

Some norms have moral importance: they represent what is "true" and "right." In this case, they are known as **mores**, or moral rules. Mores are ways of behaving that most members of a society believe are essential to its welfare. Folkways are ways one *should* act, but mores are ways one *must* act. American mores, for example, require sending one's children to school and helping a sick or injured person. Since most people believe that their mores are necessary to maintain a decent society, these moral requirements are vigorously enforced. Violation of folkways (such as loud singing on a crowded street) will probably incur only mild disapproval or ridicule; violations of mores (such as cheating at cards) might mean expulsion from the group or a punch in the nose.

Mores are enforced by group disapproval and punishment, and most mores are also enforced by laws. Legal prohibitions against such acts as theft, rape, and fraud formally define violations of a society's rules as crimes and set penalties (imprisonment, fines, execution) for them. In short, folkways plus moral importance are mores, and mores plus organized formal enforcement are laws.

Sumner divided norms into folkways and mores according to how much moral importance is attached to them. Robert Merton has analyzed norms by dividing them according to whether they represent positive or negative rules — "dos" or "don'ts."

Positive norms define what we must do and what we should do. Everyone is required by law and custom to put clothes on before appearing in public, for example. Reporting a fire is not legally required, but it is considered something we should do.

Bowing is an ancient Japanese custom with an elaborate etiquette. Saleswomen in Tokyo department stores undergo rigorous training to learn how to bend exactly 30 degrees when welcoming customers, 15 degrees when encouraging them to look around, and 45 degrees when saying goodbye.

Negative norms define what we should not do and what we must not do. Drunkenness and minor tax evasion, for example, are widely tolerated, but they are still violations of American ideas about what people should do. Absolutely forbidden behavior (treason, murder) is almost always illegal, and the prohibitions against it are enforced by government officials. Other proscriptive norms are **taboos**, deeply held beliefs that make some kinds of behavior simply unthinkable. For example, in most societies the moral prohibitions against incest and cannibalism are so strong that laws against them are unnecessary.

The existence of so many "dos" and "don'ts" may seem oppressive, but generally accepted norms are essential to keep society from falling apart. When people lose faith in the values and norms of their society, they feel they have no worthwhile goals to strive for and no dependable ways of knowing how to behave.

Durkheim noted that periods of social upheaval give rise to feelings of anomie, the sense that society's rules are not being enforced and that life has lost its meaning. Anomie is also likely to occur during adolescence, a period of great biological and social adjustment, when childhood norms are replaced with adult standards of behavior. As Durkheim might have predicted, teenagers appear to be especially prone to anomic suicide. Among Americans under the age of 25, suicide is the second leading cause of death (after traffic accidents, which are often suspected suicides).[9] Suicide rates among adolescents are highest in Phoenix, Dallas, and other rapidly growing areas of the Sun Belt. The sprawling new suburbs of the South and West, most of them populated by strangers transplanted from northern states, are often troubled by symptoms of anomie: rootlessness, isolation, restlessness, and boredom.[10]

THE SELF: IDEAS ABOUT OURSELVES

Our ideas about ourselves are also learned from other people. The culture in which we grow up becomes part of our inner selves: its values become our ideals, its norms our standards of behavior. Chapter 5, "Socialization," discusses how our self-identities are shaped by seeing ourselves as others see us, and Chapter 10, "The Sexes," explores just how deeply our personalities are affected by seeing ourselves as women or as men.

Finally, the shared ideas of culture allow human beings to see themselves objectively. Unlike any other animal, men and women are able to reflect upon their actions and to try to improve them. It is precisely this capacity for self-appraisal and self-control that makes human beings uniquely free to transform their environment and to change their destiny.

CULTURAL DIVERSITY

Of course not everyone shares the same ideas, and human culture varies enormously. The Japanese, the Arabs, the ancient Greeks, the Sioux—any people, past or present, that one can name—have distinctive values, behaviors, perceptions, and views of themselves. A specific **culture** is thus defined as the particular ideas which a number of people share because they belong to a certain society. The differences among human cultures are so great that strangers in foreign lands often experience the disturbing feeling of disorientation known as *culture shock*. At home, one can be rather certain how others will behave and what to expect of them. Transplanted to a different culture, however, one finds these expectations unreliable; suddenly the behavior of others becomes strange and unpredictable. A familiar portrayal of culture shock occurs in Lewis Carroll's *Alice in Wonderland*, when the bewildered heroine is confronted by such puzzling new rules of behavior as "Sentence first—verdict afterwards," and "Jam tomorrow and jam yesterday—but never jam today."

---

[9] Statistical Abstract of the United States 1989 (Washington, D.C.: U.S. Government Printing Office, 1989), Table 118.

[10] Mary Giffin and Carol Felsenthal, *A Cry for Help* (Garden City, N.Y.: Doubleday, 1983).

The diversity of human cultures is so enormous that in their research most early anthropologists simply recorded the immense variety of human behavior in virtually every aspect of social life. They found, for instance, that there are some 2,800 distinct languages in the world, most of which have no words in common with most of the others. They also found startling differences in the rules for sexual initiation, marriage, and family life. In one tribe in New Guinea, a youth is not accepted as a man until he kills a member of another tribe, cuts off his head, and brings it home; among religious Jews, in contrast, a boy's passage to manhood is marked by a ritual chanting of a passage from the Hebrew prophets. Anthropologists found that even what is beautiful and desirable in a woman, which might seem to depend on obvious physical attributes, is defined very differently in different cultures: modern Westerners generally prefer slender women, but some African societies find fat women very sexy. Some peoples think that a woman's eyes determine how beautiful she is, while others consider the mouth, nose, or ankles more important. Evidences of cultural diversity are so numerous that many social scientists used to believe that no aspect of human social behavior was invariable from place to place. The human being, they thought, was a blank slate written on by culture.

On the other hand, across the ages there have always been people who believe that all human beings are basically alike. Many commonplace phrases — "to err is human," "it's only human nature," "the human condition" — express the belief that all of us have similar feelings, thoughts, and experiences.

The unity of humankind is not just a matter of idle philosophical debate. Exaggerating the differences between two peoples can lead each to mistrust or hate the other. But the simplistic belief that "people are people" fails to explain why differences do exist; worse still, it offers no way to understand and get along with others whose ways are unlike our own. To the extent that aspects of culture vary from one people to another, there is little or no similarity among human beings. But if there are **cultural universals**, types of social behavior that exist in much the same form in all cultures, then the human species is, after all, one.

THE SEARCH FOR CULTURAL UNIVERSALS

While most anthropologists were bemused by the seemingly endless diversity of human cultures, others began to notice certain similarities among them. Broadly speaking, there did seem to be some cultural universals — language, for instance, and music and terms describing kinship. After reviewing the published accounts of numerous cultures, George Murdock drew up a list of over seventy cultural universals, including "athletic sports, cooking, courtship, a division of labor, family, funeral rites, joking, language, modesty concerning natural functions, penal sanctions, personal names, property rights, religious ritual, toolmaking, and visiting." [11] Other anthropologists objected that these were only "empty frames," to be filled with practices that actually varied widely from culture to culture. Murdock's list contained, to put it

---

[11] George P. Murdock, *Social Structure* (New York: Macmillan, 1949), p. 124.

Styles in adornment vary tremendously from culture to culture. Women in India, Kenya, and Japan have very different ways of enhancing their beauty.

bluntly, "fake universals." [12] Joking, for example, may be universal, but what is funny to one people is not funny to another; religion is universal, but the worship of spirits that dwell in trees has almost nothing in common with the worship of a single, all-powerful God.

When anthropologists tried to be more specific, they could agree on very few traits that were common to all cultures. Among them were marriage and courtship; the concept of murder (as distinguished from such legitimate killings as the slaying of enemies in war); prohibitions against lying, stealing, and violence within the group; mutual obligations between parents and children; and the prohibition against incest. Yet even these cultural traits are not the same everywhere. Incest, for instance, is sometimes defined as sexual relations between members of the immediate family, sometimes between cousins, and sometimes between people with the same family name.

---

[12] A. L. Kroeber, "The Concept of Culture in Science," *Journal of General Education* 35 (1949): 188.

SOCIOBIOLOGY

Sociobiology, the study of the biological basis of social behavior, is the latest attempt to locate an essential human nature amid the vast diversity of local customs and circumstances. Led by Edward O. Wilson, a biologist at Harvard, sociobiologists maintain that the behavior of human beings is determined primarily by biology, not culture. They believe that common, genetically controlled behavior patterns evolved in human beings through the Darwinian principle of natural selection. According to this view, the anthropologists' cultural universals are genetically transmitted traits which improve an individual's or a society's fitness to survive and reproduce. Wilson claims that a "new Adam and Eve," totally isolated from any cultural influence, would eventually create a society with property laws, rules against incest, religious beliefs, and so on through the list of cultural universals.[13]

---

[13] Edward O. Wilson, *On Human Nature* (Cambridge, Mass.: Harvard University Press, 1978), p. 24.

Critics of sociobiology argue that human beings, of all creatures, depend the least on biological programming to guide their behavior. Wilson's "instinct" to avoid incest, for example, has no effect in the thousands of cases that are estimated to occur every year in the United States.[14] Furthermore, any plausible theory of human nature must encompass cultural differences as well as cultural universals. The slow pace of Darwinian evolution makes it an unlikely explanation for the enormous variety of human societies or the astonishing speed of cultural change.[15] Most geneticists and evolutionists therefore conclude that biology alone cannot account for behavior, and that all human phenomena are the unique combination of inseparable genetic and environmental factors.[16]

From the sociological perspective, only culture offers a plausible explanation of why human behavior is far more flexible and diverse than that of any other animal. Culture, as Geertz argues, is an essential part of human nature. (See "Culture and Human Nature.") Undirected by established cultural patterns, the behavior of a "new Adam and Eve," he writes, "would be virtually ungovernable, a mere chaos of pointless acts and exploding emotions, . . . [their] experience virtually shapeless. Culture . . . is not just an ornament of human existence but . . . an essential condition for it." [17]

Given humanity's lack of specific biological programming, it seems most unlikely that the universals of social behavior come from the direct action of our genes. Nor can scientists know how any of these patterns originated, since they have existed in all known societies since prehistoric times. What we do know, from direct observation, is that human beings in every society have certain fundamental requirements in common — the need for nurture during infancy, for food and shelter, for sex, for companionship, and so on. We can infer that only certain behavior patterns meet these needs effectively. The virtually universal prohibition against incest, for example, seems to eliminate sexual rivalry within the family; to keep parental authority undisputed; and, by making marriages outside the family necessary, to promote social ties with other families and other larger groups (see Chapter 11, "The Family"). In a similar way other cultural universals meet other social and individual requirements and thus contribute to the survival of the species. In many respects culture makes humankind many; but in a few respects culture makes us one.

ETHNOCENTRISM: INSIDERS AND OUTSIDERS

It is the most natural thing in the world for Americans to eat hot dogs, sleep in beds, work from nine to five, ride in elevators, and shake hands. But doing what comes naturally is usually doing what comes culturally. Many other peoples would disapprove of the same behavior as strange and "unnatural." In fact, they would probably

---

[14] Ten percent of the women interviewed in a study at Harvard, for example, said they had been involved in an incestuous relationship. See Judith Herman, "Father-Daughter Incest," *Professional Psychology* 12 (February 1984): 76–80.

[15] Stephen Jay Gould, "Cardboard Darwinism," *New York Review of Books* (Sept. 25, 1986), p. 47.

[16] R. C. Lewontin, Steven Rose, and Leon J. Kamin, *Not in Our Genes* (New York: Pantheon, 1984); Arthur L. Caplin, ed., *The Sociobiology Debate* (New York: Harper & Row, 1976).

[17] Geertz, *The Interpretation of Cultures*, p. 46.

CULTURE AND HUMAN NATURE

The gifted anthropologist Clifford Geertz explains that human beings live in an "information gap" between the few things we know instinctively and the many things we need to know in order to survive. This gap is filled by our ability to think and learn symbolically. Since our central nervous system evolved largely in interaction with culture, Geertz says, the human brain cannot direct our behavior without the guidance provided by cultural sources of information. In his view, the great diversity of cultures is explained by the fact that human beings are incomplete animals who are obliged to finish creating themselves.

There is no such thing as a human nature independent of culture. Men without culture would not be the clever savages of Golding's *Lord of the Flies* thrown back upon the cruel wisdom of their animal instincts; nor would they be the nature's noblemen of Enlightenment primitivism or even, as classical anthropological theory would imply, intrinsically talented apes who had somehow failed to find themselves. They would be unworkable monstrosities with very few useful instincts, fewer recognizable sentiments, and no intellect: mental basket cases. . . . What happened to us in the Ice Age is that we were obliged to abandon the regularity and precision of detailed genetic control over our conduct for the flexibility and adaptability of a more generalized, though of course no less real, genetic control over it. To supply the additional information necessary to be able to act, we were forced, in turn, to rely more and more heavily on cultural sources — the accumulated fund of significant symbols. . . .

We are, in sum, incomplete or unfinished animals who complete or finish ourselves through culture — and not through culture in general but through highly particular forms of it: Dobuan and Javanese, Hopi and Italian, upper-class and lower-class, academic and commercial. . . . Between what our body tells us and what we have to know in order to function, there is a vacuum we must fill ourselves, and we fill it with information (or misinformation) provided by our culture. The boundary between what is innately controlled and what is culturally controlled in human behavior is an ill-defined and wavering one. Some things are, for all intents and purposes, entirely controlled intrinsically: we need no more cultural guidance to learn how to breathe than a fish needs to learn how to swim. Others are almost certainly largely cultural; we do not attempt to explain on a genetic basis why some men put their trust in centralized planning and others in the free market, though it might be an amusing exercise. Almost all complex human behavior is, of course, the interactive, nonadditive outcome of the two. Our capacity to speak is surely innate; our capacity to speak English is surely cultural. Smiling at pleasing stimuli and frowning at unpleasing ones are surely in some degree genetically determined (even apes screw up their faces at noxious odors); but sardonic smiling and burlesque frowning are equally surely predominantly cultural, as is perhaps demonstrated by the Balinese definition of a madman as someone who, like an American, smiles when there is nothing to laugh at. Between the basic ground plans for our life that our genes lay down — the capacity to speak or to smile — and the precise behavior we in fact execute — speaking English in a certain tone of voice, smiling enigmatically in a delicate social situation — lies a complex set of significant symbols under whose direction we transform the first into the second, the ground plans into the activity.

Our ideas, our values, our acts, even our emotions, are, like our nervous system itself, cultural products — products manufactured, indeed, out of tendencies, capacities, and dispositions with which we were born, but manufactured nonetheless. Chartres is made of stone and glass. But it is not just stone and glass; it is a cathedral, and not only a cathedral, but a particular cathedral built at a particular time by certain members of a particular society. To understand what it means, to perceive it for what it is, you need to know rather more than the generic properties of stone and glass and rather more than what is common to all cathedrals. You need to understand also — and, in my opinion, most critically — the specific concepts of the relations among God, man, and architecture that, since they have governed its creation, it consequently embodies. It is no different with men: they, too, every last one of them, are cultural artifacts.

SOURCE: Clifford Geertz, *The Interpretation of Cultures* (New York: Basic Books, 1973), pp. 49–51.

Ethno - cen Trism

consider their own ways of eating, sleeping, and greeting far superior to any other. This phenomenon is known as **ethnocentrism**. In *Folkways* (1906) the sociologist William Graham Sumner (1840–1910) defined it as "the view of things in which one's own group is the center of everything . . . . Each group nourishes its own pride and vanity, boasts itself superior, exalts its own divinities and looks with contempt on outsiders.[18]

Nearly every society in human history has considered its own language finer, its own food tastier, its own manners more refined (or more honest), its own morals better (or more sensible), and its own religion the one true religion. In smaller groups ethnocentrism takes the form of "team spirit," "local pride," and "company morale." To find out just how widespread ethnocentrism is in various groups, Theodore Caplow asked members of over 300 organizations — including fraternities, churches, high schools and colleges, restaurants, banks, and trucking crews — how they thought outsiders would rate their organizations compared to others of the same type. Then he asked outsiders how they actually rated the same organizations. The insiders — the members of the groups — were eight times as likely to overestimate as to underestimate what outsiders thought of their groups.[19] In another study, Caplow and his collaborator asked 122 university department chairpersons to rate their own departments: 51 percent thought that their departments were among the first five in the country![20]

Taken to extremes, ethnocentrism easily leads to *chauvinism* (the glorification of one's own group along with fear and hatred of others), racial and religious oppression, warfare, and even genocide. In moderate forms, however, ethnocentrism makes for high morale and effective cooperation within a group. Whether in a football team before a big game or in a nation at war, ethnocentric feelings have the beneficial effect of mobilizing and uniting a threatened group against its enemy. Finally, ethnocentrism can provide satisfaction and comfort. People often make themselves feel better by believing in others' inferiority. "At least I'm not a grind," they say when someone else gets a better grade, or "I may be poor, but I'm not like that riffraff." An important step in the uphill struggle of American blacks and women to win social equality was the increased self-esteem generated by such ethnocentric slogans as "Black is beautiful" and "Sisterhood is powerful."

Nevertheless, ethnocentrism is not universal. Some groups show a reverse ethnocentrism, or *xenocentrism*, when its members find their own culture inferior. Some underprivileged or lower-ranking groups, for example, believe that another group is superior to their own and wish to belong to it. Some members of racial or ethnic minorities despise their own group and want to be part of the majority.

CULTURAL RELATIVISM

As soon as it became clear that ethnocentrism was a common phenomenon, social scientists realized that they themselves might be unfairly judging the behavior of different peoples according to their own cultural values. To avoid any taint of ethno-

[18] William Graham Sumner, *Folkways* (Boston: Ginn, 1906), p. 12.
[19] Theodore Caplow, *Principles of Organization* (New York: Harcourt Brace Jovanovich, 1964), pp. 213–14.
[20] Theodore Caplow and Reece McGee, *The Academic Marketplace* (New York: Basic Books, 1958), p. 45.

centric prejudice, anthropologists began to adopt an attitude of *cultural relativism*, the view that human thoughts and deeds should be judged not by any outside standards but only by those of the society or group in which they take place.

Ethnocentric football fans consider their team superior to any other.

At first, some anthropologists interpreted cultural relativism so rigidly that they refused to make any judgments whatever about human behavior. In the 1930s, the anthropologist Ruth Benedict maintained, for instance, that the cultures of the world were all equally valid patterns of life and nothing any people did was invalid if it was in harmony with the rest of their culture. Paradoxically, the extreme cultural relativists, who wanted to give all other peoples due respect and resist all tendencies toward ethnocentrism in themselves, were drawn to the logical conclusion that anything goes—infanticide, headhunting, slavery, torture, ritual mutilation—provided only that it is in accord with the culture in which it occurs.

History soon exposed the fallacy of this doctrine of total objectivity. Under Stalin's regime, the Soviet authorities butchered or imprisoned vast numbers of their own people, ostensibly for the good of the social system. Under Hitler, the Nazis enslaved millions and put millions more to death. After the 1930s it was no longer possible for scholars to maintain the stance of total cultural relativism. While contemporary anthropologists and sociologists continue to believe that the practices of another people cannot be judged on the same terms as their own culture, they also believe that those practices can be judged in the light of universal values and basic human rights.

CULTURAL INCONSISTENCY

Cultural differences exist not only between cultures but also within them. A large, rapidly changing society like the United States, where people come from many different cultural backgrounds, is likely to have far greater diversity of beliefs and behavior than a small, homogeneous society like Sikkim or Sweden. In virtually every society, moreover, what people say they believe is often quite different from what they actually do. In sociological terms, the *ideal culture* — the values and norms that are formally accepted — conflicts with the *real culture*, or what is actually practiced. Staying together "till death do us part" is an ideal norm in Christian marriage, for example, but the real, or statistical, norm for one-third of American couples is getting divorced. According to Philip Slater, those neighbors who philosophize over the back fence are completely sincere when they agree that you-can't-take-it-with-you and success-doesn't-make-you-happy-it-just-gives-you-ulcers-and-a-heart-condition, but they would be horrified if their children took their views seriously.[21] These are examples of **cultural inconsistency**, a characteristic of a society that holds contradictory values and norms.

SOURCES OF INCONSISTENCY

The values and norms of a culture guide individuals toward the "right" or appropriate behavior in a particular social situation. When there is only one rule of conduct for every situation, it is easy to know how to act. If there are competing or inconsistent rules, however, individuals will have trouble deciding what to do. If the inconsistency is severe enough, serious social conflict will result. The current controversy over abortion reflects a conflict between the value placed upon an unborn child's right to life and the value placed upon a woman's right to control her own body. Other social conflicts have arisen from the strain between contradictory values. For example:

- During the Vietnam War, hundreds of thousands of young men were torn between the values of national loyalty and obedience to law on the one hand and humanitarianism and antimilitarism on the other. The norms dictated by those values were incompatible: military service and combat duty versus draft evasion or flight into exile.

- Candidates for political office often have to choose between the contradictory norms based on the competing values of success and honesty. To succeed, candidates may have to state opinions they do not hold, level unfair accusations against their opponents, and make secret deals with potential supporters; if they are completely honest, they risk losing the election.

- Police are sometimes under pressure to obtain evidence against suspected criminals by illegal means (such as searching a home without a warrant) and then to perjure themselves in explaining how they got it. In such a case, they are forced to choose between the value of uncovering criminal behavior and the value of telling the truth under oath.

The causes of such moral conflicts can be found in the social forces leading to cultural inconsistency: the influence of subcultures, the intrusion of new ideas from other cultures, and the phenomenon known as "culture lag."

---

[21] Philip Slater, *The Pursuit of Loneliness*, rev. ed. (Boston: Beacon Press, 1976), pp. 6–7.

SUBCULTURAL LANGUAGES

Special ways of thinking have special languages all their own. Members of some subcultures speak a nearly foreign tongue, which must be translated for outsiders. The following examples are from American occupational subcultures.

Bureaucratese

A quarantine notice in the Federal Register deals with Japanese beetles:

Regarding the area removed from regulations, the provisions of the regulations with respect to the interstate movement of regulated articles from regulated areas in quarantined States will not apply to the interstate movement of such articles from the specified counties but the provisions with respect to the interstate movement of regulated articles from nonregulated areas in the quarantined States will be applicable.

SOURCE: Quoted in Robert Sherrill, James David Barber, Benjamin I. Page, and Virginia W. Joyner, *Governing America: An Introduction* (New York: Harcourt Brace Jovanovich, 1978), p. 417.

The Language of Astronauts

The use of "we" was discouraged. "A joint exercise has demonstrated" became the substitution. "Other choices" became "peripheral secondary objectives." "Doing our best" was "obtaining maximum advantage possible." "Confidence" became "very high confidence level." "Ability to move" was a "mobility study." "Turn off" was "disable"; "turn on" became "enable."

SOURCE: Normal Mailer. *Of a Fire on the Moon* (Boston: Little, Brown, 1970), p. 39.

High-Tech Babble

Computer jargon is rapidly becoming part of everyday language, especially among workers in the electronics industries of California. Here are a few of the phrases heard around Silicon Valley (with their English translations):

"I'm interrupt driven." (My life is hectic and disorganized.)

"He's a read-only memory." (He never learns anything; he just keeps saying the same thing over and over.)

"He's pushing things on the stack." (He's overwhelmed and getting behind.)

John A. Barry, a former columnist for *Info-World* magazine, envisions a new language combining two California tongues — "computerese" and "psychobabble." It would go like this:

BABBLER 1: "I'm starting to relate to what you're saying. At first I was as down as my computer is when power spikes and bad vibes surge through the lines and don't go with the data flow, but now I think I'm beginning to feel a sense of wellness about this thing."

BABBLER 2: "Yeah, and you know, if you think of bad vibes on a power line as an analogue to bad vibes in the central nervous system, you've really accessed something important. People are really computers. They feel good; they feel bad — just like you and me. They relate to each other and interface with each other; people interface with each other; people interface with computers. Really cosmic parameters!"

BABBLER 1: "Wow! I'm accessing it!"

SOURCE: Robert Reinhold, "Computer People Are Creating a Valley of Babble in California," *The New York Times*, February 19, 1984, p. 30.

SUBCULTURES. Not only do people in all the different societies of the world share their own distinctive ideas, but groups of people within the same society also have their own ways of doing things. For instance, Italian-Americans as a group share distinctive ideas about religion, politics, and family life; they have a subculture, or particular ideas which they share because they belong to a certain group. Any identifiable ethnic group is a subculture because it has such distinctive cultural traits as a religion, a language, (see "Subcultural Languages") and particular customs in food and dress. In the United

States there are also regional subcultures, such as those found in the rural South, the urban industrial Midwest, and suburban California. In addition, certain occupations and professions are sometimes called subcultures because they have distinctive norms and values: physicians and lawyers have a special code of ethics, for example, and rock musicians and army officers have an identifying dress and language all their own. Some sociologists speak of the subcultures of still other groups — the very rich and the very poor, blue-collar workers and white-collar workers, homosexuals, young people, and the disabled. Even a single family can be considered a subculture if its members have special customs and words that only they use.

In *National Defense* (1981) James Fallows refers to a "culture of procurement" in the Department of Defense. Pentagon subculture teaches young officers that the way to get ahead is to manage a fully funded weapons program. In such a situation officers will fight for their country less fiercely than they will fight a threatened budget cut. Like other government bureaucracies the Department of Defense has no profit-and-loss sheet, and so it has no incentive to lower costs and produce more effective weapons. The central purpose of the peacetime military, Fallows finds, is to spend money: its goal is procurement, not defense. The most elaborate and expensive weapons are chosen because of their great cost, not in spite of it. And, in the words of one navy scientist, "nobody cares much what is bought as long as the money gets spent." [22] The values and norms of this subculture might astonish a civilian accustomed to those of the society at large.

While subcultures have some distinctive characteristics that conflict with the primary culture, they generally share most of the same practices and beliefs. *Counter-cultures*, in contrast, repudiate the basic norms and values of the larger culture. The term "counterculture" has most often been used to describe radically dissenting social or political groups (such as the Hare Krishna religious movement or the Ku Klux Klan).

EXTERNAL INFLUENCES.   The spread of ideas within a culture promotes consistency, but the intrusion of borrowed ideas from outside a culture promotes inconsistency. Modernization of developing countries, for example, breaks down traditional values and attitudes by introducing cultural elements from industrial societies — cash wages, birth control devices, universal education, technical machinery, and liberal political ideas. The social disorder that preceded the 1979 revolution in Iran is an outstanding example of the way a traditional culture can be shaken by the impact of alien norms and values.

CULTURE LAG.   Over fifty years ago, William Ogburn used the term **culture lag** for the maladjustment that occurs when one aspect of a culture changes more rapidly than other, related aspects.[23] In the last few years, for instance, rapid changes in medical technology have provoked troubling moral and legal questions about the "right to die." Artificial life support systems and the ability to slow the progress of incurable disease

---

[22] James Fallows, *National Defense* (New York: Random House, 1981), p. 64.
[23] William F. Ogburn, *Social Change with Respect to Culture and Original Nature* (1922) (New York: Dell, 1966), pp. 220–21.

have delayed the process of dying to the point where the gravely ill can be kept alive indefinitely. Cultural values and customs have not kept up with these medical advances. Because of the culture gap between technology and the law, doctors, relatives, judges, and the dying themselves do not have a shared idea about when life should end.

RESPONSES TO INCONSISTENCY

It is not unusual for social institutions to have inconsistent norms. Welfare and unemployment agencies, for example, exist to help individuals with their personal problems, yet they cannot do so efficiently without impersonal rules and regulations. The people who work there are thus pulled in one direction by the norms of sympathy and helpfulness, and in the other direction by the norms of loyalty to the agency and obedience to its regulations. Many institutions, in fact, operate more effectively just *because* they have to compromise between inconsistent sets of norms. If schools, welfare agencies, or hospitals were to act entirely on the basis of sympathy, they would become hopelessly bogged down, but if they were to function inflexibly according to the rules, they often would fail to provide the kind of help they are intended to give.

In other situations official norms interfere with the effort to reach goals that most people consider legitimate. In this case, there are likely to be *patterned evasions* — that is, regular deviations from the established norms. Many patterned evasions benefit the individual at the expense of other people. "Bending the rules" to get something one wants may result in ticket scalping, kickbacks to politicians on state contracts, fee splitting among physicians, expense account padding, or failure to report earnings on income tax returns. But patterned evasions also develop when official norms frustrate personal desires that are not harmful to others or even conflict with goals that people consider socially valuable. When most states had restrictive divorce laws, for example, married couples commonly offered false evidence in court in order to meet the legal requirements for a divorce. Lawyers and judges, though well aware of what was happening, regarded their dishonesty as a regrettable necessity.

Another patterned legal evasion is known as "plea bargaining." In this informal deal, an accused criminal agrees to plead guilty without a trial if the prosecutor will agree to charge him or her with a less serious crime. A famous example of plea bargaining was the case of former Vice-president Spiro T. Agnew, who resigned in 1973 after pleading *nolo contendere* ("I am not willing to contest it") to violating federal income tax laws. In return for this plea, Agnew received a suspended sentence and avoided prosecution for the real crime of which he was accused — taking bribes from highway contractors when he was governor of Maryland. Today, nine out of ten criminal convictions in the United States are obtained in this streamlined way. Given the present overload of the courts, nearly everyone agrees that the entire criminal justice system would collapse if plea bargaining were no longer used. Nevertheless, it clearly evades the official norms regarding crime and punishment.

INCONSISTENCIES IN AMERICAN CULTURE

Some of the values Americans hold most deeply are incompatible with each other. For example:

INDIVIDUALISM VERSUS COMMUNITY.   A cultural emphasis on individual rights and achievement has made "rugged individualism" an American tradition. The heroes of popular films and fiction have frequently been solitary characters who depended only on their own wits and strength to survive. Familiar examples include frontiersmen like Daniel Boone, wandering cowboys like the Lone Ranger, amoral gangsters like the Godfather, and independent private eyes like Sam Spade. At the same time, American society has traditionally had a strong sense of community. In the 1830s Tocqueville remarked on the great number and variety of voluntary associations to which Americans belonged, but he feared that their pursuit of democratic individualism would confine each "entirely within the solitude of his own heart." [24]

In recent years sociologists have repeated Tocqueville's warning: our private lives will become distorted and meaningless if we fail to link our self-interest to the larger community. In *The Pursuit of Loneliness,* Philip Slater argued that "the belief that everyone should pursue his own destiny" has forced us to become emotionally detached from our social and physical environment. The more "free" we are, he found, the more we feel "bored, lonely, unprotected, unnecessary, and unsafe." [25] Christopher Lasch angrily denounced the American "culture of narcissism," [26] and Richard Sennett mourned the erosion of public life through a narrow preoccupation with the private self.[27] In *Habits of the Heart,* Robert Bellah and his associates concluded that the individualistic language of "looking out for #1" and "being your own best friend" fails to provide Americans with a way to understand and articulate their deepest commitments to other people.[28]

SELF-DENIAL VERSUS CONSUMPTION.   Max Weber identified the Protestant ethic of hard work and self-denial as the spirit of capitalism. The virtues of work, thrift, and prosperity also represent traditional American values. The maxims in Benjamin Franklin's *Poor Richard's Almanac* (1757) have taught generations of Americans that "a sleeping fox catches no poultry," "he that goes a-borrowing goes a-sorrowing," and "early to bed and early to rise makes a man healthy, wealthy, and wise." But in the contemporary United States, other voices are trying to drown out Poor Richard: "Fly now, pay later," "You deserve a break today. . . . We do it all for you," "Yes, you can have it all!" Instead of producing and saving, commercial advertising urges everyone to consume and spend. The cultural message is thus contradictory: be industrious and thrifty, but have fun and buy things. The sociologist Daniel Bell has called these inconsistent values "the cultural contradictions of capitalism." [29]

Through mass production and mass consumption, Bell argues, capitalism destroyed the Protestant ethic by promoting self-indulgence. Today the American eco-

---

[24] Alexis de Tocqueville, *Democracy in America,* Part II (1840), Book II, Chapter 2.

[25] Philip Slater, *The Pursuit of Loneliness,* rev. ed. (Boston: Beacon Press, 1976), pp. 25–26.

[26] Christopher Lasch, *The Culture of Narcissism: American Life in an Age of Diminishing Expectations* (New York: Norton, 1979).

[27] Richard Sennett, *The Fall of Public Man* (New York: Knopf, 1977).

[28] Robert N. Bellah et al., *Habits of the Heart: Individualism and Commitment in American Life* (Berkeley: University of California Press, 1985).

[29] Daniel Bell, *The Cultural Contradictions of Capitalism* (New York: Basic Books, 1976).

Cultural inconsistency arises from contradictory norms and values. American culture places a high value on both self-denial and consumption.

nomic system is justified not by the values of hard work and self-control but by the high value American culture places on pleasure and material possessions.

According to Tom Wolfe, an acute observer of the American social scene, three decades of unprecedented prosperity after World War II produced the "Me" decade of the 1970s.[30] With the important exception of the very poor, every level of the population now has enough surplus income, leisure, and personal freedom to pursue happiness through self-fulfillment. The result, he said, is such self-absorbed "Me" movements as group therapy, transcendental meditation, Oriental philosophy and evangelical religions, feminism, and sexual permissiveness.

COMPETITION VERSUS CONCERN FOR OTHERS. Since Americans believe in activity and achievement, it is not surprising that they love competition. Sports, especially professional football and baseball, are a national obsession. But most of all, Americans admire winners. Joseph P. Kennedy, the father of two U.S. senators and of a president of the United States, used to tell his children that there is no such thing as second place; there is only winning and losing.[31] Although the result of this attitude frequently has been callous treatment of "losers" like native Americans, segregated blacks, and welfare families, Americans also have a tendency to sympathize with the underdog. They are proud of their country's reputation as a haven for the poor and oppressed, and they are often quick to offer aid to victims of war and natural disasters.

In *The Cycles of American History* (1986)[32] the historian Arthur M. Schlesinger, Jr. described the alternating periods of public concern and private interest in American

---

[30] Tom Wolfe, "The 'Me' Decade and the Third Great Awakening," *New York,* August 23, 1976, pp. 26–40.
[31] Richard J. Whalen, *The Founding Father* (New York: New American Library/Signet, 1964), p. 168.
[32] Boston: Houghton Mifflin, 1986.

The Russians have adopted some American customs, but they have not given up their own cultural values and practices.

society. He found that a period of growing responsibility to the community, sustained by liberal ideas of freedom and equality, is followed approximately every generation by a period of retrenchment, when conservative values and individual self-interest are emphasized.

In terms of Schlesinger's analysis, the last generation has been a period when me-first attitudes predominated. During the 1980s the public interest was abused again and again by scandals involving stock market manipulations in Wall Street, fraud in the savings and loan industry, and influence peddling in the Department of Housing and Urban Development.

In spite of this "age of avarice," many Americans continued to hold strong altruistic values. In fact, Daniel Yankelovich's surveys during this period reported increasing concern with community and caring relationships and less emphasis on competition and "keeping up with the Joneses." As economic growth has slowed, Yankelovich believes, both the traditional value of self-denial and the "free-to-be-me" style of self-fulfillment are giving way to a new social ethic of commitment. In his 1980 survey, 47 percent of the respondents said they felt a "hungering for a community," compared with 32 percent in 1973.[33] In a 1978 poll, only 13 percent (compared with 34 percent in 1970) said that "work is the center of my life."[34] Moreover, Yankelovich reports that the number of Americans engaged in community activities with neighbors, fellow church members, coworkers, and other groups has grown by nearly 50 percent.[35]

As they enter the decade of the 1990s, Americans once again appear to be searching for ways of reconciling the contradictory values of individualism and community, self-denial and self-expression, competition for material well-being and commitment to others.

CULTURAL INTEGRITY

In the 1970s a team of social researchers replicated the classic study that Robert and Helen Lynd had made of Muncie, Indiana (renamed "Middletown"), in 1923. As expected, the researchers found widespread evidence of cultural change: Muncie had more divorce, more pornography, and more marijuana in the 1970s than in the 1920s. The surprising finding, however, was not change but continuity. In spite of all the social upheavals of the past 50 years, Muncie high school students replied to certain questions in the same way their grandparents had. The same proportion (47 percent) agreed that "it is entirely the fault of a man himself if he does not succeed."[36] Similar numbers of adolescents said they had disputes with their parents over getting home late at night, and a majority still found the Bible a "sufficient guide to all the problems of modern life."[37]

The major change in the later Middletown study was a loosening of traditional norms concerning religion and women's roles. In 1924 an overwhelming majority (94 percent) of Muncie residents believed that "Christianity is the one true religion" and "everyone should be converted to it." By 1977 only 41 percent agreed, indicating a strong shift toward tolerance of others' religious beliefs.[38] In the 1920s the Lynds had found that 52 percent of teenage girls thought that being a good cook and housekeeper were the most desirable qualities for a mother, but by 1977 only 24 percent of their granddaughters' generation agreed.[39]

---

[33] Daniel Yankelovich, *New Rules: Searching for Self-Fulfillment in a World Turned Upside Down* (New York: Random House, 1981), p. 95.

[34] Ibid., p. 11.

[35] Ibid., p. 94.

[36] Theodore Caplow and Howard M. Bahr, "Half a Century of Change in Adolescent Attitudes: Replication of a Middletown Survey by the Lynds," *Public Opinion Quarterly* 43 (1979): 1–17.

[37] Howard M. Bahr, "Changes in Family Life in Middletown, 1924–77," *Public Opinion Quarterly* 44 (Spring 1980): 24.

[38] Theodore Caplow, "The Measurement of Social Change in Middletown," *Indiana Magazine of History* (December 1979).

[39] Howard M. Bahr, "Changes in Family Life in Middletown, 1924–1977," Middletown III Project Paper #6 (1978).

FIGURE 3-1 AMERICAN VALUES: CONTINUITY AND CHANGE

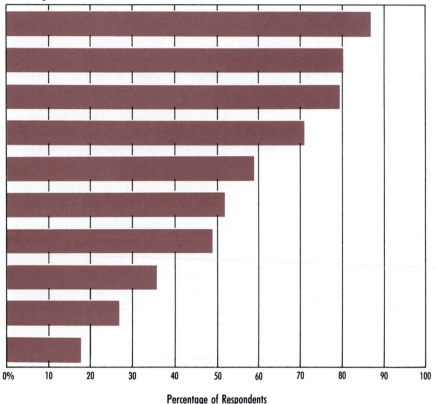

The Strength of Traditional Norms in the Late 1980s

Favor sex education in the public schools

Agree it is sometimes necessary to discipline children with a good, hard spanking

Believe extramarital sex is always wrong

Would continue to work even if they were to get enough money to live comfortably the rest of their lives

Believe birth control should be made available to 14 to 16 year olds, even if parents disapprove

Believe people have the right to commit suicide if they have an incurable disease

Believe the most important thing for a child to learn to prepare for life is "to think for himself or herself"

Believe it should be legal for a woman to have an abortion for any reason

Agree that women should take care of running their homes and leave running the country to men

Favor the legalization of marijuana

0% 10 20 30 40 50 60 70 80 90 100

Percentage of Respondents

Although change is often said to be the one constant feature of American life, many distinctive aspects of American culture have persisted generation after generation. (See Figure 3-1). Many of the features of the society Tocqueville described in the 1830s have survived, and today Americans still hold most of the same basic values and obey many of the same norms that their grandparents did. Like other cultures, American culture continues to have a unity and reality all its own.

THE STRAIN TOWARD CONSISTENCY

The Chinese drink Coca-Cola, the Japanese are wild about baseball, and rock music and denim jeans are the latest fads in the Soviet Union. Millions of Americans own German cars and Japanese television sets. "Merchants," as Thomas Jefferson said, "have no country."

As international trade and economic development have spread Western culture across the world, traditional non-Western attitudes and values appear to be breaking down. Industrialization and the growth of bureaucracy have given the developing

FIGURE 3-1   (cont'd)

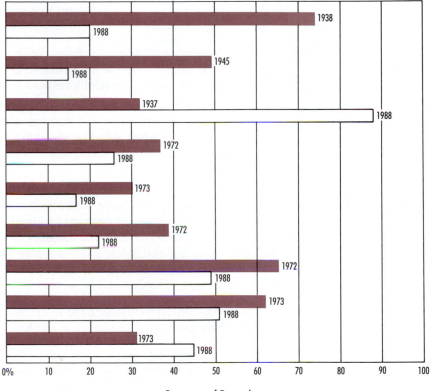

Changes in Social Norms

Percentage of Respondents

countries of Asia and Africa some of the same customs and many of the same business-oriented values as those in the West share. Some people have speculated that these developments could eventually result in a world culture based on advanced technology and rational organization. According to this view, the Western emphasis on efficiency and practicality will replace the "outmoded" values of the feudal Indian caste system and the Islamic theocracies of Iran and Saudi Arabia.

On the other hand, the intrusion of Western ideas and values has been strongly resisted by other peoples since the fifteenth century. African and Asian cultures are complex ways of life that rest on assumptions quite different from Western ideas of scientific progress, the desirability of material comforts, and the value of worldly accomplishment. Religious values usually convey the essence of a culture, and the opposition to Western influences has frequently come from religious sources. Iran, which once seemed to offer a lesson in how a "backward" society could be rapidly modernized, now demonstrates how traditional religious groups can successfully resist an attack on their most deeply held values and customs.

In Iran, as in nearly every other society, cultural consistency is the rule and inconsistency the exception. Culture shows what Sumner called a "strain toward consistency," a natural tendency to make the norms in one area of life harmonize with those in other areas. During periods of social change, when norms and values are in flux, several processes limit the inconsistencies that would otherwise arise. Those processes are

1. *Constraint:* As some parts of a culture change, other parts constrain, or prevent, intolerable conflicts. In the 1979 Iranian revolution, the Shah's land reform and modernization policies were successfully resisted by large landowners and the religious establishment.

2. *Diffusion:* The spread of new ideas and customs eventually dissolves cultural differences. In modern societies, diffusion through the mass media is especially rapid and thorough. Watching American sports on television undoubtedly encouraged the Japanese passion for baseball.

3. *Ranking:* Some values and norms are considered more important, or higher in rank, than others, making the choice between them less difficult and reducing inconsistency. For the Chinese, the decision to drink Coca-Cola is not in the same category as the decision to convert to Christianity or capitalism. Trivial cultural ideas are often easily diffused, while those of higher rank meet far greater resistance. For this reason, most Asian and African cultures remain inconsistent with the modern industrial way of life.

In an article on economic development, the writer William Pfaff notes the importance of cultural differences:

> The religious values, moral assumptions, and social structures of . . . (Asian and African) societies are at best alien, and sometimes hostile, to the values and practices of industrialism. This situation cannot be changed by the injection of money, machines, or technical instructors. For these societies to "develop" . . . would require a radical and destructive remaking of life and society, and, often, a reinterpretation of the meaning of existence itself. . . . What often is put forward as a simple transfer of resources, techniques, and information is, in fact, a revolutionary enterprise of the most momentous consequence.[40]

---

[40] William Pfaff, "Reflections: Economic Development," *The New Yorker,* December 25, 1978, pp. 44–47.

SUMMARY

1. Culture is shared ideas — the customs, beliefs, and knowledge that are learned from others and passed from generation to generation. A specific culture is the set of ideas which a number of people share because they belong to a certain society.

2. Only human beings have the capacity for culture, and only they can communicate through symbols,

especially language. Animals can be taught to communicate in crude and limited ways, but so far they have not been known to pass their knowledge to their offspring.

3. People experience the world around them in terms of their culture and language. According to the Sapir-Whorf hypothesis, differences in language lead people to think differently.

4. Culture influences behavior through shared ideas about reality. What is real to us depends on how we interpret our sense experiences, and people in different cultures do not give the same meaning to their experiences.

5. Values are shared ideas about what is morally right and desirable. American values include achievement and success, activity and work, and equality.

6. Norms are shared ideas about how to behave. Folkways, or cresive norms, arise spontaneously; enacted norms are official rules and laws. Mores are norms defining how one *must* act.

7. The self is also a cultural product because our values, standards, and ideas about ourselves are learned from others.

8. Social scientists have found few cultural universals in the enormous diversity of human cultures. Sociobiology, which argues that social behavior is genetically controlled, has been criticized by scientists who argue that genetic and environmental factors are inseparable. Common patterns of behavior apparently exist because they meet basic human needs and thus contribute to the survival of the species.

9. Ethnocentrism, the belief that one's own culture or group is superior to others, is extremely common. Some groups, however, exhibit xenocentrism, the belief that their way of life is inferior.

10. To avoid ethnocentrism, anthropologists before World War II adopted the practice of cultural relativism: they tried to be totally objective about the behavior of different peoples. Contemporary researchers are more likely to judge cultural practices according to universal humanistic values.

11. Cultural inconsistency arises in part from the contradiction between ideal culture and real culture. Inconsistency increases when new norms and values are introduced by subcultures and countercultures, by external influences, and by differing rates of cultural change (culture lag).

12. American culture shows contradictions between individualism and community, self-denial and consumption, and competition and concern for others.

13. Cultures nearly always have more consistency than inconsistency. According to Sumner, people in a society reduce inconsistency through constraint, diffusion, and ranking of norms. These processes have allowed many Asian and African cultures to maintain their traditional way of life.

KEY TERMS

culture 64, 74
symbol 66
value 70
norms 72

folkways 72
mores 72
taboos 73
cultural universals 75

ethnocentrism 80
cultural inconsistency 82
subculture 83
culture lag 84

SUGGESTED READING

* Robert N. Bellah et al. *Habits of the Heart: Individualism and Commitment in American Life.* Berkeley, CA: University of California Press, 1985.
* Ruth Benedict. *Patterns of Culture* (1934). Boston: Houghton Mifflin, 1961.
* Edward T. Hall. *The Silent Language.* Garden City, NY: Doubleday/Mentor, 1973.
* Marvin Harris. *Cows, Pigs, Wars, and Witches: The Riddles of Culture.* New York: Random House/ Vintage, 1974.

* Eugene Linden. *Apes, Men and Language.* Baltimore: Penguin, 1976.
Ralph Linton. *The Cultural Background of Personality.* New York: Appleton-Century-Crofts, 1945.
* Philip Slater. *The Pursuit of Loneliness: American Culture at the Breaking Point,* rev. ed. Boston: Beacon Press, 1976.

* Available in paperback.

If every man
could act as he
chose, the whole
of history would
be a tissue of
disconnected
accidents.

Leo Tolstoy

CHAPTER 4

SOCIAL STRUCTURE

During the 1960s, the government of Uganda created a national park and game preserve out of the ancient hunting grounds of a local tribe, the Ik. No longer allowed to hunt game in the park, the Ik were forced to leave the plains and attempt farming in the barren mountains beyond. Not surprisingly, they were unable to adjust to this completely new way of life, and soon the whole tribe was on the brink of starvation. The desperate search for food turned tribal members into mortal enemies. Parents sent their 3-year-old children out to fend for themselves, and the strong stole food from the old and sick. The Ik even built their huts with low doorways so that thieves entering in search of food could be speared in the back of the neck. Hunger had turned their society into a warring collection of isolated individuals. The tribe had literally been reduced to the unsocial condition that the seventeenth-century philosopher Thomas Hobbes described as "solitary, poor, nasty, brutish, and short."

Colin Turnbull, an anthropologist who studied the Ik, came to the melancholy conclusion that enduring human values like love and loyalty are really only luxuries that can quickly be given up.[1] However, another conclusion can be drawn from the Ik's disaster: social structure is indispensable to social life. Without their customary relationships based on hunting, the tribe could not be an organized whole. When the social bonds connecting the Ik hunters were severed, their sense of common purpose and affiliation was also lost. Without a social structure, in other words, the Ik became an assortment of hostile individuals instead of a unified society.

---

[1] Colin Turnbull, *The Mountain People* (New York: Simon and Schuster, 1972).

This boy and girl have already learned what kind of behavior is expected of the statuses "male" and "female." Would he react in the same way if she were pouring water over him?

Social structure is the stable set of relationships among individuals and groups that enables them to function as a society. Disparate individuals are linked to the larger social order by their acceptance of rules controlling their behavior and by their willingness to carry out the important tasks that benefit the group as a whole. While conflicts are inevitable in social life, there must also be predictable patterns of interaction between such groups as parents and children, workers and managers, and producers and consumers. Whether they belong to simple Stone Age tribes or live in complex industrial societies, human beings would not long survive without the dependable relationships that govern their lives together.

This chapter begins with a discussion of the basic elements of social structure: the assignment of social position *(status)* and the behavior expected of people in different social positions *(roles)*. Much of our social life is spent in rather structured groups: our families, our school classes, our work groups. The following sections explore how our membership in various groups affects the way we think, feel, and act; the way we see the world; and the way we see ourselves.

THE ELEMENTS OF SOCIAL STRUCTURE

Two small girls are playing a game. One says to the other, "I'll be the mommy and you be the baby." Although she would hardly understand the sociological term, this little girl has just built, in play, a tiny social structure.

In its simplest form, a social structure is an arrangement of individuals in various positions. These positions are linked to one another to form a network, like the one shown below. The strands of the network represent relationships between individuals and among groups. Each position is a status, and the strands are roles that link the individual in that position to people in other positions.

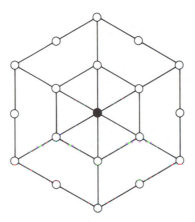

In sociology, **status** refers to any position, high or low, that has socially defined rights and obligations. A **role** is the cluster of norms that go with a certain status; that is, the behavior expected of a person in a particular social position. Even young children understand that "mommy" and "baby" are statuses that involve very different kinds of behavior.

Status and role are associated, but they are not the same thing. The roles assigned to certain statuses, for example, can be reassigned to others. The nurturant role in child care (feeding, bathing, diapering) has traditionally belonged to the status of mother, but it has recently begun to shift to the status of father as well. The money-earning role traditionally belonged to the status of husband, but today it often belongs to both the husband and wife. Changing sex roles — the new behavior expected of the status of "man" and "woman" — are the most interesting contemporary example of the way different roles can become attached to a status (see Chapter 10, "The Sexes").

From the cultural perspective social life is possible because most members of a society agree on the norms of behavior. From the structural perspective social life is possible because most members of a society can rely on people in various statuses to act in known and predictable ways. If we could not count on most people to carry out the roles connected with their statuses, life would be hopelessly chaotic. We rely on the manager of the supermarket to have food on hand for us to buy, but what if he decided not to open the store when he felt like going fishing instead, or if he sometimes stocked only housewares and newspapers? We rely on doctors and nurses to be at the hospital when we need them, but what if they showed up only when they were in the mood, or if they refused to take care of patients they didn't like? If most of us couldn't trust others to act as they are supposed to, social life would be uncertain and extremely inefficient.

STATUS AND THE SELF

In the beginning, human infants have no conception of their identity and no self-image. Gradually, month by month and year by year, they learn what other people think of them and they begin to think of themselves in the same way. Much of what others see and respond to in us, however, is not our innate, or "real," being but the statuses we occupy (as child, daughter, sister, first grader, and so on) and the roles they call for. The male child and the female one, the black child and the white one, the poor child and the rich one, the Catholic child and the Jewish one — all slowly realize how the world regards them and tend to adopt the world's view of themselves. Each acquires what sociologists call the **self** — a conception of one's own identity and personal characteristics based largely on how other people define one's place in society (status) and what behavior (role) they expect of an individual in that status.

The process of self-definition continues beyond childhood. When a woman graduates from college or gets married or is elected to public office, people see her in a different way and she learns to see herself in this new way. On the other hand, if she flunks out of college or gets a divorce or is indicted for a crime, her own view of herself is likely to change according to how others see her — as a college dropout, a divorcée, or a criminal. In sociological terms her self-image changes along with her status.

OUR SOCIAL SELVES.   Everyone, of course, occupies more than one status. A typical college student could probably list a dozen along the lines of son, brother, Protestant, roommate, undergraduate, English major, member of the basketball team, and so on. Each individual thus fills an array of social positions called a **status-set**.[2]

The diagram on page 97 of one individual's social network is therefore far too simple. Each dot (status) should be a cluster of dots (status-set), and each dot in the cluster should have its own relationships to others (roles). Suppose the central dot in the diagram represents Jane Doe, a married woman with two children, a schoolteacher, a representative of the teachers' union, and an officer in the women's organization of her church. Under a higher-powered sociological microscope, her dot is a complicated status-set like the one shown in Figure 4-1.

Clearly, Jane Doe's social self, like that of every other adult, is complex and multifaceted. This complex self is sometimes simplified when it is governed by one important "master status." A judge, for example, might be dignified even in the locker room, and an older woman could be motherly toward her co-workers at the office. Nevertheless, most people tend to see themselves as a slightly different person in each of their statuses and behave accordingly.

ASCRIBED AND ACHIEVED STATUS.   Like the rest of us, Jane Doe was born with some of her statuses (daughter) and acquired others (teacher) as she grew up. An **ascribed status** is one assigned to us without regard for our innate differences or individual abilities. Sex, age, and race are ascribed statuses: very few individuals have been able to change their sex, or disguise their age, or join another racial group. An **achieved status**, in contrast, is acquired through personal effort, or sometimes by chance. In the United States, for example, occupations are achieved statuses: people choose to become miners or weight lifters according to their opportunities and abilities.[3]

---

[2] Robert K. Merton, *Social Theory and Social Structure*, enl. ed. (New York: Free Press, 1968), pp. 422–38.
[3] Ralph Linton, *The Study of Man* (New York: Appleton-Century-Crofts, 1936), p. 115.

JANE DOE'S STATUS-SET   FIGURE 4-1

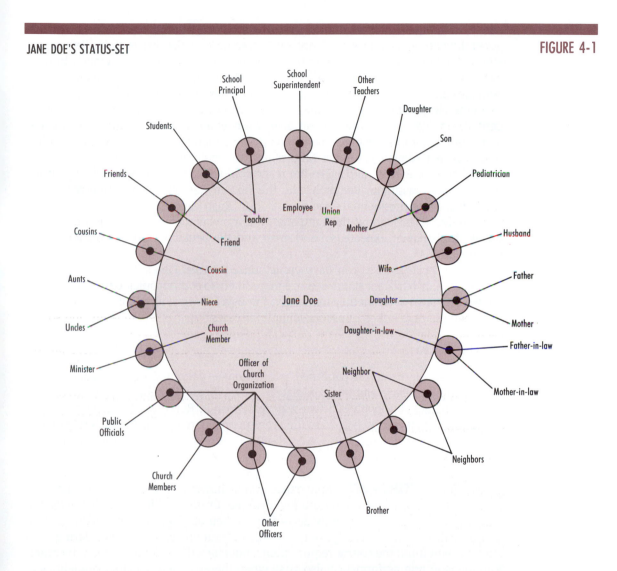

The social structures of most simple societies are based on ascribed status. In feudal systems, for example, everyone's position and functions are rigidly set at birth, and few people manage — or even try — to change them. In medieval Europe, the sons of serfs did not become knights and the daughters of aristocrats did not become members of weavers' guilds. In complex industrial societies, however, many occupational statuses are acquired through specialized training. The sons of the poor can become generals, and the daughters of the rich can be fashion designers. Industrial societies are thus characterized by their *social mobility*, or freedom to move from status to status, both upward and downward.

Most societies have a strong tendency toward **status consistency**. A status-set is said to be consistent when the statuses in it make compatible demands of the individual and offer compatible opportunities and rewards. People who take on new statuses generally choose only those that are easy to acquire or that cause them little social strain. A town's mayor is far more likely to become president of the Lions Club, for example, than the head of a nudist society. *Status inconsistency,* or incompatible demands and rewards in a status-set, is often the cost of social mobility.

When Representative Geraldine Ferraro became the first woman to be a vice-presidential candidate, there was a great deal of uncertainty about whether to treat her according to her inferior status as woman or her superior status as powerful political figure. In her campaign tour of Mississippi, the male commissioner of agriculture called her "young lady" and asked her if she could bake blueberry muffins; in a press conference in Scranton, Pennsylvania, the Roman Catholic bishop referred to the Republican vice-presidential candidate as "Mr. Bush" and to the Democratic one as "Geraldine."[4] Throughout the campaign, Ferraro was forced to walk a fine line between the behavior expected of a woman and the behavior expected of a national candidate.

These social stresses can have grave consequences. One study has shown that people with inconsistent status-sets are more likely to commit suicide than those with consistent status-sets; another found that the psychological stress of occupying conflicting statuses is linked to psychosomatic diseases.[5]

SOCIAL ROLES

All social life is based on patterned interactions — patterned because each person knows how to behave and (approximately) how others will behave; and interactions because the activity involves a two-way relationship. Roles are the socially defined expectations that link each of us to the other people in our lives. All of us rely on our knowledge of social structure for clues about what to expect of the people we meet and how to cope with them.

ENFORCING ROLE PERFORMANCE.   Role expectations, however, are not a straitjacket, and society permits some variation from the ideal. For example, different individuals will perform the same role differently according to their abilities and personalities. Two drivers will both drive legally, but one will be cautious and the other daring; two students will fulfill the course requirements, but one will work harder than the other. Variations in role performance also arise when there are contradictory guidelines to behavior. When we tell a "little white lie" to protect another person's feelings, for example, we are obeying the norm of being polite instead of the norm of being truthful.

Society cannot operate smoothly if too many individuals stray too far from their prescribed roles. Routine daily pressures thus keep us conforming to expectations. Sometimes these pressures are exerted directly. Many wives tell their husbands, "If you ever cheat on me, I'll leave you," when they mean, in sociological terms, "I regard

---

[4] Maureen Dowd, "Ferraro Campaign: Perspectives that Startle," *The New York Times,* October 10, 1984, p. A21.

[5] Jack P. Gibbs and Walter Martin, "A Theory of Status Integration and Its Relationship to Suicide," *American Sociological Review* 23 (April 1958): 140–47; Elton F. Jackson, "Status Consistency and Symptoms of Stress," *American Sociological Review* 27:4 (August 1962): 469–80.

Prince Charles, the heir to the British throne, was born with the ascribed status of royal prince, but he acquired the achieved statuses of husband and father.

sexual infidelity as an intolerable departure from your role as husband." Sometimes social pressures are exerted indirectly. Work groups in factories, for instance, usually have informal quotas for their output, and any worker who outperforms the others is punished for "rate busting": other members of the group pass nonconformists more work than they can possibly keep up with, supposedly as a joke, but actually as a way of embarrassing or pressuring them until they step back into line.[6]

People have even more subtle ways of letting others know how to behave. We all use our facial expressions, tone of voice, and style of speech to signal someone we are meeting for the first time what role we are playing and what role we expect the other person to play in return. This "front," as sociologist Erving Goffman called it, defines the situation and assigns the roles. Depending on whether the person we are meeting

[6] Erving Goffman, *Encounters: Two Studies in the Sociology of Interaction* (Indianapolis: Bobbs-Merrill, 1961), p. 77.

for the first time says "Hi, Mary!" "Please sit down, Miss Smith," or "Next!" we know immediately what kind of behavior to expect and what kind is expected from us.[7]

ROLE SETS.   Just as each person has not one status but a complex status-set, each of those statuses has not one associated role but a whole array of them — a **role-set**.[8] Thus Figure 4-1, showing Jane Doe's status-set, is far from a complete picture of her connections with other people. In Figure 4-2 we can see that just one of her statuses, "mother," has a complicated set of roles connected to it. This is the role-set of only one of Jane Doe's statuses. Other role-sets exist for all her other statuses — wife, teacher, daughter, and so on. An average adult like Mrs. Doe probably performs about one hundred roles in all; a preschool child might have only a handful of roles; the president of the United States, with his many statuses, might have several hundred.

ROLE CONFLICT.   Some roles are inherently difficult to perform. No amount of training can make it easy to lead a foot patrol through a jungle or nurse a sick child. Sometimes a person is unsuited for an achieved role: some actors suffer terribly from stage fright. Sometimes a person is forced to perform a new role without any preparation; widows, for example, usually have trouble adjusting to the unmarried role thrust upon them. Difficulty in performing a social role is called **role strain**.

The most widespread form of role strain comes from **role conflict**, the incompatibility or competition between different roles. If a policeman investigating a crime finds that his own son is one of the culprits, for example, he will have a severe role conflict: if

---

[7] Erving Goffman, *The Presentation of Self in Everyday Life* (New York: Doubleday/Anchor, 1959), p. 22.
[8] Merton, *Social Theory and Social Structure,* p. 423.

FIGURE 4-2   THE ROLE-SET FOR ONE OF JANE DOE'S STATUSES

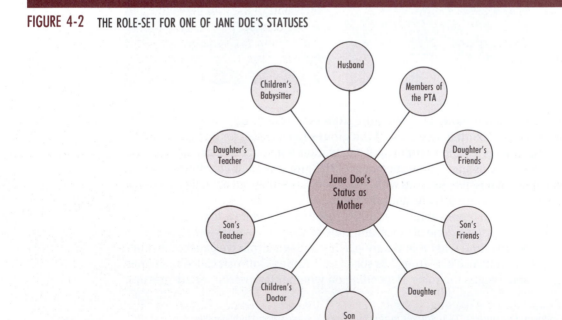

he acts according to his role as a policeman, he cannot act as a father, and if he acts according to his role as a father, he cannot act as a policeman.

Most role conflicts fall into two categories. In the first category are conflicts that arise because of status inconsistency. The competing demands of the status of physician and the status of wife, for example, leads to a conflict between the roles a woman doctor performs in meeting her obligations to her patients and to her husband. In the second category are conflicts that arise because the roles within a single status are contradictory. A factory foreman, for example, may be pulled in opposite directions by his relationship to his supervisors, who expect him to enforce the rules, and his relationship to the workers he supervises, who expect him to be a "good guy" and bend the rules a little.

Most people think of role conflicts as their own personal problems. They try to decide which is the "right" thing to do — see a daughter act in the school play or be at work; try to please the boss or help out the other guys; cram for an exam or go to football practice. From the sociological perspective, however, it is clear that these dilemmas are not just personal problems. They are built into the social structure. Considering the number of potential conflicts between the roles of all our separate statuses, and then adding to them the number of potential conflicts between the roles of *each* status, we can only wonder how anyone can endure social life at all.

The answer is rather simple. We manage the inherent conflicts of social life by a number of coping mechanisms.[9] For example, most of us juggle our role relationships by spending more time and energy on one and cutting back on another. The salesman, therefore, will give up an evening with customers to celebrate his wife's birthday — or decide that success is more important and neglect his family roles. Role conflict is sometimes reduced by giving part of one role to someone else. Working mothers, for example, hire housekeepers and babysitters to perform part of their homemaking and child-care roles. Finally, people sometimes solve a role conflict by breaking off one relationship or abandoning an inconsistent status. Politicians, for example, occasionally retire from public life so that they can pursue other interests or spend more time at home.

Mechanisms like these generally reduce role conflict, but they cannot eliminate it entirely. When the mechanisms fail, and if the conflict is severe enough, conflicting roles can lead to family problems, suicide, and criminal behavior.

As we have seen, the structure of society is a network of different statuses, linked to each other by interconnecting roles. The individual's relationship to various groups as well as the bonds between members of separate groups are the strands that hold the society together. We turn now to the question of how different kinds of groups affect society and the behavior of the individual.

SOCIAL GROUPS

When most people say "group," they mean any number of persons who happen to be together — commuters waiting at a bus stop, or a theater audience. We also use the

---

[9] Ibid., pp. 425 – 38.

term informally for statistical purposes. Census takers report that there are so many million people in the 18-to-20 age group; pollsters break down voting patterns by income groups. To a sociologist, none of these so-called groups is a group at all. A **social group** consists of a number of people who define themselves as members of a group; who interact frequently according to established and enduring patterns; who expect certain behavior from other members that they don't expect from outsiders; and who are defined by both fellow members and nonmembers as belonging to a group on the basis of some shared characteristic.[10] The interaction among people in a group can be face to face and intimate, as it usually is in a family, or it can be remote and impersonal, as it typically is between the board of directors and the employees of a large corporation.

By this definition, the commuters and the theater audience are not social groups but **aggregates** (or **collectivities**). They have never met before and probably never will again, and, aside from saying "Excuse me" if they bump into each other, they do not interact at all. They do, however, have a common idea of how to behave and what is expected of them. The theater audience, for example, knows that no one should talk out loud during the performance; if anyone does, others will probably say "Sh!" or

---

[10] Ibid., pp. 339–40.

BOOTH

"Mrs. Van Lewis-Smythe, the third wife of your chairman of the board, said to me this evening at the corporate hoodingy, and twenty people within earshot, 'We all know what *Mr.* Parmalee does. He is a very important vice-president of the Hi Lee Lolly Corporation. What we are all wondering, Mrs. Parmalee, is . . . just what is it that *you* do? Do you do anything?' I said, 'Mrs. Van Lewis-Smythe, Your Grace, I fix dripping faucets around our house. I prop up sagging book shelves. I glue broken china. I clean windows, mirrors, floors, walls, pots and pans, and dishes. I jiggle the doodada on running toilets. I repair and refinish furniture. I cane chairs, I paint and sew. I do electrical work, drive nails, saw boards, and I give birth to our babies. I wash and iron and make the beds. I prepare the meals. I get the children to school. I trim the hedge, plant and maintain a vegetable garden and flower garden. I mow the lawn, clean the basement, feed the birds, cats, a dog, and a chicken, and I chauffeur a very important vice-president of the Hi Lee Lolly Corporation to and from the bar car every blessed day.' "

Drawing by Booth; © 1978 The New Yorker Magazine, Inc.

indicate disapproval in some other way. The commuters might object strenuously if one of them pushes ahead of the others waiting to get on the bus. They share norms, but not an enduring relationship.

Technically, statistical groups are not groups but **social categories**. Members are unlikely to meet face to face, and they do not necessarily have any common norms or interests. They are only lumped together according to a particular social characteristic, such as age or income.

Collectivities are potential social groups. The commuters, tired of waiting for the bus, may decide to start a car pool. Their car pool will fit the definition of a social group. Its members will get to know each other, meet frequently at a certain time and place, and call themselves members of the pool. Other people will also identify them as members of this particular group.

Social categories can also be organized into social groups. Their common social characteristic can become the basis for similar interests and values, and thus for social interaction. Airline flight attendants, for example, are a social category, but they have a common interest in keeping their jobs and improving their working conditions. If they form a union and begin to fight for the right to keep their jobs after they marry, as stewardesses once did, then they become a social group. The union members begin to know each other, to meet regularly, and to recognize each other and be recognized as members of a certain group.

In the reality of the social world the lines that separate the social group from the collectivity are roughly drawn, and the boundaries marking the group off from the category are occasionally changed. The group, however, can be distinguished by its conscious sense of identity, its endurance over time, and its effects on social behavior.

THE SIGNIFICANCE OF NUMBERS

One obvious difference among groups is their size. The relationship between two people — the smallest possible group — is bound to be quite different from the relations among fifty or five hundred people.

Georg Simmel (1858–1918), one of the founders of sociology, argued that the key distinction was between a two-person group, or dyad, and a three-person groups, or triad.[11] He thought that there was a factual basis to the old saying "Two's company and three's a crowd." Both members of a dyad know that their group cannot exist if one of them leaves, so they have to agree or dissolve the group. The introduction of a third person changes this special relationship. The members of a triad no longer have to agree, and one of them can be overrruled by the other two. As Simmel noted, triads often break down into a pair and an intruder, or "two against one." This is the "eternal triangle" that is found everywhere — in politics (the United States, the Soviet Union, and Eastern Europe), economics (manufacturer, worker, consumer), and the family (husband, wife, mother-in-law). In triads there is always pressure to form a coalition of two weaker members against the stronger third.[12]

---

[11] Georg Simmel, *The Sociology of Georg Simmel*, trans. and ed. Kurt H. Wolff (New York: Free Press, 1950), pp. 148–69.

[12] Theodore Caplow, *Two Against One* (Englewood Cliffs, N.J.: Prentice-Hall, 1968), pp. 2–18.

Large groups and small groups also have different effects on behavior. The members of a small group are much more likely to become deeply involved with each other. In a larger group, there are so many possible relationships that everyone can't get to know everyone else very well. To take an everyday example, when one person is introduced to another — "Miss Smith, this is Dr. Miller" — there are two people and one relationship. Another person is introduced to both of them — "Miss Smith and Dr. Miller, this is Mr. Jones" — and then there are three people and six relationships (Smith to Miller, Smith to Jones, Smith to Miller and Jones, Miller to Jones, Miller to Jones and Smith, Jones to Miller and Smith). Introduce another person to all three of them and there are 25 relationships; a fifth person joins the group and there are 90 possible relationships; a sixth makes 301 and a seventh makes 966 possible relationships![13]

The astronomical number of potential relationships in a large group cannot be handled informally. A large group cannot rely on spontaneity and casual agreement. It needs specific norms, roles, and responsibilities. Someone has to be in charge, someone has to be assigned important tasks, and someone has to coordinate their efforts. A group of five may be a society of equals, but a group of fifty necessarily becomes a society of unequals.

The size of a group affects its structure, leading to changes in the behavior of its members. When people are in a group of close friends they behave differently than they do in a large, impersonal organization like a corporation.

PRIMARY AND SECONDARY GROUPS

The American sociologist Charles Horton Cooley (1864–1929) defined **primary groups** as those characterized by intimate, long-lasting relationships among a small

---

[13] A. Paul Hare, *Handbook of Small Group Research* (New York: Free Press, 1962), p. 229.

Modern social encounters are more likely to take place in secondary groups than in primary groups. More and more, the friendly neighborhood grocery is being replaced by the impersonal self-service chain store.

number of people. Primary relationships are intrinsically satisfying and enjoyable; they are an end in themselves and not a means to a political, economic, or any other end. Each member of a primary group is interested in the other members as unique individuals, and their relationship is purely personal. The people involved feel free to speak their minds and express emotion. Close friends and families are the typical primary groups.

If people associated only when they liked each other, however, society would not last long. Secondary groups provide enduring relationships that are not dependent on personal attraction and intimacy. The characteristics of **secondary groups** are roughly the opposite of primary groups. Members of secondary groups have disparate rather than common goals, and they value the extrinsic political, economic, or other benefits of the relationship rather than the relationship itself. While relations in primary groups are personal and spontaneous, those in secondary groups are impersonal and constrained. Such relations exist, for example, between sales clerks and customers, employees and executives, and taxpayers and the Internal Revenue Service. Because secondary contacts are brief and formal in nature, they are not emotionally involving. When you buy toothpaste in a drugstore, whether or not you like the clerk is irrelevant. As far as you are concerned, the transaction could just as well be made by an automatic vending machine.

If this distinction sounds too simple, it is because primary and secondary groups are sociological concepts that do not exist in their pure forms in the real social world. Every primary group actually has some secondary characteristics. Husbands and wives, for example, have formal, contractual obligations to each other. Moreover, it would be difficult to find a secondary group that was completely rational and unfeeling. In fact, most secondary groups rely on the primary relationships among their members, since no group could long survive without the loyalty and cooperation of the people who belong to it.

1941 – 1945

Giant secondary groups such as the U.S. Army are sustained by the primary-group bonds among their members.

A famous research study showed the importance of primary groups in the German military during World War II. Although outnumbered and constantly defeated on all fronts, the army was able to maintain its discipline and fighting effectiveness for several years of almost continuous retreats. The rates of desertion and surrender were extremely low. Observers at the time attributed the Germans' extraordinary tenacity to their Nazi ideology, which stressed loyalty to Hitler and devotion to the fatherland. When Edward Shils and Morris Janowitz studied the situation, however, they found that these secondary-group loyalties were not the real source of the soldiers' will to resist. Primary-group life in the army turned out to be much more important for sustaining discipline and morale. The German combat soldiers they interviewed emphasized the camaraderie of their units, frequently referring to them as "one big family." As long as these close primary-group bonds were maintained, resistance was very determined, regardless of the political attitudes of the soldiers. Shils and Janowitz concluded, "Many are bound into the larger society only by primary group identifications. Only a small proportion possessing special training or rather particular kinds of personalities are capable of giving a preponderant share of their attention and concern to the symbols of the larger world." [14]

---

[14] S. A. Stouffer et al., *The American Soldier* (Princeton, N.J.: Princeton University Press, 1949).

The American Soldier, an exhaustive study of primary groups in the U.S. Army, confirmed Shils and Janowitz's hypothesis.[15] Neither hatred of the enemy nor devotion to patriotic ideals was as important in combat as "not letting the other fellow down." The primary group of "buddies" sustained the will to fight in two ways: it set group standards of behavior and it supported the individual under the stress of battle.[16] Soldiers, it seems, do not fight and die for their country alone, but for each other.

GEMEINSCHAFT AND GESELLSCHAFT

In modern times more and more of our social relationships have a secondary nature. In a largely urban, industrial, individualistic society, most of our encounters with other people are likely to be impersonal and instrumental. The sheer size and complexity of the world around us appears to be hostile to spontaneous, intimate relationships.

The German sociologist Ferdinand Tönnies (1855–1936) called a closely involved group that is held together by largely primary bonds **Gemeinschaft**, or community. Its prototypes are the family, the neighborhood, the village, and the church. In contrast,

These members of New York City's Department of Sanitation obviously have close personal relationships with their co-workers. Such informal groups thrive within the apparently "faceless" organizations that characterize urban life.

[15] Edward Shils and Morris Janowitz, "Cohesion and Disintegration in the Wehrmacht in World War II," in Edward Shils, *Center and Periphery* (Chicago: University of Chicago Press, 1975), p. 383.
[16] Edward Shils, *Center and Periphery*, p. 391.

Gesellschaft, or society, is characterized by impersonal ties of rational self-interest, or what we would call "secondary relationships." Such associations are found in the factory, the laboratory, the bureaucracy, the city. At the time that Tönnies was writing, it seemed that the modernization of the world would mean the end of *Gemeinschaft.* Urbanization and industrialization were turning society into a large, impersonal organization where individuality would be sacrificed to efficiency and reason would prevail over emotion.

However, a recent study by Claude Fischer found that *Gemeinschaft* relationships thrive in the apparently "faceless" urban environment. Since the city puts large numbers of people within reach of one another, everyone has hundreds of "next-door neighbors" to choose among. The city thus offers a shift from "neighboring of place to neighboring of taste." [17] Fischer's analysis suggests that since urban people have more freedom to select their associates than rural people, those they choose are probably more compatible.

In the urban *Gesellschaft,* Fischer found, individuals create primary relationships within secondary groups. Similar interests in politics, in art or music, or in sports and weekend activities draw people together into clubs and other small groups. Business associates become "friends from the office." Informal groups thrive within the formal organizations that characterize urban life.

The truth is that people — no matter where they are — need to belong to intimate social groups. They need friends and family on whom they can rely for emotional and moral support. City dwellers as well as villagers live in neighborhoods and belong to primary groups (see "Small Towns in a Big City"). Urban relationships do not replace the social ties of the rural community; they add to them.

THE STRENGTH OF WEAK TIES

We have noted that primary relationships alone cannot maintain the social order. According to one theory, strong interpersonal ties actually weaken a community's social organization. Mark Granovetter has proposed that a sense of community depends on weak ties between groups, not on traditional *Gemeinschaft* relationships.[18] When two people are close friends, he argues, they tend to have friends in common, and their friendship circles overlap. These mutual friends then introduce each other to their friends, leading to *cliques,* or clusters of people with strong ties to each other. In his analysis of many research studies, Granovetter found that information spreads to more people over a greater social distance when it is passed by persons without strong ties to each other. For example, if you tell a rumor to all your close friends, and they pass it along to their best friends, many of you will hear the same story two or three times. Very soon the rumor will stop being repeated, and the information will not go beyond a select group. If you tell your barber the same story, however, it will probably spread all over town. He will tell all his customers, and they will tell the people they meet, and so on. The rumor will thus pass along a wide network of weak social ties.

---

[17] S. Keller, *The Urban Neighborhood* (New York: Random House, 1961), quoted in Claude S. Fischer, *The Urban Experience,* 2nd ed. (San Diego: Harcourt Brace Jovanovich, 1984), pp. 140–41.

[18] Mark S. Granovetter, "The Strength of Weak Ties," *American Journal of Sociology* 78:6 (May, 1973): 1360–81.

SMALL TOWNS IN A BIG CITY

E. B. White's Here Is New York *begins with a celebrated statement about city life: "On any person who desires such queer prizes, New York will bestow the gift of loneliness and the gift of privacy." But, White goes on to say, New York also offers the "excitement of participation" and the sense of protection against all the "enormous and violent and wonderful events that are taking place every minute." One reason New York is able to bestow these contradictory gifts is that its city-dwellers actually live in small-town neighborhoods.*

The oft-quoted thumbnail sketch of New York is, of course: "It's a wonderful place, but I'd hate to live there." I have an idea that people from villages and small towns, people accustomed to the convenience and the friendliness of neighborhood over-the-fence living, are unaware that life in New York follows the neighborhood pattern. The city is literally a composite of tens of thousands of tiny neighborhood units. There are, of course, the big districts and big units: Chelsea and Murray Hill and Gramercy (which are residential units), Harlem (a racial unit), Greenwich Village (a unit dedicated to the arts and other matters), and there is Radio City (a commercial development), Peter Cooper Village (a housing unit), the Medical Center (a sickness unit) and many other sections each of which has some distinguishing characteristic. But the curious thing about New York is that each large geographical unit is composed of countless small neighborhoods. Each neighborhood is virtually self-sufficient. Usually it is no more than two or three blocks long and a couple of blocks wide. Each area is a city within a city within a city. Thus, no matter where you live in New York, you will find within a block or two a grocery store, a barbershop, a newsstand and shoeshine shack, an ice-coal-and-wood cellar (where you write your order on a pad outside as you walk by), a dry cleaner, a laundry, a delicatessen (beer and sandwiches delivered at any hour to your door), a flower shop, an undertaker's parlor, a movie house, a radio-repair shop, a stationer, a haberdasher, a tailor, a drugstore, a garage, a tearoom, a saloon, a hardware store, a liquor store, a shoe-repair shop. Every block or two, in most residential sections of New York, is a little main street. A man starts for work in the morning and before he has gone two hundred yards he has completed half a dozen missions: bought a paper, left a pair of shoes to be soled, picked up a pack of cigarettes, ordered a bottle of whiskey to be dispatched in the opposite direction against his home-coming, written a message to the unseen forces of the wood cellar, and notified the dry cleaner that a pair of trousers awaits call. Homeward bound eight hours later, he buys a bunch of pussy willows, a Mazda bulb, a drink, a shine—all between the corner where he steps off the bus and his apartment. So complete is each neighborhood, and so strong the sense of neighborhood, that many a New Yorker spends a lifetime within the confines of an area smaller than a country village. Let him walk two blocks from his corner and he is in a strange land and will feel uneasy till he gets back.

Storekeepers are particularly conscious of neighborhood boundary lines. A woman friend of mine moved recently from one apartment to another, a distance of three blocks. When she turned up, the day after the move, at the same grocer's that she had patronized for years, the proprietor was in ecstasy—almost in tears—at seeing her. "I was afraid," he said, "now that you've moved away I wouldn't be seeing you any more." To him, *away* was three blocks, or about seven hundred and fifty feet.

SOURCE: E. B. White, *Here Is New York* (New York: Harper & Row, 1949), pp. 27–30.

Granovetter's theory explains why Boston's close-knit Italian community was unable to unite in opposition to the urban renewal program that finally destroyed it. The Italian neighborhood was fragmented into families and cliques with such strong ties that members neither needed nor wanted any other connections. As a result, information about the urban renewal plan did not reach more than a few groups. Because each clique was isolated from the others, the community never got together to make an effective protest.

At the same time another working-class neighborhood in Boston successfully organized against the same urban renewal plan. In contrast to the Italian West End neighborhood, the Charlestown community had a number of local organizations where residents met each other. Most residents lived and worked in the same part of the city, so the friendships they made at work also carried over to their community life. Granovetter concluded that weak ties make wider networks than strong ties, which tend to be concentrated within small groups of people. Weak ties, instead of leading to isolation, appear to be necessary for integration into the community. Strong ties, although they breed cohesive groups locally, lead to fragmentation of the larger social order.

THE FORMATION OF SOCIAL GROUPS

There was once a group of twenty-four little boys who arrived at a summer camp in Connecticut. They were all about 12 years old, they all came from lower-middle-class families in New Haven, they were all Protestants, they had similar IQs and educational backgrounds, and they had no behavior problems. After three days of living together in one large bunkhouse, the campers began to form friendships, based on personal attraction and common interests. They were then deliberately divided into two groups that in most cases excluded the friends they had made. These groups were kept apart as much as possible. They lived in different bunkhouses and they swam, hiked, and camped out separately. After five days the boys were choosing their friends almost exclusively within their own groups. Boys who continued to see their friends from the other group were called "traitors" and were threatened with beatings.

"I'd like to think of you as a person, David, but it's my job to think of you as personnel."

Drawing by Victor;
© 1986 The New
Yorker Magazine, Inc.

The groups named themselves the "Bull Dogs" and the "Red Devils." Each developed special norms—nicknames, certain ways of doing things, punishments for getting out of line, favorite songs, and so on. Each group's members felt they were different and better than those of the other group. They said things like "their lousy cabin" and "our pond is better." In the next five days a series of competitive games was arranged between the two groups. Although the contests began in a spirit of good sportsmanship on both sides, they ended with bitterness and hostility between the two teams. The winners were called "dirty players" and "cheats" by the losers. A full-scale battle with knives and cups in the mess hall was stopped by the counselors, but the groups continued to insult and provoke each other.

The Bull Dogs and the Red Devils were participating in Muzafer Sherif's famous experiment in intergroup relations. Just by dividing the boys into two groups, Sherif was able to produce much of the characteristic behavior of social groups. After only five days together, the boys had developed a social structure of leaders and followers, they had agreed upon norms and sanctions, and they were showing feelings of loyalty and mutual identification. The boys also demonstrated another interesting sociological phenomenon: allegiance to one group bred hostility to the other. Along with cohesiveness, comradeship, and team spirit came intolerance, prejudice, and belligerence. Carried to extremes, loyalty to one's own group became chauvinism and hatred of outsiders.[19]

IN-GROUPS AND OUT-GROUPS

Almost ninety years ago William Graham Sumner named such hostile groups **in-groups** and **out-groups**. He distinguished between

> ourselves, the we-group, or in-group, and everybody else, or the others-groups, out-groups. . . . The relation of comradeship and peace in the we-group and that of hostility and war towards others-groups are correlative to each other. . . . Loyalty to the group, sacrifice for it, hatred and contempt for outsiders, brotherhood within, warlikeness without—all grow together, products of the same situation.[20]

Many observers have followed Sumner's lead in assuming that all groups have in-group characteristics. Indeed, the supporting evidence is all around us. The English- and French-speaking populations of Quebec, the Protestants and Catholics in Northern Ireland, and the Sunni and Shi'ite Muslims in the Middle East all exhibit hostility to each other as the out-group.

In fact, not all groups are in-groups. Membership in one group, fortunately, does not always mean ill will toward everyone else. Some groups, as we shall see, actually admire and imitate the behavior of other groups.

REFERENCE GROUPS

Some people, even members of in-groups, look to outsiders for guidance on how to behave. The group (or social category) they use as a model is called a **reference group**.

---

[19] Muzafer Sherif, "A Preliminary Experimental Study of Attitudes," *Sociometry* 1 (1937): 90–98.
[20] William Graham Sumner, *Folkways* (New York: Ginn, 1906), pp. 12–13.

If people take the norms of another group for their frame of reference, then they cease to conform to the norms of their own group. Some of them become renegades, social climbers, or turncoats.

A classic study of reference group behavior was conducted in the 1930s at Bennington, a private women's college. During the four years they were in college, most of the undergraduates showed a dramatic change in political attitudes, from freshman conservatism to senior liberalism. In a 1936 mock-presidential election, for example, 62 percent of the freshmen, but only 14 percent of the juniors and seniors, voted for the Republican candidate Alf Landon; and 9 percent of the freshmen, but *30 percent* of the upperclassmen, voted for the Socialist or Communist party candidate.

The students whose attitudes shifted had switched reference groups from family to college. They had been influenced by their most prestigious classmates, who in each class were also the most liberal politically. The students who remained conservative did not find their reference group in the college community. They referred to their families for their political attitudes. Although they admitted that "it's considered intellectually superior here to be liberal or radical," these students didn't change their conservative attitudes. One said, "I guess my family influence has been strong enough to counterbalance the college influence." [21]

THE POWER OF THE GROUP

> At the beginning, I felt the place was a cross between boot camp and a POW camp. . . . The counselors and the rules make you very dependent, like children. "Do what we say," they keep telling you. "Don't ask, just do it." . . . One reason (they limit) . . . the TV and telephoning and even reading is that they want you to form strong ties with the group of 20 people who live in your hall, and learn how to rely on them to help you with problems. . . . If a patient has very strong defenses and little trust, they make him wear a blindfold . . . for 24 hours, and he has to be led around by another patient, as an exercise in developing trust. . . . The end result was a kind of miracle. I went in there at the end of my rope, in despair, . . . and I came out, after just four weeks, feeling optimistic, courageous, and able to cope. . . . They gave me back my life.[22]

This account was written by a former patient at the Betty Ford Center for drug and alcohol rehabilitation in Rancho Mirage, California. The techniques of group therapy she describes have been used successfully to teach addicts to turn to other people instead of drugs or alcohol when they have problems.

Many experiments have shown that it is easier to change the behavior of a small group when the members are taken together than when they are treated separately as individuals.[23] In addition to being a source of new opinions and attitudes, the group

[21] Theodore M. Newcomb, "Attitude Development as a Function of Reference Groups: The Bennington Study," in *Readings in Social Psychology*, rev. ed., eds. G. E. Swanson, T. M. Newcomb, and E. L. Hartley (New York: Holt, 1952), pp. 420–30.

[22] *Newsweek*, September 24, 1984, p. 59.

[23] Kurt Lewin, "Group Decision and Social Change," in *Readings in Social Psychology*, 3rd ed., eds. Eleanor Maccoby et al. (New York: Holt, 1958), 197–211.

offers social and emotional support during critical moments of decision. The true service of many self-help groups — whether Weight Watchers, Smokenders, or Alcoholics Anonymous — may well be providing mutual support, sympathetic understanding, and friendship to their members. The formal, explicit purpose of losing weight or giving up cigarettes or alcohol may really be of lesser importance.[24]

When we look for the reasons people act as they do, we tend to forget the power of the group to affect individual behavior. We are likely to look for hidden psychological causes for people's peculiarities or to seek completely rational and logical motives for individual behavior. When some American prisoners of war in Korea collaborated with the enemy, for example, the press and public looked for the reasons in their family backgrounds, their army careers, and their psychological makeup. Going over to the

---

[24] Natalie Allon, "Latent Social Services in Group Dieting," *Social Problems* 23 (January 1975): 59–69.

In this 1944 photograph, crew members on the U.S.S. *New Jersey* humiliate a Japanese prisoner. Isolation from one's own group is a means of inducing the psychological breakdown known as "brainwashing."

enemy side was attributed either to lack of patriotism and will power or to selfishness and cowardice.

A more scientific analysis found that the Chinese induced psychological break-downs in the American prisoners by systematically destroying the structure of their groups. They broke the military chain of command by segregating the officers, so that most of the prisoners could look to no formal authority. The captors reversed the usual positions of authority by appointing squad leaders from the lowest ranks or from among prisoners who were willing to cooperate with the Chinese. They prevented the creation of primary groups by (1) outlawing any social activity, including religious services and recreation not sponsored by the Chinese, (2) discouraging and segregating informal leaders, (3) using spies and informers so that the prisoners never knew whom they could trust, and (4) weakening the prisoner's faith in their officers and fellow prisoners by showing them false evidence of their collaboration and their forced confessions to war crimes. Although the prisoners were subject to the psychological pressures of fear and uncertainty, as well as severe physical hardships, the most important feature of the Chinese prison camp was the withdrawal of social supports. The men were cut off from the opinions, beliefs, and knowledge of their fellows; they could not discuss their situation, ask advice, or weigh the consequences of their actions with people they could trust. As a result, collaboration was usually caused not by disloyalty or opportunism but by poor judgment and lack of information. The key element in their "brainwashing" appears to have been sociological rather than psychological.

LEADERSHIP

Unless they are very small, groups require leadership to accomplish their goals. Since some members will always receive more prestige and respect from their fellows, a leader soon emerges in any group. In the normal course of events, this leader will be the person who is the most active and does the best job.

It seems a matter of course that the leader would also be the best-liked member of the group. When Robert F. Bales tested this "obvious" conclusion with an experimental group, however, it turned out to be untrue. The most able member of Bales's group was not the best liked at all. In fact, the individual who emerged as the group leader on the basis of good ideas and active participation became less and less popular with each meeting. Activity, ability, and likability did not go together. These findings made Bales think that there might be *two* leaders in a group, an idea person who did the best job and a best-liked person who handled personal emotional problems. Subsequent experiments supported his hypothesis. The most active and able members of small groups became leaders who concentrated on the group's task. They tended to be aggressive, even antagonistic. The best-liked members asked more questions and reacted more positively to the others. The result was the emergence of two complementary leaders: the *instrumental leader,* who specialized in performing the task, and the *expressive leader,* who specialized in taking care of the group's feelings.[25]

---

[25] Robert F. Bales, "Task Roles and Social Roles in Problem-Solving Groups," in *Readings in Social Psychology,* pp. 437–47.

A number of studies have shown that power and influence in small groups cannot be separated from power and influence in the larger society. Studies of juries show that male jurors and jurors with higher-ranking occupations are likely to participate more, have more influence, and appear more competent to the others than women and people in low-ranking occupations. The owner of a business is three or four times as likely as a laborer to be elected foreman of a jury, and a woman has only one chance in five.[26]

Even when married couples disagree, who persuades whom is related to the husband and wife's relative power in the community. Navajo women, for example, have high social prestige, while Mormon women are completely dependent on their husbands for their social standing. Who gets her way in the family decisions? Most of the time the Navajo wife wins and the Mormon wife loses.[27]

From the sociological perspective, leadership is not so much a matter of an individual's personal charm and ability as it is a social requirement. Since most groups need a leader, someone will inevitably take on the job. Sociologists also show us that groups tend to choose leaders who already have greater prestige and power because of their class, sex, or some other social characteristic. Other members of the group, however, are not simply the "followers" they are often said to be.

The Asch experiments on conformity concluded that virtually everyone finds it difficult to disagree with a united group.

CONFORMITY

Groups don't always follow their leaders, and leaders are constantly influenced by their followers. Sherif concluded from his study of the boys' summer camp that groups do

[26] Fred L. Strodtbeck et al., "Social Status in Jury Deliberations," in *Readings in Social Psychology,* pp. 379–88.

[27] Fred L. Strodtbeck, "Husband-Wife Interaction over Revealed Differences" in *Small Groups: Studies in Social Interactions,* rev. ed., eds. A. Paul Hare, Edgar F. Borgatta, and Robert F. Bales (New York, Knopf, 1965), pp. 464–72.

GROUPTHINK CAUSES A PERFECT FAILURE: THE BAY OF PIGS DECISION

Solidarity, conformity to group norms, and striving for unanimous agreement lead to what the psychologist Irving L. Janis calls "group-think." He believes that a deterioration of logical thought and moral judgment results from the pressure to concur in cohesive groups. As Janis shows in his analysis of the 1961 Bay of Pigs fiasco, groupthink is disastrous for rational decision making.

The Kennedy administration's Bay of Pigs decision, according to Janis, "ranks among the worst fiascoes ever perpetrated by a responsible government."

> **Planned by an overambitious, eager group of American intelligence officers who had little background or experience in military matters, the attempt to place a small brigade of Cuban exiles secretly on a beachhead in Cuba with the ultimate aim of overthrowing the government of Fidel Castro proved to be a "perfect failure." The group that made the basic decision to approve the invasion plan included some of the most intelligent men ever to participate in the councils of government. Yet all the major assumptions supporting the plan were so completely wrong that the venture began to founder at the outset and failed in its earliest stages.**

How could it happen? How could a group of the "best and the brightest" be so wrong? According to Janis's theory of groupthink, members of small cohesive groups tend to maintain *esprit de corps* by unconsciously developing shared illusions and group norms that can interfere with critical, rational thought. He believes that the following illusions were held by members of the Kennedy team as they were deciding whether or not to approve the CIA's invasion plan:

1. *An illusion of invulnerability*. Optimism, faith in the new president, and confidence in their own superior abilities gave Kennedy's group of advisers a feeling that "nothing could stop us." Hand in hand with this illusion went an unrealistically low opinion of Castro's military forces, a characteristic in-group tendency.

2. *An illusion of unanimity*. Personal doubts were suppressed in an atmosphere of complete agreement. Adviser and historian Arthur Schlesinger reproached himself afterward for his failure to voice his misgivings, saying that he had been afraid of creating a nuisance by objecting to the majority decision.

3. *Self-censorship*. By never opening the agenda to opposing arguments, President Kennedy encouraged the group's docility and uncritical acceptance of the CIA's plan. He was a one-sided discussion leader: he never distributed dissenting information or pursued the issues he knew were controversial. The evidence is that the president was not interested in opposing views because he had already made up his mind that the invasion would take place.

4. *A group norm against damaging criticism*. President Kennedy and his inner circle admired Allen Dulles and Richard Bissell, the two CIA representatives who were holdovers from the Eisenhower administration. As highly prized new members of the team, they were more likely to get a favorable and uncritical reception for their plan than outsiders would have. By giving these men preferential treatment in the way he handled the meetings, President Kennedy set the group norm for going easy on the plan.

Janis notes in conclusion:

> **The failure of Kennedy's inner circle to detect any of the false assumptions behind the Bay of Pigs invasion plan can be at least partially accounted for by the group's tendency to seek concurrence at the expense of seeking information, critical appraisal, and debate. Most crucial were the symptoms that contributed to complacent overconfidence in the face of vague uncertainties and explicit warnings that should have alerted the members to the risks of the clandestine military operation — an operation so ill conceived that among literate people all over the world the name of the invasion site has become the very symbol of perfect failure.**

SOURCE: Irving L. Janis, *Victims of Groupthink* (Boston: Houghton Mifflin, 1972), pp. 14–49.

tend to go along with a dominating person, but not if the leaders stray too far from the norms of the group. Moreover, if a leader changes his or her opinion after the group's decision is settled, the group occasionally stops following the individual's lead. The leader is then in the position of the nineteenth-century socialist who said, "My followers are on the barricades. I must go lead them."

Sherif's findings indicate that even strong leaders are weaker than a united group. Even in a friendly group, when the issue isn't a burning one, everyone knows how uncomfortable it can be to stand up against the majority view. Nearly all of us, whether we give in or not, feel some pressure to go along with the others. In a well-known series of experiments, the social psychologist S. E. Asch showed that people will even contradict what they see with their own eyes in order to conform with the majority view.

The Asch experiments placed one individual in radical disagreement with all the other members of a small group. Eight male college students were told to match the length of a given line with one of three unequal lines. Each person announced his judgment in turn. Seven of the students were collaborating with the experimenter to make wrong—and unanimous—answers. Suddenly, in the middle of this monotonous "test," the subject found himself contradicted by the entire group. Everyone was saying he was wrong when he thought he was right. What did he do?

One-third of the students tested went along with the majority. They either made the same errors as the others or changed their answers in the direction of the group's response. The remaining two-thirds of the subjects resisted the pressure to conform. The subjects tended to behave very differently: some were very independent and never gave in, and some went with the majority nearly every time. Practically everyone, however, felt the pressure to conform. The independent subjects were puzzled and hesitant, and apologized for disagreeing even when they insisted they were right. Although some suspected that the test was a trick or an illusion, they were still troubled, as if disagreeing with the majority reflected badly on their judgment rather than on that of the group.[28]

What if the others in the group had not been unanimous in their judgments? Variations on the same experiment showed that if one other person in the group responded correctly, the power of the majority was reduced, even destroyed. The subjects acted more independently and made significantly fewer errors. It turned out that a unanimous judgment of three persons had far more influence on the subject than a majority of eight with one dissenter. The experiments thus demonstrated the power of social support as well as the power of social opposition. (For a discussion of some dangers of conformity, see "Groupthink Causes a Perfect Failure.")

The results of the Asch experiments also showed that it is deviation *from what is expected,* not simply deviation itself, that causes the pressure to conform. If differences of opinion are expected, then there is no conflict, no stress, no pressure to go along. The subjects in the Asch experiments thus acted much more independently when dissent appeared to be permitted—that is, when group opinion was not unanimous. It seems that social behavior need not be uniform, just dependable.

---

[28] S. E. Asch, "Effects of Group Pressure upon the Modification and Distortion of Judgments," in *Readings in Social Psychology,* pp. 174–83.

Small groups necessarily involve personal, face-to-face relationships. Their influence on behavior is thus quite different from groups with hundreds or even thousands of members. Chapter 6, "Organizations," takes up the story of large bureaucracies — what they do for us, what they do to us, and why they dominate our society. Part 4, "Social Institutions," deals with the various groups and organizations that carry out the tasks necessary for society to survive. Groups, organizations, and institutions together account for the persistent patterns of human relationships that make up the structure of society.

SUMMARY

1. Social structure is the stable set of relationships among individuals that enables them to function as a society. Its basic elements are statuses, or social positions, and roles, the behavior expected of people in various statuses.

2. A conception of one's identity, or self, is largely based on how other people define one's status and what behavior (role) they expect.

3. Everyone occupies an array of social positions, or a status-set. Some of these statuses are ascribed, or assigned without regard for individual effort or ability; others are achieved, or acquired through personal choice and effort. Most societies tend to have status consistency: the social demands on individuals are usually compatible.

4. Role performance is enforced by social pressures to conform to expectations. Individual variations arise from differing abilities and inclinations, but some deviation is socially permitted.

5. Each status has an array of different roles, collectively called a role-set. A typical adult, occupying several statuses, may perform as many as one hundred roles.

6. Role strain is difficulty in performing any one role; role conflict is competition between different roles. These difficulties are managed through role bargaining, delegation, and role elimination.

7. A social group is composed of people who interact frequently according to established and enduring patterns. Social categories and aggregates (or collectivities) are not groups by this definition.

8. The numerical size of a group affects its structure, leading to changes in the behavior of its members. Primary groups are characterized by intimate, long-lasting relationships among a small group of people. Large secondary groups have disparate goals and value the extrinsic benefits of the relationship rather than the relationship itself. Families, for example, are primary groups; corporations are secondary groups.

9. According to Tönnies' definition, *Gemeinschaft*, or community, is characterized by primary-group bonds; *Gesellschaft*, or society, is characterized by the secondary-group ties of rational self-interest.

10. In-groups are groups whose members are loyal to their fellow members and hostile to outsiders, or out-groups. Reference groups provide models of behavior, both for members and occasionally for nonmembers.

11. Small groups can have a powerful effect on changing individual behavior. The key factor in brainwashing, for example, appears to be sociological rather than psychological.

12. Groups require a leader to accomplish their goals. Small groups often have two complementary leaders: an instrumental leader, who specializes in accomplishing the group's task, and an expressive leader, who specializes in taking care of the group's feelings.

13. The Asch experiments on conformity in small groups showed how both social support and social opposition influence individual behavior.

KEY TERMS

social structure 96

status 97

role 97

self 98

status-set 98

ascribed status 98

achieved status 98

status consistency 99

role-set 102

role strain 102

role conflict 102

social group 104

aggregates (collectivities) 104

social categories 105

primary group 106

secondary group 107

Gemeinschaft 109

Gesellschaft 110

in-group 113

out-group 113

reference group 113

SUGGESTED READING

* Herbert J. Gans. *The Urban Villagers,* 2d ed. New York: Free Press, 1982.

* William Golding. *Lord of the Flies.* New York: Putnam, 1964.

Robert K. Merton, *Social Theory and Social Structure,* rev. and enl. ed. New York: Free Press, 1968.

* Theodore M. Mills. *The Sociology of Small Groups.* Englewood Cliffs, N.J.: Prentice-Hall, 1967.

Robert A. Nisbet. *The Social Bond.* New York: Knopf, 1970.

* Gerald Suttles. *The Social Order of the Slum.* Chicago: University of Chicago Press, 1968.

Louis A. Zurcher. *Social Roles: Conformity, Conflict, and Creativity.* Bevery Hills, CA: Sage Publications, 1983.

* Available in paperback.

The chief tools
of childraising
are example
and nagging.

Miss Manners

CHAPTER 5

SOCIALIZATION

I n 1787 some hunters "captured" a wild boy near Aveyron in southern France. For about a year he had been seen running naked on all fours, foraging for food in the woods. The boy was sent to Paris, where he was examined and found to be about 11 years old. Although he was unable to speak and had scars all over his body, the boy did not seem to have any serious physical disabilities. More puzzling still, he was clearly human in a biological sense, but he lacked such distinctly human traits as speech, manners, and emotional expression. Physicians at the time declared the "wild boy of Aveyron" to be hopelessly feebleminded. Others speculated that he had been abandoned by his parents as an infant and raised by wolves.

Efforts to train the boy were only partly successful. After several months he was able to master simple social skills (eating with a knife and fork, wearing clothes, using a toilet), and he began to show such emotions as gratitude and remorse. The "wild boy" lived to be over 40 years old, but he never learned to speak and never became what we would call a normal human being.[1]

Many societies have legends about feral children, or children brought up by wild animals. The twin brothers Romulus and Remus, the mythical founders of ancient

---

[1] Harlan Lane, *The Wild Boy of Aveyron.* Cambridge, Mass.: Harvard University Press, 1976.

Rome, are typically portrayed being suckled by a wolf. In our own century, Tarzan represents the myth of the lost boy who is raised by animals in the wild. These stories fascinate us because they pose the question of how much of what we are is purely biological and how much is the result of our social upbringing. Over the centuries some philosophers have believed that children raised in isolation would reveal the essentially brutish nature of all human beings, while others have argued just the opposite: that children growing up in a state of nature would be uncorrupted by human vice and hypocrisy, and therefore pure and virtuous. Whatever our theories of human nature may be, the scientific evidence is that young children who are deprived of social contact never become fully developed human beings.

The life of the wild boy of Aveyron represents a failure of socialization, the process through which people learn the behavior and attitudes appropriate to their roles in society. To understand what went wrong in this boy's case, we need to know more about what people learn during the socialization process, how they learn it, and who influences them most.

This chapter begins by noting that people have to be taught the physical, intellectual, and social skills they need to be fully human. Then it describes the leading theories of socialization, which explain how the individual self is formed through interaction with others. The third part discusses some of the ways particular groups and institutions influence an individual's socialization, especially in childhood. Socialization, however, is a lifelong process. We are continually redefining our identities in our new social roles as adults, parents, employees, and so on. The final part of this chapter discusses socialization in adolescence, adulthood, and old age.

LEARNING TO BE HUMAN

A newborn infant is a helpless creature. Unable to move around, protect itself, or perceive the world in any coherent way, a baby is more like a bundle of nerves than a human being. Unlike the offspring of other animals, the infant child inherits few biological guidelines for survival. Nevertheless, this little bundle of nerves will eventually become both a unique personality and an active member of society. The transformation occurs through **socialization**, the interactive process by which individuals acquire some of the values, attitudes, skills, and knowledge — in short, the culture — of the society to which they belong.

Socialization involves, first of all, learning social roles and being motivated to perform them. If a society is to survive, men and women have to want to have children and be good parents. The importance of family life is instilled in us as we grow up, along with the socially expected feelings of love and loyalty that sustain the commitment to husbands, wives, and children. Like actors, we are trained for our roles in the social drama. So that the show can go on, younger actors are trained to replace older performers as they leave the stage. Societies reproduce themselves in this manner, passing on a changing cultural inheritance of values and social behavior from one generation to the next.

People obviously don't take in culture from the air, nor do they invent all their own beliefs and attitudes. As we saw in Chapter 3, culture is transmitted almost exclusively

through interaction with other people. Moreover, it is through this repeated interaction with others that individuals develop their own unique sets of moral standards, habits, and beliefs—in other words, their individual personalities. Socialization thus has two functions: the transmission of culture from one generation to the next and the development of the self.

Without relationships with others, human beings do not become fully human. Kingsley Davis's famous studies of isolated children, conducted in the 1940s, show that normal physical and psychological development does not take place without human contact. Perhaps the most deprived child Davis studied was a 6-year-old American girl named Anna. Because she was born illegitimate, her grandfather kept Anna hidden alone in an attic. She rarely saw another person and received only minimal care. When she was found at the age of 6, Anna could not walk, talk, or feed herself. She was so listless and unresponsive that she was thought to be deaf and possibly blind. Moreover, the physical and mental damage Anna had suffered could not easily be overcome. After four years of training, she had barely learned to walk, to say a few words, and to be affectionate with her doll. When she died at age 11, Anna had only reached the level of a child of 2 or 3.[2]

> Children develop their own sense of self as they learn to assume adult roles. Mead called this playacting "taking the role of the other."

---

[2] Kingsley Davis, *Human Society* (New York: Macmillan, 1949), pp. 204ff.

Anna's story shows that our biological resources are not the only factors in our development as human beings. Children seem to need a close relationship with at least one adult to develop normally. Some of the children who grow up in orphanages, for example, have been found to suffer from serious personality defects. One study compared the progress of babies in a foundling home, where they had adequate care but not much loving attention, to that of babies raised at home. For the first few months, the orphans' development was similar to that of the other infants. By the time they were 2 years old, however, the babies raised in the institution were so retarded that they could have been categorized as imbeciles. Of twenty-one children between 2 and 4 years of age, only five could walk alone, only one could get dressed without help, and only one was able to talk in sentences.[3] Many other studies report that institutionalized children continue to show cognitive and emotional damage later on. They tend to have lower IQ scores, to show less initiative, and to be more aggressive toward others.[4]

The support and company of other people is important in adult life as well. Prolonged isolation has been known to cause depression, disorientation, and loss of mental capacity.[5] Indeed, the anguish of loneliness is so well known that solitary confinement of prisoners is an almost universal form of punishment.

BECOMING OURSELVES: THEORIES OF SOCIALIZATION

From the individual point of view, socialization is the process of developing a self, or a unique identity. We are the way we are largely because of the way we were brought up—socialized—by our parents, teachers, and others who trained our minds and guided our behavior. The society in which we live becomes part of us at an early age; its values and goals are the sources for our ideals, interests, dreams, ideas about ourselves, and assumptions about life. A number of theorists of socialization have analyzed the process by which our innermost selves are molded through interaction with others. We shall examine their perspectives in brief.

THE LOOKING-GLASS SELF: COOLEY

In the early years of the twentieth century, Charles Horton Cooley originated the sociological view that personality develops through social interaction. "A separate individual," Cooley pointed out, "is an abstraction unknown to experience, and so likewise is society when regarded as something apart from individuals. . . . 'Society' and 'individuals' do not denote separable phenomena, but are simply collective and distributive aspects of the same thing."[6] The individual cannot be separated from

---

[3] René Spitz, "Hospitalism," in *The Psychoanalytic Study of the Child*, I, eds. Anna Freud et al. (New York: International Universities Press, 1945), pp. 53–72.

[4] William Goldfarb, "Psychological Privation in Infancy and Subsequent Adjustment," *American Journal of Orthopsychiatry* 15 (April 1945): 247–53.

[5] Robert E.L. Faris, *Social Psychology* (New York: Ronald Press, 1953), pp. 342–43.

[6] Charles Horton Cooley, *Human Nature and the Social Order.* (1902) (New York: Schocken, 1964), pp. 36–37.

society because the self grows through interaction with other people. Society cannot be separated from the self because it is part of the individual psyche.

Cooley's theory of socialization is based on his concept of the **looking-glass self**: our self-image is a reflection of how others see us or what we believe others see us to be. According to Cooley, we think we are witty because our friends laugh at our jokes, we think we are talented because our teachers praise us, and we think we are important because our parents worry about us. We tend to accept the judgment of others as our own, and their definition of what we are like shapes our self-identity.

> As we see our face, figure, and dress in the glass, and are interested in them because they are ours, and pleased or otherwise with them according as they do or do not answer to what we should like them to be, so in imagination we perceive in another's mind some thought of our appearance, manners, aims, deeds, character, friends, and so on, and are variously affected by it.[7]

Thus, through continuous exchanges of mental impressions and judgments, society is internalized in the self.

THE SELF IN SOCIETY: MEAD

George Herbert Mead (1863–1931), one of the leading social psychologists of Cooley's time, also believed that there could be no self apart from society. Mead defined society as a process of social communication taking place symbolically through gestures and language (see Chapter 1). Human communication, he thought, largely relied on interpreting other people's words and actions. A simple gesture like an outstretched hand can have a number of symbolic meanings: "Let's shake on it"; "Could you spare a quarter?" "Let's dance"; "I'll take that for you"; "Here's your change"; and many more. Each meaning demands a different response. The people involved must continually readjust their actions according to how they interpret each other's behavior.[8]

Children develop a mind and self as they learn to assume the role of another person and to see their own behavior from another's point of view. Mead believed this happens in two stages. A young child in the *play stage*, for example, pretends to be a fireman, or Wonder Woman, or mommy or daddy. Mead referred to this playacting as "taking the role of the other." **Significant others** are especially important role models. Mothers and fathers, in particular, show children how adults behave.

Later the older child learns to imagine how other people will behave without having to act out their parts. Mead called this the *game stage.* In organized games like baseball, each player responds to what the other players are doing. Guided by the rules of the game, children can take the place of all the other players in their minds and predict their actions. Finally, the maturing child takes the role of the **generalized other**, which means the attitudes of the whole community. Since the mature individual has internalized the attitudes of the generalized other, the community is largely able to control the conduct of its members. The rules of the game and anticipated responses of other people provide guidelines for individual behavior. What began as social control,

---

[7] Ibid., p. 184.

[8] George Herbert Mead, *Mind, Self, and Society* (Chicago: University of Chicago Press, 1934), p. 73.

or control of one's behavior by others, thus becomes self-control in the fully socialized person.[9]

Although the self is rooted in society, Mead maintained that each person is a unique actor in the social process. He thought that everyone had two sides, which he called the "I" and the "Me." The "I" responds, as a creative, unique character, to the attitudes of others; the "Me" is the social side of the self that incorporates the attitudes of others. As a "Me" the individual is aware that he or she is an object of others' attention. "If I do this, people will think I'm crazy," the "Me" says. As an "I" the individual is free to have independent attitudes toward others. "I don't care what people think. They're the ones who are crazy," the "I" says. The self as a whole combines the organized attitudes of the generalized other and the unpredictable spontaneity of the individual actor. Although everyone is inevitably part of a social world, each person responds to it in a unique way.

Cooley's looking-glass self and Mead's generalized other are concepts that help us to understand how we are influenced by what others think of us. When we see ourselves from another person's point of view, we are looking into Cooley's social mirror; when we anticipate another person's reaction to our behavior, we are taking the role of Mead's other. Our responses to what we think others will think of us are more or less automatic but still conscious. The Freudian theory of socialization suggests, on the other hand, that our responses to a social situation could be unconscious, irrational, and beyond our control.

THE UNCONSCIOUS SELF: FREUD

The most influential theory of personality was developed by Cooley and Mead's famous contemporary, Sigmund Freud (1856–1939). The founder of psychoanalysis, Freud also contributed to sociological thought by providing a new analysis of the relationship between self and society.

According to Freudian theory, socialization begins at birth. At first, the infant's biological drives dominate its behavior, making it an aggressive, self-centered, amoral creature seeking only the instant gratification of its needs. The unconscious reservoir of these antisocial, biologically based drives he called the *id*. Society, operating through the child's parents, soon interferes with the impulsive demands of the id. The infant's hunger is satisfied, but on a feeding schedule; the pleasure of elimination is controlled by toilet training in early childhood; and the sexual gratification of masturbation is curtailed or forbidden entirely. As the child grows up, Freud believed that his or her experiences during these *oral, anal,* and *phallic* stages deeply affect the adult personality.

These critical periods constitute phases of the socialization process. As children actively try to satisfy their biological urges, they are rewarded or punished for their behavior by their parents. They thus learn to control their impulses and obey the wishes of others. In sociological terms, children learn to conform to social norms through interaction with people who are important to them. As children internalize their parents' values and attitudes, they develop a *superego,* or conscience. They

---

[9] Ibid., pp. 150–55.

repress socially unacceptable impulses so that they become part of the unconscious mind, and they attempt to redirect their sexual and aggressive energies into channels that their parents would approve. The Freudian socialization process takes place as the *ego*—the rational, conscious part of the self—seeks to resolve the conflict between the id and the superego by finding appropriate realistic ways to satisfy the demands of both.[10]

Although they have been driven from the conscious mind and channeled in socially acceptable ways, unconscious desires in the id continue to demand gratification. Childhood fears of punishment for forbidden pleasures reappear in dreams or take overt form in irrational behavior. If the superego is too demanding, if too much must be repressed, these anxieties become overwhelming and destructive of the self. Far more than Cooley and Mead, Freud emphasized how social requirements can damage the personality. He saw the possibility that socialization could be overdone and believed that too much concern with meeting other people's standards could be unhealthy. Freud also thought that the compromise between biology and society could never be entirely successful. In his view the conflict between unconscious desires and social demands would make the civilized person forever discontented.

THE RATIONAL SELF: PIAGET

Developmental psychologists give us yet another view of the socialization process. They see children not as pliable creatures constantly being shaped by other people's demands but as independent beings actively engaged in ordering the world according to their own perceptions of it.

The great child psychologist Jean Piaget (1896–1980) devoted a lifetime of study to the ways in which children perceive and react to their environment. His experiments showed that there are stages of intellectual development, each of them characterized by the kind of mental "operations" that a child can perform at that stage.

In the first two years of their lives, children have *sensory-motor intelligence*, or knowledge of the physical environment. They are chiefly interested in mastering objects — toys, cups and spoons, household furniture. From age 2 to 6, children are able to think imaginatively, or make *intuitive operations*. By this time they have developed a rudimentary memory, which enables them to retain a mental image of people and objects. They are mainly involved in manipulating symbols, particularly language. Play at this stage often deals with fantasies and imaginary characters. In the next five or six years, elementary schoolchildren begin to think logically and to coordinate their behavior with others, as children do in Mead's game stage. Piaget called this the period of *concrete operations*. The ability to think abstractly begins in adolescence. Instead of accepting without question what others think, children from 12 to 15 make what Piaget called *formal operations*. In this stage, they develop logical thought and opinions of their own.[11] Now that they are able to comprehend such abstractions as justice and honesty, adolescents often see differences between what adults tell them to do and what they do themselves — one reason parents find this age so difficult.

---

[10] Anna Freud, "The Concept of Developmental Lines," in *The Process of Child Development*, ed. Peter B. Neubauer (New York: New American Library/Meridian, 1976), pp. 25–45; Talcott Parsons, *Social Structure and Personality* (New York: Free Press, 1964), pp. 78–111.

[11] Jean Piaget and Barbel Inhelder, *The Psychology of the Child* (New York: Basic Books, 1969).

According to Piaget, intellectual development takes place in stages. The 1-year-old boy is learning to cope with his physical environment, or making *sensory-motor operations*; the 5-year-old child, imagining himself as an adult, is making *intuitive* operations; the schoolchildren are able to think logically and to coordinate their play, or make *concrete operations*; the adolescents are thinking abstractly, or making *formal operations*.

Recent studies of how we learn language[12] bear out Piaget's contention that children do not imitate others' behavior as much as they initiate their own. When they first learn to talk, children do not speak in the conventional English they hear around them. The 18- to 24-month-old child uses a large number of two-word utterances, including such strange constructions as "more high," "no down," and "other fix." Since all the children studied used such phrases, it is very unlikely that they were imitating adult speech. Rather, they seem to have been using a grammar peculiar to their own stage of linguistic development. The human capacity for language, it appears, is part of the developmental process.

Piaget's work challenged a number of theories of learning: that children learn by imitation, that children have the same thought processes as adults, and that learning is only a matter of rewards and punishments.

THE MORAL SELF: KOHLBERG

Piaget believed that people's ideas of right and wrong also develop in stages. His studies of children found that the child's conception of morality changes from the early belief that moral rules are absolute to the mature knowledge that they are the result of mutual agreement and negotiations. Recently, Lawrence Kohlberg has elaborated Piaget's insights into a theory that children find their own moral values as they grow up.

Kohlberg's research — in the United States, Great Britain, Taiwan, Turkey, and Mexico — convinced him that children are taught basically the same moral values in every culture in the world. He found that different societies may hold different specific beliefs about what is wrong (eating pork, smoking opium), but they have the same larger moral principles of empathy (concern for others) and justice (concern for equality and reciprocity). According to Kohlberg, people differ in their moral judgments because they have reached different levels of maturity.

---

[12] Ben G. Blount, "Studies in Child Language," *American Anthropologist 77* (October 1975): 580–90.

Children in different parts of the world were asked to interpret this story:

A man's wife was dying of cancer and there was only one drug that might save her. The pharmacist who had discovered the drug was charging ten times its cost to him, or $2000 for a small dose. The sick woman's husband tried to borrow the money, but he could raise only about $1000. He told the pharmacist that his wife was dying and asked him to sell it cheaper or let him pay later. The druggist refused. In desperation, the man broke into the drugstore and stole the drug for his wife. Should he have done that?

Kohlberg was not interested in whether or not the children thought the man should have stolen the drug. He wanted to learn the *reasons* they thought so. He decided that there were three levels of moral development, each representing a more complex way of resolving moral dilemmas. Children pass through these levels as they mature, but their moral development may end at any one of them. A person at any level may answer either yes or no to the question at the end of the story, but the reasons for doing so will be different.

Young children, Kohlberg found, tend to have a *preconventional* morality. They define right and wrong as obedience and disobedience to authority and are thus concerned with the consequences of an act rather than the intentions behind it. Breaking the law, for whatever reason, is considered bad because the lawbreaker will be punished.

People generally reach the next, or *conventional,* level of moral development in adolescence. They begin to adopt a good-boy (or good-girl) morality based on socially approved values. Because they trust some authority to define right and wrong for them, people at the conventional level show a high regard for the "rules." Breaking the law is all right only if there is a socially acceptable reason — to save a life, for example. People at this level will go to great lengths to deny that a moral dilemma exists at all.

People who reach the third, *postconventional* level accept the possibility of conflicting values, and they try to make a rational decision between them. At this level each person becomes a moral philosopher, making choices between legitimate alternatives on the basis of moral principles — the Golden Rule, for example, or "the greatest good for the greatest number." Breaking the law is justified if the law is personally judged unjust according to a higher principle.[13]

In ordinary daily life, people are rarely faced with complex moral dilemmas that cannot be resolved by conventional definitions of justice and respect for life. An exception was the My Lai massacre during the war in Vietnam, when hundreds of Vietnamese women and children were shot by American soldiers. Kohlberg and his associate interviewed the single soldier who had refused to shoot civilians and concluded that his reasoning about the moral conflict showed principled, postconventional thought. The other soldiers had reached only the conventional level of moral judgment: they reasoned that they had to obey the command to shoot, even if the targets were unarmed civilians.

Kohlberg's theory of moral development has been criticized for failing to show a connection between moral judgment and moral action.[14] Some of the soldiers at My Lai, for example, probably knew they were committing an immoral act. They may have been obeying orders not because they thought it was the right thing to do but because they were afraid to disobey, because they were angry about their unit's heavy casualties, or because they feared and hated the Vietnamese. The ability to know what is right, in other words, does not necessarily deter people from doing something they know is wrong.

MALE-FEMALE DIFFERENCES.   Later researchers have reinterpreted Kohlberg's findings to show that girls and boys do not always see moral choices in the same way. When psychologist Carol Gilligan presented the same moral dilemma to children of both sexes (who had the same age, intelligence, education, and social class background), she found that boys and girls saw the problem in very different ways.[15] An eleven-year-old boy, for example, responded just as many of Kohlberg's postconventional subjects did. The man should steal the drug, the boy said, because "a human life is worth more than money." He saw the dilemma as a conflict between two values — property and life — and chose what he considered the higher value.

An eleven-year-old girl, however, put the dilemma in different terms. She replied that the man should not steal the drug, but he should save his wife by borrowing the money. When asked why the man should not steal the drug, the girl did not mention either the law or the druggist's right to his property. She was concerned instead with the relationship between the man and his wife:

> If he stole the drug, he might save his wife then, but if he did he might have to go to jail and then his wife might get sicker again, and he couldn't get more of the drug, and it might not be good. So, they should really just talk it out and find some other way to make the money.[16]

---

[13] Lawrence Kohlberg, "The Development of Children's Orientations Toward a Moral Order," in *The Process of Child Development,* pp. 143–63; Lawrence Kohlberg, "Stage and Sequence: The Cognitive Development Approach to Socialization," in *Handbook of Socialization Theory and Research,* ed. D. A. Goslin (Chicago: Rand McNally, 1969).

[14] William Kurtines and Esther Blank Greif, "The Development of Moral Thought," *Psychological Bulletin* 81 (August 1974): 453–70.

[15] Carol Gilligan, *In a Different Voice: Psychological Theory and Women's Development* (Cambridge, Mass.: Harvard University Press, 1982), pp. 26–29.

[16] Ibid., p. 28.

For this girl, the moral issue was the druggist's refusal to help a sick person, not the legal and individual rights of the husband, wife, and druggist. Instead of using abstract principles to decide whether the act was right or wrong, she asked who would suffer from it.

According to Gilligan, Kohlberg's sequence of stages is not the only path to moral development, and his postconventional level is not necessarily the highest order of morality. She suggests that the feminine concern for human relationships and personal responsibility represents an equally mature level of moral development, one that complements masculine concern for rational principles of logic and justice.[17]

Gilligan argues that boys and girls have different viewpoints because they live in different kinds of social worlds. Males are more likely to experience the world as a rational hierarchy, with some people logically placed at the top and others at the bottom. Females are more likely to view the world as a web of relationships in which they are embedded. As a result, men tend to rely on impersonal rules to reach agreement, while women tend to rely on communication in personal relationships.

THE SELF IN TRANSITION: ERIKSON

Erik H. Erikson, a student of Freud, extended the concept of a developing self to a theory of lifelong socialization. In *Childhood and Society* (1950), Erikson described eight developmental stages each characterized by an **identity crisis**, or a changing definition of the self. If all goes well, the maturing person finds positive solutions to the problems in each new stage of the life cycle; if the person fails to adjust to the new social demands, he or she can develop psychiatric symptoms. Although the concerns of each stage are constant throughout life, they are particularly acute at certain ages. Erikson described his eight stages of development, discussed below, as sets of alternative basic attitudes.[18]

TRUST VERSUS MISTRUST (INFANCY).   To the helpless infant, the world is totally unfamiliar and unpredictable. If the baby's physical needs are lovingly and consistently met, very young children develop a sense of ego identity based on the link between their own feelings of comfort and the people and things that provide food and warmth. The infant's first social achievement, then, is to develop the sense of trust that permits it to let its parents out of sight without feeling undue anxiety or rage.

AUTONOMY VERSUS SHAME AND DOUBT (EARLY CHILDHOOD).   In the period equivalent to Freud's anal stage, children face the conflict entailed by having control over their actions. They must learn to suppress their aggressive impulses, but they must also be protected from feeling shame and doubt when they lose control. This stage is decisive for balancing love against hate, cooperation against willfulness, and self-esteem and pride in self-control against doubt and shame from loss of control or from overly strict control by others.

---

[17] Carol Gilligan et al., eds., *Mapping the Moral Domain: A Contribution of Women's Thinking to Psychological Theory and Education.* Cambridge, Mass.: Harvard University Press, 1989.
[18] Erik H. Erikson, *Childhood and Society,* 2d ed., rev. and enl. (New York: Norton, 1963), pp. 247–74.

INITIATIVE VERSUS GUILT (LATER CHILDHOOD).   At the age of 4 or 5, children enjoy testing their new physical and mental powers. As Mead and Piaget also noted, they play at imaginary games and "dressing up" fantasies. As they try out new roles, children risk being ridiculed or punished for their initiatives; the danger at this stage is that they will develop a sense of guilt over their attempts to try out new behaviors. As some of their wildest fantasies are inhibited and repressed, children learn the limits of permissible behavior and begin to attach their dreams to conventional adult goals.

INDUSTRY VERSUS INFERIORITY (SCHOOL AGE).   School-age children earn recognition by producing things. They learn the pleasures of using tools, acquiring new skills, and working with others. The danger at this stage lies in the sense of inadequacy and inferiority that results from failure. If a child's family life is insufficient preparation for school, or if the child fails to perform successfully, he or she may lose the ability to fit into the world of work.

IDENTITY VERSUS ROLE CONFUSION (ADOLESCENCE).   Erikson's most famous insights pertain to the adolescent identity crisis. Faced with rapid physical growth and new sexual maturity, young people in this stage are concerned primarily with the question of how they appear to others compared with their own ideas of themselves. They must also deal with the pressing question of how to connect their roles and skills to an adult occupation. Role confusion, or inability to settle on an identity, is the result of leaving these questions unresolved. "To keep themselves together," Erikson wrote, adolescents

> temporarily overidentify, to the point of apparent complete loss of identity, with the heroes of cliques and crowds. This initiates the stage of "falling in love," which is by no means entirely, or even primarily a sexual matter. . . . To a considerable extent adolescent love is an attempt to arrive at a definition of one's identity by projecting one's diffused ego image on another and by seeing it thus reflected and gradually clarified. This is why so much of young love is conversation.[19]

ADULT STAGES.   Identity struggles in adulthood, Erikson finds, concern *intimacy versus isolation* (young adulthood), or giving oneself to others as opposed to being self-absorbed and avoiding commitment; *generativity versus stagnation* (middle age), or establishing and guiding the next generation as opposed to failing to meet the "need to be needed"; and *ego integrity versus despair* (old age), or accepting in a mature way the order and meaning of one's life as opposed to being disgusted with life and fearful of death.

SUMMARY

From the sociological perspective, identity is formed in and by society. People do not become human all by themselves, nor do they maintain their self-image without constant confirmation from the social looking glass. Drastic changes in social role—from small businessman to U.S. senator, for example, or from high school student to

---

[19] Ibid., p. 262.

mother or unemployed actor to movie star—produce equally drastic changes in personal identity. To a great extent, what we are is what others expect us to be.

Theories of socialization explain how social expectations are internalized in the self. For Cooley and Mead, socialization is part of the continuous interaction between individuals and the people around them: the self develops from the social experience of evaluating one's behavior from another's point of view. Freud's contribution was to emphasize that the emerging self is often antagonistic to the demands of others and that the imposition of social controls leads to unconscious conflicts that have an effect on adult behavior.

Human beings are distinguished from other animals by their ability to reason, to communicate in language, and to make moral judgments. The newborn infant, however, does not reason, does not talk, and has no morals. Developmental theorists such as Piaget and Kohlberg defined the goals of socialization in terms of reaching the final stage of intellectual and moral capacity. Like other developmental theorists, Erikson viewed socialization as a process that proceeds in stages. He believed, however, that socialization never ends, and each period of life has new crises to be met and new roles to be learned. Since the requirements of social life are not the same at all ages, a person's identity changes throughout the life cycle.

At different times in our lives, different kinds of people influence our behavior. The next section considers some of the most important agents of our socialization in childhood and beyond.

AGENTS OF SOCIALIZATION

In every society, there are certain groups and institutions with which children interact most often and most intimately. They are the primary agents of socialization, or the significant others.

THE FAMILY

The family is the child's first reference group. Parents construct and filter the way children see the world, and they provide the most important models for their behavior. The family also gives each child an ascribed status, or social position, which strongly affects the way he or she is treated. Moreover, a famous research study has shown that parents in different social classes do not teach their children the same values because they have different concepts of what their children's lives will be like.

In *Class and Conformity* (1969), Melvin Kohn explored the way class differences in socialization pass along social advantages or disadvantages from generation to generation. In an international survey, middle- and lower-class parents were asked which characteristics they thought were most important for their children to have. Not surprisingly, parents of both classes wanted their children to be honest, happy, considerate, obedient, and dependable. Middle-class parents, however, were inclined to encourage their children to act according to their own judgment and moral standards. Lower-class parents, on the other hand, more often stressed obedience to authority.

Middle-class children and poor children are raised in ways that tend to perpetuate class differences from generation to generation.

Kohn interpreted these findings to mean that parents are likely to emphasize values they think will be important to their children's future. For the lower class, "staying out of trouble" means conforming to other people's standards, and obeying parents, teachers, or the police. Such parents tend to stress **behavioral conformity**, or outward compliance with the prevailing norms regardless of one's personal beliefs. Middle-class parents are more likely to value self-control and consideration of others. Middle-class children are supposed to behave correctly, not because they are told to but because they want to. Their parents emphasize **attitudinal conformity**, or personal commitment to the prevailing norms. "The essence of higher class position," Kohn writes, "is the expectation that one's decisions and actions can be consequential; the essence of lower class position is the belief that one is at the mercy of forces and people beyond one's control, often, beyond one's understanding."[20]

These class differences in socialization, Kohn found, are partly responsible for the perpetuation of job inequalities from generation to generation. Obviously, middle-class parents have higher aspirations for their children and command greater resources to help them get ahead (see Chapter 13, "Education"). Less obvious perhaps is the way parents' values influence their children's abilities to perform certain roles. Lack of freedom and the feeling that one cannot control one's life give rise to authoritarian attitudes: obedience to the letter of the law, traditional morality, intolerance of dissent, distrust of others. These lower-class values are adequate for routine, repetitive work that requires little intellectual skill. Most low-ranking, "dead-end" jobs — typing, fac-

[20] Melvin L. Kohn, *Class and Conformity* (Homewood, Ill.: Dorsey Press, 1969), p. 189.

tory work, waiting on tables, truck driving — fall into this category. Conformist values are inadequate, however, for work that requires imagination and initiative. Consideration of others, trust in one's own judgment, and commitment to one's work are important qualities for doctors, lawyers, scientists, and executives at the upper levels of the educational and occupational hierarchy. Without these middle-class values and skills, the opportunity to reach these levels is severely limited. As Kohn somberly concluded, "Whether consciously or not, parents tend to impart to their children lessons derived from the conditions of life of their own social class — and thus help prepare their children for a similar class position."[21]

Just by growing up rich or poor, children develop different images of themselves and learn to have different expectations of life.

Robert Coles, a child psychiatrist, made the effect of social class on personality the theme of the last two volumes of his study, *Children of Crisis* (1977)[22] (see "The Important Things"). Poor children from disadvantaged minority groups, he found, are discouraged from being independent and self-assertive. Their parents teach them at an early age that "standing up for themselves" will only bring trouble and that they must be resigned to a life of poverty and deprivation. Privileged middle- and upper-class children, in contrast, are taught to be self-sufficient and to speak up for what they want. Their parents encourage them to develop their abilities and personalities. As adults, their self-absorption may be expressed in their devotion to therapeutic exercise, health foods, and popular self-help manuals.

---

[21] Ibid., p. 200.
[22] Robert Coles, *Children of Crisis*, vol. IV, *Eskimos, Chicanos, Indians*; vol. V, *Privileged Ones: The Well-off and the Rich in America* (Boston: Little, Brown, 1977).

THE IMPORTANT THINGS: TWO AMERICAN CHILDREN LEARN THE VALUES OF THEIR CLASS

Robert Coles, a pediatrician and child psychiatrist, spent two decades studying children from many ethnic and social groups throughout the United States. He got to know the children by visiting their homes regularly for several years, talking with them and their families. In the passages that follow, two 12-year-old American children talk about the important things their fathers have taught them.

THE DAUGHTER OF A CHICANO FARM WORKER IN TEXAS:

I was told that it's a waste of time to be in school. The teacher said so; the principal said the same thing when I went to her office. They told me I should only go to school if I thought that I was going to use my education. But I wouldn't be doing that, they said; I'd be in the fields. I fooled them though; I'm in this house, and it's a good place to be. {She dropped out of school at the age of 10 and now helps her mother cook and do housework for an Anglo family.}

• • •

I was nine and I was ready to go and march, when the union people came here. I was ready to go tell the grower and his foreman that they are bad people. My father heard me talking with my brother. My mother did too. They were listening in. I was swearing. I can't remember the words. I only remember my father's words: 'Don't let me ever hear you talk like that again!'

• • •

{My father} has said that he'd punish us very hard if we ever spoke back to an Anglo—if we ever had anything to do with them. He doesn't even like us going to school: the Anglo teachers are mean, and they can get you in a lot of trouble if they don't like you. They can report you; they can pick up the phone, and the next thing you know, the sheriff is there, and some other Anglos, and they are looking at your house, and saying it's dirty, and your mother and your father, they're dirty, and no good, and you have to go leave. That's what happened to our cousins; they were taken away, and their mother cried and cried, and our priest tried to get the children back, and he couldn't. He went to see the bishop—he lives far away—and I think he helped out. They brought our cousins back, but they told my aunt and uncle that they should be careful, and not to cause trouble, and not join a union, or it could happen again. My uncle works with my father. They both pick the crops. My father says: no one is safe as long as he's one of us—not an Anglo.

THE SON OF A VERY WEALTHY FAMILY IN NEW ORLEANS:

I'd like to know about the stock market. You can't inherit money and just forget about it. My father goes over the financial pages with me. He points out what's been happening to our money. I have to tell him whether we've lost or gained—the total. He bought me a little calculator, a pocket one, made in Japan. It's great fun, but it's very important business. If you have money, you have to know how to keep it, or you're in big trouble. I have my animals to take care of. I have a dog and I have three white mice. I used to have a snake, but my mother didn't want it around. The maid can't touch my mice, and only I feed the dog and take her for a walk. I have my homework, and that's *very* important. You have to have good marks to get into Princeton. Daddy says he was lucky. When he was young he could just know he'd go there. If I do my work, I will. But I've got to do my work.

SOURCE: Robert Coles, *Eskimos, Chicanos, Indians.* Vol. IV of *Children of Crisis* (Boston: Little, Brown, 1977), pp. 327, 329–30, 338; and Robert Coles, *Privileged Ones: The Well-Off and the Rich in America*, Vol. V of *Children of Crisis* (Boston: Little, Brown, 1977), p. 107.

Coles's rather impressionistic study comes to much the same conclusion as Kohn's more systematic research: just by growing up rich or poor, children develop different self-images and different expectations for the future. Poor children are taught self-denial to prepare them for a life that will probably be marred by poverty and injustice.

Rich children are taught self-concern in anticipation of a way of life that rewards independent ability and a pleasing personality.

THE SCHOOL

The educational system is specifically given responsibility for socializing the younger generation. Schools are charged with teaching young people the skills and knowledge they will need to be useful citizens. The school also introduces children, usually for the first time, to the impersonal rules and regulations of the formal organization. Other lessons are also ingrained in children at school: be polite; be on time; give teachers the answers they want; compete for grades by beating out your classmates (see Chapter 13, "Education").

Schools are also a means of social selection. By labeling and sorting students according to their IQ test scores, by grading and tracking, and by failing or promoting, schools separate children according to their accomplishments. In the United States education is supposed to break down class barriers by giving poor children the skills they need to get middle-class jobs. There is strong evidence, however, that the selective processes of modern schooling tend to reinforce rather than overcome students' class origins.

Many studies have found that class background has a pervasive effect on the way schools evaluate their students. Soon after children enter kindergarten or first grade, they are placed in separate groups according to their abilities. Teachers decide which students are the brightest and most highly motivated and then assign them to a higher track for reading, math, and so on. Since there are few reliable indicators of ability among five- and six-year-olds, elementary teachers must often rely on their subjective impressions of a child's behavior in school. In general, teachers are favorably impressed with children who are polite, who are willing to follow directions, and who use "correct" grammar and language. Middle-class teachers thus tend to evaluate middle-class children as brighter and more promising than children who come from disadvantaged backgrounds.[23]

When a child is considered "bright" or "slow" by teachers and fellow students, their judgment becomes part of the child's developing self.[24] Children begin to think of themselves as good students or poor students and to act accordingly. Children who are thought to be less able are asked to do less, and their performance usually reinforces the original low evaluation of their abilities. Moreover, children in different tracks are being taught to aspire to different futures. "Bright" students often expect to go on to college and white-collar work, while "slow" students settle for secretarial school or a blue-collar job. The reason children rarely move from a low-ability to a high-ability track is largely because the effects of being in the lower track help make their teachers' predictions into a self-fulfilling prophecy.[25]

---

[23] R. P. McDermott, "Social Relations as Contexts for Learning," *Harvard Educational Review* 47 (1977): 198–213.

[24] Frederick Elkin and Gerald Handel, *The Child and Society*, 4th ed. (New York: Random House, 1984), p. 156.

[25] Christopher J. Hurn, *The Limits and Possibilities of Schooling*, 2d ed. (Boston: Allyn and Bacon, 1985), pp. 187–90.

PEERS

After childhood, social interaction takes place increasingly among **peer groups**—equals in age, sex, occupational level, and so on. Members of peer groups tend to become friends because of their equal status and mutual interests. Friends do not intentionally set out to change each other, but friendship leads to shared opinions and values. Peers influence each other and become significant others in the socialization process.

The choice of peers in childhood and adolescence is largely determined by the school. If schools separate students according to class position, as the evidence indicates, then they will choose their friends and companions on the basis of class and reinforce that socializing effect.

In adult life other organizations often choose our peer groups for us. We make our friends in college, in the army, at the office, on the assembly line, at the club. Our "equals" are the people we feel comfortable with, and they are likely to come from similar backgrounds and have similar jobs.

In *Tally's Corner* (1967), a famous study of streetcorner men, Elliot Liebow argued that the conditions of lower-class life virtually guaranteed that the poor would fail as husbands and breadwinners. In such a situation the male peer group offers an alternate set of values to the middle-class ethic of hard work, saving, and striving for success.

After childhood most socialization takes place in peer groups.

Among his streetcorner companions, Liebow wrote, a man can forget he married because he wanted to assume the duties and status of manhood. His friends see him instead as a put-upon male who married because his girl was pregnant or because he was talked into it. He can forget that his marriage failed because he was not a good provider. Like others in the group, he can justify the failure by saying that his wife refused to put up with his manly appetite for whiskey and other women.[26]

The peer group, in this case, is socializing its members to adjust to failure. By denying the goals and values of a largely middle-class society, the streetcorner subculture offers its members a way of keeping a measure of dignity and self-esteem.

TELEVISION

In addition to being our principal source of information and entertainment, television is an important socializing agent. Preschool children, for whom television acts as a babysitter, spend an average of 30 hours a week — or nearly a third of their waking hours — in front of the set.[27] By the time the typical American child graduates from high school, he or she will have spent 11,000 hours in school and 15,000 hours in front of the television set. During all those thousands of hours, TV is socializing children by presenting them with images of American society. Children learn what it means to be a policeman or a doctor, to be rich or powerful, to be single, married, or divorced. Unless they are contradicted by some other source, these images will likely determine what children perceive society to be like.[28] Nicholas Johnson, a former member of the Federal Communications Commission, described the situation this way: "All television is educational television. The question is: What is it teaching?"[29]

According to many professional observers, the first lesson television teaches is that "might makes right." In order to appeal to a large audience and attract commercial sponsors, the TV networks tend to schedule violent, action-packed dramas, and parents and educators have long worried about the impact of such programs on the socialization of children.[30] About 2,500 studies were conducted during the 1970s on the behavioral effects of television viewing. Summarizing this research in 1982, a report prepared by the National Institute of Mental Health concluded that there is now overwhelming scientific evidence that excessive violence on television leads directly to aggressive and violent behavior in children and adolescents. The report called television a "beguiling" and "formidable" educator that has become a "major socializing agent of American children."[31]

---

[26] Elliot Liebow, *Tally's Corner* (Boston: Little, Brown, 1967), p. 214.

[27] J. Lyle and H.R. Hoffman, "Children's Use of Television and Other Media," in *Television and Social Behavior*, vol. 4 *Television in Everyday Life*, E. A. Rubenstein, G. A. Comstock, and J. P. Murray, eds., Washington, D.C.: U.S. Government Printing Office, 1972.

[28] Elkin and Handel, *The Child and Society*, p. 175.

[29] Quoted in Edward B. Fiske, "The Schools and TV: Two Kinds of Teachers," *The New York Times*, April 20, 1980, Spring Survey of Education, p. 1.

[30] In fact, cartoons and other children's programs have three times as much violence as adult programs. See George Gerbner, "Violence and Television Drama: Trends and Symbolic Functions," in *Television and Social Behavior: Media Content and Control*, G. Comstock and E. Rubenstein, eds., Washington, D. C.: U.S. Government Printing Office, 1972.

[31] National Institute of Mental Health, *Television and Behavior: 10 Years of Scientific Progress and Implications for the Eighties*, vol. 1 (Washington, D.C.: U.S. Government Printing Office, 1982).

Television also has the potential — so far hardly realized — for developing positive attitudes. Such programs as "Sesame Street" and "Mister Rogers' Neighborhood" have been found to encourage cooperation, self-control, and acceptance of different races. Apparently, children copy the attitudes they see on TV when they believe them appropriate.[32]

While no one knows how harmful televised violence actually is, most social scientists agree that it is not doing young viewers any good. One study found that children who watch a lot of TV are less popular with their peers and have lower achievement test scores than other children, although in this case it is hard to tell which is cause and which is effect.[33] Nevertheless, daily exposure to the brutal, often immoral society shown on television cannot help but affect children's attitudes toward other people and the world in which they live.

LIFE ACCORDING TO TV.   In the opinion of George Gerbner, dean of the University of Pennsylvania's Annenberg School of Communications, children are not the only ones being socialized by television.[34] For more than 15 years, Gerbner and his associates have studied the content of prime-time programs and its effects on the television audience. Their disturbing conclusion is that heavy television viewers tend to accept

---

[32] Aimee Dorr Leifer, Neal J. Gordon, and Sherryl Browne Graves, "Children's Television More Than Mere Entertainment," *Harvard Educational Review* 44 (May 1974): 213, 217, 219–20.

[33] A. Dorr, *Television and Children.* Beverly Hills, CA: Sage, 1986.

[34] Harry F. Waters, "Life According to TV," *Newsweek.* December 6, 1982, pp. 136–40D; George Gerber, ed. *Mass Media Policies in Changing Cultures* (New York: Wiley, 1977).

What is this child learning? Daily exposure to television may teach children that the world is a frightening and uncertain place.

the distorted version of reality that these programs offer more readily than the "real world" of their own experience.

Gerbner's studies found that one of television's lessons is the reinforcement of cultural stereotypes. Men in prime-time programs outnumber women by three to one, and they play a variety of roles. With the exception of a few spunky female detectives, women are almost always portrayed as weak, passive, or incompetent creatures who are dependent on powerful men. They are usually limited to roles as lovers or mothers, and fewer than 20 percent of TV's married mothers have jobs outside the home (compared with 50 percent in real life). People over 65 are also underrepresented on TV and their portrayals are likely to be negative and inaccurate. Elderly characters are usually shown to be sick and helpless or foolish and eccentric. A handful of black television characters are portrayed positively, but the rest play comic or supporting roles. Most of the important people on TV are young white males, and Gerbner believes this teaches black children that minority status is inevitable and even deserved.

To measure the effect of these distortions, Gerbner's researchers devised multiple-choice questionnaires with answers that reflected both an accurate picture of American society and the misconceptions of it presented on TV. Their sample covered an unusually large cross-section of ages, incomes, educational levels, and ethnic backgrounds. Heavy television viewers (those who watched more than four hours a day) nearly always chose the TV-influenced answers while light viewers (who watched TV less than two hours a day) chose the answers that correspond more closely to real life. Heavy viewers — who make up 30 percent of the population and are found in all social and economic categories — were far more likely than light viewers to agree with such statements as "Women should take care of running their homes and leave running the country to men" and "White people have the right to keep blacks out of their neighborhoods."

The version of reality that TV offers is shaped by the networks' peculiar situation in American society. Television is above all a commercial industry which provides popular entertainment in return for advertising revenues. The audience that prime-time sponsors most want to reach is white, middle-class, and relatively young — in other words, the people who buy most of the products advertised on TV. Popular television programs appeal to this audience by reinforcing their beliefs and norms of behavior. While network executives think they are only providing the kind of entertainment that sells best, they are unintentionally selling a point of view as well. The risk is that the distortions of the "world according to TV" will begin to define reality for the rest of us.

SOCIALIZATION THROUGH THE LIFE CYCLE

Getting older is a social as well as a biological process. Over the course of a lifetime, a person changes roles many times: from baby to schoolchild, from bachelor to husband, from wife to widow. Each change involves a transformation of identity as the old way of life is forgotten and the new way learned. Many societies have ritual celebrations, or **rites of passage**, in which a former identity (being a child, for example) is put aside and a new one (being an adult) is adopted. As people approach the transition from one age to another, they need to learn the requirements and limits of the new role. Each turning point in the life cycle thus involves **resocialization**.

In many cases, what Robert Merton and Alice Rossi described as **anticipatory socialization**, or the informal learning of future roles, eases the transition from stage to stage.[35] Medical school training, for example, involves not only formal instruction in specific techniques but also informal guidance in the ethical values and norms of the medical profession to which the student will belong. In other cases the socialization process fails to prepare us for a new stage of life. A striking example is the failure of American culture to provide guidelines on how to "act your age" when you are suddenly no longer young. The expectations of others are unclear, and there are few opportunities to learn how to be old from other people. As at any stage, when resocialization is inadequate, anxiety and confusion result (see "The Resocialization of Vietnam Veterans").

Adolescence, adulthood, and old age are the major stages of the life cycle and will be treated here in some detail. All three are periods of resocialization when new roles must be learned and old ones given up.

ADOLESCENCE

Adolescence as a separate stage of life is almost entirely an invention of industrial society. Before the end of the nineteenth century the years between puberty and adulthood were few and unimportant; many children this age were already at work on farms, aboard ships, and in coal mines. The introduction of child labor laws and compulsory education prolonged childhood by keeping youths under 16 in school and out of the work force. During the course of the twentieth century this period of dependency has been lengthened further by the increasing need for highly trained workers in technologically advanced societies. For many people today the necessity of having a college and even a graduate school education postpones full adult status to well past the age of 20.

Modern societies thus created the gap between physical maturity and full social adulthood known as adolescence. The prolonging of childlike status is also largely responsible for the psychological characteristics of adolescents: their urge to be independent from their parents, their search for identity, their questioning of adult values. For the last fifty years or so, sociologists have explained adolescent behavior in two ways: as a response to the ambiguous social role of being half-child, half-adult, and as conformity to the subculture of the adolescent peer group.

"JUST A STAGE." The ambiguity of the adolescent role was analyzed by the anthropologist Ruth Benedict.[36] In American society, Benedict argued, children are socialized to certain kinds of behavior: they are not given much independence or responsibility, they are taught to obey their parents and teachers, and they are usually not allowed to express themselves sexually. What is forbidden in childhood, however, is required in adulthood. Grown men and women are expected to take on responsibilities at home

---

[35] Robert K. Merton (with Alice S. Rossi), "Contributions to the Theory of Reference Group Behavior," in Merton, *Social Theory and Social Structure,* enl. ed. (New York: Free Press, 1968), pp. 319–22.

[36] Ruth Benedict, "Continuities and Discontinuities in Cultural Conditioning," *Psychiatry* 1 (1938): 1–8.

and at work, to be assertive rather than submissive, and to marry and raise families themselves. If an adolescent is to grow up, the lessons so well learned as a child must be almost completely unlearned.

The emotional stresses and strains of this period result from uncertainty about how to behave in new roles and from a sense of loss over giving up old familiar ones. Bewildered and unsure, many young people run away from home, drop out of school, indulge in irresponsible escapades, or withdraw into moody silences. In this ill-defined situation, maturing adolescents must work out crucial developmental problems: becoming independent, getting an education, making sexual adjustments, choosing a career, and — in many cases — getting married and starting a family of their own.

THE YOUTH SUBCULTURE.   Some sociologists view adolescence as more than just a stage on the way to adult life. They emphasize that socializing experiences during this critical period can have a long-lasting effect on personality. In these formative years, they say, adolescents learn values and attitudes from other youths that can seriously hinder their adaptations to the adult world.

The adolescent peer group has long been considered a subculture, the **youth culture**, because its members have a way of life at odds with prevailing norms. In a widely quoted article published in 1942, Talcott Parsons described the youth culture as "irresponsible," concerned mainly with "having a good time," and characterized by

These two portraits of adolescents were taken less than 80 years apart. In 1909 breaker boys took on adult roles at an early age. Today the necessity of having a college education is prolonging childhood dependency past the age of 20.

THE RESOCIALIZATION OF VIETNAM VETERANS

Vietnam was America's longest, bloodiest, and saddest war. As the fighting dragged on, and official predictions of imminent victory were again and again proven wrong, popular opposition to the war grew more bitter and divisive. Returning soldiers were treated with indifference and even hostility by their countrymen. Today, more than a decade after U.S. involvement in Vietnam ended in humiliating defeat, Americans remain ambivalent about the meaning and purpose of a war that most people view as a tragic mistake.

Like other returning veterans, the soldiers who came home from Vietnam felt the culture shock of strangers in an alien land. Not only was the behavior they had learned in the military irrelevant in "The World," as Vietnam veterans called the United States, but civilian roles had to be reestablished or learned for the first time. However, the special nature of the Vietnam conflict made these veterans' passage from combat soldier to civilian an especially difficult and painful period of resocialization.

AN UNSHAREABLE EXPERIENCE

For many soldiers Vietnam marked the beginning of adulthood. (The average age of American troops in Vietnam was 19, compared to 26 in World War II.) Becoming a man thus meant becoming a soldier: learning to accept duty and responsibility, learning to kill, learning to live in constant fear, learning to witness the horrible wounds and meaningless deaths that are the commonplace atrocities of war. In addition to these experiences, combat soldiers had to adjust to the peculiar norms of Viet-

nam: the body counts as a measure of military success; the "fragging," or fragmentation bombing of unpopular officers; the escape into drugs; the bizarre acts of rebellion against a losing war. To an unusual degree, Vietnam veterans felt that their war experiences had changed them in ways that civilians could never understand. One said,

There's a very limited number of people who have shared this experience with me . . . and I feel like I've been through something that was so intense, that unless somebody else has been through it, they're going to have a hard time understanding where I'm coming from. I've gone beyond the age of innocence and {the other kids in school} are still in that age.

LACK OF TRANSITION

Thanks to the military rotation system and the jet airplane, the transition between "Nam" and "The World" was unusually abrupt. There was no rite of passage, no period of adjustment to help Vietnam veterans become accustomed to civilian life. As one soldier put it,

You're in the Army one day and out on the streets the next, bye now. . . . That's it. . . . You really need some pasture time to think about where you've been and where you're going. It just happens too quick, you're really not prepared, even though you're counting all the time for the day of leaving . . . and coming home.

behavior on the "borderline of parental behavior or beyond the pale."[37] In its many and rapidly changing varieties, the youth culture is, first of all, a creation of the young and, secondly, fun-loving, irreverent, and expressive in behavior.

More recently, David Matza argued that the rather conventional forms of youthful rebellion help reduce the tensions and frustrations of adolescence.[38] Moreover, much of this behavior is tolerated in the spirit of "you're only young once." Enthusiasm for the youth culture is not limited to youth. Many adults mimic youthful styles and

---

[37] Talcott Parsons, "Age and Sex in the Social Structure of the United States," *American Sociological Review* 7:5 (October 1942): 604–20.

[38] David Matza, "Subterranean Traditions of Youth," in *The Sociology of Youth*, ed. Harry Silverstein (New York: Macmillan, 1973), pp. 119–23.

EXCLUSION FROM CIVILIAN SOCIETY

Vietnam veterans not only felt that they were un-like other civilians, they believed they were being unjustly treated by an indifferent society. As they saw it, soldiers returning from World War II received much more gratitude and affection. Besides the parades and dockside bands, they were given better job opportunities and more generous veterans' benefits than soldiers returning from Vietnam. More importantly, the older veterans had come home victorious and, most of the time, together. Many Vietnam veterans felt anger and resentment:

> *When I first got back, no one cared, really, what went on in your head, what you experienced. . . . I was at a party and someone really attacked me for going to Vietnam in the first place. . . . I went at her, she was a little girl— . . . and lucky it was broken up, but . . . I just snapped. It was too personal for me to listen to an attack from someone who didn't know anything about it.*

American society's failure to provide ways of resocializing its Vietnam veterans has led to serious social problems. According to the federal government's 1981 study, *Legacies of Vietnam*, a disproportionately high number of Vietnam veterans turn to violence. Former combat soldiers are more likely to engage in violent behavior than comparable nonveterans, and, among those who have never before shown antisocial tendencies, combat experi-

ence is strongly linked to violence in civilian life. A 1985 study found that two out of five Vietnam veterans in New York have trouble holding a job, and two out of three veterans of heavy combat are divorced or separated. Moreover, nearly half of the combat veterans have shown symptoms of post-traumatic stress disorder, a mental illness touched off by an event that resembles a wartime trauma.

The veterans who did succeed in getting their "heads out of Nam" were helped by the socializing effects of strong personal relationships and new commitments to school and work. Close ties with family and friends outside of the war culture were essential for helping the veteran get back his "civilian head" and "buy into" the norms of his society. Veterans who made it through this resocialization process were able to accept new responsibilities and regain a feeling of self-sufficiency. One put it like this:

> *Things must get done, life must be lived. The world is not peachy-keen to live in, OK, accept it for what it is. If people don't always treat you so well, it does little good to cry about it. Stop the crying.*

SOURCES: Robert R. Faulkner and Douglas B. McGaw, "Uneasy Homecoming: Stages in the Reentry Transition of Vietnam Veterans," *Urban Life* 6:3 (October 1977): 303–28; David Margolick, "Many Veterans Cite Trauma of Vietnam in Trials," *The New York Times*, May 11, 1985, pp. 1 and 11; and Ghislaine Boulanger and Charles Kadushin, eds., *The Vietnam Veteran Redefined: Fact and Fiction* (Hillsdale, N.J.: Erlbaum, 1985).

activities in an effort to be "with it." By doing so, they help make the youth culture acceptable to the larger society.

As their elders expect, adolescents do "grow out of it." Most leave the youth culture when they leave school and take on adult roles. Of course, some adolescents are not part of the youth culture at all. They get along well with their parents, they believe in work first and fun afterwards, and they fit right into the system and its values while they are still in school. This kind of youth was so prevalent in the "silent generation" of the 1950s that one leading sociologist thought that anticipatory socialization in high school was causing adolescence to disappear as a separate stage of life.[39] Then came the

---

[39] Edgar Z. Friedenberg, *The Vanishing Adolescent* (Boston: Beacon Press, 1959).

student activism of the 1960s and early 1970s, and "youth" again meant self-expression, rebellion, and militant idealism. The serious, politically conservative, career-oriented young people of the 1980s appeared to have much in common with the youth culture of the 1950s.

On the other hand, a few adults still behave like adolescents, possibly because they were so effectively socialized into the youth culture. In extreme cases they are middle-aged dropouts or adult delinquents like the Hell's Angels. By their own accounts, some of the young protesters of the 1970s also found they had trouble adopting the ordinary responsibilities of adult life.[40] For some people, fitting too well into the adolescent way of life means being unable to fit into adult roles. Successful socialization into the youth culture carries a risk of inadequate socialization for adulthood.

ADULTHOOD

For most of human history nearly everyone spent the adult years working and raising children. Not only did young people go to work as soon as they were physically able, but old people continued working virtually until they died. Until the twentieth century parenthood was also a lifelong process: married couples had more children and died younger, often when their last child was still living at home. In contrast, most people today retire from work at about 65, leaving them at least fourteen years to live; most parents end active child rearing with fully a third of their lives still ahead of them. These changes have divided adulthood into stages that require new, often troubling redefinitions of self.

GETTING STARTED. Getting married and having a job are the most important socializing experiences in early adulthood. "Husband" and "wife" are new roles for most young couples, and achieving intimacy with another person, as Erikson noted, is itself one of the great challenges of adult life.

Parenthood is likely to be an even more difficult adjustment than marriage.[41] When their first child is born, young parents are forced to accept full adult responsibilities: he is expected to be a successful breadwinner, supporting a family; she is still usually expected to put her role as a mother ahead of her work or educational goals (see Chapter 10, "The Sexes"). Without much anticipatory socialization, many married couples have to learn parenting by being parents. More often than not, their baby teaches them when to feed it and how to make it stop crying. Moreover, the patterns of behavior established during the mutual socialization of husband and wife are bound to be disrupted by their additional roles as parents. The feeling of being "tied down," fatigue, and financial problems frequently increase the stress of the parental transition.

Considering that most of our waking hours are spent in occupational roles, it is not surprising that the kind of work people do affects their characters. Some socialized differences are reflected in occupational stereotypes: the fussy accountant, the argumentative lawyer, the pedantic teacher, the materialistic business person, the superfi-

---

[40] James S. Kunen, "The Rebels of 1970," *New York Times Magazine*, October 28, 1973, pp. 22–23, 67–79.

[41] Reuben Hill and Joan Aldous, "Socialization for Marriage and Parenthood," in *Handbook of Socialization Theory and Research*, ed. David A. Goslin (Chicago: Rand McNally, 1969), pp. 923–25.

cial advertising executive.[42] These popular observations were borne out by an influential article, "Bureaucratic Structure and Personality," in which Robert Merton showed that the rigidly rules-minded, faceless bureaucrat is largely a creature formed by the large organization's emphasis on formal regulations and their impersonal application[43] (see Chapter 6, "Organizations").

Since the professions demand greater commitment of the whole personality, they have an even greater socializing effect than other kinds of work. Moreover, some professional schools enhance socialization by isolating their students in special areas (military academies, theological seminaries) or cutting them off from the rest of the world by the amount of work they require (medical and law schools, schools of music). Technical language, specialized training, and different ethical codes all give professionals a sense of their separate identities.

Young adults find that they must adjust to changes in their childhood relationships as parents age, friends marry or divorce, and close relatives die or move away. Early adulthood is also the time when youthful aspirations are compared to the realities of life, and people must evaluate their lives in terms of the present, not some distant future.[44]

THE MIDLIFE CRISIS.   Middle age is often called the best part of the life cycle — the prime of life. Yet middle-aged men and women often feel "let down" or trapped in the routines of boring jobs and marriages. Once the early challenges have been overcome, even a successful career can lose its interest. For those who haven't "made it," there is the fear of losing even an unsatisfying job and not being able to get another. As children grow up and leave home, mothers lose much of the purpose of their lives; fathers, in contrast, often regret having been too involved with work to spend much time with them. The result of these changes is called the **midlife crisis** — a middle-aged person's feeling of estrangement from his or her children, boredom with married life, and lack of fulfillment in work.[45]

Like adolescence, the forties and fifties are a time when familiar roles must be put aside and new ones learned. The adolescent identity crisis is relieved by many kinds of social support: parents, teachers, and friends usually encourage the young person to be independent, to decide on a job and a mate, and generally to "settle down" into adult life. Little social support is available, however, for the middle-aged person who decides to get a divorce or to make a radical change of occupation. The usual socializing agents for this age group are peers. Single parents' clubs, for instance, help the newly divorced learn to be single again.

According to David Riesman, the midlife identity crisis occurs when people follow the "socially provided script" too closely, so that they lose their sense of self and forget that they are not merely spouses, parents, and breadwinners.[46] The people who are

---

[42] Wilbert E. Moore, "Occupational Socialization," in *Handbook of Socialization Theory and Research,* p. 881.

[43] Merton, "Bureaucratic Structure and Personality," in *Social Theory and Social Structure,* pp. 249–60.

[44] Russel A. Ward, *The Aging Experience.* New York: Harper & Row, 1984.

[45] Zena Smith Blau, *Old Age in a Changing Society* (New York: New Viewpoints, 1973), pp. 184–85.

[46] David Riesman, "Some Clinical and Cultural Aspects of the Aging Process," *American Journal of Sociology* 59 (1954): 381.

"True, you're a
butterfly now, but
you still think like
a caterpillar."

Drawing by Levin;
© 1984 The New
Yorker Magazine,
Inc.

most often bored and weary in middle age are those who have most exclusively devoted themselves to traditional adult roles: women who have been only full-time home-makers; men who have pursued occupational success to the exclusion of other inter-ests.[47] For middle-class men middle age is often a time when they feel "burnt out" by a demanding career; for middle-class women the loss of the child-rearing role is thought to cause an emotional depression known as the "empty-nest syndrome."

One study of middle age concludes, however, that the empty-nest syndrome is largely a myth. In *Women of a Certain Age* (1979), Lillian Rubin found that middle-aged women are not depressed because their children grow up and leave home; in fact, they are relieved that their child-rearing years are over. She argues that their midlife crisis comes from trying to decide what to do next and finding only lukewarm support for their efforts to go back to work or to school. For women whose most important role in life has been raising children, the critical midlife question is "What am I going to do with the next thirty years of my life?"[48]

On the other hand, gerontologist Lillian Troll argues that there is no midlife crisis. She finds that the most stressful period in the life cycle is adolescence, when the physical and psychological changes are so great that they can properly be said to cause a "crisis." Troll notes that the challenges of midlife may be new, but an older person's resources for meeting them are usually greater. After age 40 people are better able to cope with life and thus are more likely to weather the storms of middle age without suffering any profound unhappiness or distress.[49]

---

[47] Blau, *Old Age in a Changing Society*, p. 187.

[48] Lillian B. Rubin, *Women of a Certain Age: The Midlife Search for Self* (New York: Harper & Row, 1979), p. 40.

[49] Lillian E. Troll, *Continuations: Adult Development and Aging* (Monterey, Calif.: Brooks/Cole, 1982), p. 249.

OLD AGE

The United States is growing older. At the beginning of the twentieth century only 40 percent of the population lived to be 65, and now 75 percent live at least that long. As a result of this "graying of America," one out of nine Americans is over 65 and officially defined as "old."[50]

In a culture that places such a high value on youthful vitality and good looks, few want to be "old." Americans spend hundreds of millions of dollars a year on efforts to disguise the aging process through cosmetics, hair dyes, wigs, face lifts, and exercise. Compared to social expectations for younger adults, the roles for elderly parents and retired workers are only vaguely defined. Moreover, resocialization for the aged is usually inadequate. Only one in five old people do volunteer work, few can afford travel or other expensive leisure activities, and few belong to senior citizens' organizations.[51] As a result, old age is a role that most Americans are not prepared to play. When it is thrust upon them unexpectedly, people receive only the most ambiguous social signals about how to behave. At this important stage in the life cycle, the socialization process breaks down, leaving many old people feeling rejected, confused, and useless.

LOSS OF VALUED ROLES.   Like the other stages of life, old age is primarily a social definition. In the 1930s the age of 65 was arbitrarily chosen as the time when Americans would be eligible for Social Security payments. This official starting point for retirement has little to do with a decline in health, productivity, or any other aspect of the aging process, but it marks a change in social roles. People whom psychologist Bernice Neugarten has called the "young old" — those who are still vigorous and productive — must look for new purposes in life after their child-rearing and working years are over; the disabled and isolated "old old" must adjust to their unwelcome dependency on others.[52]

American society has given people more years to live, but it often takes away their most rewarding, useful roles in those years.[53] Retirement from work, for example, is personally and socially defined as less valuable than employment. Most Americans believe in working and measure social usefulness and productivity in material terms. To be considered unfit for a job for which one has been trained, and in which one has had years of experience, is a terrible blow to an individual's self-image. Yet this is what happens to thousands of 65-year-old workers every year. Besides loss of income and self-respect, retirement can also mean lack of companionship and disruption of a familiar daily routine.

Old age means the loss of other socially rewarded roles too. As children become adults with lives of their own, the role of parent becomes less important. Since women live almost nine years longer than men, and since women tend to marry older men,

---

[50] U.S. Bureau of the Census, *Statistical Abstract of the United States,* 1985 (Washington D.C.: U.S. Government Printing Office, 1985).

[51] Matilda White Riley and Joan Waring, "Age and Aging," in *Contemporary Social Problems,* 4th ed., Robert K. Merton and Robert Nisbet, eds. (New York: Harcourt Brace Jovanovich, 1976), p. 43.

[52] Bernice Neugarten (interviewed by Elizabeth Hall), "Acting One's Age: New Rules for Old," *Psychology Today* 13:11 (April 1980): 66–80.

[53] Leonard Pearlin, "Life Strains and Psychological Distress Among Adults," in N. Smelser and E. Erikson, eds., *Themes of Work and Love* in Adulthood, Cambridge, Mass.: Harvard University Press, 1980.

Old age is primarily a social definition. The vigorous and productive "young-old" must look for new purposes in life after retirement from work and childrearing.

many wives must face the personal loss of their husbands as well as the end of their role as wife. The adjustment to widowhood is therefore doubly painful.

Because most elderly people lose friends and family over the years, the available research generally supports the view that aging is a process of disengagement from social roles and responsibilities. Yet research has also shown that the people who are most active and socially engaged in old age are also the happiest.[54]

Looking on the bright side, we can clearly see that the "graying of America" is changing attitudes toward old age and the kinds of behavior considered appropriate for older people. Elderly people who act in youthful ways are not criticized as severely as they were only a few years ago. According to Neugarten, the United States is becoming an "age-irrelevant" society, in which there is no longer a particular age at which one marries or goes to work or has children or goes to college. She finds that public attitudes toward "acting one's age" have relaxed to the point where most people are no longer shocked to hear of a 70-year-old attending college or a 30-year-old becoming a big city's mayor.[55] Certainly the public perception of the "young-old" was enhanced by the election of an energetic 69-year-old president in 1980.

Old age remains, however, the most troublesome period of the life cycle. Attitudes toward the elderly are still deeply ambivalent. On the one hand, they are expected to play the elder statesman role — to be wise, kind, and deserving of respect. On the other

---

[54] Troll, *Continuations*, p. 6.
[55] Neugarten, "Acting One's Age." pp. 66–80.

hand, they are often thought to be too foolish or decrepit to fulfill useful adult roles as parents, workers, and community leaders. Moreover, old age has emotional stresses of its own: the deaths of friends and family, loss of income, failing health, and the approaching end of one's own life.

LEARNING TO DIE.   Death is a most obvious part of life, yet most Americans deny its existence in their own lives. There is hardly any social support available for this final transition, and many people end their lives lonely and afraid in hospitals and nursing homes. Yet even at this ultimate point in the life cycle, socialization goes on. People can and do learn to die.

The pioneering study of how people die was written by Elisabeth Kübler-Ross, a psychiatrist who worked with dying patients. She suggested that dying is a developmental process with five successive stages. The dying person first denies the possibility of death, then tries to bargain for a way out, then becomes angry, then depressed. Finally, in fortunate cases, the patient acknowledges the reality of death and accepts the end.[56]

Socialization has been known to help people through this process. Retirement communities, for example, often prepare their elderly residents for death. Moving to a community for the aged is itself an acknowledgment that one will die there, and the reality of death cannot be denied when it is a frequent occurrence among acquaintances. Social support for the dying is provided by the elderly peer group, whose members are often better able than the young to deal with death realistically.

Acceptance of death need not mean resignation and defeat. The challenges of this last transition can be met triumphantly. "Heavens!" an 81-year-old resident of a retirement community said. "I've lived my life. I'd be delighted to have it end. . . . No, I don't want to mourn when I go. I've had a good life. It's time."[57]

---

[56] Elisabeth Kübler-Ross, *On Death and Dying* (New York: Macmillan, 1969). See also John W. Riley, Jr., "Dying and the Meanings of Death: Sociological Inquiries," *Annual Review of Sociology* 9 (1983): 191–216.

[57] Victor W. Marshall, "Socialization for Impending Death in a Retirement Village," *American Journal of Sociology* 80:5 (March 1975): 1127.

SUMMARY

1. Socialization is the interactive process by which people learn some of the values, attitudes, skills, and knowledge appropriate to their roles in society. Socialization has two functions: the transmission of culture and the development of the self.

2. Without repeated interaction with others, human beings do not become fully human. Studies of isolated children show that normal physical and psychological development does not take place without human contact.

3. Theories of socialization analyze the process by which our innermost selves are molded through interaction with others.

4. According to Cooley's theory of the looking-glass self, a person's self-image is a reflection of what others see or are believed to see that person to be.

5. Mead proposed that children develop a self as they "take the role of the other." Significant others are important models for behavior; the generalized

other represents the attitudes of the whole community.

6. The Freudian theory of socialization emphasizes that the emerging self is often antagonistic to the demands of others.

7. Developmental psychologists study the way children order the world according to their own perceptions of it. Piaget's experiments found that there are stages of cognitive development and that children can perform different kinds of mental operations at each stage. Kohlberg elaborated Piaget's insights into a theory that there are also different levels of moral development.

8. Erikson's theory of lifelong socialization describes eight stages of development, each representing an identity crisis brought on by a new situation in the life cycle.

9. Parents and other family members are the most important agents of socialization in childhood. Lower-class parents tend to stress behavioral conformity, while middle-class parents emphasize attitudinal conformity. Class differences in socialization influence children's self-image and their abilities to perform adult occupational roles.

10. Schools are officially designated agents of socialization. There is also evidence that schools socialize children for different class levels by helping to decide what kind of jobs they will get and how they feel about themselves.

11. After childhood peers are significant others in the socialization process. Television socializes both children and adults by showing them images of American society. Watching violent television programs leads directly to aggressive and violent behavior in children. Studies also indicate that prime-time programs reinforce negative stereotypes of women, blacks, and the elderly.

12. Each stage in the life cycle involves resocialization. If social expectations are not clear, or if there are few opportunities to learn new roles from others, people are likely to feel anxious and confused.

13. The irresponsible, rebellious behavior associated with adolescence has been explained in two ways: as a response to an ambiguous social role, and as conformity to the norms of the youth culture.

14. Social changes in the twentieth century have divided adulthood into stages that demand redefinitions of self. The midlife crisis is a particularly difficult transition to a new stage of family and occupational life.

15. Elderly people lose socially valued roles and are often confused by conflicting social expectations of how they should behave. Since anticipatory socialization and resocialization are usually inadequate during this period, old age remains the most troublesome stage of the life cycle.

KEY TERMS

socialization 124
looking-glass self 127
significant others 127
generalized other 127
identity crisis 133

behavioral conformity 136
attitudinal conformity 136
peer group 140
rites of passage 143

resocialization 144
anticipatory socialization 144
youth culture 145
midlife crisis 149

SUGGESTED READING

* Philippe Ariès. *Centuries of Childhood: A Social History of Family Life.* McGraw-Hill, 1965.
*Howard S. Becker et al. *Boys in White: Student Culture in Medical School.* Rev. ed. New Brunswick, NJ: Transaction Books, 1976.
* Ronald Blythe. *The View in Winter: Reflections on Old Age.* New York: Harcourt Brace Jovanovich, 1979.
* Peter W. Cookson, Jr. and Caroline H. Persell. *Preparing for Power: America's Elite Boarding Schools.* New York: Basic Books, 1987.

Helen Keller. *The Story of My Life.* Garden City, New York: Doubleday, 1954.
* Margaret Mead. *Coming of Age in Samoa.* New York: Morrow, 1971.
* Peter I. Rose, ed. *Socialization and the Life Cycle.* New York: St. Martin's Press, 1979.

* Available in paperback.

We shape our
buildings, and
afterwards
our buildings
shape us.

Winston Churchill

CHAPTER 6

ORGANIZATIONS

Neil Armstrong, the first man to set foot on the moon, has often been compared to Christopher Columbus, traditionally considered the first European to set foot in the New World. The twentieth-century astronaut and the fifteenth-century sea captain were both daring and skillful explorers, but their situations were entirely different. Columbus set out into the unknown on the basis of the speculation that the fabled Indies could be reached by sailing west. His three small ships were largely untested, his crew fearful and superstitious. Cautious homebodies told him he would never make it. He had no idea what dangers might lie ahead or what strange lands and cultures he might find. Armstrong, in contrast, was an employee of the National Aeronautics and Space Administration, a large, complex, and centralized organization. He faced few unknowns on his voyage and had hardly any independent decisions to make. There was only one Columbus, but there were at least ten astronauts who could have done Armstrong's job, and hundreds of technical experts to tell him what to do. In the twentieth century, a hero is much more likely to be an organization man.

In the fifteenth-century world in which Columbus lived, people conducted much of their business on a personal basis. Columbus was able to appeal directly to the Spanish king and queen for the money to finance his mission. He didn't need a government agency to command his ships; he dealt with the crew face to face. A modern Columbus, however, would not be able to set sail without the support and permission of large organizations. He would have to apply, through channels, for a government research and development grant, filling out all the forms and waiting for the authorities in charge to act on his request. Huge corporations would build and outfit

157

Until about a century ago, primary groups of friends and family members supplied their own entertainment. Leisure-time activities today are provided by such large organizations as television networks and amusement parks.

his ships. His crew, having passed their qualifying exams at school, would have degrees in navigation and seamanship. He could not leave the harbor without an official license to operate a ship, owner's certificates for his vessels, a passport for foreign travel, customs papers for his cargo, and proof that every sailor had been inoculated against all the diseases of the Indies.

One reason for so many regulations and restrictions is that modern societies depend on large, complex organizations to accomplish common goals. In Columbus's time, for example, most education consisted of little more than a brief apprenticeship served under a neighbor or relative. Average workers learned the skills they needed in a short period of time and then passed them on to others. This kind of educational system would obviously be inadequate in a modern city, where most residents are strangers to each other and millions of workers need a wide variety of skills. In such a situation primary-group relationships are no longer enough. Meeting everyone's educational needs requires an organization run by specialized teachers and administrators according to established rules. This type of organization, designed to accomplish large-scale tasks by coordinating the work of many individuals, is called a **bureaucracy**.[1]

Little more than a century ago, nearly all social life took place in primary groups. Families and close neighbors provided many necessities of life — food, cloth-

[1] Peter M. Blau and Marshall W. Meyer, *Bureaucracy in Modern Society,* 2d ed. (New York: Random House, 1971), p. 14.

ing, education, protection, employment, and entertainment. Today all these needs typically are met by people we may never see face to face. Large formal organizations based on secondary-group relationships dominate more and more of our lives: corporations, public schools and universities, television networks, government agencies, and scientific and cultural foundations. Since modern life is so dependent on the operations of these large organizations, it is important for us to understand how bureaucracies work and what effect they have on the rest of society.

This chapter begins by describing the distinctive features of modern bureaucracies and some of the reasons they control so much of our daily life. Designed for logic and efficiency, bureaucracies nevertheless are sometimes notoriously illogical and inefficient. We discuss next how the larger society interferes with organizational goals, as well as how some inefficiencies are inherent in the bureaucratic structure itself. We then consider the effect of bureaucracies on the individuals who belong to them, and, finally, assess the social consequences of the bureaucratic way of life.

AN ORGANIZED WAY OF LIFE

Bureaucracies are not new. They appear throughout human history whenever large numbers of people must be coordinated to achieve a complex objective. No other form of organization could have accomplished such massive building projects as the pyramids of Egypt, the Great Wall of China, or the cathedral at Chartres. Bureaucracies also arise when the efforts of many people must be coordinated to perform a routine task. To collect taxes from subjects scattered all over the known world, the Roman Empire required a bureaucracy. When the goal was getting every Christian soul into heaven, the medieval church developed bureaucratic procedures to accomplish it.

The existence of bureaucracies is not new, but the extent to which they prevail is indeed unique to modern social life. In the early years of the twentieth century, Max Weber was among the first to see the unprecedented scope and number of bureaucracies in modern society. He also made the classic analysis of the distinction between bureaucracies and other forms of organization.

CHARACTERISTICS OF BUREAUCRACY

To Weber the growth of bureaucracy was part of the triumph of a purposive, rational mentality. While tradition or family loyalties guided human action at other times in history, Weber believed, people in modern societies are more often motivated by the claims of logic and efficiency. Ancient bureaucracies probably developed largely through trial and error; modern bureaucracies are deliberately created as the rational means for achieving some large-scale goal.

Weber identified five characteristics that distinguish modern bureaucracies from traditional forms of organization.[2] Together, these characteristics amount to what he called an **ideal-type,** or conceptual model, for analyzing bureaucratic structure. Not all

---

[2] H. H. Gerth and C. Wright Mills, eds. *From Max Weber: Essays in Sociology* (New York: Oxford University Press, 1967), Chapter 8.

bureaucracies have these features to the degree described below, but all are similar enough to be studied together as a special kind of organization.

A HIERARCHY OF AUTHORITY.   In a bureaucracy there are fixed hierarchical positions, each under the control and supervision of a higher one. The organizational structure is shaped like a pyramid, with the positions at the very top directing the rest. This reliable chain of command resolves disputes among subordinates and makes coordinated decision making possible. President Harry S Truman used to keep a sign on his desk that read "The buck stops here." As the man at the top of the pyramid, he alone had the authority to decide questions that had been passed all the way up the chain of command.

Bureaucratic authority rests in the office, not in the officeholder. When an executive asks his secretary to do his Christmas shopping, he is overstepping the boundaries of his legitimate power or authority. When a subordinate "steps out of line," a superior can "pull rank." The boss's boss can reprimand him for asking his secretary to do favors beyond the duties of the position.

The limited nature of bureaucratic authority contrasts with the relatively unlimited nature of traditional authority. When Louis XV was offended by what Voltaire was writing, he had him imprisoned for impertinence. There was no separation between the king as an insulted individual and the king as the head of state, or between the office and the person holding that office.

UNIVERSALISTIC STANDARDS.   The success of a bureaucratic career is determined mainly by *achieved* characteristics (professional education, technical skills), not by *ascribed*

Like all bureaucracies, the army has hierarchies of authority to direct and coordinate the actions of large numbers of people.

characteristics such as sex, race, or family background. Employees are hired on the basis of their abilities, as measured by **universalistic standards** (applied impartially to everyone), and are promoted according to merit and seniority. Such regulations protect employees against arbitrary dismissal, favoritism, and personal animosity.

The traditional spoils system, in contrast, rewarded friends and got rid of enemies. In the eighteenth and nineteenth centuries the federal government operated on a partisan patronage system. Government jobs were sold to the highest bidder or distributed as rewards to party workers. To the winning party belonged the spoils of office. The system was reformed at the end of the nineteenth century by being bureaucratized: today, under the Civil Service Commission, employees are selected on the basis of competitive examinations, and office seekers are chosen according to merit.

SPECIALIZATION OF LABOR.   Bureaucracies tend to have a far more specialized division of labor than other forms of organization. Craftspeople like dressmakers and silversmiths need a variety of skills to produce a complete product; bureaucratic workers specialize in one task (for example, word processing or teaching modern poetry) that contributes to only part of an organizational goal. The *Dictionary of Occupational Titles,* published by the U.S. Department of Labor, now lists some 30,000 different jobs. Instead of "jacks-of-all-trades," there are now — at least theoretically — tens of thousands of "masters of one."

In a bureaucracy a clearly defined division of labor establishes specific responsibilities for each position and assigns a specialist to handle them. Training and experience on the job make for competent performance at all levels of the hierarchy. What is more, a relatively unskilled worker can become proficient at a single specialized task with a minimum of training. Industrial development has depended on the bureaucracy's ability to turn a farm hand into a factory worker practically overnight.

RULES AND REGULATIONS.   The rule book is the basis of bureaucratic administration. Written rules determine the salary for each position, set working procedures, specify requirements for promotion, and spell out impersonal criteria for dealing with people and problems. Regulations ensure that individuals will put aside their personal inclinations and perform routine tasks predictably and reliably. Formal rules and universalistic standards enable people who don't know or like each other to work together effectively.

According to an old saying, there are three ways of doing something: the right way, the wrong way, and the navy way. Right and wrong are highly personal concepts that can be applied a little differently in every case. The navy way is impersonal and absolute. The navy, like all bureaucracies, "goes by the book."

WRITTEN RECORDS AND COMMUNICATIONS.   Bureaucracies require a great many records to control their operations. Orders have to be given to subordinates, and superiors have to receive progress reports to make informed decisions. Objective standards for hiring and firing mean examinations and evaluations of performance, and these generate personnel files and supervisors' reports. Written records themselves require more memos, files, and correspondence. Computerized storage and retrieval systems, which permit reams of data to be filed and consulted instantaneously, have enormously increased the bureaucracy's record-keeping capacity.

Organizations that rely on fallible human memory are much less efficient. Many of the doctrinal disputes of the early Christian church arose, for example, over questions of what exactly Jesus had taught. The Gospels, written from memory long after his death, provided fragmentary and occasionally conflicting reports on which to base church policy. As a bureaucratic form of organization developed in the medieval church, however, these questions were settled in great detail.

ADVANTAGES OF BUREAUCRACY

"The Navy is a master plan designed by geniuses for execution by idiots." Keefer's flippant description of the navy in Herman Wouk's novel *The Caine Mutiny*[3] tells us an important truth about bureaucracies. Bureaucracies provide a way to transcend human limitations. Their peculiar features are meant to organize the abilities of ordinary people for extraordinary purposes.

Bureaucracies improve human reliability and competence by dividing work into small tasks and training specialists to do them according to standard procedures. Regulations and detailed reports minimize errors while a hierarchy of supervisors exercises control over the work process. In a bureaucracy, it does not take geniuses to carry on highly technical and complex enterprises like building a supersonic plane or

---

[3] Herman Wouk, *The Caine Mutiny* (New York: Pocket Books, 1973), p. 121.

running the telephone company. The bureaucratic division of labor breaks the task down into jobs that most people can perform adequately. Bureaucracy may limit a talented person's ability to do a superior job, but it also reduces the chance for an inept person to make a disastrous mistake. People who might otherwise be incompetent — Keefer's "idiots" — are thus able to contribute to society.[4]

According to Weber, bureaucracies are the tools for carrying out the rational, purposive actions that are the guiding force in modern societies. Compared to other forms of organization, bureaucracies are highly reliable and efficient. In the feudal system of prerevolutionary France, for example, there was no particular connection between the competence of officeholders and their responsibilities. The nobility held inherited positions of power, regardless of ability. Since the individual in the office was considered more important than the office itself, ministers of state could act on personal whim. Officeholders had no clearly defined sphere of activity. The king's mistress could direct military strategy, as Madame de Pompadour did. Salaries were not fixed, and employees had no job security. The employee's normal inclination under these circumstances was to make as much as possible out of the job while it lasted and to make it last as long as possible. As a result bribery and graft were common. Finally, since there were no objective criteria for employment, getting a job was a matter of who you were or whom you knew. Offices were often bought or obtained in return for favors. Many of these statements about eighteenth-century France also apply to contemporary Latin American, Middle Eastern, and Asian societies that are not fully bureaucratized.

Feudal systems lack the rationality that makes bureaucracies so efficient. Trained personnel, chosen by objective standards and promoted according to merit and experience, are more likely to do a good job than untrained workers. Impersonal rules and specific duties make people predictable in doing their work. Salaries and job security discourage corruption. The whole bureaucratic structure is designed to make a large number of individuals work together effectively to achieve a complex goal in a logical and efficient way.

As much as we might wish that our social ties were more personal, there are many good reasons to prefer bureaucracies to other forms of organization. Bureaucratic hierarchies enable individuals to develop expertise and to coordinate their efforts effectively. Fixed salaries and the separation of organizational from personal affairs protect the rights of individuals from abuse by their superiors. Finally, bureaucracies are far more democratic than other organizations. Bureaucratic service is a career, with opportunities for promotion on the basis of achievement and seniority; the authority of superiors to demote or dismiss is limited; and there is usually a right to appeal decisions and voice grievances.[5]

In spite of these advantages, bureaucracies are less well known for their impartiality and consistency than for their rigidity and inertia. Next we will consider why the "master plan" goes wrong.

---

[4] William J. Goode, "The Protection of the Inept." *American Sociological Review* 32:1 (February 1967): 17.

[5] Charles Perrow, *Complex Organizations: A Critical Essay*, 2d ed. (Glenview, Ill.: Scott, Foresman, 1979), pp. 56–57.

PROBLEMS OF BUREAUCRACY

Weber compared bureaucracies to highly efficient machines. "The fully developed bureaucratic mechanism," he wrote, "compares with other organizations exactly as does the machine with nonmechanical modes of production."[6] Yet bureaucracies are made up of people, and people are not machines. No matter how rationally structured an organization is, the individuals who belong to it are subject to social forces that can disrupt its smooth operation.

THE BUREAUCRAT'S DIVIDED LOYALTIES

Some of the complaints about bureaucracies are actually complaints that bureaucratic principles are not being followed. Because bureaucracies do not operate in a social vacuum, nonbureaucratic values intrude into the system and undermine its carefully laid out plan. When a group of file clerks decides to take a longer lunch hour, an administrative rule is being broken. When the president appoints an old friend to a cabinet post, impartial standards are not being enforced. There are many reasons why bureaucratic procedures are not always followed to the letter. Among them are conflicts between personal and bureaucratic values, goals, and norms.

COMPETING VALUES.   Many other social values conflict with purely objective standards of merit. Discrimination on the basis of age, race, and sex is found in bureaucracies just as it is in the rest of society. Few men, for example, believe that any woman should be promoted over them. Despite the rules incompetent workers are rarely fired. Competing values — loyalty, sympathy, friendship — intervene and new posts are found for them instead. These nonbureaucratic considerations "protect the inept" in ways that undermine the system.[7]

COMPETING GOALS.   Informal groups within a bureaucracy tend to defend their own interests against those of the organization.The specialized division of labor is violated by trading off routine jobs; informal leaders sometimes have more authority than unpopular supervisors; the grapevine occasionally outperforms regular channels of communication; and administrative rules are bent in particular cases. Loyalty to one's own group can lead to departmental competition that interferes with rational administration. Nurses, clerks, and police officers, for example, often try to protect each other against exposure by hiding mistakes from outsiders.[8]

Professional or personal standards of conduct may also take precedence over organizational goals. Occasionally, federal employees who disagreed with their superiors on a policy matter have "blown the whistle" or complained in public. In one such case, a scientist in the Public Health Service insisted that certain industrial chemicals

---

[6] Gerth and Mills, *From Max Weber: Essays in Sociology*, p. 214.

[7] Goode, "The Protection of the Inept." pp. 5–19; Alvin W. Gouldner, "Organizational Analysis," in *Sociology Today*, eds. Robert K. Merton et al. (New York: Basic Books, 1959), pp. 400–421.

[8] Erving Goffman, *The Presentation of Self in Everyday Life* (Garden City, N.Y.: Doubleday/Anchor, 1961), Chapter 2.

were dangerous and might cause cancer. When his superiors resisted his efforts to develop new plant safety standards, he wrote letters of protest to members of Congress. His criticism found its way into the newspapers, and the scientist was fired for "marginal and substandard performance" and "insubordination," two peculiarly bureaucratic sins.[9]

COMPETING NORMS. While bureaucracies operate according to universalistic standards, everyone participates in groups that have **particularistic standards**, criteria for making judgments based on each individual case. We treat our friends and families, for example, as "exceptions to the rule" who deserve special consideration.Bureaucrats too are often tempted to use their influence to promote their brothers-in-law or help out a friend.

Conflicts of this sort are especially likely to arise when a bureaucratic organization is imposed on a traditional society where particularistic norms prevail. It is a traditional African custom, for example, for men in high political positions to use their power to benefit themselves, their families, their clan, and — if they are able — even their village and their tribe. The prestige of "taking care of your people" often outweighs the shame of abusing a public trust. Kickbacks and bribes, as these terms are defined in the bureaucratic West, are therefore common. Before the civilian government of President Shehu Shagari came to power in Nigeria in 1979, a mark-up of 6 percent on the cost of goods and services was considered an acceptable amount to pay for doing business with government officials. The new government, however, overstepped these self-imposed limits. The unprecedented scope and style of the civilian regime's corruption — which included, rumor had it, one official's solid gold bathtub — were the principal reasons that President Shagari was overthrown by senior army officers at the end of 1983.[10]

Many of the norms peculiar to bureaucracy compete in a similar way with the norms that govern the rest of social life. Even within the bureaucracy itself, conformity to impersonal standards is likely to be a matter of degree.

BUREAUCRACY'S INTERNAL CONTRADICTIONS

We have just seen how social influences from outside the organization can undermine bureaucratic goals. Aside from these the organization also has internal contradictions that reduce its effectiveness. In fact, the very features that make bureaucracies so efficient also produce inefficiencies by generating internal stresses and strains. The logic of centralization, rationality, and impersonality sometimes has illogical results. Some of these unintended consequences of bureaucratic organization are discussed below.

CONFLICT BETWEEN STAFF AND LINE. In spite of the beautifully laid out pyramids of power shown in organization charts, bureaucratic hierarchies have competing sources

---

[9] Helen Dudar, "The Price of Blowing the Whistle," *New York Times Magazine,* October 30, 1977, pp. 41, 46.

[10] Clifford D. May, "Ousted Rulers' Nigeria Called Garden of Graft," *New York Times,* January 20, 1984, pp. A1, A9.

A stranger in a foreign country is usually in a situation that calls for sympathy and help from others. The clerks in this U.S. Immigration Service office, however, were trained to be impartial and to obey the rules. New immigrants are likely to interpret this ordinary bureaucratic behavior as callous indifference to their problems.

of authority. Bureaucratic offices are generally divided into staff and line positions. Staff members are specialists of various kinds — personnel directors, public relations officers, and accountants. They make no direct contribution to the output of the organization, but they are necessary to its smooth operation. Line officers are administrators — the factory foremen, school administrators, and executive vice-presidents whose job is to manage the actual production of the organization's output. Conflict is inherent in the situation because (1) staff specialists usually want authority over policy decisions, and (2) line administrators do not usually welcome the staff members' advice or follow their suggestions to the letter.[11]

In her study of a Boston mental hospital, Rose Laub Coser analyzed a basic contradiction in the goals of many service organizations: the hospital is supposed to control the behavior of its mentally ill patients and also to treat them. This dual purpose leads to a division of labor between hospital administrators and psychotherapists, thus creating two contending centers of authority. The administrator's hierarchical authority in the hospital bureaucracy conflicts with the therapist's professional authority to treat the patients. Psychotherapists complain that the administrators' decisions about patients are too restrictive to be therapeutic, while hospital administrators often feel that a certain patient is misbehaving because the therapist is too permissive and the "psychotherapy is not going well."[12]

[11] Melville Dalton, "Conflict Between Staff and Line Managerial Officers," in *A Sociological Reader on Complex Organizations,* ed. Amitai Etzioni (New York: Holt, Rinehart & Winston, 1961).
[12] Rose Laub Coser, *Training in Ambiguity: Learning Through Doing in a Mental Hospital* (New York: The Free Press, 1979), pp. 35–47.

A similar organizational strain between administrators and professional experts occurs in the military, where line officers have to rely on staff specialists to operate complex new weapons systems. Senior line officers do not usually have enough technical knowledge to know whether the specialists under their command are doing a good job. Staff officers have no administrative authority, yet they are responsible for technical operations. If they fail to interfere when a soldier is doing something wrong, they are not doing their job as technical specialists. If they do interfere, they are overstepping their authority and stepping on the line officer's toes. The two groups' different status systems — the military command's, based on seniority, and the staff specialist's, based on knowledge — worsen the conflict by making each jealous and suspicious of the other.[13]

Conflict between staff and line officers is inherent not only in the social structures of mental hospitals and armies, but also in such service organizations as schools, reformatories, and social welfare agencies.

INDIFFERENCE TO HUMAN NEEDS.   The stereotype of the "faceless bureaucrat," the drone without a human personality, grows out of the bureaucratic requirement for impartiality. In situations that usually call for personal interest or sympathy, the bureaucrat is trained to be impersonal and unemotional. Clients may regard their problems as emergencies, but to the bureaucrat they are routine. Clients find this attitude unsympathetic, even hostile, and are hurt and annoyed. The same rationality that makes bureaucracies work also makes them resented and despised.[14]

For efficiency's sake, bureaucrats are trained to ignore the peculiarities of particular cases. People and problems are placed in categories — "premedical student," for example, or "widow over 65 years old," or "Ohio licensed driver." Ignoring individual exceptions to the rule, however, can also be inefficient for accomplishing the organization's goals. The purpose of the welfare bureaucracy, for example, is to relieve poverty. But poverty is defined so narrowly that couples who had less than $2,400 to their names were not officially poor in 1986. To qualify for Supplemental Security Income, a federal program for the aged and disabled who cannot work, a single elderly person had to reduce his or her life savings to less than $1,700. Many were naturally unwilling to do so. Thus a bureaucratic goal — helping those who cannot work — is being frustrated by an impersonal rule.

RITUALISM AND INERTIA.   According to Robert Merton, bureaucrats have a trained incapacity to handle certain problems.[15] The bureaucratic structure requires officials to be methodical, cautious about overstepping their limited authority, and emotionally disciplined. These qualities create blind spots: the same training and skills that make bureaucrats precise and reliable in dealing with routine problems also make them inflexible in dealing with changing or extraordinary situations.

[13] Morris Janovitz, "Hierarchy and Authority in the Military Establishment," in *A Sociological Reader*, pp. 198–212.

[14] Robert K. Merton, "Bureaucratic Structure and Personality," in *Social Theory and Social Structure*, enlarged ed. (New York: Free Press, 1968), pp. 256–57.

[15] Ibid., pp. 251–52.

This 45-foot-long string of forms represents one year's paperwork on a single child in New York's Aid to Dependent Children program. Such enormous amounts of red tape are generated by the bureaucratic requirement for written records and centralized decision making.

The price of predictability is often overconformity to bureaucratic regulations. Breaking a rule (or showing some flexibility) is frowned upon; being prompt and accurate (or conforming to the rules) is highly regarded.[16] Since bureaucratic standards take precedence over service to the client, bureaucrats are likely to find that obeying the rules is more important than the reasons for them in the first place. A **displacement of goals** takes place: sticking to the rules becomes an end in itself instead of a means to a larger goal of the organization. The emphasis on conformity turns into rigidity, timidity, and resistance to change. Slavish obedience to regulations and obsessive concern with forms and procedures are the symptoms of bureaucratic *ritualism*.

---

[16] Laurence J. Peter and Raymond Hull, *The Peter Principle* (New York: Bantam Books, 1970), p. 25.

PARKINSON'S LAW AND THE PETER PRINCIPLE

Work expands so as to fill the time available for its completion." The British historian C. Northcote Parkinson distilled his humorous observations of bureaucratic proliferation and inefficiency into this well-known statement, Parkinson's Law. He examined how job appointments are made, how committees operate, what role cocktail parties play in bureaucratic life, and why large corporations tend to be stagnant and uncreative.

According to Parkinson's description, the expansion of bureaucracy and its paperwork begins when a senior official finds his or her workload too heavy. To avoid setting up a single powerful rival, the official appoints two assistants who pose no threat to their boss. Eventually the two assistants each appoint their own two assistants, making a total of seven people doing the original job. By now they all necessarily spend a good deal of time writing memos to each other. Everyone is working all the time, but no additional productive work is being done.

. . .

"In a hierarchy every employee tends to rise to his level of incompetence." Laurence J. Peter, an American educator, wondered why incompetence seemed rampant in every area of modern life—in schools, churches, businesses, government, and so on. He observed that individuals tend to be promoted as long as they do a good enough job. Their final promotion, however, is to a job they cannot do well; and there they stay. Fortunately, not all jobs are occupied all the time by people who have reached their limit of competence, so some work is done properly. In addition, although Peter does not point this out, some people (most secretaries, for example) are not promoted for doing their jobs well.

SOURCE: Based on information in C. Northcote Parkinson, *Parkinson's Law and Other Studies in Administration* (Boston: Houghton Mifflin, 1957); and Laurence J. Peter and Raymond Hull, *The Peter Principle* (New York: Morrow, 1969).

The conditions for achieving success in a bureaucratic career also lead to conservatism. Obeying the rules and staying out of trouble mean seniority, promotion, and all the security of a graded career. Why risk failure by sticking your neck out? In such a situation loyal "yes-men" tend to be rewarded while creative, unconventional leaders are frequently feared and resented.[17]

RED TAPE AND PAPER PUSHING. Files, reports, memos, forms in quadruplicate, correspondence with carbon copies—all this proliferation of paper grows out of the bureaucratic requirement for written records and centralized decision making. Parkinson's Law—"Work expands so as to fill the time available for its completion"—mainly applies to the huge amounts of time and energy that go into such paper pushing (see "Parkinson's Law and the Peter Principle").[18]

Complex official procedures—so-called red tape—make it far more difficult to stop a program than to start one. Thus, there are congressional committees with large staffs that never meet, outmoded research studies that continue to receive public funding, and review boards that haven't reviewed anything in years. Perhaps the most extreme example of bureaucratic resistance to change was provided by the British government. In 1803 the British civil service created a position for a man who was to

---

[17] Ibid., pp. 53–54.
[18] C. Northcote Parkinson, *Parkinson's Law* (Boston: Houghton Mifflin, 1957), Chapter 1.

stand on the cliffs of Dover with a spyglass. He was supposed to ring an alarm bell if he saw Napoleon coming. The job was not abolished until 1945.[19]

Many readers would conclude from this discussion that bureaucrats are inflexible conformists, followers who resist change and obey regulations to the letter. The sociologist Melvin Kohn disagrees. He describes bureaucrats as independent individuals who are intellectually flexible and receptive to change. In his research, Kohn found that bureaucrats are more innovative, morally self-directed, and open to new experience than other kinds of workers. The fact that bureaucrats are more highly educated has something to do with this finding, but Kohn concluded that these traits are even more likely to be related to the bureaucrat's working conditions — job security, relatively high income, and complex work. In spite of their creativity and independence, however, bureaucrats are typically closely supervised or trapped in a routine of simple tasks.[20]

REFORMING THE BUREAUCRACY

Stung by increasing competition from Japanese manufacturers, many American corporations are looking for ways to make their organizations more innovative and productive (see "Is Bureaucracy the Problem? Or the Solution?"). Rosabeth Moss Kanter, a sociologist and management consultant, diagnoses their problem this way:

> The traditional corporate bureaucracy {is} weighted down . . . with too much hierarchy, too little opportunity, overly concentrated power, a variety of nonmeritocratic inequities in the treatment of women and minorities — and the difficulty of changing itself.[21]

In traditionally segmented bureaucracies, Kanter finds, the isolation of different levels and departments means that people see only a small part of the project and are not encouraged to think about tasks beyond their own. Each segment is supposed to do its job without bothering another segment. If the job is secure and routine, then people who call attention to a problem are going to create more work for themselves — a strong disincentive to say anything. Once a problem is identified, it is sorted into a category and sent to a certain place on the organizational chart. The specialists handling the problem have very little incentive to consult with specialists in other categories. Engineers rarely talk things over with salespeople, and a clerk is not likely to take a bright idea for a new filing system to a vice-president. In short, a segmented structure creates barriers to the communication of new ideas and information and usually prevents joint efforts to solve problems. Segmentation also fosters the bureaucratic failings already discussed: loyalty to one's own group of specialists and suspicion of outside ideas; fear of making an independent decision; conservatism; inertia; ritualism.

In *The Change Masters* Kanter recommends that corporations create the cultural and structural conditions which encourage rather than discourage the bureaucrat's

---

[19] Robert Townsend, *Up the Organization* (New York: Fawcett, 1970), pp. 75.

[20] Melvin L. Kohn, "Bureaucratic Man: A Portrait and an Interpretation," *American Sociological Review* 36 (June 1971): 461–74.

[21] Rosabeth Moss Kanter, *The Change Masters: Innovation and Entrepreneurship in the American Corporation* (New York: Simon and Schuster (Touchstone), 1983), p. 24.

capacity for initiative and innovation. She argues that incentives to be imaginative and independent come from an integrated organization in which jobs are broadly defined and intersect with other people's work, assignments are not routine, and people are free to act without constant higher-level interference. Other incentives to be enterprising come from what Kanter calls a "climate of success." People who feel they are members of a community, not just employees, are more likely to be committed to the larger goals of the corporation. When an organization's norms favor change rather than tradition, and when its leaders stress the value of coming up with new ideas, then there is also a "culture of pride" in which better ways of doing things are rewarded.

THE INDIVIDUAL IN THE ORGANIZATION

As we have already seen, bureaucratic structures deeply affect the behavior of the people who belong to them. The rules and regulations of a university, for example, have a powerful influence over the day-to-day lives of students. Few undergraduates would choose to stand in long lines to register for classes, decide on their own to take difficult courses in subjects that do not interest them, or voluntarily study long hours for final exams. They do so only because the university bureaucracy has set the manner in which students must register for classes, determined that certain courses must be completed, and ruled that passing grades are required to earn a university degree. Such rules are not really necessary to meet the individual student's need for an education; they serve the organization's requirement for orderly procedures, universalistic criteria, and detailed record keeping.

Furthermore, bureaucracies shape personalities. They encourage some traits that many of us find distasteful — unthinking obedience to petty rules, a tendency to "pass the buck," and lack of imagination. Still, nearly everyone belongs to some large organizations — corporations, schools, political parties, churches, charitable groups, and professional associations. This section discusses why organizations have so much power over our lives, how people defend themselves against that power, and some of the ways organizations change the personalities of the men and women who work in them.

WHY DO WE OBEY THE RULES?

Obviously, not all of our relationships with organizations are the same. The relationship between the sales clerk and the company president is quite different from the relationship between the priest and the parishioner, and both are different from the relationship between the warden and the prisoner.

Amitai Etzioni classified our relationship to different sorts of organizations in terms of the kind of power they have over us.[22] Imagine, for example, an organization whose goal is the regular collection of garbage. Picking up garbage is a strenuous activity involving large numbers of people. The organization must persuade someone

---

[22] Amitai Etzioni, *A Comparative Analysis of Complex Organizations* (New York: Free Press, 1961).

IS BUREAUCRACY THE PROBLEM? OR THE SOLUTION?

The computer—and the technology associated with it—has been hailed as the wave of the American economic future. Although high-speed microprocessing systems have been in use barely 15 years, the semiconductor industry has already created many thousands of new jobs, new markets, and vast new wealth for American business.

This new industry developed largely in Silicon Valley, the Santa Clara County, California location of hundreds of small electronics companies whose success is based on the silicon (semiconductor) chip, the heart of the modern computer. Most of these companies were founded by one or two adventurous individuals who left large corporations to start "spin-off" businesses with their own personal savings. The most famous example is probably Steven Jobs, the founder of Apple Computer, who left Hewlitt-Packard to develop the idea of a personal home computer in his garage.

Silicon Valley symbolizes more than "clean" (environmentally safe) manufacturing plants and high profits. It has also become the symbol for an American ideal—the inventive individual entrepreneur. According to George Gilder, an economic analyst and presidential advisor, Jobs succeeded because he was not held back by a huge, cumbersome bureaucracy. He claims that large corporations inhibit innovation because they are not willing to venture into risky new businesses where profits are uncertain.

> *"One of the key principles of entrepreneurship—the business of breaking the settled mold—is the absence of clear and fast rules. It is nearly impossible to capture an industry from the top. Proof of value and profitability—major assets of (large, bureaucratic) firms—virtually define an absence of opportunity. With no such proofs, a whole industry may be yours for the asking. Starting from the bottom, you do not have to capture the top; you, like Jobs, become it. All of us are dependent for our livelihood and progress not on a vast and predictable machine, but on the creativity and courage of the particular men who accept the risks which generate our riches."[1]*

All in all, Gilder finds that the "machine"—bureaucracy—is a hindrance to sustained growth and vitality, not a cause of them.

Despite the great promise Gilder sees in entrepreneurism, the industry in which it has flourished is now in trouble:

- Since 1980 the U.S. semiconductor industry's share of the world market has declined from 60 to 40 percent, while Japan's share has grown to nearly 50 percent. The Japanese imported American technology, invested enormous resources in mastering it, and then manufactured new products faster than their competitors.[2]

- The United States is now a worldwide net importer of high-technology products. (It was a $27 billion net exporter in 1981.) When the Defense Science Board surveyed 25 microelectronic technologies in 1987, it found that the United States was the leading manufacturer of only three. American entrepreneurs appear to be of minor and declining importance in the global market.[3]

- The dominant companies in the semiconductor industry are huge, diversified firms, not small entrepreneurships. In fact, large businesses developed the original transistors and silicon chips in the first place.[4]

- Americans continue to lead the world in breakthroughs and cutting-edge scientific discoveries, but their innovations quickly travel abroad for development and improvement. Foreign competitors translate American ideas into products that often outsell and outperform those produced in the United States.[5] According to microelectronics analyst Charles H. Ferguson,

> *"Our competitors seem not to share America's passion for fragmentation and entrepreneurial zeal. U.S. industry falls victim not to nimble, small companies but to huge, industrial complexes embedded in stable, strategically coordinated alliances often supported by protectionist governments—exactly by the kind of political and economic structures that, according to the free-market entrepreneurship argument, give rise to stagnant cartels"[6]*

The solution appears to lie not in small entrepreneurial companies, but in large bureaucracies organized to allow continual incremental innovation—or what the political economist Robert Reich terms "collective entrepreneurship."[7] Reich calls for restructuring traditional bureaucracies so that every employee is better able to contribute new ideas.

The debate between the critics who call for more entrepreneurship and those who want more reliance on bureaucratic organizations (even with modified structures) highlights the issues raised in this chapter. As we have seen, bureaucracies are efficient, but they limit personal freedom. Bureaucracies have great economies of scale, but they also generate considerable waste. Although the ideal of the unfettered, rugged individual is widely held, and the lack of rules and rigid structures is appealing to business people, long-term success appears to depend on bureaucratic organizations. The key to success is not just individual genius but the translation of ideas into marketable products by coordinated groups.

Bureaucracies are often criticized for having too many rules and too much red tape. These complaints are more likely to be symptoms of another problem: too much distance between levels of the organization. Production workers, for example, often cannot communicate their ideas for improving the product to design engineers. As Kanter noted earlier in this chapter, innovation is not incompatible with bureaucracy if the structure of the organization permits it. Furthermore, huge size is not always an obstacle and often a requirement for sustained competitiveness. Huge productive capacity brings huge economies of scale and enormous size can be enormously efficient (see the discussion of vertical integration in Chapter 12, "The Economy").

American microelectronics firms appear to be losing the international competition not because they are excessively bureaucratic but because they are not competitive. In short, the semiconductor industry is not bureaucratic enough. As Ferguson put it,

"Fragmentation, instability, and entrepreneurialism are not signs of well-being. In fact, . . . fragmentation [has] discouraged badly needed coordinated action."[8]

The executives of computer technology firms seem to agree. In June, 1989 *The Wall Street Journal* ran a front-page story entitled "Computer Firms Make Bold Pitch to Retake Market Lost to Japan."[9] What was this "bold pitch"? Was it more entrepreneurs? Was it the elimination of cumbersome bureaucratic rules? Was it smaller organizations? Nothing of the sort. It was a superbureaucracy, an immense organization that combined the resources of the six largest American silicon chip manufacturers to produce DRAMs (dynamic random-access memories) — the basic chips invented by U.S. firms, but now produced and marketed almost exclusively by the Japanese. The *Journal* noted that " it is rare, almost unAmerican, for U.S. manufacturers to band together this way."

It is indeed rare for American firms to cooperate in manufacturing ventures, and this particular effort to combine forces failed six months after it began. The chairman of one of the firms involved declared that "the consortia idea is too large a leap for the entrepreneurial mentality."[10] Another member of the ill-fated consortium immediately formed a separate joint venture with a Japanese semiconductor firm to manufacture and sell DRAMs.

As we have seen, reliance on huge bureaucracies for efficiency is not rare at all. Genius and entrepreneurship are vital to the U.S. economy, but stable organizations are the hallmark of American success.

---

[1] George Gilder, *The Spirit of Enterprise* (New York: Simon and Schuster, 1984), pp. 147, 246–47.

[2] Charles H. Ferguson, "From the People Who Brought You Voodoo Economics," *Harvard Business Review* (May–June, 1988): 57.

[3] Ibid., p. 56–59.

[4] Roger Kaplan, "Entrepreneurship Reconsidered: The Antimanagement Bias," *Harvard Business Review* (May–June, 1988): 84–89.

[5] Robert B. Reich, "Entrepreneurship Reconsidered: The Team as Hero," *Harvard Business Review* (May June, 1988): 77–83.

[6] Ferguson, p. 57.

[7] Reich, p. 81.

[8] Ferguson, pp. 61–62.

[9] G. Christian Hill and Michael W. Miller, "Computer Firms Make Bold Pitch to Retake Market Lost to Japan," *The Wall Street Journal*, June 22, 1989, p. 1.

[10] Robert D. Hof, "'This Will Surely Come Back to Haunt Us'" *Business Week*, January 29, 1990, p. 72.

who ordinarily would not touch other people's garbage to work toward this common goal. According to Etzioni, there are three ways of doing it.

1. The organization can compel the acceptance of its goal by punishing any failure to perform. Compulsion is the motivating force in such organizations as prisons, forced labor camps, and military training camps. They have what Etzioni described as **coercive power**. The garbage collectors in this case are *inmates*.

2. The organization can buy acceptance of its goal by paying its members for picking up garbage. Instead of the negative reward of punishment, there is the positive reward of cash. Motivation is achieved through **remunerative power**, and the organization is a business or a government department. The garbage collectors are now *employees*.

3. Individuals can accept the goal of the organization as a personal goal. They might find garbage collecting a worthwhile activity because they believe in the value of sanitation or because they personally prefer clean sidewalks and fresh air. In this case motivation comes from identification with the organizational goal, and the rewards are psychological and emotional. This organization has **normative power**, and the garbage collectors are *voluntary participants*. Garbage collecting may not attract many volunteers, but amateur rock music groups, softball teams, and community service organizations do.

Etzioni found that an organization typically relies on one type of power to motivate its members. Workers in an automobile plant, for example, are paid for their work (remunerative power). They may identify with the company's goals, but the company does not depend on this identification (normative power) to get them to work in the morning. Prisons, on the other hand, use coercive power. Some inmates may identify with the goals of the prison and others may be paid for their labors, but the prison does not depend on its normative or remunerative power to motivate them. While many organizations exercise all three types of power, each relies primarily on only one.

To make certain that the rules are obeyed, bureaucratic organizations centralize decision making and decentralize execution. The superior decides that something should be done, and the subordinate does it. If every action of the subordinate had to wait for the direct order of the superior, however, there would have to be one supervisor for every four or five workers. If each worker had to be told individually to tighten a particular bolt every time an automobile came down the assembly line, for example, the costs in time and effort would be high and productivity would be low. Bureaucracies are efficient partly because they delegate responsibility and save the costs of close supervision. Rules and regulations take the place of supervisor's orders, and control is exercised from a distance. Once a rule is learned — "secure muffler to chassis by tightening all bolts" — one person can supervise the work of a hundred. Control by rules and regulations is most suitable for repetitive, simple work that does not provide much opportunity for creativity or the exercise of authority. Much factory work, for example, falls into this category. The lower levels of the bureaucracy are most likely to have this type of control over behavior.

A more highly trained and educated work force needs even less direct supervision. Routine decision making can be delegated because the guidelines for making the decision have been set from above. The traffic police officer decides which driver to arrest according to the rule that *everyone* who exceeds the speed limit by 10 MPH is speeding. The decision to give a particular driver a ticket may be delegated, but the police officer's behavior is still predictable. He or she can be depended upon not to give tickets to drivers who stay within the speed limit. Decentralized decision making actually increases organizational control in this way. Moreover, bureaucratic rules make personal supervision unnecessary. Whether a supervisor is there or not, the police officer will continue to make arrests for speeding. The result is greater efficiency, greater control, and lower costs for the organization.[23]

BEATING THE SYSTEM

In spite of the built-in checks on individual behavior, enforcing the rules is always a problem for bureaucracies. In 1931, for example, the Central Committee of the Communist party, the highest bureaucratic authority in the Soviet Union, tried to halt the growth of Moscow's population by ordering that no new factories be built in the city. During the next eight years, however, plants continued to be built and the population

---

[23] Charles Perrow, *Complex Organizations*, 3d ed. New York: Random House, 1986.

According to Erving Goffman, bureaucratic control is never complete. Even in total institutions such as the San Quentin penitentiary, inmates survive by asserting themselves against a nearly all-powerful organization.

of Moscow increased by 50 percent. At that point, the Soviet government's highest policy-making body, the Party Congress, demanded that the 1931 order be enforced. Nonetheless, by 1956 the size of the Moscow labor force had grown by another one-third.

Apparently, the highest-ranking officials in the Soviet bureaucracy did not have the final say in this matter. Much lower down in the chain of command, there must have been executives who felt that their own pet projects should be exceptions to party policy. Even more remarkably, their superiors must have known that the policy was being frustrated. After all, the outlawed new construction was going on in Moscow, right under the noses of all the top party officials.[24]

Even in such a highly centralized and tightly controlled organization as the Soviet government, bureaucrats are not robots. People insist on being unpredictable, no matter how little room they are given to express themselves. That is one of the conclusions reached by Erving Goffman in *Asylums,* a study of institutions that extend bureaucratic control to every aspect of human life.

According to Goffman, such organizations as prisons, monasteries, old-age homes, and mental hospitals are **total institutions**—"total" because all the inmates' activities take place within the organization and are controlled by it. In such organizations the rules of behavior are designed to destroy self-identity and make individuals part of an anonymous mass. When the draftee joins the army and the novice enters the convent, for example, they leave all personal possessions behind. New arrivals are stripped of distinctive clothing and hair styles and given a drab uniform. Even their names may be taken away and replaced by a new name or a serial number. Inmates of total institutions are often forced to obey irrational orders, do meaningless work, and submit to verbal abuse. Mental patients and prisoners are deprived of privacy and placed under constant surveillance. Rules govern every activity and reduce individual freedom to its absolute minimum.[25]

Even in a total institution like a prison, however, bureaucratic control is never complete. Goffman found that individuals are still able to assert themselves against the organization. Inmates survive by "making out," or getting around the rules and making informal adjustments to the system. "Removal activities" offer some intellectual escape and release. By losing themselves temporarily in other pursuits, inmates are able to blot out the sense of their real environment. A remarkable example of this behavior is the work of the "Birdman of Alcatraz," a prisoner who devoted himself to the study of the birds outside his window. Through a long process of finagling and "making out," he was able to build a scientific laboratory and become a leading ornithologist, all in his prison cell.

Such removal activities as art courses in old-age homes and sports in mental hospitals are more or less authorized, but undercover practices are not. Inmates engage in some activities only because they are forbidden. Patients smuggle food and liquor not just for their own sakes but to "score" against the hospital. Games of this sort demonstrate to the patient that he or she has some autonomy beyond the reach of the organization.

---

[24] David Granick, *The Red Executive* (Garden City, N.Y.: Doubleday, 1960), pp. 146–47.
[25] Erving Goffman, *Asylums* (Garden City, N.Y.: Doubleday/Anchor, 1961), pp. 3–48.

Ritual insubordination, expressed in griping and insolent remarks, is a familiar response of the powerless. Schoolchildren cross their fingers or make faces behind the teacher's back to show their contempt for authority. Prisoners mutter insults when a guard passes, but not quite loud enough to provoke retaliation. Such gestures show that inmates are people in their own right but they are not serious enough to get the offender into trouble.[26]

The power of individuals to assert themselves against the organization seems feeble indeed compared to the organization's power to command their obedience. But as Goffman has shown, even total institutions cannot completely submerge individual identity. In more loosely structured organizations, people are often encouraged to be creative. Most bureaucratic work requires some spontaneity, and bureaucracies do occasionally find new solutions to nonroutine problems. Outstanding individuals are still able to come up with fresh ideas and change the organization to accommodate them.

ORGANIZATION MEN AND WOMEN

As Goffman put it, organizations are places for "generating assumptions about identity."[27] When you join an organization and involve yourself in its activities, you accept being a particular kind of person. You begin to define yourself in terms of the organization to which you belong. Moreover, certain positions create identities of their own. Picture a hospital nurse, a marine drill sergeant, or a life insurance salesman, and you will find that you have a definite idea of what the person is like because of the position he or she has in an organization. Of course, the kinds of people who become nurses and drill sergeants and life insurance salesmen probably already have some of the appropriate character traits. But organizations also change people. Different roles demand different kinds of behavior and attitudes (see "A Person Disguised as a Secretary"). Through the selective process of hiring and promotion, organizations choose individuals whose personalities already fit their needs and then train them to be organization men and women.

CORPORATE CULTURES AND PERSONALITIES.   When people choose to work for a company, they often choose a way of life. Every organization has its own culture, which is explained to the newcomer as the "way we do things around here." Corporations, for example, have norms and values which influence how people act at work. The corporate culture includes standards of conduct which define what employees should wear (Are tight pants for women appropriate? Do men always wear ties?), how they should address each other (Is the boss called Mr. Jones or Fred?), and what kinds of behavior are acceptable (Are office romances frowned upon? Are expense accounts padded a little?). Rituals (the company picnic, the retirement dinner) are part of the corporate culture, and so are slogans that emphasize the company's values (Dupont's "Better things for better living through chemistry"; Ford's "Quality is job 1").

---

[26] Ibid., pp. 309–18.
[27] Ibid., p. 186.

A PERSON DISGUISED AS A SECRETARY

Organizations demand certain kinds of behavior from the people who belong to them. Secretaries, for example, are often expected not only to do their jobs but to play the role of a devoted office wife—making coffee, running errands, sending personal letters and Christmas cards, and listening sympathetically to the boss's problems. In the following passage one woman finds that becoming a secretary means being seen—and eventually seeing oneself—as a certain kind of person.

Recently I took a job as a part-time secretary in a department office of a university. I thought the financial security would be nice (writers never have this) and I needed the sense of community a job can bring. . . . I felt a bit like the author of "Black Like Me," a Caucasian who had his skin darkened by dye and went into the South, where he experienced what it was like to be black. Here I was, "a person," disguised as "a secretary." This move from being a newly published author to being a secretary made it very clear to me that the same people who are regarded as creative human beings in one role will be demeaned and ignored in another.

I was asked one day to make some Xerox invitations to a party, then told I could keep one (not exactly a cordial invitation, I thought). The next day I was asked, "Are you coming to the party?" I brightened and said, "Well, maybe I will." I was then told, "Well, then, would you pick up the pizza and we'll reimburse you."

A friend of mine who is an "administrative assistant" told me about a campus party she attended. She was engaged in a lively, interesting conversation with a faculty wife. The wife then asked my friend, "Are you teaching here?" When my friend replied, "Well, no, actually I'm a secretary," the other woman's jaw dropped. She then said, "Don't worry. Nobody will ever guess."

I heard secretaries making "grateful" remarks like, "They really treat us like human beings here." To be grateful for bottom-line treatment was, I felt, a sorry comment.

We think we have freed our slaves, but we have not. We just call them by a different name. Every time people reach a certain status in life they seem to take pride in the fact that they now have a secretary.

It is a fact that it has to be written very carefully into a job description just what a secretary's duties are, or she will be told to clean off the desk, pick up cleaning and the like. Women in these jobs are often seen as surrogate wives, mothers and servants—even to other women.

Many times, when a secretary makes creative contributions she is not given her due. The work is changed slightly by the person in charge, who takes the credit. Most secretaries live in an area between being too assertive and being too passive. Often a secretary feels she has to think twice before stepping in and correcting the grammar, even when she knows her "superior" can't frame a good sentence.

■ ■ ■

When after three months I announced to my co-workers that I was quitting, I was met with kind goodbyes. In some I caught a glimpse of perhaps a gentle envy, not filled with vindictiveness at all, but tinged with some remorse. "I'm just a little jealous that someone is getting out of prison," admitted one woman. "I wish I'd done that years ago," said another.

Their faces remain in my heart. They stand for all the people locked into jobs because they need the money, because they don't know where else to go, afraid there's no place else, because they don't have the confidence or feel they have the chance to do anything else.

I was lucky. I escaped before lethargy or repressed anger or extreme eagerness to please took over. Before I was drawn over the line, seduced by the daily rewards of talk over coffee, exchanged recipes, the photos of family members thumbtacked to the wall near the desk, the occasional lunches to mark birthdays and departures. . . .

As I see it, the slave mentality is alive and well. It manicures its nails. It walks in little pumps on tiny cat feet. It's there every time a secretary says, "Yes, I'll do that. I don't mind" or finds ashtrays for the people who come to talk to someone else. The secretary has often forgotten her own dream. She is too busy helping others to realize theirs.

SOURCE: Karen Kenyon, "A Pink-Collar Worker's Blues," *Newsweek,* October 4, 1982, p. 15.

According to management consultants Terrence Deal and Allen Kennedy, McDonald's dominates the fast-food industry because it has a strong corporate culture which binds together the company's 8,000 worldwide franchisees. McDonald's cultural beliefs — Quality, Service, Convenience, Value (QSCV) — are taught to new franchisees at its Hamburger University training program and are constantly drummed into the work force. These corporate values are celebrated in ceremonies honoring the most successful franchisees and in contests to determine who best fulfills McDonald's standards. The corporate culture also has its heroes: employee of the month, franchisee of the year, the creator of Egg McMuffin, and, especially, McDonald's founder, the late Ray Kroc.[28]

One result of corporate socialization, as William H. Whyte, Jr., noted in the 1950s, is the "organization man." Like the IBM typewriter salesperson who is proud to say "I work for IBM," Whyte's organization man is a conformist whose sense of identity comes from being part of a powerful, protective organization. He not only works for the organization, but *belongs* to it as well. The "company way" extends into his intimate personal life: where he lives, the kind of person he marries, what church he joins, and how he raises his children.[29] Whyte's prototype was the suburban male junior executive, but career diplomats and clergymen tend to have some of the same characteristics.

The high-tech entrepreneur of the 1990s provides a striking contrast to the devoted organization man. In Silicon Valley, an area of California dominated by the electronics industry, executives are dedicated to the individualistic pursuit of profits. Here small, adventurous engineering companies have mushroomed into $40 billion a year businesses that depend on research in advanced technology. New inventions — lasers, video games, home computers, digital watches, cordless telephones — succeed each other at breakneck speed. Silicon Valley's distinctive lifestyle is based on the credo of "work hard, play hard, and don't worry about the difference between work and play. There isn't any." Engineers typically put in 15-hour days and 7-day weeks and many expect to retire as millionaires after 10 years.[30]

CORPORATE EXPERIENCES AND INDIVIDUAL IDENTITY.   The kinds of experiences people have in their work also shape their attitudes and behavior. The successful, powerful person is likely to feel and act differently than the person who hasn't "made it." The woman with managerial responsibilities is not treated the same as her secretary; they tend to develop different kinds of personalities simply because of their different locations in the organization.

One of the themes of Rosabeth Kanter's study, *Men and Women of the Corporation,* is that what we call the "typical" behavior of people who work in corporations is really a response to their situations. For both men and women, Kanter found, the structural factors that determine behavior in organizations are opportunity, power, and relative numbers.

---

[28] Terrence E. Deal and Allen A. Kennedy, *Corporate Cultures:The Rites and Rituals of Corporate Life* (Reading, Mass.: Addison-Wesley, 1982), pp. 193–94.
[29] William H. Whyte, Jr., *The Organization Man* (New York: Simon and Schuster (Touchstone), 1956).
[30] Everett M. Rogers and Judith K. Larsen, *Silicon Valley Fever: Growth of High-Technology Culture* (New York: Basic Books, 1984), p. 29.

The experiences that people have at work tend to change their personalities. The nature of the secretary's job encourages her to be unassertive, unambitious, and dependent on her boss.

OPPORTUNITY. Since the corporate hierarchy is the path of achievement, movement up the hierarchy implies personal success. The corporation's message is "You are not really successful, you do not mean much to the company, unless you move up the ladder." People who expect to succeed are likely to be competitive, to identify with their superiors, and to be excessively committed to their jobs. People whose progress is blocked, on the other hand, have a sense of failure. They lack interest in their dead-end jobs and look for social recognition from their friends at work or from outside activities. They are likely to develop an antisuccess attitude that keeps them from even trying to do better. When the system says "You can't," the response is "I don't want to."

POWER. Power is the ability to get things done, to act effectively within the organizational structure. In a large bureaucracy, legitimate power is necessary to carry out one's responsibilities. Powerful people are in a position to be cooperative and open-minded. They are able to delegate authority and help subordinates along.

First-line supervisors of routine work, on the other hand, typically have responsibility but lack power. Executive secretaries, head tellers, and chief accountants are often caught between the demands of the managerial hierarchy and the resistance of the workers under them. "I'm afraid to confront the employees because they have the power to slack, to slouch, to take too much time," a supervisor of clerical workers said, "and I need them for results. I'm measured on *results* — . . . output, certain attendance levels, number of reports filed. They have to do it for me."[31]

People who don't wield much power turn to rigid, rule-minded behavior in order to carry out their responsibilities effectively. They become petty, critical, and bossy. These symptoms of bureaucratic ritualism are signs of organizational powerlessness.

RELATIVE NUMBERS. The numbers and proportions of different kinds of people in the work force affect the behavior of both the minority and the majority. "Tokens" — members of social groups who are represented in very small proportions — tend to be seen as representatives of their category rather than as unique individuals. They are under pressure to conform to the majority, to be just like everyone else is, yet they find it hard to fit into informal groups. Rarity itself creates a very different situation for the one who is rare.

Members of the dominant majority, on the other hand, are preferred for managerial jobs because they have "credibility": they easily join informal groups and enter close working relationships. Since most positions at the top of the corporate hierarchy are held by white men, the few women and blacks who do become managers find themselves in the token's situation.

According to Kanter's thesis, the experiences that people have at work tend to alter their identities. The "devoted" secretary, for example, is locked into a position of dependency on her boss for raises and better working conditions. The nature of her job encourages her to be unassertive, emotionally dependent, and limited in ability and knowledge. The devoted secretary develops just the qualities that will keep her from moving up to higher pay and status and, at the same time, will make her more indispensable as a secretary.

In sum, bureaucracies affect individual identities by requiring certain kinds of behavior and determining the kinds of socializing experiences people have during their working hours. To conclude that there is a "bureaucratic personality," however, would be an exaggeration. Every bureaucrat is a unique person, with particular beliefs, attitudes, and values. No organization, no matter how powerful, is likely to eradicate all individuality; it is rather the individual who adapts his or her identity to fit the needs of the organization.

BUREAUCRACY AND SOCIETY

As early as 1904 Weber saw that bureaucracy was to be our fate. Bureaucratic organization, he wrote, had already shaped the government, the economy, and the development of technology. Further bureaucratization, further rationalization of what had once been spontaneous and unpredictable, seemed inevitable. Humanity would be imprisoned in an "iron cage" of its own making, Weber warned. Future society would be as rigidly

---

[31] Rosabeth Moss Kanter, *Men and Women of the Corporation* (New York: Basic Books, 1977), p. 170.

Who should be held responsible for Mexico City's horrendous traffic jams? Many of the frustrations of modern life can only be blamed on faceless bureaucrats in remote corporations and government agencies.

controlled as ancient Egypt, only it would be more mechanized and technically advanced. The problem, he said, "is not: how can this evolution be changed? — for that is impossible, but: what will come of it?"[32]

DEPERSONALIZATION

Weber feared that bureaucrats would become mere cogs in a wheel because they had to deny their personal identities and emotions to meet the organization's demands. One of the themes of Goffman's *Asylums* is this conflict between humane standards and bureaucratic efficiency. By carrying a bureaucratic principle to extremes, total institutions deny inmates their individuality and treat them as objects. Smooth operation of the mental hospital Goffman studied required treating all the patients impersonally. It was more efficient for the hospital to launder everyone's clothes together and return them according to size instead of ownership; it was more important to keep the patients clean by shaving their heads than to protect their appearances and self-identities.

Most bureaucracies, of course, are not total institutions. By emphasizing impersonal standards, however, they offer inappropriate solutions to many human problems. Rationality and impersonality are incompatible with certain organizational goals, such

---

[32] Quoted in J. P. Mayer, *Max Weber and German Politics*, 2d ed. (London: Faber and Faber, 1956), pp. 126–27.

as the treatment of hospital patients on an individual basis. Nor can bureaucracies resolve questions that do not have routine answers: What is a good parent? What makes an effective teacher? Who should get welfare? When is a person too old to work? No wonder bureaucracies have proved inadequate in dealing with such problems.

The impersonality of bureaucratic structures has also contributed to the sense of powerlessness that pervades much of modern life. In earlier ages people usually knew who was responsible for doing them harm, even if they couldn't do much about it. If a peasant were robbed by a nobleman, at least he would know who to blame. But in 1985, when 520 people were killed in a Japanese airplane crash because part of the jet's tail section fell off in midair, where should the blame have been placed? On Boeing, the corporation that designed and built the 747? On the Japanese Transport Ministry, the government agency that supervised its flight? On Japan Air Lines, which serviced and operated the plane?

Many of the minor irritations of daily life—strikes, traffic jams, disconnected telephones, airline overbookings, recalled automobiles, computer errors, and so on— can be traced to huge, remote organizations that seem to have nothing against us personally. People feel powerless to influence these bureaucracies, not only because they are so large and complex, but because it is so difficult to discover who exactly is responsible for the problem.[33]

IRRATIONALITY

Karl Mannheim, in his analysis of modern industrial society, noted that bureaucracies replace substantial rationality with functional rationality. By **substantial rationality** he meant the capacity to act intelligently on the basis of one's own interpretation of events and to be aware of the consequences of one's actions. Bureaucracies, however, are characterized by **functional rationality**: every individual action leads logically and predictably to the achievement of some ultimate aim.[34]

Mannheim contended that the growth of bureaucracy implies that there will be more and more functional rationality and less and less substantial rationality in modern societies. In the past, he noted, workers were substantially rational: shoemakers knew exactly what product they were making, how to make it from beginning to end, and what its uses and capabilities were. Modern workers in the electronics industry, on the other hand, never see more than a small part of the whole production process. They don't have to know exactly how a computer works or how it can be used. Because they cannot see all the consequences of their actions, Mannheim believed, they can act only according to the requirements of the organization to which they belong.

The danger of a functionally rational system is that it permits people to surrender personal responsibility for their behavior. Specialization, which is one of the characteristics of bureaucracy, confines workers to a restricted area of responsibility and insulates them from the consequences of their actions. People doing highly specialized jobs lose sight of the larger goals of the organization. They are often not sure exactly what

[33] Philip Slater, *The Pursuit of Loneliness*, rev. ed. (Boston: Beacon Press, 1976), p. 43.

[34] Karl Mannheim, *Man and Society in an Age of Reconstruction* (London: Routledge & Kegan Paul, 1940), pp. 53–59.

their contribution has been or what they are accomplishing through their work. The specialist's surrender of personal responsibility for the results of his or her work is well expressed in Tom Lehrer's song about a physicist:

> "Once the rockets are up
> Who cares where they come down?
> That's not my department,"
> Says Wernher von Braun.[35]

In a world that is becoming more bureaucratic and less substantially rational, people lose control over the forces that shape their lives. They feel powerless to solve the problems that threaten them most: inflation, overpopulation, unemployment, toxic wastes, nuclear war. Human beings now have more rational control over the natural world than ever before. Yet the forces at work in their social world often appear as mysterious to men and women today as the forces of nature did to medieval peasants.

ABUSE OF BUREAUCRATIC POWER

Bureaucracies combine logic, rationality, and efficiency with tremendous centralized power. This power rests in the organization, but it is controlled by the people at the top. There is obviously a strong temptation to confuse that bureaucratic authority with personal prerogative, and organizational power is sometimes abused. When National Security Council aide Oliver North admitted that he had illegally destroyed official documents and lied to Congress about the Iran-Contra affair, he defended his actions by claiming that he was carrying out the orders of his superiors — including President Ronald Reagan himself. North constantly confused the bureaucratic power given to government officials with their personal power to advance their own political interests; he believed that he had been legally authorized to commit acts that he knew were wrong. In 1989 a jury found North guilty on three charges, but acquitted him of criminal responsibility for following what they interpreted to be direct orders from the White House.

The potential abuse of bureaucratic power has worried many observers. Weber himself feared that bureaucracies were concentrating social resources in the hands of a few, offering a vast power base that could be taken over for a leader's own purposes. Since Hitler and Stalin could control their nations' bureaucracies, for example, their destructiveness was astronomically greater than a tribal chieftain's or a feudal baron's ever could have been.

Despite these problems, bureaucracies have many positive advantages that other forms of organization do not have. No other arrangement could harness the talents of so many people to accomplish the complex tasks that make modern society possible. The problems will be solved not by doing away with bureaucracies but by making them more innovative and more responsive. The bureaucratic "iron cage" thus poses one of the most important challenges to the sociological imagination.

---

[35] "Wernher von Braun," from *Too Many Songs by Tom Lehrer with Not Enough Drawings by Ronald Searle* (New York: Pantheon, 1981), p. 125. © 1965 Tom Lehrer. Von Braun developed liquid-fuel rockets, first for Nazi Germany and then for the United States. He worked on the propulsion systems for both the V2, a German rocket that was fired on London during World War II, and the Saturn V, the launch vehicle that sent American astronauts to the moon.

Bureaucracies are tools that can be used for good or evil purposes. The Iran-Contra scandal revealed that Oliver North and other White House aides had misused their bureaucratic authority for personal and political gain.

SUMMARY

1. Modern societies depend on large, complex organizations to achieve many common goals. The type of organization designed to accomplish large-scale tasks by systematically coordinating the work of many persons is called a "bureaucracy."

2. To Weber, the growth of bureaucracy was part of the triumph of a purposive, rational mentality in modern life. He identified five characteristics that distinguish bureaucracy from traditional forms of organization: a hierarchy of authority, universalistic standards, the specialization of labor, rules and regulations, and written records and communications.

3. Bureaucracies have several advantages. They improve human reliability and competence; they are highly efficient; they discourage corruption and abuse of individual rights; and they are impartial and democratic.

4. The problems with bureaucracy arise mainly for two reasons: bureaucratic principles are not always followed, and the bureaucratic structure itself has built-in contradictions.

5. Competing values, goals, and norms interfere with bureaucratic logic and efficiency. Impersonal standards of behavior conflict with discriminatory practices, professional or personal ethics, primary-group loyalties, and particularistic standards.

6. Bureaucracy's inherent contradictions also reduce its effectiveness. Conflict between staff and line positions alter the hierarchy of authority; insistence on impersonal rules not only makes bureaucrats resented and despised but often interferes with efficiency in meeting human needs; following the rules tends to become an end in itself, leading to a displacement of goals and a trained incapacity to respond to changing or extraordinary situations; and the necessity for detailed records becomes red tape and paper pushing.

7. Nevertheless, Kohn's study concluded that bureaucrats are typically flexible and creative individuals who are often trapped in closely supervised, routine jobs.

8. Efforts to reform the corporate bureaucracy have been spurred by competition from Japanese manufacturers. Kanter argues that segmented organizational hierarchies discourage innovation and initiative. She recommends creating integrated organizations with cultural and structural conditions that foster incentives to be enterprising, a sense of community, and values favoring change.

9. Etzioni classified different kinds of organizations according to the power they have over the individuals in them. Prisons, for example, have coercive power over their inmates; businesses have remunerative power over their employees; and community service organizations have normative power over voluntary participants.

10. To make sure the rules are obeyed, bureaucracies centralize decision making and decentralize execution. Control is exercised by rules and regulations, which make direct supervision unnecessary and improve efficiency. High-level decisions, however, can be frustrated by subordinates, and control is always a problem for bureaucracies.

11. Even in what Goffman has called total institutions, bureaucratic control is never complete. Individuals assert themselves against the organization through "making out," removal activities, and ritual insubordination.

12. Membership in an organization shapes individual behavior and self-identity. Corporations choose people whose personalities already fit the organizations' needs and then train them to behave according to its own norms and values. The organization man and the high-tech entrepreneur have personalities that fit a particular type of corporate culture.

13. The kinds of experiences people have at work also change their attitudes and behavior. Kanter has identified opportunity, power, and relative numbers as structural factors that affect individual personality.

14. The unprecedented size and number of bureaucracies have contributed to depersonalization and a sense of powerlessness in modern societies. Mannheim argued that bureaucracies replace substantial rationality with functional rationality, leading to the surrender of personal responsibility for one's actions and a loss of control over larger social forces. Bureaucracies also concentrate great power, which can be abused for personal gain. Since bureaucracies are necessary arrangements in modern societies, solving the problems of the "iron cage" poses an important challenge to the sociological imagination.

KEY TERMS

bureaucracy 158	displacement of goals 168	total institutions 176
ideal-type 159	coercive power 174	substantial rationality 183
universalistic standards 161	remunerative power 174	functional rationality 183
particularistic standards 165	normative power 174	

SUGGESTED READINGS

* Peter M. Blau and Marshall W. Meyer. *Bureaucracy in Modern Society*, 3rd ed. New York: McGraw-Hill, 1987.

Lewis A. Coser. *Greedy Institutions*. New York: Free Press, 1974.

* Eli Ginzberg and George Vojta. *Beyond Human Scale: The Large Corporation at Risk*. New York: Basic Books, 1987.

Myron P. Glazer and Penina M. Glazer. *Whistleblowers: Exposing Corruption in Government and Industry*. New York: Basic Books, 1989.

* Joseph Heller. *Catch-22*. New York: Dell, 1989.
* C. Northcote Parkinson. *Parkinson's Law*. Boston: Houghton Mifflin, 1957.
* William H. Whyte, Jr. *The Organization Man*. New York: Simon and Schuster/Touchstone Books, 1972.

* Available in paperback.

PART 3

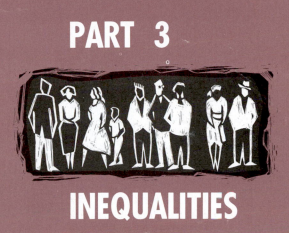

INEQUALITIES

The difference between a lady and a flower girl is not how she behaves, but how she's treated.

George Bernard Shaw

CHAPTER 7

SOCIAL INEQUALITY

Jimmy and Bobby are second-graders in the same town, but at different schools. Both boys like school and pay attention in class. Their test scores show that they are both reading slightly above grade level and have slightly better than average I.Q.s. In spite of their similar abilities, Bobby is certain to go to college — more than 4 times as likely as Jimmy — and almost certain to finish — more than 12 times as likely as Jimmy. As a result, Bobby will probably have 4 years more schooling than Jimmy. Bobby is also 27 times as likely to get a job which will put him in the top 10% of all incomes in the country by the time he is in his late forties. Jimmy has about one chance in 8 of earning even a median income.

These unequal futures of two equally bright students are forecast on the basis of just two facts: Bobby's father is a lawyer making $35,000 a year; Jimmy's father is a high-school dropout who works as a part-time messenger or janitor and earns $4,800 a year.[1]

---

[1] Richard H. de Lone, *Small Futures: Children, Inequality, and the Limits of Liberal Reform* (New York: Harcourt Brace Jovanovich, 1979), pp. 3–4.

ocial equality has been a guiding principle of American life since the signers of the Declaration of Independence boldly stated that "all men are created equal." Yet for almost a century after the document was signed, slavery was common in much of the United States, and legal infringement of the rights of women and black Americans continued for almost two centuries. Today the "inalienable right" to "life, liberty, and the pursuit of happiness" is still not equally awarded. As the passage above shows, two equally promising little boys actually have very unequal chances for success. For the one child in five who is born into a poor family, the odds of leading a healthy and happy life are slim indeed.

The signers of the Declaration of Independence, themselves members of a wealthy and privileged elite, left later generations with a traditional belief in the American Dream of unlimited opportunities for all. Reality, however, has been closer to the underlying principle of the barnyard society found in George Orwell's *Animal Farm:* "All animals are equal, but some animals are more equal than others."

Like nearly every other society, American society treats its members unequally by ranking them on various rungs of the social ladder. The higher the rung, the greater the group's share of whatever the society considers desirable. Typically, the most desirable advantages a society has to offer are wealth, social prestige, and power. Since wealth and other social advantages can be inherited, children born into the upper levels have greater access to society's rewards. **Stratification** is the sociological term for the ranking of members of a society according to the unequal distribution of whatever is considered to be valuable. The key word is "unequal," for if some have more, then others must have less. The study of stratification is thus the study of inequality.

This chapter is about social inequality — why it exists, how it affects our everyday life, and why it is tolerated in a society dedicated to the ideal of equality. Obviously, inequalities of wealth and power underlie many of the world's problems, from the hunger of Africa's impoverished millions to the wars in Afghanistan and El Salvador. Not so obviously, social rank affects nearly every aspect of human life. To a great extent your standing in the social hierarchy influences how healthy you are, what kind of education you have, whether you enjoy your job, and even how long you will live.

THE DIMENSIONS OF STRATIFICATION

It would be difficult to list all the ways human beings are unequal. Some are tall and some short, some are male and some female, some are black and some white. Some people are older or more athletic or make more money than others. Many of these differences hardly matter at all, but others are tremendously important. Most of the time, adults who were born a year or two apart are not treated very differently, but people who have had twelve years of schooling are generally considered more able than people who have had only ten. Even innate differences are not given the same weight. In the United States inherited differences in skin color have often been considered vitally important, while inherited differences in hair color have mattered very little. Inequalities in education and skin color, in other words, are important only because they are the basis for social distinctions.

Social inequalities are differences among people that are considered important in the society in which they live. In American society most people seem to think that social inequality results from differences in personal abilities. If some individuals are more powerful and successful than others, the theory goes, it must be because they are just "naturally" smarter and more talented than other people. If one person is a vice-president of IBM and another is an unemployed welfare recipient, the tendency among Americans is to explain such inequality by the differences in the ability, ambition, and effort of the individuals.

There have been many attempts over the years to prove that some people are born inferior. Some scholars have theorized that an apish physique, a smaller skull, or a low IQ represents "natural" causes of low social rank.[2] The stubborn fact is that highly intelligent and gifted people are found at all levels of the social hierarchy, and so are people who have apish physiques, small skulls, and low IQ scores. Large differences in ability are also found among people who are considered social equals. Not all IBM vice-presidents are equally talented, nor are all welfare recipients equally untalented. For these reasons most scientists are not convinced that there are any innate causes of social inferiority.

While differences in personal ability may be important for particular individuals, sociologists do not believe that they account for broad patterns of social inequality. Sociologists agree that the nature of society, not the nature of human beings, largely determines whether some people are richer or more powerful than others. This approach originated with the founders of sociology, especially Karl Marx and Max Weber. During their lifetimes the industrialization of Europe and the United States had made social differences impossible to ignore. At the end of the nineteenth century newly rich industrialists were amassing tremendous fortunes and enjoying a lavish life style, while factory workers were barely surviving on subsistence-level wages in squalid urban slums. Faced with this shocking disparity, Marx and Weber each sought an answer to the question, How is so much inequality produced?

MARX: THE INEQUALITIES OF CLASS

For Marx, inequality stems from the way human beings organize themselves to extract a living from nature. The primary goal of the human race at the dawn of history was to obtain enough food, clothing, and shelter, and Marx believed that these needs remain the central motivating force in complex modern societies. In every age, the *forces of production* are the technology and machines that increase the efficiency of human labor; the *relations of production* are the social arrangements by which the products of this labor are distributed. In the Middle Ages hand tools (looms, saws, farm implements) were the principal forces of production, and the relations of production were among such feudal groups as the church, the nobility, and the peasantry. But as the relationship of human beings to nature changes, the relationship of human beings to each other also changes. In the modern era advances in technology replaced hand tools with steam-powered machinery, and the new relations of production were between

---

[2] See Stephen Jay Gould, *The Mismeasure of Man* (New York: W. W. Norton, 1981).

In turn-of-the-century New York the splendor of John Jacob Astor's mansion provided a stark contrast to the squalor of the slums. Marx and Weber argued that the nature of industrial society, not the nature of human beings, created such vast differences between rich and poor.

factory workers and capitalist owners. Marx called a society's organization of its productive activities (both the forces and the relations of production) the **mode of production**. Slave societies, feudal societies, and capitalist societies all have different modes of production.[3]

Marx argued that social inequality arises because some members of a society own the means of production and others do not. The owners of land and factories can sell the food and goods produced; the peasants and workers have only their labor to sell. According to Marx, the value of this labor is determined by the cost of feeding, housing, and clothing the laborer's household. The laborer, however, is producing goods that are sold to pay the cost of producing them *and* to make a profit for the owner. In a pre-industrial workshop, for example, a cobbler might be able to produce three pairs of shoes a day. When the shoes are sold, there is more than enough money to pay the cobbler his daily wage; the rest is profit for the owner. In an industrial system machine technology vastly increases the productivity of labor: every factory worker can produce thirty pairs of shoes a day, yet the cost of maintaining the laborer — and hence, the daily wage — is relatively unchanged. No matter how many shoes the workers make, they cannot profit because they are still selling labor, not shoes. Greater productivity brings far greater profits for the capitalist owner but no benefit at all to workers. The forces of production in modern societies thus produce relations of production that pit the owners of the means of production, or **bourgeoisie**, against the wage laborers, or

---

[3] Karl Marx and Friedrich Engels, *The German Ideology* (New York: International Publishers, 1930), p. 18.

↓ Questions

proletariat. Marx thought of the bourgeoisie and proletariat not just as economic categories but as social classes, groups of individuals with opposing interests and different views of the world.

Furthermore, the economic division between owners and workers carries over into every other sphere of life. The powerful capitalists dominate not only the system of material production but the production of ideas and beliefs as well. Marx wrote,

> The ideas of the ruling class are in every age the ruling ideas, i.e., the class which is the dominant material force in society is at the same time its dominant intellectual force. The class which has the means of material production at its disposal has control at the same time over the means of mental production.[4]

In Marx's view all aspects of capitalist society — its political system, its laws (especially property laws), its philosophical values and moral beliefs, its literary and artistic works — justify and support the exploitation of the working class.

Marx's concept of social class certainly offers a different perspective on inequality than one that finds individuals responsible for their own fates. Although his theory has been widely discussed and debated since the nineteenth century, few social scientists accept Marx's view that inequality derives solely from the confrontation between "haves" and "have nots." We turn now to Weber, who modified Marx's ideas in what is now considered the classical analysis of social inequality.

WEBER: INEQUALITIES OF WEALTH, PRESTIGE, AND POWER

Weber agreed with Marx that economic forces are the most important factors in social inequality. However, he also believed that cultural considerations were important, and that a society's values, religious beliefs, and customs can determine how its social advantages will be distributed.

Instead of a single economic dimension, Weber suggested three ways of measuring inequality: by **wealth**, or material possessions and economic opportunities; by **prestige**, or the favorable opinion of others; and by **power**, or the ability to get what one wants even when opposed by others.[5]

WEALTH.   Economic factors affect what Weber called a person's **life chances**, or the likelihood of having a particular standard of living. A relatively high income provides better life chances from childhood to old age — better doctors, better schools, a better job with a higher salary, a more comfortable life style, and possibly even a longer life in which to enjoy these advantages.

PRESTIGE.   While objective criteria such as income determine economic standing, other people's subjective opinions produce differences in honor and esteem. Prestige does not always accompany wealth. In fact, the combination of high esteem and low income

---

[4] Karl Marx, *Selected Writings in Sociology and Social Philosophy*. trans. T. B. Bottomore and Maximilien Rubel (London: Watts, 1961), p. 78.
[5] Weber referred to these dimensions as "class," "status," and "party." To avoid confusion, we shall use the looser translations of the German terms.

Wealth, prestige, and power do not always go together. Sister Teresa has great prestige but no wealth and little power; Elizabeth Taylor has great wealth but hardly any prestige or power; Colonel Qaddafi has great power but no known wealth and only limited prestige.

is so common that there is a phrase for it — the "genteel poverty" of poor but socially prominent families.

Social prestige is also related to life style. How you spend your money can be as important as how much you have. About ninety years ago the American economist Thorstein Veblen described the competition for *status symbols*, or material goods associated with superior social rank. In *The Theory of the Leisure Class* (1899), Veblen listed conspicuous consumption, conspicuous leisure, and conspicuous display of status symbols as the ways in which people try to bolster self-esteem by gaining the admiration of their neighbors[6] (see "Classy Neckties").

POWER.   Power is the ability to determine how other people will behave, even against their wills. Powerful people are able to set economic policies, put new laws into effect, and run their own lives the way they want. The chairman of the board of Exxon, for example, wields tremendous economic power in American life. But power can be independent of wealth and prestige, as it often is in bureaucracies. The faceless government bureaucrats who read our income tax forms, issue or withhold building permits and drivers' licenses, and decide when George Washington's birthday will be celebrated may have great power over us, but they do not receive great prestige or great financial rewards.

Wealth, prestige, and power tend to overlap, but they do not always go together. As Max Weber's analysis shows us, social inequality is a more complex phenomenon than it appeared to Marx. In fact, inequality in many societies is determined primarily not by economic factors but by relative prestige and power.

---

[6] Thorstein Veblen, *The Theory of the Leisure Class* (1899) (New York: Modern Library, 1934).

Social ranking is a system for distributing the things that are scarce and valuable in every society — not only the food, shelter, and other goods produced by the economy, but also such intangibles as honor and power. Although we can imagine a society with so much material abundance that no stratification system is required, the respect of others will always be scarce and unevenly divided.

The basis for social ranking is a combination of ascribed and achieved characteristics. Some social positions are ascribed at birth according to sex, race, or other characteristics over which the individual has little or no control. Others are achieved through individual failure or accomplishment. Depending on what kinds of characteristics are considered most important, stratification systems fall into three categories: caste, estate, and class.

CASTE SYSTEMS

In **caste stratification** systems individuals are permanently assigned a social position purely on the basis of race, religion, or some other ascribed characteristic. Although the Indian government has made caste barriers illegal, India is still the most famous example of a caste system. Until a century ago, Indian society was broadly divided into four major castes and the lowest-ranking group, the *untouchables.* The ruling castes were the *Brahmans* (priests), the *Kahatriyas* (warriors), and the *Vaisyas* (merchants and peasants). The fourth caste, the *Pariahs,* served these rulers. The untouchables were considered so inferior that they were forbidden to mingle with higher castes on streets, ferries, and trains. The basis of this rigid system is the Hindu religion, which assigns believers to unalterable social positions at birth. Hindus believe that they can hope to improve their caste in the next life through reincarnation but that they must accept their lot during their present lifetimes.[7]

South Africa's *apartheid* is a caste system based on strict racial segregation. Every citizen is assigned at birth to a racial category — white, "colored" (mixed race), African, or Asian. Each category is segregated in its own residential section, with its own schools, hospitals, movie theaters, beaches, and so on. White, colored, and Asian legislators have separate chambers in the South African Parliament, and Africans are not formally represented in the government at all. Only blacks with work permits can enter the "white towns" of South Africa's cities, and whites need passes to visit the black townships, or urban districts. Until 1985 marriages and sexual relationships between whites and nonwhites were legally prohibited. Whites are a minority (16 percent) of the population, but they are ranked highest in the social hierarchy and the African majority (72 percent) is ranked lowest. Whites automatically receive higher salaries than blacks in the same jobs, and white schools receive 90 percent of the tax revenues for education.[8]

---

[7] David Mandelbaum, *Society in India* (Berkeley: University of California Press, 1970).
[8] American Friends Service Committee, "South Africa: Challenge and Hope" (Philadelphia, 1982), pp. 11–13.

CLASSY NECKTIES

John T. Molloy, author of Dress for Success, *calls the necktie "the heraldic shield of corporate America." He claims that one glance at the pattern of a man's tie will tell the knowledgeable executive whether the wearer has the social background to get to the top, and that "the average person who wears a bow tie is distrusted by almost everyone."*[1]

The following excerpt discusses the class implications of choosing a certain kind of necktie. The author is Paul Fussell, a professor of English who shares Molloy's interest in decoding the symbolic messages that clothes convey.

The necktie's association with responsibility, good employeeship, and other presumed attributes of the obedient middle class is well documented by an experiment conducted by Molloy. He had a series of men interviewed for good jobs. Some wore ties, others did not. "Invariably," he found,

> *those men who wore their ties to interviews were offered jobs; those without them were turned down. And in one almost incredible situation, the interviewer . . . was made so uncomfortable by the applicant's lack of a tie that he gave the man $6.50, told him to go out and buy a tie, put it on, and then come back to complete the interview. He still didn't get the job.*

The same suggestion that the necktie is an important marker of the division between the middle and the prole classes emerges from another of Molloy's experiments, this one performed at the horrible Port Authority Bus Terminal in New York, a traditional locus of every imaginable vice, menace, and outrage. He himself posed as a middle-class man who had left his wallet home and had somehow to get back to the suburbs. At the rush hour, he tried to borrow 75 cents for his bus fare; the first hour wearing a suit but no tie, the second hour properly dressed, tie and all. "In the first hour," he reports, "I made $7.23, but in the second, with my tie on, I made $26, and one man even gave me extra money for a newspaper."

The principle that clothing moves lower in status the more legible it becomes applies to neckties with a vengeance. The ties worn by the top classes eschew the more obvious forms of verbal or even too crudely symbolic statement, relying on stripes, amoeba-like foulard blobs, or small dots to make the point that the wearer possesses too much class to care to specify right out in front what it's based on. . . . Small white dots against a dark background, perhaps the most conservative tie possible, are favored both by uppers and upper-middles and, defensively, by those nervous about being thought low, coarse, drunken, or cynical, like journalists and TV news readers and sportscasters, and by those whose fiduciary honor must be thought beyond question, like the trust officers working for the better metropolitan banks.

Moving down from stripes, blobs, or dots, we come to necktie patterns with a more overt and precise semiotic function. Some, designed to announce that the upper-middle-class wearer is a sport, will display diagonal patterns of little flying

ESTATE SYSTEMS

In **estate stratification** systems social position depends on family membership. Each major social stratum, or estate, has certain rights and privileges passed on through inheritance.

Estate stratification is characteristic of feudal societies, in which land is the most important basis for social rank. In medieval Europe, for example, members of the nobility were at the top of the social order. They did the fighting (a highly prestigious activity), administered huge landholdings, and enforced the law. Nobles were often related to the king, who was himself a member of the nobility. The priests of the medieval church had similarly high position; below them were the commoners—

pheasants, or small yachts, signal flags, and sextants. ("I hunt and own a yacht. Me rich and sporty!") Just below these are the "milieu" patterns, designed to celebrate the profession of the wearer and to congratulate him on having so fine a profession. These are worn either by insecure members of the upper-middle class (like surgeons) or by members of the middle class aspiring to upper-middle status (like accountants). Thus a tie covered with tiny caduceuses proclaims "Hot damn! I am a physician."

. . . As we move further down the class hierarchy, actual words begin to appear on ties, and these are meant to be commented on by viewers. One such exhibitionist artifact is the Grandfather's Tie in dark blue with grandchildren's names hand-painted on it, diagonally, in white. . . . Another kind reads "I'd rather be sailing," "skiing," etc., and these can also be effective underminers of privacy —"conversation-starters," and thus useful adjuncts to comfy middle-class status, in the tradition of expecting neighbors to drop in without warning.

. . . At the bottom of the middle class, just before it turns to high prole, we encounter ties depicting large flowers in brilliant colors, or simply bright "artistic" splotches. The message is frequently "I'm a merry dog." These wearers are the ones Molloy is addressing when, discussing neckties, he warns, "Avoid purple under all circumstances."

Further down still, where questions of yacht ownership or merry doghood are too preposterous to be claimed even on a necktie, we come upon the high- or mid-prole "bola" tie, a woven or leather thong with a slide (often of turquoise or silver), affected largely by retired persons residing in Sun Belt places like New Mexico. Like any other sort of tie, this one makes a statement, saying: "Despite appearances, I'm really as good as you are, and my 'necktie,' though perhaps unconventional, is really better than your traditional tie, because it suggests the primitive and therefore the unpretentious, pure, and virtuous.". . . Like many things bought by proles, these bola ties can be very expensive, especially when the slide is made of precious metal or displays "artwork." The point again is that money, although important, is not always the most important criterion of class. Below the bola wearers, at the very bottom, stand the low proles, the destitute, and the bottom-out-of-sight, who never wear a tie, or wear one—and one is all they own—so rarely that the day is memorable for that reason. Down here, the tie is an emblem of affectation and even effeminacy, and you can earn a reputation for being la-di-da by appearing in one, as if you thought yourself better than other people. One prole wife says of her spouse: "I'm going to bury my husband in his T-shirt if the undertaker will allow it."

[1] John T. Molloy, "Tie One On," *Success* 33:1 (January/February 1986): 70–71.

SOURCE: Paul Fussell, *Class: A Guide Through the American Status System* (New York: Summit Books, 1983), pp. 66–69.

merchants, artisans, peasants, and serfs. Each estate had different rights, and each was subject to a different set of laws.

Unlike caste systems, estate systems permit some changes in social rank through intermarriage or achievement. Commoners could be knighted, or made members of the nobility, as a reward for serving the king; devout serfs could become priests; and rich merchants occasionally could purchase high office. In most cases, however, one's inherited position continued for life.

Estate stratification disappeared in the modern era, but many European societies retain vestiges of the old system. Great Britain, for example, still has a nobility whose wealth was originally based on ownership of land. The queen continues to observe many medieval customs, including the granting of knighthoods and peerages, and the

House of Lords retains a remnant of its former power in Parliament. Impoverished descendants of the English gentry still occupy "stately homes" which were built with separate staircases, chapels, and living quarters for the family and their servants.[9] Since the industrial era, however, Great Britain has had a class stratification system.

CLASS SYSTEMS

In **class stratification** systems social position is largely determined by achievement, especially the economic achievement of individuals. Virtually every industrial society has a class stratification system. Specialized education and occupational skills are more important than family background in all industrial societies, including such culturally diverse countries as the Soviet Union, France, and Japan. Marriage between members of different classes is more acceptable than in caste or estate systems, and it is not unusual to find sons and daughters in different class positions than their parents.

For convenience social scientists generally divide the social hierarchy into three classes based on occupation and income: (1) the upper class, whose large income comes mainly from property, (2) the middle class of nonpropertied professionals and white-collar workers who depend on their jobs for their incomes, and (3) the lower class of low-income manual workers. These categories are necessarily arbitrary. American manual workers in the construction industry, for example, earn more money than middle-class teachers. Some researchers identify five major classes (with many subclasses): (1) the upper class (the rich who have inherited property), (2) the upper-middle class (professionals who earn large salaries), (3) the lower-middle class (educated white-collar workers and professionals with lower salaries), (4) the working class (skilled blue-collar workers who earn hourly wages), and (5) the lower class (unskilled workers and the poor).

Using a Marxist perspective, Erik Olin Wright and his colleagues have painted quite a different picture of the American class structure.[10] Instead of defining class in terms of occupation, they used Marx's definition of class as a social relationship. Class standing is determined not by the technical content of a job, but by how much control workers have over decision-making, over other workers, and over their own work. A carpenter, for example, could be a proletarian wage laborer, a largely self-directed employee, a manager of other workers, or a bourgeois, self-employed artisan. By this definition white-collar clerical occupations are more proletarian than skilled manual occupations. Data from Wright's national telephone survey indicate that the working class is by far the largest class, and that over 60 percent of all working-class jobs are held by women and members of minority groups. Clearly, the usual occupational hierarchy does not accurately reflect other kinds of class divisions, especially those based on sex and race.

---

[9] Jill Franklin, *The Gentleman's Country House and its Plan, 1835–1914* (London: Routledge and Kegan Paul, 1981).

[10] Erik Olin Wright, David Hachen, Cynthia Costello, and Joey Sprague, "The American Class Structure," *American Sociological Review* 47 (December 1982): 709–726.

SUMMARY

In caste systems social rank depends primarily on prestige. Higher castes are not necessarily more wealthy, but they are given greater honor and respect. In estate systems the focus is power. The ranking of estates involves prestige, of course, but the nobility's control of the law and the military is even more important. In class systems prestige and power tend to be less significant than the economic dimension of social inequality.[11] The following section discusses each dimension of social stratification in American society.

INEQUALITY IN THE UNITED STATES

Americans like to think that they belong to a classless society, one in which privileges and rewards are equally available to all. Most surveys find that people are reluctant to place themselves at either the top or the bottom of the social ladder. In a 1988 poll, only 2 percent identified themselves as members of the upper class, 5 percent put themselves in the lower class, and the rest split almost evenly between a middle-class and a working-class identification. Even these class differences varied widely: 34 percent of those earning less than $20,000 called themselves middle class, as did 63 percent of those earning more than $35,000.[12] People often define the social classes according to the values they think each class has. In another poll, respondents who identified with the middle class considered themselves "better informed about current events," more interested in participating in the community, and more likely to appreciate classical music and the theater than the lower class. They described lower-class members as people who spent their time watching TV soap operas, who were less obligated to participate in community life, and who were more interested in sports. Middle-class respondents criticized upper-class members as "primarily concerned about their own income" and as people who "travel and squander their money."[13]

Inequality in the United States is clearly not just a matter of income. Money does not automatically bring power and prestige with it. Some Americans are wealthy yet have little power (million-dollar lottery winners). Others have great prestige but very little wealth (the clergy). Still others have political power or wealth yet little prestige (political bosses and gangsters). Social rank in the American class system obviously depends on the multiple dimensions of wealth, prestige, and power.

INCOME

Most Americans get what they have from their work; that is, they earn an income from wages or salaries. By far the largest share of this income is earned by the relatively few

---

[11] Daniel W. Rossides, *The American Class System* (Boston: Houghton Mifflin, 1976), p. 42.

[12] NORC, *General Social Survey*, (Chicago: National Opinion Research Center, University of Chicago, 1988).

[13] The New York Times/CBS News Poll, reported in *The New York Times*, April 24, 1978, pp. 1, 10.

people at the top of the economic ladder. In 1987 the richest 5 percent of American families received 17 percent of all income, while the poorest 20 percent received only 5 percent, mainly from Social Security and other government transfer payments.[14]

The most striking aspect of income distribution is that it has not changed significantly since the end of World War II. Although economic growth has roughly doubled real disposable family income (the money left after taxes and adjusted for inflation) over the last generation, the size of the shares given to each income level is about the same and the gap between rich and poor is slowly widening (see Figure 7-1). By any measure economic inequality in the United States is very great.

The reality behind these statistics is that a large number of Americans are poor. In 1987, 13.5 percent of the population was living below the federal government's **poverty line**, which at that time was an annual income of $11,611 for a family of four. In other words, about one out of seven Americans — over 33 million people — was officially considered unable to buy the basic necessities of food, clothing, and shelter.[15]

The government's definition of poverty is absolute deprivation, or lack of the means for survival. The poverty line is calculated on the assumption that a poor family spends one-third of its income on food; if the U.S. Department of Agriculture estimates a "nutritionally adequate" diet for a family of four at $3,300 a year, then poverty is defined as an income below $9,900. In 1982, however, when the poverty line was set at $9,862, New York City's Department of Consumer Affairs estimated that the weekly "food basket" for an average family of four cost about $107 — about $44 more than the Department of Agriculture allowed a poor urban family to spend.

[14] *Statistical Abstract of the United States, 1989* (Washington, D.C.: U.S. Government Printing Office, 1989): Table 722.
[15] U.S. Bureau of Census, *Statistical Abstract of the United States,* p. 420 and Table 734.

FIGURE 7-1   **DISTRIBUTION OF INCOME AMONG U.S. FAMILIES, 1966, 1976, AND 1987**

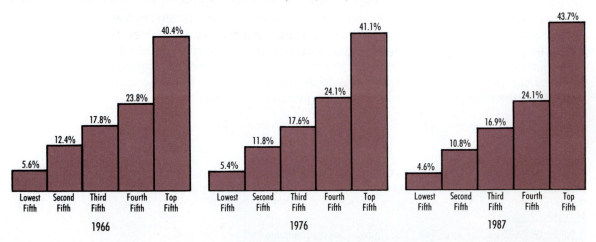

SOURCE: Bureau of the Census, *Social Indicators III* (Washington, D.C.: U.S. Government Printing Office, 1980), Table 9/15; *Statistical Abstract of the United States* (Washington, D.C.: U.S. Government Printing Office, 1989), Table 722.

Since the government's definition of poverty appears unrealistic, some critics have suggested that half the median income would be a more accurate measure. In 1987 the **median income** was $31,135 — half the families in the United States earned more than that amount and half earned less. The suggested poverty line in 1987 would have been an income of about $15,568 for a family of four. By this relative definition of poverty, which takes into account the standard of living of the whole society, one out of five American families is poor.[16]

PRESTIGE

Stratification based on prestige involves the awarding of honor or respect. Some people are highly regarded simply because they were born into a certain family: the children of a Supreme Court justice, for example, have this kind of ascribed prestige. Studies have consistently shown, however, that most Americans value personal achievement more highly than ascribed characteristics.[17] Even race, which is usually very significant, has surprisingly little effect on how highly a person is regarded by the community.[18] In short, prestige in the United States largely depends on the achievements of individuals. And the most important source of achievement in American society is occupation.

Since 1947, studies of occupational prestige have had remarkably consistent results (see Table 7-1). Not surprisingly, Americans think most highly of occupations associated with professional skills, political power, and large incomes. Judges, physicians, and scientists have some of the highest ranking occupations, while day laborers have the least prestigious jobs. Not only has the ranking of different occupations changed very little in the last fifty years; there is also very little disagreement over how occupations are ranked. Even people in low-ranking occupations agree that their jobs have little prestige. Finally, studies of occupational prestige find that the rating for particular jobs is similar in all industrial societies.[19]

Studies of occupational prestige measure the respect given to certain social positions, not necessarily to the individuals in those positions. Some people in highly regarded occupations are not respected. In 1989, for example, Samuel Pierce, the Secretary of Housing and Urban Development, lost the honor due a cabinet officer when allegations of fraud and mismanagement were directed at his department. Nevertheless, most individuals receive the prestige associated with the kind of work they do.

POWER

Power refers to the ability to take actions that affect how other people will behave. In American society power is exercised primarily by large corporations and the government.

---

[16] U.S. Bureau of the Census, *Statistical Abstract of the United States* (Washington, D.C.: U.S. Government Printing Office, 1989), Table 715.

[17] Steven L. Nock and Peter H. Rossi, "Family Types and Social Standing," *Social Forces* 57:4 (1979): 1325–45.

[18] Steven L. Nock and Peter H. Rossi, "Ascription Versus Achievement in the Attribution of Family Social Status," *American Journal of Sociology* 84 (November 1978): 565–90.

[19] Robert Hodge, D. Treiman, and Peter Rossi, "A Comparative Study of Occupational Prestige," in *Class, Status, and Power*, 2d ed., eds. Reinhard Bendix and Seymour M. Lipset (New York: Free Press, 1966).

TABLE 7-1   OCCUPATIONAL PRESTIGE RATINGS IN THE UNITED STATES

Occupation	Score	Occupation	Score
U.S. Supreme Court justice	94	Newspaper columnist	73
Physician	93	Police officer	72
Nuclear physicist	92	Radio announcer	70
Scientist	92	Bookkeeper	70
State governor	91	Insurance agent	69
Cabinet member in the federal government	90	Carpenter	68
College professor	90	Manager of a small store in a city	67
U.S. representative in Congress	90	Local official of a labor union	67
Lawyer	89	Mail carrier	66
Diplomat in U.S. Foreign Service	89	Traveling sales representative for a wholesale concern	66
Dentist	88	Plumber	65
Architect	88	Playground director	63
Psychologist	87	Barber	63
Minister	87	Machine operator in a factory	63
Member of the board of directors of a large corporation	87	Owner-operator of a lunch stand	63
Mayor of a large city	87	Corporal in the regular army	62
Priest	86	Garage mechanic	62
Civil engineer	86	Truck driver	59
Airline pilot	86	Fisherman who owns his own boat	58
Banker	85	Clerk in a store	56
Biologist	85	Lumberjack	55
Sociologist	83	Restaurant cook	55
Instructor in public schools	82	Singer in a nightclub	54
Captain in the regular army	82	Filling station attendant	51
Accountant for a large business	81	Dockworker	50
Public school teacher	81	Night watchman	50
Building contractor	80	Coal miner	50
Musician in a symphony orchestra	78	Restaurant waiter	49
Author of novels	78	Taxi driver	49
Economist	78	Farmhand	48
Official of an international labor union	77	Janitor	48
Electrician	76	Bartender	48
Trained machinist	75	Clothes presser in a laundry	45
Farm owner and operator	74	Sharecropper — one who owns no livestock or equipment and does not manage farm	42
Undertaker	74	Garbage collector	39
Welfare worker for a city government	74		

Prestige in American society is closely related to occupation. Where do you think these real estate brokers rank in prestige ratings?

CORPORATE POWER.   Business firms have always had a great deal of power over the lives of the men and women who work for them. The American steel industry offers a recent example of how decisions made in corporate boardrooms affect the public.[20]

The profits of U.S. Steel and other steel companies soared after World War II, when the destruction of German and Japanese industry during the war left them without serious international competition. When the steel plants of Germany and Japan were rebuilt with the latest technology, however, those nations began to dominate the world market. At the end of the war American workers produced almost 50 percent of the world's steel; in 1980 they produced 14 percent. The decline in the sales led to widespread unemployment in the industrial Midwest. Since 1979 U.S. Steel has shut down more than 150 plants and facilities, laying off some 100,000 workers and making ghost towns out of mill communities in Pennsylvania and Ohio.[21] In 1982 the unemployment

---

[20] William Serrin, "Collapse of Our Industrial Heartland," *The New York Times Magazine,* June 6, 1982, pp. 45, 48, 52.

[21] *Business Week,* February 25, 1985, p. 50.

rate for the whole steel industry was 30 percent. Nevertheless, in the last twenty years not a single company has built a major steel mill using the same advanced technology as its foreign competitors.

Steel executives say that profits have been low and there has been little capital available for modernization. However, some people wonder how deeply American manufacturers are committed to producing steel, rather than making other — perhaps more profitable — investments. In 1982, for example, U.S. Steel spent $6.4 billion to acquire the Marathon Oil Company. A few years later, the word "steel" was taken out of the company's name and replaced with an "X". Steel now accounts for less than one-third of USX's revenues.

Meanwhile, declining steel production has had a "ripple effect" on the Midwest. Not only tens of thousands of steelworkers but an indeterminate number of tradespeople and service workers who depended on their business have moved away. The decline of the Midwest — once the core of the U.S. industrial base — is partly the result of economic change, but it is also partly the result of management decisions made by a few steel and automobile executives.

LEGISLATIVE POWER.   Governments also exercise power by making the laws that everyone must obey. These laws, for example, determine how much individuals and corporations pay in taxes, define the government's responsibility to support the aged and unemployed, and establish other rules and regulations that affect the daily life of every citizen. Governments enforce these laws through the courts, the police, and other public officials. They also set the penalties for breaking the law, which range from a few dollars in fines to years of imprisonment or even death. Obviously, governments play a crucial role in creating and maintaining social inequality.

Lawmaking in the United States is a complex process of pulling and shoving that involves a number of special interest groups (see Chapter 16, "Politics"). Legislators and officials in regulatory agencies frequently are barraged with information from lobbyists who wish to have special laws and regulations (or exceptions to them) passed. Interest groups typically influence government decision making by a combination of threats and promises: threats of loss of votes and political support, promises of votes and campaign contributions. The most notorious example of political lobbying is the activity of the National Rifle Association, which for twenty-five years has successfully blocked effective gun-control legislation in spite of the American public's overwhelming support for restrictions on the sale of guns.

While it is most helpful to have friends among the rule makers, it is also useful to have friends among the rule enforcers. Rita Lavelle, an Environmental Protection Agency official in charge of toxic waste disposal, was convicted and sent to prison in 1985 for lying under oath about her blatant favoritism to a company where she used to work. Finally, judges often have great discretion in setting penalties, and they are sometimes more lenient toward "respectable" white-collar criminals than toward the disreputable poor (see Chapter 8, "Deviance and Social Control").

THE POWER OF ELITES.   Many sociologists have been interested in the power of certain groups to influence the political process. In *The Power Elite* (1956) C. Wright Mills argued that the most powerful people are found at the top of three dominant bureau-

Some special interest groups wield a great deal of power in the political process. Although most Americans favor restrictions on the sale of firearms, the National Rifle Association has successfully blocked gun control legislation for over twenty years.

cracies: corporations, the military, and the government. The power of members of this "elite" resides in their positions, not in their abilities as individuals. Because the interests and attitudes of these top executives, military officers, and politicians tend to coincide, Mills believed that they constitute a powerful ruling group.[22]

Other observers see the power structure of the United States differently. Instead of a society dominated by a single institution or set of individuals, they see a society made up of a multitude of groups with conflicting goals and interests. This pluralist view also stresses the importance of decision making at the community level.

The truth about how power is distributed probably lies somewhere between these two views. Much decision making clearly does take place at the local level, but even there power is usually concentrated in a few hands. In American society, however, power appears to be exercised by many groups rather than by a single power elite.

THE COSTS OF INEQUALITY

By maintaining an unequal distribution of wealth, prestige, and power, stratification systems affect everyone's opportunity to have a comfortable, satisfying life. Furthermore, there are so many disadvantages to life at the bottom of the social ladder that the chances of the poor are drastically reduced. This section considers some of the ways lower-class standing limits "life, liberty, and the pursuit of happiness."

HEALTH.   The farther down one is in the social hierarchy, the fewer chances one has of living a long and healthy life, or even of surviving at all. Infant mortality is nearly 40

---

[22] C. Wright Mills, *The Power Elite* (New York: Oxford University Press, 1956).

percent greater in the lower class than it is in the middle class, and the rates of premature births and mental deficiency are also higher. Poor nutrition and inadequate housing cause lower-class children to grow up unhealthy; as adults they have higher than average rates of diphtheria, polio, lung and heart disease, and arthritis.[23] Lower-class people also lead more dangerous lives. Compared to individuals in the middle class, they are more often killed or injured in violent attacks, including military combat. In Korea and Vietnam, soldiers from poor families were almost twice as likely to be casualties of war. All in all, the poor lead such risky and unhealthy lives that their average life expectancy is six years shorter than that of the wealthiest.[24]

OPPORTUNITY.   The deprivations of poverty exact a further cost in missed opportunities to get a good education and a decent job. Richard H. de Lone, in a report for the Carnegie Council on Children, describes the penalties of poverty:

> It is a penalty to be born to parents with little education. It is a further penalty to be born to parents who are frequently unemployed and whose employment opportunities are limited to relatively uninteresting, dead-end jobs. . . . Some of the penalties are immediate—the physical deprivations of poor nutrition, poor health, poor housing, inadequate medical care; some accumulate slowly, influencing the development of adult skills, aspirations, and opportunities.[25]

Together these penalties produce the almost insurmountable odds against millions of children who are growing up in poverty.

Paul Fussell, an observer of the American class system, comments on the destructive effects that the myth of equal opportunity has on people who never "make it":

> Because the myth conveys the impression that you can readily earn your way upward, disillusion and bitterness are particularly strong when you find yourself trapped in a class system you've been half persuaded isn't important. When in early middle life some people discover that certain limits have been placed on their capacity to ascend socially by such apparent irrelevancies as heredity, early environment, and the social class of their immediate forebears, they go into something like despair, which, if generally secret, is no less destructive. . . . The force of sheer class envy behind vile and even criminal behavior in this country, the result in part of disillusion over the official myth of classlessness, should never be underestimated.[26]

HAPPINESS.   Does money buy happiness? Sociological data show again and again that the chances for a successful "pursuit of happiness" vary a great deal from class to class. In a 1988 national survey that asked people how happy they were, 42 percent of those with family incomes over $35,000 said they were "very happy." The proportion of "very happy" people dropped to 34 percent in the $20,000 to $35,000 range, and to 27 percent among people whose income was less than $20,000.[27]

[23] Oscar Ornati, *Poverty amid Affluence* (New York: Twentieth Century Fund, 1966), pp. 73, 84.

[24] Aaron Antonovosky, "Social Class, Life Expectancy and Overall Mortality," in *The Impact of Social Class,* ed. Paul Blumberg (New York: Crowell, 1972), p. 472.

[25] Richard H. de Lone, *Small Futures: Children, Inequality, and the Limits of Liberal Reform* pp. 3–4.

[26] Paul Fussell, *Class: A Guide Through the American Class System* (New York: Summit Books, 1983), p. 20.

[27] National Opinion Research Center, *General Social Survey* (Chicago: University of Chicago Press, 1988).

Other measures of contentment show similar class patterns. We may think that rich people have more per capita divorces, but it only looks that way. In fact, the upper class — as it is measured by occupation, education, and income — has a lower rate of divorce than the lower class. Upper-class couples also seem to be more happily married, perhaps because there are fewer strains on the marriage from external events — the loss of a job, for instance, or an illness or accident.[28]

Low-income people also appear to lead lonelier lives. One study reported that nearly one-third of unskilled workers said they had no close friends, compared to only one-tenth of professionals and executives.[29] Moreover, people are much more likely to say that they like their jobs if they are in the upper end of the occupational hierarchy. Happiness at work appears to be closely tied to a good salary and a chance to be independent and creative — all characteristics of middle-class rather than lower-class occupations (see Chapter 19, "Work and Leisure").

Besides affecting our objective experience of life, the stratification system affects how other people feel about us and how we feel about ourselves. The higher the regard in which society holds us, the more people will defer to us and our opinions. The lower our social rank, the more likely it is that people will belittle us and our abilities. Other people's ideas of us are important: they help form our own self-images as competent or incompetent, successful or unsuccessful, superior or inferior (see Chapter 5, "Socialization").

EXPLANATIONS OF INEQUALITY

In a democratic society like the United States, which enjoys one of the highest standards of living in the world, it is particularly difficult to find reasons why millions of families do not have enough to survive. Theories of social inequality attempt to answer this question: Why are virtually all societies structured so that some people get more and some people get less than their fair share?

A FUNCTIONAL EXPLANATION

From one functional perspective social inequality is both inevitable and necessary for allocating individuals to important social roles. The most persuasive argument for the functional theory of stratification was made over forty years ago by Kingsley Davis and Wilbert E. Moore. They contended that people are motivated to perform demanding or difficult roles through the unequal distribution of rewards. If surgeons did not have such high occupational prestige and incomes, Davis and Moore argued, not enough people would put up with the long years of training, life-and-death responsibilities, or personal sacrifices that the surgeon's role requires. On the other hand, plumbers fulfill a social role that demands less effort and training, make less money, and enjoy less prestige. "Social inequality," according to Davis and Moore, "is thus an unconsciously evolved device by which societies insure that the most important positions are con-

---

[28] William J. Goode, "Marital Satisfaction and Instability," in *Class, Status, and Power*, pp. 377–87.

[29] Joseph Alan Kahl, *The American Class Structure* (New York: Rinehart, 1959).

scientiously filled by the most qualified persons. Hence every society, no matter how simple or complex, must . . . possess a certain amount of institutionalized inequality." [30]

This functional explanation has been criticized on several grounds. First, it is impossible to say which social positions are more important than others. Which society would function better, the critics ask — one with no surgeons or one with no plumbers? Defining highly paid positions as functionally more important comes dangerously close to the circular argument that certain positions pay more because they are functionally more important because they pay more. It is quite possible that some relatively unrewarded positions (schoolteachers, farmhands, housewives) contribute more to the survival of society than some highly rewarded positions (professional athletes, movie stars, advertising executives).

Secondly, it is difficult to argue that only a small proportion of the population has the motivation and talent necessary to fill important positions. Supporters of Davis and Moore are forced to the silly conclusion that CBS news anchorman Dan Rather, who earned $2.2 million in 1984, and Philip Caldwell, the chairman of Ford Motor Company, who earned $1.6 million, have such rare qualifications that they command such extraordinary rewards.[31]

Finally, in Davis and Moore's world everyone with the right talents has an opportunity to attain a highly rewarded social position. As we know, in the real world the access to these positions is very limited. A medical school education, for example, is available only to relatively few people. For this reason, the conflict theorist Melvin Tumin has turned Davis and Moore's theory around: he finds that stratification is dysfunctional for society because it prevents talented people from filling important positions.[32]

CONFLICT THEORY

While Davis and Moore argue that inequality benefits the society as a whole, other theorists point out that it benefits some people more than others. According to this conflict perspective, stratification exists because certain groups are able to exploit and dominate others through force or through traditional inherited privileges. Some sociologists argue that surgeons are highly paid because the American Medical Association has the power to keep the supply of medical school graduates smaller than the public's demand for physicians' services (see Chapter 14, "Health Care"). Conflict theorists see classes as conflicting groups — rulers against ruled, "haves" against "have nots."

Ironically, the communist countries of eastern Europe provide good examples of class stratification. In order to achieve Marx's ideal of economic equality, the Soviet Union and its satellites attempted to do away with social stratification based on wealth. Instead of becoming classless societies, however, these socialist systems became tightly structured along political lines, with ruling groups made up of Communist party officials. Many privileges became reserved for party members and their families

---

[30] Kingsley Davis and Wilbert E. Moore, "Some Principles of Stratification," *American Sociological Review* 10 (April 1945): 243.

[31] *Business Week*, May 6, 1985, pp. 87, 79.

[32] Melvin M. Tumin, ed., *Readings on Social Stratification* (Englewood Cliffs, N.J.: Prentice-Hall, 1970), p. 380.

— opportunities to be well educated, to have a good job with a high income, and even to be rich. High officials and professionals in these societies have a life style that includes country houses, servants, and all the other rewards of power and affluence. In fact, these party bureaucrats have been called a "new class" more similar to the dominant groups in capitalist countries than to a ruling proletariat.[33]

Conflict theory also stresses the cultural beliefs that sustain stratification systems. People who are relatively well-off tend to believe that they deserve their advantages and that the poor deserve their disadvantages. Most cultures have myths explaining why some people are rich and powerful: they have a divine right to rule, for example, or they are smarter or more hard working. Because the ideology justifying inequality is part of the society's culture, it is generally accepted by rich and poor alike.

In American society the stratification system is justified by an ideology that stresses individual effort as the means to success. Not everyone is equally successful, according to this myth, but everyone has an equal opportunity to succeed. Although Americans accept the notion that an individual's success may be due to a privileged background, they are likely to think failure is caused by stupidity, laziness, or some other purely personal characteristic. Those who succeed usually take personal credit for their success; those who fail often blame themselves for their failure.

ECONOMIC EXPLANATIONS

Other explanations of inequality cite economic factors, especially changes in the kinds of jobs available (see Chapter 19, "Work and Leisure"). Since World War II the American economy has shifted from producing goods to producing services — from farming and manufacturing, in other words, to such fields as data processing, teaching, and health care. The service revolution has brought an increase in white-collar jobs for the educated and technically skilled, but it has caused a rising rate of unemployment among relatively unskilled workers in such heavy industries as steel and automobile production. The pace of this economic change accelerated during the 1980s, when the strong dollar contributed to a rising trade deficit. Between 1980 and 1985, the American economy lost 2.3 million manufacturing jobs — the result of foreign competition, continuing automation and computerization, and the flight of American manufacturers to the cheap labor markets of Latin America and East Asia.[34]

Job inequalities also arise from what economists call the "dual labor market." The *primary market* is dominated by large corporations, which employ workers with specialized skills and offer them good wages and working conditions, job security, and a fair chance of promotion. The primary market also includes jobs for unionized blue-collar workers, independent craftsmen, technical workers and specialists, government bureaucrats, and professionals.

In contrast, the *secondary market* is dominated by small manufacturing companies and service establishments (restaurants, stores), which employ unskilled or semi-skilled workers in low-paying, temporary, or dead-end jobs. The secondary labor

[33] Milovan Djilas, *The New Class* (New York: Praeger, 1959).
[34] Clyde Farnsworth, "The Too-Mighty Dollar Takes a Toll of Manufacturing Jobs," *The New York Times*, September 23, 1984, p. E3.

market also provides jobs for nonunion manual workers, women in "pink collar" occupations (clerical work, sales jobs), and migrant farm laborers. A number of institutional barriers prevent these workers from entering the primary market. Some lack specialized education or a professional degree; others cannot meet the requirements for union membership; still others are considered too old or too young to work. As a result, many of the working poor are trapped in badly paid, dead-end jobs.

Theories of stratification explain inequality by showing that structural and cultural forces put certain people in certain social positions. The next section discusses theories of social mobility, which explain how certain people are able to change from one position to another.

SOCIAL MOBILITY

Social mobility is the movement of individuals and groups from one social position to another. Because there are several dimensions to social rank, or status, people are able to change position by gaining or losing wealth, prestige, and power. *Upward mobility* refers to movement up the social ladder, or a gain in status; *downward mobility* refers to a movement down the social ladder, or a loss of status. Individuals can also have a higher or lower status than their parents, or experience *intergenerational mobility*.

In an open stratification system, such as the American class system, there are supposed to be few obstacles to social mobility: status ideally depends on individual

"Ed, as you know, is the product of a fine heritage, traditional values, a topnotch education, devoted parents, a cultured environment, and an I.B.M. training program."

Drawing by H. Martin; © 1983 The New Yorker Magazine, Inc.

merit and achievement. Because there are many different ways of evaluating a person's social position, class lines tend to be blurred and overlapping. (Indeed, some sociologists reject the term "class" as too restrictive, preferring the term "socioeconomic status" instead.) The opposite is true of a closed stratification system, in which status is assigned more or less permanently at birth. Caste systems such as South Africa's apartheid, in which social ranks are rigidly defined, obviously allow much less social mobility than open systems like those of the Soviet Union and Great Britain.

STRUCTURAL FACTORS IN SOCIAL MOBILITY

Occupational mobility does not depend only on having the talent and social background to get ahead. It also depends on the social structure being climbed and how much room there is at the top. For a society to have a high rate of upward mobility, the opportunity to move up the ladder must be open to a large number of people.

For this reason industrial societies allow more upward mobility than pre-industrial, agrarian societies. Industrial technology causes a shift from a manual to a white-collar labor force and a corresponding rise in status. Table 7-2 shows that farm laborers made up 38 percent of the American labor force in 1900, but only 3 percent in 1988. The trend toward white-collar work is equally impressive: from 17 percent of the labor force at the turn of the century to 56 percent today. The industrialization of the United States has drastically changed the occupational hierarchy, creating many more prestigious, well-paid positions and eliminating low-paying manual jobs. In such a situation the opportunity to get ahead is greatly enhanced, and upward mobility is just about guaranteed for a large proportion of the labor force.

Education is no longer the privilege of an elite in industrial economies but a necessity for earning a living. Because education is a major factor in gaining status and occupational success, the expansion of educational opportunities in industrializing societies brings a corresponding increase in social mobility.

Another effect of industrialization is a huge increase in total income. An ever larger production of goods and services multiplies the per capita income, making successive generations of American children approximately twice as rich as their parents. The

THE DISTRIBUTION OF THE AMERICAN ADULT POPULATION AMONG OCCUPATIONAL CLASSES TABLE 7-2

Occupational Class	Both Sexes	
	1900	1988
Upper white-collar	10%	25%
Lower white-collar	7	31
Upper blue-collar	11	13
Middle blue-collar	13	12
Lower blue-collar	21	16
Farmer and farm laborer	38	3

SOURCE: U.S. Bureau of the Census, *Historical Statistics of the United States, Colonial Times to 1974* (Washington, D.C.: U.S. Government Printing Office, 1975); U.S. Bureau of Labor Statistics. *Handbook of Labor Statistics:* Table 17 (Washington, D.C.: U.S. Government Printing Office, 1989).

shift from low-paid jobs in agriculture and the growth of an educated middle class tend to spread this larger income more widely across the population.

All in all, industrialization tends to favor upward mobility by distributing more widely the three major determinants of higher status — prestigious occupation, education, and income — and thus giving more people greater opportunities to get ahead. These social consequences of industrialization account for the fact that all industrial societies — no matter how different their politics and cultural values — have similarly high rates of upward mobility. Many readers will be surprised to learn that during the 1950s Switzerland, France, and Japan all had higher percentages of upward mobility than the United States, and that Sweden and West Germany were not far behind.[35]

CLASS FACTORS IN SOCIAL MOBILITY

In American society, as we have seen, class is usually judged by occupation. Like all industrial societies the United States has a high rate of upward occupational mobility. In other words, people generally are able to get better jobs and move to a higher class position than their grandparents and parents. Even so, upward mobility is still limited; many people do not change class, and others lose social rank.

Research on social mobility shows that inequality is to a large extent inherited. In Peter Blau and Otis Duncan's classic study of the subject, a model of mobility showed that the amount of education a man receives is influenced by his father's occupation and that his level of education in turn affects his own occupation. In practical terms Blau and Duncan found that the sons of fathers in upper-level jobs are more likely than others to go to college and graduate school; sons of fathers in lower-ranking jobs are less likely than their upperclass peers to get the kind of advanced education that will enable them to attain a higher status.[36] Other statistics show how important education is to socioeconomic standing. In 1987, for example, households headed by individuals with fewer than eight years of schooling earned a median income of $10,884, but high school graduates earned $25,910 and college graduates earned $43,952.[37] Blau and Duncan found, however, that the training and early career experiences of the men they studied had an even greater influence than their father's occupation on their occupational rank.

The United States does appear to have more long-distance, or rags-to-riches, mobility than other countries. Blau and Duncan's research confirmed the moral of Horatio Alger's stories: a poor person with "pluck and luck" can climb to the top of the social ladder. About one out of ten sons of manual laborers in the United States attains a managerial or professional occupation, a larger proportion than Japan (1 in 14), Sweden (1 in 30), France (1 in 67), and Italy (1 in 300). A 1964 *Scientific American* survey of top executives in large corporations found that only 10 percent came from wealthy families, fewer than half had fathers who were managers or professionals, and 23

---

[35] Seymour M. Lipset and Reinhard Bendix, *Social Mobility in Industrial Society* (Berkeley: University of California Press, 1959).

[36] Peter M. Blau and Otis Dudly Duncan, *The American Occupational Structure* (New York: Wiley, 1967), pp. 401–3.

[37] U.S. Bureau of the Census, *Statistical Abstract of the United States* (Washington D.C.: U.S. Government Printing Office, 1989), Table 713.

percent came from lower-class backgrounds.[38] The growth of corporate bureaucracies (with their impersonal standards for promotion) and the spread of higher education for working-class children have undoubtedly contributed to the success of these "self-made" men and women.

INHERITING INEQUALITY. If family background, years of education, and early job experience are the key factors in upward mobility, and if they are interrelated, then poor children have several handicaps in moving up the social ladder. Not only do they come from lower-class backgrounds and have relatively less education, but they often enter the occupational structure at the bottom.

There is much evidence to support the theory that inequality is transmitted from generation to generation through the socialization process. Melvin Kohn's research, for example, found that middle-class and lower-class families teach their children different attitudes and values and that these class differences in upbringing influence the children's abilities to perform occupational roles. Because middle-class parents stress the development of independence and creativity, their children are more likely to learn skills appropriate to professional and managerial jobs (see Chapter 5, "Socialization").

School tracking systems are another means of reinforcing class origins. By selecting students for vocational or college careers partly on the basis of their family backgrounds, high schools frequently increase the effect of the parents' occupational status on the kind of education a child will get (see Chapter 13, "Education"). In short, education appears to be less an explanation of social mobility than a reflection of the social position one already has.

Obviously there is more to getting ahead than ability and hard work. Americans place such a high value on individual achievement that they generally fail to see the structural factors underlying personal success and failure. Family background is more important than most Americans like to think, and many crucial advantages and disadvantages are passed from generation to generation. Increasing educational and occupational opportunities for those at the middle of the social ladder have not diminished the upper class's share of wealth and power, nor have they given much hope to people at the bottom. The next part of this chapter assesses the extent of poverty in American society, as well as some efforts to alleviate it.

POVERTY IN THE UNITED STATES

Public concern about poverty became a national issue during the 1960s. In *The Other America* (1963) the socialist writer Michael Harrington shocked the public with his finding that between 40 and 50 million Americans were being denied the bare essentials of food, housing, education, and health care. The discovery of this "other America" led to an enormous increase in government spending on welfare. "This Administration today, here and now," President Lyndon B. Johnson said in his 1967 State of the Union

---

[38] Seymour Martin Lipset, "Equality and Inequality," in *Contemporary Social Problems*, 4th ed., Robert K. Merton and Robert Nisbet, eds. (New York: Harcourt Brace Jovanovich, 1976), p. 319.

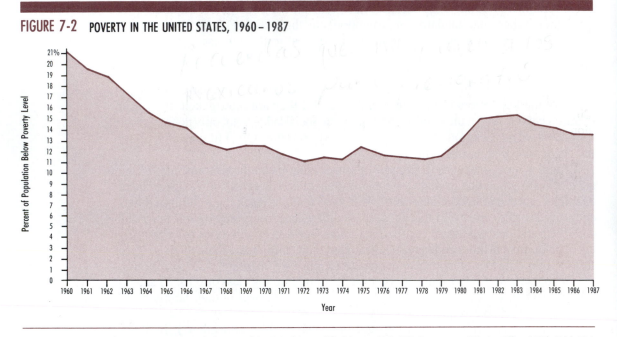

FIGURE 7-2   POVERTY IN THE UNITED STATES, 1960–1987

SOURCE: U.S. Bureau of the Census, *Statistical Abstract of the United States* (Washington, D.C.: U.S. Government Printing Office, 1989), Table 734.

message, "declares unconditional war on poverty in America." In only ten years total spending on social welfare in the United States quadrupled — from $77.2 billion in 1965 to $286.5 billion in 1975. By 1972 welfare payments and Social Security benefits had reduced the official number of poor people from nearly 40 million to about 23 million — the lowest figure in fifteen years.

Between 1980 and 1984, however, the rate of poverty in the United States rose sharply (see Figure 7-2). Median family income, adjusted for inflation, declined from $23,005 in 1979 to $20,885 in 1983 — the largest drop since the Great Depression. In the cities, the ragged homeless became symbols of increasing deprivation and neglect, and a presidential commission concluded that hunger was "a real and significant problem throughout our nation." [39] By the end of 1983 the poverty rate had reached 15.3 percent, the highest level since the "war on poverty" began.

There are several reasons why poverty increased in the early 1980s. As we have already noted, economic changes produced many more low-paying service jobs and many fewer middle-income manufacturing jobs. Workers who were laid off in the steel and textile industries, for example, were often forced into the ranks of the "working poor" — those whose minimum-wage jobs provide incomes below the poverty line. The entry into the labor force of young people born during the post-Second World War

---

[39] Robert Pear, "U.S. Hunger: A New Focus," *The New York Times*, January 12, 1984, p. A27.

baby boom, combined with increasing immigration, made competition for these low-level jobs even tougher.

The rising poverty rate was also linked to a rising rate of divorce. Since most mothers have custody of the children, and since single women generally cannot earn as much as their husbands, the family's income drops dramatically.

These long-term trends were intensified by political developments in the 1980s. Citing welfare abuses and the need to cut domestic spending, the Reagan administration tightened eligibility requirements and reduced social programs for the poor. As a result, a federal unemployment benefits program with an estimated 340,000 recipients was allowed to expire, and over 200,000 were dropped from the rolls of the Supplementary Security Income program alone. Without these cash allowances many more households fell below the official poverty line.

The latest Census Bureau figures paint a slightly brighter picture. In 1987 the rate of poverty was 13.5 percent — the lowest level since 1978. This good news was generally attributed to a strong economic recovery from the 1982 recession, but the bad news was that the new prosperity was unevenly distributed. Even as the median income was rising dramatically, the gap between rich and poor was widening: the average family income of the poorest fifth of the population declined by 6.1 percent between 1979 and 1987, while the family income of the richest fifth increased by 11.1 percent.[40] Furthermore, the earnings gap between blacks and whites continued its steady increase (see Figure 7-3).

---

[40] House Ways and Means Committee, "Background Material and Data on Programs Within the Jurisdiction of the Committee on Ways and Means" (Washington, D.C.: U.S. Government Printing Office, 1989).

MONEY INCOMES OF HOUSEHOLDS, BY RACE: 1970–1987   FIGURE 7-3

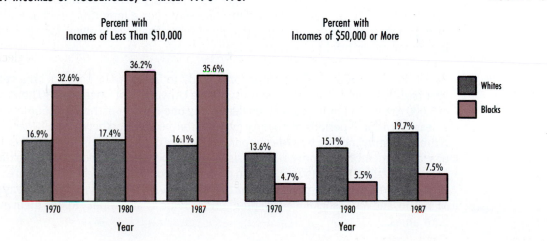

SOURCE: U.S. Bureau of the Census, 1989 Statistical Abstract of the United States (Washington, D.C.: U.S. Government Printing Office: Table 711).

Social welfare has actually done little to reduce inequality in the United States.

WHO IS POOR?

Although the official poverty rate changes from year to year, most Americans think that people with incomes below the poverty line stay poor a long time, perhaps all their lives. A new study found, however, that poverty is usually only a temporary condition lasting for rather brief periods of time.

THE OCCASIONALLY POOR.   The first national study to follow poor families on a year-to-year basis was conducted by economists at the University of Michigan.[41] Their survey of 5,000 American families indicated that nearly one-quarter of the U.S. population had at least occasional periods of poverty over the ten-year period between 1969 and 1978. A drop in family income was the temporary result of divorce, loss of a job, illness, death of a family member, or some other crisis. Since the occasionally poor resemble the rest of the population in most ways, certain groups of people do not seem to be more prone to poverty than other Americans. For these families, unemployment compensation, Medicaid, and other social welfare programs provide a "safety net" to tide them over in hard times.

---

[41] Grey J. Duncan, *Years of Poverty, Years of Plenty: The Changing Economic Fortunes of American Workers and Families* (Ann Arbor: University of Michigan, 1984).

THE PERSISTENTLY POOR.   The same study found that a smaller number of American families are poor for long periods of time. While the occasionally poor are spread rather evenly across the population, the persistently poor are concentrated in certain groups. Over half belong to families headed by women, and a third live in families headed by a black woman. Compared with the occasionally poor, the persistently poor are more likely to live in rural areas, particularly the South. Unlike the rest of the poor they are usually unable to do much about their plight. Some suffer from physical handicaps or mental illness. Others are elderly and still others are the mothers of small children.

THE FEMINIZATION OF POVERTY.   Focusing on the official poverty rate obscures the question of who is poor. More and more the answer is "women and their children." Women are almost twice as likely as men to have incomes below the poverty line, and about two out of five poor people are children.

While poor women in the past were likely to be the wives of poor men, today they are much more likely to be the heads of their own households.[42] A small fraction are unwed teenage mothers — not because there are more teenage pregnancies (these have declined along with the overall birth rate) but because pregnant teenagers today are half as likely to get married. Other poor women are "displaced homemakers" — divorced, deserted, or widowed women who are ineligible for welfare and too young to receive Social Security payments. Still others are elderly women with Social Security benefits below the poverty line. However, most attention has lately been given to the 11 percent of the poor who are female heads of households: the women without husbands who typically have one or two children under 18. Given the fact that only one single mother in three receives any child support at all from the absent father (with the average annual payment at $2,215 in 1985),[43] as well as the obstacles to employment

Lower-class background and educational experiences severely limit poor children's chances of moving up the social ladder.

---

[42] Irwin Garfinkel and Sara McLanahan, *Single Mothers and Their Children* (Washington, D.C.: The Urban Institute Press, 1986).

[43] U.S. Bureau of the Census, "Child Support and Alimony, 1985" (Washington, D.C.: U.S. Government Printing Office, 1987).

(low wages, inadequate child care, lack of job opportunities), most of these women are entirely dependent on help from the Aid to Families with Dependent Children program. These "welfare mothers" are the primary subject of the current welfare debate.

THE WELFARE DEBATE

The great increases in social welfare spending during the 1970s helped establish a minimum standard of living, but they have not eliminated poverty. One reason is that most of the money is spent on programs that benefit people at all income levels, not just the poor. Social Security pensions, veterans' pensions, and unemployment insurance together paid out $383 billion in 1987, or about 38 percent of all government expenditures. Only one-third of this money went to families at the bottom fifth of the income scale. Nevertheless, Social Security has been successful in reducing poverty among the aged.[44]

Second, the amount spent on cash assistance to the poor is rather small. In 1987 social welfare for the poor — Supplementary Security Income (SSI), Aid to Families with Dependent Children (AFDC), food stamps, and Medicaid accounted for only about 8 percent of the federal budget (see Figure 7-4). SSI reaches the blind, the permanently and totally disabled, and the indigent aged. AFDC, the most controversial of all welfare programs, is partially funded by the federal government but administered by the states. The qualifications for AFDC and the size of the payments vary erratically across the country. The maximum benefit California pays a needy family of four is $734 a month (an income that still falls below the poverty line), while Mississippi pays only $144. Since its benefits are set so low, the AFDC program fails in its explicit purpose of supporting children.

Third, social welfare programs do not reach all the poor. Fewer than half the occasionally poor receive any public assistance at all, and only about half of the elderly who are eligible for SSI benefits ever receive them.[45] Many poor people never claim the benefits to which they are entitled because they do not know they are eligible, because they are too proud to "go on relief," or because they are defeated by the intricacies of the application process.

Finally, in-kind aid — or help in acquiring the basic necessities of shelter, food, and health care — can be counted only a limited success. Most states offer a housing subsidy to poor families, but it is still not usually enough to pay the rent. Eligibility for food stamps, one of the most effective aid programs, was drastically reduced by the Reagan administration. Medicare, which lowers medical costs for senior citizens at all income levels, and Medicaid, a program for the poor, have unquestionably improved health care, yet we have seen that the health of the poor is still far worse than average.

In spite of the inadequacy of these efforts to relieve poverty, 43 percent of the American public believes that the government spends too much on welfare.[46] During the 1970s surveys found that four out of five respondents (including 81 percent of

---

[44] Congressional Budget Office, "Poverty Status of Families Under Alternative Definitions Income," Background Paper No. 17 (June 1977); U.S. Bureau of the Census, *Statistical Abstract of the United States, 1989, Table 565.*

[45] C. I. Waxman, *The Stigma of Poverty* (Elmsford, N.Y.: Pergamon, 1977), p. 72.

[46] NORC, *General Social Survey* (Chicago: National Opinion Research Center, University of Chicago, 1988.

SOCIAL WELFARE IN THE UNITED STATES   FIGURE 7-4

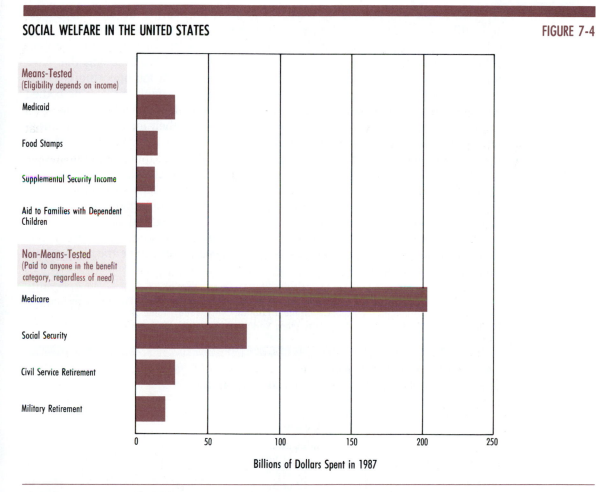

Means-Tested
(Eligibility depends on income)

Medicaid

Food Stamps

Supplemental Security Income

Aid to Families with Dependent Children

Non-Means-Tested
(Paid to anyone in the benefit category, regardless of need)

Medicare

Social Security

Civil Service Retirement

Military Retirement

0   50   100   150   200   250

Billions of Dollars Spent in 1987

SOURCE: Congressional Budget Office

whites and 78 percent of blacks in one study) agreed that "there are too many people receiving welfare who should be working." [47]

In *Losing Ground* (1984)[48] Charles Murray claims that welfare does more harm than good. He argues that the expansion of social welfare in the 1960s — particularly AFDC – encourages illegitimacy and unemployment and discourages self-sufficiency and work. Murray's views were used to justify the Reagan administration's attempts to curb social welfare spending and deny benefits to the "undeserving poor" — those who are thought to prefer living on welfare to working. Like other conservatives, President Reagan was convinced that welfare should be limited to the "truly needy" — the "deserving poor" who are too old or too disabled to help themselves.

[47] Richard D. Coe, "Participation in the Food Stamp Program Among the Poverty Population," in G. J. Duncan and J. N. Morgan, eds., *Five Thousand American Families—Patterns of Economic Progress*, Vol. 7 (Ann Arbor: Institute for Social Research, 1979).

[48] Charles Murray, *Losing Ground: American Social Policy, 1950–80* (New York: Basic Books, 1984).

The trouble with this approach is its assumption that many of the poor can become self-sufficient if they want to. But, as we have just seen, most of the officially poor are self-sufficient most of the time and only become poor occasionally because of unemployment or a family crisis. Most of the persistently poor have problems that have nothing to do with willingness to work—ill health, lack of job opportunities, low wages, responsibility for young children. Another welfare myth is that able-bodied men are loafing on the taxpayers' money, but the fact is that men who can work are excluded from most public assistance no matter how low their incomes are. Willingness to work does not always mean escape from poverty. In 1986, 31 percent of poor families with male heads had at least one member with a full-time, year-round job.[49]

In *The Culture of Inequality* (1978) Michael Lewis suggested that most Americans explain the persistence of poverty by referring to the personal failings or disabilities of the poor. Liberals believe that poverty is caused by lack of skills and other disadvantages; they want to give the poor more education, job training, and family counseling services. Conservatives think that poverty is caused by immoral and irresponsible individuals; they want to cut back government spending on people they believe are unwilling to help themselves.[50]

---

[49] U.S. Bureau of the Census, *Current Population Reports*, Series P-60, No. 160, "Poverty in the United States: 1986" (Washington, D.C.: U.S. Government Printing Office, 1988), Table 20.

[50] Michael Lewis, *The Culture of Inequality* (New York: New American Library/Meridian, 1978).

TABLE 7-3   **THE POOR IN THE UNITED STATES, 1987**
TOTAL NUMBER OF PERSONS BELOW THE POVERTY LINE = 32,546,000

Characteristics	Percentage of the Poor	Characteristics	Percentage of the Poor
Age		Education	
under 18	40	0–11 years	54
18–64	49	12 years	31
65 and over	11	13 or more	15
Race		Work Experience	
white	69	work full-time	24
black	28	work part-time	17
spanish*	16	not working: ill/disabled	13
		not working: housekeeping	18
Sex		not working: in school	10
male	49	not working: cannot find work	6
female	51	not working: retired	10
		not working: other reasons	2
Region		Family Status	
northeast	17	head of family	22
midwest	23	children in families	38
south	41	other family members	17
west	19	not in families	23

*Spanish origin may be any race: thus percentages do not add up to 100%.
SOURCE: U.S. Bureau of the Census, *Money Income and Poverty Status in the United States: 1987.* Current Population Reports, Series P-60, No. 161, 1988. Washington, DC: U.S. Government Printing Office; and Current Population Reports, Series P-60, No. 160, *Poverty in the United States: 1986.*

IDENTIFYING THE POOR

"What is to be done about the poor?" In one form or another, this question has been asked by virtually every politician, clergyman, philosopher, and national leader—not to mention most taxpayers. Although the answers to this age-old dilemma are debated endlessly, we must recognize that they are often based on specific definitions of who is poor and what accounts for poverty.

■ ■ ■

Using the official definition of poverty and Census Bureau survey data, we can outline a quick portrait of the poor (see Table 7-3). These data reveal the following facts.

- Slightly more than one-half (51%) of the poor are younger than the working age or older than the standard retirement age of 65.
- More than two-thirds of all people below the poverty line are white. Poverty is not confined to racial minorities, although they *are* more likely to be poor. One-tenth of whites, slightly more than one-quarter (27%) of Hispanics, and one-third (33%) of blacks are poor.
- The poor are almost evenly split between males and females.
- More than 40 percent of poor people aged 15 and older work, and almost one-quarter of this group works full-time. Work is no salvation from poverty—many jobs pay poverty wages. Having

one full-time minimum-wage worker does not lift a family of three above the poverty line.

- Most of the nonworking poor are unable to work. Eighteen percent of poor people keep house, 6 percent are unable to find work, and the rest cannot work because of illness, age, or school.
- The poor are spread throughout the country, although poverty is worst in the South. Approximately 60 percent of the poor live in urban areas; most of the rest live in rural areas far removed from city ghettos.
- Thirty-eight percent of poor people are children in families. Twenty-three percent live alone or in nonfamily arrangements.
- Twenty-five percent of adult poor have less than eight years of schooling. Almost one-half (46%) have at least a high school education.

■ ■ ■

Keep these facts about poverty in mind as you evaluate the sociological theories about its causes and the government policies that are intended to reduce the poverty rate in the United States. You may find that some of the assumptions we make about the poor do not quite fit the sociological facts.

SOURCE: Steven L. Nock and Paul W. Kingston, *The Sociology of Public Issues*. Belmont, CA: Wadsworth, 1990, p. 73 and 78–80.

These attitudes have lent wide popular support to *workfare,* or programs that require welfare recipients to work or accept job training in return for their benefits. The federal Family Security Act of 1988, for example, requires single parents of children over three years old to participate in either education, job training, or state-organized jobs. According to one of its sponsors, this latest attempt at welfare reform aims to "get these people off the welfare rolls and onto the payrolls."[51] Since most of "these people" are mothers of young children, the bill includes measures to enforce the collection of child support and to underwrite the costs of transportation and child care. Given the modest amount of money appropriated ($3.34 billion), the quality of child care and job training the program will be able to offer is very much in doubt.

Supporters of workfare assume that work is the answer to poverty. We have seen, however, that most welfare recipients cannot work because of age or poor health (see "Identifying the Poor"). Moreover, most studies of workfare programs find that the

---

[51] Andrew Hacker, "Getting Rough on the Poor," *The New York Review of Books* (October 13, 1988), p. 12.

participants would have found jobs anyway, and that the jobs they do find are so badly paid that AFDC payments are reduced by less than 10 percent at best.[52]

Although workfare may be more acceptable to the public than welfare "handouts," poverty in the United States will not be eliminated as long as Americans continue to blame the victims of poverty for their plight. The myth of equal opportunity obscures the fact that the true causes of inequality lie not in individual differences but in an economic and social situation that gives the poor a less-than-equal chance to succeed. Even in a society traditionally considered the land of opportunity, the workings of the stratification system continue to deny many the equality promised by the Declaration of Independence.

---

[52] Marci Jo Williams, "Is Workfare the Answer?" *Fortune* 114 (October, 1986), p. 27, 109.

SUMMARY

1. Stratification is the ranking of members of a society according to the unequal distribution of desirable rewards, which are typically wealth, prestige, and power.

2. Social inequalities are differences among people that are considered important by the society in which they live. Beginning with Marx and Weber, sociologists have argued that the nature of society, not the abilities of individuals, largely determines that some people will be richer or more powerful than others.

3. Marx believed inequality arises from a society's mode of production. In capitalist societies the bourgeoisie profit from the greater productivity of machine technology and the low cost of labor. Marx thought of the bourgeoisie and proletariat as social classes with conflicting interests. The powerful capitalists constitute a ruling class that dominates every aspect of society, including its philosophical beliefs and intellectual life.

4. Weber viewed social inequality as a more complex phenomenon based not only on economic standing but also on relative amounts of prestige and power. He agreed with Marx that wealth is the most important factor, but he believed that cultural values, beliefs, and customs have a separate influence in determining which groups have greater advantages than others.

5. In caste stratification systems, social rank depends primarily on prestige; in estate stratification systems, the social hierarchy is based on relative amounts of power; in class stratification systems, power and prestige are less important than wealth and income.

6. Social rank in the American class system is determined by multiple dimensions of wealth, power, and prestige. Economic inequality is very great: income is concentrated at the top of the economic ladder and 13.5 percent of the population lives on incomes below the official poverty line. Prestige depends largely on individual achievement, and most people are esteemed on the basis of their occupation. Power is the ability to take actions that affect how others will behave. In the United States, power is exercised primarily by large corporations and the government. Special interest groups are often able to influence the political process, but power in American society appears to be distributed among many groups rather than a single ruling elite.

7. The costs of social inequality are paid by disadvantaged groups in poor health, lack of opportunity, unhappiness at home and at work, and low self-esteem.

8. According to one functional theory, inequality is inevitable and necessary to ensure that the most important positions are filled by the most qualified individuals. Critics find that some relatively unrewarded positions are essential, while some highly rewarded positions do not contribute to the survival of society.

9. Conflict theorists argue that inequality exists because some groups are able to exploit and dominate others. In this view inequality is sustained by ideologies that are accepted by rich and poor alike.

10. Economic explanations of inequality focus on the patterns of unemployment caused by the service revolution and the dual labor market.

11. All industrial societies have similarly high rates of social mobility. Industrialization favors upward mobility by distributing more widely the three major determinants of higher status—white-collar occupations, education, and income. Class factors limit educational and occupational opportunities, however, and many advantages and disadvantages are passed from generation to generation through the socialization process.

12. In spite of the expansion of social welfare spending in the 1960s and 1970s, poverty in the United States increased in the early 1980s. Social and economic change, intensified by the Reagan administration's cuts in social programs, caused more families to fall below the official poverty line. Efforts to reduce poverty have had limited success because most social welfare benefits all income levels, public assistance has been ineffective in reaching all the poor, and welfare payments are inadequate.

13. A new study of poor families indicates that one-quarter of the U.S. population has at least occasional periods of poverty. Unlike the occasionally poor, the persistently poor are concentrated in certain groups: women who head their own households, especially black women; children in these families; and residents of rural areas, especially the South.

14. Disapproval of welfare for the "undeserving poor" is based on the false assumption that many poor people could be self-supporting if they wanted to. The truth is that poverty usually has nothing to do with willingness to work. Social inequality will be largely tolerated in the United States as long as most Americans believe that poverty is caused by the personal failings or disabilities of the poor.

KEY TERMS

stratification 190
social inequalities 191
mode of production 192
bourgeoisie 192
proletariat 193

wealth 193
prestige 193
power 193
life chances 193
caste stratification 195

estate stratification 196
class stratification 198
poverty line 200
median income 201
social mobility 210

SUGGESTED READING

* E. Digby Baltzell. *Philadelphia Gentlemen: The Making of a National Upper Class.* New Brunswick, NJ: Transaction Publications, 1989.

Reinhard Bendix and Seymour M. Lipset, eds. *Class, Status, and Power: A Reader in Stratification.* Rev. ed. New York: Free Press, 1966.

* Sheldon H. Danziger and Daniel H. Weinberg, eds. *Fighting Poverty: What Works and What Doesn't.* Cambridge, MA: Harvard University Press, 1987.

* David T. Ellwood, *Poor Support: Poverty in the American Family.* New York: Basic Books, 1989.

* Irwin Garfinkel and Sara McLanahan, *Single Mothers and Their Children: A New American Dilemma.* Washington, DC: The Urban Institute Press, 1986.

Christopher Jencks et al. *Who Gets Ahead?* New York: Basic, 1979.

* Gerhard Lenski. *Power and Privilege: A Theory of Social Stratification.* Chapel Hill, NC: University of North Carolina Press, 1984.

* Jonathan Cobb and Richard Sennett, *The Hidden Injuries of Class.* New York: Random House, 1973.

* Lester Thurow. *The Zero-Sum Society.* New York: Simon and Schuster/Touchstone Books, 1986.

---

* Available in paperback.

Morality is the custom of one's country and the current feeling of one's peers. Cannibalism is moral in a cannibal country.

Samuel Butler

CHAPTER 8

DEVIANCE AND SOCIAL CONTROL

A few years ago, *The Wall Street Journal* commissioned a Gallup poll entitled "Ethics in America." The survey compared the moral beliefs and behavior of business executives with the general public's. Some of the *Journal's* editors must have been startled by the results (see Table 8-1). A large majority of executives admitted to stealing office supplies, making personal long-distance calls on their company's telephones, and driving while drunk. Of the executives under 50 years of age, 29 percent had smoked marijuana and 41 percent said they had cheated on their income tax. Lying, pilfering, and illegal drug use also appear to be common among the general public.[1]

The sociological term for any illegal, immoral, or merely eccentric behavior is **deviance**. Deviance is usually defined as any significant departure from social norms. It is important to note that deviant behavior is not necessarily good or bad; the saint and the sinner are both social deviants because both are violating the norms of their society. Deviance includes acts that are merely unconventional, such as going barefoot on city streets, as well as serious social problems, such as crime and drug abuse.

---

[1] *The Wall Street Journal*, October 31, 1983, pp. 33, 42.

TABLE 8-1   **DEVIANCE IN AMERICAN SOCIETY**

Activity	Percent Who Have Ever Done Each Activity	
	Business Executives	General Public
Taken home work supplies	74%	40%
Called in sick to work when not ill	14	31
Used company telephones for personal long-distance calls	78	15
Overstated deductions somewhat on tax form	35	13
Driven while drunk	80	33
Smoked marijuana	17	25
Used cocaine	2	8

SOURCE: *The Wall Street Journal*, October 31, 1983, p. 33.

The sociological definition of deviance calls our attention to the fact that societies do not regard all nonconformity as harmful. In fact, social groups choose which kinds of deviance to punish and which to tolerate. The use of heroin is legal and acceptable in Italy, for example, but illegal and strongly condemned in the United States. Americans who use other addictive and harmful drugs, such as alcohol and nicotine, are still generally tolerated and even encouraged through advertising to do so. The definition of who and what is deviant is always socially determined.

Social control refers to the practices all societies adopt to enforce conformity. People who violate the norms of their society risk being frowned upon, beaten up, imprisoned, and even killed. Yet in every society some people continue to break the rules and everyone occasionally bends them a little.

Students of society are interested in deviance for two reasons. First, the existence of any social group depends on conformity to its norms. If people could not rely on others to drive on the right side of the road, then all traffic would soon come to a halt. Similarly, members of a society rely on people to do other things: pay their taxes, do an honest day's work, tell the truth, and so on. By studying the reasons why some people depart from these social expectations, sociologists hope to learn more about why most people conform to them. Second, social scientists are interested in certain kinds of deviance because they want to reduce or eliminate them. Knowing what causes deviant behavior makes it easier to find practical means of preventing crime and the other forms of deviance that are considered threatening to society.

This chapter begins by discussing the kinds of rules that define deviance and then presents the main sociological theories explaining why some people break them. The sociological insights of the first two sections are next applied to an understanding of crime, the most disturbing form of deviance. A concluding section suggests how the sociological perspective can help public policy makers deal with crime and other forms of deviant behavior.

DEFINING DEVIANCE

No behavior is inherently deviant. What appears weird and unnatural to some people frequently seems normal and sensible to others. Each group regards its own way of doing things as normal and finds departures from its own particular norms abnormal, or deviant.

We can all probably think of exotic or extreme forms of behavior that are not considered deviant in some cultures. Cannibalism, for example, although shocking to us, was a conventional religious practice among the Aztecs. Polygamy, the practice of having more than one spouse at a time, is still officially acceptable for Moslems. While women in India wear jewelry in their noses and men in New Guinea paint themselves blue, Americans of both sexes dye their hair and suntan their skins in order to look their best. Even more interesting than the differences between cultures, perhaps, is the fact that deviance is also relative to its social setting *within* each culture.

In the history of the United States, differing standards of conduct have contributed to conflicts between religious groups (Protestants and Mormons in the Midwest), racial

The question of who and what is deviant is a matter of social definition. In 1922 these women were arrested for wearing "abbreviated" bathing suits on a Chicago beach.

groups (whites and the Chinese in California), age groups (youthful protest marchers and older supporters of the status quo), and sex groups (feminists and the male establishment). Dominant groups have an advantage in the struggle over *whose* behavior will be officially accepted as normal, for they are usually able to have their views of acceptable conduct written into law. Laws regarding the age at which young people can get married or buy liquor are not geared to adolescent sexual behavior or drinking customs but to adults' ideas of what is right and proper. Similarly, in most societies men have usually decided how women should behave and upper- and middle-class legislators have written the laws that every citizen must obey. Once the dominant group's norms are made into laws, then another group's departures from these norms become *crimes*.

R. F. Bales has described how nineteenth-century Irish immigrants to America brought with them cultural traditions supporting the heavy use of alcohol.[2] Too poor to marry and have a family, yet forbidden by the Catholic church to have sexual relations outside of marriage, a large number of young Irishmen were kept dependent on their parents and sexually deprived throughout adulthood. In the Irish culture frequent heavy drinking was a socially acceptable outlet for male hostility and frustration. Hard drinking became identified with "being a man."[3]

While he may not have been generally regarded as deviant in his own ethnic subculture, the drunken Irishman was condemned as shiftless and irresponsible by other Americans. The temperance movement largely represented the views of rural American Protestants, who saw drinking as a defiance of norms that were important to them — sobriety, industry, responsibility.[4] Their particular norms were enforced against other subcultures not only by the **informal sanctions** of public disapproval, but also by **formal** (legal) **sanctions.** Protestant clergymen preached against the sins of drink and the depravity of the drunkard, and state legislators passed blue laws limiting and regulating the sale of alcohol. A similar situation has existed in recent years, with laws against marijuana use directed not so much against the drug as against the user, reflecting opposition to a youthful, pleasure-seeking subculture.[5] Once again, the same behavior (smoking pot) that is expected and approved in one subculture (rebellious youth) is being condemned as deviant by other subcultures (older, more conservative groups). As these examples show, deviance from one group's norms is often conformity to another's.

TYPES OF NORMS

Definitions of deviant behavior depend not only on *whose* rule is being broken but also on *which* rule it is. We react with ridicule when a quarterback drops the ball (dumb klutz!), with anger when another driver cuts ahead of us in line (rude so-and-so!), and

---

[2] Robert Freed Bales, "Cultural Differences in Rates of Alcoholism," *Quarterly Journal of Studies on Alcohol* 6 (March 1946): 480–99.

[3] Richard Stivers, *A Hair of the Dog: Irish Drinking and American Stereotype* (University Park: Pennsylvania State University Press, 1976), Chapter 5.

[4] J. R. Gusfield, *Symbolic Crusade: Status Politics and the Temperance Movement* (Urbana, Ill.: University of Illinois Press, 1963).

[5] Elane Nuehring and Gerald E. Markle, "Nicotine and Norms: The Re-emergence of a Deviant Behavior," *Social Problems* 21:4 (April 1974): 513–14.

with outrage when a mugger attacks an old woman (filthy animal!). The varying reactions indicate that different kinds of norms are being violated.

Violations of folkways are not regarded as vitally important, and these everyday customs are enforced by such informal social controls as gossip and ridicule. Nevertheless, people who fail to use proper manners can be punished with social disapproval: they may not be asked to join a sorority or they may be turned down for a job.

Mores, however, are norms that a group considers essential to its well-being. Breaking these rules is thus a more serious matter, and the punishment for doing so is more severe. American history shows over and over that people who go against the mores of a particular group frequently risk financial loss and sometimes physical harm. Because they violated the norms of the group in which they found themselves, sheepherders have been driven out of cattle country, radicals have been blacklisted from government jobs, and northern civil rights workers have been attacked and murdered in segregated areas of the South.

Finally, **laws** are norms that are enforced by the formal sanctions of the state. Violations of the laws against rape, murder, and treason are considered so threatening to society that they are punished by long imprisonment and even death. Although laws are influenced by the prevailing mores (laws against prostitution and burglary) and folkways (laws against public nudity and littering), they can be independent of such popular sentiments and traditions. Many laws — including tax laws, fire codes, and traffic regulations — are on the books simply for the sake of enforcing an administrative rule.

TYPES OF VIOLATORS

As we have seen, ordinary citizens sometimes engage in illegal behavior, and most people occasionally deviate from social norms without getting into serious trouble. In fact, if you are a typical American, you have probably committed a crime for which you could have been imprisoned. Far from being rare and abnormal, deviant behavior appears to be a fact of everyday social life.

As these advertisements from a California newspaper indicate, deviance is a rather "normal" part of everyday life.

Although everyone deviates from social norms at one time or another, distinctions are made between different kinds of violators as well as between different kinds of norms. Also, not everyone is held equally responsible for deviant acts. Youthful age, mental incompetence, and insanity are all excuses in the eyes of the law and the general public. Extreme circumstances can also excuse violators. The marooned survivors of a plane crash in the Andes who ate their dead companions were not considered "real" cannibals but victims of a life-or-death ordeal.

Perhaps the most important distinction between different types of violators relates to the motives for their behavior. Robert K. Merton used the terms **nonconforming behavior** and **aberrant behavior** to describe the two principal types of deviance. Draft resisters in the 1960s, for example, were nonconformers. They publicized their cause by burning their draft cards in front of television cameras. Draft dodgers in the 1940s were aberrants: they hid from government officials and tried to escape public attention. Nonconformers challenge the legitimacy of the norms they reject and attempt to change them, voluntarily risking punishment. Unauthorized protest marches, sit-down strikes, and work slowdowns are some examples of nonconforming behavior. People who engage in aberrant behavior are chiefly concerned with escaping public notice and consequent punishment.

Nonconforming behavior and aberrant behavior bring different social reactions. Conventional people usually admit, however reluctantly, that nonconformers are not acting purely for personal gain but for some moral principle. Hardly anyone has this view of aberrant behavior, which is almost always motivated by self interest.[6]

SOCIAL CONSEQUENCES OF DEVIANCE

Not all deviance is destructive or criminal. Such nonconformers as Mahatma Gandhi and Martin Luther King, Jr., may have been called common criminals by their enemies, but they led social movements that changed their societies in ways that are generally viewed as beneficial. Social change can also make today's deviant into tomorrow's conformist. "Career women" were considered deviant when few women worked outside the home; today, with a large proportion of married women in the work force, some groups feel that choosing to be "just a housewife" is deviant. Such long-term considerations are yet another way of classifying deviant acts.

SUMMARY

Behavior is defined as deviant if it departs from a group's norms. It is called unconventional, immoral, or criminal deviance depending on whether the norms violated are folkways, mores, or laws. Deviance may be excused if special characteristics of the violator and the situation are taken into account. According to how its social consequences are evaluated, deviance can be considered constructive rather than destructive. Having explored the various ways of perceiving deviant behavior, we now turn to the major theories explaining its prevalence in society.

---

[6] Robert K. Merton, "The Sociology of Social Problems," in *Contemporary Social Problems*, 4th ed., eds. Robert K. Merton and Robert Nisbet (New York: Harcourt Brace Jovanovich, 1976), pp. 29–30.

THE CAUSES OF DEVIANCE

Explaining deviant behavior is complicated by the fact that there are many more ways to deviate from a norm than to conform to it. There is only one correct way to stop for a red light, for example, but there are many ways of *not* stopping: speeding through a red light while driving drunk, running through it in the middle of the night when there are no other cars on the road, roaring through it in a fire engine, and so on. Theories of deviance must account for the actions of every type of offender — from alcoholics and suicides to bank robbers, terrorists, and vandals — all of whom appear to have little in common apart from their deviance. Sociological theories focus on the circumstances that give rise to deviance. Biological and psychological theories, however, attempt to explain the reasons certain individuals commit deviant acts. These theories might be called kinds-of-people theories, and we shall look first at them.

KINDS-OF-PEOPLE THEORIES

> Psychopathy, possibly more than any other mental disorder, threatens the safety, the serenity, and the security of American life. From the ranks of the psychopaths come political demagogues, the most violent criminals, the riot leaders, sexual misfits, and drug addicts.[7]

To many observers, the causes of deviance seem simple enough: because ordinary, sensible people do not cheat or steal, people who do must not be ordinary and sensible. There must be something wrong with them. To test this assumption, much research over the years has been devoted to finding out if there is such a thing as the "born criminal" and the "criminal mind."

BIOLOGICAL EXPLANATIONS.   Cesare Lombroso, an Italian physician working in the 1870s, developed the theory that criminals are a biologically inferior lot.[8] He believed that dangerous offenders could be identified by peculiar physical traits, especially the primitive shape of their skulls.

Although Lombroso's theory has been completely discredited, the scientific search for a biological explanation of deviance has continued.[9] Researchers have examined family histories to find out whether criminal traits might be inherited. The famous study of the Jukes family discovered that its 1,200 members included 140 criminals.[10] A comparison study of the descendants of Jonathan Edwards, a colonial American preacher, failed to turn up a single criminal. Instead, the Edwards family included presidents of the United States and justices of the Supreme Court, as well as many well-known writers, judges, and clergymen. This particular comparison, however, had a fatal flaw: some of Jonathan Edwards's *ancestors* had been convicted of crimes. If

---

[7] William McCord and Joan McCord, *Psychopathy and Delinquency* (New York: Grune & Stratton, 1956).
[8] Cesare Lombroso, *Crime: Its Causes and Remedies* (Boston: Little, Brown, 1911).
[9] See Robert K. Merton and Ashley Montagu, "Crime and the Anthropologist," *Advances in Forensic Psychology and Psychiatry*, 1 (1984): 147–70.
[10] Richard Dugdale, *The Jukes, A Study in Crime, Pauperism and Heredity* (New York: Putnam, 1877); A. H. Estabrook, *The Jukes in 1915* (Washington, D.C.: Carnegie Institution, 1916).

criminal traits are inherited, then some of his descendants should have been criminals too.[11] Moreover, it is nearly impossible to separate inherited characteristics from social experience. While children in the Jukes family grew up among thieves and prostitutes, children in the Edwards family were raised by judges and preachers. Under these conditions who can tell whether heredity or environment is more conducive to crime?

In the 1940s William H. Sheldon claimed that there was a connection between a muscular, energetic physique and delinquent behavior.[12] Sheldon assumed that delinquents were inferior to nondelinquents and that this inferiority was inherited. Critics who made a close inspection of his data found that Sheldon's findings failed to justify these conclusions. On the contrary, delinquents do not appear to be physically much different from nondelinquents, and their physical inferiority is unproven. Moreover, Sheldon's critics suggested, strong and energetic boys may be attracted to delinquent gang activities for the same reason that they are attracted to competitive team sports — because they are good at them.[13]

Interest in biological theories of criminality was revived by the discovery that Richard Speck, who murdered eight student nurses in Chicago in 1966, had an extra Y chromosome. Normal males have an XY chromosome combination, but some violent criminals were subsequently found to have an XYY pattern. Although most men who have this extra Y chromosome appear to be law-abiding citizens, one study found an unusual number of XYY males among prison populations. However, further research failed to find evidence that XYY males are more inclined to crime and violence than normal males. Studies with larger samples have not turned up a disproportionate number of XYY males in prisons, and Speck was later discovered to have a normal XY pattern after all.[14]

Biological inheritance does appear to be a factor in mental illness. Studies of identical twins who were raised apart have found a genetic tendency toward schizophrenia and depressive disorders.[15] Other scientists are attempting to find out whether there is any inherited disposition to alcoholism, drug abuse, and aggressive and impulsive acts. Although researchers continue to explore the possibility that deviant behavior can be inherited, there is still no proof that biological factors necessarily lead to social deviance as it is usually defined.

PSYCHOLOGICAL EXPLANATIONS.   Other kinds-of-people theories point to the psychological causes of deviance. When we say that criminals must be "crazy" or "sick," we are suggesting psychological reasons for deviant behavior.

According to classical Freudian theory, social behavior is motivated by basic biological drives (the id), socialized experience (the superego), and intellectual capacity (the ego). The demands of the id for physical gratification are curbed by the superego, which acts as the instrument of social control, and by the ego, which represents the

[11] Edwin H. Sutherland and Donald R. Cressey, *Principles of Criminology*, 5th ed. (Chicago: Lippincott, 1955), pp. 98–99.
[12] William H. Sheldon et al., *Varieties of Delinquent Youth* (New York: Harper & Row, 1949).
[13] Albert K. Cohen, *Deviance and Control* (Englewood Cliffs, N.J.: Prentice-Hall, 1966), pp. 51–53.
[14] Herman A. Witkin et al., "Criminality in XYY and XXY Men," *Science* 193 (August 1979): 547–55.
[15] D. M. Barnes, "Schizophrenia Genetics a Mixed Bag," *Science* 242 (November 1988): 1009.

ability to make rational judgments. If early childhood socialization does not proceed normally, the theory does, the superego will be defective and the individual will not develop conventional moral standards. If the superego fails to develop at all, the result is a "psychopathic personality," or a completely amoral person.

Psychological theories provide a plausible explanation for some of the spectacular crimes we read about in the newspapers. When James Huberty, an unemployed security guard, shot 21 strangers to death in a McDonald's restaurant in California in 1984, for example, the causes of his behavior appeared to be mainly psychological. One of the reasons such mass-murder cases are sensational, however, is that they are so rare. In comparison to Huberty's behavior, most deviance is quite unspectacular, even commonplace. Ordinary crimes like auto theft and burglary are not the obvious result of mental illness. Indeed, much deviance is actually a rational response to need: a prostitute makes more money than a typist; an army deserter runs to save his life; a building contractor bribes a fire inspector to escape a fine. Many criminals do show symptoms of mental illness after they are caught, but it is hard to say whether mental illness is the cause of their deviance or the result of their arrest and imprisonment. It may also be that psychologically incapacitated criminals are more likely to be found out and arrested than sane lawbreakers.

The behavior of these men would not seem strange to other bodybuilders. Deviance from one group's rules of conduct is often conformity to another's.

Another difficulty with psychological theories is that individuals engage in deviant behavior only in certain situations. Even professional criminals deviate from social norms only some of the time. The con man can be a good father and the gangster a regular Democrat. Many convicted criminals have otherwise been models of decorum and self-control as public officials, corporate executives, doctors, and bank officers. All in all, psychological theories explain only a small percentage of all deviant behavior.

Instead of seeking the causes of deviance in differences among individuals, sociologists look for differences among the social situations in which deviance occurs. Sociological explanations do not replace psychological explanations; rather, they answer different questions about the same kinds of behavior.

DEVIANCE AS CONFORMITY

(Johnny, a fence for stolen goods,) used to tell us a whole lot of things that we didn't know about. He told us how to steal furs and what to do with them afterward, how to steal silver, and how to go downtown to the places where few Negroes went and steal stuff. Johnny told us how to dress. He'd tell us things about looking like a delivery boy when you went down on Park Avenue to steal something or looking like a working boy when you went down to the garment center to steal things. He knew a lot about stealing and all kinds of crime.[16]

While kinds-of-people theories hold that abnormal people behave in abnormal ways, social learning theories stress that ordinary people learn to be deviant in ordinary

---

[16] Claude Brown, *Manchild in the Promised Land* (New York: New American Library/Signet, 1965), p. 118.

ways. As we have seen, deviance from one group's standards is often conformity to another's. It follows that people can learn deviant behavior in the same way they learn conforming behavior — from other people.

Edwin H. Sutherland, a leading member of the "Chicago school" of American sociology, proposed a general theory of criminal behavior based on the concept of **differential association,** or membership in deviant groups. If the people with whom we associate, especially our best friends, define certain laws as "stupid" or unimportant, then we tend to take their definitions as our own. Sutherland's principle of differential association states that a person will become a criminal if he or she is surrounded by more definitions favorable to breaking the law than definitions unfavorable to breaking it.

Sutherland's theory of differential association is firmly grounded in major sociological theories of socialization and social learning. When members of a peer group approve of certain activities — whether it is a group of salespeople padding their expense accounts or a college football team taking steroids — new members of the group tend to adopt the same attitudes and behavior. People who disobey minor rules by telling "little white lies" or by exceeding the speed limit, as well as people who commit major crimes, have often learned such behavior from their friends and associates.

The strength of the differential association theory is that it explains why psychologically healthy people engage in "crazy" behavior — why they vandalize public buildings, for instance, or experiment with dangerous drugs. Such learning theories explain how normal individuals become deviant by associating with deviant groups, but they do not explain how these groups developed in the first place.

DEVIANCE AND OPPORTUNITY STRUCTURES

> I was about fifteen, going on sixteen. I was sitting in a coffee shop in the Village, and a friend of mine came by. She said: "I've got a cab waiting. Hurry up. You can make fifty dollars in twenty minutes." . . . We took a cab to midtown Manhattan, we went to a penthouse. The guy up there was quite well known. . . . It was barely sex. . . . He barely touched me and we were finished. . . .
>
> It was a tremendous kick. Here I was doing absolutely nothing, feeling nothing, and in twenty minutes I was going to walk out with fifty dollars in my pocket. That just made me feel absolutely marvelous. . . . How many people could make fifty dollars for twenty minutes' work? Folks work for eighty dollars take-home pay. I worked twenty minutes for fifty dollars clear, no taxes, no nothing! . . . It was terrific.[18]

According to Merton's **theory of anomie and opportunity structures,** the rate of deviant behavior is higher in situations where people have little chance of achieving their ambitions through legitimate means and thus turn to illegitimate means of getting what they want. The discrepancy between what people want and what they can get creates social pressures that lead to deviance.[19]

---

[17] Sutherland and Cressey, *Principles of Criminology,* Chapter 4.

[18] Roberta Victor, prostitute, quoted in Studs Terkel, *Working* (New York: Pantheon, 1974), pp. 57–59.

[19] Robert K. Merton, *Social Theory and Social Structure,* rev. and enl. ed. (New York: Free Press, 1968), Chapters 6 and 7.

What do people want? Usually, they want to have whatever their culture defines as worth having; in other words, they want to achieve success. In American culture the paths to success are supposed to be a good education and a job with a "future." Merton believes, however, that the strong emphasis on material success in American culture is not always linked with individuals' access to the conventional means of "making it." When, as football coach Vince Lombardi put it, "winning is the only thing," it matters little how the game is won.

In describing this situation, Merton used Durkheim's term, "anomie," to refer to the normless state that results from the conflict between culture and social structure. The usual norms of behavior lose their force, he found, when culturally valued goods (money, material comfort, success) are incompatible with access to the socially approved means of achieving them (a professional degree, a good job). In the American ideology, everyone can succeed, no matter what his or her station in life may be. The fact is, of course, that most people have only limited chances of becoming rich.

Some groups have even less chance of achieving success than others. Compared to their middle-class counterparts, lower-class persons generally have fewer opportunities to get an advanced education, join a profession, and get a desirable job (see Chapter 7, "Social Inequality"). The opportunity structure of society gives the poor little hope of success. In a society where "getting ahead" and "making it" are widely accepted goals, large numbers of people are denied the opportunity to achieve them. Their failure, Merton found, is doubly painful. Not only can they not enjoy the comforts of affluence and social prestige; they are also likely to be personally blamed for being poor and good-for-nothing. In this situation the temptation to succeed by any means is strong and the probability of deviance is higher (see "Deviance and Conformity in the Struggle for Success").

Merton's theory deals with the opportunity structure for achieving cultural goals in conventional ways. There is also an opportunity structure for achieving the same goals in deviant ways. Just as people in certain places in the social structure have limited access to legitimate opportunities, they also have limited access to illegitimate opportunities. A lower-class child in a big city, for example, has many more opportunities to learn the ways of criminals and drug addicts than a lower-class child in a small town. Just as accountants have more opportunities to embezzle and politicians have more opportunities to take graft, people living in high-crime neighborhoods have more opportunities to join a burglary ring, push drugs, or run a numbers racket.

Richard A. Cloward and Lloyd E. Ohlin combined Merton's and Sutherland's theories in their research on delinquent gangs. The members of the gangs they studied all had very limited chances of achieving success legitimately. Their responses to this situation varied according to the kinds of illegitimate means available. Wherever a criminal organization existed, delinquency took the form of shoplifting and other types of petty theft. Fences for stolen goods, bail bondsmen, and older criminals provided the necessary market, protection, and training. In a disorganized slum that lacked this kind of criminal structure, however, the delinquent subculture was marked by vandalism and gang warfare.[20] As Albert K. Cohen noted in another study, success in this type of

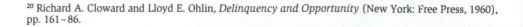

[20] Richard A. Cloward and Lloyd E. Ohlin, *Delinquency and Opportunity* (New York: Free Press, 1960), pp. 161–86.

DEVIANCE AND CONFORMITY IN THE STRUGGLE FOR SUCCESS

Most Americans strive to get ahead, to make lots of money, and thus to achieve success. Some of us do reach these goals, but many do not. What happens to the people who fail to "make it"? According to Robert K. Merton's theory of anomie and opportunity structures, people react in various ways when their paths to success are blocked.

Some people never give up. They continue to strive for success by working hard and denying themselves material comforts. They remain "poor but honest." When both the cultural goals (money and success) and the legitimate means of access to them (hard work and self-denial) are accepted, the result is *conformity.*

There are also a number of deviant adaptations available to people who cannot make it by legitimate means. The first is *innovation,* or acceptance of the goal but rejection of the approved means of attaining it. Innovative behavior includes armed robbery, drug trafficking, or any other offense aimed at material gain. The incidence of this sort of deviance is likely to be high in disadvantaged groups, where lack of education and occupational skills limit the chances to succeed. It may be as frequent, however, in higher-income groups striving to achieve or maintain an affluent life style. In these groups innovative behavior is more likely to take the form of tax evasion, insider trading, or fraud.

Merton used the term *ritualism* to describe rejection of culturally defined ambitions combined with compulsive attachment to social rules. Although ritualistic people realize that they are never going to be very successful, they go through the motions anyway. Such behavior is often not defined as deviant.

Retreatism refers to a situation in which the individual gives up commitment to both the cultural goals and the socially accepted means of achieving them. When success of any kind seems hopelessly remote and inaccessible, some people give up the struggle entirely. Alcoholics, drug addicts, derelicts, and other "dropouts" fall into this category.

Rebellion involves the creation of both a new set of goals and a new means of attaining them. Rejection of competition for material success has characterized some political, social, and religious movements, including communism and early Christianity. Rebellion also includes some political crimes, such as terrorist hijackings and kidnappings, which attempt to overthrow governments or bring about social change by force.

SOURCE: Based on Robert K. Merton, *Social Theory and Social Structure,* rev. and enl. ed. (New York: Free Press, 1968), pp. 193–211.

delinquent subculture had been redefined in terms that lower-class boys could meet: physical strength, "street smarts," and the courage to hang tough in defiance of authority. The criminal activities of these gangs were carried out not so much for gain as to express contempt for respectable, middle-class society. Without any effective adult controls, criminal or legitimate, delinquency in this situation was typically wild, unpredictable, and violent.[21]

Another retreatist type of delinquency is drug addiction. The necessary condition here is access to a steady supply of illegal drugs from dealers and users. Cloward and Ohlin speculated that lower-class adolescents turn to drugs when they are losers in both the law-abiding and criminal worlds. When both legitimate and illegitimate opportunities are severely restricted, retreatists adapt to this double failure by abandoning the cultural goals and any effort, criminal or otherwise, to achieve them.

Given the emphasis on "winning" in American culture, it is not surprising that even the most successful sometimes resort to deviant behavior in order to stay on top. Entertainers who use cocaine before a performance, Olympic athletes who take

[21] Albert K. Cohen, *Delinquent Boys* (New York: Free Press, 1955).

According to Robert Merton's theory of anomie and opportunity structures, some people turn to deviant behavior when legitimate paths to success are blocked. During the 1983 riots in Miami, looters tried innovation to acquire the goods they could not afford to buy (*top*). The bag lady has made a retreatist adaptation to continual failure (*center*). MOVE, a radical antiestablishment group in Philadelphia, resorted to rebellion to achieve their revolutionary goals (*bottom*).

steroids, and Wall Street arbitrageurs who manipulate stock prices are all highly successful people who violate social norms rather than accept the risk of failure.

Since its original publication in 1938, Merton's theory of anomie has been the most influential single explanation of deviance. Besides making a plausible connection between crime and its social setting, Merton's argument that the causes of deviance may be found not in the individual personality but in social structures is sociologically convincing. One strength of his theory is that it explains both individual and group deviance. Groups as well as individuals fall into Merton's categories: there are innovative groups, such as the Mafia and the Iran-Contra conspirators; ritualistic groups such as the Amish and the Moral Majority; retreatist groups, such as the Hare Krishna; and rebellious groups, such as the Italian Red Brigade and the Irish Republican Army.

Anomie theory also takes into account most forms of deviance, from armed robbery and political corruption to prostitution and suicide. The question that social structural theories neglect, however, is why the legitimate opportunities are so limited for certain groups.

LABELING DEVIANCE

> The enemy (the Protestant British government) sits in mahogany rooms and makes up rules. By their rules they declare their legality to colonize people who don't want to be colonized, rules to conduct warfare by, rules to legally starve people to death, rules to carry out whatever they want to carry out. They say, with enormous pride, these rules come from the Mother of Parliaments so obviously they must be right and anyone who goes against these rules must be wrong. We are expected, as a subject people, to live by their rules, fight by their rules, and obey their rules. . . . Now, according to their rules, we are depraved . . . killers, fanatics, anarchists, gunmen, or whatever scum they so designate, and therefore fit to be destroyed by their self-declared legality.[22]

The **labeling theory** of deviance, first developed by Edwin M. Lemert and Howard S. Becker,[23] focuses on the rule makers rather than on the rule breakers. Becker argued that powerful groups are able to force other groups to conform to their norms and to impose their definitions of deviance on people who do not necessarily share the same point of view. Taking the conflict theorists' perspective, Becker found that these imposed definitions of acceptable behavior also serve the interests of the rich and powerful. By and large, rules are made by older people for younger ones, by men for women, by the ethnic majority for minorities, and by the middle classes for the poor.

According to labeling theory, the prejudices and class biases of those who enforce the law help define who and what is deviant. The official classification of certain young offenders as "delinquent" — with all that that label implies for the individuals' future — seems to be not so much a matter of what they have done as how they are perceived by police officers and judges. In his analysis of the juvenile justice system, Aaron Cicourel concluded that the delinquent's demeanor is more important than the offense committed in determining the outcome of the case. When probation officers describe a female adolescent shoplifter as a "punk" or a "bitch," she is likely to end up in a reformatory. On the other hand, if a girl arrested for shoplifting is described as "appealing and attractive," if she is "friendly" and "wants very much to be liked," she is more likely to be perceived as a nice child who is having a few problems. Instead of being sent to a reformatory, she will probably be sent home or referred for psychiatric counseling. Instead of the label "thief" she will be given the label "mixed-up kid." [24]

Several studies have also shown that the police frequently single out certain individuals for arrest while ignoring others. Older juveniles, members of known delinquent gangs, blacks, youths who dress like "tough guys," and suspects who do not show what is considered proper respect for the police tend to be more harshly treated.[25]

---

[22] Long Dan Sweeney, a fictional Irish revolutionary. Leon Uris, *Trinity* (New York: Doubleday, 1976), p. 465.
[23] Edwin M. Lemert, *Social Pathology* (New York: McGraw-Hill, 1951); Howard S. Becker, *Outsiders* (New York: Free Press, 1963).
[24] Aaron Cicourel, *The Social Organization of Juvenile Justice* (New York: Wiley, 1968), pp. 131–32.
[25] Irving Piliavin and Scott Briar, "Police Encounters with Juveniles," *American Journal of Sociology* 69 (September 1964): 206–14.

Clean-cut boys from middle-class families, on the other hand, are less likely to be arrested for the same minor infractions of the law. William Chambliss's study of two gangs, called the "Saints" and the "Roughnecks," found that "not-so-well-dressed, not-so-well-mannered, not-so-rich boys" run a greater risk than others of being labeled juvenile delinquents.[26]

The Saints came from upper-middle-class families and made good grades in high school. They liked to sneak out of class and get together for their own kind of fun: drinking, reckless driving, breaking into empty houses, and stealing things "for the hell of it." Although their favorite activities were all illegal, not one of the Saints was ever officially arrested for delinquent behavior. Members of the gang were stopped by the police only twice in two years; when caught, they were apologetic and respectful and were treated as harmless pranksters. Like the rest of the community, the police labeled them as basically good boys who got a little wild sometimes.

The Roughnecks came from lower-class backgrounds and did not do well in school. Since they could not afford to buy cars, they were usually found hanging around the local drugstore drinking from hidden bottles. Like the Saints, they stole things. The gang was in constant trouble with the police, and its members were frequently arrested. When caught, the Roughnecks were openly hostile and defiant. They got a reputation for being bad boys headed for trouble.

As adults, the Saints and the Roughnecks lived up to the community's expectations of them. Almost all the Saints went on to college and white-collar jobs, while most of the Roughnecks ended up in low-paying occupations or took up criminal careers. The fate of the Saints and the Roughnecks is a perfect demonstration of the labeling theory of deviance.

Once convicted for a crime, the labeling theory goes, a person risks being stigmatized as a criminal and therefore considered untrustworthy and immoral. A deviant reputation, whether or not it is justified, tends to be a self-fulfilling prophecy: it produces further criminal behavior by closing off opportunities to conform. A person who wears the label "homosexual" or "mentally ill" or "alcoholic" has a harder time getting a job and becoming accepted by respectable people. Since our own identity is affected by what others think of us, known offenders begin to live up to what people expect, becoming the "queer" or the "drunk" that others believe them to be. **Primary deviance**, or the original deviant act, becomes **secondary deviance**, or the deviant identity and way of life.

The labeling perspective is useful in several ways. It shifts attention away from the conditions that cause deviance to the processes that sustain it. It suggests that there is an important difference between engaging in deviant activities and being identified as a deviant individual and that this difference is largely defined by other people. By analyzing not just what the offender has done but also the response of others to the offense, labeling theory emphasizes social controls. It indicates that class factors partly determine the definition of deviant behavior and the designation of certain people as deviant.

Labeling theory does not work as an exclusive explanation of deviant behavior. Labeling theorists are not concerned with the rates of different kinds of deviance, nor

---

[26] William J. Chambliss, "The Saints and the Roughnecks," *Society* 11 (December 11, 1973): 24–31.

with the motivation for performing deviant acts in the first place. Furthermore, labeling analysis ignores the many occasions when deviance remains secret and undetected and therefore unlabeled, as well as the many cases in which the label fails to stick. It also underestimates the extent to which legal systems represent a consensus of social values, not just the interests of powerful groups.

SUMMARY

Instead of looking for the causes of deviant behavior in individual case histories, sociological theories show us that deviance results from the same social processes that shape our own "normal" behavior. Far from being irrational or extraordinary, much deviance appears to be a predictable response to the rather commonplace situations of poverty, inequality, and lack of opportunity. If we are to deal effectively with crime and the other social problems deviance causes, we must first understand the ordinary social forces that shape both conforming and deviant behavior. Gresham Sykes, a noted criminologist, has written that sociological theories help us to see that

> crime is often the pursuit of goals widely understood and accepted; and, as such, it is frequently permitted or condoned — if not actually demanded — by the norms of certain social groups. Crime, that is to say, may often not be the act of a person whom society has failed to socialize, but may be instead the behavior of a person who has absorbed society's norms all too well.[27]

CRIME

Crimes are distinguished from other deviant acts only because they are legally forbidden. Like other forms of deviant behavior, crimes are interpreted differently according to what norms are being violated and who is violating them. Some laws represent generally accepted mores, but others prohibit behavior that only some people consider immoral. In spite of the warning that "you can't legislate morality," legislators have in fact written numerous laws against adultery, homosexual relations, abortion, drug use, and other acts that violate their own standards of appropriate behavior. Many of these laws are opposed or ignored by large numbers of people. Another kind of law prohibits behavior that has little to do with underlying social values. Some are simply matters of convenience, like the law against double parking.

Finally, there are some practices generally considered immoral that are not at all illegal. A doctor who "assaults" a patient with an unnecessary operation will not be arrested, and a lawyer who charges exorbitant fees will not be imprisoned for extortion. The political scandals of the 1980s — the abuse of power revealed by the Iran-Contra affair, the misuse of federal housing funds, and the government's bailout of a corrupt savings and loan industry — raised the question of just what values and interests the law actually represents.

Since it deals with violations of every kind of norm, from widely held folkways and mores to administrative rules, and since criminal behavior is such a disturbing social

---

[27] Gresham M. Sykes, *Criminology* (New York: Harcourt Brace Jovanovich, 1978), p. 283.

Popular movie and TV heroes have often been known to shoot first and ask questions later. Romantic portrayals of gunmen encourage tolerant attitudes toward violence in American society.

problem, the study of crime is an appropriate place to test the leading theories of deviance.

WHO IS ARRESTED — AND WHO ISN'T

Much of what we know about crime is provided by the FBI's *Uniform Crime Reports*, which supply national crime statistics on the number of crimes known to the police, the number of arrests, the disposition of suspects, and so on. There are several reasons, however, why the number of crimes reported to the FBI probably has little to do with the number of crimes actually committed. First of all, some crimes are more likely to become known to the police than others. The statistics on murder, for example, are probably fairly accurate, since there is usually a body to show for it. On the other hand, some offenses are less likely to come to official attention because no one complains to the police. Many crimes — illegal gambling, illicit sexual relations between willing adults, the use of certain drugs — are seldom reported. Furthermore, many victims believe that reporting the crime will do no good or that the police cannot be of much help. Since only about one-fifth of reported crimes are "cleared by arrest," they have good reason to think that the culprit will not be caught.[28]

To overcome these limitations, the Department of Justice began collecting data on unreported crimes in 1973. Interviewers for the *National Crime Survey* ask a sample of 60,000 households every year whether one of their members has been the victim of a crime and if so whether or not it was reported to the police. According to the survey, only about one-third of the crimes committed each year are ever reported. In 1985 the victims of more than 92,000 rapes, 660,000 robberies, and 3.1 million assaults did not report them to the police.[29]

The FBI's statistics do show that members of certain groups run a greater risk of being arrested. Older adolescents and young adults are more often arrested than members of other age groups, and men are over five times as likely to be arrested as women.[30] The poor are far more likely to be charged with crimes than the middle class. Moreover, the **crime rate** — or proportion of reported crimes to the total population under consideration — is not the same across the country. The rate of reported crimes is highest among deprived minority groups, and urban crime rates are higher than rural crime rates.[31]

One simple explanation for these statistics is that lower-class crime is more visible than middle-class crime. People living in crowded tenements and urban ghettos are forced to drink, fight, and use drugs more or less in public. They are therefore more likely to disturb their neighbors and attract the attention of the police. In contrast, members of the middle class tend to have more privacy. They are more likely to have private houses and cars where illicit activities can take place out of sight.[32]

Middle-class crime is less likely to be detected for another reason, too. Occupational crimes, such as fraud and embezzlement, are harder to uncover and prove than street crimes, such as mugging and armed robbery. For these reasons, some sociologists have suggested that the upper classes actually have a higher crime rate than the lower classes.[33]

Variations in the official crime rate can readily be explained by the theories of deviance we have just discussed. A heterogeneous urban culture obviously offers more opportunities for association with vandals, drug addicts, and professional criminals

---

[28] Sykes, *Criminology,* p. 76.

[29] U.S. Department of Justice, *Criminal Victimization in the United States,* 1985 (Washington, D.C.: U.S. Government Printing Office, 1986).

[30] Federal Bureau of Investigation, *Crime in the United States, 1982* (Washington, D.C.: U.S. Government Printing Office, 1983), pp. 183–86.

[31] Albert K. Cohen and James F. Short, Jr., "Crime and Juvenile Delinquency," in *Contemporary Social Problems,* p. 63.

[32] Chambliss, "The Saints and the Roughnecks."

[33] Walter C. Reckless, *The Crime Problem,* 5th ed. (Englewood Cliffs, N.J.: Prentice-Hall, 1973).

than a homogeneous rural culture. Moreover, young males, especially members of urban minority groups, have the highest rates of unemployment in the country. In cities like New York, where Harlem is only a few blocks from Park Avenue, youthful aspirations are painfully blocked by a modern economy that offers few job opportunities for the uneducated and unskilled. Despite the risks of imprisonment and violent death, crime is often the best-paid job for ghetto youths — at least in the short run.

Finally, in an impersonal urban environment youthful offenders run a higher risk of being arrested and labeled criminals than in rural communities. Authorities in small towns are more likely to know the youths and their families personally and are probably more willing to treat their offenses "off the record."

The FBI's statistics on arrests, therefore, tell less than the whole story. They are misleading in other ways as well. By emphasizing "kinds-of-people" categories, the official figures divert public attention from the underlying causes of crime. Instead of concentrating on the individuals who are arrested, the sociological study of crime tries to determine what kinds of laws are being broken and why people are breaking them.

TYPES OF CRIME

Most serious crimes are violations of mores, the norms of behavior that are considered vital to preserving society. They fall into three broad categories: crimes against persons, crimes against property, and crimes against morality.

CRIMES AGAINST PERSONS.   Violent crime is the kind people fear most. Several surveys have shown that fear of a violent attack — being mugged, raped, or assaulted — keeps many citizens inside after dark. Violent crimes are not as common as many people think; in fact, they are the least prevalent type of crime. According to the FBI's *National Crime Survey*, crimes against persons (murder, robbery, aggravated assault, and forcible rape) made up only about 12 percent of serious crimes in 1987; all the rest were property offenses.[34]

Nevertheless, violence has been called "as American as cherry pie." It is often pointed out, for example, that the rate of violent crime in the United States is officially higher than that in comparable industrial nations and that there are more homicides in Detroit (population 1,670,000) every year than there are in all of Great Britain (population 55,500,000).

These differences exist, many sociologists believe, because violence is learned behavior. Marvin Wolfgang and Franco Ferracuti have described a "subculture of violence" in which fighting is a respected way to settle arguments and answer insults. In such a subculture the man who refuses to fight is considered deviant and is ridiculed as a coward. These sociologists think that a subculture of violence prevails in the United States among young, lower-class men, particularly blacks and Hispanics. Here the concept of machismo, or extreme masculinity, demands that male honor be defended with physical violence. Here, too, the rates of homicide and assault are consistently high.[35]

---

[34] Federal Bureau of Investigation, *Uniform Crime Reports* (Washington, D.C.: U.S. Government Printing Office, 1988), p. 41.

[35] Marvin Wolfgang and Franco Ferracuti, *The Subculture of Violence* (London: Tavistock, 1967), pp. 151–55.

Violence is also part of the larger American culture. Many prime-time television programs and popular films specialize in shootings, beatings, and car crashes. Domestic violence appears to be common at all social and economic levels, and child abuse and wife-beating have only very recently been defined as crimes. This cultural tolerance and even encouragement of violent behavior — especially in men — is surely one reason why the United States has higher rates of violent crime than other industrial societies do.

CRIMES AGAINST PROPERTY.   Theft is the most common of all crimes. A likely reason for its high incidence is that American society offers tremendous opportunities for crimes against property. Few societies have so many valuable objects to begin with, and fewer still leave them unguarded so often. (According to the FBI, the owners of four out of five stolen cars have left them unlocked, and one out of five had left the key in the ignition.) When this carelessness (or indifference, because of theft insurance) is added to the difficulty of tracing mass-produced goods and the impersonal ownership of so much property by large corporations, then it is not so surprising that many people have the opportunity and the inclination to steal.[36]

Modern computer technology has greatly increased the opportunities for embezzlement. In the last twenty years computers have become essential to the processing of bank accounts, credit cards, inventory and sales records, payrolls, welfare checks, tax payments, and the like. The number of Americans directly involved in programming and operating computers has been estimated at more than 2 million — and nearly all of them have the opportunity to falsify and manipulate financial records. The impersonality of the computer — its image of remote, uncaring power — often makes embezzlement easier to rationalize than taking money directly from the cash drawer. Other tempting features of computer crime are that it is difficult to detect (no one's handwriting appears on a computer printout) and usually very profitable. When computer crimes are detected, they are seldom prosecuted vigorously (see "How to Make Crime Pay"). Banks, for example, do not always report their losses from embezzlement. They sometimes just fire the embezzler (if they know who it is) and absorb the cost rather than risk unfavorable publicity and higher insurance rates.

A new form of computer crime involves "hacking," or electronic trespassing. Hackers use computer bulletin boards illegally to exchange access codes and technical information about how to break into government, university, and corporate computer banks. "Phone phreaks," who steal long distance telephone services, distribute credit card numbers on these boards. Other hackers duplicate computer software in violation of copyright laws, and still others are electronic vandals who devise destructive software, or "computer viruses," which erase the computer files of unsuspecting users. Prosecution of these thieves — many of whom are still in high school — is complicated by the *culture lag* between advances in electronic technology and the laws covering the use of computerized information.

CRIMES AGAINST MORALITY.   The most controversial section of the criminal law consists of the statutes enforcing conventional standards of moral behavior. Nearly every state has

---

[36] Sykes, *Criminology*, pp. 119–20.

HOW TO MAKE CRIME PAY

A nursing home operator swindles the government out of $1 million in Medicaid funds and is sentenced to four months in jail. A lawyer cheats two law firms out of $2.5 million and gets five years' probation. A man steals $1 million worth of equipment from the telephone company and serves forty days on a prison farm.

These are just a few recent examples of how crime can pay. From these and similar cases, anyone starting out on a life of crime can learn a few rules that will greatly increase the chances of success.

1. *Steal a lot of money as quietly and indirectly as possible.* The crimes people fear most are directed against their own persons or property. Impersonal and nonviolent crimes are less frightening and are taken less seriously. A few years ago, a chief teller in a New York savings bank embezzled more than $1.5 million by computer. By using the bank's computer system to transfer money through hundreds of small accounts, he was able to make it appear that the bank's books were in order while he was pocketing large amounts of cash. The teller was careful never to take more than the insured amount from each depositor, so that no one personally lost a cent. None of the money he stole, however, was ever recovered. After pleading guilty and expressing remorse for his crime, the teller received a prison sentence of twenty months. With time off for good behavior, he served only fifteen. His story is a lesson for anyone planning a criminal career.

2. *Commit a high-class crime.* Commit a crime the judge can understand. A judge cannot be expected to sympathize with armed robbers, pimps, and burglars. Pick the type of theft that a judge might have had a chance to commit himself. Failing that, choose a crime that a judge's clients might have committed, back when he was a practicing lawyer. Such crimes include tax evasion, securities fraud, bribery of foreign sales agents, and antitrust violations.

Of course, most people are not in a position to break the securities laws or to embezzle millions from a bank. You probably will have the opportunity to steal only small amounts of your employer's money or to shoplift from a department store—crimes a judge will find completely unsympathetic. The underworld has social classes, too.

3. *Save money for a lawyer.* Good legal advice is very expensive. Put aside at least 20 percent of the amount you steal for the rainy day when you will need the best lawyer money can buy. Through successful plea bargaining with the prosecutors, former Vice President Spiro Agnew's lawyers were able to get their client off with a fine for income tax evasion instead of a prison sentence for bribery and extortion. Hundreds, maybe thousands, of people would not be in jail today if they had had lawyers like Agnew's. Once again, it is important to commit a highly lucrative crime. Success in a criminal career frequently depends on the ability to pay a good lawyer.

4. *Look respectable and have a good reputation.* A prosperous appearance, a clean record, and influential character witnesses will lower your sentence and may even get you acquitted. The more like the judge and prosecutor you appear to be, the more they will identify with you and the harder it will be for them to put you behind bars. The Watergate conspirators, all of them eminently respectable public servants, were liable for thirty-year prison sentences, but they spent only a year or two in minimum-security accommodations. Their leader, the president of the United States, drew a pardon.

Of course, not everyone can occupy such high social positions.

As you may have noticed, many of the techniques for avoiding a long prison sentence depend on high class position, education, money, and powerful friends. If you lack some of these advantages in pursuing a criminal calling, maybe you had better go straight after all.

SOURCE: Based in part on Stephen Gillers, "How to Make Crime Pay," *The New York Times,* February 16, 1978; Thomas Whiteside, *Computer Capers: Tales of Electronic Thievery, Embezzlement, and Fraud* (New York: New American Library (Mentor), 1978).

laws against gambling, obscenity, prostitution, public drunkenness, and the possession of certain drugs. These offenses are often called **victimless crimes**, since they are voluntary activities that typically harm no one but the person who commits them. Especially in recent years, when traditional concepts of sexual morality and personal freedom have been changing rapidly, these questions have been debated: Should behavior that is only immoral, unhealthy, or unorthodox be considered criminal? Does it do any good to put alcoholics, homosexuals, and gamblers in jail? Don't people have the right to be different?

On one side of the argument are those who say that the state should not interfere in activities that do not hurt others and that if some people want to ruin their lives or their health, then that is their business. Besides, the argument goes on, the police and the courts spend too much time and money on these trivial offenses when they could be going after real criminals. Two of every five arrests are for drunkenness, disorderly conduct, vagrancy, gambling, and minor sexual deviations.[37]

Furthermore, the argument continues, the laws against drugs, gambling, and prostitution are unenforceable. People are always going to want certain kinds of thrills, and making them illegal causes serious problems. First, because there is usually no victim to testify in court, the police frequently resort to illegal methods to get evidence. Moreover, most police corruption from bribes and payoffs is associated with victimless crimes. Second, the public demand for gambling, prostitution, and narcotics is the principal support of organized crime. Instead of making a lot of gangsters rich, some people argue that these goods and services should be provided by legitimate, taxable businesses. Finally, attempts to enforce moral laws that no longer have strong public support not only are ineffective but undermine respect for the law. The lack of public consensus on marijuana, for example, has bred contempt both for the laws prohibiting its use and for the police who enforce them.

At first glance these arguments are rather persuasive. Most of us would agree that enforcing moral standards is expensive, problematical, and occasionally unjustified. On the other hand, some so-called victimless crimes are not really victimless after all. Even if the injuries are self-inflicted, drug addicts and compulsive gamblers could certainly be considered victims. And the fact that people have always gambled and used drugs is not a logical justification for legally permitting them to do so. Politicians are constantly "legislating morality" by deciding what is right and wrong in other human affairs, and the question of what is the state's business and what is invasion of privacy is still an open one. Finally, immoral activities that are declared to be crimes violate a society's most deeply held convictions about human life. Even if the self is the only victim, a fundamental social value is still being challenged. Many people believe that such challenges are crimes that society should not allow to go unpunished.[38]

TYPES OF CRIMINALS

Since so many people have so many opportunities to break all kinds of laws, the question is, Why do only some people commit only a certain type of crime? To prevent

---

[37] FBI, *Uniform Crime Reports*, 1983, p. 186.
[38] Sykes, *Criminology*, p. 192.

A prostitute looks for business during the evening rush hour. Laws against the "oldest profession" are ineffective because of public demand for its services.

crime, we must understand not only what kinds of laws are being broken but also the different reasons people become criminals.

RESPECTABLES. Amateur thieves are quite often white-collar workers who steal on the job. White-collar crime includes embezzlement, expense-account padding, and taking bribes and kickbacks from suppliers. In a well-known study of embezzlement, *Other People's Money,* Donald Cressey found that employees are more likely to steal if (1) they know the techniques of embezzlement and (2) they have a secret, urgent reason to do so—a gambling debt, for example.[39] Even more important than opportunity and motive is having an excuse they can use to rationalize their behavior and deny that they have done anything wrong. Typical excuses are "I was just borrowing the

[39] Donald Cressey, *Other People's Money* (New York: Free Press, 1953).

money. I was going to pay it back," and "The company owes it to me. They've never paid me enough for everything I've done for them."

Embezzlers and other white-collar criminals don't earn their living by stealing. They rarely have a criminal record or associate with people who do. Many occasional shoplifters are housewives who consider themselves respectable and generally law-abiding. They excuse their conduct by saying that the stolen goods are not worth much and that a large store can easily absorb the loss.[40] "Respectable" crimes do add up, however. The theft of souvenirs like towels and ashtrays are estimated to cost hotel and motel owners hundreds of millions of dollars a year.

Another common amateur crime is tax evasion. Many ordinary citizens criminally evade income taxes by failing to report their earnings from part-time jobs and "moonlighting." Undeclared — and therefore untaxed — income from this underground economy has been estimated at around $80 billion a year.[41]

PROFESSIONALS. Professional criminals do not commit crimes on impulse or as an occasional sideline but as a regular way of making a living. Some are highly skilled technicians who have made a career out of such crimes as safecracking and confidence games. Like other professionals in other lines of work, they are dedicated to their jobs and take pride in their accomplishments.[42]

Edwin Sutherland's *The Professional Thief*, published in 1937, provided an influential account of the criminal subculture to which the professional thief belongs. According to Sutherland, professional criminals differ from casual offenders in several ways: they never have an honest job, but devote all their working time to their illegal occupations; they plan their crimes carefully; they have specialized skills and training; and they share certain underworld values with other professionals — loyalty, mutual aid, and contempt for conventional, "straight" society.[43]

CRIMINAL ORGANIZATIONS. Criminal syndicates, often referred to as "organized crime," are groups of criminals organized for illegal purposes — to distribute drugs or to operate a numbers racket, for example. The Mafia, probably the largest and easily the best-known criminal organization, is associated in the popular mind with spectacular gangland killings, a mysterious code of honor, and the colorful names of its leaders.

In reality, there is nothing romantic about organized crime. The Mafia appears to be run much like any other business — although it is a particularly savage and competitive one.[44] Major sources of revenue are illegal gambling (bookmaking, casinos, and numbers rackets), importing and distributing narcotics, and "loan sharking," or lending money at illegally high rates. Profits from organized crime are frequently used to infiltrate legitimate businesses, which provide a tax cover and a means of "laundering" (hiding the real source of) illegal profits.

---

[40] Richard Quinney, *The Social Reality of Crime* (Boston: Little, Brown, 1970), p. 252.

[41] Joint Economic Committee of the Congress of the United States, *Growth of the Underground Economy, 1950–1981* (Washington, D.C.: U.S. Government Printing Office, 1983), p. 14.

[42] Peter Letkemann, *Crime as Work* (Englewood Cliffs, N.J.: Prentice-Hall, 1973), pp. 23–26.

[43] Edwin H. Sutherland, *The Professional Thief* (Chicago: University of Chicago Press, 1937), Chapter 1.

[44] Donald R. Cressey, "The Functions and Structures of Criminal Syndicates," in President's Commission on Law Enforcement and Administration of Justice, Task Force Report, *Organized Crime* (Washington, D.C.: U.S. Government Printing Office, 1967), p. 29.

Organized crime could not exist without the help of millions of respectable Americans. Without its steady customers — the otherwise honest people who play the numbers, use hard drugs occasionally, and see little harm done by bookies and loan sharks — the Mafia would go out of business. Such huge illegal enterprises could not thrive without the cooperation of their partners in crime: the legitimate business people, police officers, and politicians who also benefit from their criminal activities. Romantic notions about gangsters — and public tolerance of their services — help create social attitudes that indirectly support widespread criminal behavior.

CORPORATIONS. In 1985 federal investigators found that some of the country's largest military contractors were routinely bilking the U.S. government by filing fraudulent claims for overhead expenses. One corporation billed the Pentagon $12,333 for two season sports tickets at the Los Angeles Forum, another charged off $10,713 in operating losses for its executive barbershop, and still another billed the taxpayer for a $1 million loss on its company cafeteria.[45] This sort of fraud was so extensive that it obviously had to have been approved or initiated at the highest levels of management. How could so many prominent executives stoop to such shenanigans?

Over thirty years earlier, Sutherland had proposed an answer to this question in his famous book, *White Collar Crime* (1961). The corporate executive, he argued, is inclined to commit criminal acts by the competitive nature of American business. The incentive to increase profits by any means is always strong, and there are usually many opportunities for doing so illegally. Just as a delinquent learns criminal behavior from other delinquents, Sutherland found, business people learn criminal attitudes and techniques from their associates. In a peer group that regularly juggles the books to avoid taxes, for example, the executive is led into breaking the law and then into rationalizing his or her behavior as the price of staying in business. In Sutherland's view, this combination of illegitimate opportunities and criminal definitions creates a situation favorable to breaking the law.[46]

Although a few highly publicized white-collar criminals have drawn stiffer sentences since the Watergate scandal, most corporate crime receives very lenient treatment. Not a single individual was prosecuted, for example, when the Wall Street brokerage firm of E. F. Hutton & Company recently pleaded guilty to 2,000 felony counts in an elaborate fraud to obtain interest-free bank loans. The firm itself was let off with a $2 million fine and an agreement to pay back the banks it had cheated — a penalty that the columnist William Safire called equivalent to putting a parking ticket on a bank robber's getaway car.

From the labeling theory perspective, public attitudes toward corporate crime help business people avoid being stigmatized as criminals. Such offenses as price fixing and antitrust violations do not appear to the public to be serious crimes. Furthermore, corporate executives hardly look like crooks. On the contrary, they are often respected members of the community.

POLITICAL GROUPS. Political organizations commit crimes not for purely personal gain but in support of an idea or a principle: national security, an independent Sikh state,

[45] Wayne Biddle, "Audit Cites Pentagon Contractors," *The New York Times,* April 24, 1985, p. D1.
[46] Edwin H. Sutherland, *White Collar Crime* (New York: Holt, Rinehart & Winston, 1961).

"Here's the story, gentlemen. Sometime last night, an eleven-year-old kid in Akron, Ohio, got into our computer and transferred all our assets to a bank in Zurich."

Drawing by Stevenson; © 1983 The New Yorker Magazine, Inc.

Palestinian liberation, the Third Reich, the Islamic revolution. Political crimes take two major forms: (1) illegal attacks on the existing social order, such as terrorist bombings and kidnappings, and (2) illegal uses of political authority, such as torturing a suspect to obtain evidence. The first type of political crime can sometimes be described as nonconforming behavior, as it is in the case of Soviet dissidents who criticize the government. The second type of political crime, on the other hand, is usually defined as aberrant behavior. To serve their own private interests or prejudices, government officials have been known to engage in job discrimination, unlawful arrests, manufacturing of evidence, police brutality, repression of lawful dissent, and military war crimes.

THE CAUSES OF CRIME

When crimes are classified according to what kinds of offenses are committed for what reasons, it is clear that different explanations are needed to account for apparently identical crimes. The respectable teller who embezzles from the bank, for example, denies that the theft is wrong and tries to justify it with a good excuse. When the same crime is committed by an expert forger, however, the motives and justifications are very different: theft is a way of making a living. Since the underlying causes of the two criminal acts are so different, each is best explained by a different theory. The theory of anomie accounts for the embezzler's theft: a low-paid bank teller wants money and uses an innovative, or illegitimate, means to get it. The professional forger fits Sutherland's theory that criminals learn their deviant behavior from their associates in the underworld.

Furthermore, the different causes of crime call for different social responses. A man who murders his wife in a blind rage is not treated the same way as a Mafia hit man who kills on the job, and neither is regarded in the same light as the corporate executives responsible for killing their customers with unsafe products. Attempts to prevent such murders also take different forms: for the violent husband, a crisis intervention program to help him cope with family problems; for the professional killer, prison or other radical punishment; for the indifferent manufacturer, a stiff fine for violating product safety standards. The next section considers some of the available strategies for controlling crime and other forms of deviance.

SOCIAL CONTROL OF DEVIANCE

Although many of the statistics are unreliable, it is clear that reported crime in the United States increased at an alarming rate between 1965 and 1980 (see Figure 8-1). The rate of both reported and unreported crime has fallen in the 1980s, probably because the large post-Second World War generation has outgrown their late teens and early 20s—statistically the crime-prone years (see Figure 8-2). Nevertheless, the National Crime Survey reported that one out of three American households was victimized by a crime against persons or property in 1987.[47] Control of crime remains a most urgent problem for the sociological imagination.

From the sociological perspective the causes of crime and violence lie deep within the social structure. Poverty, unequal opportunities for minorities, a cultural emphasis on competition for material success, tolerance of organized crime, approval of male violence, and acceptance of "respectable" crimes—all these factors contribute to an unusually high rate of criminal behavior in American society. More police and more prisons would treat the symptoms of crime, but they cannot reach its social roots.

Although "solving" the crime problem would require major social changes, a number of practical remedies could be undertaken. To the sociologist the most obvious way to prevent deviance is to promote conformity. Two approaches can be taken: (1) eliminate some norms, so that certain acts are no longer defined as deviant; and (2) eliminate the causes of deviance by making it easier to conform and painful not to.

Laws are the easiest of all norms to eliminate. Decriminalizing public drunkenness[48] and possession of marijuana alone would significantly reduce crime rates. Social change has also made some laws obsolete. The sexual revolution, for example, has

---

[47] U.S. Department of Justice, *Criminal Victimization in the United States, 1987*.

[48] Twelve percent of all arrests in 1982, according to the FBI. *Uniform Crime Reports* (Washington, D.C.: U.S. Government Printing Office, 1983), p. 186.

CRIMES REPORTED TO THE FBI, 1965–1985

FIGURE 8-1

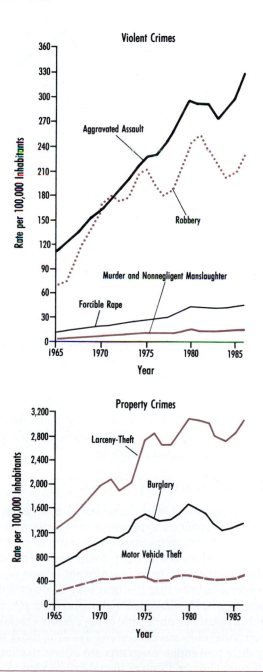

SOURCE: Bureau of the Census, *Social Indicators III* (Washington, D.C.: U.S. Government Printing Office, 1980), pp. 217, 218; *Statistical Abstract of the United States* (Washington, D.C.: U.S. Government Printing Office, 1988), p. 154.

FIGURE 8-2   TRENDS IN VICTIMIZATION RATES FOR 1973–1985

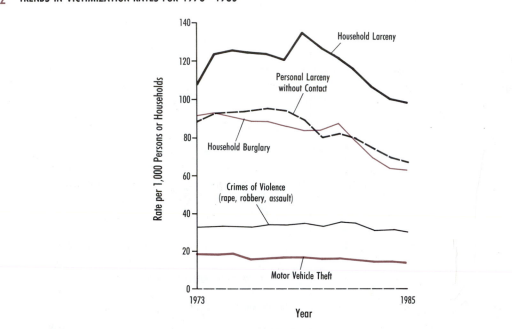

SOURCE: Bureau of Justice Statistics Bulletin, "Criminal Victimization 1985." U.S. Department of Justice, Bureau of Justice Statistics, p. 1.

brought greater public tolerance of such deviant behavior as premarital sexual relations, homosexuality, and the sale of pornographic films and literature. As behavior that was once considered shocking becomes acceptable, the laws enforcing traditional sexual mores are no longer appropriate.

ELIMINATING THE CAUSES OF DEVIANCE

Theories about the causes of deviance could also be applied to preventing it. Crime could obviously be reduced by relieving the economic hardships that lead to it. From Merton's structural perspective, the solution lies in opening up more opportunities to succeed by legitimate means. A sharp decline in unemployment among urban youths, for example, would clearly have a significant impact on crime and delinquency.

Most experts believe that the best way to control drug abuse is to change the culture that supports it. Reducing the demand for crack, cocaine, and other dangerous drugs would obviously be preferable to the current crackdown on suppliers, which has so far proved dangerous and ineffective. Treating those who are already addicted and developing drug prevention programs are efforts to eliminate the causes of crime by making the smuggling and sale of illegal drugs a less profitable business.

Another way to control deviance is to make crime more difficult to commit. This is the method we all use whenever we lock our doors, chain our bicycles, and stay off deserted streets at night. Surveillance by the police and by private guards is also thought to reduce the opportunities to commit such crimes as robbery and shoplifting. The effect, if any, of these measures on controlling crime is as yet unknown.

The theory of differential association is the basis for other preventative tactics that may prove to be more successful. Public service campaigns against drunken driving and drug use, for example, teach potential alcoholics and addicts the dangers (unfavorable definitions) of deviant behavior. Suicide prevention "hotlines," drug treatment centers, and such organizations as Alcoholics Anonymous and Gamblers Anonymous try to return former deviants to normal behavior.

From the labeling perspective more effective rehabilitation is the most practical way to prevent secondary deviance. Through job counseling and out-patient services, the community attempts to help former prisoners, mental patients, and drug addicts lose the deviant label. These strategies, however, have not been extensively applied. The most widely used method of preventing crime is the threat of punishment. Imprisonment is supposed to be a form of retribution imposed by society for wrongdoing, a means of deterring potential criminals, and a way of preventing future crimes by the same offender. There is no doubt in the public mind that retribution, or "just deserts," is a powerful argument for imprisonment. Much controversy, however, surrounds the question of whether punishment deters crime. Although many exconvicts commit new crimes after their release from prison, the fear of imprisonment may still act as a general restraint upon the law-abiding.

In addition to punishing and preventing crime, imprisonment is intended ideally to be a means of rehabilitation and reform. Unfortunately, very little is known about how to accomplish such contradictory goals as punishment and rehabilitation at the same time. Furthermore, by isolating petty offenders from the outside world and putting them in close contact with professional criminals, imprisonment is far more likely to encourage definitions favorable to violation of the law than socialization into normal life. The results of rehabilitation programs in such a setting have proven to be disappointing at best.

ASSESSING DEVIANCE

Although the price of controlling deviant behavior is very high, deviance cannot be overlooked for larger social reasons. Crime and delinquency do more than cause personal injuries and individual suffering. Émile Durkheim long ago pointed out that people respond to "social facts" as well as personal experience. People who constantly read about rapes and muggings in the daily newspaper are likely to feel threatened, even if they have had no direct experience of crime. Fear of being victimized by others and resentment of criminals who "get away with murder" erode the fragile bonds of trust and good will that hold a society together. Other forms of deviant behavior, such as prostitution, threaten shared values connected with sexual relationships and family life. Drug addiction and alcoholism are viewed as evils partly because they violate many people's beliefs about individual responsibility and morality. Although public consensus is weakening on some of these issues, many people still feel that such moral offenses cannot safely be tolerated.

On the other hand, deviance has some positive functions for society. According to Durkheim, deviance serves a useful purpose by defining the boundaries of acceptable behavior. Every society is a moral community, or a group of people who identify with each other because they share certain norms, values, and laws. Without this moral consensus, there is no group identity and no real community. Since the moral boundaries of the community are continually being redefined by changing attitudes and beliefs, the public identification and punishment of deviant behavior reestablishes consensus and strengthens social bonds among the law abiding. For this reason, accounts of deviance receive prominent attention in the newspapers and on television. Public executions, whippings, dunkings, and "scarlet letters" served the same purpose in the past.[49]

Tolerance of some social deviance is also a healthy sign, since a society that enforced total conformity would probably not survive long. Rigid social controls that permit no deviation pose as great a threat to a society's well-being as any deviant behavior they might prevent. Besides, the totalitarian solution to deviance has never been completely successful either. Whenever a fanatical political or religious group attempts to suppress all dissent in the name of ideological purity, history has shown that its efforts will end in failure.

---

[49] Kai T. Erikson, *Wayward Puritans* (New York: Wiley, 1966), pp. 12–13.

SUMMARY

1. Deviance is any significant departure from social norms; social control is the effort all societies make to enforce conformity. Deviant behavior is not necessarily good or bad; it includes merely unconventional acts as well as serious crimes. The definition of who and what is deviant is always socially determined.

2. Groups define behavior as deviant if it departs from their own norms. Dominant groups are usually able to have their particular definitions of unacceptable conduct written into law.

3. Responses to deviance depend on what kind of norm is being violated. Folkways are enforced by such informal sanctions as gossip and ridicule; violations of mores are usually more severely punished; and laws are enforced by the formal sanctions of the state.

4. Distinctions are also made between different types of violators and different types of consequences. Merton distinguished between nonconforming and aberrant behaviors on the basis of motive.

5. Biological and psychological theories of deviance, which explain the reasons why certain individuals

commit deviant acts, cannot account for most types of deviance. Sociological theories look for differences among the social situations in which deviance occurs.

6. Sutherland's theory of differential association, based on the concepts of social learning, argues that people learn to be deviant by associating with deviant groups.

7. Merton's theory of anomie and opportunity structures proposes that the rate of deviant behavior is higher in situations where people have little chance of achieving success in legitimate ways. Merton used Durkheim's term, "anomie," to describe the normless state that results when cultural goals (money, material rewards) are not achieved in socially approved ways (hard work, a good job). When people have few legitimate opportunities to succeed, they may turn to deviant behavior. The form their deviance takes depends on what illegitimate opportunities are available.

8. The labeling theory of deviance contends that powerful groups force others to conform to their norms. Once labeled deviant, individuals have fewer opportunities to behave in acceptable ways.

By a self-fulfilling prophecy, primary deviance, the original deviant act, becomes secondary deviance, or a deviant identity and way of life.

9. The FBI's *Uniform Crime Reports,* which supply data on crimes reported to the police, show that young males, the poor, and members of minority groups are more likely to be arrested. Certain parts of the country, especially urban areas, have higher crime rates than others. There is reason to believe that most crime is never reported and that middle-class criminals are less often arrested.

10. Violent crimes account for only about 12 percent of serious crimes, but the rate of violent crime is higher in the United States than in other industrial societies. Property crimes are the most common offenses. Some people argue that victimless crimes are matters of personal morality and should not be illegal.

11. "Respectable" people, professional criminals, and organizations commit crimes for different reasons. Their deviance calls for different kinds of responses.

12. Although the official statistics are often misleading, crime is a serious social problem in the United States. The causes of crime are deeply embedded in the social structure, but, barring major social changes, some practical steps could be taken to promote conformity and eliminate the causes of criminal deviance.

13. Deviance is inevitable in any society. By clarifying the norms of acceptable behavior, Durkheim found that deviance often has the positive effect of defining moral boundaries and strengthening social bonds.

KEY TERMS

deviance 225
social control 226
informal sanctions 228
formal sanctions 228
laws 229
nonconforming behavior 230

aberrant behavior 230
differential association theory 235
theory of anomie and opportunity
    structures 235
labeling theory 239

primary deviance 240
secondary deviance 240
crime 241
crime rate 243
victimless crimes 247
white-collar crime 248

SUGGESTED READING

Malin Akerstrom. *Crooks and Squares: Lifestyles of Thieves and Addicts in Comparison to Conventional People.* New Brunswick, NJ: Transaction Publications, 1985.

* Howard S. Becker, ed. *The Other Side: Perspectives on Deviance.* New York: Free Press, 1967.

* Kai T. Erikson. *Wayward Puritans: A Study in the Sociology of Deviance.* New York: MacMillan, 1968.

* George V. Higgins. *The Friends of Eddie Coyle.* New York: Penguin Books, 1987.

* Charles E. Silberman. *Criminal Violence, Criminal Justice.* New York: Random House, 1980.

* Gresham Sykes. *Criminology.* San Diego, CA: Harcourt Brace Jovanovich, 1978.

George B. Vold and Thomas J. Bernard. *Theoretical Criminology,* 3rd ed. New York: Oxford University Press, 1985.

* James Q. Wilson and Richard J. Herrnstein. *Crime and Human Nature.* New York: Simon & Schuster Touchstone Books, 1986.

* Available in paperback.

Only a peace
between equals
can last.

Woodrow Wilson

CHAPTER 9

RACE AND ETHNICITY

The 1985 winner of the National Spelling Bee in Washington, D.C., was a 13-year-old Chicago schoolboy who bested 167 other competitors by correctly spelling the word "milieu." His name is Balu Natarajan, he was born in India, and he speaks Tamil at home.

The fact that an Indian immigrant can achieve success in his adopted country by mastering its customs and language (including a word with French origins) is a triumph of the melting pot, or the melding of diverse peoples into the larger American culture. On the other hand, Balu remains a member of a group that is both physically and culturally distinct. Many other Americans would identify him as a foreigner because of his name, his appearance, and his family's national origins. Instead of being

259

absorbed into the mainstream, immigrant groups like Balu's have often preferred to transplant their own traditions to American soil. And, instead of willingly accepting cultural differences, native-born Americans have frequently reacted to the new arrivals with suspicion, if not outright hostility.

While the American immigrant experience is unique in some respects, racial hatreds and nationalistic rivalries are found in all corners of the world — between Basques and Spanish, Christians and Arabs, Sikhs and Indians, Uzbeks and Russians, Cambodians and Vietnamese. Racial and ethnic differences have also been implicated in virtually all the great wars and tyrannies of human history.

By sociological definition, a **race** is a number of people sharing genetically inherited characteristics who are thought of as a distinctive group and think of themselves as such. An **ethnic group** is a number of people sharing a common origin or a separate subculture who are thought of (and who think of themselves) as a distinctive group because of their origins or subculture. Many ethnic groups have both racial and cultural characteristics. White Anglo-Saxon Protestants (once jokingly, now conventionally, known as WASPs) are an ethnic group in the United States, as are Pakistanis in Great Britain, French-Canadians in Canada, and Russians in the Soviet Union. The term **ethnicity** refers to the distinctive characteristics of an ethnic group.

Race and ethnicity are interesting to the sociologist for two reasons. First, intergroup hostilities are obviously the source of serious social problems. The most destructive conflicts of the last generation have not been between nations but between such ethnic groups as the Moslems and Hindus in India, the Ibo and Hausa tribes in Nigeria, and Sunni and Shiite Moslems in the Middle East. Furthermore, discrimination on the basis of ethnic identity deprives millions of people of the social benefits to which they are entitled. In the United States the cost of belonging to some ethnic groups can be measured in loss of income, education, health care, and occupational achievement.

Sociologists are also interested in racial and ethnic divisions because such distinctions are not supposed to matter in modern societies. Theories of modernization have predicted that the requirements of industrial technology and bureaucratic organization will do away with old-fashioned tribal loyalties and antagonisms. In our rationalized, computerized era, there should be no room for racial hatred and religious fanaticism. Moreover, democratic ideologies specifically ignore ethnic differences. The American creed, for example, proclaims that every citizen — regardless of race, religion, or ethnic

Blacks are a minority group in South African society even though they out-number whites. The laws of apartheid require that blacks and whites be treated differently simply because they have different racial characteristics.

background — has a chance to succeed on individual merit. Nevertheless, ethnic differences persist even in advanced industrial societies. In Northern Ireland conflict between Catholics and Protestants has caused devastating riots and widespread terrorism. In South Africa a whole social system has been based on the oppression and segregation of black people. And in the United States, where supposedly any child can grow up to be president, no Catholic was considered eligible for the presidency until John F. Kennedy was elected in 1960; whether a black could be elected is still uncertain. Clearly, ethnic antagonisms have not been eliminated by either social modernization or democratic idealism.

This chapter discusses the meaning of race and ethnicity, the interaction of ethnic groups in society, and some of the social costs and consequences of ethnic diversity. It also examines assimilation, both as a social goal and as a sociological theory, and considers the most important exception to the melting pot process — the history of black Americans. Sociological insights into the black experience are then applied to the situations of four other American ethnic groups. The question here is: Why have some groups made it into the mainstream of American life, while others have not? A final part explores the implications of this chapter's findings for current issues in race and ethnic relations.

RACES, ETHNIC GROUPS, AND MINORITIES

To a biologist races are human subgroups that developed common physical characteristics over thousands of years of inbreeding in separated areas of the globe. The human species has traditionally been divided into three broad racial categories: *Negroid,* referring to most of the peoples of Africa; *Caucasoid,* including the peoples of Europe and India; and *Mongoloid,* defining the Oriental and Eskimo populations. The only trouble with this classification, and others like it, is that it is useless. The peoples of the world have been migrating and crossbreeding for so long that they no longer fit neatly into racial categories. In fact, the variations *within* these three racial categories are probably greater than the differences between them. If a "pure" race ever existed, which is unproven, it no longer exists. Biologically, the concept of race is unimportant.

THE SOCIOLOGY OF RACE AND ETHNICITY

To a sociologist the idea of race is important only when it is made the basis for social distinctions. There is no distinction made between the "tall race" and the "short race," for example, although height is an obvious, genetically transmitted characteristic. Skin color, however, has frequently been selected as a basis for discrimination. As we noted in Chapter 7, race is an important factor in inequalities of income, power, and prestige. Ethnic identity, too, is important only when it is a basis for treating people differently. A Jewish identity in the Netherlands is socially rather insignificant. Jews in the Soviet Union, by contrast, are treated as second-class citizens simply because they are Jews.

Because they are treated unfairly on the basis of their ethnic identity, Soviet Jews are considered a minority group. A **minority group** has been defined as a "group of people who, because of their physical or cultural characteristics, are singled out from others in the society in which they live for differential and unequal treatment, and who therefore regard themselves as objects of collective discrimination." [1] A minority group is not necessarily outnumbered by the dominant group. Black people, who represent a majority of the population of the Union of South Africa, are still a minority group; they have far less political and economic power than white people. Blacks and Chicanos continue to be minority groups in the United States not because they are a numerical minority, but because they are treated differently on the basis of their physical and cultural characteristics.

The subordination of minority groups is frequently justified by an ideology that affirms the ruler's right to rule. Privileged groups tend to believe that they are entitled to their privileges because the people they dominate are "too stupid" or "too lazy" to be trusted. When the minority groups appear to be racially distinct, the ideology justifying domination is called "racism." **Racism** is a systematized belief that biological differences cause members of different races to behave in different ways. For instance, the British rulers of colonial India held the complacent belief (like many whites in the United States) that a dark skin indicated mental or moral inferiority while a white skin was a sign of a person's intelligence and high moral character.

FORMS OF ETHNIC RELATIONS

When two ethnic groups come together in a society, one of four things can happen: (1) **exclusion**, if one group voluntarily withdraws or is forced to withdraw from further interaction; (2) **assimilation**, if one group loses its ethnic identity and blends into the other group; (3) **pluralism**, if the two groups continue to interact on an equal basis; or (4) **ethnic stratification**, if the two groups continue to interact on an unequal basis.

EXCLUSION. Physical removal, or exclusion, occurs when one ethnic group simply eliminates the other or when one group withdraws from social contact with the other. Some societies have practiced the most extreme and brutal form of exclusion — *extermination,* or *genocide.* In the 1930s and 1940s the Nazi regime in Germany decided upon extermination as its "final solution" to the "question" of ethnic minorities. To prevent contamination of the so-called Aryan master race, the Nazis transferred millions of Jews, Gypsies, and other minorities to concentration camps, used them as slave labor, and then murdered them. Genocide, however, did not begin or end with Hitler. At the turn of the twentieth century, the Turks carried out a systematic plan for exterminating the Armenian people; in 1972, in the African state of Burundi, 100,000 members of the Hutu tribe were slaughtered by their enemies, the Tutsis.

The physical *expulsion* of an ethnic group is a less extreme form of exclusion than extermination, but it can amount to the same thing. When the communist government of Vietnam expelled ethnic Chinese residents in 1979, tens of thousands of refugees were stripped of their possessions and forced to leave the country, frequently in overcrowded boats. Some of these "boat people" were rescued and taken in by other countries, but many others drowned.

---

[1] Louis Wirth, "The Problem of Minority Groups," in *The Science of Man in the World Crisis,* ed. Ralph Linton (New York: Columbia University Press, 1945), p. 347.

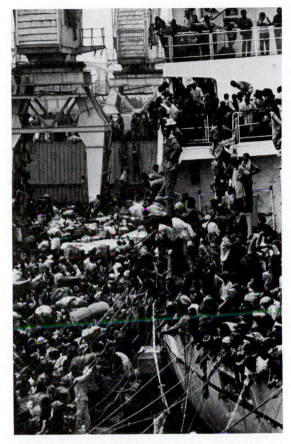

In 1983 the Nigerian government expelled about two million foreigners, many of them guest workers from Ghana. Some were lucky enough to force their way aboard this Ghanaian boat, but most crossed the border in trucks or on foot.

Finally, an ethnic group may choose *voluntary isolation,* or secession from the larger society. The Puritans came to Massachusetts partly to escape persecution in England but also to fulfill what they saw as their divine mission in the New World. In the 1920s Marcus Garvey, an American black leader, proposed a similar exodus from the United States with his "Back to Africa" movement.

ASSIMILATION.   The opposite of exclusion is assimilation, the "process by which diverse ethnic and racial groups come to share a common culture and have equal access to the opportunity structure of a society." [2] When they are fully assimilated, different ethnic groups lose their distinctive features. In the United States the Scotch-Irish have long since abandoned their cultural traditions and are now completely absorbed into the dominant American culture. *Amalgamation* occurs when racially distinct groups disappear through crossbreeding. Brazil and Hawaii are largely amalgamated societies in which people of different races mingle rather freely and intermarry. In a fully assimilated society, whether Miss Kelly, of Irish descent, marries Mr. Eisenhower, of

---

[2] Joseph Hraba, *American Ethnicity* (Itaska, Ill.: Peacock, 1979), p. 29.

German descent, is purely a matter of personal choice. There are no social pressures to keep them apart. In an amalgamated society, however, Miss Kelly and Mr. Eisenhower would not even be aware that they belonged to different ethnic groups.

Both exclusion and assimilation end the interaction between two ethnic groups by causing one of them to disappear. Two other forms of interethnic relationships, pluralism and ethnic stratification, fall in between. They represent different power relationships among different groups.

PLURALISM. Ethnic groups retain their distinctive identities but participate equally in a pluralist society. Pluralism exists in Switzerland, where ethnic French, Italians, and Germans share power on an equal basis. Pluralist policies appeal to many people because they permit cultural variety without discrimination.

Pluralism is difficult to achieve, however. Even Switzerland has been described as "a miracle of inter-group harmony which depends on a complex and sometimes precarious institutional balance of hostile forces."[3] In Canada pluralist policies have not prevented a bitter rivalry between the French- and English-speaking populations.

ETHNIC STRATIFICATION. While pluralism is a condition of equality between groups, ethnic stratification refers to the inequality that more often exists. In an ethnically stratified society, one group represents the majority, or dominant elite, and the other is the minority, or subordinate group. South African *apartheid* is an elaborate racial stratification system, in which 4.5 million whites are assigned the richest 87 percent of the country and about 24 million blacks are granted rights only in impoverished tribal reservations. Ethnic stratification is maintained through **discrimination**, or the unequal treatment of certain people on the basis of their race or ethnicity. Until 1986 a rigid system of segregation was legitimized in South Africa through "pass laws," which prevented blacks from working in white areas without identity cards. Discriminatory practices are not always so formal. The 1964 Civil Rights Act made discrimination illegal in the United States, but "unwritten laws" still keep minority groups from being promoted to certain jobs, joining certain clubs, or buying houses in certain residential areas. In this case, the result is **de facto discrimination**, or discrimination in practice, rather than **de jure discrimination**, or discrimination by law.

ASSIMILATION IN AMERICA

During the course of its history, the United States has experienced all four patterns of ethnic relations. Exclusion has been the official policy toward native Americans, many of whom are still relegated to isolated reservations. An ethnic stratification system has always placed certain groups at the bottom of the social ladder, though the groups have changed: in the past the Irish and Chinese were exploited as underpaid workers; today, blacks and Hispanic Americans are the largest underprivileged minorities. In recent years pluralism has become a popular goal for ethnic groups wishing to preserve their

---

[3] Nathan Glazer and Daniel P. Moynihan, eds., *Ethnicity* (Cambridge, Mass.: Harvard University Press, 1975), p. 90.

cultural heritage. Nevertheless, assimilation has always been the predominant pattern of American ethnic relations. In this "nation of immigrants," the melting pot has long been a national ideal as well as a fact of history.

THE HISTORICAL EXPERIENCE

Compared to other nations, the United States has had little difficulty accommodating many different ethnic groups. The history of immigration to the United States provides some reasons why assimilation has been relatively successful here.

THE COLONIAL MOSAIC.   The first American settlers were a motley group. Some came to the New World to escape religious persecution; others were adventurers looking for gold or trade in exotic goods. Many did not want to come at all: hundreds of thousands of African slaves were shipped to America in chains, and thousands of English paupers and convicts were banished to the colonies as undesirables. The majority, however, came voluntarily, principally out of economic need. Between one-half and two-thirds of the early white immigrants were indentured servants — poor people who paid their

A Hungarian mother and her children pose uneasily for their picture after arrival at Ellis Island in 1909. Between 1892 and 1924, 16 million people immigrated to the United States through New York.

passage to the New World by selling themselves as laborers for a fixed number of years.[4]

Although early America was a mosaic of different nationalities, the colonists were still a rather homogeneous population. First, the colonists had similar cultural origins. The great majority were British Protestants; the rest were mainly Protestants from such northwestern European countries as Holland, Germany, Sweden, and France. Second, the American continent was rich in natural resources, particularly land. If minor differences did cause trouble, dissident groups could avoid conflict by moving further west. Since there was a chronic need for farm labor, there was hardly any job competition between the new arrivals and the established settlers. Finally, frontier wars with the native Indians gave the colonists a sense of common identity and a feeling of "us against them." A situation favorable to assimilation had thus already developed by the end of the colonial period.

By the time of the Revolution, the colonists themselves had realized that they were no longer English or German or Swedish but "American." An observer during that time, J. Hector St. Jean Crèvecoeur, saw in America the birth of a new people. Who, he asked, is the American?

> He is either an European, or the descendant of an European, hence that strange mixture of blood, which you will find in no other country. . . . Here individuals of all nations are melted into a new race of men, whose labours and posterity will one day cause great changes in the world.[5]

THE GREAT MIGRATION.   In the century between 1820 and 1920, some 33 million immigrants entered the United States in a migration extraordinary in both size and duration. The immigrants were motivated by a combination of "push" and "pull" factors. The strongest push factor was the huge surplus of labor in Europe — the result of population growth, more efficient farming methods, and the replacement of domestic handicrafts by mechanized industry. Political upheavals and religious discrimination also contributed to widespread discontent. Besides the push of mass unemployment, there was the pull of abundant land and paying jobs in America. (Since immigration fell off sharply during periods of economic depression in the United States, the pull of American opportunities appears to have been the stronger motive.)[6] At first, these millions of newcomers were able to assimilate rather easily. They were culturally similar to the original settlers, and land and jobs were still readily available.

In the 1880s a second wave of immigrants began. They came from southern and eastern Europe, especially from Italy, Russia, and the Austro-Hungarian Empire. These "new" immigrants were ethnically very different from other Americans. Many were Catholic or Jewish. Moreover, the New World in which they found themselves had changed in fifty years from a largely agrarian society to an industrial one. These differences made assimilation of the new arrivals harder, though some of their problems had been foreshadowed by the experiences of the Irish a few decades earlier.

---

[4] Maldwyn Allen Jones, *American Immigration* (Chicago: University of Chicago Press, 1960), p. 9.

[5] J. Hector St. Jean Crèvecoeur, *Letters from an American Farmer* (New York: Albert and Charles Boni, 1925; reprinted from the 1st ed., London, 1792), pp. 54–55.

[6] Jones, *American Immigration*, p. 100.

Even before the Statue of Liberty was dedicated in 1886, Americans were having second thoughts about her invitation to "give me your poor." This late-nineteenth-century cartoon reflects nativist hostility to Irish immigrants.

Ireland's Great Famine is perhaps the most dramatic example of a push factor in immigration. Between 1845 and 1849, successive potato blights destroyed the staple of the Irish peasants' diet, causing such widespread starvation and suffering that 1.5 million people left the country in the next decade. Unlike other immigrants of rural origin, the American Irish generally settled in the coastal cities where they landed and rarely moved out to the farmlands beyond. Partly because they were too poor to buy farms and needed work desperately, partly because farming to them meant a life of misery and want, and partly because they were Catholics who wanted to be near their own churches, the Irish congregated in Boston, New York, and Philadelphia. There they lived miserably in filthy, overcrowded tenements and worked at whatever unskilled jobs they could get.

To other Americans the Irish represented a triple threat. Not only was their extreme poverty and their religion disturbing to the relatively well-off Protestants, but their "cheap labor" was taking jobs away from other unskilled urban workers. The Irish were thus the first white immigrant group to be the target of widespread prejudice and discrimination. By the end of the century, negative stereotypes of the "shanty Irish" and the "drunken Irishman" were common. Notices of job vacancies often stated "No Irish need apply"; one advertisement for a cook or chambermaid said "must be American, Scotch, Swiss, or African — no Irish." Far from being passive or helpless victims, the Irish began to protect their own interests through the rough-and-tumble politics of

[7] George Potter, *To the Golden Door: The Story of the Irish in Ireland and America* (Boston: Little, Brown, 1960), p. 168.

the time. Taking advantage of their concentrated numbers and their knowledge of democratic government, the Irish shortly gained control of the big-city political machines. With the help of their leaders, Irish immigrants began to predominate in such city jobs as policeman and fireman.

CLOSING THE DOOR.   The Irish experience became the pattern for later immigrant groups. After the closing of the western frontier, most of the new arrivals congregated in cities, where they found work in the factories of the newly industrialized economy. Little Italies, Chinatowns, and other ethnic neighborhoods were found in most American cities. By 1910 one-third of the population of the eight largest cities was foreign-born. To many Americans this huge influx of foreigners (more than a million a year between 1900 and 1914) was a cultural and economic threat. Because job opportunities in northern and midwestern cities were now attracting workers from rural areas of the United States, the demand for imported labor declined. Immigrants frequently found themselves competing with other ethnic groups for industrial jobs. Furthermore, to Anglo-Saxons the new immigrants appeared illiterate and politically subversive. *Nativism,* a backlash movement against free immigration, began to gain momentum. As early as 1882, Congress had responded to public pressure by halting Chinese immigration; in 1897 it approved a literacy test for immigrants (passed into law over President Woodrow Wilson's veto in 1917); and during the 1920s it instituted immigration quotas that discriminated against southern and eastern Europeans. America's ambivalent attitude toward immigration is perhaps best expressed in the Statue of Liberty's backhanded welcome to other countries' "huddled masses" and "wretched refuse." The United States was no longer a nation of immigrants; it was now a nation of natives.

Nevertheless, Crèvecoeur's vision of Americans as a "new race of men" continued to inspire. In 1908 a character in Israel Zangwill's popular play *The Melting Pot* described the "real American" as a "fusion of all the races, the coming Superman." The melding of diverse cultural traits into a superior American character is still a national ideal. And, by and large, the melting pot has worked. In 1980 the U.S. Census reported that Americans belong to 31 major ethnic groups, and that 40 percent of the population identify themselves with more than one group.[8] Furthermore, in spite of their early difficulties, most immigrant groups have eventually moved up the social and economic ladder.[9] Sociological theories of assimilation attempt to explain the melting pot process, or how diverse racial and ethnic groups are absorbed into modern industrial societies.

THE MELTING POT IN SOCIOLOGICAL PERSPECTIVE

Assimilation theories grew out of nineteenth-century concepts of social evolution and modernization, especially the ideas of Karl Marx and Émile Durkheim. Marx argued that the modern capitalist system would eventually make workers loyal to their occupational class, rather than to their family, village, or nationality. In *Division of Labor in*

---

[8] Stanley Lieberson and Mary Waters, *From Many Strands: Ethnic and Racial Groups in Contemporary America* (New York: Russell Sage Foundation, 1988), pp. 1, 11, 34.
[9] Nathan Glazer and Daniel P. Moynihan, *Beyond the Melting Pot,* 2d rev. ed. (Cambridge, Mass.: MIT Press, 1970).

Society (1893) Durkheim predicted that folk communities would disappear as industrialization made the division of labor more complex. In a highly diversified, urban society, Durkheim thought, traditional ethnic ties would inevitably give way to the stronger bonds between co-workers, neighbors, and other groups with shared interests. With ideas such as these in mind, American sociologists looked at ethnicity in their own society and sought to explain how and why it would disappear.

THE CONTACT HYPOTHESIS. Modern assimilation theory is closely associated with the Chicago school of sociology, particularly the theories of Robert Park (1864–1944). According to Park the lesson of the melting pot is that diverse groups that are thrown together will eventually assimilate. As people left the land and moved into modern cities, Park thought that they would come into contact with each other, compete for a while, then reach an accommodation, and eventually assimilate. Park's **contact hypothesis** holds that personal intimacy between ethnic groups in the end proves stronger than impersonal competition and that ethnic relations thus always evolve toward accommodation and finally assimilation.[10]

In reply to the assimilationist argument that ethnicity will eventually disappear in modern societies, the pluralist school of sociology cites the evidence that ethnicity is almost as prominent in industrial societies as it is in traditional communities. Pluralists note that, far from disappearing, ethnic groups remain important sources of social identity and a sense of community, as well as the basis for political mobilization. Assimilation and pluralism, however, are not entirely incompatible points of view. Milton Gordon, a leader of the pluralist school, ingeniously used Park's assimilation theory to explain why ethnicity has continued to survive.[11] Like Park, Gordon found that assimilation proceeds in stages. He called the first stage *cultural assimilation,* or acculturation. At this stage one ethnic group adopts the cultural patterns of another group — its language, values, and customs. Second-generation immigrants have usually adopted the American life style, while their parents continue to use their native language and customs.

During the second stage of *structural assimilation,* many members of an ethnic group enter the dominant group's institutions. Most immigrant groups have been absorbed rather quickly into the public schools, but desirable jobs, clubs, and political offices are still closed to some of them. One measure of an ethnic group's assimilation is the proportion of its members who have prestigious occupations (see "Puttermesser on Wall Street"). This stage can continue indefinitely.

The final stage is *identificational assimilation.* After generations of intermarriage about 15 percent of white Americans have such mixed backgrounds that they no longer identify with any particular ethnic group.[12] They now think of themselves as "100 percent American."

Since different ethnic groups remain at different stages of assimilation, Gordon described the United States as a pluralistic society made up of diverse ethnic subcultures. According to this view pluralism is incomplete assimilation.

---

[10] Robert Ezra Park, *Race and Culture* (New York: Free Press, 1950).
[11] Milton M. Gordon, *Assimilation in American Life* (New York: Oxford University Press, 1964).
[12] Lieberson and Waters, p. 35.

PUTTERMESSER ON WALL STREET

The fictional heroine of several of Cynthia Ozick's stories is a Jewish woman lawyer named Puttermesser. In Women in Law *sociologist Cynthia Fuchs Epstein quotes part of the following passage as an illustration of how a young associate moves into the elite of a WASP law firm. Notice that Puttermesser is more often put into the category "woman" than "Jew," although in her case the two identities cannot long be separated.*

Immediately after law school, Puttermesser entered the firm of Midland, Reid & Cockleberry. It was a blueblood Wall Street firm, and Puttermesser, hired for her brains and ingratiating (read: immigrant-like) industry, was put into a back office to hunt up all-fours cases for the men up front. Though a Jew and a woman, she felt little discrimination: the back office was chiefly the repository of unmitigated drudgery and therefore of usable youth. Often enough it kept its lights burning till three in the morning. It was right that the Top Rung of law school should earn you the Bottom of the Ladder in the actual world of all-fours. The wonderful thing was the fact of the Ladder itself. And though she was the only woman, Puttermesser was not the only Jew. Three Jews a year joined the back precincts of Midland, Reid (four the year Puttermesser came, which meant they thought "woman" more than "Jew" at the sight of her). Three Jews a year left—not the same three. Lunchtime was difficult. Most of the young men went to one or two athletic clubs nearby to "work out"; Puttermesser ate from a paper bag at her desk, along with the other Jews, and this was strange: the young male Jews appeared to be as committed to the squash courts as the others. Alas, the athletic clubs would not have them, and this too was preternatural—the young Jews were indistinguishable from the others.

■ ■ ■

Only their accents fell short of being identical: the "a" a shade too far into the nose, the "i" with its telltale elongation, had long ago spread from Brooklyn to Great Neck, from Puttermesser's Bronx to Scarsdale. These two influential vowels had the uncanny faculty of disqualifying them for promotion. The squash players, meanwhile, moved out of the back offices into the front offices. One or two of them were groomed—curried, fed sugar, led out by the muzzle—for partnership: were called out to lunch with thin and easeful clients, spent an afternoon in the dining room of one of the big sleek banks, and, in short, developed the creamy cheeks and bland habits of the always-comfortable.

The Jews, by contrast, grew more anxious, . . . became perfectionist and uncasual, quibbled bitterly, with stabbing forefingers, over principles, and all in all began to look and act less like superannuated college athletes and more like Jews. Then they left. They left of their own choice; no one shut them out.

Puttermesser left too, weary of so much chivalry—the partners in particular were excessively gracious to her, and treated her like a fellow-aristocrat. Puttermesser supposed this was because *she* did not say "a" in her nose or elongate her "i". . . . Long ago her speech had been "standardized" by the drilling of fanatical teachers, elocutionary missionaries hired out of the Midwest by Puttermesser's prize high school, until almost all the regionalism was drained out; except for the pace of her syllables, which had a New York deliberateness, Puttermesser could have come from anywhere. It seemed to her the partners felt this.

■ ■ ■

For farewell she was taken out to a public restaurant—the clubs the partners belonged to (they explained) did not allow women—and apologized to.

"We're sorry to lose you," one said, and the other said, "No one for you in this outfit for under the canvas, hah?"

"The canvas?" Puttermesser said.

"Wedding canopy," said the partner, with a wink. "Or do they make them out of sheepskin—I forget."

"An interesting custom. I hear you people break the dishes at a wedding too," said the second partner.

An anthropological meal. They explored the rites of her tribe. She had not known she was strange to them. Their beautiful manners were the cautiousness you adopt when you visit the interior: Dr. Livingstone, I presume? They shook hands and wished her luck. . . . They were pleased though not regretful. She was replaceable: a clever black had been hired only that morning.

SOURCE: Cynthia Ozick, *Levitation: Five Fictions* (New York: Knopf, 1982), pp. 24–28.

Sociological theories of assimilation try to explain how diverse racial and ethnic groups are absorbed into modern industrial societies.

THE THEORY OF CULTURAL CONSISTENCY.   In *An American Dilemma* (1944), the Swedish social scientist Gunnar Myrdal proposed another influential theory of assimilation, **cultural consistency**. The "dilemma" he saw was the conflict between the American creed that "all men are created equal" and the American practice of racial discrimination. While most white Americans believe in human equality as a moral principle, he found, they nevertheless have racist beliefs that affect their attitudes toward black Americans. Myrdal optimistically predicted that this cultural inconsistency could not be maintained. He was certain the further modernization of American society would eventually overcome white racism, resolve the moral dilemma, and permit blacks to assimilate at last.[13]

LIMITATIONS OF ASSIMILATION THEORIES.   While theories of assimilation offer plausible explanations for the melting pot process, they also have some obvious shortcomings. Park and Myrdal both asserted, for instance, that assimilation will eventually take place, but they did not say when that will be. Does assimilation take a few years or a few centuries? Moreover, the hypothesis that assimilation is inevitable is impossible to test empirically: in the very long run anything can happen.

Another limitation of assimilation theories is their assumption that ethnic groups *want* to join the cultural mainstream and that successful assimilation depends on their acceptance by the larger society. But what about American Jews, many of whom have

---

[13] Gunnar Myrdal, *An American Dilemma* (New York: Harper & Brothers, 1944).

maintained their distinctive ethnic heritage while becoming structurally assimilated at the highest professional levels? The theories also fail to account for ethnic separatist movements, such as that of the Amish community, and for the revival of ethnic consciousness that such modern societies as Bulgaria and the Soviet Union have recently experienced.

Finally, theories of assimilation cannot explain the one glaring exception to the melting pot ideal—the persistent failure, after 350 years, of American society to assimilate its black population.

THE BLACK EXPERIENCE IN AMERICA

African Americans are the largest and one of the oldest ethnic groups in the United States. They have lived in close contact with whites for centuries, yet they have not "melted" into the larger American society. Furthermore, blacks have suffered from discrimination and economic deprivation far longer and more intensely than other immigrants. The black experience is therefore unlike that of any other American ethnic group.

Of course, there is one essential difference between blacks and other immigrants: blacks were the only group to be enslaved. A popular explanation of the black experience contends that slavery was such a catastrophe that its effects have never been overcome. Recent research on slavery, on the other hand, appears to refute this "catastrophe theory." What impact has the history of African Americans had on their situation today?

THE NATURE OF AMERICAN SLAVERY, 1619–1865

Slavery, like any other system of domination, existed because a certain group had a reason for seeking dominance and an opportunity to achieve it. Since it involved two ethnic groups, American slavery was essentially a system of ethnic domination.[14]

In the southern colonies of English North America, the reason for slavery was purely economic: the cultivation of tobacco, rice, and cotton demanded a large, dependable labor force. Opportunity lay in the powerlessness of imported blacks. Uprooted from different regions of Africa and scattered about the colonies, first-generation slaves lacked a tribal basis for organization or even a common language. Unlike white indentured servants, they were not granted any rights under English law. Finally, the cultural and racial differences between seventeenth-century Africans and northern Europeans could hardly have been more extreme. As a result of this combination of factors, slavery was so widespread by 1700 that the work force on southern plantations had changed from predominantly white to almost exclusively black. Racial differences now coincided with social and economic divisions, and whites began to view blacks as a totally different and inferior people.[15]

---

[14] Donald L. Noel, "A Theory of the Origin of Ethnic Stratification," *Social Problems* 16 (Fall 1968): 157–72.
[15] Winthrop D. Jordan, *White Over Black: American Attitudes Toward the Negro, 1550–1812* (Baltimore: Penguin, 1969), Chapters 1 and 2.

It is one of the ironies of history that a society based on democratic idealism produced as rigid and fanatical a form of domination as American slavery. If "all men are created equal" — and the belief existed long before Thomas Jefferson wrote the words — the enslavement of blacks could be rationalized only if they were defined as not truly "men." By defining blacks as "chattel," or property, founding fathers like George Washington and Thomas Jefferson could believe sincerely in the "blessings of liberty" and still be slaveholders. The United States at this time was thus a *Herrenvolk*[16] *democracy,* a society that is egalitarian for the master race but tyrannical for the subordinate group.

A great deal of controversy surrounds the question of just how bad slavery was — both as an economic system and as a way of life. Most scholars, however, agree that slavery was first and foremost an economically efficient arrangement, providing cheap labor for large-scale production.[17] To the planters slaves represented both a large capital investment and an essential labor force. Not surprisingly, the physical welfare of this valuable property appears to have been important to them. As far as we can tell from contemporary records, American slaves were as well fed and sheltered as most European peasants and American laborers. At least by nineteenth-century standards, which included fourteen-hour working days and subsistence-level wages, historians have concluded that the slaves were not deliberately overworked. Furthermore, some slaves held skilled jobs. Most large plantations had black overseers, or managers. Slave labor was used in railroad construction and in the tobacco and iron industries. In 1865 a remarkable 83 percent of southern mechanics and artisans were black.[18]

Even in its historical context, however, slavery was a uniquely horrible system of exploitation. "No matter how degraded the factory hand," as the first great black sociologist, W. E. B. DuBois, put it, "he is not real estate." [19] The slaveholders' power over their slaves was absolute, and brutal masters were free to indulge in cruelty, sexual abuse, and injustices of every kind. Nearly every slaveholder relied on the fear of physical punishment to enforce complete submission. Moreover, the slave system undermined black family ties and encouraged passivity. Finally, slavery shamefully deprived a whole race of the basic right to be treated as human beings.

Nevertheless, the Marxist historian Eugene Genovese has argued that the dehumanizing effects of slavery should not be exaggerated.[20] He finds that the slave system, like all social arrangements, was a negotiated order, an accommodation between slaves and slaveholders. Slaves fulfilled their obligations to their masters in return for certain customary rights and privileges — the granting of reasonable working hours and days off, retirement in old age, permission to hold religious services, and the right to raise chickens and vegetables. This paternalistic compromise allowed whites to regard themselves as the benevolent guardians of a docile, contented work force and left blacks free to develop a community and culture of their own.

---

[16] In Dutch the "dominant ethnic group." Pierre L. van den Burghe coined the term from a similar racial pattern in South Africa. See his *Race and Racism,* 2d ed. (New York: Wiley, 1978), p. 18.

[17] Robert William Fogel and Stanley L. Engerman, *Time on the Cross* (Boston: Little, Brown, 1974), pp. 191–209.

[18] Hraba, *American Ethnicity,* p. 261.

[19] W. E. B. DuBois, *Black Reconstruction* (New York: Harcourt Brace Jovanovich, 1935), p. 10.

[20] Eugene D. Genovese, *Roll, Jordan, Roll: The World the Slaves Made* (New York: Pantheon, 1975).

An 1859 handbill advertises slaves and other property for sale. By defining blacks as not-quite-human "chattel," white Americans could believe sincerely that "all men are created equal" while continuing to buy and sell slaves.

NEGROES
FOR SALE.

I will sell by Public Auction, on Tuesday of next Court, being the **29**th of November, *Eight Valuable Family Servants*, consisting of one Negro Man, a first-rate field hand, one No. 1 Boy, **17** years of age, a trusty house servant, one excellent Cook, one House-Maid, and one Seamstress. The balance are under **12** years of age. They are sold for no fault, but in consequence of my going to reside North. Also a quantity of Household and Kitchen Furniture, Stable Lot, &c. Terms accommodating, and made known on day of sale.

Jacob August.
P. J. TURNBULL, *Auctioneer.*
Warrenton, October **28, 1859.**

Printed at the *News* office, Warrenton, North Carolina.

In some ways the black slave population on the eve of emancipation was better equipped for assimilation than most immigrants. As native-born,[21] English-speaking Protestants, they were culturally similar to other Americans. Many of them had managerial and mechanical skills, and their way of life had already been adapted to the American setting. In 1865 many observers predicted that the newly freed blacks would have little trouble becoming independent farmers and industrial workers. But this prediction failed to come true. What went wrong?

INDUSTRIALIZATION AND JIM CROW, 1865–1915

Instead of assimilation, the collapse of slavery produced an entirely new separation of the races, known as *Jim Crow.* The system, named for a figure in a minstrel show, originated not in the South but in the free states of the North and Midwest. In the years before the Civil War, racial segregation there was enforced by legal codes and social customs that systematically separated blacks from whites in virtually every area of life. In *North of Slavery* Leon Litwack described how free blacks were

either excluded from railway cars, omnibuses, stagecoaches, and steamboats or assigned to special "Jim Crow" sections; they sat, when permitted, in secluded and remote corners of theaters and lecture halls; they could not enter most hotels, restaurants, and resorts, except as servants; they prayed in "Negro pews" in the

---

[21] By 1860 all but 1 percent of the 4 million American slaves were native-born. See Fogel and Engerman, *Time on the Cross.* pp. 23–24.

white churches, and if partaking of the sacrament of the Lord's Supper, they waited until the whites had been served the bread and wine. Moreover, they were often educated in segregated schools, nursed in segregated hospitals, and buried in segregated cemeteries.[22]

After the Civil War the economic and social conditions that had produced segregation in the free states prevailed for the first time in the South. Two new groups were challenging the power of the old slaveholding aristocracy: the rich business elite and the poor white working class. In the industrializing postwar economy, poor whites had essentially two different interests. As members of the working class, they were interested in improving the condition of all workers through higher wages and increased political power. However, as members of the *Herrenvolk* (the dominant race), they could not tolerate competing for jobs on an equal basis with former slaves.

In politics, the southern populist movement represented the class interests of poor whites, often in alliance with poor blacks. To meet this threat to their own political power, southern planters and businessmen made what amounted to a deal for the support of the white working class. They saw to it that blacks were excluded from all trades except farm labor and domestic service. They denied political participation to black voters through such devices as the "white primary" and the poll tax. Through a combination of legal strategems and sheer terrorism, blacks were almost completely disenfranchised. Louisiana, for example, had only 1,342 black voters in 1904, compared with 130,334 in 1896.[23] With the passage of Jim Crow legislation in the 1880s and 1890s, blacks were removed from the white school system, forbidden to work at certain occupations or to serve on juries, and segregated in all public facilities. By 1890 almost 90 percent of black workers were engaged in agriculture or domestic service; by 1900 the proportion of black artisans in the South had dropped from 83 percent to 5 percent.[24] Southern blacks had been turned into a powerless subordinate class.

Although poor whites did gain some protection from the economic competition of black labor, it was the former slaveholding class that benefited most from the racial caste system. By dividing the labor market between blacks and whites, the planters kept their cheap black farm labor and let the industrialists (many of whom were Yankees) have the more expensive white labor. They also broke the populist alliance between black and white workers and thus retained political and economic control over the South.[25]

MIGRATION FROM THE SOUTH AND THE STRUGGLE FOR EQUALITY, 1915–1990

Two historical changes have shaped recent black history: the migration of millions of blacks from the rural South to the cities of the North and West; and the civil rights movement, which destroyed the legal basis of Jim Crow and gave blacks new opportunities to assimilate.

[22] Leon F. Litwack, *North of Slavery: The Negro in the Free States, 1790–1860* (1961). Quoted in C. Vann Woodward, *The Strange Career of Jim Crow*, 3d ed. (New York: Oxford University Press, 1974), p. 21.

[23] Woodward, *The Strange Career of Jim Crow*, p. 85.

[24] Leonard Broom and Norval Glenn, *Transformation of the Negro American* (New York: Harper & Row, 1965), p. 107; and Bart Landry, "The Economic Position of Black Americans." in *American Minorities and Economic Opportunity*, ed. H. Roy Kaplan (Itaska, Ill.: Peacock, 1977), pp. 50–108.

[25] Hraba, *American Ethnicity*, p. 272.

In 1910 almost 90 percent of all black Americans lived in the South, mostly in rural areas. By the 1980s only half the black population lived in the South, and four out of five blacks — North and South — lived in metropolitan areas. In little more than two generations, an extraordinary social transformation had taken place. From a largely rural class of farm laborers and domestic servants, black Americans had become a largely urban class of industrial and white-collar workers.

Southern blacks moved off the farm for the same basic reasons that European immigrants came to America: the push of agricultural depression at home and the pull of jobs in the cities. After European immigration was restricted in the 1920s, southern blacks (and whites) met the demand for new workers in the mines and heavy industries of St. Louis, Chicago, and Los Angeles.

To northern industrialists black labor offered an attractive alternative to higher-priced union labor. They frequently used black workers to break strikes, creating racial antagonisms in the 1910s and 1920s. When blacks began to move into poor white neighborhoods, these tensions erupted in bloody race riots in East St. Louis in 1917 and in Chicago in 1919. Nevertheless, whites never united against blacks in the North as they did in the South. During the New Deal era northern white workers served their own class interests by actively recruiting black workers into labor unions.[26] The focus of racial conflict shifted instead to the social and political arenas.

---

[26] William Julius Wilson, *The Declining Significance of Race* (Chicago: University of Chicago, 1978), p. 147.

These World War II soldiers fought in segregated units under the command of white officers. Until about forty years ago the United States was largely a segregated society in which blacks had few opportunities to meet whites on an equal basis.

SOCIOECONOMIC STATUS BY RACE AND ETHNICITY — 1987   TABLE 9-1

	White	African-American	Hispanic*
Percent completing college	20.5%	10.7%	8.6%
Percent unemployed	5.3%	13.0%	8.8%
Median household income	$27,427	$15,475	$19,305
Percent below poverty	10.5%	33.1%	28.2%
Percent homeowners (1985)	66.8%	42.8%	39.6%

* Hispanics may be any race.

SOURCE: U.S. Bureau of the Census, *Statistical Abstract of the United States: 1989* (109th ed.), Washington, D.C.: U.S. Government Printing Office, 1989: Tables 212, 647, 712, 734, 1243.

The Supreme Court's 1954 decision outlawing segregation in public schools, followed by the Civil Rights Act of 1964 and the Voting Rights Act of 1965, effectively ended the Jim Crow legal system (see Chapter 17, "Social Movements and Collective Behavior"). The triumphs of the civil rights movement over de jure segregation, however, have not greatly affected de facto segregation. Most African Americans continue to live in mainly black neighborhoods, to send their children to schools with large black enrollments, and to have little sustained interaction with whites.[27] This social isolation, especially in the inner city, leads to further inequalities in housing, education, and job opportunities (see Chapter 7, "Social Inequality").

While a growing black middle class has prospered from the occupational and political gains of the last 20 years, poor blacks still suffer the consequences of a heritage of poverty and discrimination (see Table 9-1). Partly because many of them cannot afford adequate medical care, and partly because they lead more dangerous lives, black Americans on the average do not live as long as white Americans (69.7 years of age vs. 75.5 years).[28] And, although blacks make up 12 percent of the population, they account for 30 percent of the poor.[29]

More than a hundred years after emancipation, blacks remain a marked exception to the usual assimilationist pattern. As internal immigrants to northern cities from the agrarian South, African Americans confronted some of the same difficulties as the Irish had a century before. Poverty, discrimination, and ethnic differences have similarly hindered black assimilation. In a segregated society blacks have had little opportunity for close contacts with whites on an equal basis. Assimilation theories of modernization, contact, and cultural consistency all fail to apply to the black experience. As more and more blacks have taken advantage of equal opportunities in education and employment, this situation has begun to change. According to assimilation theories, further modernization and closer contact between the races should create a more favorable environment for assimilation.

---

[27] Reynolds Farley and Walter Allen, *The Color Line and the Quality of Life in America* (New York: Russell Sage Foundation, 1987), p. 141.

[28] *Statistical Abstract of the U.S.: 1989*, Table 106.

[29] U.S. Bureau of the Census, "Poverty in the United States: 1987." Current Population Reports, Series P-60, No. 163, Washington, D.C.: U.S. Government Printing Office, Table 1.

The following section takes up the question of how much of the "black problem" today is due to white racism and how much to other — perhaps more intractable — social factors.

THE PERSISTENCE OF RACIAL AND ETHNIC INEQUALITY

In 1968 the National Advisory Commission on Civil Disorders ended its investigation of the racial violence that had swept the black ghettos of the nation's cities. Its report, known as the Kerner Commission report, concluded that the United States was moving toward two societies, one black, one white — separate and unequal. The commission found that the civil rights movement for racial equality had failed because of white racism — the ingrained system of attitudes and behavior that denies blacks a fully equal position in American society. The days of slavery and Jim Crow have ended, but the history of racial conflict and injustice is not over. How can this inequality be explained today?

PREJUDICE: THE PSYCHOLOGY OF DISCRIMINATION

One key ingredient in racial and ethnic conflict is **prejudice** — literally, a "prejudgment," an opinion based on insufficient evidence. Prejudice is a judgment (usually unfavorable) of an individual that is formed solely on the basis of his or her membership in a category. The social psychologist Gordon Allport defined it as "an aversive or [a] hostile attitude toward a person who belongs to a group, simply because he belongs to that group, and is therefore presumed to have the objectionable qualities ascribed to that group."[30]

In many social situations we have to prejudge people we do not know personally according to their membership in a certain category. If we did not assume that all fire fighters were helpful in a crisis, we would never call the fire department. If our judgment turns out to be incorrect, we will probably revise our opinion of fire fighters. A truly prejudiced person, however, will go on making incorrect judgments *even in the face of contrary evidence.* That is because prejudiced people judge others only on the basis of **stereotypes**, or simplified, rigid mental images of what members of a certain group are like. Ethnic and racial stereotypes are mental pictures of people based not on their individual differences but on attitudes or beliefs about their group's shared characteristics. Truly prejudiced people will go on believing that "you can't trust a Jew" or that "blacks are welfare bums" no matter how many trustworthy Jews or hard-working blacks they meet. People who have such stereotyped views will often go to great lengths to deny the evidence against them (see "In-Group Virtues and Out-Group Vices").

When psychologists studied these "faulty and inflexible generalizations" (Gordon Allport's phrase), they found several mechanisms underlying prejudice. The first is *displacement,* or the venting of anger on an unrelated object. When people are denied something they want but are afraid to confront the real source of their frustration, they

---

[30] Gordon W. Allport, *The Nature of Prejudice* (Reading, Mass.: Addison-Wesley, 1954), p. 7.

IN-GROUP VIRTUES AND OUT-GROUP VICES

Ethnic out-groups are condemned if they lack the obvious characteristics admired by an in-group. But they are also condemned if they do have in-group virtues. Robert K. Merton analyzes the damned-if-you-do-damned-if-you-don't quality of prejudice.

Superficial appearances notwithstanding, prejudice and discrimination aimed at the out-group are not a result of what the out-group does, but are rooted deep in the structure of our society and the social psychology of its members.

To understand how this happens, we must examine the moral alchemy through which the in-group readily transmutes virtue into vice and vice into virtue, as the occasion may demand. Our studies will proceed by the case-method.

We begin with the engagingly simple formula of moral alchemy: the same behavior must be differently evaluated according to the person who exhibits it. For example, the proficient alchemist will at once know that the word "firm" is properly declined as follows:

I am firm,
Thou art obstinate,
He is pigheaded. . . .

With this experiment in mind, we are prepared to observe how the very same behavior undergoes a complete change of evaluation in its transition from the in-group Abe Lincoln to the out-group Abe Cohen or Abe Kurokawa. We proceed systematically. Did Lincoln work far into the night? This testifies that he was industrious, resolute, perseverant, and eager to realize his capacities to the full. Do the out-group Jews or Japanese keep these same hours? This only bears witness to their sweatshop mentality, their ruthless undercutting of American standards, their unfair competitive practices. Is the in-group here frugal, thrifty, and sparing? Then the out-group villain is stingy, miserly and penny-pinching. All honor is due the in-group Abe for his having been smart, shrewd, and intelligent and, by the same token, all contempt is owing the out-group Abes for their being sharp, cunning, crafty, and too clever by far. Did the indomitable Lincoln refuse to remain content with a life of work with the hands? Did he prefer to make use of his brain? Then, all praise for his plucky climb up the shaky ladder of opportunity. But, of course, the eschewing of manual work for brain work among the merchants and lawyers of the out-group deserves nothing but censure for a parasitic way of life. Was Abe Lincoln eager to learn the accumulated wisdom of the ages by unending study? The trouble with the Jew is that he's a greasy grind, with his head always in a book, while decent people are going to a show or a ball game. Was the resolute Lincoln unwilling to limit his standards to those of his provincial community? That is what we should expect of a man of vision. And if the out-groupers criticize the vulnerable areas in our society, then send 'em back where they came from. Did Lincoln, rising high above his origins, never forget the rights of the common man and applaud the right of workers to strike? This testifies only that, like all real Americans, this greatest of Americans was deathlessly devoted to the cause of freedom. But, as you examine the statistics on strikes, remember that these un-American practices are the result of out-groupers pursuing their evil agitation among otherwise contented workers.

SOURCE: Robert K. Merton, *Social Theory and Social Structure*, enl. ed. (New York: Free Press, 1968), pp. 482–83.

may take out their anger on a relatively defenseless person, or *scapegoat*. When minority groups are used as scapegoats, stereotypes become the rationalization for abusing them. The ethnic scapegoating of Jews in Nazi Germany provides perhaps the most infamous example. By shifting the blame for Germany's economic collapse to the Jews, the Nazis displaced popular anger from the government to a traditionally "objectionable" group.

The actual content of stereotypes is thought to derive from the *projection* of one's own sins onto others. People who are afraid to recognize their inner feelings, according to this theory, deny them by attributing them to people who are completely unlike themselves.

Like other attitudes prejudice is also learned from the surrounding culture. Children are taught stereotypes by their parents, schoolmates, and television programs. Much of American humor depends on ethnic stereotypes, such as "dumb" Poles, "smart" Jews, and Italian "gangsters."

Prejudice alone, however, cannot account for the way certain ethnic groups are treated. First of all, prejudiced *attitudes* do not always result in discriminatory *behavior*. No matter how white storekeepers feel about the Chinese, for example, they are unlikely to turn away Chinese customers. On the other hand, unprejudiced people can discriminate by belonging to restricted clubs or by refusing to hire black workers because they say "it's bad for business." Robert K. Merton has identified four possible combinations of prejudiced attitudes and discriminatory behavior:

1. Type I: *Unprejudiced nondiscriminators, or all-weather liberals,* act on their unprejudiced beliefs in every situation, except when it is truly dangerous to do so.

2. Type II: *Unprejudiced discriminators, or fairweather liberals,* take the easier or more profitable course. Though not prejudiced themselves, they support discrimination for fear of losing business, social esteem, or votes.

3. Type III: *Prejudiced nondiscriminators, or fair-weather illiberals,* are reluctant conformists to nondiscriminatory practices. Since the passage of the 1964 Civil Rights Act, which made discrimination illegal, many prejudiced people have fallen into this category.

4. Type IV: *Prejudiced discriminators, or all-weather illiberals,* are confirmed, consistent bigots. Like the all-weather liberals, they will act on their beliefs unless they have very strong reasons not to do so.[31]

Most of us are probably Type II or Type III, the people whose behavior changes under social pressure. Research on prejudice also confirms Merton's hypothesis that most Americans are not very devoted bigots.

In a study of the Pocahontas Coal Field, for example, Ralph Minard found that the white miners' behavior toward black miners was inconsistent. During working hours the miners had no trouble cooperating, but off the job, in the segregated community in which they lived, the whites behaved in a prejudiced manner toward blacks. About 20 percent of the whites, he estimated, were unprejudiced (Type I) and about 20 percent appeared to be prejudiced both inside and outside the mine (Type IV). The remaining 60 percent tended to shift their attitudes toward blacks as they went from the mine to the outside world.[32]

Like the Pocahontas miners, most people adjust their behavior to the situations in which they find themselves. If discrimination is appropriate, most Americans will discriminate; if prejudice is frowned upon, they are likely to be more tolerant. Many studies show that most prejudiced people will conform to nondiscriminatory norms even if they do not agree with them. It is not necessary, in other words, to reform

---

[31] Robert K. Merton, "Discrimination and the American Creed," *Sociological Ambivalence and Other Essays* (New York: Free Press, 1976), pp. 190–99.

[32] Ralph D. Minard, "Race Relationships in the Pocahontas Coal Field," *Journal of Social Issues* 8 (1952): 29–44.

prejudiced attitudes in order to eliminate discriminatory behavior. In fact, one way to reform prejudiced attitudes is to eliminate discrimination.

In the 1950s, after the Supreme Court outlawed racial segregation in public schools, many people agreed with President Dwight D. Eisenhower when he said that the "hearts and minds of men" could not be changed through legislation. But this is just what happened. Desegregation changed not only American legal norms but attitudes as well. In 1978 a *New York Times*/CBS News poll replicated a survey of racial attitudes that the University of Michigan conducted for the Kerner Commission ten years before. The second survey reported a dramatic increase in white tolerance of blacks. In 1978 nine out of ten whites, compared to six out of ten in 1968, approved of integrated neighborhoods; 66 percent, compared to 46 percent in 1968, said they would mind "not at all" if a black family with a similar class standing moved next door. One out of three whites interviewed in 1968 claimed that whites "have a right to keep blacks out of their neighborhoods if they want to." Ten years after the Kerner commission report, only one in twenty held such an opinion.[33] Other polls show a sharp decline in prejudice — probably as a result of the ending of legal discrimination during the 1960s and 1970s (see Table 9-2).

Psychological theories of prejudice explain the processes underlying the distorted perceptions of prejudiced individuals, as well as some of the reasons why they cling to their stereotyped misconceptions of other people. We have seen, however, that prejudice does not always lead to discrimination. In fact, prejudiced attitudes sometimes develop *after* discriminatory practices have begun (see Muzafer Sherif's classic experiment, discussed in Chapter 4, "Social Structure"). Moreover, social factors appear to determine which groups are chosen as targets of prejudice. Sociological theories are needed to explain how discrimination actually works.

INSTITUTIONALIZED DISCRIMINATION

Many people who discriminate do not even know they are being unfair. Sometimes they are just going about their everyday routines with no intention of harming any ethnic group. **Institutionalized discrimination**, which results from simply adhering to social norms, has no direct connection to race or ethnicity, yet it is a major cause of minority problems today.

When an insurance company, for example, "red lines" an ethnic ghetto (that is, puts it off limits for property insurance), it is discriminating against the people who live there. The company, however, is not necessarily "prejudiced"; it is simply taking into account the statistical fact that buildings in that district are poor insurance risks. Discrimination of this sort is the result of unequal treatment of equals — in this case, property owners. Institutional discrimination can also result from the equal treatment of unequals, or the failure to make special provisions for people entitled to them. By treating Spanish-speaking children "just like everybody else," for example, the public schools actually discriminate against them. Because they do not understand their

---

[33] Data for 1968 from the Survey Research Center, University of Michigan; data for 1978 from *The New York Times*/CBS News poll, reported in *The New York Times*, February 26, 1978, p. 28.

TABLE 9-2   DECLINING LEVELS OF RACIAL PREJUDICE

"How strongly would you object if a member of your family wanted to bring a black friend home to dinner?"

Percent whites who would object strongly:

1963	1970	1985
31%	18%	11%

"White people have a right to keep blacks out of their neighborhood if they want to, and blacks should respect that right."

Percent whites agreeing with statement:

1963	1972	1985
55%	40%	26%

"If a black with the same income and education as you moved into your block, would it make any difference to you?"

Percent whites who would not object:

1942	1956	1972
35%	52%	84%

"Do you think there should be laws against marriage between blacks and whites?"

Percent of whites answering yes:

1963	1972	1985
61%	39%	28%

"White students and black students should go to the same schools.

Percent of Americans agreeing:

1942	1956	1963	1970	1985
30%	49%	63%	75%	90%

"If your party nominated a generally well-qualified man for president and he happened to be black, would you vote for him?"

Percent Americans answering yes:

1958	1965	1978	1983
38%	59%	77%	77%

SOURCE: Dennis Gilbert, *Compendium of American Public Opinion*. New York: Facts on File Publications, 1988.

English-speaking teachers, Hispanic students are often unfairly categorized as "slow learners" in school.

Sometimes unknowingly, sometimes with the best of intentions, Americans frequently act in ways that have discriminatory consequences for certain racial and ethnic groups. And sometimes, of course, institutionalized discrimination is just bigotry in disguise. If school officials refuse to administer IQ tests in Spanish, for example, they may be letting institutional routine cover up for personal bias.

In order to compensate for such practices, federally mandated affirmative action programs are actively recruiting minority applicants in unions, graduate schools, and business training programs. Such programs attack the results of discrimination but not its causes. In order to eliminate discrimination, we have to find out where discriminatory norms come from in the first place.

POLITICS, ECONOMICS, AND INEQUALITY

It is no secret that politics and economics — the struggle for power and money — are the roots of discrimination. White support for racial segregation, for example, began to erode after World War II, when the United States became an international power. As leader of the "free world," the United States could not afford foreign criticism of its racial policies. Under political pressure from blacks and white liberals, the federal and state governments actively opposed discrimination in employment and education during the 1950s and 1960s. The courts also played a political role by enforcing civil rights legislation and supporting minority rights. Finally, minority groups successfully used political channels to assert their claims to equal opportunities and even favored treatment.

Economic developments over the last generation have also affected the relative power of various ethnic groups. Since the 1950s the United States has been moving toward a *post-industrial economy,* a society that produces more services (for example, banking, government, entertainment) than goods (for example, coal, farm products, television sets) (see Chapter 19, "Work and Leisure"). The demand for educated white-collar workers has therefore increased and the need for unskilled laborers has declined. Furthermore, the growth of industrial unions has made blue-collar labor more expensive, encouraging manufacturers to automate their plants or to move them where labor is cheaper — in the southern states and the Far East. Since a large number of blacks and other minorities are semiskilled and unskilled workers, these groups have suffered most.

Today, the American economy is dominated by large corporations and government agencies employing skilled, unionized workers. Although there is little overt discrimination against them, minority group members usually do not have the training or education necessary for these jobs. In order to become qualified, they must compete with members of other groups for admission to graduate schools and technical training programs. The smaller manufacturing industries still employ unskilled, nonunion workers, but there are fewer and fewer of these jobs available. Moreover, wages and working conditions are often so poor that some urban workers prefer collecting unemployment compensation.

Increasing suburbanization, or population growth on the outskirts of cities, has expanded the number of jobs available beyond the urban centers where most members of minority groups are concentrated. Since public transit routes and schedules are organized on the assumption that commuters travel from the suburbs into the central cities, rather than the other way around, it is difficult for minority workers to reach the new jobs for which they are qualified.[34]

As a result of such trends black unemployment since 1954 has consistently been twice as high as white unemployment. Because these combined economic changes have hurt innercity blacks the most, they help explain the ghetto riots of the 1960s.

While the reasons people discriminate can be explained by institutional norms and individual attitudes, the underlying causes of discrimination must be traced to its social

---

[34] Paul Peterson, ed., *The New Urban Reality* (Washington, D.C.: The Brookings Institution, 1985), p. 33.

context. The importance of political and economic factors in minority problems proves once again that the true causes of discriminatory behavior lie in the social situation in which it occurs.

MINORITY ACTIVISM AGAINST DISCRIMINATION

Nearly every ethnic group in the United States has at one time or another been the target of prejudice and discrimination. Most have managed, despite the hostility of other Americans, to move up the social and economic ladder. In fact, successful ethnic groups often seem most threatening, and are therefore most feared and hated, just because they appear to be "taking over." American anti-Semitism, for example, was especially blatant during the 1880s and 1890s — just when Jewish immigrants were moving rapidly from poverty to prosperity.[35] Greater tolerance, in other words, is not necessary for assimilation. Minority groups with the resources and the opportunity to use them will advance their own interests even in the face of strong opposition.

Some ethnic groups have cultural traits and skills that help them overcome discrimination. German immigrants, for example, had no trouble applying their European farming methods to the Ohio Valley. Cuban businesspeople, Asian merchants, and other immigrants with technical and professional backgrounds are most easily assimilated today.

Other ethnic groups have been able to capitalize on a "handicap" that all minorities have in common: their exclusion from some sectors of the larger society. At a time when Jews were denied jobs in established businesses, for instance, many joined the infant movie industry and became successful actors, writers, and producers. Excluded groups have frequently entered trading and commercial occupations, where they act as middlemen (distributors, rent collectors, money lenders) between producers and consumers, landlords and tenants, or the upper and lower classes. Such *middleman minorities* provide services that are not otherwise available. When thousands of single men poured into California during the Gold Rush, for example, they found few women available to do their washing and cooking. Instead, Chinese immigrants performed these services, just as Chinese laundries and restaurants do today.

A minority's sense of ethnic identity can also be a defense against discrimination. First, ethnic unity often means political strength. In the 1960s the movement for "black power" stressed black solidarity to broaden its support. Individuals can also benefit from affirmative action programs, which attempt to reduce discrimination by opening more jobs and educational opportunities to "under-utilized" minorities. Others receive help from ethnic mutual aid organizations (the Chinese Consolidated Benevolent Association, Catholic Charities, the B'Nai B'Rith). Finally, ethnic pride may even be a stimulus to achievement, giving minority groups the underdog's determination to try harder.

SUMMARY.   A full understanding of contemporary minority problems requires a number of theoretical perspectives. Prejudice obviously underlies much interethnic conflict, and psychological tensions explain most outbursts of hostility. Injustice, however,

---

[35] Thomas Sowell, *Ethnic America* (New York: Basic Books, 1981), p. 82.

In 1973 militant members of the American Indian Movement seized the town of Wounded Knee, South Dakota, the site of a famous massacre of the Sioux, to protest the federal government's treatment. Native Americans' attempts at self-help have been hindered by the tribes' fragmentation, isolation, and extreme poverty.

does not always have psychological motives; it can result from unbiased conformity to institutional norms. Impersonal social forces are also responsible for the nearly insurmountable problems of the urban poor and unskilled. Finally, any analysis of contemporary minorities must take into account their own strivings for political power and economic security. The history of immigration shows over and over that even the underprivileged have resources they can use to overcome poverty and discrimination. The next section applies some of these theoretical perspectives — prejudice, norms, social context, and minority resources — to four American ethnic groups.

OTHER AMERICAN ETHNIC GROUPS

There are scores of ethnic groups in the United States — Estonians and Lithuanians, French Canadians and Hungarians, Armenians and Poles. Taking four of the largest American ethnic groups as examples, this section discusses how their experiences were determined by an interplay of discriminatory norms, social context, and minority self-help.

NATIVE AMERICANS

When Columbus landed in what he thought was India in 1492, the native population of North America probably numbered about 10 million.[36] Although the European explorers called all the peoples they found "Indians," the natives actually belonged to over 200 tribes, each with its own language and cultural characteristics.[37] As the white population expanded farther and farther west, the settlers took over tribal lands first by purchase and then by force. Time and again, whites in search of land and gold broke the government treaties protecting native American territories. To the invading whites, the Indians were "cruel savages" who did not deserve their own land. These racist attitudes were used to justify the exploitation and virtual extermination of the native population.

When gold was discovered on Cherokee homelands in Georgia, to take one notorious example, whites obtained a fraudulant treaty that forced the tribe to move west. As many as 4,000 Cherokees died on the way to a reservation in Oklahoma, along what became known as the "Trail of Tears."

At the end of the Indian Wars in 1886, the surviving tribes (now reduced to only 200,000 people) were expelled from their homelands and segregated on remote reservations. Disadvantaged by their tribal fragmentation, their relatively small numbers, and their lack of money and military technology, the Indians could offer no effective resistance.

Today, native Americans are the country's poorest minority. About 25 percent of the Indian population of 1.37 million live on barren, isolated reservations under appalling conditions. In 1986 a Department of Interior study reported that the unemployment rates for Indian men on reservations (including "discouraged workers" who have

---

[36] Henry F. Dobyns, "Estimating Aboriginal American Population," *Current Anthropology* 7 (October 1966): 395–416.
[37] Alvin M. Josephy, Jr., *The Indian Heritage of America* (New York: Knopf, 1969), p. 12.

stopped looking for a job) was 58 percent, compared with 12 percent for all Americans.[38] As wards of the U.S. government, reservation Indians receive free food and medical care; yet their life expectancy is only 47 years. Their suicide rate—one of Durkheim's measures of anomie—is twice the national average.[39]

As the original inhabitants of North America, the Indians confronted the invading Europeans as enemies to be expelled, not absorbed. In contrast to the uprooted black Africans, their tribal organizations and fierce early resistance made them difficult to enslave or otherwise organize into a stable labor force. As a result, the U.S. government's official policy toward the Indian tribes has always been exclusion. Physically isolated on reservations, native Americans as a group have been generally denied useful participation in the labor force, access to the educational system, and membership in other American institutions.

Unlike other rural poor who moved to the cities in search of work, most American Indians remain tied to their unproductive lands and meager life. Recently, Indian tribes in Alaska and Maine have asserted their legal rights to their ancestral homelands and the American Indian Movement (AIM) and other "red power" organizations have reaffirmed tribal identity in political activism. In 1973 members of AIM occupied Wounded Knee, South Dakota, to demand a review of federal treaties. However, the fragmentation of the native American population has made effective protest difficult to sustain.

HISPANIC AMERICANS

Spanish-speaking nationalities make up the nation's second largest and most rapidly growing ethnic group. Defining and counting the Hispanic population involves a number of problems. First, Hispanic Americans come from many different countries in South and Central America and the Caribbean. Some are new legal immigrants, some are second-generation natives, and some are illegal aliens. Some Hispanics are considered blacks, but most are white. Finally, even the name of this ethnic group varies in official and popular usage, with "Spanish origin" and "Latino" used interchangeably with "Hispanic."

The Hispanic population is officially counted at 14.6 million, or 6 percent of the total U.S. population. Since the official figures overlook illegal immigrants, the actual number is thought to be much higher. Puerto Ricans (14 percent) and Cubans (6 percent) represent substantial numbers of Hispanics, but the great majority are Mexican-Americans, or "Chicanos."[40]

About 200,000 Mexican settlers in the Southwest became Americans when the United States annexed half of Mexico in 1848. Later, the booming western economy brought millions of legal and illegal immigrants across the Mexican border as unskilled laborers. Anglo discrimination restricted the Chicanos to menial jobs, denied them equal access to public facilities, and kept them from voting. Mexican-Americans thus became a subordinate class of underpaid workers in farming, mining, and the railroad

---

[38] *The New York Times*, December 11, 1986, p. B19.

[39] *The New York Times*, November 12, 1972.

[40] Frank Bean and Marta Tienda, *The Hispanic Population of the United States* (New York: Russell Sage Foundation, 1987), pp. 38, 57–60.

The assimilation of Hispanic Americans has been slowed by their close ties to Mexico, their isolation in the *barrio*, and their concentration in low-paying farm labor or nonunion industrial jobs.

industry. In the larger cities they could live only in *barrios*, or slum neighborhoods, with inferior public schools and housing. Ethnic prejudice against Chicanos still persists in some parts of the Southwest.

The assimilation of Hispanic Americans has been hindered in several ways. Unlike other ethnic immigrants, Chicanos still have close ties to their mother country. Many continue to use Spanish as their primary language, and the majority are bilingual. The isolation of the *barrio*, the closeness of the Southwest to Mexico, and the constant movement back and forth across the border are some of the reasons for the persistence of Spanish cultural patterns and the resistance to mainstream Americanization.[41]

In addition, the economic progress of Hispanic Americans has been stymied by their concentration in low-paying farm labor and in nonunion industrial jobs. Since many Mexican residents are illegal aliens without access to welfare or unemployment benefits, they must often take the poorest jobs. Finally, like urban blacks, Hispanic Americans suffer from prejudice, institutionalized discrimination, and lack of employment opportunities. The cost of being Hispanic, in other words, is almost as high as the cost of being black (see Table 9-1).

ASIAN AMERICANS

The first Asian Americans were nearly all Chinese and Japanese, but large numbers of Filipino, Korean, Vietnamese, and Indian immigrants have recently swelled the Asian population to about 3.6 million.

The original Chinese immigrants to the United States arrived in California during the Gold Rush years. Almost all of them were single male peasants from the Canton region, brought over as short-term contract laborers to mine, construct the railroads, and farm. As white "Forty-niners" poured into California, the Chinese were forced out of these jobs and into urban areas, where they found work in sweatshops or as houseboys. Although they were excluded from most industries by white discrimination against "coolie labor," the Chinese energetically exploited the few opportunities that were left to them. In the ethnic ghettos of urban Chinatowns, they took up middleman occupations (importing, retailing) and started new service industries (restaurants, laundries). The Chinatown communities were organized around Old World ties to clans, regional ethnic groups, and secret societies, or *tongs*. These organizations looked after their members' welfare and provided job opportunities protected from white competition.

Most Chinese immigrants came as single *sojourners*, visiting laborers who planned to make some money at temporary jobs and then go home to spend it. The Japanese, in contrast, came to the West Coast in family groups and took up farming. In spite of such discriminatory acts as California's Alien Land Law, which forbade them to buy land, Japanese farmers were remarkably successful. By forming protective agricultural associations that set prices and provided credit, Japanese farmers were able to undercut their competition and offset the discrimination against them. In 1919 this very small minority of 1 percent accounted for 10 percent of California's farm production.[42]

To many whites the success of the Japanese meant they were "wily Orientals" — sneaky, dangerous, and untrustworthy. During World War II this racist attitude contributed to the decision to evacuate 110,000 Japanese residents, two-thirds of whom were U.S. citizens, from the West Coast to inland "relocation centers." Because the Japanese were not fully compensated for the loss of their farms and business,[43] the

---

[41] Leo Grebler, Joan W. Moore, and Ralph G. Guzman, *The Mexican-American People* (New York: Free Press, 1970), pp. 384, 430.

[42] Roger Daniels, "The Japanese-American Experience: 1890–1940," in *The Social Reality of Ethnic America,* eds. Rudolph Gomez et al. (Lexington, Mass.: Heath, 1974), pp. 218–19.

[43] In 1988 Congress finally authorized a $20,000 payment—and the nation's apologies—to each of 60,000 Japanese Americans who had been interned in the wartime camps.

This turn-of-the-century photograph shows a Chinese fish peddler at work in San Francisco. White discrimination against "coolie labor" led many Chinese immigrants to take up such middleman occupations.

wartime internment virtually destroyed their self-sufficient economy and dissolved their ethnic ties.[44] Once forced out into the larger society, however, they were readily assimilated. Today, Japanese-American achievements in education and income are well above the national average. Now that their rate of intermarriage is approaching 50 percent, Japanese Americans are rapidly losing their ethnicity through amalgamation.

The success of more recent Asian immigrants has also been resented; Vietnamese fishermen, for example, have been accused of unfair competition because they work longer hours. During the early 1980s the Texas state legislature passed a discriminatory

[44] William Petersen, "Chinese Americans and Japanese Americans," in *Essays and Data on American Ethnic Groups*, ed. Thomas Sowell (New York: The Urban Institute, 1978), pp. 84–85.

two-year moratorium on shrimp boat licenses and tried to limit the hours when fishermen could leave port. Crimes against Asian Americans rose sharply in Los Angeles and Boston during 1986, indicating other attempts at retaliation. Like blacks and some Hispanics, Asian Americans have distinct physical characteristics which make them easy targets of harassment.[45]

By most measures of economic and social success, Asian Americans rank higher than any other ethnic group except American Jews. Ethnic solidarity and internal protective organizations are one reason why Chinese and Japanese immigrants were able to cope with white hostility and discrimination. Another self-help factor in their achievement was the Chinese and Japanese cultural emphasis on hard work and self-discipline. These qualities helped them first to build an independent subeconomy in farming and urban commerce and then to attain a high level of education, the basis for their superior income and occupational standing.

Since recent Asian immigrants have many of the same cultural traits, they are likely to have much the same success. Traditional Confucian values emphasizing education and family obligations are probably one reason Asian students are disproportionately represented in the nation's elite colleges and universities; another is the fact that their parents are less likely to be poor peasants than middle-class refugees from oppression in their homelands.

JEWISH AMERICANS

Of all the immigrant groups that came to the United States in the 1880s, the Jews from eastern Europe were the poorest. And yet by 1910 a majority held skilled jobs, mainly in the garment industry, and relatively few (14 percent) were unskilled workers. In Boston an astonishing 45 percent were "in business," typically as peddlers and storekeepers.[46] No other immigrant group has moved as quickly into the middle class. By 1950, 75 percent of the sons of Jewish immigrants had achieved middle-class status, compared with the more typical 25 percent of second-generation Italians. Today Jews are America's highest achievers in education, income, and occupation.

There are several reasons for the legendary mobility of Jewish immigrants. First, many Jews were already skilled workers when they arrived in the United States. They came from the urban ghettos of the Old World, where they had worked in factories and belonged to trade unions. Jewish tailors, for example, readily moved into New York's garment industry. Their experiences at home also helped them build an effective union movement to protect Jewish workers. Second, the Jewish religious tradition put a high value on literacy and education. Jewish parents were thus willing to sacrifice a great deal to keep their children in school. Finally, the Jewish community had unusually effective charitable organizations. This feeling of responsibility to other Jews undoubtedly contributed to the group's extraordinary social mobility.

America's 6 million Jews are a unique ethnic group in several respects. Unlike the Chinese or Japanese they have no physical characteristics common to all Jews. Unlike

---

[45] Karl Zinsmeister, "Asians: Prejudice from Top and Bottom." *Public Opinion* 10 (July/August, 1987), pp. 8–10.

[46] Alice Kessler-Harris and Virginia Yans-McLaughlin, "European Immigrant Groups," in *Essays and Data on American Ethnic Groups*, pp. 112, 116.

most immigrant groups they come from different countries and speak different languages. Although they are distinguished by their religion, many Jews do not observe all the practices of traditional Judaism.

Anti-Semitic discrimination has hindered the assimilation of Jews to some extent, but the continued existence of the Jewish community appears to be more a matter of choice than lack of acceptance by the larger society.

NEW ISSUES IN ETHNIC RELATIONS

Until the last generation, the history of American ethnic relations was largely a history of prejudice and overt discrimination. One of the most remarkable aspects of the postwar period has been the decline of purely ethnic antagonisms and their replacement by institutionalized patterns of discrimination. Today racial and ethnic conflicts have had more to do with politics and economics than with prejudice and racism. Future ethnic relations will undoubtedly be affected by such issues as the rise in immigration and the effort to combat institutionalized discrimination through affirmative action.

RISING IMMIGRATION

About 6 million immigrants entered the United States during the 1980s, the highest number in any decade since the 1920s. In addition to these legal residents, an estimated 2 million undocumented aliens live in the country, most of them unskilled workers from the overpopulated areas of Mexico, Central America, and the Caribbean.

Before 1965, when Congress eliminated racial quotas in immigration, the majority of American immigrants came from Europe (See Figure 9-1). By 1985 only 5 percent of the legal immigrants were Europeans; nearly half were Filipinos, Koreans, Vietnamese, and Indians; and about 40 percent were Latin Americans, primarily Mexicans.[47] Miami now has districts known as Little Havana and Little Haiti; Los Angeles has Koreatown; Orange County, California, has Little Saigon; and Brooklyn, New York, has Little Odessa. Outside of the Middle East the largest concentration of Arabic-speaking people in the world — some 200,000 Lebanese, Palestinians, Yemenis, and Iraqi-Chaldeans — now live in Detroit and its nearby suburbs. Many of these new immigrants are refugees from the ravages of war, famine, poverty, and political repression.

Although the majority of American immigrants arrive legally, much public debate has focused on the question of illegal immigration, thought to be between 300,000 and 500,000 a year. Even if the United States were to abandon its humanitarian posture toward the poor and oppressed, it is doubtful that the ebb and flow of undocumented immigrants could be stopped. Since the American border with Mexico is easily crossed, and airports and harbors are equally open to illegal entry, the control of aliens is difficult to maintain, at least with current methods.

---

[47] Population Reference Bureau (Immigration) and Census Bureau sources reported in *The New York Times*, June 30, 1986, p. B5.

PATTERNS OF AMERICAN IMMIGRATION, 1820–1985   FIGURE 9-1

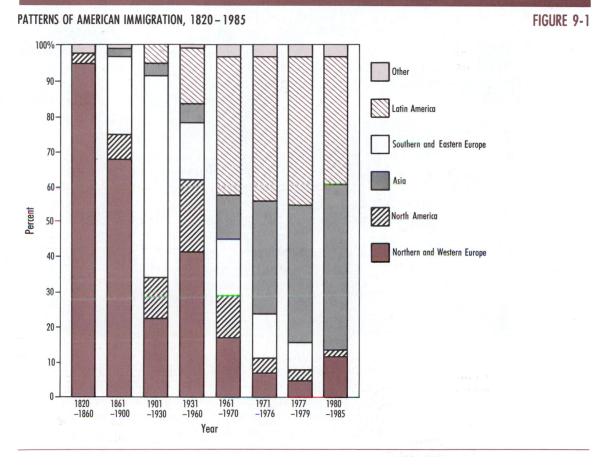

Other

Latin America

Southern and Eastern Europe

Asia

North America

Northern and Western Europe

SOURCE: Population Reference Bureau (Immigration) figures reported in *The New York Times,* June 30, 1986, p. B5.

Furthermore, American employers want illegal aliens who will do the dirty work that other workers refuse. Like the Mediterranean "guest workers" in northern Europe, illegal aliens meet the demand for cheap, unskilled labor in agriculture and in sweat-shop industries. Since they have no permanent right to live in the country, alien workers are easily exploited and deprived of their rights to minimum wages and fringe benefits.

In 1987 the United States offered legal status, or amnesty, to millions of illegal residents who could prove that they had lived in the country continuously for five years. The same legislation prohibits employers from hiring undocumented aliens, but makes it easier to bring in temporary foreign workers. The effects of this new law are not yet fully known. However, given the pull of American jobs and the push of poverty and oppression in the developing world, this new wave of immigration is likely to continue.

Like their turn-of-the-century counterparts, native-born Americans are ambiva-lent about the increasing flow of ethnically distinct immigrants. Despite widespread sympathy for the poor and oppressed, many Americans resent the new arrivals and

A parade in Los Angeles celebrates the city's large Korean community. Between 1975 and 1984 over 5 million immigrants entered the United States, the highest number of any decade since the 1920s.

strongly support limiting immigration in the future. Two-thirds of the respondents in one national poll approved of taking in victims of persecution from other countries, and a majority of those polled believed immigrants are basically good, honest people who would eventually become productive citizens. On the other hand, two-thirds of the respondents also said that immigration should be strictly limited, and a majority thought that immigrants add to the crime problem and usually end up on welfare.[48]

To some observers, such contradictory attitudes reveal an underlying fear that America is losing its white, English-speaking identity.[49] The resistance to federal affirmative action programs indicates that a nativist backlash to minority activism may have already begun.

AFFIRMATIVE ACTION

By the end of the 1960s it had become clear that simply outlawing discrimination did little to bring disadvantaged groups into the mainstream of American life. The removal of formal racial barriers to a medical school education, for example, had not significantly increased the number of minority students. Although practically everyone agreed on the need for more black doctors, all but two of the medical schools in the

[48] *Time* poll taken by Yankelovich, Skelly & White Inc. Reported in *Time*, July 8, 1985, pp. 27–28.
[49] Elizabeth Drew, *Campaign Journal: The Political Events of 1983–1984* (New York: Macmillan, 1985), pp. 681–82.

country remained virtually all white. In an attempt to compensate for such institution-alized discrimination, the federal government launched affirmative action programs requiring a large number of businesses and educational institutions to recruit racial minorities. Sometimes a fixed number of places was reserved for minorities; more often there was a "goal" to be met only if enough qualified minority candidates were available. Under affirmative action, students who would have been rejected under the traditional system were admitted to graduate schools and more minority workers were hired and promoted.

Granting preferential treatment to racial minorities obviously means that some whites will be injured—not by discriminatory practices but by the deliberate effort to overcome them. Affirmative action has thus provoked a number of lawsuits charging "reverse discrimination." In 1978 Alan Bakke, a white student who was denied admission to medical school at the University of California at Davis, won his case when the Supreme Court found the university's numerical quotas unacceptable. At the same time, however, the justices ruled that race could be used as a factor in a university's admission policy. Whatever the personal cost to individuals, the Supreme Court decided that affirmative action is consistent with democratic ideals, at least as the Constitution defines them.

During the 1980s a more conservative Supreme Court has seesawed on the issue of hiring preferences for women and minorities. By a 6 to 3 decision the court strongly endorsed the principle of affirmative action as a remedy for past job discrimination, but in three subsequent cases the divided court failed to support affirmative action policies.

Affirmative action, busing of schoolchildren, and integrated housing have clearly stirred anger and bitterness among whites who are directly affected by efforts to end institutionalized discrimination. White nativism has contributed to a conservative mood in American politics, as well as to a resurgence of turn-of-the-century problems in the assimilation of millions of new Asian and Hispanic immigrants.

SUMMARY

1. A race is defined as a number of people sharing genetically inherited characteristics who are thought of as a distinctive group and regard themselves as such. An ethnic group shares a common origin or subculture and its members are thought of (and think of themselves) as a distinctive group.

2. Race and ethnic identity are only important because they are often the basis for making social distinctions. A minority group is treated differently because of its physical or cultural characteristics. Subordination of minorities is frequently justified by racism.

3. There are four kinds of relationships between ethnic groups: exclusion, assimilation, pluralism, and ethnic stratification. Assimilation has been the predominant pattern of American ethnic relations, but because of discrimination some groups continue to stand at the bottom of the social ladder.

4. Theories of assimilation explain how the American melting pot has absorbed millions of immigrants from different ethnic backgrounds. Park's contact hypothesis holds that personal ties between ethnic groups lead to accommodation and eventual assimilation. By arguing that ethnic groups pass through three different stages of

assimilation, Gordon explained why the United States remains a pluralistic society. Myrdal predicted that the pressure toward cultural consistency would eventually overcome white racism and allow American blacks to assimilate. These theories have several shortcomings: they are impossible to test empirically, they assume that every group wants to be assimilated, they cannot account for recent revivals of ethnicity, and they do not explain the glaring exception to the melting pot process — the experience of African Americans.

5. Although the slave system left American blacks theoretically better able to assimilate than many immigrants, poverty and intensive, prolonged discrimination have hindered their passage into the mainstream of American life.

6. Psychological theories explain how prejudiced attitudes develop, but prejudice does not always lead to discrimination. In fact, prejudiced people tend to conform to nondiscriminatory norms. In the last twenty years, outlawing discriminatory behavior has actually changed prejudiced attitudes as well.

7. Institutionalized discrimination is a major cause of problems for minorities. Another is their relative lack of training and education for the jobs available.

8. The history of American ethnic groups indicates some of the ways minority groups can advance their own interests even against strong opposition. Ethnic solidarity and a cultural emphasis on hard work helped Asian Americans overcome discrimination. Similarly, American Jews benefited from cultural values that emphasize higher education and community responsibility. Native Americans, the poorest of American minorities, had the disadvantages of a fragmented population and isolation on unproductive reservations. The assimilation of Hispanic Americans has been hindered by their resistance to full Americanization, discrimination, and their concentration in low-paying jobs.

9. The future of American ethnic relations will probably be less affected by prejudice than by political and economic developments, especially the rise in immigration and federal efforts to combat institutionalized discrimination through affirmative action.

KEY TERMS

race 260
ethnic group 260
ethnicity 260
minority group 261
racism 262
exclusion 262

assimilation 262
pluralism 262
ethnic stratification 262
discrimination 264
de facto discrimination 264
de jure discrimination 264

contact hypothesis 269
cultural consistency 271
prejudice 278
stereotype 278
institutionalized
  discrimination 281

SUGGESTED READING

Frank D. Bean and Marta Tienda. *The Hispanic Population of the United States.* New York: Russell Sage Foundation, 1988.

* W. E. B. DuBois. *The Souls of Black Folk* (1903). New York: Penguin Books, 1989.

Reynolds Farley. *Blacks and Whites: Narrowing the Gap?* Cambridge: Harvard University Press, 1984.

Jacqueline Jones. *Labor of Love, Labor of Sorrow: Black Women, Work, and the Family from Slavery to the Present.* New York: Basic Books, 1985.

* Maxine Hong Kingston. *China Men.* New York: Random House, 1989.

* Howard Schuman, Charlotte Steeh, and Lawrence Bobo. *Racial Attitudes in America: Trends and*

Interpretations. Cambridge: Harvard University Press, 1988.

* Thomas Sowell. *Ethnic America: A History*. New York: Basic Books, 1983.

* Stephen Steinberg, ed. *The Ethnic Myth: Race, Ethnicity, and Class in America*. Rev. ed. Boston, MA: Beacon Press, 1989.

William J. Wilson. *The Truly Disadvantaged: The Inner City, the Underclass, and Public Policy*. Chicago: University of Chicago Press, 1987.

* Available in paperback

One is not born,
but rather
becomes, a
woman.

Simone de Beauvoir

CHAPTER 10

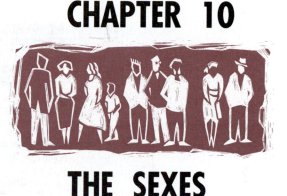

THE SEXES

In his commencement address at Smith College in 1955, Adlai E. Stevenson, the Democratic presidential candidate, told the graduating women that their task in life was to "influence us, man and boy," to "restore valid, meaningful purpose to life in your home, and to keep your husbands truly purposeful." [1] Mr. Stevenson was voicing the widely held assumption that even college-educated women could play only a supporting role in society. His view of marriage reflected the prevailing notion that husbands were the active achievers and wives only succeeded vicariously through their husbands and sons. He was speaking at a time when "career woman" was a derogatory term, a man in an apron was a standard joke, and paid employment for women was a misfortune visited primarily on the poor or unwed.

Today, a generation later, women's lives have changed so profoundly that a revolution can be said to have taken place. A majority of American women now have paying jobs, and most say they value their work and independence as much as their family life. [2] Nevertheless, many of the traditional attitudes and social arrangements to which Mr. Stevenson referred have not changed. Men are still generally expected to be more competent than women, more successful in their careers, and less concerned with household responsibilities. An ideology that reveres "motherhood and apple pie" continues to assign working women most of the traditional burdens of childrearing and homemaking.

American society, like most societies, has tended to keep the sexes separate and unequal. Like other peoples of the world, most Americans believe that men and women have different abilities and concerns and that these differences limit and define their

---

[1] *Woman's Home Companion*, September 1955, pp. 29–31.
[2] *New York Times* poll, reported in *The New York Times*, December 4, 1983, pp. 1, 66.

social roles. Sexual differences that were always accepted as facts of life have only very recently been attacked for being unnecessary and unjust. If fact, a new word — **sexism** — had to be invented to describe something that before the twentieth century had never seemed to matter much.

Sexist ideology contends that the inequalities between the sexes are based on innate characteristics and that women are "naturally" inferior to men in most respects. Sexists believe that the social roles traditionally assigned to men and women represent basic differences between the sexes and therefore cannot and should not be changed.

Nevertheless, these conventional social arrangements do seem to be breaking down. The resurgence of feminism in the 1960s and 1970s led to a questioning of social patterns that assigned the female half of the population a secondary place in American society. During the 1970s nearly two-thirds of Americans believed that it was best for men to be achievers outside the home and for women to take care of the family; by 1988 less than half agreed. The same national poll found that 57 percent of Americans in the 1970s thought it was more important for a wife to help her husband's career than to have one herself; in 1988 only 38 percent agreed.[3] Before 1972 public opinion polls showed a widespread prejudice against a woman running for president, especially among women themselves. Since then, however, a remarkable change in attitudes toward women in leadership positions has taken place. Most voters — of both sexes and all educational levels — are now willing to consider a woman for president.[4]

These changing attitudes toward "woman's place" have coincided with economic developments that have brought millions of wives and mothers out of the home and into the workplace. Women now represent 45 percent of the labor force, and they are entering fields that used to be considered strictly male preserves. In 1955 women accounted for fewer than one out of twenty medical school graduates and fewer than one out of twenty-five law school graduates; in 1986 women received nearly one out of three medical school degrees and two out of five law degrees. Female students were not even admitted to most engineering schools until the 1960s; today they represent one out of eight engineering degrees.[5] More and more young women now expect to be not just wives and mothers but professional career women as well.

Although women obviously have much higher aspirations, they do not yet have fully equal opportunities. Men still dominate the professions, the government, and the executive suites. Women continue to earn only about two-thirds as much as men, and their salaries are lower even in the *same* jobs.

The defeat of the Equal Rights Amendment (ERA), which would have guaranteed equal rights for both sexes constitutionally, indicated that many Americans are confused and ambivalent about sexual equality. Some opposed the amendment because they feared that changing the status of women would threaten the stability of the family, relieving men of their responsibility to support their wives and children and taking away legal protections for the "weaker sex." Supporters of the ERA insisted that

---

[3] National Opinion Research Center, *General Social Survey.* Chicago: University of Chicago Press, 1988.

[4] E. M. Schreiber, "Education and Change in American Opinions on a Woman for President," *Public Opinion Quarterly* 42 (Summer 1978): 178; National Opinion Research Center, *1988 General Social Survey,* op. cit.

[5] U.S. Bureau of the Census, *Statistical Abstract of the United States* (Washington, D.C.: U.S. Government Printing Office, 1989), Table 268.

Every society defines some activities as appropriate for only one sex. In the Soviet Union shopping is considered "women's work."

men and women should be equal partners in marriage and that they should have equal pay and chances for promotion on the job.

Male domination, probably the oldest and most widespread form of social stratification, does appear to be weakening in American society. The trend toward sexual equality raises all sorts of questions: How far could these changes go? Will men and women become more alike? Can they exchange roles completely? How basically different are the sexes? This chapter considers the distinctions between male and female roles and how they are changing. First it discusses the separation between women's work and men's work, both at home and on the job. Then we take up the question of whether the differences between men and women are innate and necessary or "culture bound" and susceptible to drastic change. The next section describes the limitations and conflicts built into contemporary male and female roles. The final part views the movement toward sexual equality from a larger historical perspective.

THE SEXES IN SOCIETY

Every society assigns different roles to its members according to their sex. "Being a man" means playing a certain social role; "being a woman" means playing another. These **sex roles** are sets of expectations that define how men and women are supposed to act according to the norms of their society. In addition, every culture defines some personality traits as appropriate for only one sex. **Masculinity** and **femininity** are the psychological attributes associated with the roles played by men and women. Although males and females are supposed to think and act differently in every society, the particular differences between them are not the same everywhere.

In American society, for example, a capacity for abstract and analytical thought traditionally has not been considered feminine. Girls were not generally thought to be good at math and science, and they were often discouraged from pursuing such masculine subjects. In the Soviet Union, however, scientific abilities are not **sex-typed**, or considered appropriate for only one sex. In fact, women in Soviet society make up 72 percent of the physicians, 30 percent of the engineers, and 39 percent of the scientific workers.[6]

Just as cultural notions of femininity constrain female behavior, notions of masculinity limit the range of male behavior. American men, for instance, are not generally permitted to show their emotions as freely as women are. Women who cry at sad movies or greet each other with hugs and kisses are not considered peculiar: such displays of feeling are "feminine." On the other hand, a man who sheds tears in public or embraces another man affectionately is likely to embarrass others with his "unmanly" behavior.

Other peoples of the world, however, have very different ideas about how men and women should behave. In her research on the tribes in New Guinea, the renowned anthropologist Margaret Mead provided the classic example of how culture shapes the traits often considered "eternally" feminine or masculine. Among the Arapesh Mead found that both males and females exhibited such supposedly feminine traits as gentleness, passivity, and emotional warmth. Competition and aggression were discouraged, and both men and women were responsible for child care. A second tribe, the Mundugumor, was characterized by supposedly masculine traits. Both males and females were violent, aggressive people with little time for their children. A third tribe, the Tchambuli, had sex roles exactly opposite to those in the United States. The women were the breadwinners, and the men cared for the children. Mead concluded from her work that sex roles have no inherent relationship to biological sex.[7] Other anthropologists have made similar findings in other cultures.[8]

Besides designating different personality traits as masculine or feminine, every culture assigns certain occupations and interests on the basis of sex. Dentists, for example, are usually women in Denmark and nearly always men in the United States. Certain sports are also associated with only one sex: in the United States football is for boys and field hockey for girls. These categories, however, are also subject to change. In recent years girls have played Little League baseball for the first time, and men have become telephone operators and elementary schoolteachers, positions formerly reserved for women. Vigorous physical activity—whether it is running a marathon, driving a truck, or riding a racehorse—that was once defined as exclusively masculine is now becoming acceptable for women as well.

THE ORIGIN OF THE SEXUAL HIERARCHY

Differing social expectations for men and women reflect a sex stratification system similar to the class stratification system discussed in Chapter 7, "Social Inequality."

---

[6] Rose Laub Coser, "Where Have All the Women Gone?" in *Access to Power: Cross-National Studies of Women in Elites,* Cynthia Fuchs Epstein and Rose Laub Coser, eds. (London: Allen & Unwin, 1981), pp. 16–33.

[7] Margaret Mead, *Sex and Temperament in Three Primitive Societies* (1935) (New York: Morrow, 1963).

[8] Michelle Zimbalist Rosaldo and Louise Lamphere, eds. *Women, Culture, and Society* (Stanford, CA: Stanford University Press, 1974); Alice Schlegel, ed. *Sexual Stratification: A Cross-Cultural View* (New York: Columbia University Press, 1977).

While wealth, power, and prestige can often be achieved in class systems, sex is an ascribed trait. Probably for this reason, people tend to see inequalities based on sex as "natural" differences rather than socially created ones. Nevertheless, it is possible to trace the origins of sexual inequality to the social roles that men and women have played in human history.

Using a Marxist perspective, sociologists Joan Huber and Glenna Spitze argue that male power has historically been based on control of the economy.[9] In the earliest foraging societies, childbearing and childrearing limited women to gathering small amounts of nuts and berries, while men provided most of the food from hunting. In the horticultural societies of the ancient world, women and men both cultivated the land, and women had a relatively high status. In the agricultural stage of economic development, the invention of the plough made it possible to cultivate larger, more distant fields. Since child care kept women close to home, and since men's greater size and strength gave them a monopoly on the plough, men again dominated economic production. When land became the chief source of wealth in feudal systems, women lost power. The transition to modern industrial society removed paid (men's) work even farther from home. Women were denied a major productive role and became primarily housebound consumers.

Huber and Spitze contend that people who produce and distribute surplus goods have more social power and prestige than those who consume them. According to their theory, as women became more highly educated and less constrained by constant childbearing, they began to enter the labor force in ever larger numbers. As more women became producers instead of consumers, their power and prestige increased. But as long as women continue to perform most household and child-care tasks, Huber and Spitze conclude that their economic power outside the home will not be equal to men's. In their view, equality between the sexes depends on changes within the family, not just within the world of work.

From the dawn of history, it seems, the activities of men and women have been separated primarily in two social institutions: the occupational world and the family. "Men's work" and "women's work," both at home and on the job, have always been defined differently, but the definition is constantly changing. In American society today traditional assumptions about what men and women are like and how they should behave appear to be giving way under the weight of social changes that have fundamentally altered both the family and the world of work.

MEN AND WOMEN AT WORK

Perhaps the most obvious distinction between American male and female roles is in the division of labor. Men are supposed to go to work and support their families; women's place is in the home, keeping house and raising children. In making this common distinction, it is easy to overlook the fact that most women have always contributed to the family income. In the agricultural economy of nineteenth-century America, the work done by women — milking cows, churning butter, raising chickens, and so on — brought in the "butter and egg money" that helped support the farm family. As the

---

[9] Joan Huber and Glenna Spitze, *Sex Stratification: Children, Housework, and Jobs* (New York: Academic Press, 1983).

In the past the typical working woman was young and single; today she is middle-aged and married. But today, as in 1895, most women who work are employed in sex-typed occupations.

country developed a manufacturing economy, large numbers of young women began to work outside the home. While men's jobs were still mainly agricultural, women worked in the new textile mills and factories. In the expanding service economy of the 1970s and 1980s, women have again been the pioneers. Men now dominate manufacturing, while women hold the majority of all jobs dealing with such services as banking, retail sales, health, and education.

Not only has the kind of work women do changed, but the extent to which women contribute directly to the economy has grown dramatically. Since 1900 the proportion of women in the work force has doubled; women now represent 45 percent of all workers. Even more impressive perhaps is the different age composition of the female work force today. Until the 1940s women stopped working when they married. The female labor force was thus predominantly made up of young, single workers. This work-only-until-marriage pattern changed completely in the 1960s and 1970s, when millions of married women began to go back to work after their children reached school age. Increasing numbers of younger married women with children have entered the labor force, so that well over half the mothers of preschoolers and almost three-quarters of the mothers of school-age children now work outside the home. As a result the typical working woman is no longer young and single, but middle-aged and married (see "Images of Working Women, 1900–1990").

In spite of the enormous changes that have taken place in the size and nature of the female work force, men's work and women's work are still defined differently. With few exceptions[10] male occupations and female occupations do not overlap. In 1980, just

---

[10] Some well-integrated occupations in which women represent roughly 45 percent of the workers (equal to their participation in the work force as a whole) are psychologists, secondary/college teachers, editors and reporters, painters and sculptors, real estate agents, bus drivers, and bartenders. Andrea Beller and Kee-Ok Kim Han, "Occupational Sex Segregation: Prospects for the 1980s," in Barbara Reskin, ed., *Sex Segregation in the Workplace* (Washington, D.C.: National Academy Press, 1984).

as in 1900 and 1940, about half of all working women were employed in occupations where at least 80 percent of the workers were female.[11] The separation of men's work and women's work is almost complete in such jobs as secretary (99 percent female), truck driver (97 percent male), kindergarten teacher (98 percent female), architect (96 percent male), registered nurse (96 percent female), and electrician (98 percent male).[12] Although the laws against sex discrimination in employment have brought more women into male occupations in the last few years, they still represent only a tiny fraction of the female work force.

Occupational segregation by sex is also striking within industries, firms, and professions. As you move up the hierarchy of any organization, you will usually find proportionately more men and fewer women. For example, nurses are nearly always women (97 percent), while doctors are generally men (86 percent); bank tellers tend to be women (94 percent), but the majority of bank officers are men (63 percent); elementary schoolteachers are most often women (84 percent), but school administrators are more often men (63 percent). Most of the top executives in any business are men; only a handful of full-time working women (10 percent) earned over $30,000 a year in 1987 compared with 34 percent of men.[13]

In most cases traditionally female occupations are low paying and offer little opportunity for promotion and little social prestige. The federal government's *Dictionary of Occupational Titles (DOT)*, which describes and rates the level of complexity

---

[11] Valerie Kincade Oppenheimer, *The Female Labor Force in the United States* (Berkeley: University of California Press, 1970); Nancy Rytina and Suzanne Bianchi, "Occupational Reclassification and Changes in Distribution by Gender," *Monthly Labor Review* 107 (March, 1984), pp. 11–17.

[12] Beller and Han, *op. cit.*

[13] Beller and Han, *op. cit.*; U.S. Bureau of the Census, "Money Income of Households, Families, and Persons in the United States: 1987." *Current Population Reports* Series P-60. No. 162. Washington, D.C.: U.S. Government Printing Office, (February, 1989), Table 41.

IMAGES OF WORKING WOMEN, 1900–1990

1900

Only 20 percent of women over 18 worked outside the home, mostly as household servants or factory workers. However, office employment of women was rising dramatically, corresponding to a decline in domestic occupations (maids, dressmakers, laundresses). A 1905 *Ladies Home Journal* column advised young women that marriage should take precedence over a career: "Do not suppose that the prize and success it, the business world, holds out to you will at last outweigh the nearer, dearer blessings of home and home life."[1] The typical working woman was 26 and single.

1920

The decade of the 1920s was the era of the emancipated woman. For the first time in American history, women could vote, show their legs, and get a Ph.D. Factory jobs were divided between men and women, but the thousands of new clerical jobs were held almost exclusively by women.[2] The popular image of the working girl now included the office worker who finds her true love and quits to get married.

1930

When the Great Depression of the 1930s produced mass male unemployment, many wives went to work to support their families. Nevertheless, the feminine image was still largely domestic. One of the most popular films of the decade was about a beautiful girl who keeps house for seven dwarfs and then marries a prince. By 1940, 30 percent of all women over 18 were in the labor force.[3]

1940

The decade of the 1940s was a turning point in the history of working women. The manpower shortage produced by World War II brought women into predominantly male occupations for the first time. Large numbers of older married women began to go back to work when their children started school. Popular films of the era portrayed women bosses who were more interested in their careers than in marriage.

1950

The return of millions of men to civilian jobs, the postwar baby boom, and the suburban exodus combined to keep wives at home. The media of the period celebrated the "eternal feminine" and domestic "togetherness." In his best-selling book on child care, Dr. Benjamin Spock emphasized the importance and difficulty of child rearing, advising mothers to give it priority over all other activities, including a professional career. Nevertheless, one of the most striking features of the decade was the continuing increase in the number of working mothers. By 1960, 40 percent of women over 16 held a job.

1960

Between 1960 and 1970 the number of women in the labor force went up by 8,280,000, or 36 percent. Almost half the increase occurred in clerical occu-

of about 30,000 jobs, provides some vivid examples of social attitudes toward women's work. The *DOT* rates the complexity of any job for three categories: data, people, and things. A 0 on the scale indicates the highest degree of complexity possible; an 8 means the job requires no skill in the category. In the 1977 edition, one of the highest scores was for surgeon, which received a 101 (very complex for data, most complex for people, and very complex for things). One of the lowest scores was 677 for a foster parent who, according to the *DOT*,

> Rears . . . children in home as members of family. Organizes and schedules activities, such as recreation, rest periods, and sleeping time. Insures child has nutritious diet. Instructs children in good personal and health habits. Bathes, dresses, and undresses young children. Washes and irons clothing. Accompanies children on outings and walks. Disciplines children when required. . . . May work under supervision of welfare agency. May prepare periodic reports concerning progress and behavior of children.[14]

---

[14] U.S. Department of Labor, *Dictionary of Occupational Titles*, 4th ed. (Washington D.C.: U.S. Government Printing Office, 1977), p. 224.

pations.[4] A 1970 Gallup poll found that a majority of women believed they were discriminated against in business and the professions.[5] The ideal woman, at least as she was represented by movie and television stars, appeared less maternal and dependent and more knowledgeable and athletic than ever before.

1980

Over 13 million more women went to work during the 1970s, making 1980 the first year in which over half (51.1 percent) of all American women were in the labor force. Married women with preschool children represented the largest increase of any category: from 19 percent in 1960 to 30 percent in 1970 to 45 percent in 1980.[6] Women were both pulled and pushed into the labor market during this decade. The women's movement was highly visible in the mass media, and lawsuits and federal affirmative action programs helped open better educational and employment opportunities for women. At the same time high rates of inflation and a rising divorce rate pushed more women into the labor force. The latest films and television programs showed the woman with a paying job to be the rule, not the exception.

1990

The proportion of married women who worked outside the home continued to increase during the 1980s. By the end of the decade, two-thirds of all mothers were in the workforce, including more than half the mothers of infants. While nearly every young woman aspired to be a "superwoman" who combined family and career, many older women felt worn out and discontented with the role of working mother. Others worried about the trade-off between the rewards of independence and self-expression and the rewards of close relationships with their husbands and children and a stable family life. Women's issues in the 1980s shifted from equal rights to abortion policies and to such bread-and-butter issues as equal pay for jobs of "comparable worth," maternity leaves, "palimony" after the break-up of live-in arrangements, and quality day care programs. The glamorous heroines of the new films and television series were now likely to have exciting professional careers—even if they pursued them off-camera.

[1] Quoted in Rosabeth Moss Kanter, *Men and Women of the Corporation* (New York: Basic, 1977), p. 27.
[2] Ibid., p. 26.
[3] Valerie K. Oppenheimer, *The Female Labor Force in the United States,* Population Monograph Series, no. 5 (Berkeley: University of California Press, 1970).
[4] U.S. Bureau of the Census, "Population Profile of the U.S.: 1980," *Current Population Reports,* Special Studies, P-20, No. 363 (Washington, D.C.: U.S. Government Printing Office, 1981).
[5] Cited in William H. Chafe, *The American Woman* (New York: Oxford University Press, 1972), p. 240.
[6] U.S. Bureau of the Census, *Current Population Reports* (Washington, D.C.: U.S. Government Printing Office, 1981), Table 22.

Nursery school attendant ("organizes and leads activities of children, maintains discipline") also received a 677, slightly higher than coin machine collector (687 . . . "collects coins . . . from parking meters or telephone pay stations") but slightly lower than driver helper (667 . . . "loads and unloads truck").[15] Such blatant discrimination would be funny if it were not so serious. The undervaluing of female occupations continues to be translated into low rewards—both in money and social prestige—for most women who work.

Not only are traditionally female occupations badly paid, but women earn less than men in the *same* occupations. Jobs in which women are concentrated—secretaries, preschool teachers, cashiers—pay much less than jobs that have a high concentration of men—engineers, firefighters, dentists. A steady wage gap persists even in occupations where men and women are more equally represented—bus driver, college teacher, financial manager, for example (see Table 10-1).[16]

[15] Ibid., p. 217.
[16] U.S. Bureau of the Census, "Money Income: 1987"; Table 39.

Laws against sex discrimination have brought more women into predominantly male occupations, but women like these New York City fire fighters still represent only a tiny minority of the female work force. Largely because of occupational segregation, women on average earn about one-third less than men make.

Federal legislation passed in the 1960s made it illegal to pay men and women different salaries for the same jobs. Yet these inequalities continue to exist, largely because of differences in seniority and education, occupational segregation, and the persistence of sexist discrimination. As a result, the average American woman makes only 65 percent as much as the average American man, or, in 1987, a yearly salary of $16,909 compared to $26,008 for men. In spite of the recent and well-publicized "firsts" for women — the first woman vice-presidential candidate, the first woman astronaut, the first woman justice on the Supreme Court — the earnings gap between men and women is the same as it was in 1955.[17] Moreover, this situation is not unique to the United States. All over the industrialized world women earn from one-half to two-thirds as much as men.[18]

If the pay and the jobs are so bad, the question arises: What brought so many women into the work force in the first place? The answer is that most women, today as in 1900, work because they have to. More than two of every five working women are single — either unmarried, widowed, divorced, or separated from their husbands.[19] Among working wives, one out of eight is married to a man who is unemployed or earns less than she does.[20] Over half the couples in the median income range ($20,000–

---

[17] Ibid.

[18] Patricia Roos, *Gender and Work: A Comparative Analysis of Industrial Societies* (Albany: State University of New York Press, 1985).

[19] U.S. Bureau of the Census, *Statistical Abstract of the United States (1987), Table 653.*

[20] Suzanne Bianchi, "Wives Who Earn More Than Their Husbands," *Special Demographic Analyses* CDS-80-9 (Washington, D.C.: U.S. Bureau of the Census, 1983).

WOMEN'S VS. MEN'S EARNINGS
(Median Annual Earnings for Full-Time Employment)

TABLE 10-1

Occupation	Women	Men	Women's Earnings per $1,000 for Men
Executives, administrators, managers	$21,874	$36,055	$610
Accountants and auditors	22,960	34,867	$660
Engineers	32,506	40,309	$810
College teachers	28,522	39,842	$720
Lawyers and judges	38,650	54,190	$710
Retail sales workers	10,592	17,726	$600
Cashiers	9,902	12,294	$800
Secretaries	16,237	a	N.A.
Police and firefighters	a	30,614	N.A.
Carpenters	a	20,005	N.A.
Machine operators	12,395	20,493	$600
Motor vehicle operators	11,882	21,830	$540
Construction laborers	a	16,327	N.A.
Farm operators and managers	3,110	12,638	$250

[a] Fewer than 75,000 in occupation.

SOURCE: U.S. Bureau of the Census "Money Income of Households, Families, and Persons in the United States: 1987" *Current Population Reports* Series P-60, No. 162. Washington, D.C.: U.S. Government Printing Office (February 1989): Table 39.

$30,000) are both employed, and so are two-thirds of the couples with incomes between $30,000 and $50,000.[21] Without that second paycheck, many families could not afford a new car, a suburban house, or a college education for their children. In 1981 a national survey reported that over 80 percent of working women gave as important reasons for working "helping to make ends meet" and "improving the family's standard of living."[22] Moreover, between 1960 and 1980 a lower birth rate reduced child care to less than a full-time, lifelong occupation for many middle-class women. Under these circumstances it is not surprising that so many are willing and able to work outside the home.

Valerie Oppenheimer argues convincingly, however, that it is not just the increasing supply of women who want to work but the rising demand for female labor that brought ever-larger numbers of women into the work force. By 1940, she notes, women had virtually monopolized several occupations that were to expand enormously after World War II. First of all, the postwar baby boom increased the need for teachers, librarians, and nurses — all traditionally female occupations. Second, economic development shifted the demand for labor away from farming and manufacturing and

[21] Internal Revenue statistics, reported in *The New York Times*, June 17, 1985, p. D1.
[22] Louis Harris and Associates, *The General Mills American Family Report 1980–81: Families at Work* (Minneapolis, Minn.: General Mills, Inc., 1981).

toward white-collar occupations, thus increasing the demand for women to work in other sex-typed jobs as secretaries, telephone operators, and clerical workers.[23]

During the 1970s there was another rapid expansion in jobs available to women. More than 70 percent of the new, nongovernment jobs created between 1970 and 1980 were in retail trade and services (provided by nursing homes, fast-food restaurants, data-processing firms, and the like) — all traditionally women's work.[24] The service economy's huge new demand for female labor could only be satisfied by bringing previously ineligible women into the work force — first older married women with school-age children and then, as the demand continued to increase, younger mothers with preschool children.

If female labor is in such great demand, why is women's work still underpaid and undervalued? Oppenheimer's analysis suggests an answer. Because they are responding to a demand for female labor, most women who enter the work force go into sex-typed occupations. Because these jobs typically offer low-paid, dead-end, or part-time work, women are still not usually found at upper-income levels.

MEN AND WOMEN AT HOME

Work and marriage have different meanings for each sex. Men tend to view their jobs as central to their existence and to look for fulfillment and excitement from their work. Until very recently women were more likely to think that their jobs had little to do with the real point of their lives, which was the well-being of their husbands and children. Unlike men, women who pursue a professional career have to face a conflict between the demands of their work and the traditional roles society assigns them.

Whether they have a job or not, women are expected to take responsibility for child care and domestic chores. The traditional division of labor in the family between the husband/breadwinner and wife/homemaker, no matter how outmoded it may appear for millions of two-income families, is still strongly supported by American attitudes and values. Most people, including women themselves, believe that a woman's first duty is to her family. As recently as 1968, at a time when millions of wives and mothers were in the labor force, only 47 percent of American woman thought that a wife should contribute to the family income.[25]

More recent polls indicate a growing acceptance of working wives, especially among women. A 1988 nationwide survey reported that two out of three Americans believe that working mothers can have "as warm and secure a relationship" with their children as mothers who do not work.[26] Nevertheless, many young women have mixed feelings about working outside the home. In Brown University's recent study of 3,000 college students, 77 percent of the women (and 84 percent of the men) agreed that mothers should not work full-time until their children were in school. "If I can't give

[23] Valerie Kincade Oppenheimer, "Demographic Influence on Female Employment and the States of Women," in *Changing Women in a Changing Society*, ed. Joan Huber (Chicago: University of Chicago Press, 1973), pp. 184–99.

[24] U.S. Department of Labor, *Employment and Earnings* (Washington, D.C.: U.S. Government Printing Office, 1980), Tables B1, B2.

[25] Hazel Gaudet Erskine, "The Polls: Women's Role," *Public Opinion Quarterly* 34 (Summer 1971): 275–90.

[26] National Opinion Research Center, *1988 General Social Survey*, op. cit.

my children 100 percent," one Princeton senior said, "I'd rather not be a mother at all." [27]

Most women, then, accept almost full responsibility for housework and child care as part of the female role. Even when they work full-time, married women do not expect — or get — much help from their husbands. Studies by four advertising agencies in 1980 concluded that a sizable minority of husbands are willing to help out around the house, but the majority still expect their wives to be primarily responsible for household chores, shopping, and child rearing.[28] Other studies have found that employed women spend about half as much time on domestic chores (twenty-six hours a week) as other housewives, but they still do 80 percent of the housework. Working wives are no more likely to have paid help than other wives, and they get only slightly more help from their husbands.[29] Apparently, they just do not have the time to do as much housework, and so less cooking, cleaning, and laundry are done. As many observers have pointed out, the increasing popularity of fast-food restaurants, polyester fabrics, and microwave ovens are social side effects of the working wife's dilemma.

In an era when half of all American women have jobs, the assumption that man is the breadwinner and woman is the dependent homemaker is becoming more and more unrealistic. Sex roles in the family, however, are not changing as fast as economic facts. The traditional pattern is still strongly supported by men and women in their own lives and in their attitudes toward work and family life.

SEX DIFFERENCES: REAL AND IMAGINARY

What are men like? — Self-reliant, independent, athletic, assertive, analytical, decisive, dominant, ambitious.

What are women like? — Affectionate, compassionate, loyal, sympathetic, sensitive, gentle, yielding, fond of children.

These are the words that people usually use to describe the "typical" male and female personalities. They also describe real men and women. In fact, although individuals often show characteristics associated with the opposite sex, the sexes *as groups* tend to bear out these generalizations.[30] This section discusses where the differences come from.

MALE AND FEMALE: BIOLOGICAL DIFFERENCES

The disagreement between sexists and feminists often comes down to the question of whether biological characteristics or social influences are more important in determining human behavior. Among social scientists this disagreement is known as the

---

[27] Quoted in *The New York Times,* December 28, 1980, p. 1.

[28] *The New York Times,* November 1, 1980, p. 52.

[29] Philip Blumstein and Pepper Schwartz, *American Couples: Money, Work, Sex* (New York: Morrow, 1983).

[30] Sandra Lipsitz Bem, "The Measurement of Psychological Androgyny," *Journal of Consulting and Clinical Psychology* 42 (1974): 155–62. The descriptive adjectives are based on her androgyny scale.

nature/nurture controversy. Advocates for the nature side argue that hormones and other physiological factors account for the differences between men and women. Those on the nurture side of the debate emphasize the role of social learning in producing sex differences.

According to the evolutionary view, citizens of today's industrialized societies are walking around with an ancient genetic heritage that best equips them for hunting and fighting if they are male and for child rearing and food gathering if they are female. Over millions of years of natural selection our primate ancestors are thought to have adapted to their living conditions both physically and psychologically. The female developed manual dexterity, physical stamina, and emotional endurance; the male became tall, strong-shouldered, and visually acute. While women gradually developed nurturant and submissive personalities, men became aggressive and dominant.[31]

Most sociologists, on the other hand, ridicule the idea that "man the hunter" has much to do with man the tax accountant or man the factory worker. They emphasize the fact that cultural factors can override inherited physical traits. In American society, for example, men are assigned to work that requires a high degree of manual skill (performing brain surgery, changing a fuel pump), while women are sometimes expected to shoulder heavy burdens (carrying children, lifting loaded trays as waitresses). From the "nurture" point of view, if boys and girls were raised in exactly the

---

[31] B. A. Hamburg, "The Psychobiology of Sex Differences: An Evolutionary Perspective," in *Sex Differences in Behavior*, eds. R. C. Friedman, R. M. Richart, and R. L. Vande Wiele (New York: Krieger, 1974), pp. 373–92; and B. A. Hamburg, "The Biosocial Bases of Sex Differences," in *Human Evolution: Biological Perspectives*, eds. Stanley L. Washburn and Elizabeth McCown (New York: Benjamin, 1978).

Child care in every society is primarily the mother's job, even though fathers too appear to have a "maternal" impulse toward their children.

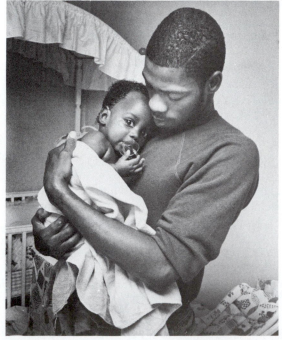

same way, they would be *androgynous,* possessing bisexual personality traits, as adults.

AGGRESSIVENESS.   Because male aggressiveness shows up in subhuman primates and in all human cultures, there is reason to think that it does have a biological basis. War is a male pastime; so, for the most part, is violent crime. Among suicides, men are likely to shoot themselves, while women typically choose sleeping pills. Boys are more aggressive than girls both physically and verbally; they play at fighting more frequently and have more aggressive fantasies than girls do.[32]

Girls are more likely to run away from a fight than boys are, but dominance over a group does not seem to be as important to them.[33] (Of course, there are many ways of expressing aggression that are harder to study than physical and verbal abuse. Girls, for example, might use the "silent treatment" more often to get their own way.) At least one writer has argued that their greater aggressiveness is the reason why men generally dominate women and occupy most of the high positions in any social organization.[34] Others think that this claim goes too far. Aggression may be the way apes and little boys dominate each other, but it is not the usual means of attaining positions of leadership among adult human beings.[35] If dominance depends more often on argument and persuasion than on brute force, then women should have an equal chance to achieve positions of power.

The role of male aggressiveness, as opposed to social factors, in warfare has probably been exaggerated as well. Rather than hordes of killers driven by primitive instincts, armies are much more likely to be made up of weary and frightened men who would rather not be there at all.

THE "MATERNAL INSTINCT."   When it comes to reproducing the species, the biological difference between the sexes is unquestionable: pregnancy, childbirth, and lactation are exclusively female functions. In theory, there is nothing to prevent the father from participating in child care, but in practice it is always primarily the mother's job.

Does this "fact of life" mean that there is a maternal instinct guiding women to a nurturing role? Alice Rossi, a sociologist who favors complete sex-role equality, answers yes. She argues that biological factors make the mother-infant bond uniquely close and that women consequently do have a greater emotional investment than men in their children. As evidence Rossi cites studies showing that new mothers have many unlearned responses to their babies. Without being aware of it, nearly every mother cradles her child in her left arm, where the newborn can be soothed by the familiar sound of her heartbeat. When mothers talk to their babies, they use similar cooing sounds and exaggerated facial expressions.[36]

Rossi's argument has been criticized on two grounds. The first is that she has failed to prove that only women have an instinct for child care. At least two studies have

---

[32] Eleanor Emmons Maccoby and Carol Nagy Jacklin, *The Psychology of Sex Differences* (Stanford, Calif.: Stanford University Press, 1974), p. 352.

[33] Ibid., pp. 353–55.

[34] Steven Goldberg, *The Inevitability of Patriarchy* (New York: Morrow, 1973).

[35] Maccoby and Jacklin, *The Psychology of Sex Differences,* p. 368.

[36] Alice S. Rossi, "A Biosocial Perspective on Parenting," *Daedalus* 106:2 (Spring 1977): 1–31; and Carol Gilligan, "Women's Place in Men's Life Cycle," *Harvard Educational Review* 49 (1979): 431–36.

found that fathers of newborn babies behave much the same way mothers do.[37] New fathers are also preoccupied with their infants; they hold them and watch them just as lovingly as the babies' mothers. Single fathers in particular become adept at "mothering" their children.

Second, Rossi's critics are not convinced that positive responses to infants are unlearned rather than learned.[38] As the statistics on child abuse show, any innate predisposition to child care has not prevented mothers from harming and even killing their babies. In fact, historians have suggested that the high infant mortality rate in premodern Europe was due in part to maternal indifference and child neglect.[39] Such cases provide evidence that an inclination to care for one's children is not inherited but learned from others.

Other evidence supports the position that maternal behavior is affected more by culture than by biology. In many societies the barren (childless) woman is stigmatized, and child rearing is the only acceptable adult role for women. The desire for social approval, then, may be a better explanation than maternal instinct for the motivation to have children and take good care of them.

Whatever the biological differences between the sexes, it is clear that they must be expressed in a social and cultural context that can enhance or dilute their effect.

PERSONALITY AND ABILITY: PSYCHOLOGICAL DIFFERENCES

Many people think that girls are more "social" than boys. They are supposed to be more interested in other people, and more likely to go along with the suggestions of others. Many people also think that boys are better at math and science than girls. They are supposed to care less about understanding people and more about understanding things and ideas. Many of us believe in these differences, but do they really exist?

Two psychologists, Eleanor Maccoby and Carol Jacklin,[40] set out to answer this question by analyzing the results of over 2,000 current research studies on sex differences in social behavior and intellectual ability. Although most of the research was done with children and thus does not measure differences that might show up later, Maccoby and Jacklin's summary is the most complete source of information available on sex differences in psychology and personality. They found that many myths regarding sex differences have no scientific basis. For example,

■ *Girls are not more "social" than boys.* Girls are *not* more likely than boys to be concerned with people rather than objects or abstract ideas. Both sexes are sociable, but in different ways. Boys tend to play in larger groups than girls: they congregate in gangs of playmates, while girls prefer to play with one or two best friends. Boys'

---

[37] R. Parke and S. O'Leary, "Father-Mother-Infant Interaction in the Newborn Period," in *The Developing Individual in a Changing World*, eds. K. Riegal and J. Meacham, Vol. II of *Social and Environment Issues* (The Hague: Mouton, 1975); M. Greenberg and N. Morris, "Engrossment: The Newborn's Impact upon the Father," *American Journal of Orthopsychiatry* 44 (1974): 520–31; Barbara Risman, "Can Men 'Mother'? Life as a Single Father," Chapter 13 in Barbara Risman and Pepper Schwartz, eds., *Gender in Intimate Relationships* (Belmont, CA: Wadsworth, 1989).

[38] Nancy Chodorov, *The Reproduction of Mothering* (Berkeley: University of California Press, 1978), pp. 18–19.

[39] Edward Shorter, *The Making of the Modern Family* (New York: Basic, 1975).

[40] Maccoby and Jacklin, *The Psychology of Sex Differences.*

games — football, soccer, and other team sports — enhance this tendency to associate in larger groups. Girls' games, on the other hand, are more likely to be individual sports like skating, tennis, and gymnastics. Some observers believe that this difference in the games children play has long-run consequences for male and female personalities. Since girls tend to have exclusive friendships, they are more likely to develop social skills involving intimacy, or the intuition of other people's needs and the disclosure of their own. Boys, on the other hand, are "team players." They learn to play ball with people they do not particularly like, developing social skills related to group decision making and leadership.[41] Although this theory seems rather speculative, it has interesting implications for male and female occupational roles. Since managers and executives in most organizations must cooperate with others effectively, male "gamesmanship" is a useful skill that puts women at a relative disadvantage.[42]

- *Girls are not more suggestible than boys.* Boys are just as likely as girls to imitate other people spontaneously, and they are just as susceptible to social pressure. If anything, boys seem to be more willing to conform to the values of their peer group when these conflict with their own.

- *Girls do not have lower self-esteem than boys.* Boys and girls are both generally self-confident and satisfied with their abilities in childhood and adolescence. Girls, however, consider themselves socially more competent, less shy and more attractive than boys rate themselves; boys more often see themselves as physically strong and dominant.

On the other hand, Maccoby and Jacklin found some sex differences to be fairly well established:

- *Girls have greater verbal ability than boys.* The sexes are very similar in verbal abilities until they are about 11 years old. After that point girls become increasingly superior in both high-level verbal tasks (reading comprehension and creative writing) and low-level skills (language fluency and spelling).

- *Boys have greater visual-spatial ability than girls.* Boys excel in tasks that involve the visual perception of figures and how they are related to each other. Male superiority in such tasks is found even in childhood, but it increases during the high school years. Starting at about the same age, boys' mathematical skills also increase faster than girls' skills do. This greater rate of improvement does not seem to be entirely due to the fact that boys take more math courses in high school, although the matter has not been extensively studied.

In any discussion of male and female differences, it is important to remember that the term "sex difference" refers to a **mean difference,** that is, the difference between the average scores of men and women. It should not be interpreted to say that every man is different from every woman; in fact, there is usually a wide overlap, with most

---

[41] Donna Eder and Maureen T. Hallinan, "Sex Differences in Children's Friendships," *American Sociological Review* 43:2 (April 1978): 237–50.

[42] See Margaret Hennig and Anne Jardim, *The Managerial Woman* (Garden City, N.Y.: Anchor/Doubleday, 1977), pp. 20–26.

Parents, schools, and peers convey definite ideas about what kinds of behavior are appropriate for each sex. By the time they reach high school, most girls do not want to play football and most boys do not aspire to be cheerleaders.

men and most women scoring in the same range. Sex differences in ability and personality should also not be interpreted as the only reasons men and women behave differently.

The finding that males, by and large, have superior visual-spatial ability has sometimes been cited to explain why there are relatively few female scientists and mathematicians. Many studies have concluded, however, that ability is not necessarily the most important factor in the choice of a professional career. From a sample of 1,300 students in California schools, for example, researchers were surprised to find that math was the only subject that boys and girls liked equally well. Thirty percent of the boys and 29 percent of the girls said they liked math best, while 27 percent of the boys and 29 percent of the girls said it was the subject they liked least. As the students progressed in school, however, math became established as a male domain. In contrast to the fairly even amount of parental help that children get in English, the study found that, beginning in the sixth grade, fathers became the authority on math homework. In high school one-third of the students thought boys did better in math than girls, while about half thought there was no difference.[43]

To a sociologist, the key question is not whether men and women have different abilities, but why American society values ''male'' ability in math more highly than ''female'' ability in language. Mastering math and science is considered difficult, and it leads to such prestigious occupations as engineering and finance. The verbal ability to

---

[43] John Ernest, ''Mathematics and Sex'' (unpublished manuscript, Department of Mathematics, University of California at Santa Barbara, 1976). A supporting published work is Ralph Norman, ''Sex Differences in Attitudes Toward Arithmetic-Mathematics from Early Elementary School to College Levels,'' *Journal of Psychology* 97 (1977): 247–56.

communicate is not considered as difficult or important, and it leads to less prestigious occupations — teaching, for example.

In sum, it seems that many, perhaps most, personality differences between the sexes are better explained by social factors than by innate biological and psychological characteristics.

MASCULINITY AND FEMININITY: SOCIALIZED DIFFERENCES

Once a child's sex is known, he or she becomes identified with cultural concepts of what a boy or girl should be like. **Sex**, the biological fact of maleness or femaleness, thus connotes **gender**, the social and psychological characteristics associated with masculinity and femininity. No one is born knowing that crying is unmanly or that playing football is unladylike. Children are born male or female, but they have to learn to be masculine or feminine.

Sex-role socialization begins early. Studies have shown that parents respond to their new babies differently: they tend to smile at and talk to infant girls, but they rock and handle infant boys more often.[44] By the age of 3 or 4, the child's sense of gender is so deeply ingrained that it can only be changed with great difficulty.

John Money, a psychologist at the Johns Hopkins Medical School, has done extensive research on children whose ambiguous genitals caused them to be assigned to the wrong sex at birth. He has found that male or female identity is fixed early in life and that a child who has been raised in the wrong role resists changing just as strongly as a

[44] H. Lewis and M. Weintraub, "Sex of Parent × Sex of Child: Socioemotional Development," in *Sex Differences in Behavior,* eds. R. C. Friedman et al. (New York: Wiley, 1974), pp. 165–90.

child who has been raised in the right one. If a boy, for example, is brought up as a girl by mistake, it is usually easier to change him into a girl physically through surgery than to change his sense of himself as a girl. Money believes that both nature and nurture determine how men and women behave. Although cultural upbringing probably cannot override biological differences entirely, he thinks that it can reinforce them. Society, he has found, can also cause men and women to behave in similar ways, leading them toward a "unisex."[45]

Ideas about how men and women should behave come from other people, especially the people who are important to us in childhood. Fathers and mothers are uniquely able to shape their children's lives, both because they treat daughters and sons differently and because they themselves represent sex-role models with which their children identify. Parents usually have definite ideas about what kinds of behavior are appropriate for each sex, and they have both subtle and not so subtle ways of conveying them. Boys, for example, are usually given trucks and soldiers to play with; the toys' message is that "boys are active and mechanically inclined, and strong and brave." Girls' toys are dolls and dollhouses; they mean that "girls are interested in babies and homemaking."

There is some evidence, however, that this traditional upbringing is going out of style. A 1980 Roper poll reported that three out of four mothers no longer thought it "feminine" for boys to wash dishes or "masculine" for girls to take out the garbage.[46] When these sons and daughters grow up, they will probably be less inclined to define masculinity and femininity so strictly.

Schools also transmit different expectations for each sex. Nursery schoolrooms are often arranged so that there is a doll corner for girls and a block corner for boys. Teachers may emphasize sex-role distinctions by asking boys to move chairs and girls to clean blackboards. The curriculum, too, is usually sex-typed: shop is for boys and home economics is for girls.

From early school age on, most children play with friends of their own sex. These same-sex peer groups tend to emphasize distinctions between boys' and girls' activities and interests and to enforce them with threats of social isolation. Little girls who do not want to play with dolls have little recourse to other games; little boys who dislike baseball risk being left out altogether. After parents the peer subculture is probably the most influential socializing agent for sex-stereotyped values and attitudes.

SEXUAL STEREOTYPES.   We all know her. She smiles at us from billboards or stares seductively out from magazine covers. She is beautiful and sexually available, but she never seems to be doing anything. Once married and settled down, however, she loses her allure. When faced with dirty floors and clogged drains, she is completely helpless until a male voice tells her what to do. She worries a lot about why she can't make a decent cup of coffee or get her husband's shirts clean. She is lovable but just plain dumb.

---

[45] John Money and Anke Ehrhardt, *Man and Woman, Boy and Girl* (Baltimore: Johns Hopkins University Press, 1972); Richard Green and John Money, *Transsexualism and Sex Reassignment* (Baltimore: Johns Hopkins University Press, 1969).
[46] Roper Organization, *Virginia Slims American Women's Opinion Poll, 1970–1980.*

We all know him, too. He is fearless, adventurous, competent in every field. Whether facing down a gunslinger in a saloon or ordering champagne in a nightclub, he is always in control of the situation. He also plays it cool with women. He might let a woman lean on him for a while, but he refuses to be domesticated and usually escapes marriage in the end. When he is not climbing a mountain or racing his sportscar, he likes to relax by drinking beer and playing games with other men.

Although we all know these people, few of us have ever met anyone like them. They are the feminine and masculine images that appear before us daily in the mass media. In thousands of war stories and adventure movies men are shown working together to overcome obstacles and to achieve some moral goal. In popular magazines and television commercials women are shown either as decorative sex objects or domestic drudges. The hidden message is clear: "Men are intelligent and active. They win the victories and get things done. Women are sexually desirable but passive and dependent. Family life and emotional ties are secondary to men but all-important to women."

These images reach children not only through television programs and commercials but through textbooks and children's books. The most extensive study of readers for children — a survey of 2,750 stories from 14 publishers — found that far more stories were about boys than girls. Boys and men in these readers were brave, clever, and curious. They showed qualities that Americans particularly admire: ambition, perseverance, and sportsmanship. They solved problems. They made things. Girls and women, on the other hand, were scared and helpless. They had to ask other people to solve their problems. They cried a lot when things went wrong. They worried constantly about their appearance. They spent their time sewing and baking cookies and watching the boys' activities. No wonder the boys in these stories ridiculed them as scaredy-cats and excluded them from their groups.[47]

An analysis of prize-winning preschool picture books also showed that women were underrepresented. The books had 11 times as many pictures of males as females, and for animals with obvious genders (for example, Peter Rabbit), the ratio was 95 to 1. When women did appear, they were pictured in sex-stereotyped activities. In most of the stories the only adult woman was a mother or a wife. The men had varied and interesting occupational roles, but not one female character in the sample had a job or profession. Once again, females were shown as passive, indoor creatures devoted solely to taking care of men and children.[48]

In the past few years these sex stereotypes have been attacked from several directions. Almost all the major textbook publishers now have guidelines on the treatment of the sexes that attempt to present a more positive and fair image of the contemporary woman. Television advertisers have only recently violated longstanding taboos by showing a woman driving a car and a man diapering a baby. Nevertheless, cultural norms and attitudes do not change overnight. The conventionally masculine hero and the conventionally feminine wife and mother are likely to be with us for some time.

---

[47] Women on Words and Images, *Dick and Jane as Victims: Sex Stereotyping in Children's Readers* (Princeton, N.J., 1972).

[48] Lenore J. Weitzman, "Sex-Role Socialization in Picture Books for Preschool Children," *American Journal of Sociology* 77:6 (1971–1972): 1125–50.

THE COSTS OF SEX-ROLE STEREOTYPING.   Sexist attitudes and practices are logical results of cultural stereotypes that depict men as the achievers and providers and women as their helpless dependents. When carried to extremes, sexism has social costs that can be measured in the growing proportion of women among the poor, as well as in the shocking statistics on wife beating and rape.

Divorce and desertion are economic disasters for women, partly because of the outmoded legal concept that wives will always have husbands to support them. Half of all female-headed households with children have incomes below the poverty line, and two out of three poor adults are women. Seventy-five percent of absent fathers pay no child support at all, even when they are legally obligated to do so.[49] Most child support is inadequate in any case; in 1985, the average yearly support payment was only $2,215.[50] A rising divorce rate, lower pay for "women's work," occupational segregation, and lack of child-care facilities for working mothers have all contributed greatly to the increasing feminization of poverty (see Chapter 7, "Social Inequality").

Physical abuse of women appears to be one result of the sexist view that women should passively accept male domination. The FBI estimates that wife beating is the nation's most common crime, but it rarely results in an arrest. Until very recently, domestic violence has been considered a family matter in which the police are reluctant to interfere. Most battered wives still fail to press charges against their husbands, either because their self-esteem is so low that they think they deserve the beatings, or because they are economically dependent on their spouses, or because they have few legal protections against a vengeful husband.[51]

Rape is another form of violence against women. The FBI's *Uniform Crime Reports* cited 91,000 forcible rapes in 1987 and estimated that many more are never reported. About one-third of rapists are known to the victim, and "date rape" — the rape of a woman by someone she knows — is increasingly common. Because a wife by long legal tradition is considered her husband's property, husbands may still legally rape their wives in most states. Five states have now made marital rape against the law, but 13 states have actually extended the rape privilege to men who are cohabiting with women, and five states legally permit date rape.[52]

The double standard for sexual conduct has contributed to the "rape myth" — the belief that the victim "asked for it" because of her supposedly provocative clothing or promiscuous behavior. As long as American culture defines "normal" sexual relations as male dominance and female passivity, rape is likely to be a continuing social problem.[53]

THE EFFECT OF SOCIALIZATION ON WOMEN.   After years of "getting the message" about how men and women should behave, American girls and boys absorb rather narrow defini-

---

[49] Carol Tavris and Carole Wade, *The Longest War: Sex Differences in Perspective.* 2d ed. (San Diego: Harcourt Brace Jovanovich, 1984), p. 27; Irwin Garfinkel and Sara McLanahan, *Single Mothers and Their Children* (Washington, D.C.: The Urban Institute Press, 1986).

[50] U.S. Bureau of the Census, "Child Support and Alimony: 1985," *Current Population Reports*, Series P-23, No. 152 (Washington, D.C.: U.S. Government Printing Office, 1987), Table D.

[51] Laura Shapiro, "Violence: The Most Obscene Fantasy." in *Women: A Feminist Perspective*, ed. Jo Freeman (Palo Alto, Calif.: Mayfield, 1979), pp. 469–73.

[52] Tavris and Wade, *The Longest War*, p. 29.

[53] Dianne Herman, "The Rape Culture," in *Women: A Feminist Perspective*, pp. 41–63.

In Beatrix Potter's classic story, Peter Rabbit's mother and sisters stay home while he has an exciting and dangerous adventure. After Peter returns safely, his mother nurses him with camomile tea and puts him to bed. Nearly all children's books reinforce sexual stereotypes by portraying boys as brave and active and girls as dependent and domestic.

tions of masculinity and femininity from the culture in which they grow up. Despite many efforts to change sex-role stereotyping in the media, television and children's books by and large still depict active boys who accomplish things and passive girls who need help. "Liberated" parents are often horrified when their daughters ask for Barbie dolls and their sons want to play with guns.

Unless these cultural messages are counteracted by parents or other mentors, young girls learn that femininity means giving up independent interests and trying to please other people, especially men. A number of studies conducted in the 1960s indicated that women considered intellectual and professional achievement a masculine preserve and that fear of seeming unfeminine kept them from doing their best.

Matina Horner, a psychologist who became president of Radcliffe College, conducted the most famous tests of the proposition that women consider intellectual achievement unfeminine. She asked women undergraduates at the University of Michigan to write a story beginning "After first-term finals, Anne finds herself at the top of her medical school class." Male students were given the same test, with "Anne" changed to "John." Ninety percent of the men approved of John's success and predicted a happy future for him: "John continues working hard and eventually graduates at the top of his class." Sixty-five percent of the women's stories, however, showed what Horner called "fear of success." Most predicted that Anne's academic achievement would make her lonely, unpopular, and unmarried. Some students solved Anne's "problem" by having her quit medical school to marry a successful doctor or to go into a predominantly female occupation like social work. Horner concluded that women are often ambivalent about success:

Consciously or unconsciously the girl equates intellectual achievement with loss of femininity. A bright woman is caught in a double bind. In testing and other achievement-oriented situations she worries not only about failure but also about success. If she fails, she is not living up to her own standards of performance; if she succeeds, she is not living up to societal expectations about the female role. Men in our society do not experience this kind of ambivalence, because they are not only permitted but actively encouraged to do well.[54]

Horner's findings have been somewhat qualified by dozens of follow-up studies. First of all, men often show as much fear of success as women do. The same study conducted at the same university with similar students found that more men than women (77 percent to 65 percent) wrote fear-of-success stories. Men, however, appear to have different reasons to question academic achievement than women do. Women associate success with social rejection, but men question the value of a professional career in the first place. In the male students' stories, John leaves medical school to write a novel, or "he graduated with honors and hates being a doctor. He wonders what it was all for." [55] Anne is unpopular and unmarried, but John drops dead prematurely.[56]

New interpretations of Horner's findings conclude that it is not success that women fear but nonconformity to traditional sex roles. The stories may only be describing what women believe outstanding women can realistically expect. Moreover, they are often correct in thinking that men will reject the unconventional woman. Other studies show that men seem to be more disturbed by Anne's success than women are and that they write more negative stories about her than women do.[57] Even against these odds, fear of success does not seem to keep women from succeeding. A follow-up study of Horner's subjects found that most of the students who had high fear-of-success scores went on to get advanced degrees anyway.[58]

Nevertheless, both sexes in these studies seem to agree that Anne's modern role as a professional woman is unusual and unfeminine. In a period of changing cultural expectations for women, the conflict between modern roles and traditional values has made both sexes ambivalent and uncertain (see "Why Young Women Aren't Feminists").

SEX ROLES IN TRANSITION

In the 1970s women's demands for greater equality produced new definitions of what men and women are like and how they should behave. In an era when the working wife has become the rule rather than the exception, it is often the traditional housewife who

---

[54] Matina Horner, "Fail: Bright Women," *Psychology Today* 3 (November 1969): 38.

[55] Lois Wladis Hoffman, "Fear of Success in Males and Females: 1965 and 1971," *Journal of Consulting and Clinical Psychology* 42 (1974): 353–58.

[56] Lillian Robbins and Edwin Robbins, "Comment on 'Toward an Understanding of Achievement-related Conflicts in Women,'" *Journal of Social Issues* 29:1 (1973): 133–37.

[57] Tavris and Wade, *The Longest War*, p. 247.

[58] Lois Wladis Hoffman, "Fear of Success in 1965 and 1974: A Follow-Up Study," *Journal of Consulting and Clinical Psychology* 42 (1977): 310–21.

feels she is not living up to what is socially expected of her. On the other hand, the effort to reconcile domestic responsibilities with the demands of a job or career leads to a number of problems and compromises for the contemporary woman.

For men, changing sex roles have not meant relief from many of the burdens of traditional masculinity. Men in American society are still generally expected to be more able and more successful than women, especially their wives. At a time when the feminist movement is encouraging women to claim more power and freedom, however, the privileges that have assured male superiority are not so easily taken for granted. Moreover, the discrepancy between the masculine ideal and the demands of modern life is often a source of confusion and ambivalence for the contemporary man.

THE NEW WOMAN

Modern American women want it all: husbands, babies, equal job opportunities, political power, economic rewards, professional careers. In one sample of seniors at a prestigious women's college, 85 percent said they would like to be a married career woman with children.[59]

The combination of occupational and family roles represents the New Woman's dilemma. If she is an educated, middle-class woman, she has two simultaneous and contradictory goals: motherhood *and* a full-time career. If she is a working-class woman, she has to reconcile two inconsistent demands: domestic obligations *and* a paying job. She can attempt to solve her dilemma in one of three ways: (1) by leaving her job for the traditional homemaker role; (2) by taking a part-time or nine-to-five job while her children are in school; or (3) by trying to have it all: a marriage, a career, and children.

"JUST A HOUSEWIFE."   In recent years the role of full-time housewife has become a more and more unpopular one. The number of working wives and mothers has increased greatly, and this, combined with the feminist description of housework as uncreative drudgery, has tended to put the housewife on the defensive. A generation ago it was the "career woman" who often had to justify spending so much time away from home. Now it is the full-time homemaker who often feels that she must explain why she is not fulfilling herself in paid employment.

This change in social expectations has tended to diminish the housewife's sense of accomplishment and satisfaction in her work. Although her job is important and difficult, it is unpaid, and unpaid work is held in low esteem in American society. Housekeeping skills go unrewarded in other ways. The housewife, no matter how competent and efficient, receives little outside recognition for a job well done. The *Dictionary of Occupational Titles* has no description for her work, instructing the reader to "see maid." Although a wife contributes services to her family worth upwards of $40,000 a year, some dictionaries still define a housewife as someone "who does not work for a living."[60]

---

[59] Mirra Komarovsky, *Women in College: Shaping New Feminine Identities* (New York: Basic Books, 1985), p. 118.

[60] Michael Minton and Jean Libman Block, *What Is a Wife Worth?* (New York: Morrow, 1984).

WHY YOUNG WOMEN AREN'T FEMINISTS

Gloria Steinem, a leading feminist writer, explains why many women reverse the usual pattern of "brave exploring youth and cowardly conservative old age." She argues that feminist activists tend to be older women because college students have not yet been through the radicalizing experience of sexist discrimination in their working and married lives.

If you had asked me a decade or more ago, I certainly would have said the campus was the first place to look for the feminist or any other revolution. I also would have assumed that student-age women, like student-age men, were much more likely to be activist and open to change than their parents. . . .

   It has taken me many years of traveling as a feminist speaker and organizer to understand that I was wrong about women; at least, about women acting on their own behalf. In activism, as in so many other things, I had been educated to assume that men's cultural pattern was the natural or the only one. If student years were the peak time of rebellion and openness to change for men, then the same must be true for women. In fact, . . . women may be the one group that grows more radical with age. Though some students are big exceptions to this rule, women in general don't begin to challenge the politics of our own lives until later.

   . . . Though every generalization based on female culture has many exceptions, and should never be used as a crutch or excuse, I think we might be less hard on ourselves and each other as students, feel better about our potential for change as we grow older — and educate reporters who announce feminism's demise because its red-hot

center is not on campus — if we figured out that for most of us as women, the traditional college period is an unrealistic and cautious time. Consider a few of the reasons.

   As students, women are probably treated with more equality than we ever will be again. For one thing, we're consumers. The school is only too glad to get the tuitions we pay, or that our families or government grants pay on our behalf. With population rates declining because of women's increased power over childbearing, that money is even more vital to a school's existence. Yet more than most consumers, we're too transient to have much power as a group. If our families are paying our tuition, we may have even less power.

   As young women, whether students or not, . . . we haven't yet experienced the life events that are most radicalizing for women: entering the paid-labor force and discovering how women are treated there; marrying and finding out that it is not yet an equal partnership; having children and discovering who is responsible for them and who is not; and aging, still a greater penalty for women than for men.

   Furthermore, new ambitions nourished by the rebirth of feminism may make young women feel and behave a little like a classical immigrant group. We are determined to prove ourselves, to achieve academic excellence, and to prepare for interesting and successful careers.

* * *

Like most groups of the newly arrived or awakened, our faith in education and paper degrees also has yet to be shaken. . . . Though we may know intellectually that we need to have new

---

On the other hand, the housewife's work does have some intrinsic rewards. When researchers asked housewives themselves how they liked their work, the great majority (71 percent) said they were very happy with the job as a whole.[61] Not surprisingly, taking care of children and cooking were their favorite household tasks, but even regular housework was on average more liked than disliked. As their education and

---

[61] Kathryn E. Walker, "Household Work: Can We Add It to the GNP?" *Journal of Home Economics* (October 1973); Carolyn Jarmon, "Relationship Between Homemakers' Attitudes Toward Specific Household Tasks and Family Composition, Other Situational Variables and Time Allocation" (Master's Thesis, Cornell University, 1972).

games with new rules, we probably haven't quite absorbed such facts as the high unemployment rate among female Ph.D.s; the lower average salary among women college graduates of all races than among counterpart males who graduated from high school or less; the middle-management ceiling against which even those eagerly hired new business-school graduates seem to bump their heads after five or ten years; and the barrier-breaking women in nontraditional fields who become the first fired when recession hits. Sadly enough, we may have to personally experience some of these reality checks before we accept the idea that lawsuits, activism, and group pressure will have to accompany our individual excellence and crisp new degrees.

Then there is the female guilt trip, student edition. If we're not sailing along as planned, it must be *our* fault. If our mothers didn't "do anything" with their educations, it must have been *their* fault. If we can't study as hard as we think we must (because women still have to be better prepared than men), and have a substantial personal and sexual life at the same time (because women are supposed to care more about relationships than men do), then we feel inadequate, as if each of us were individually at fault for a problem that is actually culture-wide.

■ ■ ■

With all that pressure combined with little experience, it's no wonder that younger women are often less able to support each other. Even young women who espouse feminist goals as individuals may refrain from identifying themselves as "feminist": it's okay to want equal pay for yourself (just one small reform) but it's not okay to want equal pay for women as a group (an economic revolution). Some retreat into individualized career obsessions as a way of avoiding this dangerous discovery of shared experience with women as a group. Others retreat into the safe middle ground of "I'm not a feminist but . . ."

■ ■ ■

None of this should denigrate the courageous efforts of young women, especially women on campus, and the many changes they've pioneered. On the contrary, they should be seen as even more remarkable for surviving the conservative pressures, recognizing societal problems they haven't yet fully experienced, and organizing successfully in the midst of a transient student population. Every women's history course, rape hot line, or campus newspaper that is finally covering *all* the news; every feminist professor whose job has been created or tenure saved by student pressure, or male administrator whose consciousness has been permanently changed; every counselor who's stopped guiding women one way and men another; every lawsuit that's been fueled by student energies against unequal athletic funds or graduate school requirements: all those accomplishments are even more impressive when seen against the backdrop of the female pattern of activism.

SOURCE: Gloria Steinem, "Why Young Women Are More Conservative," in *Outrageous Acts and Everyday Rebellions* (New York: New American Library, 1983), pp. 211–16.

income level increased, however, the women were less positive about physical tasks at home and more inclined toward paid work. Moreover, most working women surveyed say that they prefer full-time jobs to staying home.[62] So do their counterparts in the Soviet Union, perhaps for the same reason:

> The married woman who works {in the Soviet Union} bears a double burden, but her position in society is superior to that of the woman who does not work. I once asked

[62] John R. Shea et al. *Dual Careers: A Longitudinal Study of the Labor Market Experience of Women,* Vol. 1 (Columbus: Ohio State University, Center for Human Resource Research, 1970), p. 213.

Television programs provide images of what men and women are like, socializing girls and boys (and adults) to behave in ways that are shown to be appropriate for their sex.

several women in a factory why they worked. I deliberately chose women whose earnings were low and whose work was more monotonous than housework. They replied that no matter how hard they worked in the home, they never got credit for it. Here they received respect and appreciation.[63]

"JUST A SECRETARY."   The married woman who works has two jobs, one inside and one outside the home. To relieve the strain of playing both occupational and domestic roles,

----

[63] *Current Digest of the Soviet Press*, December 1968, p. 11.

most working women either (1) work for a few years before marrying or before having children and then remain full-time homemakers for the rest of their lives; or (2) work until they have children, stay home for a few years, and then go back to work at jobs that do not interfere with family responsibilities. The first pattern was predominant until World War II, but the second pattern is now the typical one.

This working pattern by itself is probably a major factor in relegating women to the lower level of most occupations. By interrupting or changing her job, the working mother loses seniority benefits and opportunities for advancement. By accepting only part-time or seasonal work, the working wife fails to learn the skills and get the experience necessary for higher-level positions. Women managers with family responsibilities are left in the "mommy track" of dead-end, lower paying jobs, while women who put their careers first move ahead in the executive "fast lane".[64] According to a Labor Department analysis of women's work patterns, nearly one-third of American women 30 to 44 years of age are still in the occupation in which they started. More married women had moved down than up and were holding jobs that were not as good as their first ones. The average single woman, however, had moved up to a better one.[65]

Even before they marry, many women anticipate conflicts between family and career and thus do not seek demanding work. In her research on adolescent girls, for example, Gisela Konopka noted that many thought it would be difficult to combine marriage with a career. As one 15-year-old girl described her future plans:

> Maybe a secretary or something like that. Hopefully I will be married with some children. That's what I want to do, I guess that's the way I've been brought up. I don't want to have any career. . . . I do want to have something that I can do and I do want to get married and have children. I do want to have something to fall back on if something happens, or if I decide to go back to work.[66]

"SUPERWOMAN."   The third possibility for the working wife is a business or professional career. For the talented and educated middle-class woman, this option is rapidly becoming the socially approved one. At a time when many women are eager to prove their competence on an equal basis with men, there are more and more nontraditional women who aspire to be a superwoman who can handle it all — a satisfying career on the male pattern and family responsibilities. This choice, however, rarely solves the problem. A New York magazine editor described the "Superwoman's" role strain:

> I felt insecure as a mother and yet deeply guilty because I wanted to go back to work. Nothing worked out. I wasn't happy at work. And I wasn't happy at home. I always felt as though I was doing the wrong thing.[67]

---

[64] See Felice N. Schwartz, "Management Women and the New Facts of Life," *Harvard Business Review* (January/February, 1989).

[65] Shea et al. *Duel Careers* (also published as Manpower Research Monograph No. 21, Vol. 1, by the Manpower Administration, U.S. Department of Labor, 1970); Mary Corcoran, Greg Duncan, and Michael Ponza, "Work Experience, Job Segregation, and Wages," Chapter 10 in Barbara Reskin, ed., *Sex Segregation in the Workplace* (Washington, D.C.: National Academy Press, 1984).

[66] Quoted in Gisela Konopka, *Young Girls: A Portrait of Adolescence* (Englewood Cliffs, N.J.: Prentice-Hall, 1976), pp. 15–16.

[67] Anita Shreve, "Careers and the Lure of Motherhood," *The New York Times Magazine*, November 21, 1982, p. 43.

A professional career — with all its demands on time and energy — is in many ways incompatible with the equally demanding family roles. First of all, motherhood leaves the professional woman less time for her occupation. Regardless of education or occupation, numerous studies have shown that employed wives perform the majority of household and child care tasks.[68] In a predominantly male business or profession, occupational obligations are expected to take priority over others. Women executives are required to take business trips and women doctors are duty-bound to treat their patients at all hours, just as their male colleagues are. Moreover, professional wives can rarely count on their husbands, who have occupational responsibilities of their own, to provide the usual "wifely" support and assistance that would promote their careers. The result is frequently a head-on collision between irreconcilable professional and domestic responsibilities.[69]

Second, the nontraditional woman may still be seen by other people, especially her employer, in terms of traditional female roles (see "The Double Standard at Work"). According to a survey of 1,500 *Harvard Business Review* subscribers, the married woman, even if she is not burdened with family duties, is not likely to be accepted on the same basis as a man. Respondents in the survey, all of whom were managers themselves, were asked to make decisions regarding male and female employees in a hypothetical organization. The responses showed that the managers (5 percent of whom were women) were (1) clearly biased in favor of men in their decisions to develop and promote employees, and (2) skeptical about women's abilities to balance work and family demands. If an employee's personal conduct threatened his or her job, managers tried harder to keep a qualified man than an equally valuable woman. They expected male employees to give top priority to their jobs when there was a conflict between career and family, but they expected female employees to sacrifice their careers to family responsibilities.[70] No matter how untraditional the woman herself, and no matter how skilled she may be, it appears that traditional attitudes toward "woman's place" may still impede her success in a business career. Marya Mannes, an astute observer of contemporary manners, once commented on the incompatible roles of the superwoman:

> Nobody objects to a woman's being a good writer or sculptor or geneticist if at the same time she manages to be a good wife, a good mother, good-looking, good-tempered, well dressed, well groomed, and unaggressive.[71]

THE NEW MAN

While contemporary women have some choice of goals in life, contemporary men generally do not. Men in American society are expected to put their careers ahead of almost every other obligation or aspiration. Since a woman's social role is viewed as

---

[68] Richard A. Berk and Sarah B. Berk, *Labor and Leisure at Home* (Beverly Hills: Sage Publications, 1979); Huber and Spitze, *Sex Stratification.*

[69] Kathleen Gerson, *Hard Choices* (Berkeley: University of California Press, 1985).

[70] Benson Rosen and Thomas H. Jerdee, "Sex Stereotyping in the Executive Suite," *Harvard Business Review* 52 (March – April 1974): 45 – 58.

[71] Marya Mannes, "The Problems of Creative Women," in *The Potential of Women,* eds. Seymour M. Farber and Roger H. L. Wilson (New York: McGraw-Hill, 1963), p. 122.

THE DOUBLE STANDARD AT WORK

Even when men and women have comparable jobs, supervisors and co-workers are likely to accept the stereotyped view that women are more emotional and less efficient than men. Here is one version of the office double standard.

The family picture is on HIS desk:
  Ah, a solid, responsible family man.
HIS desk is cluttered:
  He's obviously a hard worker and a busy man.
HE's talking with co-workers:
  He must be discussing the latest deal.
HE's not at his desk:
  He must be at a meeting.
HE's not in the office:
  He's meeting customers.
HE's having lunch with the boss:
  He's on his way up.
The boss criticized HIM:
  He'll improve his performance.
HE got an unfair deal:
  Did he get angry?
HE's getting married:
  He'll get more settled.
HE's having a baby:
  He'll need a raise.
HE's going on a business trip:
  It's good for his career.
HE's leaving for a better job:
  He recognizes a good opportunity.

The family picture is on HER desk:
  Hmm, her family will come before her career.
HER desk is cluttered:
  She's obviously a disorganized scatterbrain.
SHE's talking with co-workers:
  She must be gossiping.
SHE's not at her desk:
  She must be in the ladies' room.
SHE's not in the office:
  She must be out shopping.
SHE's having lunch with the boss:
  They must be having an affair.
The boss criticized HER:
  She'll be very upset.
SHE got an unfair deal:
  Did she cry?
SHE's getting married:
  She'll get pregnant and leave.
SHE's having a baby:
  She'll cost the company money in maternity
    benefits.
SHE's going on a business trip:
  What does her husband say?
SHE's leaving for a better job:
  Women are undependable.

SOURCE: Natasha Josefowitz, *Paths to Power* (Reading, Mass.: Addison-Wesley, 1980) p. 60.

primarily domestic, her identity depends more on her family than on her occupation. The opposite is true for a man: his social role is viewed as primarily economic, and his sense of identity by and large depends on his occupation. Just as women find that their work conflicts with their primary responsibility to be good wives and mothers, men find that their family roles conflict with their primary responsibility to be good providers.

THE BREADWINNER TRAP. In spite of the American cultural emphasis on men's work as a source of satisfaction, most men say that their families are far more important to them than their work. While it is clear that employed husbands spend much less time on household chores and child care than employed wives, it is equally clear that the roles of husband and father are the most significant part of men's lives. Study after study shows that family life contributes more to men's happiness and well-being than their experiences at work.[72]

Because male identity depends so heavily on the provider role, husbands and fathers are caught in the "breadwinner trap." There is much evidence to show that men's jobs leave them little time for family life. According to a 1976[73] survey of 1,300 upper New York State couples, husbands employed less than 40 hours per week do an average of 2.1 hours of family work a day, husbands employed 40 to 49 hours do 1.7 hours a day, and husbands employed 50 or more hours do 1.2 hours per day. On average, national time-budget data have shown that men's family work amounts to 96 minutes a day, including 12 minutes for child care.[74]

Men themselves acknowledge that their work and family roles conflict. According to a study made in the late 1960s, highly educated men feel that they are inadequate parents because they have to spend so much time at their work.[75] Many were torn between wanting to establish a close relationship with their children and wanting to establish financial security for the family. Because the male family role is primarily defined in terms of economic support, the breadwinner role may indeed be just as confining for men as the homemaker role is for women.

MEN'S LIBERATION.   In recent years, social critics have drawn attention to the harmful effects of defining masculinity only in terms of achievement, competition, and emotional inexpressiveness. The high incidence of stress-related diseases (heart attacks, ulcers) among men has been called one of the costs of the "rat race," or the competitive struggle for success. When men are required to devote so much energy and time to their work, the critics claim, their intimate relationships suffer.

The obligation to be tough and self-sufficient, for example, allows very little freedom to express the qualities of sympathy and trust that enable people to feel close to others. Since child care is largely defined as the mother's responsibility, the father's involvement with his family is sometimes limited and unsatisfying. Overly dependent on their occupation for self-esteem and a sense of accomplishment, many men are ill-equipped for periods of unemployment or retirement from work. One study found that men who were out of work felt less masculine: most of them felt small, unwanted, ashamed.[76] The data on aging also indicate that men see themselves as manly, and life as worthwhile, only when they are employed.[77]

In attacking the restrictions of the female role, the women's liberation movement of the 1960s undoubtedly had a consciousness-raising effect on men as well. Many men

---

[72] Joseph Pleck, "The Contemporary Man," in Michael Kimmel and Michael Messner, eds., *Men's Lives* (New York: Macmillan, 1989), pp. 591–6.

[73] K. Walker and M. Woods, *Time Use: A Measure of Household Production of Goods and Services* (Washington, D.C.: American Home Economics Association, 1976).

[74] John Robinson, *How Americans Use Time* (New York: Praeger, 1977).

[75] Joseph Veroff and Sheila Feld, *Marriage and Work in America* (New York: Van Nostrand-Reinhold, 1970).

[76] D. D. Braginsky and B. M. Braginsky, "Surplus People: Their Lost Faith in Self and System," *Psychology Today* (August 1975): 69–72.

[77] Sidney M. Jourard, "Some Lethal Aspects of the Male Role," in *Men and Masculinity*, eds. Joseph H. Pleck and Jack Sawyer (Englewood Cliffs, N.J.: Prentice-Hall, 1974), pp. 21–29; Jessie Bernard, "The Good Provider Role: Its Rise and Fall," in Michael Kimmel and Michael Messner, eds., *Men's Lives* (New York: Macmillan, 1989), pp. 223–40.

The traditional masculine ideal — represented by the intrepid, lady-killing James Bond — pervades American culture. Even "liberated" men usually judge themselves according to this image of the dominant, undomesticated male.

have since realized that they can also be oppressed by traditional sex-role definitions requiring them to be all-powerful achievers and providers. The fear-of-success research indicates that some men are beginning to question whether the benefits of traditional masculinity outweigh the penalties. Very recent studies showing that fathers have what had always been called a "maternal instinct" offer evidence that young men today feel more comfortable in nurturing and expressive roles. There are also signs that men's family behavior, too, is beginning to change. In 1977 a national survey of employed persons found — *for the first time* — that husbands are doing appreciably more housework and child care when their wives work than they used to.[78] This finding

---

[78] Joseph Pleck, "The Contemporary Man," *op. cit.*

was the first hint that homemaking may be losing its "for women only" label. Finally, the current masculine image in the mass media is not exclusively that of a superhero. Although the tough guys still predominate in movies and on television, the male lead is more often permitted to be sensitive as well as strong, tender as well as dominant.

Nevertheless, even "liberated" men tend to judge themselves by conventional standards of masculinity. Mirra Komarovsky's study of college men — although it represents a small, elite sample — is probably an accurate portrayal of the New Man's dilemma. The young men she interviewed (sixty-two seniors at Columbia University) held fast to the traditional view of masculinity. They described the ideal man as assertive, strong, courageous, and aggressive. At the same time they had a great deal of difficulty living up to this ideal in their relationships with women. One senior said, "One thing that bothers me is the way they always picture men as dominant and strong. That puts a lot of strain on a man." [79] The nonphysical nature of most work and the modern two-income family does not provide many occasions for the New Man to express traditional masculinity in other ways. Furthermore, other cultural norms interfere. The modern male ideal now includes the traditionally "feminine" qualities of patience, sensitivity, and artistic appreciation.

Many of the young men Komarovsky studied were sympathetic to feminist goals, but they still personally preferred traditional women. When they were asked what they wanted in a woman, the seniors' replies showed a startling conflict between a desire for intellectual companionship and traditional role expectations. Many showed ambivalence toward intelligent women. They disapproved of women who played dumb with men, but they also felt threatened by intellectually superior women. "I enjoy talking to more intelligent girls," one said, "but I have no desire for a deep relationship with them. I guess I still believe that the man should be more intelligent." The college men were also ambivalent toward full-time homemakers and career wives. On the one hand, they did not have much respect for housewives; on the other hand, they did not think a wife's career should interfere with her housekeeping or her husband's career. "It's only fair," declared one senior, "to let a woman do her own thing, if she wants a career. Personally, though, I would want my wife at home." [80]

HALF A REVOLUTION?

After two decades of activism for women's rights, the feminist revolution appears to be stalled at the halfway mark. The enormous, rapid social changes that have transformed women's lives so dramatically have hardly affected men's lives at all. Even with most mothers — including a majority of mothers of babies and preschool children — in the labor force, the working wife and mother is still widely considered an exception to the rule that a woman's usual place is in the home. No one refers to "working fathers" or the "daddy track," and women who work are still being pressed to fulfill nearly all their traditional responsibilities to home and family. This half-revolution leaves working

---

[79] Mirra Komarovsky, *Dilemmas of Masculinity* (New York: Norton, 1976), p. 154.
[80] Ibid., pp. 34, 49.

THE POLITICS OF ABORTION

In the historic *Roe v. Wade* decision in 1973, the Supreme Court declared, by a 7 to 2 majority, that women have a constitutional right to abortion in the early stages of pregnancy. Although many states had already legalized abortions, the court's ruling aroused public outrage and vigorous political opposition. The anti-abortion "Right-to-Life" movement and other conservative organizations have campaigned singlemindedly to reverse the *Roe v. Wade* decision. These groups have unsuccessfully proposed constitutional amendments against abortion, sponsored congressional legislation declaring that life begins at conception, demanded that anti-abortion judges be appointed to the federal courts, campaigned against candidates supporting a woman's right to abortion, and even resorted to disrupting and bombing abortion clinics.

"Pro-choice" activists argue that overturning *Roe v. Wade* will force millions of women to risk illegal — and sometimes fatal — abortions. Their campaigns have used the symbol of a bent coat hanger to remind the public of the dangers of back-alley abortions. In 1989 such groups as the National Organization for Women, the National Abortion Rights Action League, and Planned Parenthood organized a pro-choice rally in Washington, D.C. which drew hundreds of thousands of demonstrators — more than either the 1963 civil rights march or the anti-war demonstrations of the 1970s.

Why is the debate over legalized abortion so heated? The sociologist Kristen Luker argues that the right to a legal abortion threatens strongly held beliefs about women's social roles. In *Abortion and the Politics of Motherhood** Luker contends that people who join the "pro-life" and the "pro-choice" movements come from different positions in the American social structure.

According to Luker, the typical anti-abortion activist is a married woman with several children who is not employed outside the home. The majority are devout Catholics. Household income for pro-life women is relatively low, and most have only a high school education. Although many women are now active in the Right-to-Life movement, it was started originally by male lawyers and clergymen.

The typical pro-choice activist, in contrast, is a college-educated woman who works outside the home. These women tend to have smaller families and higher incomes than pro-life activists. They are more likely to be single or divorced, and they do not find religion to be an important influence in their lives. While pro-life activists report little firsthand experience with abortion, many pro-choice activists have faced the abortion dilemma themselves or have friends who have had abortions. Finally, women have been the leaders of the pro-choice movement from the start.

Luker argues that these differences in education, employment, income, religious beliefs, and life experience shape social attitudes toward women's roles. Pro-life activists think that a woman's main purpose in life is to be a wife and mother. Pro-choice women view motherhood as only one of the many options in their lives; they believe women should be able to plan their pregnancies. One side believes abortion is murder, the other side believes abortion is a "reproductive right." Each group of activists feels that their deepest beliefs — as well as their sources of social power — are threatened by the other group.

In May 1989 a more conservative Supreme Court upheld, by a 5 to 4 decision, the constitutionality of a Missouri law sharply restricting publicly funded abortions. Chief Justice William Rehnquist's majority opinion strongly suggested that *Roe v. Wade* no longer represented the court's views. The court's decisions in pending abortion cases will almost certainly set legal precedents that will make legal abortions more difficult to obtain. Luker predicts, however, that the political battle over abortion will continue as long as there is such profound disagreement over the role of women in American society.

* Berkeley: University of California Press, 1984.

mothers in the typical domestic bind of the 1980s: juggling jobs, child care, and domestic chores.

On the political front there has lately been strong, organized resistance to feminist goals from those who have the most to lose from changes in male and female roles (see "The Politics of Abortion"). Women who have spent their adult lives as homemakers

Drawing by
D. Reilly; © 1985
The New Yorker
Magazine, Inc.

are deeply offended by the suggestion that they have been wasting their time and talents in unproductive activities. To men accustomed to the privileges of male supremacy at home and work, feminists appear to threaten their roles as breadwinners and family heads. By mobilizing such men and women in political protests, fundamentalist churches and other conservative groups have successfully blocked two feminist proposals: passage of the ERA and Medicaid abortions for the poor.[81]

There is little doubt, however, that the resurgence of feminism in the 1960s has stimulated a reappraisal of American values. Opinion polls show that the majority of young people today believe that women should receive equal pay for equal work and that men and women have the same essential human nature ("It's the way they are brought up that makes them different."). The younger generation is no longer committed to the idea that the man must be the main decision maker in the family and that men should always take the initiative in sexual matters. Unlike earlier women's rights movements, the women's liberation movement of the 1960s coincided with social and economic trends that were taking women away from home and into the work force (see "The Woman's Movement, 1848–1990," in Chapter 17). By the 1970s married women were consistently departing from the traditional pattern. The fertility rate in the middle of the decade was at a new low of 1.9 children per woman, the proportion of women in the labor force was approaching 50 percent, and half the freshman class in college was female. For the first time the feminist ideology of equal rights and equal opportunities was relevant to the lives of millions of women who felt thwarted by their place in American society.

New social values, however, have not yet resulted in many new social practices. Very little has actually been done about changing American institutions to promote

[81] Jane Dehart Mathews and Donald Mathews, "The Cultural Politics of the ERA's Defeat," in Laurel Richardson and Verta Taylor, *Feminist Frontiers II* (New York: Random House, 1989), pp. 458–63.

equal rights for women. So far, only a few businesses and government agencies have experimented with flexible working hours that permit men and women to share family and occupational responsibilities more equally. Partly because of its ambivalence about working mothers, the United States remains the only industrial society that does not have a national day-care program for children. Such **institutionalized sexism** is rooted in a social structure that assigns different places to men and women and in the cultural values that support these arrangements. It is the real obstacle to women's achieving equality with men.

Nevertheless, rather dramatic shifts in behavior and attitudes have taken place in the last twenty years. Some of these changes have already undermined the basis of inequality by loosening rigid definitions of masculinity and femininity; by changing the role models that parents, especially mothers, provide their children; and by breaking down the barriers separating male and female activities and interests. If these changes have not brought equality between the sexes, there is still reason to believe that the movement toward it will not soon end.

SUMMARY

1. American society, like societies in general, has tended to keep the social roles of men and women separate and unequal. Sexist ideology contends that these inequalities are based on innate characteristics, that women are "naturally" inferior to men, and that their separate social roles should not be changed. Nevertheless, these sex roles are changing because of the impact of the feminist movement and the economic developments that have brought a majority of American women into the work force.

2. Women's aspirations are higher today, but they still do not have fully equal opportunities at work. Occupational segregation in low-paying, dead-end jobs is one reason women earn only about two-thirds as much as men.

3. At home women traditionally have been assigned the primary responsibility for housekeeping and child care. Even when they work full-time, married women do not expect or get much help from their husbands.

4. The differences between men and women, as groups, appear to be more influenced by nurture, or cultural factors, than by nature, or innate biological and psychological characteristics.

5. There is reason to think that males are generally more aggressive because of biological factors, but greater aggressiveness is not an adequate explanation for male domination. The so-called maternal instinct is apparently learned rather than innate.

6. The personalities and abilities of boys and girls are similar in their early years, but they begin to differ markedly in adolescence. Girls as a group develop greater verbal ability than boys, and boys have greater visual-spatial ability than girls. On the whole, American society values "male" ability in math more highly than "female" ability in language.

7. The most important differences between the sexes are learned through the socialization process. Money's research found that cultural upbringing fixes male or female identity at a very young age. Parents, teachers, and playmates are influential socializing agents in childhood. The mass media and children's books transmit stereotyped ideas of how men and women behave.

8. When carried to extremes, sex-role stereotyping leads to sexist attitudes and practices. Some of the social consequences of sexism are the feminization of poverty and the physical abuse of women through wife beating and rape.

9. Changing sex roles cause problems for both sexes. The conflict between occupational and family roles is the New Woman's dilemma. Some solve it

by leaving their jobs to be full-time housewives, but the majority stay home until their children are in school and take jobs that do not interfere with domestic responsibilities. This interrupted working pattern is a major reason women stay on the lower rungs of the occupational ladder. Superwomen, who combine motherhood with demanding careers, find that conflicts between professional and family roles are difficult to resolve. Traditional attitudes about women's place also lead to discrimination against the unconventional woman.

10. The New Man has the dilemma of meeting both traditional expectations and new definitions of masculinity. Work and family roles conflict, leaving men in a breadwinner trap, with little time for their families. Even liberated men, who question the value of putting their work ahead of other goals, still tend to judge themselves (and women) by traditional standards.

11. After 20 years of activism for women's rights, the feminist revolution appears to be stalled. Rapid changes in women's roles have not yet had much effect on men's roles, and changing views of masculinity and femininity have not yet resulted in institutional changes that would promote sexual equality. Feminist goals have lately met strong political resistance, but the real barriers to women's rights lie in a social structure that assigns different places to men and women and in the cultural values that support these arrangements.

KEY TERMS

sexism 300
sex roles 301
masculinity 301
femininity 301

sex-typed 302
nature/nurture controversy 312
mean difference 315

sex 317
gender 317
institutionalized sexism 335

SUGGESTED READING

*Cynthia Fuchs Epstein. *Deceptive Distinctions: Sex, Gender, and the Social Order.* Yale University Press and Russell Sage Foundation, 1988.

Clyde W. Franklin II. *The Changing Definition of Masculinity.* New York: Plenum Press, 1984.

Joan Huber. *Sex Stratification: Children, Housework, and Jobs: Monograph.* Ed. Glenna Spitze. San Diego, CA: Academic Press, 1983.

* Louise Kapp Howe. *Pink Collar Workers.* New York: Putnam's, 1977.

* Jean Lipman-Blumen. *Gender Roles and Power.* New York: Prentice-Hall, 1984.

* Gerda Lerner. *The Creation of Patriarchy.* New York: Oxford University Press, 1987.

* Kristin Luker. *Abortion and the Politics of Motherhood.* Berkeley, CA: University of California Press, 1984.

* Margaret Mead. *Sex and Temperament in Three Primitive Societies.* New York: Morrow, 1963; originally published in 1935.

* Alice S. Rossi, ed. *Gender and the Life Course.* New York: Aldine, 1985.

* Lillian B. Rubin. *Worlds of Pain: Life in the Working Class Family.* New York: Basic, 1977.

* Available in paperback.

PART 4

SOCIAL INSTITUTIONS

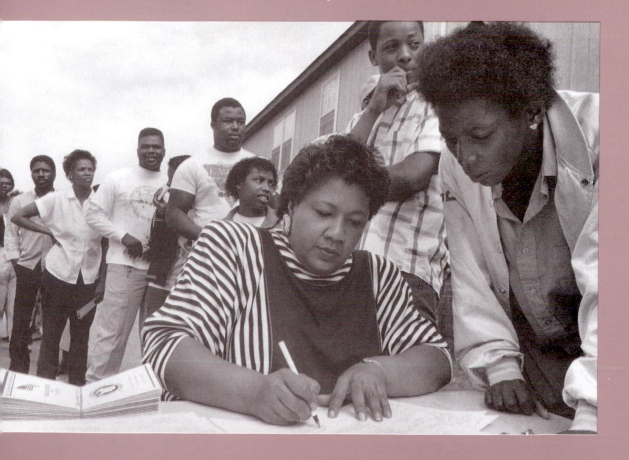

"Oh, 'tis love,
'tis love, 'tis
love, that makes
the world go
round."
"Somebody
said," Alice
whispered, "that
it's done
by everybody
minding their
own business!"
"Ah, well! It
means much the
same thing,"
said the Duchess.

Lewis Carroll

CHAPTER 11

THE FAMILY

Tea for two
And two for tea.
Me for you
And you for me
  Alone. . . .

We will raise a family,
A boy for you, a girl for me.
Can't you see
How happy we will be?

T his familiar love song is a classic expression of the American ideal of family life. Like the songwriter, most Americans dream of marriage as "me for you and you for me alone"—an entirely personal relationship. Yet the family is an ancient and universal institution. There is no record of any society, no matter how simple, that does not have marriage as one of the basic elements of its social structure.

Although families exist in all human societies, they appear in so many different forms that it is difficult to say exactly what a family is. Webster's dictionary has 22 separate definitions, which the Census Bureau boils down to "two or more persons related by birth, marriage or adoption who reside in the same household." In its most general sense, a **family** is usually defined as two or more persons who are linked by marriage or descent and who engage in common activities. The family envisioned in "Tea for Two" is a **nuclear family**: a married couple and their children. Of course, not all families fit this model. A family can take many forms: it might be a single-parent household; or a married couple sharing their home with a relative who has moved in temporarily; or a large group of parents, children, and in-laws who live together on a permanent basis. When relatives outside the nuclear family share the same household, then this family group is known as an **extended family**.

Even this definition of the family varies enormously in different societies. Among the Nayar of India wives live with their mothers instead of their husbands; in some Israeli kibbutzim, children are raised separately from their parents and visit them on weekends. Marriage also takes different forms in different cultures. Under the Ottoman Empire the sultans kept their many wives secluded in harems; in ancient China the gentry arranged marriages for their sons and daughters when they were still small children. Because it is impossible to define exactly what families *are*, sociologists concentrate on what families *do*—in other words, what social functions they perform.

This chapter is about the functions and structures of the human family in general and the American family in particular. As everyone knows, patterns of family life in the United States have been changing rapidly. Only a generation ago, the traditional family —working father, stay-at-home mother, and one or more children—represented 70 percent of all American households; today it accounts for just *9 percent* of them. Only a small majority (58 percent) of households include a married couple, and most wives (52 percent) are now employed outside the home.[1]

There has been a great deal of speculation, much of it pessimistic, about this profound change in American family life. Compared to earlier generations, the modern family has been called weak, unstable, and less able to meet vital social needs. In assessing these criticisms, we focus here on the problems that result when the family's needs conflict with those of other institutions. Finally, we discuss some alternatives to the nuclear family and consider the prospects for family life in the future.

WHY MARRIAGE?: THE UNIVERSAL FUNCTIONS OF THE FAMILY

Ask people who are engaged why they are getting married and they will probably say "We love each other" and perhaps "We want to have children." But of course it is not

---

[1] U.S. Bureau of the Census, "Household and Family Characteristics: 1988," *Current Population Reports,* Series P-20, No. 437 (Washington, D.C.: U.S. Government Printing Office, 1989).

necessary to be married in order to have sexual relations or to care for any offspring that may result. As a matter of fact, people everywhere have always *limited* their sexual activity by getting married. Evidently the biological needs for sex and infant care do not explain the universality of the family. The family must be meeting universal *social* needs instead.

THE REGULATION OF SEX

Every society has rules about what sorts of people are permitted to marry each other. The strongest, most ancient prohibition against marriage within a certain group is the **incest taboo**. This rule strictly prohibits sexual intercourse between precisely those people who would ordinarily be the natural and most accessible partners — close family members. Parents and children and brothers and sisters are never allowed to marry; first cousins are sometimes included in the taboo as well. An extremely rare exception is the society of ancient Egypt, where incest was acceptable for gods; because the kings were believed divine, several of them were legally married to their sisters or daughters.

According to popular belief, the incest taboo is a universal way of preventing the genetic deformities that result from inbreeding. Because primitive peoples did not always understand the direct relationship between sexual intercourse and pregnancy, and because only a few people in modern societies know how such disabilities are inherited, it is hardly possible that a fear of inbreeding accounts for the fact that incest has been prohibited in every society. Furthermore, any breeder of animals knows that inbreeding is just as likely to result in desirable traits as undesirable ones. As we shall see, the incest taboo meets universal social — not biological — requirements.

The incest taboo requires that the exchange of sexual partners must take place *between* and not *within* families. The rule thus ensures that every member of society who marries will be linked to two families: the family into which he or she is born, and the family which is established by marriage. Instead of being emotionally and socially tied to only a few members of the same small group, everyone is in effect made part of a larger social structure. On a broader social level the prohibition of incest ensures that every marriage will unite not just two people but two previously unrelated families. The anthropologist Bronislaw Malinowski called this rule of family exchange the **principle of reciprocity**.[3]

The unifying social function of marriage, though usually unremarkable, is quite obvious when warring families are reconciled. The wedding of King Ferdinand and Queen Isabella brought peace to Spain by uniting the great ruling houses of Aragon and Castile. And a love match finally settled the disastrous feud between the humble Hatfield and McCoy families in the rural United States. Marriage thus creates a network of affiliations that helps bind the social structure together.

The incest taboo also helps maintain clear social identities. If a mother and son were permitted to marry and produce children, for example, the family's relationships would become hopelessly tangled. The children's father would also be their brother,

---

[2] Russell Middleton, "A Deviant Case: Brother-Sister and Father-Daughter Marriage in Ancient Egypt," *American Sociological Review* 27:5 (October 1962): 603–11.

[3] Bronislaw Malinowski, "Parenthood, the Basis of Social Structure," in *The New Generation*, eds. V. F. Calverton and S. D. Schmalhausen (Secaucus, N.J.: Macauley/Citadel, 1930), pp. 113–68.

their mother would be their grandmother, their sisters and brothers would be their nieces and nephews, and so forth into endless confusion. In this way social necessity overrides biological possibilities.

CHILD REARING

If biological considerations were all-important, there would be no good reason for both parents to raise a family. The father's biological role ends with conception, and a mother and her children could theoretically make a complete family unit. Children, however, inherit a social status, a particular place in the complex of social relationships. Every society has a concept of fatherhood, which is usually — but not always — the same as biological paternity (see "The Meaning of Parenthood"). Biology usually settles the question of who the mother of a child might be, but fatherhood is a social role that involves giving children their initial status in the world. This heritage, or ascription of social position, assures every child a clearly defined place in the social structure. The social process of linking a father to every child is known as **legitimacy**.

According to Malinowski's **principle of legitimacy**, each child must have a social father — a guardian who provides the male link between the child and the community. Biological fathers who refuse to accept their responsibilities as social fathers deny the child their "name" and consequently the right to a certain status. Children who lack a social father are thus said to be illegitimate. Throughout history bastards have been disapproved of socially because their incomplete heritage gives them an ambiguous status. A mother and her children, no matter how self-sufficient they may be biologically, have always been considered an incomplete social unit.[4]

According to the principle of legitimacy, the second function of the family is the orderly placement of new members in society. As William J. Goode, an authority on family organization, has noted,

> In all known societies, almost everyone lives his life enmeshed in a network of family rights and obligations. . . . A person is made aware of (these) through a long period of socialization during his childhood, a process in which he learns how others in the family expect him to behave, and in which he himself comes to feel this is both the right and the desirable way to act.[5]

The family, Goode contends, is the principal link between the individual and the larger society. Its "mediating function" is to prepare children for their roles in the community and to motivate them to perform these roles as well as they can. The family thus helps a society to survive by producing new members who are willing and able to carry on its cultural traditions and social institutions. The family, in other words, is the primary means of social reproduction as well as biological reproduction.

Since in every society a father is expected to provide for his children, the male link to the community is more than symbolic. Higher American rates of illegitimacy are troubling mainly because children born out of wedlock are more likely to suffer

---

[4] Rose Laub Coser, *The Family: Its Structures and Functions,* 2d ed. (New York: St. Martin's Press, 1974), p. xviii.

[5] William J. Goode, *The Family* (Englewood Cliffs, N.J.: Prentice-Hall, 1964), pp. 1–2.

THE MEANING OF PARENTHOOD

"If King Solomon were alive today, he would be sorely vexed. It is now possible for a child to have up to five individuals claiming to be parents: a sperm donor, an egg (ovum) donor, the woman providing a womb for gestation, and the couple raising the child."[1]

Modern technologies solve problems of infertility by permitting men and women to have children in ways that separate sex from procreation. Today it is possible for a man to have a child he has not "fathered"; it is also possible for a pregnant woman to be carrying a child that is not her own — at least in the sense that she and the fetus share no genetic links. When sex and procreation are unrelated, questions arise about kinship: What is a father? What is a mother?

The following technologies are redefining the meaning of parenthood:

Artificial insemination. In this procedure, a donor's semen is inserted into a woman during the period of ovulation. Since the sperm is not usually from the woman's husband, artificial insemination produces an "illegitimate" baby. Nevertheless, most states have declared a child born through this method to be the husband's legal offspring. The "real" or biological father is not considered kin.

In vitro fertilization. So-called "test-tube" babies are conceived by removing 5 to 7 ova from a woman and fertilizing them outside her body. Two or three are then inserted into her uterus for normal development and birth. The others may be destroyed, used for research, or frozen and implanted later, either in the same woman or another woman. But who has the right to decide what to do with these embryos? Should they be treated as property or human lives? Until recently, U.S. courts have usually considered fertilized ova as the joint property of the donors, giving them the right to decide what should happen. However, after the Supreme Court's 1989 decision in *Webster v. Reproductive Services,* which validated a Missouri law declaring that life begins at conception, a court in Tennessee granted custody of 7 frozen embryos to the wife in a divorce case.

Surrogate motherhood. In the famous "Baby M" case, Mary Beth Whitehead agreed to be artificially inseminated with the sperm of William Stern with the understanding that Mr. and Mrs. Stern would take legal custody of the child at birth. Mrs. Whitehead changed her mind during the pregnancy and refused to accept the $10,000 for which she had contracted. When Baby M was born, whose baby was it? Clearly, Baby M is genetically half Mary Beth Whitehead's and half William Stern's. At first the contractual agreement was upheld. A New Jersey judge gave the Sterns custody of the child and denied Mrs. Whitehead any rights as a parent. Finally, in 1988, the New Jersey Supreme Court unanimously overturned this decision and declared that surrogacy for money is illegal. The Sterns now have custody of Baby M, but Mrs. Whitehead is considered her legal mother and has been granted visiting rights.

Every technological improvement brings moral questions in its wake. Indeed, the most troubling aspect of these solutions to infertility is their *social* meaning. Families — mothers, fathers, children — are not only biological and legal definitions but social relationships. When these definitions and relationships are changing, as they are now, then everyone is likely to feel puzzled and confused.

[1] Stephen L. Issacs and Rene J. Holt, "Redefining Procreation: Facing the Issues," *Population Bulletin* 42. Washington, D.C.: Population Reference Bureau, Inc., 1987, p. 3.

numerous problems as they grow up: poverty, low educational achievement, and high rates of divorce and welfare dependency.[6] Although more than one out of five births were illegitimate in 1988,* American society is no closer to finding a successful alternative to fatherhood than any other society has been.

---

[6] Irwin Garfinkel and Sara S. McLanahan, *Single Mothers and Their Children* (Washington, D.C.: Urban Institute Press, 1986.)

* Including 15 percent of white, 56 percent of black, and 26 percent of Hispanic children.

The family is an ancient and universal social institution. This relief depicts the Pharaoh Tutankhamon's family, who lived about 1350 BC.

A "HAVEN IN A HEARTLESS WORLD"

Industrial societies have been called a "heartless world" in which the family is uniquely able to provide a private haven of intimate companionship and emotional support.[7] At work and at school, in hospitals and in courts of law, people in modern societies are subject to impersonal rules and bureaucratic regulations. Other modern institutions are expected to treat all their members equally on the basis of **universalistic norms** — objective criteria such as years of seniority or IQ scores. But the family is expected to treat each member as an individual according to **particularistic norms**, standards based on faith and love that apply to only particular people: *my* wife, *my* child, *my* brother. When other institutions seem less and less able to provide emotional satisfactions, the family becomes more and more important as a "safety-valve institution" for blowing off the built-up tensions and frustrations of daily life.

Of course, husbands and wives do not always give each other unconditional love, acceptance, and companionship. Some marriages are unhappy and some families erupt in violent conflict or drift into sullen indifference. When it is the only institution where personal feelings can be freely expressed, the family can also suffer from "emotional overload." Many people depend solely on their spouses or children for the emotional

---

[7] Christopher Lasch's phrase, in *Haven in a Heartless World: The Family Besieged* (New York: Basic, 1977).

rewards that others find in their religion or their work. The family is frequently unable to support such a heavy burden, and the ties among its members may break down.

Nevertheless, families provide most of us with love and affection. Three out of five people in a national survey said the family was the most important aspect of their lives, and another one out of the five said it was among the most important.[8]

ECONOMIC FUNCTIONS OF THE FAMILY

Randall Collins, a conflict theorist, argues that the concept of property is a basic organizing principle for the family.[9] Owning something means that members of a society have agreed that one person has a right to use it, other people do not have a similar right to use it, and, if called upon, agents of society (police, government) will enforce that individual's rights of ownership. According to Collins, the family is based on three types of property relationships:

Sexual property. In every society marriage establishes rights of sexual intercourse (sexual property) between husbands and wives. Each spouse is entitled to have sex with the other spouse, others (generally) do not, and adultery is almost universally defined as a crime. Collins believes that the incest taboo is part of this system of property relationships, since incest is sometimes a form of adultery that violates one spouse's property rights.

Household economic property. Families everywhere provide food, shelter, nursing, child care, and many other products and services.

Intergenerational property. All parents have the right to control their children; all children have the right to inherit material goods from their parents.

As Collins points out, families almost always perform special economic functions. In agricultural societies many families are nearly self-sufficient units, producing most of what they need themselves and "paying" their members in room and board. In industrial societies, however, families are primarily economic consumers rather than producers. Adult members work for pay outside the family, and children and unemployed housewives are "dependents" who rarely earn any wages at all. Nevertheless, the family functions as an economic unit that provides innumerable services ranging from child care and food production to transportation and secretarial help.[10] An almost universal division of labor gives female members the primary responsibility for unpaid work at home and male members the primary responsibility for paid work in the outside world. Such job specialization according to sex is breaking down somewhat in Western societies, but husbands and wives still share the family's basic economic functions, even if they are dividing them differently (see Chapter 10, "The Sexes").

Moreover, all families take on special responsibilities for their members' material needs. Today, in addition to food, clothing, and shelter, family members are also likely to pay for such contemporary requirements as higher education and professional

---

[8] White House Conference on Families, *Families and Major Institutions* (Washington, D.C.: U.S. Government Printing Office, 1980).

[9] Randall Collins, *Sociology of Marriage and the Family,* 2d ed. (Chicago: Nelson Hall, 1988), p. 66.

[10] According to the Congressional Budget Office, the average American wife contributes 34 hours a week in household services and the average husband contributes 15 hours. If this labor were purchased for $5.00 an hour, wives would earn a yearly salary of $8840 and husbands would be paid $3900. See Janet Peskin, "Measuring Household Production for the GNP," *Family Economics Review* 3 (1982): 16–25.

In the nineteenth century many families were nearly self-sufficient economic units, producing most of their own goods and services. Although families today are primarily economic consumers, they still produce vital services for their members.

medical care. People who are poor or disabled frequently receive assistance from their families in the form of money or nursing services. The family's willingness to meet such obligations benefits society by providing care and protection for its weakest members.

THE CHANGING FUNCTIONS OF THE FAMILY

As society has grown more complex, other institutions have assumed responsibility for many tasks traditionally performed by families. Of course, the production of most consumer goods and services now takes place outside the home. In addition, schools now play a much greater role in socializing children than they did in preindustrial times: schoolteachers are supposed to teach vocational skills, form character, and instill society's values. Hospitals and nursing homes have assumed much of the family's role in caring for the aged and sick. And social welfare institutions are increasingly called upon to provide support for the poor.

If marriage is no longer necessary, it is still just as popular. A growing proportion of Americans eventually marry, although they are doing so at a slightly older age than their parents (see Figures 11-1 and 11-2). Modernization has removed many of the family's traditional responsibilities but has increased its importance as a unique source of special care and attention in a largely cold and impersonal world. People continue to marry and have children, not just because it is convenient but because they need to love and be loved as individual human beings.

FIGURE 11-1

PERCENT NEVER MARRIED BY AGE 40

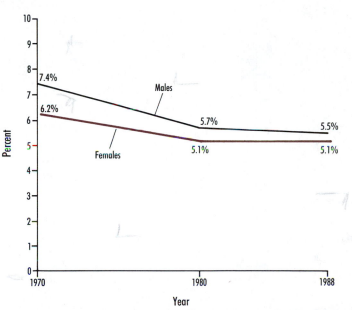

SOURCE: U.S. Bureau of the Census, "Marital Status and Living Arrangements: March 1988," *Current Population Reports*. Series P-20, No. 433 (Washington, D.C.: U.S. Government Printing Office, 1989), Table A-1.

FORMS OF THE FAMILY

While the family serves the same basic functions everywhere, its particular structure changes in response to different situations. Old practices that Americans find exotic — like the sultans' harems of wives or the childhood marriages of the Chinese gentry — turn out to have been solutions in other social environments to the same personal and social needs served by the Western form of marriage.

FORMS OF MARRIAGE

Because families everywhere regulate sexual relationships, and because there are roughly as many men as women in most societies, it is hardly surprising that the most common form of marriage is **monogamy,** or marriage between one man and one woman. Societies with a shortage of eligible mates frequently also permit **polygamy**, or marriage to more than one partner.

Polygyny, the most common form of polygamy, is the marriage of one man to two or more women. The anthropologist George Murdock found that polygyny was permitted in 75 percent of the 565 mostly tribal societies he studied.[11] In such societies

---

[11] George P. Murdock, "World Ethnographic Sample," *American Anthropologist* 59 (1957): 664–87.

FIGURE 11-2   MEDIAN AGE AT FIRST MARRIAGE

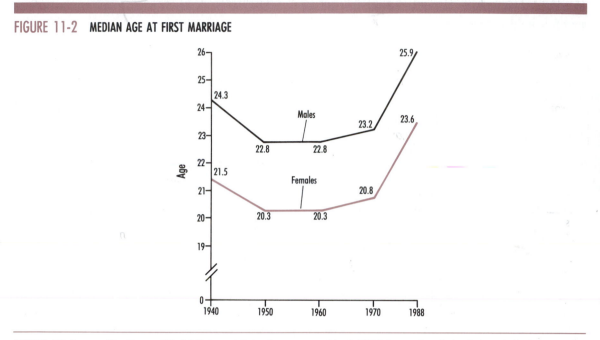

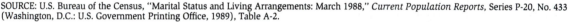

SOURCE: U.S. Bureau of the Census, "Marital Status and Living Arrangements: March 1988," *Current Population Reports,* Series P-20, No. 433 (Washington, D.C.: U.S. Government Printing Office, 1989), Table A-2.

wives are generally a sign of wealth, which brings a man prestige in the community; more wives also produce more children, who provide extra labor. The hard economic fact that additional wives and children cost more to support, however, usually limits polygyny to a wealthy elite, like the sultans of the Ottoman Empire.

Polyandry, the marriage of one women to more than one man, occurs only under unusually severe economic conditions. The most frequent type of polyandry is the sharing of a wife by brothers who are too poor to support separate households.

MATE SELECTION

Marriages may be "made in heaven," but they are always made according to two rules: **exogamy,** the rule requiring marriage *outside* a certain group; and **endogamy,** the rule requiring marriage *inside* a certain group. As we have seen, the incest taboo is a virtually universal rule of exogamy, necessitating marriage outside the family circle. (Although cases of incest are not uncommon, there are still moral, religious, or legal prohibitions against it in every society.) All societies also have rules of endogamy that restrict the field of eligible mates to members of a certain social circle, especially a class or ethnic group. These rules of mate selection are often unrecognized applications of the principle of reciprocity, through which desirable family connections are made (see "Wanted — A Wife"). In agrarian societies such as ancient China, members of the upper class typically accumulated their landholdings through intermarriage with the

WANTED — A WIFE

Matchmaking is an age-old practice in China, India, and many other countries. In traditional societies that offer few opportunities for boys and girls to meet, friends, relatives, and even professional matchmakers arrange introductions between suitable partners. This excerpt describes how modern Indians negotiate the value of a prospective mate.

[A] ritual connected with Hindu marriage, which even today occasionally creates sensational headlines in both the national and the foreign press, is the notorious practice of dowry. This is a custom in which the bride's father is required to pay a certain amount in cash, and often in goods, too, at the time of the wedding to the groom or his parents.

The sum of money is negotiated in advance, and the actual figure will depend upon several variables, which will be determined by the market value of the would-be husband. At the top of the scale will be a "foreign-returned" boy (usually a graduate from a British or American university), who may command as much as $45,000 within an average middle-class milieu. Lower down the scale will be members of the prestigious foreign or civil service (as their jobs will be secure, even if they don't earn a great deal), then an ordinary graduate from an Indian university, and so on. If the man is wholly uneducated but runs a little stall in a village or small town, he may still demand and get as much as $1,500 to $2,000.

Several other factors may determine the size of the dowry: the skin complexion of the groom (the fairer he is the higher the price), his job status, the social standing of his family, and finally, the bargaining power of the middleman who brings the two families together.

Attempts are now being made to eliminate the services of the go-between by advertising in newspapers; there are whole pages devoted to husband-and wife-hunting in the English and native press. A typical ad might read:

WANTED—FOR HANDSOME, ENGLAND-RETURNED, FAIR-COMPLEXIONED BOY, 26, WITH BRILLIANT PROSPECTS, A REALLY BEAUTIFUL VIRGIN FROM RESPECTABLE SOUTH INDIAN BRAHMIN FAMILY, WITH WELL-TO-DO BACKGROUND AND ECONOMIC CAPACITY.

That last phrase, "economic capacity," is a coded signal, indicating that a fairly fat dowry is being demanded, since it is against the law to do so openly. The Dowry Prohibition Act of 1961 expressly forbids the giving or taking of dowries. But the law is more frequently breached than observed, because when the giver and the taker are in collusion, it is almost impossible to prove that an illegal transaction has taken place.

The practice of dowry is as often condoned as condemned. It is motivated by greed, a craving for the ostentatious display of social and economic status, and ultimately underlines the implicit assumption that a woman is a burden. It is the girl's father who pays for the wedding, however lavish or modest it may be. It is he who is the supplicant to the groom's family, it is he who has to beg, borrow, or steal to scrape up enough cash so that his daughter may have a suitable marriage.

Supporters of dowry make sophisticated pleas about the facility of social mobility that the practice of dowry affords. A beautiful girl from a lowly background may climb several steps up the social ladder if the boy is less than handsome but comes from a high-class family. A boy who has done brilliantly at the university but does not have the economic backup to mix on equal social terms with his colleagues may be given a head start in life with the right sort of dowry. The trade-offs are not exclusively financial, either: If a boy is handicapped while the girl is healthy as a rose, the dowry demand will be correspondingly low.

SOURCE: Sasthi Brata, *India: Labyrinths in the Lotus Land.* New York: William Morrow and Company, Inc., 1985, pp. 133–34.

neighboring gentry. By limiting marriage partners to one's own group, endogamy preserves ethnic solidarity or class status and assures the group's survival by renewing its membership.

COURTSHIP.   Because marriage serves such important social functions, it has usually been considered too important to be left to the young. Parents in most societies have selected their children's mates for them, frequently without concern for whether the boy and girl liked or even knew each other. The most restrictive form of parental control is *child marriage*, in which the couple's elders arrange a union long before puberty. This system is common in India and Saudi Arabia, where women are hidden behind veils and secluded from the outside world.

In other societies, *kinship rules* limit the choice of a spouse to a small group of relatives—cousins, for example. Still other social arrangements *isolate* young people from each other in single-sex schools and public events so that close relationships cannot easily develop between inappropriate pairs. Courtship in some modern societies is still supervised by a *chaperone*—a parent or other elder who is present when boys and girls get together. Finally, the least restrictive method of controlling marriage is to *limit the range of contacts* that young people have, so that they will meet and marry only the "right" kind of people. This last pattern is typical of American society, where marriage is primarily a union of two individuals rather than two families.[12]

In the United States *dating* is the only socially recognized form of courtship. Few young people date just to find a spouse, yet dating is as highly ritualized and socially controlled as other types of mate selection. A century ago, couples did not typically go out on dates; they courted under the watchful eyes of their parents or other chaperones. A generation ago, the boy usually called the girl several days beforehand, invited her out, suggested the agenda for the evening, and assumed all its costs. According to the rules of the 1960s, premarital sex was permitted only among couples who were in love and considering marriage. Today, dating is more informal. Young people "hang out," or get together in groups, and some pair off afterwards. Sexual intimacy is more widely accepted as part of a dating relationship.

Within this cultural setting the choice of a mate is formally free, with extremely few exogamous rules about who can marry whom. Most American young people have virtually unlimited opportunities to meet members of the opposite sex in school or at work. Special social activities, such as dances and mixers, provide settings for falling in love. In practice, however, most people marry not only persons of the same age, race, ethnicity, and religion, but also members of the same social class and even from the same region of the country. **Homogamy**, the tendency of similar kinds of people to marry each other, is no accident. Instead of locking up their daughters, American parents subtly and not so subtly persuade them to go out only with "nice boys" who are acceptable to them. In the upper classes, where the stakes are higher, young people are thrown together at debutante balls, exclusive clubs, and expensive schools and colleges. Less affluent parents make financial sacrifices so that they can live in neighborhoods where their children will meet the "right people." Through their indirect control of these informal relationships, American parents can be almost as successful in enforcing endogamous rules of mate selection as any ancient Chinese lord.

The modernization of the world has thus given people more freedom to choose a mate. Yet the result is about the same: the vast majority of marriages still take place within the endogamous bounds of race, religion, and social class.

---

[12] William J. Goode, "The Theoretical Importance of Love," *American Sociological Review* 24 (1959): 38–47.

An affluent Nigerian magician with eight wives poses with his three favorites. Polygamy is found in many societies, but it is usually limited to a wealthy few who can afford the added family responsibilities.

POWER AND DESCENT

According to the principle of legitimacy, status is assigned to new members of society through the kinship system. **Kinship** is a social rather than a biological relationship. We are biologically related to all our ancestors and distant cousins, but only some of these relatives are socially defined as our kin. Kinship rules everywhere limit the number of people to whom an individual is related. For example, Americans have no kinship term for the relationship between a man and his wife's brother-in-law; he can only be called "my wife's brother-in-law."

Most of the world's societies trace descent through the male line in a *patrilineal descent* system. Under this system a man gets his "name," his social identity, from his father, his paternal grandfather, and so on. A woman marries into her husband's family and takes his name. The relationship of their children to her biological kin tends to be ignored.

The second most common rule of descent is *bilateral descent,* a system that traces a child's heritage through both parents. In this case kinship is claimed only with very close relatives on both sides. Bilateral descent is the usual practice in the United States.

In societies that use *matrilineal descent,* or descent traced through the female line, a child's status is determined by the mother, and the father has little authority. As a result children are more closely tied to their maternal uncles, who usually run the household, than to their fathers.

In most families of the world the father or male head exercises the greatest power. His authority comes from the customary deference shown to the oldest male of the family and from his legal right to control the family's property and the fate of its members. This system of male dominance is known as **patriarchy.** Its logical opposite, **matriarchy,** appears to exist only in theory. No true matriarchy, in which women run the family by law and custom, has yet been discovered.

In advanced industrial societies patriarchal arrangements tend to break down. American men, for instance, no longer have a monopoly over money, education, and social prestige. When the husband was the only wage-earner, his control of the family's resources gave him virtually unquestioned power to make decisions for his wife and children. Now that more women are earning salaries and going to college, their husbands are less able to dominate the family's decision making. A number of studies have shown that working wives have more power at home than other wives.[13] Even in more egalitarian middle-class families, however, husbands usually make the big decisions: what kind of car to buy, where the family will live, and whether or not to buy a house. In day-to-day decision making wives typically exercise far greater authority than their husbands over children and households.[14] But when husbands and wives disagree, it is usually the man who wins. In working-class families, especially, the husband almost always has the final say.[15]

At least in the middle class, children also have a great deal of power. Either by themselves or in coalitions with one parent against the other, older children frequently are able to "swing the vote" their way on such family decisions as where to go on vacations and whether to buy a television set or a washing machine.

NUCLEAR AND EXTENDED FAMILIES

Families vary in size, from the small nuclear family of "Tea for Two" to the larger extended family of kin groups who share the same household. The extended family usually includes a married couple and their children, their children's spouses, and their grandchildren.

The extended family form appears in some agrarian societies, where it operates as an efficient economic unit for working the fields and producing household goods. There are two reasons to doubt, however, that the extended family was ever the *typical* form in any society. The first reason is biological: most people in the world, past and

---

[13] Stephen Bahr, "The Economics of Family Life: An Overview," *Journal of Family Issues* 3:2 (1984): 139–46.

[14] Richard R. Clayton, *The Family, Marriage, and Social Change,* 2d ed. (Lexington, Mass.: Heath, 1979), pp. 402–403.

[15] Lillian Breslow Rubin, *Worlds of Pain* (New York: Basic, 1976), p. 113.

present, do not live long enough to preside over a family encompassing three generations. The second reason is sociological: such a large group of people is very difficult to
organize and support without extraordinary managerial skills and financial resources.
For as far into the past as scholars can go, most human beings have lived in nuclear
families that rarely included more than two generations (parents and children), with an
average size of only five or six members.[16] In sum, the nuclear family is the only family
most people, including most Americans, have ever had.

THE AMERICAN FAMILY

Two major social changes have deeply affected the American family in the twentieth
century: industrialization and the changing status of women. Industrialization, which
separated the home from the workplace, changed relationships within the family by
casting the husband in the role of wage earner. When men went off to work for most of
the day in a distant factory or office, husbands lost much of their influence on their
wives and children (see "Life Without Father"). The movement for sexual equality, by
giving women greater independence from men, has altered the traditional family
division of labor between male breadwinner and female homemaker. The entry of
growing numbers of women into the labor force has meant that mothers as well as
fathers now leave home for hours at a time.

Industrialization and greater sexual equality have brought more freedom for individuals, but their effect on the family has often been deplored. Many observers think
that the low birth rate and high divorce rate in the United States show a declining
commitment to family life. Has the American family become weak and unstable compared to the way it was in the "good old days"?

THE MYTH OF THE EXTENDED FAMILY

People who lament recent changes in family life often have an unrealistic idea of what it
was like. As it is portrayed in the paintings of Norman Rockwell and Grandma Moses,
the American family was a friendly collection of relatives of all ages who lived under
the same roof and cheerfully shared the household chores. The disappearance of the
extended family is said to have caused many of the contemporary family's problems.
Without all those helpful grandmothers and maiden aunts, today's mothers are thought
to be overburdened with housework and child care. Without the company of their
relatives, Americans are supposed to be deprived of the companionship of their kin and
to have lost their sense of responsibility for other family members. In contrast to the
homey extended family of the past, the modern nuclear family has often been described
as isolated and lonely.

According to Mary Jo Bane, a sociologist who has sifted the historical evidence, this
portrait of the extended family is more nostalgic than factual. While some extended
families have always existed, the typical American family has consisted of parents

---

[16] William J. Goode, *World Revolution and Family Patterns* (New York: Free Press, 1963).

LIFE WITHOUT FATHER

The Industrial Revolution profoundly altered family relationships. As the workplace changed from farm to factory, fathers had to give up many of their family roles to "go to work." Mothers became primarily responsible for household chores, and the bumbling, domestically unskilled father became a popular figure of fun.

The following newspaper article summarizes a discussion, "Issues in Paternity," at a meeting of the American Psychoanalytic Association. Dr. John Demos, professor of history at Brandeis University, led the session.

He is the bumbling father, the perfect fool of a dad. He has been humored, cajoled, patronized and just plain put up with by long-suffering wives and clever children. As a figure of fun he is a hallowed character in our culture: Dagwood Bumstead of the "Blondie" comic strip, Ozzie Nelson of the radio and television show "Ozzie and Harriet" or the faintly ridiculous hero of Clarence Day's Broadway play "Life With Father."

Though this image — the father as klutz — has shaped the way fathering has been portrayed in America, it is a relatively recent concept, according to new research by historians. This view of the American father arose only in the last century, when men began working away from the home and became, in sociological parlance, secondary caretakers.

■ ■ ■

During the early 1800s, Dr. Demos said, vast numbers of men, caught up in the Industrial Revolution, were drawn out of their families to pursue income-producing work. As the century progressed, he said, a new posture and responsibility emerged for fathers: he became the one who brought home the bacon. "Fathers had always been involved in the provision of goods and services to their families," Dr. Demos said, "but before the 19th century such activity was embedded in a larger matrix of domestic sharing. With modernization it became the chief, if not the exclusive, province of adult men."

The pattern of fathering before this time in America was hardly idyllic, given the rates of infant mortality and the trials of Colonial existence. Nevertheless, once infants were past the age of breast-feeding, Dr. Demos said, most fathers spent most of their time in the presence of their children. "It is a picture, above all, of active, encompassing fatherhood, woven into the whole fabric of domestic and productive life," he explained.

The changes wrought by the Industrial Revolution altered women's roles, too. "Mother was now the primary parent," Dr. Demos said. "On her fell the chief responsibilities for proper rearing of the young."

Throughout the 1800s, he said, virtually all human relationships were reshaped by a vast system of what modern sociologists would call sex-role stereotyping. Women and men were thought to occupy different "spheres" appropriate to entirely different characters.

Under this system, Dr. Demos said, the father mostly had "duties" — to set a standard of morality, to conduct family prayers, to be the final arbiter of discipline. "Distance and part-time involvement came to characterize fatherhood," he said.

■ ■ ■

Since fathers spent so little time at home, he continued, they could not acquire skills in "domestic employment." Ultimately they became figures of fun like Dagwood Bumstead or W. C. Fields's incomparable distracted dad, Egbert Souse.

SOURCE: Glenn Collins, "Perspectives on Father and His Role," *The New York Times,* May 17, 1982, p. B10.

living with their own children and no other adults. The first national census, taken in 1790, reported that the average household had 5.8 people — too small a figure to include large numbers of extended families. Given the high fertility of colonial women, it is very likely that most of those family members were children. Furthermore, the families of sisters and brothers almost never lived together, and parents and married children have rarely shared a household. Although few extended families have ever existed in the United States, Bane notes that American families have always expanded

This 1823 sampler lists the members of the Porter family. Early American households generally included more children, but they had much the same nuclear family form that they have today.

to take in needy relatives. During the nineteenth century, when both farm and factory wages were extremely low, perhaps one out of five families took in relatives as boarders.[17]

American families today continue to take in relatives who are in distress, but when the situation improves those relatives generally move out. Although families still feel responsibility for their members, social welfare programs have made this kind of help less prevalent than it was in the past. Without relatives and with few children, American families tend to be rather small. In 1987 the average was only 2.66 persons (see Table 11-1).

While some sociologists have been exposing the myth of the extended family, others have been showing that the American nuclear family is not as isolated from kin as it is thought to be. In a 1988 national survey, for example, 55 percent of the respondents said that they spent a social evening with relatives several times a month.[18]

---

[17] Mary Jo Bane, *Here to Stay: American Families in the Twentieth Century* (New York: Basic, 1976), p. 37.
[18] NORC, *General Social Survey* (Princeton, N.J.: National Opinion Research Center, 1988).

TABLE 11-1   SELECTED CHARACTERISTICS OF AMERICAN HOUSEHOLDS, 1987

	Percent of Households
Marital Status	
Married — Husband and wife present	57.6
Married — Spouse absent-separated	4.7
Widowed	12.6
Divorced	11.6
Never married	13.5
Size	
One Person	23.6
2	32.0
3	18.1
4	15.6
5	6.9
6	2.4
7 or more	1.4
Average persons per household	2.66
Race	
White	86.4
Black	11.1
Spanish origin*	6.1
Presence of Children	
No children under 18	64.4
With children under 18	7.1
All children under 6	9.3
All children 7 to 17	19.2

SOURCE: U.S. Bureau of the Census, "Household and Family Characteristics: March, 1987," *Current Population Reports.* Series P-20, No. 424 (Washington, D.C.: U.S. Government Printing Office, 1989), Tables 1, 21.
*Spanish origin may be any race.

LOVE AND MARRIAGE

When Margaret Mead told the story of Romeo and Juliet in Samoa, everyone laughed at the idea of dying for love. Under the Roman Empire moralists disapproved of the new trend toward marrying for love. The design of the traditional Chinese willow plate tells the sad story of two rebellious lovers who escaped their angry parents by turning into doves.

As these examples suggest, romantic love is a recognized force in many societies, but marrying for love alone is usually thought to be either ridiculous or tragic. Because men and women can be strongly attracted to each other in any society, and because every society has rules about who can marry whom, all societies attempt to channel love in the right directions. The usual method in traditional societies is to limit the opportunity to fall in love, either by arranging marriages between children or by segregating boys and girls until their elders find suitable mates for them. In modern societies, however, family alliances and tribal loyalties are less important. Social position depends more on individual achievement than on family background, and young people frequently live long distances from their parents. As a result, a new husband and

"One of the ten best authors in historical romance fiction."
—*Barbra Critiques*

Rebecca Brandewyne

author of the bestselling *And Gold Was Ours* and *Love, Cherish Me*

The **Outlaw Hearts**

The saga of a renegade, a lady, and a love that became a legend.

American culture has traditionally encouraged romantic love. Without this encouragement many people might not want to marry.

wife must depend primarily on each other instead of on their families. In this situation strong feelings of mutual attachment between husbands and wives are useful, even necessary.[19]

In contrast to other cultures of the world, American culture actually encourages romantic love as a preliminary to marriage. Movies, love songs, and popular literature all tell us that romantic love alone makes life worth living. Whatever its emotional delights may be, love is important in modern societies because it provides the motivation to marry. In traditional societies marriage served so many functions that it was a

---

[19] Rose Laub Coser, *The Family: Its Structure and Functions*, p. xx.

practical necessity in adult life. A century ago it wasn't necessary to persuade Americans that marriage would also provide them with romance, intellectual companionship, and a satisfying sex life. In modern societies, however, marriage is less economically and socially convenient, and young people are far more independent of their parents' authority. A cultural emphasis on romantic love as a basis for marriage, therefore, appears more often in industrial societies. Without it many people might not want to marry at all.

Given the emphasis on romantic love in American culture, a certain amount of disillusionment with marriage is probably inevitable. Romantic idealism is hardly compatible with the day-to-day reality of paying bills and changing diapers. But when people are asked why they got married, they hardly ever say that love was the only reason. Here is what some working-class husbands and wives told an interviewer:

> After we were going together for almost a year, it just seemed like the thing to do. So we did.

> I guess the biggest thing was that there was no other way if I wanted to get away from that house and be a person in myself instead of just a kid in that family.

> By the time we graduated, everybody was just expecting us to get married.

> I was just a dumb kid.

> I guess the reason we got married was because he was out of job, and he was being kicked out of his boardinghouse.

> I got pregnant.[20]

Love is only one of many reasons for marriage. In many cases it is apparently not even the most important one. The search for intimacy and security is certainly a motivating force, but the social norms supporting the family — the expectation that everyone gets married sometime — are more often mentioned. "So we come together," Lillian Rubin writes of the working-class couples she studied, "because we need to feel close to someone; because it's what most of us do at a certain stage of life; because it's the accepted and the expected, the thing to do if one is finally to be grown up."[21]

Nevertheless, love and marriage are still strongly linked in our minds. Americans expect from marriage what they expect from love — companionship, comfort, security, sexual excitement, lifelong devotion. It is not surprising that few marriages live up to these lofty ideals.

WIVES AT WORK

One of the major changes affecting American life in the last generation has been the growing number of married women who work outside the home. The majority (52 percent) of wives now hold down two jobs: housewife and employee. A still more startling statistic is that 65 percent of the mothers of school-age children (and 57

---

[20] Rubin, *Worlds of Pain*, Chapter 4.
[21] Ibid., pp. 53–54.

percent of the mothers of pre-schoolers) have an outside job.[22] These women are juggling three demanding roles: housewife, mother, and employee.

The reasons why so many married women have entered the labor force are discussed in detail in Chapter 10, "The Sexes," but some of them should be mentioned here. The first reason is that most mothers can no longer contribute "butter and egg" money, nor do they produce such necessities as food and clothing. Most women work because they are out of a job at home and because their families need the income.

The second reason is that women today have greater opportunities to work outside the home. Wives who were born during the post–World War II baby boom postponed having children and then gave birth to fewer of them than their mothers had. Because they spent less time raising a family, wives in the 1960s and 1970s had more time to work. And they had a better chance of getting a job. During the same period the expanding service industries more than doubled the demand for workers in such traditionally female occupations as clerical work, teaching, nursing, and food preparation. Economic pressures, combined with new economic opportunities, have made it both desirable and possible for mothers to work.

Like other social pioneers who have overturned traditional expectations, working mothers have been criticized for being selfish and immoral. Many people still believe that working outside the home is bad for marriage and bad for children (see Chapter 10, "The Sexes"). The research on working wives, however, concludes that a wife's job can actually be good for her marriage. After reviewing hundreds of articles, Glenna Spitze found substantial evidence for only four consequences of a wife's employment:

1. Family income increases. The family obviously benefits from the wife's earnings, which typically amount to about 30 percent of the family's income.

2. Divorce rates are higher. Since working wives are better able to support themselves, they are more likely to end unhappy marriages. Employed wives thus have higher divorce rates than traditional homemakers.

3. Husbands do slightly more child care. Studies show repeatedly that husbands do very little housework or child care whether or not their wives have a job. But when wives go to work, there is typically a very small increase in the time their husbands spend on child care. Husbands usually say they are "helping" their wives — as if the tasks of homemaking and childrearing naturally fell on the female partner.

4. Marital happiness is not much affected. A wife's job is good for both spouses when both want her to work. Marriages tend to be less happy when the wife is working out of necessity or the husband does not approve of his wife working.[23]

Despite the difficulties of reconciling the demanding roles of housewife and full-time employee, working seems to provide stimulation, opportunities, and a sense of personal fulfillment for women.

---

[22] "Half of Mothers with Children under 3 Now in Labor Force," Press Release, U.S. Bureau of Labor Statistics, 1987; "Over Half of Mothers with Children One Year Old or Under in the Labor Force," Press Release, U.S. Bureau of Labor Statistics, 1987.

[23] Glenna Spitze, "Women's Employment and Family Relations: A Review." *Journal of Marriage and the Family* 50 (August, 1988), pp. 595–618.

There appears to be little basis for the criticism that working mothers "neglect" their children. Nearly every couple staggers their working hours so that one spouse is at home while the other works — an arrangement that costs them much of their time together.[24] Other studies find that a mother's job has no effect either on preschool or school-age children's intellectual development and emotional adjustment.[25] In fact, child-care arrangements have changed so dramatically in the last century that whether or not mothers work makes relatively little difference. Whether their mothers are at home or not, the major activity of contemporary children is watching television. Preschoolers apparently watch TV about thirty-three hours a week, or one-third of their waking hours. Sixth graders watch an average of thirty-one hours a week. Television is thus by far the most important new development in the care of children.[26]

The second most important change in child care is the amount of time spent in school. A larger percentage of children of all ages goes to school now than ever before. Children also start school at an earlier age and stay in school longer. In the 1880s the average student went to school only 80 days a year; in the 1980s the typical school year was 180 days. Furthermore, increasing numbers of very young children are in nursery school and kindergarten. In 1965 about 27 percent of 3- to 5-year-old children were enrolled; by 1983, 53 percent of these preschoolers were actually going to school.[27]

Under these conditions, it is hard to say what difference a working mother makes to the life of a contemporary child. Some mothers are able to arrange their schedules so that they work only when the children are in school or when their husbands are at home to take care of them. In most cases, however, a relative or a babysitter stays with the children in their own home. Only about one-quarter of the preschool children of working mothers go to day care centers or nursery schools (see Figure 11-3).

There is no evidence that having a working mother is in itself a bad thing for children. Studies have found, for example, that the difference in the amount of time that both working and nonworking mothers spend exclusively with their children is surprisingly small. Although they spend less time on child care, working mothers — especially in the middle class — set aside time for special activities with their children. In families where the mother has to work because the father is unemployed or poorly paid, children may indeed suffer from these family troubles. But in families where the mother works for other reasons, her children do not appear to turn out differently from other children.[28]

THE NEW STATUS OF THE CHILD

Another change in the family in the last century has been the declining fertility of American women. Although fewer wives have no children at all, there has been a

---

24 Paul W. Kingston and Steven L. Nock, "Time Together Among Dual-Earner Couples." *American Sociological Review* 52 (June, 1987), pp. 391–400.

25 M. A. Easterbrooks and W. A. Goldberg, "Effects of Early Maternal Employment on Toddlers, Mothers, and Fathers." *Child Development* 56 (1985), pp. 361–75.

26 Bane, *Here to Stay*, p. 15.

27 U.S. Bureau of the Census, *Statistical Abstract of the United States* (Washington, D.C.: U.S. Government Printing Office, 1984), Table 212.

28 Gail Howrigan, *The Effects of Working Mothers on Children* (Cambridge, Mass.: Center for the Study of Public Policy, 1973); Alison Clarke-Steward, *Child Care in the Family* (New York: Academic Press, 1977).

CHILD CARE ARRANGEMENTS USED BY EMPLOYED MOTHERS WITH CHILDREN UNDER AGE 5 — 1985   FIGURE 11-3

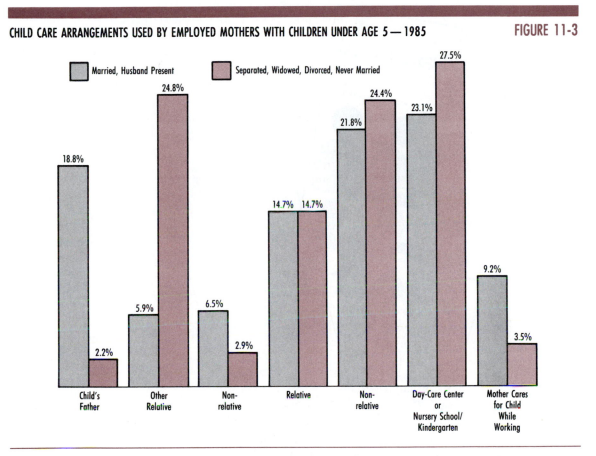

SOURCE: U.S. Bureau of the Census, "Who's Minding the Kids? Child-Care Arrangements: Winter 1984–85." *Current Population Reports,* Series P-70, No. 9 (Washington, D.C.: U.S. Government Printing Office, 1987).

dramatic decrease in the number of children each mother has. The average mother born in the mid-nineteenth century had 5.7 children; mothers born on the eve of World War I had an average of 2.9 children. After World War II the "baby boom" brought the rate up to 3.4 children for mothers born in the 1930s, but it is now falling again.

During the same period, the proportion of married women without children steadily declined — from over 20 percent of women born between 1901 and 1910, when the birth rate fell during the Great Depression, to 7.3 percent of women born between 1931 and 1935, who had babies during the affluent 1950s and 1960s.[29] In the present generation a majority of young (18-to-24-year-old) American women say they expect to have only two children. About 12 percent expect to have one child, and 11 percent expect to be childless.[30] Unless the women who do not expect to have children change their minds, there will be more childlessness in the future than there is today.

[29] Bureau of the Census data, reported in Bane, *Here to Stay*, p. 8.

[30] U.S. Bureau of the Census, "Fertility of American Women: 1983," *Current Population Reports*, Series P-20, No. 386 (Washington, D.C.: U.S. Government Printing Office, 1984), Table 2.

These brochures from the National Alliance for Optional Parenthood reflect changing American attitudes toward mariage and the family.

Undoubtedly, low fertility rates are partly the result of changing attitudes toward large families. In traditional societies children are considered valuable helping hands, but in industrial societies they are more often seen as extra mouths to feed. The average cost of housing, feeding, clothing, and educating one child through high school was estimated at over $107,000 for an urban worker's family in 1988.[31] In the middle class

---

[31] "Updated Estimates of the Cost of Raising a Child." *Family Economics Review* 2 (May, 1989), p. 24.

the financial drain of having children is likely to continue through their college years. At the same time that smaller families became more desirable, more effective contraception made a small family easier to achieve. The fact that parents today decide to have children *despite* their economic cost is nothing less than a revolutionary change.

It is practically certain, therefore, that the children born in the next decade will grow up in small families. On the whole, this will be good for them. A number of studies have found that children in small families do better in school and score higher on standardized tests than children in large families. Even when the families are equally well-off financially, the children in a small family will still get more education, better jobs, and higher incomes.[32] Researchers have speculated that children in small families benefit from more adult care and attention and they get a larger share of the family's financial resources for their education. Far from being a sign of indifference to children, the trend toward smaller families indicates that most children will receive more parental attention and support.

PRIVATE TROUBLES AND PUBLIC ISSUES

When families have problems, the individuals involved are frequently blamed. "She started working and she started getting too independent," they say of a wife.[33] When people are unhappy or in trouble, they also tend to blame themselves: "Other women seem to be happy with being married and having a house and kids. What's the matter with me?"[34] Private troubles, as the American sociologist C. Wright Mills pointed out, are often reflections of public issues.[35] Families are frequently unhappy for social reasons outside the control of any individual member.

One source of trouble is an uncomfortable "fit" between the family and other social institutions. A demanding teaching career, for example, may cause problems for the family by taking a wife's time and energy away from her family roles. A wife's full-time commitment to family roles, on the other hand, denies society the contributions of a talented teacher. Whenever the fit between the family and other institutions is poor, social problems result, either for the family or for the larger society. Here we shall examine some of the private troubles that are also public issues.

DIVORCE

In the first year of the reign of King Julief, two thousand married couples were separated, by the magistrate, with their own consent. The emperor was so indignant, on learning these particulars, that he abolished the privilege of divorce. In the course of the following year, the number of marriages in Agra was less than before by three

---

[32] Otis Dudley Duncan, David Featherman, and Beverly Duncan, *Socioeconomic Background and Achievement* (New York: Seminar Press, 1972).

[33] Rubin, *Worlds of Pain*, p. 177.

[34] Ibid., p. 115.

[35] C. Wright Mills, *The Sociological Imagination* (New York: Grove Press, 1961), p. 8.

thousand; the number of adulteries was greater by seven thousand; three hundred women were burned alive for poisoning their husbands; seventy-five men were burned for the murder of their wives; and the quantity of furniture broken and destroyed, in the interior of private families, amounted to the value of three million rupees. The emperor re-established the privilege of divorce.[36]

Divorce, as this Indian ruler discovered, is not all bad. Tolerant attitudes toward divorce mean that couples can more easily end a miserable marriage without suffering social ostracism and legal reprisals. Some divorces can be counted successful — some adults are happier and some children do better than children in unhappy, intact families. However, the breakup of a marriage often causes financial and emotional problems, especially for women. Divorced mothers are frequently unable to support a family and take care of children adequately. Most husbands, even middle-class ones, fail to keep up their child-support payments, and divorced mothers often end up on welfare. Moreover, divorced women have fewer economic and social opportunities than divorced men and are less likely to remarry. The psychological costs of separation from a spouse or a parent are more difficult to measure than the financial costs, but are probably equally difficult to bear. Finally, there is much evidence to show that the process of separation, divorce, and — more often than not — remarriage of one of the partners is a wrenching experience with lasting emotional effects for all concerned.[37]

A rising rate of divorce is thus as much a matter of public concern today as it was to the Indian emperor. Yet no one knows exactly how many marriages are ending in divorce. Most statisticians rely on the **divorce rate**, or the number of divorced persons for every 1,000 married persons. The United States divorce rate in 1960 was 35; in 1970 it was 47, and in 1980 it was 100. Between 1985 and 1988 the divorce rate appears to have leveled off at 133.[38] The trouble with this calculation is that it tends to underestimate the number of divorces in a growing population. When more people are getting married, then the proportion of divorced persons goes down even if more marriages from previous years are ending in divorce. Because the large post–World War II baby boom generation reached their 20s (or marrying age) in the 1970s, it is possible that an increase in married persons caused the official divorce rate to underestimate the number of divorces that were actually taking place.

A more accurate measure of divorce can be estimated by calculating the outcome of marriages made in the past. Of those married in the period between 1970 and 1974, 23 percent were divorced before their fifth wedding anniversary; of those married between 1975 and 1979, 30 percent were divorced within five years; and of those married between 1980 and 1985, 31 percent are expected to be divorced before the same five years are up. Assuming that divorce rates have reached their maximum in the last few

[36] Niles Register 229 (June 11, 1825), cited in Doris Jonas Freed and Henry H. Foster, Jr., "Divorce American Style," *Annals of the American Academy of Political and Social Science* 383 (May 1969): 88.

[37] David Demo and Alan Acock, "The Impact of Divorce on Children." *Journal of Marriage and the Family* 50 (August, 1988), pp. 619–48; Judith S. Wallerstein and Sandra Blakeslee, *Second Chances: Men, Women and Children A Decade after Divorce.* New York: Ticknor & Fields, 1989.

[38] U.S. Bureau of the Census, "Marital Status and Living Arrangements: March, 1988, *Current Population Reports,* Series P-20, No. 389 (Washington, D.C.: U.S. Government Printing Office, 1989).

"Bad news, kids. Daddy's leaving government in order to devote more time to his family."

Drawing by D. Reilly; © 1985 The New York Magazine, Inc.

years, demographers predict that 64 percent of the marriages made in the mid-1980s will end in divorce.[39]

How this high divorce rate is assessed depends on one's point of view. To the extent that a rising divorce rate means that unhappy marriages are being ended more often, it is a healthy sign. But if a rising divorce rate is an indication that more marriages are unbearable, then it means that many families are failing to provide adequately for the physical and emotional care of their members.

CAUSES OF DIVORCE.   The most widely accepted explanation for divorce comes from **exchange theory**, or the trade-off between the costs and rewards of staying married. According to the social psychologist George Levinger, couples stay together as long as the attractions of marriage (love, companionship, social prestige, economic security) and barriers to divorce (children, social disapproval, religious principles) outweigh the attractions of some alternative (going home to mother, living alone, marrying someone else).[40] Levinger's hypothesis helps explain why divorce rates are highest among the

---

[39] Teresa Martin and Larry Bumpass, "Recent Trends in Marital Disruption." *Demography* 26 (February, 1989), pp. 37–52.

[40] George Levinger, "A Social Psychological Perspective on Marital Dissolution," *Journal of Social Issues* 32 (1976): 21–47.

young and the poor. For both husbands and wives, marriage is less attractive in low-income families. Moreover, teenage couples are more likely to have the alternative of moving back in with their parents. Unstable jobs, little money, and unsatisfying work strain many lower-class marriages to the breaking point.

WHY THE INCREASE IN DIVORCE?   Clearly, there are fewer reasons to stay married today than there were in the past. When the family served more economic and social functions, the end of a marriage deprived husbands and wives of much more than companionship. The loss of a spouse left a man without essential "female services" such as cooking, laundry, and gardening, and left a woman without financial support for herself and her children. As a result, sexual or temperamental conflicts may have caused as much misery as they do today, but they led to divorce more rarely. Today, when emotional satisfaction is the primary expectation from marriage, there are fewer reasons for an unhappy couple to stay married. Finally, because schools and other institutions provide continuity in children's lives, "staying together for the children's sake" is considered less important in modern society.[41]

As the benefits of marriage have been reduced, women's alternatives to marriage have expanded. The traditional housewife in the 1950s was less likely to have a job and thus was more dependent on her husband. Since then many more women have entered the labor force, and millions of working wives have become financially independent of their husbands. Some observers conclude that this change in women's roles is the single most important factor in the rising divorce rate.

Finally, as the number of divorced people has increased, American society has become more tolerant of them. Divorce no longer carries the social stigma it did when "divorcée" meant social outcast. As divorce has become more socially acceptable, it has also become easier to obtain. Until recently, it was almost impossible to get divorced in most states without a great deal of expense and usually some fraud as well.[42] Most divorce proceedings were adversarial: one spouse sued the other on the ground that some offense had been committed. Many couples had to resort to false charges of "mental cruelty" or "desertion" to obtain a divorce. Nonadversary (no-fault) proceedings, community property laws, and joint custody of children have made divorce simpler and less painful to arrange. The lowering of these social barriers against divorce has undoubtedly contributed to the rise in the divorce rate.

MARRIAGE: AN ASSESSMENT.   Concentrating on divorce statistics, however, leads many people to overlook the underlying strength of American family life. Other statistics show that the rate of remarriage has generally kept up with the rate of divorce. This means that, for most people, only a particular marriage partner, not marriage itself, is being rejected. Of those who divorce, 75 percent of the women and 83 percent of the men remarry within three years.[43] Most married couples still stay married, and very few marry more than twice.[44] Furthermore, a high divorce rate does not mean that more

---

[41] Keniston, *All Our Children,* pp. 21–22.
[42] Bane, *Here to Stay,* p. 32.
[43] Glick and Norton, *Marrying, Divorcing, and Living Together in the U.S. Today.*
[44] Bane, *Here to Stay,* p. 35.

MEN AND WOMEN AGES 25–39 WHO SAID THEY WERE "VERY HAPPY," 1972–1976 AND 1982–1986						TABLE 11-2
	Men			Women		
	1972–1976	1982–1986	Change	1972–1976	1982–1986	Change
Marital Status						
Never married	13.2	24.3	+11.1	13.7	24.4	+10.7
Married	33.7	30.0	−3.7	42.9	36.6	−6.3
Separated or divorced	12.7	15.8	+3.1	15.7	17.4	+1.7
Total	29.1	27.0	−2.1	37.0	30.2	−6.8

SOURCE: Norval D. Glenn and Charles N. Weaver, "The Changing Relationship of Marital Satisfaction to Reported Happiness." *Journal of Marriage and the Family* 50 (May 1988), p. 319.

children are being separated from their parents than in the past. Gradually declining death rates mean that fewer families today are disrupted by the death of a parent, and better jobs for women mean that mothers are more often able to keep their families together. By 1988 only 3 percent of children under 18 were not living with either parent.[45] Present rates of death and divorce indicate, however, that one-half of all black children and one-fifth of all white children born since 1980 will live in a one-parent family at some point.[46] And, while research studies so far have not established that divorce is worse for children than marital unhappiness, hardly anyone has argued that a broken home is good for them.

Marriage can also be counted a qualified success in other ways. Married men and women are much more likely than single, widowed, or divorced people to say they are "very happy." Marriage is especially good for men: married men enjoy better physical and mental health, live longer, and are more financially successful. Marriage seems to be less beneficial to women. Many wives find traditional housekeeping roles unsatisfying, while others find it difficult to combine family and occupational roles successfully. Nevertheless, most wives consider themselves and their marriages to be happy.[47]

While happiness and marriage are still strongly correlated, surveys of marital happiness over the last 15 years show that marriage today is not as rewarding as it used to be, especially for women. Between the mid-1970s and the mid-1980s, the proportion of "very happy" married women declined from 43 to 40 percent, with a much sharper decline (from 43 to 37 percent) for younger wives. During the same period the proportion of "very happy" single men under 40 increased from 13 to 24 percent—an indication that married life is not as important to men's happiness as it once was (see Table 11-2).[48]

---

[45] U.S. Bureau of the Census, "Marital Status and Living Arrangements: March, 1988," *Current Population Reports* (1989), Table 4.

[46] Larry Bumpass, "Children and Marital Disruption: A Replication and Update." *Demography* 21 (1984), pp. 71–82.

[47] Bane, *Here to Stay,* p. 35.

[48] Norval D. Glenn and Charles N. Weaver, "The Changing Relationship of Marital Satisfaction to Reported Happiness." *Journal of Marriage and the Family* 50 (May 1988), pp. 317–24.

WOMEN'S RIGHTS AND THE FAMILY

As the social movement toward sexual equality has gained momentum, changing cultural definitions of masculinity and femininity have disrupted traditional family roles. Now that so many wives work full-time outside the home, more of them expect their husbands to help around the house. Most men, however, resist any change from the old-fashioned male breadwinner and female homemaker roles. "That's just the way it is," one working-class husband said. "It's her job to keep the house and children and my job to earn the money."[49] Even among the professional middle class, men talk about how willing they are to share the housework, but their wives actually do it (see Chapter 10, "The Sexes," p. 311).

For working mothers the result is sometimes called "role overload." Career woman, mother, and housewife are too heavy a load for many women to bear. Some compromise by taking undemanding jobs that do not interfere with their family responsibilities. Others feel guilty when they fail to do everything well. In the conflict between individual fulfillment and family roles — between what is good for a woman and what is good for her husband and children — the family often wins and the individual woman loses. In this case, problems arise because the demands of the family are incompatible with the need for personal achievement and sexual equality.

CHILDREN'S RIGHTS AND THE FAMILY

The family also conflicts with other kinds of social equality. Families, as we have seen, do not treat their members "just like anybody else": they treat them according to particularistic standards of affection and loyalty. Therefore, as long as children are raised in families, they will never have equal opportunities. Some children will always start out with the advantages their families can give them in the form of greater wealth, better schooling, or more tender loving care. Money, class status, and access to jobs in the family business are passed from generation to generation through inheritance. In addition, the admissions policies of prestigious schools and universities benefit certain family members by giving the children and siblings of graduates priority over other applicants.

Other children inherit disadvantages from their families. Poverty and neglect at home, for example, are associated with poor performance in school. Although some children obviously suffer from a deprived family background, attempts to intervene in private family matters are often fiercely resisted. Today, for instance, child abuse is considered a serious social problem in the United States. Nearly one in 50 children was a victim of extreme violence (being kicked, punched, shot, or stabbed) in 1985, and a significant number died from their injuries.[50] Protecting these children from their parents involves a conflict of values that has proved very difficult to resolve. Concern for family privacy and for the rights of parents to treat their children as they see fit has

---

[49] Quoted in Rubin, *Worlds of Pain*, p. 100.

[50] Murray A. Straus and Richard J. Gelles, "Societal Change and Change in Family Violence from 1975 to 1985 as Revealed by Two National Surveys." *Journal of Marriage and the Family* 48 (August 1986), pp. 465–79.

hindered the investigation of injuries that would normally be considered criminal assault. The family's rights are also strongly upheld by public opinion. Two-thirds of the respondents in a national survey opposed any punishment of parents who committed violent acts against their children, and over half of them thought that an abused child should be separated from his or her parents only as a last resort.[51]

The conflict between family rights and educational opportunities is equally difficult to resolve. For example, should parents be allowed to deprive their children of educational advantages? The answer so far is yes: a recent Supreme Court decision upheld the rights of Amish parents to prevent their children, for religious reasons, from going to high school.

In sum, commitment to the family is a source of continuing tension between competing social values. The intervention of government agencies on behalf of universalistic values (sexual equality, protection of children from abuse, equal educational opportunities) is resisted because of loyalty to the family's particularistic values and belief in the privacy of parent-child relationships. For this reason, some people have argued that the family is incompatible with the demands of modern life and that its function would be better performed by other kinds of institutions. Some of these proposals are taken up in the next section.

THE FUTURE OF THE FAMILY

Many alternatives to the traditional family have been suggested. Perhaps the most sweeping attempt to do away with the family was made in the Soviet Union in the 1920s. Because the Bolsheviks considered the basis of the family to be inherited property and male dominance, they believed that it perpetuated social inequalities that socialism was intended to abolish. Therefore, the new government made drastic changes in sexual, marital, and parental relationships. Because marriage was to be based on equality instead of property, marriages were performed and divorces were granted simply by registration. Any man and woman who lived together were also considered legitimately married with respect to property rights and inheritance. Parents were no longer responsible for their children's behavior or financial support, and children were not responsible for their aging parents. All children were considered equally "legal," and no distinction was made between legitimate and illegitimate offspring. Young children were to be kept in child-care centers so that their mothers could work, or they were to be sent to boarding schools, away from their parents' influence.

The result of these policies was not at all what the Soviet leaders intended. Bigamy became widespread and parents could not control their children. Government boarding schools turned out to be too expensive, and there were not enough child-care centers. After 1935 the family began to be reinstated. Parents were again made responsible for

---

[51] David Gil, *Violence Against Children* (Cambridge, Mass.: Harvard University Press, 1970), pp. 92–98.

While the form and functions of the American family have changed dramatically, marriage remains the primary source of love and companionship in a largely impersonal and bureaucratic world.

the disorderly conduct of their children, and the Soviet newspaper *Pravda* proclaimed the new doctrine that sexual freedom was bourgeois and against socialist principles. Since 1944 only registered marriages have been legal in the Soviet Union, and divorces are difficult to obtain. The principle of legitimacy is again in effect: only children born in legal marriages can claim their family's name and property. Bastards again carry the stigma of their "fatherless" status. Today, family life in the Soviet Union is apparently more stable than in the United States.[52]

As the Soviet experiment showed, the family is not easy to replace. Its structure, however, does change rather rapidly in response to external social pressures. In the 1970s new forms of the family appeared, reflecting changing American attitudes toward sex, marriage, divorce, and childbearing. Some of these functional alternatives to the nuclear family are discussed below.

COHABITATION

In the last ten years unmarried couples have become more socially acceptable. In 1988 the Census Bureau counted 2.5 million unmarried men and women sharing the same household — a million more than in 1980.[53] Some (14 percent) are young adults under 25, but more (25 percent) are 25 to 34 years old. At least one member of half these

[52] Rose Laub Coser and Lewis A. Coser, "The Principle of Legitimacy and Its Patterned Infringement in Social Revolutions," in *The Family: Its Structure and Function*, pp. 99–102.

[53] U.S. Bureau of the Census, "Marital Status and Living Arrangements: March 1988," *Current Population Reports* (1989).

couples is divorced, and only about one-third have never been married. Contrary to popular belief, most cohabiting couples are not young adults who are postponing marriage, but older men and women who have been married and divorced.

Nevertheless, many young people do live together before they decide to break up or get married. About one-third of all adults under the age of 24 have cohabited, and one-third of the women and half of the men who marry before the age of 24 have lived with their spouses beforehand.[54]

Some observers have suggested that cohabitation leads to more stable marriages. This does not seem to be the case, however. Couples who have lived with their spouses before marriage tend to be less happily married and almost twice as likely to get divorced.[55]

As we have already seen, Americans today are marrying later than their parents (see Figure 11-2). Many young adults are postponing marriage and children in order to finish graduate school or pursue a career. Others are divorced and reluctant to enter another marriage for economic reasons. For many men and women cohabitation offers the benefits of marriage without its obligations. Now that extramarital sex is widely tolerated and contraception or abortion is more readily available, simply living together is a feasible alternative to marriage.

STAYING SINGLE

The recent trend toward later marriages plus the increased rate of divorce mean that many more people are now single and living alone. In 1987 the Census Bureau found that 24 percent of American households consisted of just one person—a very large increase over 1970's rate.[56] Most people who live alone are not "swinging singles" but elderly widows—a statistic that reflects the fact that women usually outlive their husbands by several years. The huge increase in single households, however, came from the under-35 age group. The proportion of women in their late twenties who have never married rose to 25 percent (from 10 percent in 1960), and the proportion of unmarried men the same age increased to 38 percent. The average age at first marriage in 1988 was 23.6 years for women (20.3 in 1960) and 25.9 for men (22.8 in 1960) (see Figure 11-2).[57] Later marriages mainly reflect the fact that more young people (especially women) are going to college and waiting until after graduation to settle down. Furthermore, changing mores have made other people more tolerant of sexual relationships outside of marriage. Nearly everyone, however, still gets married at one time or another. If the past is any guide to the future, between 85 and 90 percent of today's young Americans will marry at least once.

---

[54] Arland Thornton, "Cohabitation and Marriage in the 1980's." *Demography* 25 (November, 1988), pp. 497–508.

[55] Alan Booth and David Johnson, "Premarital Cohabitation and Marital Success." *Journal of Family Issues* (June 1988), pp. 225–72.

[56] U.S. Bureau of the Census, "Household and Family Characteristics: March, 1987," *Current Population Reports* (1988).

[57] U.S. Bureau of the Census, "Marital Status and Living Arrangements: March 1988," *Current Population Reports* (1989), Table A-2.

A rising divorce rate has made single parenthood a new form of the American family.

SINGLE PARENTHOOD

After unmarried households, the fastest-growing new form of the family is the single-parent household. One out of four families with children under 18 is now headed by a single adult, usually the mother. If divorce and out-of-wedlock children are both considered, 74 percent of the black children and 26 percent of the white children born in the 1980s will spend at least part of their childhood living with one parent.[58]

Single parenthood was a major factor in the feminization of poverty during the 1980s. Half the single-parent families headed by a woman were living below the poverty line in 1987 (see Chapter 7, "Social Inequality"). Besides the financial demands of raising a family alone, single parents face a number of social and psychological difficulties. With few guidelines to follow, single mothers and fathers must create their own rules for childrearing, dating, and family activities. Moreover, single parents must be both father and mother to children who have often been left angry and

---

[58] U.S. Bureau of the Census, "Poverty in the United States: 1987". *Current Population Reports,* Series P-60, No. 163, Table 2, 1988.

disoriented by a divorce. Although most single parents eventually remarry, single parenthood is rapidly becoming recognized as a new kind of American family.

SERIAL MONOGAMY

Given the present rates of divorce and remarriage, one of the most popular forms of the family in the future may well be a series of monogamous unions. Changing partners is one way of serving the family's primary function of providing intimacy and emotional support; when one marriage becomes unsatisfying, it would easily be ended and another begun. As yet, however, most American marriages still consist of one lifelong partnership.

There is no doubt that the American family is changing in profound, even revolutionary ways. If present trends continue through the 1980s, divorce rates will remain high, fewer children will be born, and more mothers will leave the house for a demanding full-time job. For many people, these developments will spell the decline of marriage and family life. In spite of dire predictions about the end of the nuclear family, however, the amount of change that can reasonably be expected seems limited. We can predict for instance, that the family will continue to show great flexibility of form. Single-parent households will probably become common. Changing sex roles will bring new divisions of power and labor for husbands and wives. But it is unlikely that families will entirely disappear. Although the family is losing some of its traditional functions, it remains the primary institution for love and companionship in an otherwise "heartless world." Thus, no matter what new forms it may take, the family is certain to remain the source of the tender care and attention we all need to survive.

SUMMARY

1. A family consists of two or more persons who are linked by marriage or descent and who engage in common activities. Some form of the family has been found in every known society.

2. Sociologists find that the family is a universal institution because it meets certain social needs. First, the family regulates sexual relationships. The incest taboo requires that the exchange of sexual partners take place between and not within families. According to Malinowski's principle of reciprocity, nearly every marriage unites two previously unrelated families and helps create affiliations that bind society together.

3. A second function of the family is the placement of children in the social structure. Malinowski's principle of legitimacy holds that every child must have a social father to provide him or her with an inherited social status, or legitimacy.

4. Families also provide their members with intimacy and social support. Other functions of the family include socialization of children, economic production and consumption, and care of the sick and needy.

5. In industrial societies other institutions have taken over many of the family's traditional functions, but its importance as a source of special care and attention has increased.

6. The structure of the family changes in response to different situations. The most common form of marriage is monogamy, but societies with a shortage of eligible mates frequently permit polygamy. The choice of partners is regulated by rules of exogamy and endogamy. Kinship is a social relationship traced through patrilineal, matrilineal, or bilateral descent. Most families of the world have patriarchal authority structures, but in industrial

societies decision making is more often shared. Most people have always lived in nuclear families, but the extended family form appears in some agrarian societies.

7. Industrialization and the changing status of women have deeply affected the American family. Some people deplore the changes, but the historical evidence indicates that American families have always been very much what they are now: small in size and flexible in providing companionship and help to their members.

8. In contrast to the restrictive practices of many societies, American culture emphasizes romantic love as the motivation to marry. Nevertheless, most American marriages are homogamous, and the social norms supporting the family appear to be as important a reason to get married as the search for intimacy and security.

9. The majority of wives now work outside the home because housewives can make fewer economic contributions, because modern women are spending less time raising children, and because women today have greater job opportunities. Working mothers are frequently criticized for neglecting their families. A wife's job can benefit a marriage under certain conditions, however, and there is no evidence that having a working mother is in itself a bad thing for children. Whether a mother works or not, most of her children's time is spent watching television or going to school.

10. Another change in the American family is a dramatic decrease in the number of children each mother has. The higher cost of raising children has helped change social attitudes in favor of smaller families, and more effective contraception has made it easier to control family size. Rather than being a sign of indifference to children, the trend toward smaller families indicates that children will receive more parental attention and support.

11. A higher divorce rate reflects changes in American society. According to the exchange theory of divorce, there are fewer reasons to stay married than in the past, and working women have more financial independence and are better able to leave their husbands. Moreover, divorce has become more socially acceptable and easier to arrange. Marriage can still be considered a qualified success, though. The rate of remarriage is as high as the divorce rate, fewer children are being separated from their parents by death or economic need, and married men and women are more likely than single persons to describe themselves as "very happy."

12. The demands of the family are sometimes incompatible with those of other institutions. Commitment to the family may conflict with such social values as equal rights for women and equal educational opportunities for children.

13. Changing American attitudes have led to an increase in single-person households and to new forms of the family: cohabitation, single parenthood, and serial monogamy.

KEY TERMS

family 340
nuclear family 340
extended family 340
incest taboo 341
principle of reciprocity 341
legitimacy 342
principle of legitimacy 342

universalistic norms 344
particularistic norms 344
monogamy 347
polygamy 347
exogamy 348
endogamy 348
homogamy 350

kinship 351
patriarchy 352
matriarchy 352
divorce rate 364
exchange theory 365

SUGGESTED READING

* Mary J. Bane. *Here to Stay: American Families in the Twentieth Century.* New York: Basic, 1978.

* Urie Bronfenbrenner. *Two Worlds of Childhood: U.S. and U.S.S.R.* New York: Pocket Books, 1972.

Theodore Caplow et al. *Middletown Families: Fifty Years of Change and Continuity.* Minneapolis: University of Minnesota Press, 1982.

David Demo and Alan Acock. "The Impact of Divorce on Children." *Journal of Marriage and the Family* 50 (August 1988): 619–48.

* Irwin Garfinkel and Sara S. McLanahan. *Single Mothers and Their Children: A New American Dilemma.* Washington, DC: Urban Institute Press, 1986.

* William J. Goode. *World Revolution and Family Patterns.* New York: Free Press, 1970.

Teresa Martin and Larry Bumpass. "Recent Trends in Marital Disruption." *Demography* 26 (February 1989): 37–52.

* Available in paperback.

Merchants have
no country.

Thomas Jefferson

CHAPTER 12

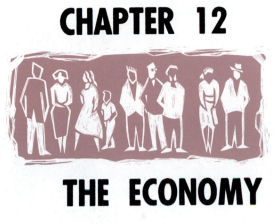

THE ECONOMY

According to Sigmund Freud, human beings fulfill themselves in two activities: love and work. If the family can be called the institution for love, the economy is the institution for work. More specifically, the economy is the social institution that specializes in the production and exchange of goods and services to satisfy the wants and needs of a population. *Work*, by its narrowest definition, is the performance of specialized roles in the economy. After the family, the economy probably has a greater influence on our lives than any other institution. Nearly all the world's people spend most of their time working to produce such goods as food and clothing or to distribute such services as education and medical care. Human beings not only spend most of their lives in economic pursuits, but the kind of work they do largely determines whether the life they lead is poor and deprived or healthy and comfortable.

For most of human history the economy was not a separate institution representing a clashing set of interests. Before the Industrial Revolution separated the workplace from the home, economic activities were a part of family life. In simple societies production and exchange are still inseparable from family roles. When hunting and fishing and gathering fruits and vegetables produce enough goods for the family's

Fishermen on the Ivory Coast haul in the daily catch. Members of simple hunting and gathering societies do not sell the goods they produce; they share them according to established custom.

subsistence, the workday is over. Members of these **custom economies** exchange scarce goods and services according to established tradition. Families share their food supplies and labor without expecting anything particular in return: a brother is simply *entitled* to half the daily catch of fish; a sister-in-law is *expected* to help repair the nets.

Other economies are organized not by custom but by command. In this case economic activities are inseparable from political institutions. Industrial production in the Soviet Union, for example, has been largely directed by government plans that set the type and amount of goods to be distributed. The state owns the means of production (factories, farms, mines), hires the workers, and determines their wages. In **command economies** centralized planning, directed by an authoritarian regime, replaces the haphazard, inefficient exchanges of hunting and gathering societies.

From the dawn of civilization until about 1750 all the world's economies were guided by either custom or command. Nearly all the available goods and services were used by the people who produced them, their families, or a landholding elite who confiscated whatever surplus was left. In the eighteenth century, when the Industrial

Revolution began, the dominant economic pattern in western European societies was *mercantilism,* an elaborate, state-regulated system of controls over trade. Since wealth was measured by the amount of gold and silver a country had, the national governments encouraged new revenues from abroad by granting monopolies to certain large firms that produced goods for export. Small, unsponsored businessmen could hardly compete with these enterprises. They naturally resented the interference of the state in the normal course of business. When the government of Louis XIV asked what it could do to help them, the French merchants replied, "Laissez nous faire (Leave us alone)!"[1] The industrialists' plea was to receive support from an unlikely source, a Scottish professor of moral philosophy named Adam Smith and his new theory of a market economy.

Over 200 years ago Smith envisioned a new economic system that would greatly increase human productivity and bring general prosperity to the world. His theory of a free market was to become not only the basis for Western capitalism but also the justification for the sweeping social changes that followed industrialization. The economic structures Smith proposed, with all their historic implications for the human condition, are now to be found to some degree in all industrial societies.

This chapter begins with a summary of classical economic theory. The next two sections explore some of the social consequences — both expected and unexpected — that flowed from the development of the modern economic institution. The fourth part discusses the spread of industrialization and the development of a world economy. A final section, "Capitalism and Socialism," takes a look at some alternatives to the free market system.

THE WEALTH OF NATIONS: CLASSICAL ECONOMIC THEORY

In one of the most famous works of all social science, *An Inquiry into the Nature and Causes of the Wealth of Nations* (coincidentally published in 1776), Adam Smith declared the independence of the economy from other social institutions. A nation's true wealth, he said, lies not in its hoard of gold and silver but in the amount of goods and services available to its people — what today we call its "Gross National Product." Nations could increase their wealth by "liberating" economic activity from all other considerations and allowing everyone to pursue economic goals with neither protection nor hindrance from the government. Smith's justification of a **laissez-faire**, or unregulated, **economy** had an immediate influence. It benefited the rising class of businessmen and dealt an eventually fatal blow to mercantilism. But his book had implications that were far more revolutionary. The principles of the **free**, or competitive, **market** that Smith elaborated in *The Wealth of Nations* have guided economic thought ever since. In essence they are the principle of self-interest, the principle of rationality, and the principle of supply and demand.

---

[1] Robert L. Heilbroner, *The Economic Transformation of America* (New York: Harcourt Brace Jovanovich, 1977), p. 168

THE INVISIBLE HAND: THE PRINCIPLE OF SELF-INTEREST

Throughout the ages work has ordinarily been regarded as the "curse of Adam": an unpleasant duty or a necessity of life. At the time *The Wealth of Nations* was published, popular wisdom held that people would not work any longer than they absolutely had to. Moralists argued that wages had to be kept at barely subsistence level: a hungry man would work only until he earned enough money to buy a meal, and then he would walk off the job.

In contrast to his contemporaries, Adam Smith took the view that people are enthusiastic about working only when they *want* to work — when they are motivated not by necessity or duty but by simple greed. "It is not from the benevolence of the butcher, the brewer, or the baker that we expect our dinner," he wrote, "but from their regard to their own interest." The desire for profit, if left unchecked, might urge the butcher and the baker to charge intolerably high prices for their products while paying starvation wages to their employees. Smith argued that the check on greed is competition, the conflicting self-interests of all the members of society. A baker who charges too much for bread will lose customers to another baker; a butcher who pays employees too little will find that they will go to work for someone else. And if all the butchers and bakers get together and agree to set prices high and wages low, they risk losing their employees to other industries and their customers to any enterprising person who decides to open a "discount" butcher shop or bakery. In this highly competitive system an individual who "intends only his own gain" is thus "led by an **invisible hand**" — the laws of the free market — to promote the public good.[2]

Today classical economists continue to admire the way self-interest promotes voluntary cooperation for mutual benefits. The Nobel Prize–winning advocate of laissez faire, Milton Friedman, wrote in 1980 that "self-interest is not myopic selfishness," because people pursue their own objectives by collaborating with others to produce the goods and services society needs. "No external force, no coercion, no violation of freedom is necessary to produce cooperation among individuals all of whom can benefit"[3] Neither concern for tradition nor moral principle should be allowed to interfere — at least in theory — with the workings of the invisible hand. This belief justified the nineteenth-century capitalist's vast wealth and the wage laborer's degradation; in the twentieth century it made the "profit motive" as legitimate as other common interests — the public need for clean air and water, for example.

THE PIN FACTORY: THE PRINCIPLE OF RATIONALITY

Adam Smith reasoned that once people were free to make as much profit as they could, they would naturally seek the most rational means of doing so. Furthermore, the spur of competition would force industrialists to use the most efficient production techniques. For if they did not, their competitors might find a cheaper way to produce the same goods and either undersell them or put them out of business. So, for Smith,

---

[2] Adam Smith, *An Inquiry into the Nature and Causes of the Wealth of Nations* (1776) (New York: Modern Library, 1965), pp. 14, 423.

[3] Milton Friedman and Rose Friedman, *Free to Choose* (New York: Harcourt Brace Jovanovich, 1980), pp. 27, 2.

competition encouraged, and even required, efficiency and technological innovation.

The best example of how rationality enhances productivity and profit making is still the famous description of the pin factory with which *The Wealth of Nations* begins. One worker by himself, Smith found, could barely make as many as 20 pins a day. If the task was broken down into many simple operations, however, ten workers doing specialized jobs — from drawing out the wire to packaging the finished product — could make more than 48,000 pins a day. Instead of 20 pins per worker, the daily production rate would now be 4,800 pins per worker, with each specialist producing at least 240 times what he could do alone. The application of the principles of rationality and efficiency to human effort greatly increases **productivity** (the condition of getting more for less) and hence the number of goods available. Thanks to the specialization and cooperation of thousands of different kinds of workers in producing hundreds of different household products, Smith was delighted to observe, "the very meanest person in a civilized country" had a higher standard of living than "many an African king, the absolute master of the lives and liberties of ten thousand naked savages."[4]

The moving assembly line is the modern application of Smith's principle of rationality in its most extreme form. At the General Motors plant in Lordstown, Ohio, for example, 101 cars pass by every hour. A worker has exactly thirty-six seconds to

The rational pursuit of efficiency has revolutionized how most people work. The haphazard procedures of individual artisans were replaced during the nineteenth century by a highly controlled and specialized division of labor. This computer assembly line is a contemporary version of Adam Smith's pin factory.

[4] Smith, *The Wealth of Nations,* pp. 4–5, 12.

complete a single task, such as attaching a side-window trim, before the next car comes along.

The fragmentation of the industrial work process had enormous human consequences. Smith himself feared that the repetitious routines of the pin factory would have a stupefying effect on the people who worked there. And, as we shall see in Chapter 19, Marx believed that one of the most devastating social effects of industrialization was the alienation of workers from their work. The emphasis on efficiency has caused this human factor in industrial production to be largely neglected. As Weber noted, the triumph of rational calculation has been the hallmark of the modern era.

THE FREE MARKET: THE PRINCIPLE OF SUPPLY AND DEMAND

In the principles of self-interest and rationality, Smith argued that the desire for profit, combined with efficiency in producing goods, would solve the problem of supply in a competitive market system. The butcher, the brewer, and the baker would be only too glad to sell us our dinners for a profit, and efficient production methods would ensure that there would be enough beef, beer, and bread to go around. But what guarantee have these hardworking individuals that enough people will want to buy what they have to sell? Smith's answer to this question is perhaps his most startling innovation: if producers and consumers follow their own self-interest, then all the goods for sale in the market will automatically find a buyer!

According to the classical theory of market equilibrium, everything has a price: goods, services, and labor all command different prices. If people want more of a product — shoes, for example — shoe factories will receive more orders than they can handle and the demand for shoes will be greater than the supply. Some customers will want new shoes so much that they will be willing to pay more for them, and the price of shoes will go up. Larger orders will motivate shoe manufacturers to increase production, the higher profits on shoes will encourage enterprising business people to go into shoe manufacturing, and more shoes will be produced to meet the buyers' demand. As the output of shoes increases, the price will go down to a level consistent with the cost of producing them plus an acceptable profit. Since the supply of shoes now balances the demand for them, market equilibrium will have been restored. The same principle of supply and demand applies to the services of laborers. When more workers are needed in shoe factories than on farms, the hourly wage for shoemakers will rise and farm wages will go down. As laborers leave the farm for factory work, factory wages will go down and farm wages will go up until the distribution of labor balances out.

Smith argued forcibly that what is true at home is also true of international markets and that mercantilist barriers to free trade should be removed. He believed that unrestrained competition would allow international production and consumption to reach equilibrium, giving every nation the highest possible productivity and greatest wealth — hence, "The Wealth of Nations."

According to this classical model the competitive market system will always provide us with the goods we want at the prices we are willing to pay for them. Supply always meets demand because sellers' self-interest leads to the production of just the kind and amount of goods that can be sold at a profit. In "the wonderful world of Adam

Smith,"[5] as one economic historian calls it, the market is a self-regulating mechanism that automatically promotes the best interests of society.

Whatever merits and limitations the competitive market may have, there is no doubt that the free-enterprise system unleashed a huge surge in economic growth. Once European governments adopted laissez faire as official policy in the nineteenth century, production and consumption soared. For the first time in human history utopian philosophers could predict an end to the age-old problem of scarcity and want. Like Adam Smith they saw in industrialization the dawn of a new age of freedom, equality, and prosperity for all.

Today, some consequences of the industrial economy appear far from utopian. Poverty and the inequalities of wealth and power are with us still, along with new problems of environmental damage, the social indifference of huge corporations, recurring inflation and unemployment, and an oppressive sense of futility and helplessness. An economic system that was thought to be independent of other institutions turned out instead to have far-reaching consequences for nearly every aspect of social life. All the carefully reasoned interpretations of classical economic theory failed to appreciate the social side effects of industrialization. What happened to the wonderful world of Adam Smith?

THE DEVELOPMENT OF MODERN CAPITALISM

In the 200 years since the publication of *The Wealth of Nations,* industrial economies have developed along the lines Adam Smith predicted. For every market economy the **Gross National Product (GNP)** — the total national production of goods and services, valued at market prices — has shown a steady, if irregular, upward climb, raising per capita income at a rate that has made every generation of children approximately twice as rich as their parents.[6] This ever-increasing output of goods and services has given industrial societies a standard of living undreamed of in Smith's day. The competitive market that he advocated has become the basis for modern **capitalism** — an economic system in which the means of production are owned by private firms and individuals, and in which the distribution of income is primarily determined by the competition of the marketplace.[7] Through the capitalist system the Industrial Revolution was developed to its fullest extent, and classical economic theory was most consistently and successfully applied.

Yet all has not gone as well as the classical theorists expected. The industrial success story has not had an entirely happy ending. Furthermore, even critics who acknowledge the productive power of the free-enterprise system argue that laissez faire is no longer a suitable policy for modern industrialized societies. The next two

---

[5] Robert L. Heilbroner, *The Worldly Philosophers,* 5th ed. (New York: Simon and Schuster/Touchstone, 1980), Chapter 3.

[6] At a per capita growth rate of 2.3 percent a year, income doubles about every generation. After World War II yearly per capita growth rates of 3, 4, and 5 percent were common in the West; in Japan the rate has been as high as 9 percent.

[7] Robert L. Heilbroner's definition, in *Business Civilization in Decline* (New York: Norton, 1976) p. 22.

sections examine some of the historical developments that have called capitalism into question.

OUTGROWING THE FREE MARKET

At the heart of the capitalist system is a fundamental contradiction. In order to work properly the free market depends on constant, no-holds-barred competition. In order to enter the market the entrepreneur must want to make money. But the same self-interest that leads people to compete vigorously in the free market also leads them to try to protect themselves from competition. The same is true of the free labor market: employed workers understandably want to protect their jobs from competition from the unemployed or underpaid. Throughout history, therefore, both workers and business people have sought shelter from the insecurity of the free market, usually by attempting to gain a monopoly over the supply of certain kinds of goods and labor.

Adam Smith himself recognized that the greatest threat to the free market was the advancement of self-interest through monopoly. "People of the same trade seldom meet together," he wrote, "but the conversation ends in a conspiracy against the public, or in some diversion to raise prices."[8] Many familiar anti-competitive devices have come into use since Smith's time: protective tariffs and quotas on low-priced foreign goods (Japanese cars), price cartels (OPEC), legal price fixing (government regulated rates for interstate trucking), and restrictions on the entry of new firms and workers into the market (licensing of new businesses, professional qualifications for accountants and teachers). From the beginning of capitalism, then, the conflict between competition and self-interest has kept free enterprise from ever being entirely free.

Even if individuals did not have good reasons to avoid competition, the capitalist economy has certain inherent features that explain why free markets will disappear anyway.

RETURNS TO SCALE. As Adam Smith's description of the pin factory indicates, large enterprises employing many workers are generally more efficient than small workshops with only a few artisans. When manufacturing became more highly mechanized and automated, large-scale production runs lowered unit costs and thus increased profits. In the warfare of the open market these returns to scale gave larger firms the advantage over their competitors. Continued to its logical conclusion the process of weeding out smaller companies would eventually result in the domination of major markets by a few monopolistic survivors.

In modern capitalist systems the advantages of large size have concentrated production in oligopolies, the technical term for a market dominated by relatively few companies. In the United States, for example, most of the soft drinks, beer, cigarettes, and automobiles sold in the country are produced by only two or three giant corporations.[9] Eight airlines dominate the market, and service to many large cities is provided by only one or two companies. Air fares have risen since federal regulations were lifted

---

[8] Quoted in Heilbroner, *The Worldly Philosophers*, p. 67.
[9] *Standard & Poor's Industry Surveys* (New York: Standard & Poor's Corporation, 1989).

in 1978, in part because such carriers as United and Northwest control the price of air travel to and from major "hubs."

INTEGRATION.   Another feature of the pin factory's operations is the need to relieve the uncertainties of supply and demand. Profit-making enterprises achieve maximum efficiency only when they have a reliable supply of raw materials and a predictable demand for the finished goods. A firm that is independent on an important mineral or product — as U.S. Steel depends on iron ore and Sears depends on household appliances — cannot be sure that the free market will always supply enough ore and toasters at the price it is willing to pay. A fluctuation in demand for their particular products is also uncomfortably difficult to predict. Such firms tend, therefore, to eliminate these risks by absorbing, or integrating, their important suppliers and whole-sale customers. An integrated producer such as Exxon owns oil fields, oil refineries, and the gas stations that distribute the finished product. *Vertical integration* — the absorption of supplier firms and distributors — is one way of reducing the uncertainties of the market; another is *horizontal integration*, or the absorption of competing firms. The great multinational corporations extend their control even to foreign markets: Michelin, the French tire company, owns rubber plantations in Asia (vertical integration); it recently acquired Uniroyal Goodrich, the second largest American tire maker (horizontal integration).

The Exxon oil refinery at Baytown, Texas, is part of a huge, vertically integrated corporation. The growth of such multinational giants has reduced competition in major industries to a handful of firms.

FINANCIAL NEEDS.   The basis of capitalism is obviously capital. Even in Smith's time pin factories needed financial backing, but the amount of capital required to start a new business was relatively small and entrepreneurs could move in and out of the market rather easily. As late as 1903 the Ford Motor Company was formed with only $28,500 in cash and produced its first automobile just four months later. In 1988, however, Ford was a multinational corporation with over $143 billion in assets and nearly 360,000 employees.[10] In markets dominated by such giant, publicly owned companies, no one without financial reserves at least as large could seriously challenge Ford or IBM or Lockheed.

Perhaps a completely free and ruggedly individualistic market economy would be as the nineteenth-century historian Thomas Carlyle described it: "anarchy plus a constable." [11] No one knows what it would be like because the risks of a true free-enterprise system have kept it from ever being tried. Even in the heyday of competitive capitalism, in the 1880s and 1890s, the great fortunes of the Rockefellers, Vanderbilts, and Carnegies were made not in a free market but from oligopolistic trusts in such vital industries as oil, railroads, and steel. These capitalists eliminated their competition by using ruthless business practices, including outright fraud and manipulation of government resources. As John D. Rockefeller once explained the process to a Sunday school class: "The growth of a large business is merely the survival of the fittest. . . . The American Beauty rose can be produced in the splendor and fragrance which bring cheer to its beholder only by sacrificing the early buds which grow up around it." [12]

If Rockefeller's natural law of monopoly seems a long way from classical economic theory, the rules governing the modern marketplace seem farther still. In every capitalist society the requirements of productive efficiency and rational planning, as well as the need for large pools of capital, have given rise to giant oligopolistic enterprises. Rather than being guided by the buyers' demand for certain products at certain prices, the modern market is more likely to be influenced by the sellers' ability to set prices and manipulate public preferences through advertising.

THE PECULIAR SPIRIT OF CAPITALISM

Max Weber proposed another view of capitalism. He argued that the economic principles that Adam Smith took to be eternal laws of nature really represent only a temporary phase of human history.

In 1904, when Rockefeller and Carnegie were at the peak of their careers, Weber attacked the basic premise of classical economics — the assumption that the "profit motive" is an intrinsic part of human nature. In probably the most famous and provocative sociological work ever written, *The Protestant Ethic and the Spirit of Capitalism*, Weber analyzed the cultural and social conditions that had given rise to a capitalist economy.

Weber took capitalism to be as Adam Smith described it: an economic system in which the unrestricted competition for personal wealth, pursued with strict rationality, accidentally produces great common wealth. He was curious, though, about the traditional assumption that capitalists are ruthlessly competitive by nature, that they would rather invest than spend what they earn, and that they are coldly rational decision

---

[10] "*Fortune's* Directory of the 500 Largest Industrial Corporations," *Fortune*, April 24, 1989, p. 354–58.
[11] Quoted in John Kenneth Galbraith, *The New Industrial State* (New York: New American Library/Signet, 1967), pp. 23–24.
[12] Quoted in Richard Hofstadter, *Social Darwinism in American Thought* (Boston: Beacon Press, 1955), p. 45.

makers. Most of all, Weber wondered whether the desire for unlimited wealth drove all human beings, or only capitalists. Most people in history, he decided, do not "'by nature' wish to earn more and more money, but simply to live as [they are] accustomed to live and to earn as much money as necessary for that purpose."[13] In Adam Smith's time conventional wisdom assumed the opposite: people would only work as long as they were poor. But long after they had accumulated their great fortunes, capitalists like Rockefeller and Carnegie continued to work as hard as ever. Unlimited wants, then, are not part of human nature, Weber concluded, but must be explained historically.

Weber found the explanation in the **Protestant ethic**, the belief that hard work is a moral obligation. To the early Protestants work was a "calling," or service to God. Since work was God's wish, the pursuit of gain had to be morally good. Benjamin Franklin's rules of business conduct, for example, were moral maxims: "A penny saved is a penny earned," so a penny *should* be saved; "time is money," so it *should not* be wasted.

The Calvinist doctrine of predestination, Weber argued, is the historical source of the compulsive acquisitiveness of capitalists. According to this doctrine human beings are predestined to spend eternity in heaven or hell. The followers of John Calvin believed that their fate was already settled and that nothing could be done to change it. Neither good works not piety could bring salvation, which was an arbitrary gift of God. This Calvinist doctrine was very harsh indeed, and it generated a great deal of anxiety in the seventeenth century. Imagine how students today would feel if they knew that it had already been decided whether they would graduate or not, but no one would tell them! For graduation, substitute eternal bliss or damnation, and you have a psychologically intolerable situation.

People who are anxious about their fate look for signs: students worried about their grades are crushed by a curt word from their professor and hopeful if they get a smile instead. Calvinists, too, desperately grasped for straws, looking for signs that they were among the elect. It is understandable that they came to view financial success as a sign of God's favor. No one, however, could be sure that the sign had been read correctly. Protestants constantly sought reassurance through more and more business success.

The psychology of the Protestant ethic is thus Weber's explanation for the capitalists' frantic, insatiable pursuit of money. Because Calvinists still considered self-indulgence sinful, the actual possession of wealth brought little pleasure. Capitalists are not satisfied to be rich; they must always be richer. By elevating work to a sacred duty, the Protestant Reformation in Scotland and Puritan England (where Calvinism had its greatest effect) provided the cultural setting necessary for the Industrial Revolution and the rise of capitalism. The spirit of capitalism, Weber found, is not inherent in human nature but only in the special mentality of the self-disciplined, hard-working men and women who transformed the medieval world into the modern industrial one.

THE VISIBLE HAND: SOCIAL CONSEQUENCES OF CAPITALISM

In the capitalist system a competitive market is supposed to produce the most efficient allocation of resources. Consumers and producers, intent only on benefiting them-

---

[13] Max Weber, *The Protestant Ethic and the Spirit of Capitalism* (New York: Scribner's, 1956), p. 60.

selves, will be led by an invisible hand to benefit society by demanding and supplying just the right amount of goods and services at just the right prices. As capitalism has developed, however, some visible social effects of the invisible hand have caused some misgivings about how well the free market actually works.

ECONOMIC INEQUALITY

Not all the participants in the free market are evenly matched. Smith himself realized that the distribution of wealth depended on whether the employer or the worker had greater bargaining power, and it was not difficult for him "to foresee which of the two parties must . . . have the advantage in the dispute, and force the other into a compliance with their terms." [14] The superior strength of the industrialists, merchants, and landlords, he believed, would eventually press the wages of the working masses down to survival level.

In the early days of capitalism, there was indeed a tremendous disparity between the economic rewards given to capitalists and laborers. Between 1892 and 1899, for example, John D. Rockefeller's dividends from his investment in Standard Oil came to between $30 and $40 million; Andrew Carnegie's income from his steel companies in 1900 alone was $23 million.[15] In 1892, while his boss was accumulating a great personal fortune, an assistant roller in Carnegie's Homestead, Pennsylvania, steel mill was earning $65 a month.[16]

Smith foresaw two situations in which wages would rise: a scarcity of workers or steady economic growth. "It is not the actual greatness of national wealth," he wrote, "but its continual increase, which occasions a rise in the wages of labour." [17] Once again, Smith was right. The average worker eventually received a higher income not because of any significant reduction in inequality but because of an ever-increasing GNP. In the decade between 1900 and 1909 American workers received 55 percent of all income. Since the 1930s their share has been about 12 percentage points higher. But the country's income in 1987 was about *thirty times* what it was in 1929, giving workers a little bit larger slice of a very much larger pie.[18] While economic expansion has brought increasing prosperity to the average wage earner, however, the invisible hand has still not touched those at the bottom of the income scale.

DEPRESSION AND RECESSION

Throughout the nineteenth and early twentieth centuries financial panics and depressions were so frequent in capitalist economies that they were considered a normal part of the "business cycle." About every ten years a growth in demand, such as the British economy experienced during World War I, would cause a sharp rise in the GNP. When the demand for labor and materials fell off, as it did at the end of the war, the "boom"

---

[14] Smith, *The Wealth of Nations,* p. 66.
[15] *The New York Times,* March 4, 1957.
[16] Heilbroner, *The Economic Transformation of America,* p. 126.
[17] Smith, *The Wealth of Nations,* p. 69.
[18] Gale Johnson, "The Functional Distribution of Income in the United States, 1850-1952," *Review of Economics and Statistics 26* (May 1954); U.S. Bureau of the Census, *Statistical Abstract of the United States* (Washington, D.C.: U.S. Government Printing Office), 1989, Table 689.

was followed by a "bust"—a period of bankruptcies, wage cuts, and mass unemployment. Finally, in the 1930s, the boom-and-bust cycle led to a disastrous breakdown in industrial economies. In the United States the Great Depression brought economic growth to a standstill, left one quarter of the work force unemployed, and put 85,000 companies and 11,000 banks out of business. Production in the businesses that survived was often reduced to half the volume of the previous decade, and wages in some industries dropped to barely subsistence levels.[19] After the Great Depression governments found that they could no longer rely on the invisible hand alone to ensure continuing prosperity.

Since World War II, government intervention to stimulate economic growth has become public policy in industrial societies, both socialist and capitalist. Partly under the influence of the British economist John Maynard Keynes,[20] governments try to "fine-tune" the economy by raising or lowering interest rates, increasing or reducing public spending, creating new tax incentives, and so on. Large national budgets keep general demand high and encourage business investment, while spending on social welfare programs—health care, education, Social Security, and welfare—maintain private purchasing power and offset the economically depressing effects of poverty and unemployment.

After Ronald Reagan was elected president in 1980, American economic policy took a different turn. The old, politically conservative virtues of laissez faire were rebottled as *supply-side economics*, a theory that drastic tax cuts would stimulate economic growth by increasing savings for capital investment. In 1981 Congress passed across-the-board reductions in income tax rates and other "supply-side" tax breaks that were estimated to total between $600 and $750 billion over the next five years. Since neither Congress nor the president (Reagan or his successor, George Bush) was willing to match these reductions in revenues with reductions in spending, the result was huge federal budget deficits and a corresponding increase in the federal debt.

Keynesian economists contended that "Reaganomics"—Reagan's program for lower taxes and higher military spending—had actually had a Keynesian effect. The huge budget deficits caused by these policies were a form of dis-saving that stimulated economic activity. Critics of Reaganomics suspected that its main objective was not primarily to stimulate new economic growth but to deprive the government of the tax revenues needed to finance social welfare programs.

Whatever the reason in theory, economic recovery was the practical result. After a typical boom-and-bust period, when the wild inflation of the 1970s was stopped by the worst recession since the 1930s, the American economy again entered a period of expansion in the mid-1980s. By the end of the decade economists were predicting a period of stagnation, or slowing of economic growth. Increased borrowing by the federal government (to cover budget deficits), business (to finance a wave of highly leveraged mergers and acquisitions), and consumers (to maintain living standards when household income has stopped rising) generated higher interest rates at the end

---

[19] Heilbroner, *The Economic Transformation of America*, p. 179.

[20] In order to stimulate economic growth in a depression, Keynes argued that the government must supplement insufficient business investment and thus increase the country's general buying power.

FIGURE 12-1   U.S. PER CAPITA GROSS NATIONAL PRODUCT, 1965-1987

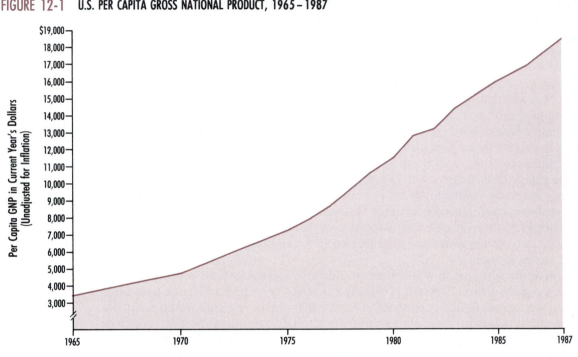

SOURCE: U.S. Bureau of the Census, *Statistical Abstract of the United States* (Washington, D.C.: U.S. Government Printing Office, 1989), Table 690.

of the 1980s. The higher cost of borrowing money is likely to reduce capital investment in new plants and equipment, which in turn reduces gains in productivity. Economic growth alone, however, has not solved the recurring problems of capitalist economies — inflation and unemployment.

INFLATION

Perhaps the most troublesome economic problem for capitalism today is not depression but inflation, the general rise in prices set off by increasing demand. In the last two decades every capitalist country has experienced a high rate of inflation, which can be measured by how much less the British pound, the Japanese yen, and the American dollar can now buy (see Figure 12-1). The reasons for this worldwide inflationary trend lie in the same postwar economic changes we have just discussed. First, capitalist governments have assumed more responsibility for their citizens' economic well-being. In the United States in 1929 all government spending amounted to barely 8 percent of GNP. Today it is about 30 percent, and in many European countries it is 40 and even 50 percent. As the economist Robert L. Heilbroner points out, when the budget for "welfare or warfare is added to vigorous private spending, the economy is pushed along faster, and prices naturally move upward as a consequence." [21]

Second, government-sponsored growth encourages private borrowing and spending by removing the fear of a severe depression. When every boom was followed by a bust, both business people and consumers were more cautious about building a new plant or investing in a house. And, without recurring panics and depressions, there are no sharp declines in demand to send prices down.

Finally, in an economy where oligopolies predominate, prices are sheltered from shifts in public demand. All-out price competition ceases to exist in an expanding economy: big corporations are able to set prices at a markup over costs with less risk of losing their customers. At the same time labor unions have given workers greater bargaining power in increasing wages to offset higher prices, and non-union workers have the choice of taking government unemployment payments instead of a low-paying job.

Capitalist governments have tried several methods of controlling inflation — tightening the money supply so that borrowing money becomes more difficult and expensive; raising taxes; imposing wage and price controls. Such efforts to ensure price stability by reducing demand often alternate with efforts to ensure full employment by encouraging economic expansion. This stop-go pattern — in which the stop phase brings down the inflation rate but increases unemployment, and the go phase brings down the unemployment rate but increases inflationary pressures — is one of the capitalist economy's most difficult dilemmas.[22]

UNEMPLOYMENT

When U.S. Steel shut down its South Chicago works in 1984, 7,000 workers suddenly lost their jobs. The day of the closing a long line of cars, bearing such signs as "Welding Shop Rest in Peace" and "Machine Shop Rest in Peace," drove from the union hall to the plant in a mock funeral procession. The steelworkers were mourning not just the end of their jobs but the death of a way of life.

The South Chicago steelworkers were victims of **structural unemployment**, or the loss of jobs from a restructuring of the economy. The closing of their particular steel plant is partly the result of one such restructuring — the American economy's shift from manufacturing to service occupations (see Chapter 19, "Work and Leisure"). At the end of World War II, half of all employed Americans held jobs that provided services — in education, banking, health care, government, sales, advertising, and so on. Today, three out of four workers are in service occupations, and fewer than one in five are in manufacturing.[23] Industries based on new electronic technologies have created some jobs, but many more jobs in older industries (steel, textiles) have been permanently lost because of foreign competition, automation, and relocation abroad.

---

[21] Heilbroner, *The Worldly Philosophers*, p. 291.

[22] Ibid., pp. 291–94.

[23] U.S. Bureau of the Census, *Statistical Abstract of the United States* (Washington, D.C.: U.S. Government Printing Office, 1988).

Unemployed workers stand in a breadline during the 1930s. After the Great Depression, governments decided they could no longer rely entirely on the invisible hand of the free market to ensure prosperity.

For the employer, closing an obsolete manufacturing plant is an inevitable result of the need to stay competitive and profitable. If the money is invested elsewhere, South Chicago's loss may be another community's gain in new employment opportunities. The mobility of capital — the ability to move money easily from one kind of investment to another, and from one location to another — is a basic feature of the capitalist system. In recent years many American corporations have moved away from the "rust belt" — the industrial areas of the Northeast and Midwest — to the "sun belt" of the South and West, where profits tend to be higher because wages and business taxes are generally lower.

This movement of capital, or *capital flight*, has had a devastating effect on the industrial labor force. Between 1981 and 1986, nearly 11 million workers lost their jobs because of plant closings or employee cutbacks. Two-thirds of them (67 percent) found new jobs during that period, but 14 percent left the labor force, and the rest were still looking for work. The largest group of displaced workers had held manufacturing jobs in the industrial Midwest. The average worker was out of a job for four months, and two out of three had not received any unemployment benefits. Most (55 percent) of these displaced workers took up different occupations, and about two out of five had to take pay cuts.[24]

---

[24] Francis W. Horvath, "The Pulse of Economic Change: Displaced Workers of 1981–1985," *Monthly Labor Review* (June 1987), pp. 3–12.

Plant closings also have a ripple effect on the community. Unemployment eventually spreads to retail businesses, supplier firms, and even the public schools and hospitals dependent on corporate income and property tax revenues. What began as a private business decision ends by affecting nearly everyone in town.[25] The tendency to neglect such "external" concerns is another visible effect of the free-market system.

ENVIRONMENTAL AND SOCIAL NEGLECT

According to the economic theory on which capitalism is based, the free market is the most reliable and efficient way to allocate goods and services for the benefit of society. Competition forces producers to make only goods that will sell, and rational producers look for the most efficient way to increase productivity and maximize profits.

Unfortunately, the most efficient production methods and the most profitable goods are not always the most socially beneficial. The ecologist Garrett Hardin describes, in "The Tragedy of the Commons," how individual self-interest leads to collective disaster:

> Picture a pasture open to all. It is to be expected that each herdsmen will try to keep as many cattle as possible on the commons. Such an arrangement may work reasonably satisfactorily for centuries because tribal wars, poaching, and disease keep the numbers of both man and beast well below the carrying capacity of the land. Finally, however, comes the day of reckoning {when the land will be overgrazed and ruined by the addition of more animals}. . . . As a rational being, each herdsman seeks to maximize his gain.
>
> ■ ■ ■
>
> {He} concludes that the only sensible course for him to pursue is to add another animal to his herd. And another and another. . . . But this is the conclusion reached by each and every rational herdsman sharing a commons. . . . Each man is locked into a system that compels him to increase his herd without limit — in a world that is limited. Ruin is the destination toward which all men rush, each pursuing his own best interest in a society that believes in the freedom of the commons.[26]

The tragedy of the commons is that the pursuit of maximum profit destroys the natural resources on which profit is based. Killing whales, for example, is profitable until there are no more whales; pumping as much crude oil as possible is very profitable for this generation but depletes energy supplies for the next.

The tragedy of the commons lies also in the poisoning of the environment. Rational, enterprising executives found that the cheapest and most efficient way to dispose of toxic chemicals was to discharge them into Lake Erie, for example, or into the Atlantic Ocean or the air over Los Angeles. Although these methods of waste disposal are cheap for a few, the high public cost is shared by all and may be paid by generations to come. Concentration on the "bottom line," or selling only what is most

---

[25] Barry Bluestone and Bennett Harrison, *The Deindustrialization of America* (New York: Basic Books, 1982), p. 67.

[26] Garrett Hardin, "The Tragedy of the Commons," *Science 64* (December 13, 1968): 1245–46.

HOW MUCH IS A LIFE WORTH?

Scientists, politicians, and corporate executives must deal with processes that have catastrophic potential: nuclear power plants, explosive and toxic chemicals, air travel, nuclear weapons, the launching of missiles into space. Undertaking any of these processes involves assessing the risk for third and fourth parties — the innocent bystanders and future generations who will be the victims of a disastrous accident. The sociologist Charles Perrow, an authority on complex organizations, describes how the benefits and costs of such risks are analyzed by professionals.

The field {of risk assessment} acknowledges the difference between voluntary risks such as skiing and hang-gliding, and involuntary ones such as leaching of chemical wastes. But it does not acknowledge the difference between the *imposition* of risks by profit-making firms who could reduce that risk, and the *acceptance* of risk by the public where private pleasures are involved (skiing) or some control can be exercised (driving). All are bundled up in a vague reference to market principles, as if we would not have heat and light without X number of dead miners or irradiated nuclear glow boys. The literature reflects a rational, calculative marketplace theory of cost-benefit analysis. The technical literature is fond of pointing out that we spend millions of dollars in safety devices to save one nuclear power worker, but refuse to spend $80,000 to save the driver of an automobile. (That is, the benefits from, say, an emergency core cooling system and an automatic seat belt are figured on the basis of how many lives one expects to save, and of course the cost of the ECCS and the seat belt are vastly different, as is the number of lives to be saved.) It is thus irrational to spend that much

money on the nuclear plant; we should spend it on seat belts, highway guardrails or anti-smoking literature. It is as if there were a fixed budget category for safety, regardless of whether corporation profits or private needs are involved, and the budget, being fixed, cannot be enlarged when new risks come along.

Reading this discussion can lead one to imagine a scenario such as this: At the board meeting of a large corporation, the vice president for finance has received advice from the risk assessors. He announces that by not installing some safety devices we will kill one more worker per year. This will not affect the supply of candidates for this death, since workers will still take jobs at the plant because the labor market is depressed, and each worker decides there is a very good chance that someone else will be killed. On the benefit side, killing that worker will mean that the corporation will avoid a cost of $50 million for the safety devices. This avoids a price rise or a cut in the dividends or management bonuses. The vice president might estimate that they can avoid a one-dollar price rise on 20 million items, and avoid a cut in dividends of $30 million. By killing the worker, the public and the stockholders will obviously greatly benefit. What is a life worth? Well, he figures, 50 million is pretty high for a random, anonymous worker, so let's do it. The vice president for finance is correct; in risk analysis terms, it is a good bargain. Something similar took place at the Ford Motor Company when it decided not to buffer the fuel tank in the Pinto, and at the General Motors Company when it rejected warnings from engineers that the Corvair would flip over for the lack of a $15 stabilizing bar.

SOURCE: Charles Perrow, *Normal Accidents: Living with High-Risk Technologies* (New York: Basic, 1984), pp. 309–10.

profitable, also makes capitalists blind to the socially harmful effects of such products as cigarettes, high-powered automobiles, and chemically colored and flavored junk foods (see "How Much Is a Life Worth?").

The tendency to measure what is "good" by what is profitable is not limited to capitalist societies. The ministries in charge of production in the Soviet Union are also required to produce the greatest amount of goods at the lowest possible cost. One result has been the pollution of Lake Baikal, the world's largest body of fresh water, with wastes from the paper mills on its shores. According to the manager of one of these

Chemical waste from a paper mill spills into a river in Ontario, Canada. Concentration on the "bottom line" has made capitalists generally indifferent to the environmental consequences of industrial production.

plants, purifying filters have not been installed because they are too expensive: reducing pollution would mean reducing the return on the capital invested in the plant.[27]

While industrial systems have been most successful in meeting the demand for profitable goods and services, they have often failed to supply such nonprofit-making necessities as clean air, good schools, and safe streets. Whether we are indeed getting an efficient allocation of resources has long been questioned. "A country that spends money on champagne before it has provided milk for its babies," George Bernard Shaw scolded in 1928, "is a badly managed, silly, vain, stupid, ignorant nation."[28]

THE WORLD ECONOMY

The worldwide spread of industrial development is evident in virtually every society. More and more, the world is a single economic system in which huge, multinational corporations compete for larger shares of the global market for goods and labor. World-system theory offers one explanation for the development of a world economy.

---

[27] Marshall Goldman, *The Spoils of Progress: Environmental Pollution in the Soviet Union* (Cambridge, Mass.: Massachusetts Institute of Technology Press, 1972).

[28] George Bernard Shaw, *The Intelligent Woman's Guide to Socialism and Capitalism* (New York: Brentano's, 1928), p. 50.

WORLD-SYSTEM THEORY

In *Imperialism* (1902) J. A. Hobson, an English economist, made the first analysis of world capitalism.[29] He argued that the industrial European nations were looting their colonies by buying their raw materials at low prices and selling manufactured goods back to them at high prices. Later, Lenin and other Marxist writers charged that capitalist nations exploit less developed countries and keep them from modernizing. Immanuel Wallerstein elaborated this approach a few years ago in what is known as **world-system theory**

According to Wallerstein, the Industrial Revolution was a result of the international economy which had already developed from the European explorations and conquests of the sixteenth century.[30] By 1900 this colonization had produced a worldwide division of labor. The modern, industrialized Western European societies acted as an international upper class of owners and managers; other less-developed societies acted as an international lower class which provided cheap labor and raw materials. In between were a few countries which were trying to join the rich societies by using poor societies in the same way. Modern, industrialized countries benefited from this relationship while less developed countries remained weak and economically dependent on one or at best very few export products. This arrangement was not necessarily a plot by the rich against the poor (although it often looks that way), but a result of the structure of the international economic system.

Wallerstein used the term *core societies* to describe the capitalist countries of Western Europe and the United States. He called the poor countries *peripheral societies*. Many countries of Latin America, Asia, and Africa are still less developed, relatively weak, and dependent on the export of a few raw materials (coffee, oil, beef, minerals). These peripheral societies are usually dominated by a core society's economic interests, producing relatively unprofitable raw materials which are exported to the core nations for manufacture into very profitable finished goods.[31] *Semiperipheral* societies, such as Taiwan and the Philippines, are not as highly industrialized as the core nations. Japan is a rare example of a semiperipheral society that has achieved core status, perhaps because its economy was never dominated by a core society.[32]

World-system theory provides a useful explanation for the uneven industrial development of the world. For example, Wallerstein argued that the industrialization of Hungary and Poland was thwarted because the core societies already dominated the market for manufactured goods. Today the Hungarian and Polish economies continue to rely on the export of food in return for manufactures — the characteristic situation of peripheral societies.

Most sociologists agree, however, that Wallerstein underestimated the effect of local internal problems on industrial development.[33] For example, the population

---

[29] Rodney Stark, *Sociology* (Belmont, Calif.: Wadsworth, 1985), p. 399.

[30] Immanuel Wallerstein, *The Modern World-System* (New York: Academic Press, 1974).

[31] Christopher Chase-Dunn, "The Effects of International Economic Dependence on Development and Inequality: A Cross-National Study," *American Sociological Review* 40 (1975), pp. 720–38.

[32] Daniel Chirot, *Social Change in the Twentieth Century* (New York: Harcourt Brace Jovanovich, 1977), pp. 9–11.

[33] Carlos Diaz-Alejandro et al., *Rich and Poor Nations in the World Economy* (New York: McGraw-Hill, 1978).

The spread of industrial development has created a worldwide market for goods and labor. These automobiles are being manufactured in Japan, but they will probably be driven by Europeans or Americans.

explosion in developing countries created a tremendous drain on capital that would otherwise be available for investment (see Chapter 20, "Population, Ecology, and Urbanization"). Other critics of world-system theory point to the exceptions to the rule that peripheral societies export food and other raw materials and core societies export manufactured goods. The United States and Canada are advanced industrial societies, yet they are the world's leading exporters of grain; by some definitions, Taiwan and

South Korea are peripheral societies, yet they import oil and other raw materials and export manufactured electronic equipment, clothing, and automobiles. Clearly, the economies of the world in the twentieth century are more complex and interdependent than world-system theory indicates.

THE GLOBAL MARKET

The rapid spread of new transportation and communications technologies has created a worldwide marketplace for goods and labor. Manufacturing components can now be shipped by jet across the globe in a day or two, and managers can relay orders and information instantaneously by telephone or fax machine. New inventions are soon bought, borrowed, or stolen by foreign competitors, and developing nations are now able to install the most up-to-date steel-rolling mills, fertilizer plants, paper machines, and computer systems.[34] While it took 63 years for the first steam-powered cotton mill to be built in the United States after its invention in Great Britain, computer microchips were being produced all over the industrialized world less than 10 years after their invention in the United States.[35]

As a result of these new technologies, capital is more mobile than ever before. In the highly competitive global marketplace, manufacturing companies cut production costs by relocating their operations to the low-wage, low-tax areas of the developing world. When the Chrysler Corporation found it less profitable to make cars in the high-wage labor market of Detroit, for example, they moved their assembly plants to Mexico, where there are over 1,100 "maquiladoras," or American-owned plants along the border. In an age of jet air cargo, computerized production control, and telecommunications, highly specialized operations can be performed in far-flung corners of the world. Leather covers, yarn, and thread are regularly shipped from the United States to Haiti, where local women are employed for a few cents an hour to make them into baseballs; wafers for semiconductors are made in California, sent to Singapore where gold thread is soldered to the terminal, and then flown back to the United States.[36] This export of manufacturing jobs to low-wage labor markets is a contributing factor in the chronically high unemployment rate among American unskilled workers in the "smokestack" industries of the Northeast and Middle West.

New technologies are beginning to create a "global office" for service operations as well. To take advantage of lower pay rates and business costs, New York Life processes insurance claims via a computer link from New Jersey to a village in Ireland, and American Airlines sends its ticket stubs to Barbados for data processing.[37]

In a world economy every country depends on others for essential goods and services. Events that take place in a single country are now likely to affect everyone.

---

[34] Robert B. Reich, "Global Change," in F. Hearn, ed., *The Transformation of Industrial Organization* (Belmont, CA: Wadsworth, 1988), p. 114.

[35] D. Stanley Eitzen and Maxine Baca Zinn, *The Forces Reshaping America* (Englewood Cliffs, N.J.: Prentice-Hall, 1989), p. 10.

[36] Richard J. Barnet, *The Lean Years: Politics in an Age of Scarcity* (New York: Simon and Schuster, 1980), p. 245.

[37] Steve Lohr, "The Growth of the Global Office," *The New York Times*, October 18, 1988, pp. D1, D25.

By replacing the free market with centralized control, socialist systems have created notorious inefficiencies. Because the supply of consumer goods rarely meets the demand for them, shoppers in the Soviet Union are accustomed to waiting in long lines to buy scarce foods, clothing, and household appliances.

The price of oil in Saudi Arabia, a surplus of wheat in the United States, the cost of borrowing money to finance factories in Brazil or Czechoslovakia, a change in the relative value of the Japanese yen or the German deutsche mark — all have repercussions for the world market to which every nation now belongs.

CAPITALISM AND SOCIALISM

While Adam Smith saw government interference with the free market as a hindrance to economic efficiency, Americans are more likely to see government control as a threat to their individual freedoms in a democracy. For many people, the alternative to economic freedom is socialism — an imprecise term for a system of public ownership and management of the means of production and distribution of goods. The dangers of centralized economic and political power are clearly seen in the totalitarian socialist states of Eastern Europe. In 1985, when Mikhail Gorbachev came to power in the Soviet Union, Communist command economies were part of a repressive political system in which personal as well as economic freedom was severely restricted. By reducing

THE TRIUMPH OF CAPITALISM

According to the noted economic historian Robert Heilbroner, the political and economic changes sweeping Eastern Europe mean that capitalism is now generally accepted as the most successful means of distributing goods and services. The trend toward a free market in socialist states also raises the possibility that the two systems could converge in a way that would combine capitalism's economic freedom and socialism's political responsibility.

Less than seventy-five years after it officially began, the contest between capitalism and socialism is over: capitalism has won. The Soviet Union, China, and Eastern Europe have given us the clearest possible proof that capitalism organizes the material affairs of humankind more satisfactorily than socialism: that however inequitably or irresponsibly the marketplace may distribute goods, it does so better than the queues of a planned economy; however mindless the culture of commercialism, it is more attractive than state moralism; and however deceptive the ideology of a business civilization, it is more believable than that of a socialist one. Indeed, it is difficult to observe the changes taking place in the world today and not conclude that the nose of the capitalist camel has been pushed so far under the socialist tent that the great question now seems how rapid will be the transformation of socialism into capitalism, and not the other way around, as things looked only a half century ago.

Yet I doubt whether the historic drama will conclude, like a great morality play, in the unequivocal victory of one side and the ignominious defeat of the other.

■ ■ ■

The collapse of centralized planning shows that at this moment socialism has no plausible economic framework, but the word has always meant more than a system of economic organization. At its core, it has stood for a commitment to social goals that have seemed incompatible with, or at least unattainable under, capitalism — above all, the moral, not just the material, elevation of humankind. However battered that conception may be from the designation of bloody and cruel regimes as "socialist," the vision has retained its inspirational potential, just as that of Christianity has survived countless autos-da-fé and vicious persecutions. At a more down-to-earth level, the great question seems to be whether the still centralized economies can duplicate the remarkable coexistence of realms which has provided so much of the success of capitalism. As the Soviet Union, China, and Eastern Europe allow an increased autonomy to their managerial cadres and encourage the growth of entrepreneurial activity in the crevices of their economies, we find the ingredients of a new universal class; but if socialism is truly to make way for such a class, more will have to be ceded than the capacity for acting without consultation with the authorities. What is crucially at issue is whether socialism can accept a second republic within its own borders — a republic of economic affairs with its own rewards, punishments, imperatives, and ideology, without which the republic of political affairs seems unlikely to acquiesce in the all-important limitation of its powers.

Would this mean, in effect, the transformation of socialism into capitalism? This is to ask how closely capitalism, under its most democratic impulse, could approach socialism, under its most economically open arrangements. Sweden has always been the living example, real or slightly imaginary, of a system whose economic realm is unmistakably capitalist but whose political leaders have often declared their admiration for socialism, and sought — successfully, on the whole — to move toward its egalitarian standards. This raises the vision, once popular with political scientists and economists, of a historic "convergence" of systems that has grown increasingly less plausible in the light of the immense gulf between the performances of the two social orders. Perhaps the vision will again become a matter for serious consideration if the extraordinarily difficult movement of centralized socialism toward economic and political liberation is not derailed, and if the drift of capitalism toward a more responsible amalgam of economic freedom and political responsibility continues its slow historical advance. Mutterings of both right and left to the contrary, there is no evidence that at least some capitalisms could not progress in this direction. Whether that will be possible for centralized socialism we simply do not know. Meanwhile, for both sides the immediate aim is to create systems that will work well enough. Despite the triumph of capitalism, that is not a matter to be taken for granted, least of all by us.

Source: Robert Heilbroner, "The Triumph of Capitalism," *The New Yorker* (January 23, 1989), pp. 98, 109.

competition, these socialist systems often produced notorious inefficiencies. When free enterprise is replaced by highly centralized bureaucracies, as it was in the Soviet Union, a typical displacement of goals takes place: the rules and procedures for meeting production goals are followed to the letter without as much concern for the quality and quantity of consumer goods being produced. Furthermore, in a society where everyone is guaranteed a job, there is little incentive to improve workmanship and productivity. As a result, shoddy goods, haphazard distribution, and unpredictable shortages plagued the Soviet economy.

Gorbachev's policy of *perestroika,* or restructuring, was an attempt to reform the Soviet economy by decentralizing decision making so that local managers, not bureaucrats in Moscow, decide how and what to produce. Gorbachev's reforms helped to bring about stunning political and economic changes in Eastern Europe. Popular uprisings in Poland, East Germany, Czechoslovakia, Bulgaria, and Rumania ended the rule of authoritarian Communist parties which had held power for over 40 years. A tentative kind of free-market capitalism is now emerging in Poland and Hungary, and ideological support for the state-run Communist economy is waning throughout Eastern Europe (see "The Triumph of Capitalism"). For workers accustomed to job security and equality of income, however, the shift to a free-enterprise economy will probably mean a painful adjustment to its problems: unemployment, inflation, and a society of "winners and losers."

Classical economists share Adam Smith's belief that the invisible hand should not be hampered by government interference in the market. We have seen, however, that laissez-faire policies eventually led to monopolistic concentration and the Great Depression, and that the government has usually intervened to protect rather than oppose the competition of the free market. All capitalist countries have **mixed economies** which combine a relatively free market with some government controls. In the American free enterprise system — probably the least regulated of all capitalist economies — the federal government supports farm prices, limits foreign imports, sets minimum wages, provides Social Security benefits, and influences economic activities through its tax and budget policies. Even if we wanted to go back to the "good old days" of competitive capitalism, we could hardly do so. Today corporate giants like the "Fortune 500" are well protected against the pressures of the market. Futhermore, a return to laissez faire would not necessarily unleash the creative energies of individual self-interest. Almost all modern workers are now employees: freeing IBM or General Motors from government control would not give corporate bureaucrats much incentive to try harder. A successful return to Adam Smith's policies would require a return to Adam Smith's world, and that world has disappeared forever.

Nevertheless, there are many ways of rearranging the mixture of mixed economies. Industrial managers in the Soviet Union now offer pay incentives to increase productivity, and socialist Yugoslavia is developing a genuinely competitive market for its state-owned enterprises. The progressive capitalist countries of Europe have tried almost every possible mix of public and private ownership, central planning and open market, monopoly and competition, and worker and management control. These experiments with the mixed economy will probably continue, as one kind of system tries to control the instability inherent in capitalism and the other tries to reduce the inefficiencies inherent in socialism.

SUMMARY

1. The economy is the social institution specializing in the production and exchange of goods and services. Until about 1750 all the world's economies were organized on the basis of custom or command. Most industrial economies are based instead on the principles of the free market.

2. Adam Smith formulated classical economic theory, which became the basis and justification for the capitalist free-enterprise system. In *The Wealth of Nations* Smith proposed that people who pursue their own self-interest are led by an "invisible hand" to benefit society by producing necessary goods and services. He thought that the competitive free market would automatically balance supply and demand for the best interests of society. In his famous description of the specialization of labor in a pin factory, Smith argued that the rational control of the work process would increase efficiency and productivity.

3. As Smith predicted, the competitive market system in industrial societies has brought steady economic growth and a huge increase in human productivity. The "free market," however, has never been completely free. The principle of self-interest has led to anticompetitive measures and attempts to form monopolies. The requirements of productive efficiency and rational planning have given rise to giant oligopolistic enterprises that tend to dominate major markets and discourage competition.

4. In *The Protestant Ethic and the Spirit of Capitalism,* Weber argued that the economic behavior Smith took to be "human nature" was actually typical of only a certain period of history. In Weber's view, by elevating work to a sacred duty the Protestant ethic provided the cultural setting necessary for the Industrial Revolution and the rise of capitalism.

5. Modern capitalist societies have steadily increased their GNPs, but this wealth has been unevenly distributed. Free enterprise has not solved the recurring problems of recession and inflation, and the capitalist labor market has produced chronically high rates of unemployment. In both capitalist and socialist economies, the emphasis on profit-making has often outweighed concern for its harmful environmental and social effects.

6. Technological change and the spread of industrial development has created a world economy. According to world-system theory, the Industrial Revolution was based on European colonial trade. In Wallerstein's theory, rich, industrialized core societies imported raw materials from poor, dependent peripheral societies and exported manufactured goods to them in return. Today the world economy is a complex system of interdependent countries, where multi-national enterprises compete in a world-wide market for goods and labor.

7. Capitalist economies today are mixed economies which combine a relatively free market with government controls. Socialist systems have public ownership and management of the means of production and distribution of goods. The economic problem for capitalism is to control the instability of the market; the economic issue for socialism is to reduce the inefficiencies and low productivity of a highly bureaucratized command economy.

KEY TERMS

the economy 377
custom economy 378
command economy 378
laissez-faire economy 379
free market 379
the invisible hand 380

productivity 381
Gross National Product (GNP) 383
capitalism 383
returns to scale 384
oligopolies 384

Protestant ethic 387
structural unemployment 391
world-system theory 396
socialism 399
mixed economy 401

SUGGESTED READING

Richard J. Barnet and Ronald E. Muller. *Global Reach: The Power of the Multinational Corporations.* New York: Simon and Schuster, 1976.

* David Bensman and Roberta Lynch. *Rusted Dreams: Hard Times in a Steel Community.* Berkeley, CA: University of California Press, 1988.

* Barry Bluestone and Bennett Harrison. *The Deindustrialization of America.* New York: Basic, 1984.

John K. Galbraith. *The New Industrial State.* Rev. ed. Boston: Houghton Mifflin, 1978.

*Robert L. Heilbroner. *The Nature and Logic of Capitalism.* New York: Norton, 1986.

* Matthew Josephson. *The Robber Barons.* New York: Harcourt, Brace, 1962.

Robert Lekachman. *The Age of Keynes.* New York: Random, 1966.

* Neil J. Smelser. *The Sociology of Economic Life,* 2d ed. Englewood Cliffs, NJ: Prentice-Hall, 1976.

* Paul D. Staudohar and Holly E. Brown, eds. *Deindustrialization and Plant Closure.* Lexington, MA: Lexington Books, 1986.

* Available in paperback

We teach what we are, not really what we know and not always what we think.

Henri Peyre

CHAPTER 13

EDUCATION

F rom the desk where I sit," President Lyndon Johnson declared, "I have learned one great truth. The answer for all our national problems—the answer for all the problems of the world—comes to a single word. That word is 'education.'" [1]

Like Lyndon Johnson, Americans have always placed great faith in the benefits of education for themselves as individuals and for society as a whole. "Getting a good education" is valued for its own sake, as self-improvement and intellectual cultivation. At the same time, American tradition emphasizes the practical uses of education as a means of "getting ahead"—as the qualification for a good job and a better life. And, in today's highly complex post-industrial society, the right educational credentials are usually essential for entry into technical and professional occupations. The American faith in education also rests on the political belief that an informed electorate makes democracy possible. At a time when American business is facing the challenges of the new "information society," a knowledgeable, well-trained workforce is thought to be the answer to continued prosperity and technological progress. Finally, the conviction that education can solve social problems by doing away with ignorance and misunderstandings has long been shared by those who advocate equal educational opportunities as the cure-all for injustice and inequality.

---

[1] Quoted in Laurence J. Peter, *Peter's Quotations: Ideas for Our Time* (New York: Morrow, 1977), p. 175.

Education obviously means many things to many people. The sociological definition of **education**, however, is the deliberate, formal transfer of knowledge, skills, and values from one person or group to another. Education is an institution for *socialization,* the universal social process by which a cultural heritage is transmitted from generation to generation. While some socialization takes place in virtually every area of social life, the institution of education is devoted specifically to teaching and learning. Education usually involves a formal teacher-student relationship, a separate classroom setting, and the use of special teaching tools, such as this textbook.

For almost all of human history only a tiny elite of scholars and bureaucrats has ever had formal schooling. Most societies have had schools to train a few specialists (scribes in ancient Greece, priests in medieval France, government officials in Mandarin China), while the rest of the population were farmers and artisans who learned whatever occupational skills they needed from their parents or other relatives. Throughout history education has largely been a family task.

The growth of education as a separate institution began after the Industrial Revolution, when the family could no longer adequately teach the younger generation everything it needed to know. Although parents could teach their children to milk a cow or build a fence, they could hardly be expected to teach them to run a bank or build a railroad. In industrial societies, moreover, nearly every citizen has to be able to read directions, fill out official forms, and add up the monthly budget. In the modern world education is not a privilege for the few but a necessity for all.

American colonists continued the European tradition of elite education for the upper classes. Elite education is still a way to maintain social class distinctions, but it also provides the credentials for social mobility.

Today formal educational institutions teach not only basic skills but social values. Sportsmanship, honesty, patriotism, and other moral values that used to be considered "family" matters are now part of the school curriculum. At the same time, such occupational skills as bookkeeping and auto mechanics, which used to be picked up at home or on the job, are now routinely taught in high school. As the institution of education grew, it adopted some of the primary-group features of the family, with its special attention to the individual, and some of the secondary-group features of the economy, in which impersonal standards prevail. As a result, modern education has two incompatible goals: the intellectual and moral development of the individual student and the practical training of productive workers and useful citizens. The clash between these two principles — particularistic concern for each child and universalistic belief in equal treatment for all — is the central dilemma of education today.

This chapter begins by describing the development of the institution of education in the United States and the functions it fulfilled in each period of history. Next we describe the socializing effects of the American school system, especially the unintentional lessons of its hidden curriculum. The rest of the chapter considers the dilemmas of mass education in a democratic society as well as some of the current efforts to improve the American school system.

THE GROWTH OF AMERICAN EDUCATION

The history of education in the United States illustrates how and why the institution of education has changed in all modern societies. It also explains why American education developed some unique features of its own.

EDUCATION IN THE NEW WORLD: 1620 – 1776

When the first settlers arrived in America, they brought with them a form of education that had been handed down from medieval times. In the rural villages from which the colonists came, the family was the most important agency of socialization. Children depended on their elders for whatever knowledge and moral values they had. Moreover, among the farm laborers and small tradesmen who made up nearly all the population of seventeenth-century Europe, family members provided all the vocational training necessary to make a living. If a boy wanted to learn a specialized skill such as cabinetmaking, he had to become an apprentice in a cabinetmaker's household.

Beyond the family the church was the institution most often involved in educating the young. As the guardian of moral and cultural values, organized religion also served as a powerful unifying force in the community. Formal education in schools and universities was supported by private donations and restricted to the small number of people who entered the professions. Although the seventeenth-century scholars and scientists certainly loved learning for its own sake, a classical education in Latin and Greek was a practical necessity for physicians, architects, politicians, and churchmen.

The colonists soon found that these medieval educational arrangements could not be maintained in the American wilderness. The unity of organized relation, the mainstay of the Old World community, eventually broke down into sectarian rivalry and competition for converts among the native Indians. Traditional family life came under tremendous pressure from the beginning. Because land was abundant and labor scarce, any energetic white man could make a living without the support of his parents. Apprentices, servants, and sons soon escaped the patriarchal household and set up their own. At first, the colonists made heroic efforts to prop up the fading authority of the family and to re-create their ancient forms of education in the New World setting. Within a decade after the first settlers landed, all the colonies had passed laws requiring that children obey their parents (on pain of death in Connecticut and Massachusetts). The Massachusetts statute of 1642 condemned the "great neglect of many parents and masters in training up their children in learning and labor" and threatened dire punishment. When even these drastic measures failed, the colonies took prompt action. Driven by the fear that civilization itself would be lost in the savage environment, the Puritan governments of Massachusetts and Connecticut ordered every town to institute compulsory schooling as early as 1647. After only a generation in the New World, the colonists were forced to transfer what the historian Bernard Bailyn has called the "maimed functions of the family" to a separate institution—education.[2]

Modern American education has many of the same functions it had from the start. The first of these is **cultural transmission**. Ever since the Puritans, American schools have passed on accumulated knowledge and protected cultural standards. Because the purpose of education is to conserve social values and prevent moral decline, schools have always been a conservative force in society. To some extent, all schools practice indoctrination: they teach the young only what their elders want them to know. American schoolchildren are not taught Marx's theories of socialism; Soviet schoolchildren do not study Jefferson's theories of democracy.

At the same time that the early settlers were inventing public education for the masses, they were continuing the European tradition of elite education for the upper classes. At the time of the Revolution, Latin and Greek were still being taught in the numerous private "grammar schools" and at Yale, Harvard, and other prestigious colleges. Even though the wealthy merchants and landowners were willing to support a rudimentary education for every child, they wanted *their* sons to attend an elite grammar school and university. Education, then as now, was a means of obtaining the credentials necessary for social mobility. A wealthy businessman sent his son to Harvard not to learn a trade but to meet the "right kind of people" and be certified as a member of the upper class.

Modern education continues this **selection and screening** process, by which students who do not "make the grade" are filtered out and directed toward vocational training courses and those who "pass the test" are selected for college. Because a college education is a prerequisite for the best-paid jobs, schools help decide who will belong to tomorrow's executive and professional classes. The family, however, continues to interfere in this selection process. For the same reasons as the colonial elite, middle- and upper-class parents are likely to insist that *their* children go to private schools and Ivy League colleges. Education thus acts both to reinforce social class distinctions for the well-to-do and to facilitate upward mobility.

---

[2] Bernard Bailyn, *Education in the Forming of American Society* (New York: Random House/Vintage, 1960), pp. 26–27.

Transmission of cultural values has been one of the functions of the American educational system throughout its history.

While the institution of education in every society transmits culture and selects people for different occupations, American education has two distinctive features that were evident from the beginning. The first is the tradition of *community control*. Schools were established outside the family setting in the seventeenth century, but they were still part of a small community that was largely controlled by the families who lived there. Compared to the national or regional systems that most countries have, education in America is heterogeneous and fragmented among thousands of local school districts.

Second, Americans have a great *faith in education* as a means of reform (see "Schooling, Textbooks, and Education"). Just as the Puritan settlers believed that schools could do what the family was failing to do, modern Americans put their trust in the power of education to overcome the disadvantages of family background. More than other peoples, Americans put heavy burdens on the educational system to change

SCHOOLING, TEXTBOOKS, AND EDUCATION

In America Revised *the Pulitzer-Prize winning journalist Frances FitzGerald examines how history textbooks have changed to reflect the particular aims and attitudes of educators. Here she questions the premises underlying American schooling.*

Americans tend to expect far too much from schooling. . . . At least since the nineteenth century, Americans have believed in the power of education in general, and schooling in particular, to improve the lot of their children and to improve society. . . . This belief in education and in the future is, however, politically ambiguous. It could signify a great openness to change and a willingness to promote reform, but it could also signify the reverse. To urge reform through education could be merely a piece of wishful thinking or could be a strategy for avoiding reform, and the social conflict it would entail, by putting it off into the future. To urge reform through the public-school system could be merely to displace responsibility from the adult institutions that could achieve it. And, in practice, Americans in this century have sometimes placed burdens on children which they themselves were unwilling to shoulder, and put far too great a weight of responsibility on the schools.

∎ ∎ ∎

Schooling is not all of education, and yet it has often been saddled with the responsibility for all of it. "Concerned citizens" groups will, for example, go to absurd lengths to take the word "damn" out of literary anthologies and anatomical drawings out of biology books, when the word is heard on every street corner and when really pornographic pictures can be found on the magazine racks of the local drugstore. This may be wishful thinking or it may be pure hypocrisy, a variation on the theme of "let us be saved but not too soon"—that is, "let us be saved by the next generation."

Not only fundamentalists but progressives as well have a strong tendency to think that the schools should present the world, or the country, as an ideal construct. The censorship of schoolbooks is simply the negative face of the demand that the books portray the world as a utopia of the eternal present—a place without conflicts, without malice or stupidity, where Dick (black or white) comes home with a smiling Jane to a nice house in the suburbs. To the extent that young people actually believe them, these bland fictions, propagated for the purpose of creating good citizens, may actually achieve the opposite; they give young people no warning of the real dangers ahead, and later they may well make these young people feel that their own experience of conflict or suffering is unique in history and perhaps un-American. To the extent that children can see the contrast between these fictions and the world around them, this kind of instruction can only make them cynical. The textbooks' naïveté about child psychology is matched only by their lack of respect for history. Indeed, to insist that children do as we say, not as we do, is to assert that the past has no influence over the future and that today peels away from yesterday like a decal. Yet, since the Progressive era, those responsible for the majority of American-history texts have been paying mere lip service to the truism that one must know history in order to understand the present and the future. To teach history with the assumption that students have the psychology of laboratory pigeons is not only to close off the avenues for thinking about the future; it is to deprive American children of their birthright.

SOURCE: Frances FitzGerald, *America Revised: History Schoolbooks in the Twentieth Century* (New York: Vintage/Random House, 1980), pp. 215–18.

prejudiced beliefs and attitudes and to solve social problems ranging from unemployment to drug abuse. In the years following the Revolution this great faith in education was to become part of American democratic ideology.

EDUCATION IN A DEMOCRACY: 1776–1865

In the era of Jacksonian democracy concern for the welfare of the "common man" led to a movement for free public education. In 1830 workers in Philadelphia stated their belief "that there can be no real liberty without a wide diffusion of real intelligence . . . [and] that until means of equal instruction shall be equally secured to all, liberty is but an unmeaning word, and equality an empty shadow." [3] By the 1850s every state was committed to making free, tax-supported elementary schools available to all children. Attendance was not compulsory and the schools provided only the barest essentials of literacy, but the principle that everyone was entitled to a good education was now firmly established.

Support for free public education came from several sources. The first was the new democratic ideology, which opposed the elitist view that education should be limited to those who could pay for it. In theory, if not yet in practice, the democratic conviction was that one person's child was as good as the next's, and both had an equal right to a good education.

A second development was the expansion of occupational opportunities in an increasingly commercial and industrial society. In 1820 seven out of ten workers were still farmers who had little need for formal education. Illiterate parents could hardly prepare their children to be the navigators, engineers, and telegraphers the economy required. A classical education at Harvard could not provide the necessary training either. Workers for the newly created jobs were trained instead at the private vocational schools that sprang up all over the country. At the same time, hardheaded businessmen saw the need for free public education to give their future employees basic reading, writing, and mathematical skills.

The third important factor in the spread of education was the familiar desire of American parents to get the best for their children. In the early nineteenth century, just as today, ambitious families believed in the power of education to give their own children definite social advantages.

During this period the American institution of education incorporated some of the democratic idealism it has today. Along with vocational training, self-development is still a major purpose of education. Gallup polls reveal that parents strongly support the school's development of their children's self-discipline, motivation, and personal moral standards. Parents also express a great deal of confidence in the public school's ability to deal with such social problems as alcohol and drug abuse, and the great majority (88 percent) believe that the educational system will be very important to determining America's future strength.[4]

The emphasis of American education continues to be highly utilitarian. While education has always been valued for its own sake, the idea that education should be *for* something usually carries more weight. About two out of three college freshmen plan to major in business, engineering, or professional and technical fields; three out of four say that one of their important objectives is to be well off financially (see Table 13-1).[5] Another poll reported that 75 percent of American parents believed that a primary purpose of education was to equip children for financial success.[6]

---

[3] Quoted in John M. Blum et al., *The National Experience,* 7th ed. (New York: Harcourt Brace Jovanovich, 1989), p. 262.

[4] Alec M. Gallup and Stanley M. Elam, "The 20th Annual Gallup/Phi Delta Kappa Education Poll," *Phi Delta Kappan* (September 1988), pp. 34–46.

[5] U.S. Bureau of the Census, *Statistical Abstract of the States* (Washington, D.C.: U.S. Government Printing Office, 1989), Table 237.

[6] "The Grolier Survey: What Parents Believe About Education," reported in *The New York Times,* September 3, 1983, p. B6.

TABLE 13-1   CHARACTERISTICS OF COLLEGE FRESHMEN, 1966–1986

Characteristic (in percent)	1966	1970	1975	1980	1981	1982	1983	1984	1985	1986
Sex: Male..	57	55	53	49	49	49	49	48	48	48
Female.......................................	43	45	47	51	51	51	51	52	52	52
Average grade in high school:										
A − to A + ...	15	16	18	21	21	21	20	20	21	23
B − to B + ...	54	58	60	60	60	60	59	58	59	56
C to C + ...	30	27	21	19	19	19	21	21	20	20
D	1	1	1	1	1	1	1	1	1	1
Political orientation:										
Liberal	(NA)	34	29	20	18	19	19	20	21	22
Middle of the road	(NA)	45	54	60	60	60	60	58	57	56
Conservative	(NA)	17	15	17	20	18	18	19	19	19
Probable field of study:										
Arts and humanities	17	16	11	9	7	8	8	8	8	9
Biological sciences	4	4	6	4	4	4	4	4	4	4
Business	14	16	19	24	24	24	24	26	27	26
Education	11	11	10	7	7	5	6	7	7	8
Engineering	10	9	8	12	12	12	12	11	11	11
Physical science	3	2	3	3	3	3	3	3	2	2
Social science	15	14	10	7	6	6	6	7	8	8
Professional	(NA)	(NA)	(NA)	15	13	13	14	14	13	12
Technical	2	4	9	6	6	7	7	5	5	4
Data processing/computer programming	(NA)	(NA)	(NA)	2	3	4	4	2	2	2
Other	(NA)	(NA)	(NA)	(NA)	14	16	16	16	16	15
Communications	(NA)	(NA)	(NA)	2	2	2	2	2	2	2
Computer science	(NA)	(NA)	(NA)	1	1	2	5	3	2	2
Essential or important objectives:										
Be very well-off financially	44	39	50	63	65	69	69	71	71	73
Develop meaningful philosophy of life	(NA)	76	64	50	49	47	44	45	43	41
Help others who are in difficulty	69	65	66	65	63	62	62	62	63	57
Become involved in programs to clean environment	(NA)	43	29	27	25	23	21	21	20	16
Attitudes—agree or strongly agree:										
Activities of married women are best confined to home and family	(NA)	48	28	27	27	26	25	23	22	20
Capital punishment should be abolished	(NA)	56	(NA)	34	30	28	29	26	27	26
Legalize marijuana	(NA)	38	47	39	34	29	26	23	22	21

SOURCE: U.S. Bureau of the Census, *Statistical Abstract of the United States* (Washington, D.C.: U.S. Government Printing Office, 1989), Table 237.

THE SPREAD OF PUBLIC EDUCATION: 1865–1954

Establishing the principle of free public education opened the schoolhouse doors to every child, but not until after the Civil War did millions of children actually begin to go through them. By 1900 nearly every state outside the South had compulsory school-attendance laws, and education was being spread more widely than ever before. The length of the school year increased, and so did the number of years spent in school. At the end of the nineteenth century there were more than 6000 public high schools (compared with 160 in 1870), and city school systems included public kindergartens, normal schools (for training teachers), night schools, and adult education programs.

The explosion in education after the Civil War was due in large part to the economy's growing demand for managerial and clerical employees with more than a third- or fourth-grade education. During the course of the twentieth century the United States changed from an economy based on small farms and family businesses to one based on large bureaucracies. As organizations grew, written orders replaced verbal ones, detailed reports replaced casual estimates, and inventory flow charts replaced guesswork. Millions of people had to be trained to handle all these papers — to write them, type them, file them, and use them.[7] The interrelationship of these developments produced far-reaching changes in the American social structure. Industrialization of the economy and the growth of large formal organizations led to an expansion of the institution of education, which in turn intensified the trend toward further industrialization and bureaucratization.

There were other reasons public education grew in importance in the last decades of the nineteenth century. Public schools became the primary agents for a special kind

[7] Martin Trow, "The Second Transformation of American Secondary Education," *International Journal of Comparative Sociology* 2 (1961): 144–65.

After the Civil War the Freedman's Bureau provided schooling to former slaves in the South. The spread of education in this period was largely due to the growing demand for clerical workers in an industrializing economy.

of socialization—the Americanization of millions of European immigrants. They offered such courses as English, health care, home economics, and citizenship, as well as vocational training. Compulsory schooling was the means both of integrating the children of the newly arrived immigrants into the American culture and of providing the basis for a dependable work force.

For reformers who worried about the alarming gulf between rich and poor, and for industrialists who feared that the antagonism between capitalist and worker would lead to class warfare, public education also offered a way to soften economic divisions and prevent violence. Education, Horace Mann preached, "is the great equalizer of the conditions of men—the balance wheel of the social machinery. . . . It does better than to disarm the poor of their hostility toward the rich; it prevents being poor." [8]

By the beginning of the twentieth century all the pieces of the American institution of education were in place. The United States was now firmly committed to the principle that every child was entitled to a good free education in the public schools. During the course of the century mass education spread upward, so that the proportion of adults with a high-school diploma has increased from 25 percent in 1940 to 70 percent in 1987 (see Figure 13-1). Mass education has also spread outward to give previously excluded women and minority groups the opportunity to have a college and graduate school education. Today more Americans have more formal education than the people in any other large society.

EDUCATION AND SOCIAL JUSTICE: 1954–PRESENT

The American belief in education as the means of social progress was affirmed in 1954 by the famous case of *Brown v. Board of Education of Topeka,* in which the Supreme Court outlawed racial segregation of the public schools. By concentrating on legal segregation, the court at first ignored the implications of residential, *de facto* segregation in neighborhood school districts. In many northern communities the courts found transporting children across district lines to be the only way to overcome segregated residential patterns and integrate the public schools.

Busing schoolchildren to achieve racial balance met with bitter resistance during the 1970s. In urban ethnic districts, such as Boston's Irish neighborhoods and San Francisco's Chinatown, court-ordered busing violated traditions of community control, aroused class antagonisms, and aggravated hostile feelings toward other racial groups. Some sociologists claimed that busing contributed to the white flight from inner cities to the suburbs, but recent studies show that busing has had little or no effect on suburban growth.[9] While the adverse effect of school desegregation remains a controversial issue, many sociologists who have studied the matter agree that integration policies led to a substantial short-term decline in white enrollment.[10]

---

[8] Horace Mann, *Report to the Massachusetts Board of Education,* 1848, quoted in Blum et al., *The National Experience,* p. 262.

[9] Christine Russell, "School Desegregation and White Flight," *Political Science Quarterly* 90 (1975): 675–95.

[10] Franklin D. Wilson, "The Impact of School Desegregation Programs on White Public-School Enrollment, 1968–1976," *Sociology of Education* 58 (July 1985): 137–53.

THE EXPANSION OF EDUCATION   FIGURE 13-1

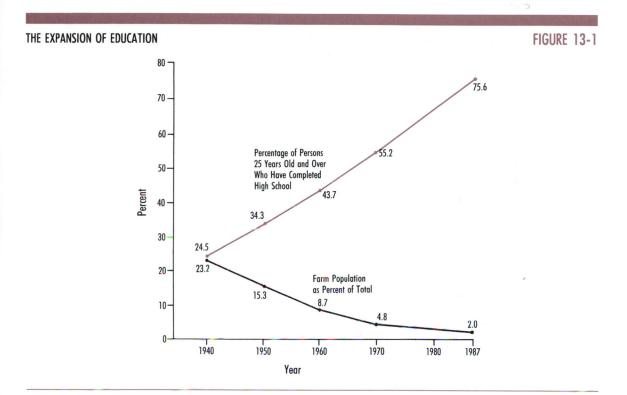

SOURCE: U.S. Bureau of the Census. *Historical Statistics of the United States: Colonial Times to 1970.* Bicentennial Edition, Part 2 (Washington, D.C.: U.S. Government Printing Office, 1975); U.S. Bureau of the Census, *Statistical Abstract of the United States* (Washington, D.C.: U.S. Government Printing Office, 1988); U.S. Bureau of the Census, *Educational Attainment in the United States: 1987 and 1986.* Current Population Reports, Series P-20, No. 4 8, Table 12. The rise in the proportion of adults who are high-school graduates has been closely related to the shift from an agricultural to an industrial society.

After the public schools were fully integrated, it became clear that racially mixed classes were not significantly improving the quality of education for blacks or reducing the differences in achievement for black and white children. Even when their IQ is the same, members of disadvantaged groups (blacks and other minorities, the poor) still generally have lower scores on achievement tests than white middle-class children.[11] In 1982 the Senate reversed its support for busing, reflecting a growing movement to challenge and overturn the federal courts on this issue.

During the 1970s minority students made significant educational gains (see Figure 13-2). The proportion of African-Americans who finish college is still rising, but the proportion of Hispanic Americans with college degrees has fallen in recent years. Today the percentage of the white population remains roughly twice the percentage of the black population receiving a college degree.[12]

---

[11] Cary Orfield, "Must We Bus? Segregated Schools and National Policy" (Washington, D.C.: The Brookings Institution, 1978).

[12] *Statistical Abstract of the United States,* 1988, Table 203.

FIGURE 13-2   THE EXTENSION OF HIGHER EDUCATION TO MINORITIES

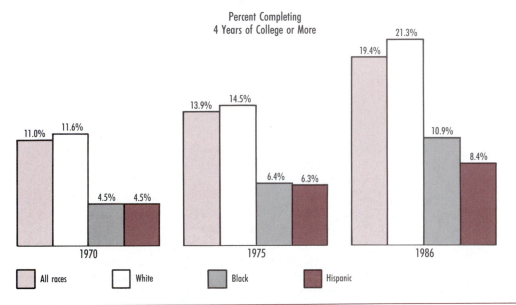

SOURCE: U.S. Bureau of the Census, "Population Profile of the United States: 1980," *Current Population Reports*. Series P-20, No. 363 (Washington, D.C.: U.S. Government Printing Office, 1981); U.S. Bureau of the Census, *Statistical Abstract of the United States* (Washington, D.C.: U.S. Government Printing Office, 1988), Table 203.

Nevertheless, most Americans continue to have faith in education as the best means of changing society for the better. More than any other institution, the educational system is the place where the ideals of equality and social justice are most often pursued.[13]

THE HIDDEN CURRICULUM

The primary aim of education remains the transmission of culture. Most parents want the schools to teach their children the skills and knowledge they need to get ahead. But cultural transmission involves more than lessons in geography and long division; it also involves instruction in values and attitudes. Students learn these lessons from all aspects of the school situation, not just from their textbooks. In schools, as in other social organizations, people learn special ways of coping with the situation in which they find themselves. This **hidden curriculum**, unofficially taught and unconsciously absorbed, is one very important consequence of American education that its founders never intended.

---

[13] Diane Ravitch, *The Troubled Crusade: American Education 1945–1980* (New York: Basic Books, 1983), pp. 323–24.

CULTURAL LESSONS

As we have already seen, socialization is best accomplished in primary groups. In schools the most influential primary group for students is their fellow students, or peer group. Young people teach each other how the school system works and how to deal with the demands of the formal curriculum. They also pass on much information to each other directly: information about sex, about drugs, and about the latest fads in clothes and music. More important, students learn the attitudes and values of their peer group.

THE STUDENT SUBCULTURE.   In any group some kinds of behavior are considered admirable and will be rewarded with praise and social esteem. To find out what kinds of behavior adolescents admire most, James Coleman investigated the status systems of ten high schools in the Midwest.[14] All the boys were asked, "How would you most like to be remembered in school: as a brilliant student, as a leader in extracurricular activities, or as most popular?" Although Coleman had expected to find that high schools in different neighborhoods would have different status systems, he discovered that the similarities were much more striking than the minor differences. Nearly every boy replied that he would rather be a star athlete than be considered popular or brilliant. In every school the "leading crowd," or highest status group, had twice as many athletes and many more popular boys than it had brilliant students.

Similarly, the girls, who were generally better students than the boys in every school, did not want to be considered "brilliant students." They had good reason not to want a reputation for brains: the girls named "best students" in each school had fewer friends and were even less likely than the best male students to be members of the leading crowd. In all the schools students admired academic achievement less than other attributes, especially being a star athlete for boys and being "good looking" for girls. To Coleman these results suggested that the values of the adolescent subculture were a deterrent to academic success. The lesson: Don't be too smart!

Another interesting finding was that students who are seen by their schoolmates as "intellectuals"—and who come to think of themselves in that way—were not necessarily the most intelligent. More important than their intellectual ability was their willingness to work hard at a relatively unrewarded activity. Coleman found a basic sociological reason for the students' low opinion of high grades. Unlike the outstanding athlete, whose victories bring glory to the school in interscholastic competition, the outstanding students' successes are purely personal triumphs usually won at the expense of their classmates. From the sociological perspective it is not surprising that academic accomplishments are undervalued and that outstanding students are often ridiculed as "grinds."

COMPETITION.   Teachers and administrators also teach students values and attitudes that are not in the school's formal curriculum. For example, what do you think is being taught in this classroom?

---

[14] James S. Coleman, "The Adolescent Subculture and Academic Achievement," *American Journal of Sociology* 65 (1960): 337–47.

Boris had trouble reducing "12/16" to the lowest terms, and could only get as far as "6/8." The teacher asked him quietly if that was as far as he could reduce it. She suggested he "think." Much heaving up and down and waving of hands by the other children, all frantic to correct him. Boris, pretty unhappy, probably mentally paralyzed. The teacher, quiet, patient, ignores the others and concentrates with looks and voice on Boris. . . . After a minute or two, she becomes more urgent, but there is no response from Boris. She then turns to the class and says, "Well, who can tell Boris what the number is?" A forest of hands appears, and the teacher calls Peggy. Peggy says that four may be divided into the numerator and the denominator. Thus Boris's failure has made it possible for Peggy to succeed; his depression is the price of her exhilaration; his misery the occasion of her rejoicing.[15]

The subject was officially mathematics, but this lesson could more accurately be called a lesson in "competition." Boris and Peggy are learning that life is competitive and that the rewards of success are to be won at the expense of others. The school system fosters competitiveness through its use of grading: the winners get prizes and promotion to a higher level, and the losers are demoted, "failed," and eventually weeded out of the system altogether. The classroom emphasis on individual competition prepares children for graduation into the larger society: competing for grades is an early version of the competition for jobs and economic advantage in a complex social world.

---

[15] Jules Henry, *Culture Against Man* (New York: Random House, 1963).

The children in this classroom are also learning to evaluate themselves according to their teacher's standards. By setting up a situation in which Peggy "wins" and Boris "loses," the school is shaping their image of themselves as "smart" or "dumb," a "good student" or a "bad student." In hundreds of formal and informal ways teachers unwittingly judge children by their own standards of behavior. Since most teachers are white and come from middle-class backgrounds, they tend to be biased in favor of students who conform to their own ethnic and class definitions of neatness, politeness, and cooperation. In such cases, many lower-class or minority-group students learn to think of themselves as people who are "rowdy," "messy," or "troublemakers" — in other words, "losers."

STRUCTURAL LESSONS

Many of the things students are required to do in school, and the rules and behavior that they learn are "normal" or "right," have nothing directly to do with education. Learning to line up quietly, for example, does not help the first grader learn to read, but it does make running the classroom easier for the teacher. These hidden organizational lessons are so much a part of the underlying assumptions of schooling that we tend to forget how pervasive and important they are.

PUNCTUALITY.   One of the first things a child learns in school is to be on time. Instead of the family's rather flexible "lunchtimes" and "bedtimes," time in school is precise and arbitrary. To meet the requirements of organizational efficiency, the school day is divided into class periods, lunch hours, and recess. These "times" need not be related to hunger, fatigue, the changing seasons, or anything else outside the organization itself. Learning to be punctual has nothing to do with learning to add and subtract, but it has a lot to do with learning to meet the strong demand for precise timing in the larger social structure. American high-school graduates, whether or not they have learned anything else, have absorbed the organizational imperative: Be on time!

OBEDIENCE.   Learning to be obedient is clearly part of learning to get along in school. The most successful students have usually learned not only to obey the rules but to please their superiors by anticipating their demands, or "giving teachers what they want." This early lesson in dealing with authority can carry over into later life, when employees try to please their bosses by agreeing with them. Of course, nearly every school permits some bending of the rules. However, most children know the second lesson of the hidden curriculum: Do as you're told!

INSTRUMENTALISM.   Children in a competitive school system soon learn to work for higher grades. While mastering the subject is certainly most important, grades can also be improved by being on time, obeying the rules, and acting interested in what the teacher is saying. Punctuality, obedience, politeness, and other aspects of "good" behavior are not so much worthwhile ends in themselves as they are the necessary means to a high-school diploma. **Instrumentalism** — or rational, goal-oriented behavior — is one of the guiding principles of bureaucracy. It is also taught as part of the school's hidden curriculum. The lesson here: Playing by the rules pays off!

What children learn in school depends on their experience of a certain social setting as well as on the content of their studies.[16] Students learn to accept the norms of their peer groups — to act according to what their schoolmates think is appropriate and desirable behavior. They also learn the organizational ropes — the norms of a bureaucratic world. These aspects of schooling were never consciously planned; they are unintended consequences of establishing an educational institution where children the same age spend most of their waking hours together in an organizational setting. Nevertheless, if the goal of the founders of the American school system was to train an orderly and obedient work force, the symbolic lessons of the hidden curriculum have probably been more effective than any textbook.

EDUCATION AND EQUALITY

Ever since Horace Mann declared education to be the "great equalizer" in 1848, American schools have been assigned the responsibility for giving every child the means to a "decent life." In the mid-1960s the American dream of equality through education became a central goal of specific social policies. The Kennedy and Johnson administrations attempted to widen access to education through the racial integration of the schools, the training of workers in special skills, and open admissions to state colleges. Up until this time equality was defined primarily as **equality of opportunity**. Since the advocates of these policies assumed that schools equalize by producing higher levels of achievement, however, it was a logical next step to the idea that equal schools could be equally effective schools. The democratic idea of equality thus came to be defined as **equality of achievement**. If only every child had equal access to schools that were equally well endowed with trained teachers and other resources (equality of opportunity) — then every group of children, in Harlem as well as Scarsdale, would perform equally well on standardized tests (equality of achievement).[17] It soon became obvious, however, that equal schools do not produce equal students.

In 1964 the Office of Education commissioned a famous research report on educational opportunity by the sociologist James Coleman. The sponsors of the project expected to find huge disparities between predominantly black and predominantly white schools and to cite them in an argument for more federal spending to reduce educational inequality. Everyone, including Coleman himself, was astonished to find that there was little overall difference between black and white schools in physical facilities, curriculum, or educational resources. Moreover, the Coleman report found that the gap between black and white children's achievement scores appeared as early as the first grade, and — even more surprising in roughly equal settings — this gap became even larger the longer the children were in school.[18] Coleman's findings shocked educators and fueled a continuing debate over the place of education in a

---

[16] Robert Dreeben, "The Contribution of Schooling to the Learning of Norms," *Harvard Educational Review* 37 (1967): 211–37.

[17] Daniel Bell, *The Coming of Post-Industrial Society* (New York: Basic/Colophon, 1976), p. 431.

[18] *Equality of Educational Opportunity,* Report of the Office of Education to the Congress and the President (Washington, D.C.: U.S. Government Printing Office, 1966).

democratic society. As later researchers found more and more evidence that schools tend to increase rather than reduce inequalities of class and race, the American faith in the equalizing effects of public education was profoundly shaken.

SCHOOLS AND SOCIAL CLASS

In spite of the family's dwindling role in the education of the young, family background is still the most important factor in educational achievement today. As the authors of the Coleman report discovered, the variation in test scores among children in the *same* school is far greater than the range between average children at *different* schools. Numerous studies have documented the rule that the higher the family's social standing, the higher a child's level of education. Compared with the influence of different family backgrounds, the school itself appears to have little effect on how well students perform and how long they stay in school. The Coleman report found three aspects of family background to be especially important: the educational level of the parents, the family's income, and the interest the parents take in their children's education. By investigating these clues, perhaps we can discover why social class is of such overwhelming importance in education.

THE INFLUENCE OF HOME AND NEIGHBORHOOD.   There is much evidence to show that the attitudes and values children bring *to* school outweigh those they learn *in* school. In *Class and Conformity,* for example, Melvin Kohn concluded that middle-class families tend to reward self-reliance and creativity, while most working-class families are more interested in obedience and respect (see Chapter 5, "Socialization").[19] These middle-class values at home give strong support to academic achievement in school.

Of course, success in school is not entirely limited to middle-class children. Everyone knows at least one child from a poor family who studied hard and became a doctor or lawyer. Joseph Kahl wondered whether or not these "achievers" had parents who had given them special encouragement. In a study of working-class parents whose sons were good students, Kahl discovered that these parents tended to be dissatisfied with their own jobs and anxious to have their sons do better than they had. They were more likely than other working-class parents to stress education as the means of getting ahead, and they took a strong interest in their sons' progress in school and rewarded them when they did well.[20]

Clearly, working-class parents can do much to motivate their children to study and encourage them to strive for advanced degrees. Middle-class children, however, already live in an environment that encourages reading and other school-related activities; they use correct grammar and develop proper manners; and they play with children who share the same values and interests. Children who come from working-class backgrounds or who live in slum neighborhoods grow up in an environment that does not usually encourage getting good grades and going to college. Their parents must therefore expend much more effort, enforce much stricter discipline, and have

---

[19] Melvin Kohn, *Class and Conformity: A Study in Values with a Reassessment* (Chicago: University of Chicago Press, 1977).

[20] Joseph A. Kahl, "Educational and Occupational Aspirations of 'Common Man' Boys," *Harvard Educational Review* 23 (Summer 1953): 186–203.

While Americans believe in educational equality, they also want their children to have the best education they can afford to give them. Family background remains the most important factor determining the quality and amount of education a child will receive.

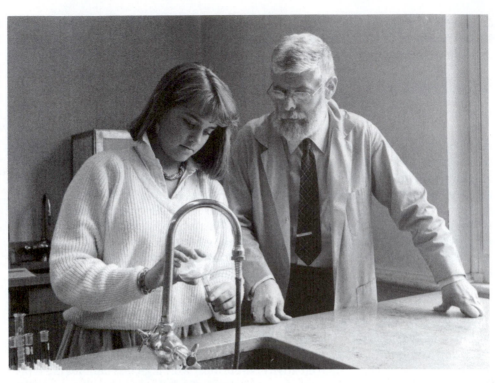

much greater motivation themselves to give them the same kind of support for educational goals as a middle-class family in a middle-class neighborhood.[21]

"THE BEST EDUCATION MONEY CAN BUY."   Although the number of students attending college has risen spectacularly, the opportunity to get a college education is not more evenly distributed than in the past. Wealthier families still send their children to better schools, and for longer periods, than poorer families. A study that followed the careers of 9,000 Wisconsin high-school students established that high-school graduates who come from less affluent backgrounds are (1) less likely to enter college immediately after high school, (2) much less likely to go to prestigious colleges, (3) more likely to drop out of college, and (4) less likely to return to college if they do drop out. On average, upper-middle-class children receive four more years of schooling than lower-class children.[22]

Obviously, wealthy families can afford to send their children to private schools and to support them while they go through college. Less obviously, middle-class families with moderate incomes are able to send their children to better public high schools because they live in neighborhoods with higher school taxes to support "quality" education. Of every dollar spent on schooling, the states pay about 39 cents, the federal

[21] James S. Coleman, "Equality of Educational Opportunity," *Integrated Education* (September–October 1968): 23.
[22] William H. Sewell, "Inequality of Opportunity for Higher Education," *American Sociological Review* 36 (1971): 793–808.

THE EDUCATIONAL PAYOFF: 1987 MEDIAN INCOME FOR YEAR-ROUND
FULL-TIME WORKERS, 25 AND OLDER

FIGURE 13-3

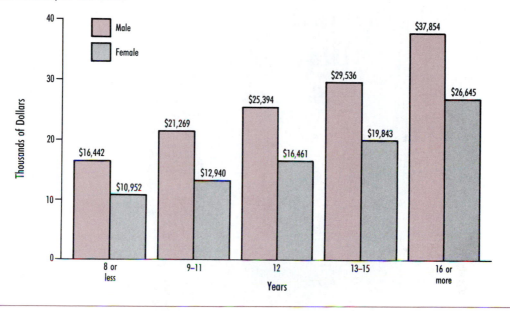

SOURCE: U.S. Bureau of the Census, *Money Income of Households, Families and Persons in the United States: 1987*, Current Population
Reports Series P-60, No. 162 (Washington, D.C.: U.S. Government Printing Office, 1989), Table 35.

government pays 9 cents, and local property taxes pay the rest. As a result, there is a
tremendous disparity in the funds available for schools in middle-class districts (where
property values are high) and schools in poor districts. Moreover, public-school
spending varies from state to state. In 1987 Utah spent an average of $2,390 on each
schoolchild, while Wyoming spent $5,144.[23]

Aside from its intangible benefits, education provides the credentials for success.
As Figure 13-3 shows, the median incomes for men and women aged 25 to 34 varies
according to how many years of schooling they completed. Since 1968 the story has
been about the same: the more years of education, the higher the income. Although
women are not rewarded as highly for their education as men, the difference between
finishing high school and finishing college is still very large for both sexes. In 1987 a
college degree was worth (for full-time, year-round workers) an average of $9,850 a
year to men and $6,945 a year to women.[24] Clearly, education pays off in American
society.

In spite of the American ideal of educational equality, children's social origins
deeply affect the amount and the quality of the education they receive. First of all,

---

[23] *Digest of Educational Statistics*, U.S. Department of Education, 1988.

[24] U.S. Bureau of the Census, "Money Income of Households, Families, and Persons in the United States:
1987," *Current Population Reports*, Series P-60, No. 162. (Washington, D.C.: U.S. Government Printing
Office, 1989), Table 35.

"Son, you're all grown up now. You owe me two hundred and fourteen thousand dollars."

Drawing by Weber; © 1983 The New Yorker Magazine.

education is expensive. College tuitions have increased by 75 percent since 1980, more than twice the increase of consumer prices (33 percent) and median family income (34 percent) over the same period. The average cost of college is now between $20,000 and $40,000 — or about three times what it was only 15 years ago.[25]

Moreover, class differences in the environment at home, the parents' attitude toward learning, and the amount of money invested in education all make it considerably more likely that children from privileged backgrounds will do well in school and acquire the credentials they need to get a good job. Besides these economic resources, well-to-do parents provide their children with "symbolic capital," [26] which can also bring them financial dividends. They introduce their sons and daughters to such cultural experiences as classical music, art museums, and the theater — all socializing institutions that can give them social advantages over the children of working-class

[25] Terry W. Hartle, "Are College Costs a Problem?" *Public Opinion* (May–June 1987), pp. 48–50.

[26] Paul D. DeMaggio, "Review Essay: On Pierre Bourdieu," *American Journal of Sociology* 84 (May 1979): 1460–74.

parents. In short, the influence of social background is so strong that most children start adult life at about the same class level as their parents. However, the family is not entirely responsible for the perpetuation of class differences. The educational system itself also tends to give children unequal treatment.

THE EQUAL TREATMENT OF UNEQUALS

Education is not a "great equalizer," the Coleman report paradoxically suggests, because the schools are homogeneous: they treat their students uniformly, or *too* equally. Future musicians are required to undergo the same training as future engineers; talented artists must study math in the same class as talented mathematicians. In other words, when unequal individuals are treated alike, people with special interests and special disabilities are bound to be overlooked.

In recent years the school system has made a number of adjustments based on the principle that the equal treatment of unequals is unjust. The Head Start program, which trained preschool children in the skills they would need to do first-grade work, was perhaps the broadest effort to eliminate the handicap of being black, Hispanic, poor, or in other ways "culturally disadvantaged."

Changed Lives, the landmark study of Head Start programs, proved that early childhood education can have a lasting effect on students' achievement.[27] The researchers followed two groups of black children from low-income families in Ypsilanti, Michigan, for nearly 20 years. They found that the group with preschool education had significantly higher rates of high-school graduation and employment and lower rates of arrest and teenage pregnancy than the group that had not participated in such programs. Even so, a report from the public schools in Montgomery County, Maryland, indicates that Head Start programs alone cannot solve the problems that many poor minority-group children have in school. In comparison with middle-class white students, children from preschool educational programs still tend to have more academic difficulties and to score lower on standard achievement tests.[28]

The educational system also tries to adjust to individual differences by providing bilingual instruction and by making special arrangements for deaf and crippled children. These efforts to deal with "exceptional" students treat only the more visible — and more publicized — tip of the iceberg of individual differences in ability and temperament. Because every child is exceptional in some way, the school's attempts to deal with unique individuals have so far been rather crude and ineffective.

GRADING AND TRACKING.   Grouping students into homogeneous classes according to different levels of achievement seems a logical way to teach people of different ages and skills, but it is actually a fairly recent practice. For most of education's history children simply progressed at their own pace from one lesson to the next. Since the modern grading system is geared to an average age and achievement level, it is in fact

---

[27] *Changed Lives* (Ypsilanti, Mich.: High/Scope Educational Research Foundation, 1984).
[28] Gene I. Maeroff, "Despite Head Start, 'Achievement Gap' Persists for Poor," *The New York Times.* June 11, 1985, pp. C1, C9.

About 3.6 million schoolchildren do not speak English well enough to cope with the regular curriculum. Bilingual education is one of the adjustments the school system has made to individual differences.

less responsive to individual differences than the old heterogeneous one-room school-house.

The second major concession to individual variation is tracking, which groups students in separate programs according to their abilities. High-school students in a college-preparatory track, for example, study advanced math and foreign languages; students in a vocational track take only basic math and English courses while studying such directly occupational subjects as stenography and auto repair. Assignment to the college, vocational, or other ability-level track is determined by IQ scores, reading and math tests, or the kind of higher education or job the student plans to have. Since only one kind of ability or interest is singled out as the basis for each category, the differences among students even *within* a track in a given grade are still enormous.

Clearly, tracking does not provide the specialized instruction that would reduce inequality. In fact, it tends to produce greater inequalities simply by limiting the kind of education an individual gets. If a vocational student should decide later to attend college, he or she will lack not only the basic academic courses required for admission but also the factual knowledge and intellectual skills needed for college-level work. Classification in a "slow" category is also a blow to a person's self-esteem and aspirations for higher education. A former delinquent who was placed in a noncollege section recalled:

I felt good when I was with my class, but when they went and separated us — that changed us. That changed our ideas, our thinking, the way we thought about each other and turned us to enemies toward each other — because they said I was dumb and they were smart.[29]

Tracking has other, more subtle effects on students' educational experiences. Some evidence suggests that a teacher's expectations for a student affect the child's performance in school. The original study of this "Pygmalion effect" was conducted by Robert Rosenthal and Lenore Jacobson in San Francisco in the 1960s. The researchers randomly selected about 20 percent of the children in each class and told the teacher that a standard intelligence test had predicted that these students would "bloom" during the course of the school year. All the children were retested at the end of the year and again in the following year. According to Rosenthal and Jacobson, the test results showed that the imaginary "bloomers" were more likely to improve their scores than their classmates.[30]

Although the San Francisco study and later follow-up studies had inconsistent results, other research has established that the teacher's expectations often constitute a self-fulfilling prophecy.[31] In one study of a ghetto school, Ray Rist found that kindergarten teachers sometimes divided children into "bright" and "slow" groups after only a few days or weeks. The "slow" group, which was made up entirely of the most disadvantaged children in the class, was placed farthest away from the teacher and the blackboard. The "bright" group, which was nearest the teacher, had more opportunity to participate and was praised more often. Not surprisingly, the group the teacher expected to do best did so, and the group expected to do worst did so too. Two years later, in second grade, supposedly "slow" children were still assigned to a low-ability group.[32]

Labeling students is a form of self-fulfilling prophecy because it places young children in social categories from which they have difficulty escaping even in adulthood. The school experience thus tends to institutionalize and justify inequalities of family background that might otherwise have been overcome. In an era of mass public education the dilemma of the American school system is how to educate children in large groups and still offer enough individual attention to guarantee truly equal educational opportunity.

THE SOCIAL ORGANIZATION OF THE SCHOOL

The dramatic growth in American public education during the twentieth century brought a corresponding increase in the organizational size and complexity of the

---

[29] Quoted in Beth E. Vanfossen, *The Structure of Social Inequality* (Boston: Little, Brown, 1979), p. 263.

[30] Robert Rosenthal and Lenore Jacobson, *Pygmalion in the Classroom* (New York: Holt, Rinehart & Winston, 1968).

[31] See Donna Eder, "Ability Groupings as a Self-fulfilling Prophecy," *Sociology of Education* 54 (July 1981): 151–62; R. P. McDermott, "Social Relations as Contexts for Learning," *Harvard Educational Review* 27 (1977): 198–213; Diane Felmlee and Donna Eder, "Contextual Effects in the Classroom," *Sociology of Education* 56 (April 1983): 77–78.

[32] Ray C. Rist, "Student Social Class and Teacher Expectations: The Self-Fulfilling Prophecy in Ghetto Education." *Harvard Educational Review* 40 (August 1970): 411–51.

Over the course of the twentieth century the one-room schoolhouse has been replaced by large people-processing organizations. The dilemma of modern public educaton is that bureaucratic school systems make education more difficult to achieve.

school. A larger youthful population, more years of schooling per student, and the concentrating effects of urbanization have all led to the consolidation of education in ever larger organizations. In 1987 nearly 80 percent of all students were in school systems that enrolled 2500 or more children.[33] Today the typical public school is a large, highly complex organization — in a word, it has become a bureaucracy.

Although we do not usually think of them in this way, modern school systems have many of the characteristics of other bureaucracies (see Chapter 6, "Organizations"). In their specialized division of labor, administrators have different jobs and qualifications than teachers. Moreover, teachers with degrees in early-childhood education do not teach high-school classes, and college English professors do not teach the modern Spanish novel. Schools have hierarchies of authority from the board of education down to the cooks and janitors, and they are run according to impersonal rules and procedures. Like other bureaucracies schools depend on written records, especially tests, grades, and reports of all kinds. Finally, schools tend to produce a standardized product — an educated human being with a basic knowledge of English, math, American history, and so on.

---

[33] *Digest of Educational Statistics,* Table 68.

The product, however, is people. Schools are people-processing organizations, similar to hospitals, prisons, and job-training centers.[34] Like these other organizations schools attempt to change and "improve" people. Unlike these organizations, however, schools process people in batches, or collectivities.[35] Students enter the organization as part of a class. Each class, one of several groups, passes through the organization in an orderly manner, year by year, from one grade to another, until the process is completed and the class graduates.

Children, then, are educated in an organization that operates according to bureaucratic principles. The dilemma for the American school system is that this kind of organization makes education more difficult to achieve.

STANDARDIZED INSTRUCTION

Since students come to school with varied abilities and progress at different rates, they presumably are best taught on an individual basis. For organizational reasons, however, schoolchildren are treated in standardized ways. What, when, and how subjects are taught often depend less on individual needs than on the organization's demand for efficiency.

In *A Place Called School* (1984), John I. Goodlad described public school classrooms as a world where teachers spend nearly all their class time lecturing to uninterested, uninvolved students. His in-depth study of schools in 13 communities revealed that the average instructional day at a junior or senior high school consisted of 143 minutes of "teacher talk" and only seven minutes of students' questions and discussion. His researchers rarely observed laughter, anger, enthusiasm, or any open display of feeling. Goodlad asked himself:

> How would I react as an adult to these ways of the classroom? I would become restless. I would groan audibly over still another seatwork assignment. My mind would wander off soon after the beginning of a lecture. It would be necessary for me to put my mind in some kind of "hold" position. This is what students do. . . . One learns passivity. Students in schools are socialized into it virtually from the beginning.[36]

EXTRINSIC MOTIVATION

Like other people-processing organizations (reformatories, mental hospitals), schools must deal with a captive audience that does not necessarily want to be there but cannot leave without permission.[37] Schools therefore have the constant problem of motivating students to study and pay attention in class. Grades, which offer the extrinsic motivation of rewards and punishments, are the principal method of encouraging students to work. Good grades can be exchanged for other benefits — praise from parents, school privileges, admission to college. Like money in a work organization, grades are the payments students receive for their efforts.

---

[34] Yesheskel Hasenfeld, "People-Processing Organizations: An Exchange Approach," *American Sociological Review* 37 (June 1972): 256–63.

[35] Stanton Wheeler, "The Structure of Formally Organized Socialization Settings," in *Socialization After Childhood*, ed. Orville Brim, Jr., and Stanton Wheeler (New York: Wiley, 1966), pp. 51–116.

[36] John I. Goodlad, *A Place Called School* (New York: McGraw-Hill, 1984), p. 233.

[37] Christopher Hurn, *The Limits and Possibilities of Schooling*, 2nd ed. (Boston: Allyn & Bacon, 1985).

The challenge of teaching is to interest students in the subject matter, which provides the intrinsic motivation to learn. Schools, however, more often rely on less effective extrinsic rewards — usually grades — to get students to study and pay attention in class.

Grades are not nearly as effective an incentive as money, however. If a student cannot — or does not want to — go to college, good grades offer little reward. The threat of poor grades does even less to motivate students who, for whatever reason, cannot perform well in school.

The challenge of teaching is to engage the students' interest in their studies, which would provide the intrinsic motivation to learn. Organizations, on the other hand, try to reduce uncertainty and make events predictable: how many pages of the history textbook will be read or how many students will be in eighth grade next year. A student's potential interest in history, which might be the intrinsic motivation to learn about the Civil War, for example, is replaced by the extrinsic motivation of rewards and punishments. A certain number of pages in a specified history textbook must be read, a test on the Civil War must be passed, or the student will not go on to the next grade. Education is thus transformed into a series of tasks to be accomplished, and learning becomes work — literally, schoolwork.

Students, when asked, are entirely practical about what their education is for — economic and social advancement. "Have your courses been helpful?" a high-school student was asked.

> Just to get into college. I need them to get into college. I do like History, though, and English.
> My main purpose is to get the diploma. . . . It's getting pretty tough to get a good job, you know. The main purpose for me and to other students who are not going on to further education is to get that diploma.[38]

Even gifted students at elite high schools show little or no intrinsic motivation. As Kahl's study of working-class boys concludes, "School and the possibility of college were viewed by all the boys as steps to jobs. None was interested in learning for the subtle pleasure it can offer; none craved intellectual understanding for its own sake." [39]

All in all, the social setting of the modern school is inappropriate for many of the educational purposes it is supposed to serve. The dilemma of American education is a sociological problem: how to organize a school system that will educate each child to the best of his or her ability.

IMPROVING AMERICAN EDUCATION

A quarter of adult Americans, given a paycheck listing deductions, cannot tell whether the amount on the check is correct. Forty-four percent, shown a number of help-wanted ads, cannot match their qualifications with the job requirements. Twenty-two percent cannot address a letter clearly enough to have it delivered, and 25 percent

---

[38] Quoted in Buford Rhea, "Institutional Paternalism in High School," in *Learning in Social Settings: New Readings in the Sociology of Education,* ed. Matthew W. Miles and W. W. Charters, Jr. (Boston: Allyn and Bacon, 1970), p. 310.

[39] Kahl, "Educational and Occupational Aspirations of 'Common Man' Boys," p. 202.

HOW CULTURALLY LITERATE ARE YOU?

According to E. D. Hirsch, Jr., "more and more of our young people don't know things we used to assume they knew." Literacy, by his definition, is a common body of knowledge — the shared ideas of the American national culture. Literate people do not just decode the words they read; they are able to infer the meanings behind them. The phrase "Pearl Harbor," for example, refers to a naval base in Hawaii, but it has important historical and emotional meanings as well. Hirsch and his colleagues at the University of Virginia compiled a list of 6,000 items a culturally literate American should know. Here are a few of them:

1066	byte	Easter	Hepburn, Katharine
Aaron, Hank	*Canterbury Tales, The*	electrolysis	hibernation
affluent society	capacitor	English Channel	Holy Roman Empire
Alas, poor Yorick . . .	Cassandra	ethics	Horace
alpha and omega	Cézanne, Paul	exponential growth	hurricane
Ankara	classicism	expressionism	hypothalamus
antimatter	class struggle	Far West	Ides of March
Appomattox Court	collateral	fief	Indian file
House	complex sentence	flying saucers	induction (philosophy)
artery	concentration camp	Fourth of July	intercontinental
art for art's sake	conspicuous	fringe benefit	ballistic missile
AT&T	consumption	From the sublime to	(ICBM)
Baa, Baa, Black Sheep	Crazy Horse	the ridiculous is but	irony
Bard of Avon, the	crocodile tears	a step.	jack-of-all-trades,
baritone	cyclotron	Garvey, Marcus	master of none
Berlin airlift	Dead Sea	Gershwin, George	Jolly Roger
Bible Belt	De gustibus non est	Give me liberty or give	justification by faith
boat people	disputadum.	me death.	kilowatt hour (kwhr)
bolt from the blue	Department of Defense	Grandma Moses	labor-intensive
Bronze Age	(DOD)	*Grinch Who Stole*	Lafayette, we are here.
Brueghel, Pieter (the	dictatorship	*Christmas, The*	law of contradiction
Elder)	Dominican Republic	gulag	Lennon, John
bubble chamber	Dow-Jones average	Hanoi	L'état c'est moi.

cannot add their own return address to the envelope. Twenty-five million American adults cannot read the poison warnings on a can of pesticide nor the front page of a daily newspaper.[40]

Functional illiteracy — the inability to perform basic reading, writing, and mathematical tasks — keeps at least one-third of American adults from full participation in their society. While it is tempting to blame individual students for their own failings or handicaps, illiteracy is so widespread that we must look for its causes in the educational system itself.

---

[40] Jonathan Kozol, *Illiterate America* (New York: Anchor Press, 1985).

Lindberg, Charles A.
lockout
Luftwaffe
Mandela, Nelson
mare's nest
mass
matrilineal
mercator projection
metamorphosis
Milan
Moby Dick
Molotov cocktail
morraine
Murphy's Law
natural selection
Neither a borrower nor
    a lender be . . .
nicotine
non sequitur
Nuremberg trials
oil sands (tar shales)
Ontario
opera

Orwell, George
parallelogram
passing the buck
Pennsylvania Dutch
personal pronoun
phoenix (myth)
Pilgrim's Progress, The
Poe, Edgar Allan
post mortem
predestination
Pride and Prejudice
proof of the pudding is
    in the eating, The
quark
Quisling
Raphael
reactionary
Restoration (of the
    British monarchy)
Rhine River
Robinson, Jackie
Rosetta stone
run-on sentence

Samson and Delilah
Scopes trial (monkey
    trial)
secular
separate but equal
Shall I compare thee to
    a summer's day?
Singapore
solipsism
sour grapes
Spare the rod and spoil
    the child.
State of the Union
    address
Strauss, Richard
suffer fools gladly
symphony
Talmud, the
tax loophole
thermostat

They shall not pass.
Thorpe, Jim
tokomak
torque
trump card
unicorn
universal gravitation
Vandals
Veni, vidi, vici.
Voltaire
wampum
wavelength
wet behind the ears
Whig party
withdrawal symptoms
Wright, Frank Lloyd
You can't go home
    again.
Zurich

SOURCE: E. D. Hirsch, Jr., *Cultural Literacy: What Every American Needs to Know* (New York: Random House, 1988), pp. 152–215.

Indeed, there is much evidence that the schools are not doing what they are traditionally supposed to do: provide every citizen with the skills and learning necessary to a full and comfortable life. In 1983 the National Commission on Excellence in Education delivered a scathing report on the schools, saying that "a tide of mediocrity" was destroying public education. The report, *A Nation at Risk*, cited inadequate teachers, low academic standards, and lack of math, science, and language requirements. Its central criticism was that

> our society and its educational institutions seem to have lost sight of the basic purposes of schooling, and of the high expectations and disciplined effort needed to attain them. . . . If only to keep and improve on the slim competitive edge we still retain in

TABLE 13-2   GETTING MORE EDUCATION AND SPENDING MORE FOR IT

	1940	1950	1960	1970	1980	1985
Percent of adults with high school diplomas	24.5	34.3	41.1	55.2	68.6	73.9
Percent of adults with college degree	4.6	6.2	7.7	11.0	17.0	19.4
Percent of U.S. population engaged in education (student, teacher, administrator)	23	21	25	30	27	26
Expenditures for elementary/secondary education (in billions of $)	3	6	17	43	103	149
Expenditures for higher education (in billions of $)	.6	3	7	25	62	98
Combined math and verbal scores on Scholastic Aptitude Test	—	970	975	948	890	906
Percent of Gross National Product devoted to education	3.5	3.4	4.8	7.1	6.6	6.6

SOURCE: U.S. Department of Education, Census Bureau, Educational Testing Service, reported in Terry Hartle, "Education Reform: We Have a Lot to Learn," *Public Opinion* (September–October, 1987), p. 48.

world markets, we must dedicate ourselves to the reform of our educational system for the benefit of all.[41]

The commission recommended tightening the basic curriculum, raising required standards of performance for students, and improving teacher preparation.

Although Americans are getting more schooling than ever before and paying much more for it, high school students know shockingly little about their own history, geography, and literature (see Table 13-2). Three out of four high school seniors can't identify Walt Whitman or Henry David Thoreau or the term Reconstruction. Two out of three cannot place the dates of the Civil War within 50 years; half are equally unsure of the date of World War I and do not recognize the name Joseph Stalin.[42]

To remedy the situation, some critics have called for a nationwide, grade-by-grade core curriculum in the elementary schools. In *Cultural Literacy* (1987), E. D. Hirsch argues that the increasing variety of what is taught, even in the same course at the same grade level, has steadily diminished the store of common information and thus fragmented American culture (see "How Culturally Literate Are You?").

A growing number of parents are also joining the back-to-basics movement, which calls for a return to traditional teaching methods and a renewed emphasis on basic skills, discipline, "good manners," and respect for authority. More than 40 state legislatures have passed laws requiring students to take more academic subjects, especially courses stressing the basic skills of reading, writing, and arithmetic.

---

[41] National Commission on Excellence in Education, *A Nation At Risk: The Full Account* (Cambridge, MA: USA Research, 1984), pp. 5 and 7.

[42] Diane Ravitch and Chester E. Finn, Jr., *What Do Our Seventeen Year Olds Know?* (New York: Harper & Row, 1988).

Some critics of the school system believe that the best way to achieve better education is with better teachers. Traditionally low salaries and little prestige are said to make teaching an undervalued profession that is unable to attract the most qualified personnel. It is unlikely, however, that much more money will be raised for teachers' salaries in the near future. A resurgence of political conservatism in the 1980s combined with voters' dissatisfaction with the public schools have killed most recent proposals for higher spending on education. The passage of California's Proposition 13, which lowered the property taxes supporting social programs, is only the best-known example of such middle-class taxpayers' revolts.

The shrill complaints often aimed at the schools should be evaluated according to the evidence on how well they are doing their job. A national survey reported that only 5 percent of personnel officers say that the high school graduates they interview do not have basic skills, and only the same 5 percent say they have trouble finding qualified applicants for the available jobs.[43]

Much of the criticism of the educational system comes from middle-class parents who find that the market value of a high school or college degree has eroded as it has become more available. For them the back-to-basics movement is a call to restore the value of educational achievement, and thus make their children better able to compete in the job market.

Furthermore, some conservative critics are making American education a scapegoat for the decline in the United States' world position, blaming the schools for loss of trade, teenage unemployment, and the size of the federal budget deficit. They prefer to ignore the social issues that affect the school system and its students — the relatively low salaries and prestige of teachers, the failure to change racist attitudes, and the neglect of the urban poor.

Any attempt to improve education must come to terms not only with these social problems, but with the inherent conflicts of the institution of education in a complex social structure. The rights of the family must be weighed against the rights of society, and the needs of individual students must be balanced with the organization's demand for uniformity. Given these contradictions, it is probably unrealistic to expect the school to carry out fully all the responsibilities with which it has been entrusted. Nevertheless, the quality of American education could clearly be improved.

---

[43] Paul W. Kingston, "Theory at Risk: Accounting for the Excellence Movement," *Sociological Forum 1* (1986), pp. 632–55.

SUMMARY

1. Education is the deliberate, formal transfer of knowledge, skills, and values from one person or group to another. The institution of education is specifically devoted to socialization, especially of the young.

2. The history of American education illustrates how and why education has changed in modern societies. The family and organized religion were responsible for education in pre-industrial times, but under the impact of social and economic

change these arrangements were replaced by a separate institution for education. From the start American education had two functions: cultural transmission and the selection and screening of candidates for occupational roles. Education both reinforced class distinctions and facilitated upward mobility. The tradition of community control and the American faith in education were established by the end of the colonial period.

3. Universal public education was introduced during the nineteenth century. The increasing demand for educated workers in an industrial society, the growth of bureaucracy, democratic idealism, the desire to "Americanize" millions of immigrants, the importance of educational achievement as a means to success, and the decline of the family's responsibility for education—all these cultural and social factors intertwined the educational system with other institutions in American society.

4. The American faith in education as a means of social progress was affirmed in the Supreme Court's 1954 decision outlawing racial segregation in the public schools. Court-ordered busing to achieve racially balanced schools has led to bitter confrontations between the values of equal education and community control, and the busing issue has still not been finally resolved. Moreover, racially integrated schools have not significantly reduced the differences in educational achievement for black and white children.

5. American education has largely met its original goals of cultural transmission and vocational training, but it has had some unintended consequences. The cultural and structural lessons of the hidden curriculum are that children should accept the norms of their peers and adjust their behavior to a bureaucratic world.

6. Until the 1960s equality in education was defined as equality of opportunity. When educators tried to translate educational opportunity into educational achievement, they found more and more evidence that schools tend to increase rather than reduce inequalities of class and race. Family background is still the most important factor in educational achievement. Middle- and upper-class parents give their children the benefit of economic and social resources that working-class parents do not have. Moreover, the school system's grading and tracking practices tend to produce greater inequalities through self-fulfilling prophecies of student differences.

7. The dilemma of organized education is how to educate children in large groups and still offer enough individual attention to guarantee equal opportunity. Modern schools are people-processing organizations that rely on standardized instruction and extrinsic motivation. The social setting of the modern school is thus inappropriate for many of the educational purposes it is supposed to serve.

8. Attempts to improve the quality of American education have focused on raising academic standards, emphasizing basic skills, and hiring better teachers. Critics usually ignore the social issues affecting the schools' performance—relatively low salaries and prestige for teachers, racism, and poverty.

KEY TERMS

education 406
cultural transmission 408
selection and screening 408

hidden curriculum 416
instrumentalism 419
equality of opportunity 420

equality of achievement 420
functional illiteracy 432
back-to-basics movement 434

SUGGESTED READING

* Alan Bloom. *The Closing of the American Mind.* New York: Simon and Schuster, 1988.

Randall Collins. *The Credential Society: A Historical Sociology of Education and Stratification.* San Diego: Academic Press, 1979.

Lawrence A. Cremin. *American Education.* Vol. I: *The Colonial Experience 1607–1783.* Vol. II: *The National Experience 1783–1876.* Vol. III: *The Metropolitan Experience 1876–1980.* New York: Harper & Row, 1972, 1980, and 1988.

James Crouse and Dale Trusheim. *The Case Against the SAT.* Chicago: University of Chicago Press, 1988.

* John I. Goodlad. *A Place Called School.* New York: McGraw-Hill, 1984.

* E. D. Hirsch, Jr. *Cultural Literacy: What Every American Needs to Know.* New York: Random House (Vintage), 1988.

Christopher Hurn. *The Limits and Possibilities of Schooling,* 2nd ed. Boston: Allyn & Bacon, 1985.

J. Anthony Lukas. *Common Ground: A Turbulent Decade in the Lives of Three American Families.* New York: Knopf, 1985.

* Available in paperback.

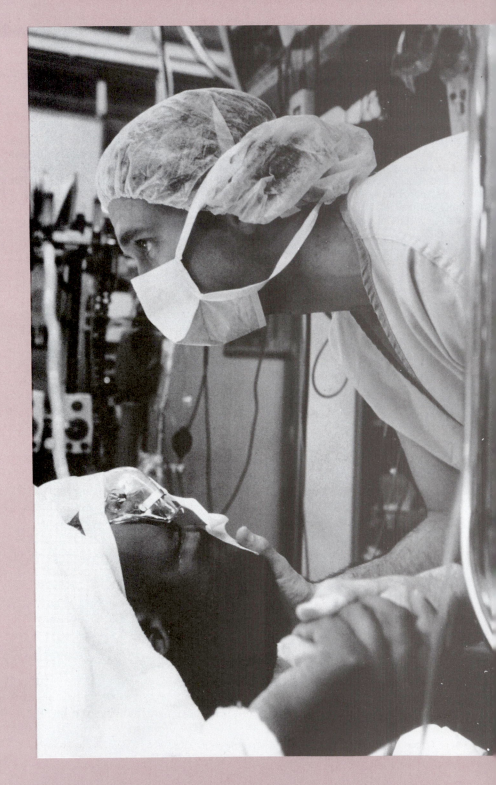

We have met
the enemy and
they is us.

Pogo

CHAPTER 14

HEALTH CARE

In 1635 the English king Charles I discovered that one of his subjects, Thomas Parr, was thought — because of church records — to be 152 years old. The king summoned "Old Parr," as he was affectionately known, to London, where he was lavishly wined and dined. Old Parr died soon afterwards, while he was still in London. An autopsy was performed by the great William Harvey, the physician who discovered the circulation of the blood and who is often called the father of modern scientific medicine. Harvey pronounced the ancient man's organs to be "as healthy as the day he was born." He attributed Old Parr's death to overindulgence and the polluted air of London.[1]

Old Parr's story shows that good health and longevity do not depend entirely on modern medical science and the effective treatment of illness. As Harvey knew 350 years ago, good health also depends to a great extent on the environmental conditions that can cause or reduce disease. All societies make some provision for maintaining health, which is defined both as the absence of illness and as a state of physical and mental well-being. In many societies the family is the institution responsible for preserving health and treating illness. When family members fall ill, their parents or other relatives care for them. Only if their efforts fail is a more knowledgeable specialist — a "medicine man" or other healer — called upon.

In Western societies until about 150 years ago, medicine, or the treatment of illness, relied almost entirely on home remedies, prayer, and such drastic cures as bleeding and purging. The modern era of scientific medicine began in Europe in the

---

[1] René Dubos, "Introduction" to *Anatomy of an Illness as Perceived by the Patient* by Norman Cousins (New York: Norton, 1979), p. 12.

A South African medicine man selects a remedy from his stock of cures. Until 150 years ago, medical treatment in Western societies was about as effective as the witch doctor's herbs and charms.

1820s and 1830s. Through careful observation of both the patients' symptoms and the history of their illnesses, scientists established that diseases had specific physical causes, which produced distinctive effects. The scientific view of disease revolutionized health care. Instead of being left to self-taught healers and family members, the practice of medicine became a profession requiring long years of training and dedication to the patient's welfare. By the beginning of the twentieth century in modern societies, the medical institution had been assigned the task of maintaining health and treating illness. Scientific medicine has unquestionably been spectacularly successful in carrying out its assigned purpose. Millions, perhaps billions, of lives have been saved by the modern medical treatment of smallpox, cholera, tuberculosis, malaria, and other diseases that were once incurable and fatal.

Today, however, the medical institution appears to be approaching the limits of its effectiveness. U.S. citizens, for example, have the benefits of the most sophisticated medical technology and the best hospital facilities in the world. Yet Americans are not the healthiest people on earth. When ranked according to average life expectancy and the rate of infant deaths — the usual measures of general health in a population — the United States is one of the *un*healthiest of all industrial societies. Fourteen countries have a longer average life expectancy than the United States and fourteen have lower infant mortality rates.[2]

---

[2] Countries with populations over 5 million with longer life expectancies are: Australia, Austria, Belgium, Canada, Denmark, France, Greece, Hong Kong, Italy, Japan, the Netherlands, Sweden, Switzerland, and West Germany. Countries with lower infant mortality rates are: Australia, Austria, Belgium, Canada, Denmark, France, Italy, Japan, the Netherlands, Norway, Sweden, Switzerland, United Kingdom, and West Germany. U.S. Bureau of the Census, *Statistical Abstract of the United States* (Washington, D.C.: U.S. Government Printing Office, 1989), Table 1405.

Poverty is one reason that a comparatively large proportion of a population dies at a young age. Statistics show that the affluent are generally healthier than the poor, that black children (who are disproportionately poor) are almost twice as likely to die in infancy as white children, and that the life expectancy of black people is five years shorter than that of white people.[3] Other comparative figures tell us that women generally live longer than men and that elderly people are not as healthy as the young. These facts are not very surprising. Youthful strength and the ability to afford medical care could conceivably be enough to give the relatively young and prosperous a health advantage. And biology appears to give women a longer lease on life than men. There are other considerations, however, less easy to explain.

Let us take the case of two adjoining states within the United States with the same climate and terrain. They also have almost identical levels of education and urbanization. Their health statistics, however, are very different. For the moment we shall call them State *A* and State *B*.

The people who live in State *A* are far healthier than the people who live in State *B*. Residents of State *A* can expect to live three to four years longer than the residents of State *B*. In every age group the **mortality rate**—or number of deaths per 100,000 people—is significantly lower in State *A* than in State *B*. Ranked with the other forty-eight states, State *A* has the third longest life expectancy and State *B* has the fifth shortest.

If sex, race, age, and poverty were the only considerations in health, we might suspect that State *B* has more people who tend to be unhealthy because they are male, black, old, or poor. In fact, State *B* does have more males and blacks, but it also has *fewer* elderly people and a *higher* per capita income than State *A*. This tipping of the balance toward health may be offset, however, by the fact that State *B*'s population includes proportionately fewer physicians and therefore has more restricted access to medical care. All in all, the demographic and economic differences between States *A* and *B* are slight—certainly not enough to account for such large differences in life expectancy. The answer must lie in other factors.

One clue to the puzzle might be found by asking what the residents of each state die from. Heart disease, cancer, strokes, and accidents are the leading causes of death in both, as they are in the United States generally. After these four the leading killers in State *B*, the unhealthy state, are suicide, cirrhosis of the liver, infant diseases, and lung disease. In "healthy" State *A* the next most common causes of death are influenza, infant diseases, diabetes, and suicide. In all age groups residents of State *B* are two to six times more likely to die from cirrhosis of the liver and lung cancer than the residents of State *A*.

Since cirrhosis of the liver is related to the consumption of alcohol, and lung cancer is linked to cigarette smoking, it is hardly surprising to learn that State *B*'s residents drink and smoke a great deal more than the people who live in State *A*. In fact, State *B* has the highest rate of alcohol consumption of all the states, while State *A* has the lowest. State *A* also has the lowest rate of cigarette smoking in the United States, and State *B* has the fourth highest. The reason for this remarkable disparity is not the cost

---

[3] Ibid., Table 106.

The way we live strongly affects how healthy we are. Different social situations — not more effective medicine — are the reason Salt Lake City residents have a longer life expectancy than the people who live in Las Vegas.

and availability of alcohol and cigarettes; they are about the same in both states. The explanation lies in the different attitudes the people of the two states have toward drinking and smoking. Ten percent of the people in State *B*, but 75 percent of the people in State *A*, are Mormons — of the Church of Jesus Christ of Latter-Day Saints — whose religious beliefs forbid the use of alcohol or tobacco. Residents of State *A* also lead rather stable family lives. In contrast to State *B*, State *A* has much lower rates of divorce and change of residence. These different social and religious norms account for the extraordinary fact that the people who live in State *A* — Utah — are so much healthier than the people who live in State *B* — Nevada.[4]

Clearly, patterns of social life have a great deal to do with health and sickness. This chapter first examines the role medicine plays in health as well as its limitations in dealing with the social factors in illness. Next we analyze how health care is distributed in the United States. The third section discusses the changing concept of mental illness in modern societies. The final part suggests that health care, having approached the limits of scientific medicine, may now be taking a fundamental change in direction.

---

[4] Leon E. Clark, *Mortality American Style: A Tale of Two States* (Washington, D.C.: Population Reference Bureau, 1977); Frederic D. Wolinsky, *The Sociology of Health* (Boston: Little, Brown, 1980), pp. 23–28.

SOCIETY AND HEALTH

As recently as the 1920s the practice of medicine was still a discouraging business. Much of medical science consisted of making an accurate diagnosis and then watching the illness run its course. Many deadly diseases were simply untreatable: whooping cough, diphtheria, polio, meningitis, typhoid fever. Doctors could only prescribe good nursing care and hope for the best. The use of drugs was limited mainly to morphine, a

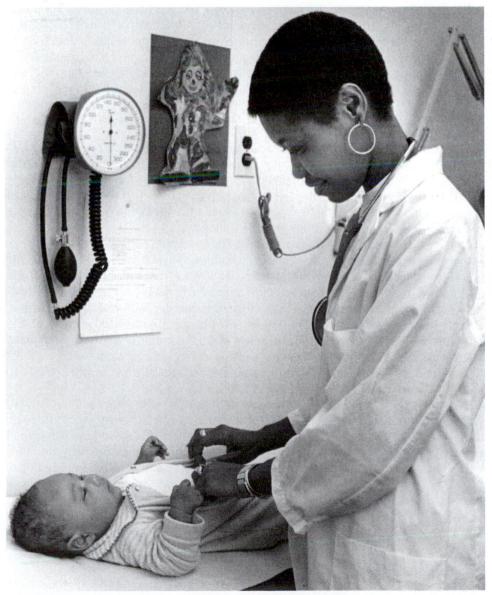

During the twentieth century, Americans' average life expectancy increased by 28 years, almost entirely because of a sharp decline in child mortality. Modern medicine's contribution to better health in childhood has been small compared with the impact of a healthier environment, which has dramatically reduced exposure to infectious diseases.

painkiller. Leading causes of death were tuberculosis, nearly always fatal, and pneumonia.[5]

At the beginning of the twentieth century infectious diseases were the major threat to health in the United States (see Table 14-1). Because so many young children died of these diseases, the average life expectancy in 1900 was only 47 years. By 1987 it had increased to 75 years (78 for women). This increase was almost entirely due to a sharp decline in infant and child mortality. Since 1900 twenty-eight years have been added to life expectancy at birth but less than five years to life expectancy at age 65.[6] The eradication of some childhood diseases and the control of others resulted partly from better medicine, especially antibiotic drugs and universal immunization. But medicine's contribution to longer life expectancy has been small compared to the impact of a healthier environment. The introduction of clean water supplies, pasteurized milk, better nutrition and personal hygiene, and more efficient sewage disposal dramatically reduced exposure to infection. Over the last century plumbers and sanitation workers have probably saved as many lives as physicians.

THE SOCIAL MODEL OF ILLNESS

In modern societies illness is usually explained by citing a disease. Once the disease is identified, we look for its physical cause. We say that a disease has been cured when its symptoms have been relieved. When we ask sick people why they don't feel well, we expect an answer in terms of this **medical model**, an explanation of illness in terms of disease. Both laypersons and physicians are likely to say "I'm down with the flu" and try to cure their illness with drugs or other therapy.

As we have seen, the medical profession has developed extremely effective treatments of illness. It is rare that doctors can do nothing to help people feel better. On the other hand, doctors can rarely do anything to remove the underlying cause of the disease. Antidepressant drugs, for example, are useful in treating depression in individual cases but do not affect the situation causing the depression. Coronary bypass surgery has been effective in repairing diseased hearts but has had no effect on the incidence of the disease itself. If the purpose of the institution of medicine is to make people healthy in a positive sense — by keeping us from getting sick — then we must look beyond the symptoms of individual patients to the social world in which they live (see "The Story of an Old Man").[7]

The **social model** describes illness not only in terms of the bodies of the individuals who are ill but also in terms of the social situation in which disease occurs. Some thirty years ago Talcott Parsons defined health as the state of having the capacity to perform social roles and illness as a disturbance of this capacity to carry out one's expected tasks. Breaking a leg, for example, would plainly hinder an acrobat's performance. Applying the same concept to psychological illness, an inability to meet deadlines would limit an adolescent's capacity to perform the role of student. A physically or

---

[5] Lewis Thomas, *The Youngest Science: Notes of a Medicine Watcher* (New York: Penguin, 1983), pp. 19–35.

[6] U.S. Bureau of the Census, *Social Indicators III*; U.S. Bureau of the Census, *Statistical Abstract of the United States* (Washington, D.C.: U.S. Government Printing Office, 1989).

[7] Eric J. Cassell, "Changing Ideas of Causality in Medicine," *Social Research* 46:4 (Winter 1979): 728–43.

THE TOP TEN KILLERS

TABLE 14-1

	Per 100,000 Population	As Percent of All Deaths		Per 100,000 Population	As Percent of All Deaths
1929			**1986**		
Heart disease	211.2	17.7	Heart disease	317.5	36.4
Pneumonia and influenza	146.5	12.3	Cancer	194.7	22.3
Cancer	95.8	8.0	Strokes	62.1	7.1
Chronic kidney infection	91.1	7.6	Accidents	39.5	4.5
Strokes	90.8	7.5	Lung disease†	31.8	3.6
Tuberculosis	75.3	6.3	Pneumonia and influenza	29.0	3.3
Accidents*	55.0	4.6	Diabetes mellitus	15.4	1.7
Certain conditions of infants	32.9	2.7	Suicides	12.8	1.5
Auto accidents	25.5	2.1	Liver disease‡	10.9	1.2
Gastrointestinal infections	23.8	1.9	Atherosclerosis§	9.4	1.1

* Includes legal executions
† Other than cancer and pneumonia
‡ Other than cancer
§ Of arteries other than those of the heart, brain, and lung
SOURCE: National Center for Health Statistics, *Vital Statistics of the United States* (Washington, D.C.: U.S. Government Printing Office, 1989).

mentally ill person is someone who cannot carry out his or her social roles, and is said instead to adopt the **sick role**.[8]

The sick role has specific components: (1) The individual is not considered responsible for his or her illness. Falling ill is thought to be beyond the individual's control, and recovery from illness is supposed to require some therapeutic treatment. (2) Illness is a legitimate excuse for not performing certain roles. Workers are allowed a day off to nurse a cold but not to go fishing. (3) Although anyone can become ill, everyone is expected to try to get well. The sick person is obliged to seek appropriate help and to follow "doctor's orders."

The sick role does not depend on having a high level of bacteria in one's system or on being injured or disabled. Some people who play the sick role are not physically ill; they may just want to have a day's rest in bed. Others ignore their symptoms and carry out ordinary social roles. Most of us do not consider a case of sunburn or a mild headache sickness, nor do people so affected consider themselves "sick."

---

[8] See three works by Talcott Parsons: "The Sick Role and the Role of the Physician Reconsidered," *Milbank Memorial Fund Quarterly* 53 (1975): 257–78; "Definitions of Health and Illness in Light of American Values and Social Structure." in *Patients, Physicians, and Illness*, 2nd ed., ed. E. G. Jaco (New York: Free Press, 1972); *The Social System* (New York: Free Press, 1951).

THE STORY OF AN OLD MAN

How important is it to identify the scientific cause of an illness? Are cause and cure always related? Eric J. Cassell, a physician and professor of public health, argues that the medical explanation of disease does not tell the whole story of an illness.

An elderly man was found unconscious in his fifth-floor walk-up apartment and brought to a New York City teaching hospital. He was found to have pneumococcal pneumonia. In addition, his right knee was greatly swollen; his physicians believed that he had a Charcot joint, a rare manifestation of late syphilis. . . .

The patient's diagnosis, in classical terms, was pneumococcal pneumonia and, perhaps, tertiary syphilis. The treatment in this case seems to get at the cause. Antibiotics will eliminate the pneumococcus and cure his pneumonia. If he has syphilis, the same antibiotics will eliminate the treponema but, unfortunately, will not make his knee better (because structural damage to the joint would already have occurred).

■ ■ ■

What else do we know of this patient? He is seventy-four years old and his wife died about a year ago; the remainder of his family lives out of New York; he has no friends. The bad knee turns out to be not syphilis but "merely" osteoarthritis — degenerative disease of the joints.

Any attempt to use the modern medical language of cause would face difficulties in describing this man's case. But, avoiding the words and difficulties of concepts of cause, there is another way in which his case can be presented. We are able to tell the *story* of his illness.

With his wife recently dead and no close friends, this man withdrew from social contact, a common happening in the lonely aged. Often, such people will stop making real meals, instead picking at food or eating what little is required to still their hunger. Any attempt this man might have made to re-establish social connections or to improve his diet, of his own desire or at the urging of his family and acquaintances, was hampered by his disabled right knee. Walking up and down his five flights of stairs was extremely painful, and he avoided it as much as possible. A previous physician, and the patient himself, had dismissed the knee problem as "old age arthritis for which nothing could be done." The combination of malnutrition and social isolation increased his susceptibility to infection. In all probability, the pneumococcus responsible for his pneumonia had been an inhabitant of his throat for a long time before the host-parasite relationship was tilted in its favor. He was found only because a neighbor had not seen or heard him in his apartment for more than a day.

■ ■ ■

Treating the pneumonia will solve only part of the problem. Experience suggests that the man will soon be ill again unless other problems are solved. For decades, we have called these other problems

In modern societies, however, the concept of sickness has expanded to cover many physical and emotional conditions that were never before considered medical problems.[9] In the early years of the twentieth century, for example, American women usually gave birth at home, with a midwife or other members of the family in attendance. As American society became more urban, people became more accustomed to depending on the specialized skills of strangers. Pregnancy and childbirth became **medicalized**, or viewed as a condition that requires — and ought to have — medical attention. Most babies are now born in hospitals, and doctors treat women as patients during their pregnancies. The modern faith in science and technological progress has also bolstered the medical profession's authority to deal with all sorts of problems. Psychological symptoms that used to be considered signs of a bad character or ex-

---

[9] Paul Starr, *The Social Transformation of American Medicine* (New York: Basic Books, 1982), pp. 18 – 19.

the "psychosocial aspects" of the case. But clearly, the man's crippled knee is not a "psychosocial aspect." Further, we do not call the lung an aspect of pneumonia — you cannot have pneumonia without it.

These things — age, widowhood, loneliness, fifth-floor walk-up, osteoarthritis, malnutrition — are not "aspects" of the case; they are *necessary parts of this story, without which the story would be different.* Furthermore, if the story were different, the disease would be different. For example, this man might have consumed aspirin because of his painful knee — and developed gastrointestinal bleeding from erosive gastritis but, because eating diminished the pain coming from his stomach, maintained his nutrition. Or, in sorrow, he might have started drinking, become intoxicated, vomited, and then aspirated the vomitus into his lungs, producing a lung abcess or aspiration pneumonia. In each instance, a different disease with a different treatment results when a feature of the story is changed. . . .

■ ■ ■

In fact, in stories of illness, there are always two protagonists — the body and the person. There are the events that take place in the body (such as the effect of malnutrition, the alterations in the knee, or the alterations that take place as part of pneumonia). And there are those events that happen to the person either before the body events (widowhood, social isolation), in mixed sequence (the malnutrition), or as a result of the direct effect of the body events or their meaning (inability to walk stairs, the connotation of helpless aging from the knee, the hospitalization, and many others). To see the story in only body terms is as inadequate as viewing it in only "psychological" or "social" terms.

In the story of the old man, *cause,* certainly as it is currently used in medicine, is an almost empty concept. What is the cause of the old man's pneumonia? His age, the fifth-floor walk-up, malnutrition, the knee, the pneumococcus? . . .

■ ■ ■

. . . Modifiers to the word "cause," such as contributing, necessary, sufficient, multifactorial, and so forth, are simply attempts to hold onto the concept of specific etiology as it evolved in the late nineteenth and early twentieth century. We are attached to the concept for historical reasons, not because that is the only or even best or most effective way of seeing things. In the case of the old man, the concept of specific etiology must be given up because it does not point to the most definitive way to make and keep him better.

SOURCE: Eric J. Cassell, "Changing Ideas of Causality in Medicine," *Social Research* 46 (Winter 1979): 732–36.

plained as "one of Aunt Lucy's spells" are now more likely to be viewed as signs of a mental illness that should receive psychiatric treatment. This social trend toward medicalization has made Americans more and more likely to depend on the health-care system and less likely to rely on other institutions when they are in trouble. Doctors — not clergymen, teachers, or family members — are now expected to help the despondent adolescent, the uncertain parent, or the disabled elderly person.

POVERTY AND HEALTH

Viewed from the sociological perspective it is clear that the impact of medical care on health is not as great as the impact of the social environment. In fact, two social factors — income and education — largely determine what kind of health we have.

As Table 14-2 indicates, the lower the family income, the higher the incidence of disabling illness. The link between poverty and poor health can be explained by the fact

TABLE 14-2   HEALTH AND INCOME

Family Income	Percentage Rating Their Health as Excellent	Restrictions Due to Acute Conditions		Percentage of Persons With One or More Chronic Conditions	
		Restricted Activity Days per 100 Persons per Year	Bed Days per 100 Persons per Year	Limitations in Person's Major Activity	Unable to Carry on Major Activity
Less than $10,000	26%	1,004	475	19%	9%
$10,000–19,000	31%	775	345	13%	6%
$20,000–34,999	40%	654	271	8%	3%
$35,000 or more	50%	585	242	5%	1.5%

SOURCE: National Center for Health Statistics, *Vital and Health Statistics: Current Estimates from the National Health Interview Survey of 1988* (Washington, D.C.: U.S. Government Printing Office, 1989).

that the poor lead riskier and unhealthier lives than other people. The conditions of poverty—a lower standard of living, less access to health care, and a more dangerous environment—all contribute to a higher rate of illness and injury among the poor.

As for the relationship of education and health, the economist Victor Fuchs has put it starkly: each additional dollar spent on education reduces mortality rates more than each additional dollar spent on medical care.[10] Fuchs's conclusion is based on studies showing that the higher the level of education in a population, the lower its mortality rate. In one such study white men with less than a high-school education had a mortality rate 64 percent higher than men who had graduated from college. Women who had not completed high school had a mortality rate more than twice as high as college graduates.[11]

Poverty contributes to ill health, but ill health also contributes to poverty by preventing people from holding down a steady job. In 1988 about 26 percent of Americans who had family incomes below $10,000 were disabled, compared to 8 percent of those with incomes over $35,000.[12]

According to estimates made by the demographer Evelyn Kitagawa, the "excess mortality" rate from the effect of socioeconomic differences is 20 percent: if everyone in the United States had been white and had had one year of college, one-fifth of all adult deaths in 1960 would not have occurred.[13] Some 300,000 deaths every year, in other words, are linked to poverty and are preventable in theory.

[10] Victor Fuchs, *The Service Economy* (New York: National Bureau of Economic Research, 1968).

[11] Evelyn Kitagawa and Philip M. Hauser, *Differential Mortality in the United States* (Cambridge, Mass.: Harvard University Press, 1973), pp. 12–14.

[12] National Center for Health Statistics, *Vital and Health Statistics: Current Estimates from the National Health Interview Survey of 1988,* (Washington, D.C.: U.S. Government Printing Office, 1989).

[13] Evelyn Kitagawa, "Socioeconomic Differences in the United States and Some Implications for Population Policy," in Commission on Population Growth and the American Future, Research Reports, Vol. I, *Demographic and Social Aspects of Population Growth,* ed. Charles F. Westoff and Robert Parke, Jr. (Washington, D.C.: U.S. Government Printing Office, 1972), pp 87–110.

In the fifteenth century, Joan of Arc's peculiar behavior was interpreted as a sign that she was a witch. Later the same behavior was deemed evidence of sainthood. Today, a woman who heard strange voices and dressed in men's clothing would probably be considered mentally ill and in need of medical treatment.

SAVING LIVES THROUGH SOCIAL ACTION

As recently as the 1920s infectious diseases were still dangerous threats to health (see Table 14-1). Modern medicine, especially the development of sulfa drugs and antibiotics, has greatly reduced the risk of death from infections. Today the most dangerous diseases are not contagious but chronic disorders. Four types of disease — heart disease, cancer, stroke, and lung disease — account for over 70 percent of all the deaths in the United States. While modern scientific medicine has been able to relieve the effects and arrest the progress of these diseases in individual cases, it cannot cure or prevent them. The findings of medical research emphatically suggest that the causes of cancer, emphysema, and circulatory disorders are not just physical but also social. The way we live is strongly affecting how healthy we are.

John Knowles, a physician and past president of the Rockefeller Foundation, believes that most Americans are born healthy and suffer from illness or premature death only because of their own misbehavior or an unhealthy environment. Prevention of disease, he argues, means giving up some "bad" habits — smoking cigarettes, eating too many fats, drinking too much, exercising too little, driving too fast.[14] Knowles's prescription was borne out by a California study that found that longer life expectancy is significantly related to a healthy life style.

For five and a half years 7,000 adults followed a few sensible rules:

> Three meals a day at regular hours and no snacking
>
> Breakfast every day
>
> Moderate exercise two or three times a week
>
> Adequate sleep (seven or eight hours a night)
>
> No smoking
>
> Moderate weight
>
> No alcohol or alcohol in moderation

The study found that a 45-year-old man who practiced three or even fewer of these healthy habits had a remaining life expectancy of 21.5 years (to age 67); if he followed four or five of the rules, he could expect to live 28.0 more years (to age 73); and if he observed six or seven, he would lengthen his life expectancy to 33.0 additional years (to age 78). The researchers also found that middle-aged people who practiced all seven habits were as healthy as people thirty years younger who practiced none of them.[15] As this study indicates, just a few simple changes in everyday living habits can apparently reduce the frequency of illness and add years to life.

Most of the leading causes of death would be affected by similar changes in the social environment. Eighty percent of the deaths from cancer and heart disease may be "premature"; that is, they occur in relatively young people and are believed to be preventable. Heart disorders and strokes (46 percent of all deaths) are related to diet, cigarette smoking, undetected hypertension, and lack of exercise. Cancer (22 percent of all deaths) is correlated with smoking, eating fatty and refined foods, and breathing chemically polluted air. Stress, the hallmark of modern urban societies, seems to play an important role in heart disease and strokes. Moreover, the emotional strain of adjusting to loss and change often precedes the onset of other illnesses. The death rate for widows and widowers, for example, is ten times higher in the first year of bereavement than it is for others the same age. In the year following a divorce those who are divorced are twelve times more likely to get sick than married people.[16]

---

[14] John H. Knowles, M.D., "The Responsibility of the Individual," in *Doing Better and Feeling Worse,* ed. John H. Knowles (New York: Norton, 1977), pp. 79, 59.

[15] See two articles by N. B. Belloc and L. Breslow: "Relationship of Health Practices and Mortality," *Preventive Medicine* 2 (1973): 67–81; "The Relation of Physical Health Status and Health Practices," *Preventative Medicine* I (August 1972): 409–21.

[16] Knowles, "The Responsibility of the Individual," p. 63.

Public campaigns against drunken driving are efforts to improve health by preventing some of the tens of thousands of deaths and injuries caused every year by automobile accidents.

Many deaths from accidents, homicide, and suicide could also be prevented. Almost half of all fatal accidents are caused by automobiles. Popular resistance to lower speed limits and such safety features as seat belts is doubtless a contributing factor. Drunken driving contributes to between 50 and 75 percent of all deaths and injuries in automobile accidents, and the excessive use of alcohol causes cirrhosis of the liver, a leading cause of death. The suicide rate is increasing generally, but it has nearly doubled among young people since the 1960s. Accidents, murders, and suicides are responsible for three out of four deaths among 15- to 25-year-olds — the only age group for which the mortality rate has *risen* since 1976.[17]

There is much evidence to show that social action would prevent many of these deaths. Let us turn to a few recent examples of how changes in social behavior have affected health.

SMOKING.   When the surgeon general's report on the link between cigarette smoking and cancer was released in 1964, 50 percent of the adult population of the United States smoked cigarettes. By 1985, in part because of public education programs and restrictions on cigarette advertising, the proportion of adult smokers had dropped to 30

---

[17] Benjamin A. Kogan, *Health,* 3rd ed. (New York: Harcourt Brace Jovanovich, 1980), p. 178.

percent. If cigarette smoking were stopped entirely, experts estimate that one out of five deaths from cancer would be prevented.[18]

ALCOHOL.   When the sale of alcoholic beverages was restricted during Prohibition, the death rate from cirrhosis of the liver dropped from 11.8 per 100,000 in 1916 to 7.2 in 1932. After the Prohibition amendment was repealed, the death rate from cirrhosis rose steadily to an all-time high of 16 deaths per 100,000 in 1973 (today the rate is 10.9).[19] In France, where wine production is the country's largest industry, alcoholism is the third most common cause of death, after heart disease and cancer.[20]

ACCIDENTS.   In 1976 Ontario, Canada, made it illegal to drive or ride in a car without wearing a seatbelt. Officials say the use of these safety devices is primarily responsible for the 40 percent drop in traffic fatalities between 1975 and 1982, even though there are many more cars on the roads.[21] In the United States new legislation and a public campaign to curb drunken driving have received some of the credit for reducing 1983 traffic deaths to their lowest level in 20 years. These measures have become less effective as public concern over the problem has waned. Traffic fatalities, including alcohol-related deaths, began to increase again in 1986, partly because of less strict enforcement of speeding laws, smaller cars, decreased use of seatbelts, and simply more driving by more people. Traffic accidents remain the chief cause of death in the 15-to-25-year-old age group.[22]

As these examples strongly suggest, many of the leading causes of death and disability are social, not medical, problems (see "The AIDS Epidemic"). Doctors cannot cure cancer or heart disease with shots and pills, as they can cure the "old killers" like diphtheria and tuberculosis. Today most Americans could improve their health not simply by passively receiving better medical treatment but by actively changing the way they live every day. The health-care system, however, has an important effect on social behavior. The role of the medical institution in American society is discussed in the next section.

HEALTH CARE IN THE UNITED STATES

After food and construction, health is the third largest industry in the United States. In 1986, $458 billion — or $1,837 for every man, woman, and child — was spent on hospitals, doctors' and dentists' fees, drugs, and other health costs. Health spending takes 11 percent of the nation's total output of goods and services — the highest percentage in

[18] Knowles, "The Responsibility of the Individual," p. 76.

[19] Ibid, p. 65.

[20] Frank J. Prial, "French Fight Alcoholism but It Keeps on Winning," *The New York Times*, July 18, 1980, p. A14.

[21] Lindsey Gruson, "Ontario's Seat-Belt Law Hailed for Saving Lives," *The New York Times*, July 13, 1984, p. B4.

[22] *Health: The United States, 1982* (Rockville, Md.: U.S. National Center for Health Statistics, 1983).

THE AIDS EPIDEMIC

AIDS (Acquired Immune Difficiency Syndrome) was first diagnosed in the United States in 1981 among homosexual men in New York City. The disease cripples the body's immune system, leaving its victims defenseless against illnesses that eventually kill them. It is caused by a virus spread through sexual intercourse or the exchange of blood, especially among intravenous drug users who share needles. Symptoms of the disease often do not develop for seven or more years after infection. By 1989 50,000 to 100,000 cases of AIDS had been diagnosed, with estimates of as many as 270,000 cases expected by 1991.[1] In New York AIDS is already the leading cause of death among men between 25 and 44 and women between 25 and 34 years old.[2]

Although the spread of the virus has been slowed, the AIDS epidemic will soon become much worse because most of the one to two million Americans infected in the early 1980s are not yet ill. According to the most recent estimates, about half of those infected will develop the disease, and all of them will die from it. So far there is no cure or vaccine for AIDS, and none is expected in the foreseeable future.[3]

More than any other disease in modern times, the AIDS epidemic demonstrates the social aspects of illness:

- The transmission of AIDS is linked to social behaviors—homosexual intercourse, promiscuous sex, and intravenous drug abuse. The spread of most other contagious diseases is not affected by the victim's way of life, and, since the advent of modern medicine, no other fatal illness can be "caught."

- The fight against AIDS has been hampered by its high incidence among homosexuals and intravenous drug addicts—two groups whose life-styles had already made them subject to abuse and discrimination. According to Parsons' theory, the sick role allows us a legitimate escape from our usual obligations because falling ill is not thought to be our fault. But some people consider AIDS victims responsible for their illness because their deviance—not a random virus—caused the illness. Newspapers and television commentators, for example, refer to the "innocent victims" of AIDS—those who are infected by their spouses, through blood transfusions, or by being born to a mother with AIDS—and thus imply that other victims are guilty in some way. Relatives of AIDS victims are often ashamed to mention the cause of death in obituaries, stating the complications of the disease instead. The popular sentiment that homosexuals and IV drug abusers are getting their "just deserts" presents a great obstacle to effort to combat the disease.

- With no effective treatment for AIDS in sight, prevention is the only available remedy. Unlike other diseases we have discussed in this chapter, prevention in this case depends entirely on changing behavior. In a society dominated by the medical model of illness, an epidemic which cannot be "cured" by modern medicine is puzzling indeed. Since transmission of AIDS has social causes, sociologists can help by devising educational programs to change the behavior of drug abusers, homosexuals, and other populations at risk. Since AIDS is a contagious disease, medical researchers can help by finding a vaccine to prevent its spread and a cure for those already infected. Since AIDS is a national problem involving extraordinary research and hospitalization costs, the state can help with political support, scientific grants, public education, and legislation. At the moment, however, none of these groups has taken full responsibility for the AIDS crisis, and each has looked to the others for a remedy. Mobilizing the resources to end the AIDS epidemic thus poses a unique challenge to the sociological imagination.

[1] U.S. Bureau of the Census, *Statistical Abstract of the United States,* Table 181.

[2] Philip M. Boffey, "Spread of AIDS Abating, But Deaths Will Still Soar," *The New York Times* (February 14, 1988), p. 36.

[3] Richard A. Berk, "Anticipating the Social Consequences of AIDS: A Position Paper," *The American Sociologist,* 18 (Fall 1987), pp. 211–27.

Expensive new technology such as this CAT scanner is one reason the costs of medical care have increased enormously in the last twenty years.

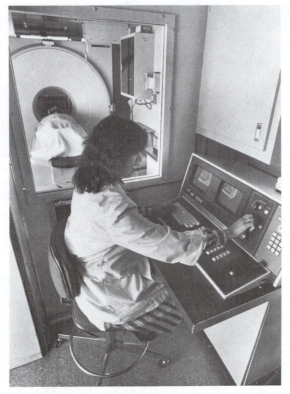

the world. As we have seen, Americans' poor health has more to do with life style than with lack of medical care. There is no doubt, however, that the state of the nation's health depends in part on the kind of medical services available to its citizens.

THE RISING COST OF HEALTH CARE

Between 1970 and 1986 the amount of money spent on health services increased from $26 billion to $458 billion — a staggering 1,700 percent. About a fourth of this money is spent by the federal government on Medicare programs for the elderly and Medicaid programs for the poor, which together represent a little more than one-tenth of the federal budget. The rest comes out of private insurance programs and individual incomes. Because much of the cost of health care is not covered by insurance, the risk of a long illness is a serious financial threat to most Americans. Moreover, the rising price of medical care shows no sign of leveling off in the future. Some of the reasons why health costs will continue to go up are discussed below.

HIGHER HOSPITAL BILLS.   Hospital charges, which represent 40 percent of all health costs, have risen faster than any other kind of medical care. The average per-patient cost of a day in the hospital was $245 in 1980; today it is about $500. One reason for this enormous increase is medical progress. Expensive new machinery — such as the computerized X-ray (CAT) scanner, which costs $750,000 to buy and about as much each year to operate — requires hospitals to make huge capital outlays. New routine procedures, such as X-rays and laboratory tests, also add to hospital costs.

Still another factor in higher hospital bills is the increasing proportion of elderly people in the population. A longer life span often means the development of chronic diseases that require longer and more frequent hospitalization. The average hospital bill for an aged patient is more than twice that for a middle-aged one.

MORE SPECIALISTS.   In 1986 the average physician's median yearly fees amounted to $200,000, about 50 percent more than they were in 1980.[23] One reason for this increase is the growing proportion of medical specialists. While 30 percent of the nation's doctors were general practitioners twenty years ago, only 13 percent are today. Physicians tend to specialize for two reasons. First, the growing body of medical knowledge means that few doctors can feel competent in every field, so most practice in such limited areas as obstetrics or anesthesiology. Doctors also enter specialized fields to make more money. Medical specialization increases health-care costs because specialists charge higher fees and because a patient must often see several doctors and pay each of them a separate fee.

HEALTH INSURANCE.   In 1965 Congress approved government health insurance for the aged (Medicare) and expanded federal assistance to state financing of medical care for the poor (Medicaid). Since physicians and hospitals are reimbursed on the basis of their fees, Medicare and Medicaid proved to be a financial windfall for the health industry. Private physicians, who had customarily adjusted fees according to their patient's ability to pay, could now charge rich and poor the same amount. Partly as a result, doctors' incomes have risen sharply since 1965. Private hospitals and profit-making nursing homes have also benefited from a flood of new business, as patients who could never before have afforded them seek semiprivate rooms and nursing services. Before Medicare and Medicaid were introduced, the poor visited a doctor and had hospital treatment less often than other income groups; now they actually use medical services more often than other groups.[24]

RISING EXPECTATIONS.   Adding to the spiraling costs of medical care is the growing belief that health is a right rather than a matter of privilege or good fortune. A more highly educated, urbanized, and affluent American population is demanding better medical care through the use of private specialists and hospitals, advanced medical techniques and laboratory tests, and special services for the aged and disabled. Moreover, the medical view of illness as a physical condition that can be cured by expert treatment is now the prevalent one. Minor ailments and psychological problems that were once tolerated or treated with home remedies are now taken to a doctor. Faith in medical progress has led to a widespread belief that there is — or should be — a cure for every malady.

---

[23] U.S. Bureau of the Census, *Statistical Abstract of the United States*, Table 155.
[24] U.S. Bureau of the Census, *Vital and Health Statistics*, Table 71.

All these factors have contributed to the enormously increased costs of health care in the last twenty years. The huge amount of spending on health, however, has not brought a corresponding proportional increase in the availability of medical care.

THE UNEQUAL DISTRIBUTION OF HEALTH CARE

There is no question that Medicare and Medicaid have given the poor greater access to medical care. In 1964, before these programs passed Congress, members of poor families visited a doctor an average of 4.3 times a year, compared with 4.6 visits for other families. By 1988 the average poor person saw a doctor 6.6 times a year, while other people visited a doctor only 5.3 times a year. This improvement, however, may not be as great as it sounds. First, the evidence indicates that the poor are more likely to be seriously ill than other people; in fact, many persons are poor just because they are disabled and cannot work. When the more severe health problems of the poor are taken into account, studies show that poor people use medical services less frequently than others. Second, two groups among the poor — children and the aged — see doctors less frequently than other age groups. Finally, outside of the northern and western states, Medicaid programs are often limited, and rural areas, especially in the South, have been neglected entirely.[25]

While Medicaid has given the poor more medical purchasing power, it has not given them more services. Hospitals and physicians are not evenly distributed across the country (see Figure 14-1). New York, for example, has 234 practicing physicians for every 100,000 people, but Alabama has only 146.[26] About 32 million people in the United States have no private or public health insurance, and hence no protection against the costs and consequences of prolonged illness.[27]

It is not clear, however, that the health of the poor could be improved with better access to medical care. One of the goals of the British National Health Service, a publicly supported program of health care, was to improve the health of lower-income groups by providing more equitable access to medical facilities. A survey of the British data concluded that this goal has not been achieved. Equalizing the distribution of medical care did not overcome the unhealthy social and environmental conditions associated with poverty — the deficient diet, rundown living quarters, exposure to disease-carrying rats and garbage, the stress of money worries, divorce, and unemployment. These conditions alone, Lee Rainwater theorized, are enough to make people sick. Rainwater also cited evidence that the poor feel old at a relatively young age and are therefore more likely than the nonpoor to accept illness and disability as normal. Finally, because the poor are more often treated with contempt or hostility by medical personnel, they may put off visiting doctors and hospitals for treatment. Even with equal access to medical care, these conditions lead to more frequent and more serious illnesses among the poor than among other income groups.[28]

---

[25] Ibid.

[26] U.S. Department of Health and Human Services, *Health: United States, 1984* (Washington, D.C.: U.S. Government Printing Office, December 1984), p. 34.

[27] U.S. Bureau of the Census, *Statistical Abstract of the United States*, Table 146.

[28] Lee Rainwater, *What Money Buys: Inequality and the Social Meaning of Income* (New York: Basic Books, 1974).

DISTRIBUTION OF PHYSICIANS BY REGION, 1985   FIGURE 14-1

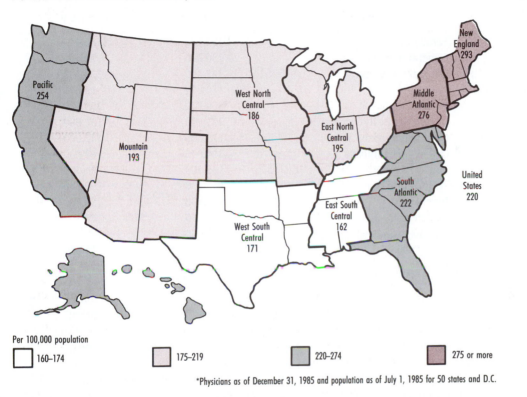

New England
293

Pacific
254

Middle Atlantic
276

West North Central
186

East North Central
195

Mountain
193

East South Central
162

South Atlantic
222

United States
220

West South Central
171

Per 100,000 population

☐ 160–174   ☐ 175–219   ☐ 220–274   ☐ 275 or more

*Physicians as of December 31, 1985 and population as of July 1, 1985 for 50 states and D.C.

SOURCE: American Medical Association, *Physician Characteristics and Distribution in the United States,* 1986; *Statistical Abstract of the United States,* 1989, Table 156.

THE AMERICAN HEALTH-CARE INDUSTRY

In *The Social Transformation of American Medicine* (1982) Paul Starr argues that the great change in medicine occurred when health care became a commodity — to be bought and sold in the marketplace — instead of a family responsibility. This transformation has made health a big business in the United States. Today the health-care industry employs millions of workers and generates billions of dollars in revenue every year. The primary goal of all this activity is not necessarily to provide the best possible medical care for the greatest number of people at the lowest possible cost. One of the goals of drug companies and private hospitals, like other businesses, is to make money. And, from the point of view of profits, the health industry is a very successful enterprise. In 1986 general practitioners earned a median net income (after expenses) of $72,800, and specialists did even better. Obstetricians made nearly $138,000, opthamologists $148,000, and plastic surgeons $180,000 (see Table 14-3). Humana, Inc., a giant chain of for-profit hospitals, spends millions on advertising and market research and uses a hard-sell, brand-name strategy to attract patients. According to its president,

TABLE 14-3   PHYSICIANS' INCOME BY SPECIALITY, 1986*

Speciality	Gross Earnings	Net Earnings
Family physicians	$181,100	$ 86,400
General practitioners	130,000	72,800
General surgeons	227,100	122,400
Internists	180,800	95,600
Neurosurgeons	359,800	203,600
Obstetricians/Gynocologists	271,800	137,800
Ophthalmologists	315,600	148,000
Orthopedic surgeons	354,000	182,600
Pediatricians	168,200	84,300
Plastic surgeons	357,200	180,200
Psychiatrists	127,900	86,700
Radiologists	187,500	147,500
Thoracic surgeons	263,900	156,500
MDs Total:	200,300	112,800

* Office-based physicians' median earnings from practice.

Humana aims to provide as uniform and as reliable a product as McDonald's.[29] Nursing-home chains are also publicly owned and often highly profitable corporations. The drug business, too, has high returns; in fact, the manufacture of drugs is regularly ranked among the top three most profitable industries in the United States.

In every other industrial society health care is a publicly supported social service; only in the United States is it also a private, profit-making business. Much of the high cost and poor distribution of medical services can be traced to the pursuit of private rather than public interests. The American Medical Association (AMA), for example, gives physicians monopoly control over the supply of their services. In the 1930s the AMA applied the classical economic theory of supply and demand: it attempted to hold down the supply of doctors to keep practices large and incomes high. By raising its licensing standards, the AMA was able to limit the number of medical schools and the number of students admitted. During the decade the total number of medical students decreased by 17 percent, and the numbers of blacks, Jews, and women decreased even more sharply. By the early 1960s physicians were in short supply: the United States had fewer doctors per capita than the Soviet Union, Bulgaria, and Argentina.[30]

When private insurance programs, such as Blue Cross and Blue Shield, and government spending on Medicare and Medicaid increased the demand for health services in the late 1960s, the AMA relaxed its restraints on the supply of physicians. More foreign doctors were admitted to practice, and the number of medical school admissions rose dramatically. In 1960 there were 151 physicians per 100,000 people; in 1975 there were 187, and in 1986 there were 246.[31] Contrary to the expectations of the

[29] Gwen Kinkead, "Humana's Hard-Sell Hospitals," *Fortune*, November 17, 1980, pp. 68–81.
[30] A. F. Ehrbar, "A Radical Prescription," *Fortune*, February 1977, p. 169.
[31] U.S. Bureau of the Census, *Statistical Abstract of the United States*, Table 149.

classical market, a larger supply of medical practitioners resulted in higher, not lower, prices; moreover, doctors' incomes rose at a faster rate than those of any other group. Because competitive practices such as advertising are condemned by the AMA as unethical, doctors are by and large able to set their own fees according to how much money they want to make. According to one survey, fees for the most common urological operation, removal of the prostate gland, range from $875 in West Virginia to $2,350 in Orange County, California. In New York, Medicare pays $1,600 for the same operation.[32] Such huge geographical disparities cannot be explained entirely by differences in the cost of living, extra professional expenses, or the quality of care. Most of the difference in fees appears to be personally determined by the physicians themselves.[33]

In addition to controlling the price and supply of their services, doctors have some control over the demand for them. No one can choose whether to be sick or not, and patients have little say about what their treatment will be. They rely on the doctor to decide whether laboratory tests, drugs, hospitalization, and surgery are necessary. Several studies conclude that the number of tonsilectomies and other elective operations increases with the number of surgeons available to do them. For example, an estimated 13 percent of coronary bypass operations — which cost, on average, between $15,000 and $25,000 — have been found to have no lifesaving value.[34] In the preface to his play *The Doctor's Dilemma*, George Bernard Shaw commented on the drawbacks of making health care a business enterprise: "That any nation, having observed that you could provide for the supply of bread by giving bakers a pecuniary interest in

---

[32] Milt Freudenheim, "Doctors' Concern: Fixing Prices and Price Fixing," *The New York Times* (December 18, 1988), p. E7.

[33] Jordan Braverman, *Crisis in Health Care* (Washington, D.C.: Acropolis, 1978), p. 21.

[34] Study by the National Heart, Lung, and Blood Institute, reported in *The New York Times*, November 1, 1983, p. C1, C4.

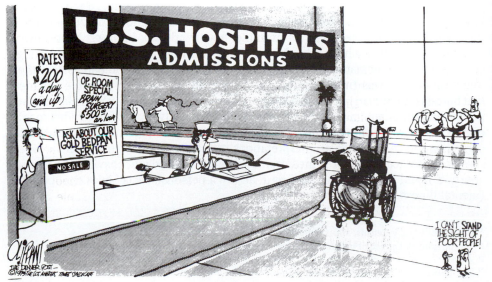

"Old, ill and broke! So, what do you want, trouble-maker?"

Drawing by Oliphant; © 1979 Universal Press Syndicate.

baking for you, should go on to give a surgeon pecuniary interest in cutting off your leg is enough to make one despair."

Although there is no longer a national shortage of doctors, there is a growing regional shortage. More and more doctors are going into practice in urban and suburban areas: 87 percent practice in metropolitan areas, where only 68 percent of the population lives. Another aspect of this maldistribution of medical services is the surplus of hospital beds. While some areas have too few hospitals, others have too many: about 3 out of 10 hospital beds are empty every day.[35] Poor distribution has also resulted in a shortage of doctors in some fields and a surplus in others. Because fewer doctors are engaged in primary care than in specialized practice, there is a national shortage of general practitioners, pediatricians, and internists. Meanwhile, the trend toward specialization has created a surplus of surgeons. Joseph A. Califano, Jr., the former secretary of Health, Education, and Welfare, summed it up: "Doctors, hospitals, pharmaceutical companies . . . act exactly as the incentives motivate them to act: conscious of quality but insensitive to cost. As a result, health care resources are neither well distributed nor efficiently organized."[36]

MENTAL HEALTH

Mental illness is often said to be the number-one health problem in the United States. About 238,000 people are hospitalized in psychiatric facilities on an average day,[37] and an estimated 10 percent of all Americans will be disabled by emotional illness at some point in their lives. Although mental health is clearly an important issue, a great deal of controversy exists about just what mental illness is and whether it is, in fact, an illness at all.

THE SOCIAL CONTEXT OF MENTAL ILLNESS

Laymen and experts alike find mental disorders hard to diagnose. If you saw a man talking to himself on the street, for example, how would you interpret his behavior? Some people might say he was "sick" — or, in psychiatric terms, that he was having a schizophrenic hallucination of carrying on a conversation with someone else. Others might say that he was "nuts" and should be "locked up" — an unfavorable judgment that his behavior was inappropriate and so offensive to others that it should be officially punished. Still others might find that the man was simply lonely and needed to talk, even if no one was listening. These three different interpretations of the same behavior correspond to three different interpretations of mental disorder: that it is an illness similar to physical illness (the medical model); that it is deviant behavior (the labeling approach); and that it is not an illness at all but a personal, social, or ethical problem (mental illness as myth).

---

[35] U.S. Bureau of the Census, *Statistical Abstract of the United States,* Table 158.
[36] "Counterattack Launched by AMA's Dr. Sammons," *American Medical News,* June 27–July 4, 1977, p. 21.
[37] U.S. Bureau of the Census, *Statistical Abstract of the United States,* Table 174.

THE MEDICAL MODEL.   The medical definition of health is a negative one: the absence of symptoms and signs of physiological disturbance and malfunctioning. By analyzing the physical symptoms, physicians are trained to diagnose the disease, eliminate what is causing its symptoms, and thus return the patient to health. Before the era of modern medicine, however, some symptoms and signs were not defined as a medical problem but as a religious or moral one. In medieval Europe hearing voices would have been interpreted not as a symptom of schizophrenia but as a sign of possession by the devil; in nineteenth-century Boston public drunkenness was seen not as a sign of possible alcoholism but as criminal behavior; and until very recently compulsive gambling and drug addiction were not considered symptoms of mental disorder but signs of a weak moral character. Like physical disabilities, mental problems have been medicalized in modern societies. As Leon Kass notes, "All kinds of problems now roll to the doctor's door, from sagging anatomies to suicides, from unwanted childlessness to unwanted pregnancy, from marital difficulties to learning difficulties, from genetic counseling to drug addiction, from laziness to crime." [38]

According to the medical model mental disorders are psychological illnesses that can be diagnosed and treated in individual cases. Anxieties, hostilities, and other kinds of abnormal behavior are viewed as signs of emotional disorders that can be remedied by relieving or removing the underlying conflicts and tensions. By redefining "sinful" and "criminal" behavior as sick behavior, the medical model of mental illness has made possible the humane treatment of the emotionally disturbed. Instead of being imprisoned or burned at the stake, alcoholics and schizophrenics now receive psychological counseling and hospital care. The medical model has also made possible rational, scientific investigation into the causes and treatment of mental disorders. By making "insanity" a medical problem, modern medicine has taken the responsibility for mental disorders out of the hands of preachers and police officers and put it into the hands of trained psychologists and physicians.

The view that mental disorders are types of illness does have some drawbacks, however. Focusing on individual cases, psychiatrists and psychotherapists have tended to overlook the social factors associated with the incidence of emotional problems. Sociologists, on the other hand, are concerned less with individual experiences and more with the link between mental illness and the structure of the larger society.

LABELING THE MENTALLY ILL.   According to Talcott Parson's analysis of the sick role, illness is a form of deviance. In the United States health is the highly valued capacity to fulfill social obligations. Illness, the nonperformance of social roles, is considered deviant behavior. Criminals, who are capable of being law-abiding, role-performing citizens but choose not to be, are held responsible for their deviant acts. But because illness is no one's fault, sick people are not held responsible for deviating from social expectations.

Nevertheless, any deviant behavior can carry a stigmatizing label. The violation of a social convention — such as talking to yourself on the street — may be tolerated as a mild eccentricity or labeled "schizophrenia" or "senile dementia." Many people — perhaps a quarter of the American population — exhibit symptoms of mental illness

---

[38] Leon R. Kass, "Regarding the End of Medicine and the Pursuit of Health," *The Public Interest* 40 (Summer 1975): 11.

LANGNER'S PSYCHIATRIC SCREENING SCORE

Responses marked with an asterisk indicate psychiatric illness, and the screening score is the sum of these responses. A score of 4 or more shows the respondent is psychiatrically im- *paired. The results of this test indicate that about one out of four Americans is troubled by symptoms of serious mental illness.*

Item	Response
1. I feel weak all over much of time	1. Yes* 2. No
2. I have had periods of days, weeks, or months when I couldn't take care of things because I couldn't "get going."	1. Yes* 2. No
3. In general, would you say that most of the time you are in high (very good) spirits, good spirits, low spirits, or very low spirits?	1. High 2. Good 3. Low* 4. Very Low*
4. Every so often I suddenly feel hot all over.	1. Yes* 2. No
5. Have you ever been bothered by your heart beating hard? Would you say: often, sometimes, or never?	1. Often* 2. Sometimes 3. Never
6. Would you say your appetite is poor, fair, good, or too good:	1. Poor* 2. Fair 3. Good 4. Too Good
7. I have periods of such great restlessness that I cannot sit long in a chair (cannot sit still very long).	1. Yes* 2. No
8. Are you the worrying type (a worrier)?	1. Yes* 2. No
9. Have you ever been bothered by shortness of breath when you were *not* exercising or working hard? Would you say: often, sometimes, or never?	1. Often* 2. Sometimes 3. Never
10. Are you ever bothered by nervousness (irritable, fidgety, tense)? Would you say: often, sometimes, or never?	1. Often* 2. Sometimes 3. Never
11. Have you ever had any fainting spells (lost consciousness)? Would you say: never, a few times, or more than a few times?	1. Never 2. A few times 3. More than a few times*

Item	Response
12. Do you ever have any trouble in getting to sleep or staying asleep? Would you say: often, sometimes, or never?	1. Often* 2. Sometimes 3. Never
13. I am bothered by acid (sour) stomach several times a week.	1. Yes* 2. No
14. My memory seems to be all right (good).	1. Yes 2. No*
15. Have you ever been bothered by "cold sweats"? Would you say: often, sometimes, or never?	1. Often* 2. Sometimes 3. Never
16. Do your hands ever tremble enough to bother you? Would you say: often, sometimes, or never?	1. Often* 2. Sometimes 3. Never
17. There seems to be a fullness (clogging) in my head or nose much of the time.	1. Yes* 2. No
18. I have personal worries that get me down physically (make me physically ill).	1. Yes* 2. No
19. Do you feel somewhat apart even among friends (apart, isolated, alone)?	1. Yes* 2. No
20. Nothing ever turns out for me the way I want it to (turns out, happens, comes about, i.e., my wishes aren't fulfilled).	1. Yes* 2. No
21. Are you ever troubled with headaches or pains in the head? Would you say: often, sometimes, or never?	1. Often* 2. Sometimes 3. Never
22. You sometimes can't help wondering if anything is worthwhile anymore.	1. Yes* 2. No

SOURCE: Thomas Langner, "A 22-Item Screening Score of Psychiatric Symptoms Indicating Impairment, *Journal of Health and Social Behavior* 3 (1962): 269–76. Copyright © 1962 by the American Sociological Association.

(see "Langner's Psychiatric Screening Score"). Whether or not these people are considered mentally ill depends on whether society labels them as such. The American Psychological Association recently acknowledged the importance of labeling when it removed homosexuality from its list of psychiatric disorders. (For a full discussion of labeling theory, see Chapter 8, "Deviance and Social Control.")

When family members, friends, or doctors tell a depressed or anxious person that he or she is "mentally ill," they are offering that person a reason to assume the sick role. Thomas Scheff, a labeling theorist, finds that once the sick role is adopted, it is hard to return to "normal," "healthy" roles. Army psychiatrists have reported, for example, that battle fatigue, a neurosis associated with the stresses of combat, often disappears after very superficial medical attention in the field. When soldiers with symptoms of battle fatigue were taken away from their unit and sent to a hospital, however, many of them become chronically impaired. Once they were diagnosed as mentally ill and in need of hospitalization, Scheff concludes, the soldiers' deviance was reinforced by the labeling process.[39]

The sociological perspective shows us that mental illness is a social role as well as a medical problem. Many people at some point in their lives are unable to meet social expectations, but whether they are mentally ill or not is often a matter of someone else's definition. Sociologists are interested in *whose* definition is accepted as authoritative. By casting nonconformists in the sick role and expecting them to "get well," physicians and social workers exert a powerful form of social control. It may be more compassionate to define homosexuals and political radicals as mentally ill rather than criminal, for example, but there is the danger that the medical model will deny some individuals the right to be different.

MENTAL ILLNESS AS MYTH.   Thomas Szasz, a psychiatrist, carries labeling theory one step further. He makes the provocative argument that mental illness is not an illness at all. In *The Myth of Mental Illness* (1974) Szasz suggests that psychiatrists treat moral, not medical, problems. Mental illness, he finds, is actually an unresolved personal, social, or ethical problem in living.

Mental illness is supposed to be a kind of disease, Szasz argues, and psychiatry is a branch of medicine. Yet people rarely think of themselves as "mentally sick" when they are in psychological distress: "A person might feel sad or elated, insignificant or grandiose, suicidal or homicidal, and so forth; he is, however, not likely to categorize himself as mentally ill or insane; that he is, is more likely to be suggested by someone else." Psychiatry is still an efficient method of helping people — "not to recover from an 'illness,' but rather to learn about themselves, others, and life."[40] Since mental illness does not exist, Szasz believes that "psychiatric treatment" must be either a moral effort by patients to change voluntarily or a political effort to change them against their will. The "mentally ill" are either people who consult psychotherapists on their own or people who are confined in mental hospitals by somebody else. Therapy,

---

[39] Thomas J. Scheff, *Being Mentally Ill: A Sociological Theory* (Chicago: Aldine, 1966).

[40] Thomas S. Szasz, M.D., *The Myth of Mental Illness* (New York: Harper and Row/Perennial Library, 1974), pp. xi, xvi.

From the sociological perspective, mental illness is an inability to perform social roles. This mental patient's message reflects an effort to "get well" by meeting others' expectations.

he warns, is thus a means of social control that enforces conformity with medical treatment, by force if necessary.[41]

THE PREVALENCE OF MENTAL ILLNESS

Because mental illness is so difficult to define and diagnose, it is impossible to know the exact state of mental health in American society. The official statistics are based only on the number of treated cases. In spite of the trend toward treating the mentally ill as out-patients, the 1980 Census reported, for example, that there are 11 hospitalized psychiatric patients for every 1000 people in the United States.[42] About half these patients were suffering from schizophrenia, depression, or alcoholism. Because researchers suspect that many psychiatric problems go untreated and do not show up in the official statistics, they have made other attempts to measure the level of mental illness in the general population. The most widely used survey device is Langner's Twenty-Two Item Psychiatric Screening Score (see p. 462). By using this test, the 1975 Midtown Manhattan Study came to the startling conclusion that 23 percent of the population of New York City was impaired by serious psychiatric problems.[43]

The Study's findings have been substantiated by the first published results of a much larger survey conducted by the National Institute of Mental Health.[44] Data from extensive household interviews of 10,000 adults in New Haven, Baltimore, and St. Louis, when projected nationally, indicate that about 19 percent of the adult population have mental disorders severe enough to be treated professionally. A second important

[41] Thomas Szasz, "Justice in the Therapeutic State," *Comprehensive Psychiatry* 11 (1970): 433–44.

[42] U.S. Bureau of the Census, "Persons in Institutions and Other Group Quarters, 1980."

[43] Leo Srole et al., *Mental Health in the Metropolis: The Midtown Manhattan Study*, rev. ed. (New York: Harper and Row, 1975).

[44] Lee N. Robins et al., "Lifetime Prevalence of Specific Psychiatric Disorders in Three Sites," *Archives of General Psychiatry* (October 1984): 949–58.

THE MENTAL STATE OF THE UNION

TABLE 14-4

Mental Disorder	Percentage Afflicted*	
	Male	Female
Substance use		
Alcohol abuse/dependency	28.9	4.3
Drug abuse/dependency	7.4	3.8
Schizophrenia	1.0	1.1
Affective disorders		
Major depression	2.5	8.1
Manic episodes	1.0	1.0
Anxiety disorders		
Phobias	4.0	9.4
Panic	.9	2.0
Obsessive/compulsive	1.1	2.6
Antisocial personality	4.9	1.2
Cognitive impairment	1.0	1.1

* Results from St. Louis in the NIHM study of five metropolitan areas.
SOURCE: Wrynn Smith, *Mental Illness and Substance Abuse* (New York: Facts on File, 1989), Table 2-1.

finding of the NIMH study is that men and women have about the same rates of mental illness, although they tend to have different types. Depression and anxiety are more common among women, while men are more likely to suffer from antisocial personality disorders, alcoholism, and drug abuse (see Table 14-4). Because previous mental health research focused on anxieties, phobias, and depression, women were assumed to be more prone to mental illness. However, the new survey did find that women are twice as likely as men to seek professional help for their problems. For both sexes, the rate of mental illness is about half as high after the age of 45, and people over 65 are emotionally the healthiest.

Although mental illness appears to be widespread, its distribution throughout the population is rather uneven. Because mental illness is often associated with emotional stress, many researchers have tested the proposition that mental disorders are caused by the pressures of modern city life or the deprivations of poverty.

URBAN LIFE.   Many people assume that the stress and strain of modern life are responsible for the high incidence of mental illness in the United States. The "rat race" for success, the impersonality of large urban organizations, and the confusion of rapid social change are all thought to make our psychological environment unhealthy. Compared to the hectic pace of life in modern cities, the traditional rural societies of the past seem to many people to be more relaxed, more comforting, and less emotionally stressful.

One way to test the effect of modern life on mental health is to compare urban and rural rates of mental illness. The Hutterite communities of Montana and the Dakotas were chosen for a rural population sample because they approximated the living conditions of the American past. Ever since they were settled by Anabaptist immigrants

Many people assume that the stress of city life is psychologically unhealthy. Studies have found, however, that the rates of severe mental illness are about the same in rural and urban areas.

from central Europe, these isolated farming communities have strongly resisted the influences of modern life. The Hutterites have no electricity or machinery, and they cling to the customs and dress of a century ago. Their close family ties, shared traditional values, and disapproval of social change provide a stark contrast to modern city life. Nevertheless, Joseph Eaton and Robert Weil's classic study found that the Hutterites have about the same rates of severe mental illness as the residents of the state of New York. The only difference is that the Hutterites prefer to treat the mentally ill at home rather than seek professional treatment in hospitals.[45]

Another way to test the proposition that modern urban society contributes to mental disorders is to look for evidence that contemporary rates of mental illness are higher than they were in the past. A careful study of the number of mentally ill people in jails, alms-houses, and other places of confinement in Massachusetts in the 1840s showed that the rate of serious psychiatric problems was at least as high then as it was in 1950.[46] Even during a century of stressful social change, modern living does not appear to have had any effect on mental health. The available research indicates that mental illness is not a new problem: the major types of mental disorders have been found in every known society, no matter what its way of life.[47]

POVERTY.   A connection between mental illness and deprived living conditions has long been suspected. One of the earliest sociological studies of social class and mental health was conducted by Robert Faris and H. Warren Dunham in 1938. By examining the home addresses of 35,000 hospitalized mental patients in Chicago, the researchers

---

[45] Joseph W. Eaton and Robert J. Weil, *Culture and Mental Disorders* (New York: Free Press, 1955).

[46] Herbert Goldhamer and Andrew Marshall, *Psychosis and Civilization* (New York: Free Press, 1953).

[47] John A. Clausen, "Mental Disorders," in *Contemporary Social Problems*, 4th ed., ed. Robert K. Merton and Robert Nisbet (New York: Harcourt Brace Jovanovich, 1976), p. 120.

found the highest rate of mental illness in the lower-class sections of the inner city, where the population came from varied ethnic backgrounds and moved frequently from place to place. Moreover, the lowest rates of treated mental illness were found at the opposite end of the socioeconomic ladder—in stable residential areas where the population had higher incomes and higher social status.[48]

A later study, by August Hollingshead and Frederick Redlich, found a similar pattern in New Haven for hospitalized patients. For patients receiving treatment in outpatient clinics or from private psychiatrists, however, the reverse was true: the highest rates of treatment outside of hospitals were in the higher social classes.[49] A further confirmation of the higher rate of hospitalization for lower-class patients was made in Washington, D.C., in 1969. By analyzing the class backgrounds of 4650 male patients who were admitted to mental hospitals over a two-year period, William Rushing discovered that the rate of hospitalization for lower-class men was higher than that of all other groups. In fact, the lower the patient's class standing, the more likely he was to be hospitalized. Rushing believed that the lowest class had the highest rate of hospitalization because the poor are more likely to come in contact with judges and social workers who will recommend hospitalization. They are also less likely to have families who can support them while they undergo outpatient treatment.[50]

In the Midtown Manhattan Study, symptoms of serious disorders were found much more frequently in the lowest economic group, where nearly half of those tested were considered impaired, and much less frequently in the highest economic group, where only about one person in eight was rated impaired. An even more interesting finding was that one-fifth of the "impaired" people at upper-income levels received psychiatric treatment, and more than one-half had formerly been treated for mental illness, mostly as outpatients. At lower-income levels, in contrast, only *1 percent* of those rated impaired received psychiatric treatment, and only 20 percent had previously been treated, almost all of them in mental hospitals.[51] At least according to this study, more poor people have symptoms of serious mental illness, but fewer of them ever receive psychiatric treatment.

In sum, there is strong evidence that mental as well as physical illness is found more often among the poor than among the privileged. It also appears that social class deeply affects how and where sick persons are treated, and even whether they receive any treatment at all.

IMPROVING HEALTH

If Americans want better health, and if medicine is not giving it to them, then many people have concluded that the quality of medical care should be improved and the

---

[48] Robert E. L. Faris and H. Warren Dunham, *Mental Disorders in Urban Areas* (Chicago: University of Chicago Press, 1939).

[49] August B. Hollingshead and Frederick C. Redlich, *Social Class and Mental Illness* (New York: Wiley, 1958).

[50] William Rushing, "Two Patterns in the Relationship Between Social Class and Mental Hospitalization," *American Sociological Review* 34 (August 1969): 533–41.

[51] Strole et al., *Mental Health in the Metropolis*, p. 246.

unhealthy aspects of the social environment should be eliminated. This section explores these two possibilities.

CHANGING THE HEALTH-CARE SYSTEM

Nearly everyone agrees that the American health-care system has three major problems: (1) medical care is too expensive, (2) it is unevenly distributed among social groups and geographical areas, and (3) it is not providing the same level of good health that citizens of many other industrialized societies enjoy. Recent efforts to change the existing system, therefore, have concentrated on decreasing costs and increasing access to medical care in order to improve the general level of health. Meanwhile, the high costs of medical services are creating pressures toward a more efficient and orderly means of distributing health care.

According to Starr's analysis, the medical profession's fee-for-service system is being challenged in two ways.[52] First, the federal government is making new efforts to control medical costs by regulating hospital and doctor's fees. Under Medicare's new payment system, adopted by Congress in 1983, hospitals and physicians receive a fixed sum for each type of case instead of a reimbursement based on the total hospitalization costs for each patient. The average stay of Medicare patients has already declined, apparently because hospitals now have a financial incentive to discharge them.

Second, large corporations are now competing with private physicians by offering another source of medical services. Prepaid health plans, called health maintenance organizations (HMOs), provide comprehensive medical care at a lower cost, mainly because their subscribers are not hospitalized as often. Hospital corporations like Humana, Inc., are becoming integrated, full-service companies which provide health insurance plans and walk-in medical services at convenient emergency centers. The growth of corporate, "over-the-counter" medicine has raised questions about the quality and accessibility of this new form of health care. Some critics say that doctors who are employed by profit-making corporations face a conflict of interest when they make decisions about expensive treatments for their patients. Others find that private hospitals and clinics cater to middle-class patients with lucrative, acute problems (broken bones, influenza) that are easily cured, while neglecting poor, uninsured, or elderly patients with chronic, long-term diseases.

Supporters of a national health insurance program believe that a universal, comprehensive health-care plan would improve access to medical care by extending benefits to millions of people who are ineligible for public welfare and cannot afford private insurance. They also expect that better access to medical care would be likely to improve the health of the poor and thus raise the nation's overall health level.

Since the cost of private insurance would be transferred to the federal budget, Congress has so far been reluctant to pass a comprehensive insurance program. Other critics have wondered whether enlarging an ineffective health-care system is really the best way to solve its three major problems. If spending $458 billion a year is not enough to give Americans good health, they doubt that more money and more medicine is the

---

[52] Paul Starr, *The Social Transformation of American Medicine,* Chapter 5.

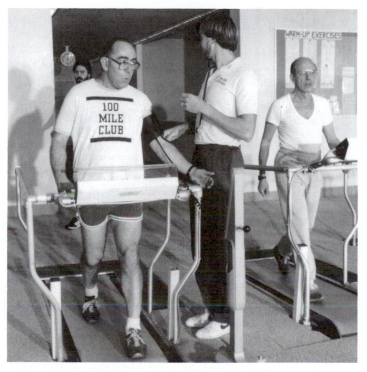

The popularity of exercise programs, natural foods, and diet books indicates that many Americans are attempting to change to a healthier life style.

answer. These misgivings have helped give rise to a new social movement and a different conception of health and health-care services.

THE SOCIAL HEALTH MOVEMENT

As the comparison between States *A* and *B* has clearly shown, the greatest potential for improving health lies with all of us as individuals. Our daily routines of eating and sleeping, our consumption of alcohol and tobacco, the amount of physical exercise we get, and the emotional stress we undergo — all these are far more important to our health and longevity than the number of physicians and hospital beds available. By expecting too much of modern medicine in curing disease, however, we have expected too little of ourselves in preventing it.

In recent years a new social movement has attempted to take the responsibility for health away from the institution of medicine and give it back to other social institutions. The social health movement springs from several different roots. One is the public health bureaucracy, especially the Department of Health and Human Services. In spite of the opposition of the Tobacco Institute and other powerful lobbies, former Secretary Califano succeeded in drawing public attention to the close correlation between smoking and lung cancer. Under his administration government-sponsored advertising campaigns urged people to stop smoking and moderate their drinking habits in order to improve their health.

By increasing public awareness of the social behavior that causes disease, such educational programs have succeeded in getting many people to change to a healthier life style. One indication of the public's interest in health is the number of self-improvement books being sold. Other signs are found in the dramatic increase in health-club memberships and the appearance of salad bars in fast-food restaurants. The middle class in particular has found a new interest — sometimes bordering on obsession — in such vigorous activities as bicycling, running, and aerobic dancing; in more nutritious "natural" foods; and in wine, soda water, and other drinks with lower or no alcoholic content. And, in response to the national concern over cholesterol, Americans now eat far less red meat, fewer eggs, and less saturated animal fat than they did ten years ago.

The social health movement also reflects changing social values. In what appears to be part of a growing rebellion against medical expertise, women's groups are questioning male doctors' decisions to perform mastectomies and hysterectomies. Some women are advocating natural childbirth and reviving the profession of midwifery. The doctor's loss of authority is also reflected in the sharply rising number of malpractice suits and in the new claim that people have a "right to die" rather than be kept alive when they have an acute disability and no hope of recovery.

Finally, advocates of consumerism and environmental protection are also interested in the social causes of disease. While the federal government has legislated industrial antipollution measures and outlawed cigarette advertising on television, a number of private organizations have vigorously advocated pollution-free automobiles and the restriction of smoking in public places.

Having entered a period of diminishing returns from modern medicine, Americans appear to be turning their attention from medical therapy to the social measures that can prevent disease. Faced with the staggering cost of the "sickness care" system, policy makers are beginning to realize that a more effective and less wasteful use of national resources lies in keeping people well instead of taking care of them after they become sick. Knowing that an adequate diet is an important part of health care, for example, government officials would obviously do better to spend money on school lunches and food stamps for the poor rather than on insurance to cover hospitalization for malnutrition and its related diseases. And if the money Americans spent on improving nutrition were equal to the money now spent on cardiac surgery, the United States would almost certainly have healthier citizens with less heart disease requiring drastic surgical treatment. Only by dealing with these social issues will tomorrow's medicine be as effective in preventing disease as yesterday's medicine was in curing it.

SUMMARY

1. Health is defined both as the absence of illness and as a state of physical and emotional well-being. All societies provide for maintaining health and treating illness.

2. Until 150 years ago medicine was practiced almost entirely by members of the patient's family and by self-taught healers. In modern societies the medical institution is given the responsibility for health care. Good health, however, has always depended to a great extent on social environment.

3. The medical model explains illness as a disease with a physical cause. The medical profession has developed very effective therapies for treating individual cases, but doctors can do little to eliminate underlying causes of disease.

4. The social model looks for the causes of illness in the social structure. According to Parsons' analysis of the sick role, illness is a disturbance of the capacity to perform social roles. Unlike others who deviate from social expectations, sick people

are not held responsible for their deviance. They have a legitimate excuse for failing to perform their usual roles, although they are expected to try to get well.

5. The social definition of sickness has been expanded to cover more and more kinds of behavior. The trend toward medicalization in modern societies has reduced the role of other institutions in caring for the sick and disabled.

6. Two social factors—income and education—largely determine what kind of health we have. Because of their relatively unhealthy living conditions, the poor are more likely to become sick, and they have a shorter life expectancy than other income groups.

7. Longer life expectancy is related to a healthy life style. The leading causes of death in the United States—heart disease, cancer, stroke, and lung disease—are correlated with such social factors as diet, cigarette smoking, and stress. A change in social behavior would also reduce the harm done by alcohol and automobile accidents.

8. The cost of health care in the United States has risen enormously in the last twenty years, mainly because of the cost of new medical technology, the growing proportion of medical specialists, the effects of Medicare and Medicaid, and the medi-

calization of minor ailments and psychological problems.

9. Much of the high cost and poor distribution of medical services can be traced to the fact that the American health-care system is a private, profit-making industry.

10. There are three interpretations of mental illness: as a disease that can be treated in individual cases (the medical model); as a form of deviance (the labeling approach); and as a moral problem (mental illness as myth).

11. Mental illness appears to be rather widespread. The rate of mental disorders does not appear to be affected by the stresses of modern life. A larger proportion of poor people have been found to have symptoms of serious mental illness.

12. The high costs of medical services are creating pressures to make the health-care system more efficient. The medical profession's fee-for-service arrangement is being challenged by the federal government's efforts to regulate hospital and doctors' fees and by the growth of corporate medicine.

13. Other suggestions for improving health care emphasize the benefits of a national health-care system. Advocates of the social health movement emphasize preventing disease by changing social behavior.

KEY TERMS

health 439

medicine 439

mortality rate 441

medical model (of illness) 444

social model (of illness) 444

sick role 445

medicalize 446

social health movement 469

SUGGESTED READING

Samuel S. Epstein. *The Politics of Cancer*. San Francisco: Sierra Club, 1978.

* Nicky Hart, *The Sociology of Health and Medicine*. Ormskirk: Causeway, 1985.

* John H. Knowles, ed. *Doing Better and Feeling Worse: Health in the United States*. New York: Norton, 1977.

* Mary A. Mendelson. *Tender Loving Greed*. New York: Vintage, 1976.

D. L. Rosenhan. "On Being Sane in Insane Places," *Science* 179 (1973): 250–59.

* Charles E. Rosenberg. *The Care of Strangers: The Rise of America's Hospital System*. New York: Basic Books, 1989.

* Paul Starr. *The Social Transformation of American Medicine*. New York: Basic Books, 1984.

Margaret Stacey. *The Sociology of Health and Healing: A Textbook*. London: Unwin Hyman, 1988.

Lewis Thomas. *The Youngest Science: Notes of a Medicine Watcher*. New York: Penguin, 1983.

* Available in paperback

Once God is dead, does not everything become permissible?

Feodor Dostoevski

CHAPTER 15

RELIGION

Edgar D. Mitchell, an American astronaut who walked on the moon in 1971, described how the experience affected him:

> When I went to the moon, I was as pragmatic a scientist-engineer as any of my colleagues. I'd spent more than a quarter of a century learning the rational-objective-experimental approach to dealing with the universe. But [during the Apollo 14 mission] . . . I underwent a religiouslike peak experience, in which the presence of divinity became almost palpable, and I knew that life in the universe was not just an accident based on random processes. This knowledge, which came directly, intuitively, was not a matter of discursive reasoning or logical abstraction. It was deduced not from information perceptible by the sensory organs. The realization was subjective, but it was knowledge every bit as real and compelling as the objective data the navigational program or the communications system was based on.[1]

Through the ages men and women have believed in a reality beyond the facts of ordinary human experience. The intuitive knowledge of which Mitchell speaks is usually called religious "faith," because it cannot be verified by empirical observation or experiment. The sociological study of religion deals not with the validity of this "knowledge of the unknowable" but with its social organization and consequences. To

---

[1] Edgar D. Mitchell, "Outer Space to Inner Space: An Astronaut's Odyssey," *Saturday Review,* February 22, 1975, p. 20.

a sociologist, a **religion** is an institution of shared beliefs and practices created by human beings as a response to forces that they cannot understand rationally and that they believe give ultimate meaning to their lives. Such forces are recognized in many ways around the world. Western religions worship a single God, while Eastern religions stress moral values that are in harmony with the guiding principles of the universe.

Religion and the family are probably the oldest of all human institutions. Every known society has had some religious beliefs and activities, and there is strong evidence that these existed even among our Neanderthal ancestors 100,000 years ago. Apparently, people have always felt the need to explain the eternal mysteries of the human condition: Why are we here? Why do we suffer? What happens when we die?

This chapter first defines religion and then shows how the human search for meaning gave rise to the religious institutions that serve both individual needs and larger social purposes. Theories of religion — especially the perspectives of Durkheim, Marx, and Weber — are discussed next. The last two sections assess the place of religion in modern societies such as the United States.

DEFINING RELIGION

Religion is both a source of personal beliefs and a powerful social force. The private side of religion concerns moral values and attitudes which affect the behavior of particular individuals. The decision to have an abortion, for example, is an exceedingly personal choice which can be guided by the religious beliefs of the individuals involved. But religion also has a public, social side. The Biblical commandment "Thou Shalt Not Kill" is a moral principle that has politically demanding implications. Religious beliefs in the sanctity of human life have provided a moral justification for laws against abortion and supported the political activism of the Right-to-Life movement. Finally, religion is a social institution that is made up of numerous churches and community organizations, each with its own special customs, loyalties, and hierarchies. Many of these groups exist to serve such social purposes as educating the young, caring for the sick and elderly, and helping the victims of war and natural disaster.

Emile Durkheim defined religion in a way that draws our attention to both its private and its public aspects:

> A religion is a unified system of beliefs and practices relative to sacred things, . . . which unite into one single moral community called a Church all those who adhere to them.[2]

For Durkheim, concern for the sacred — or what he called "things set apart and forbidden" — is the central feature of religion. The **sacred** is extrahuman and mysterious; it therefore inspires awe and respect. The **profane**, in contrast, is ordinary and understandable and thus attracts no particular attention. The difference between the sacred and the profane lies not in the intrinsic qualities of the object or event but in the

---

[2] Emile Durkheim, *The Elementary Forms of the Religious Life* (New York: Free Press, 1966), p. 62.

way the community defines them. To Catholics a cross is a sacred image and Mecca is just another city; to Moslems a cross is only two pieces of wood but Mecca is a sacred place.

The second feature of religion is the set of beliefs and practices connected with the sacred, the spiritual, and the holy as opposed to the profane, the worldly, and the secular. Religious beliefs are associated with certain symbols. In the Christian sacrament of Holy Communion the bread and wine have symbolic significance as reminders of the martyrdom of Christ; they have no importance at all on the profane level of food and drink. Religions are also characterized by **rituals**, or practices required and acts forbidden. Believers must fast on certain days or pray at certain times. They are also forbidden to do certain things. Orthodox Jews, for example, may not eat pork, and Hindus may not eat beef. Religious beliefs are separate from worldly considerations. It would be sociologically naive, for instance, to suggest to a Hindu that hunger in India could be relieved by butchering the sacred cows or to advise an Orthodox Jew that eating pork chops would be more economical than eating roast beef.

The third feature of religion is the sharing of religious beliefs and activities. An individual's private faith is not a religion until it is held by others as well. Jesus, Buddha, Confucius, and Mohammed could not have founded new religions if they had not been great teachers who persuaded their followers to accept their own beliefs about the nature of ultimate reality. In addition to a common faith that defines human life in relation to the divine purpose, communities of believers also share moral norms and

Religion is a source of moral beliefs which often have powerful political implications.

values defining human relationships in this world. Christians and Moslems, for example, have strict codes of behavior that guide nearly every aspect of their lives, from their roles in the family to their duty to the state.

All religions — primitive and modern, Western and Eastern — are searches for the meaning of human life. All try to understand and harmonize with a spiritual reality, whether it is called The Way or Allah or God. The next section explores why the search for meaning is a universal human effort and what purposes religion serves in society.

THE SEARCH FOR MEANING

Nearly seventy years ago the anthropologist Bronislaw Malinowski was studying the tribal customs of the Trobriand Islanders when he observed a curious phenomenon. Even on the same South Pacific island, different communities carried on significantly different religious activities. For example, one fishing village practiced a great many magical rituals, while another used little magic. Malinowski noted that the second village was situated on a calm lagoon, where the catch was usually large. These villagers apparently felt little need for magical rituals designed to protect the fishermen and provide an abundant food supply. The members of the first village, in contrast, went out into the stormy open sea to fish and often returned empty-handed. These fishermen relied on elaborate magical devices to help them overcome their difficulties. Malinowski concluded that people practice **magic** in order to gain a sense of control over uncertain forces. In a precarious world the Trobriand Islanders' magical rituals allayed their fears. When life was safe and predictable, the islanders had fewer fears and felt less need for magic. As Malinowski observed, whenever human knowledge and skill make an outcome more predictable, there is less use of magic.[3] Such a situation occurs, for example, when modern technology reduces the riskiness of human effort.

Religion, like magic, is a response to situations of uncertainty and danger. The difference between them is that magic aims for immediate results. The purpose of a magical love potion is to win the beloved's heart; the reason for sticking pins in a voodoo doll is to harm the enemy it represents. Magical rituals are likely to appear in situations where the outcome cannot be rationally determined. Baseball players, for example, are as inventive as Trobriand Islanders in developing taboos and fetishes: some play only in lucky uniforms, others avoid certain foods on game days, and many carry good luck charms.[4]

Religious prayers and rituals occasionally seek divine intervention in the here and now, and many have such magical components as visions and miracles. In contrast to magic, however, religions emphasize the ultimate meaning of life's rewards and frustrations rather than the effort to affect them. This search for meaning has both private and public implications.

---

[3] Bronislaw Malinowski, *Magic, Science, and Religion* (New York: Free Press, 1948).
[4] George Gmelch, "Baseball Magic," *Transactions* 8 (June 1971): 39–41, 54.

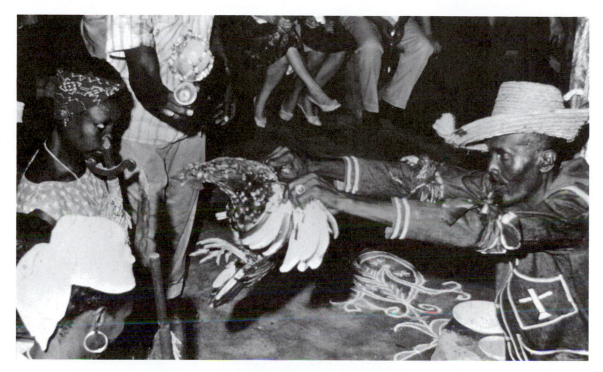

PRIVATE RELIGION

Alexis de Tocqueville, a French political writer who visited the United States in the 1830s, saw religion primarily as an influence on individual character and behavior. He believed that Christianity provided "by universal consent" the stability of a guiding moral force for a new, politically volatile society. While Tocqueville applauded the Constitutional separation of church and state, he nevertheless called Americans' religion "the first of their political institutions." In his view, the political function of religion was to support the mores that made democracy possible. Tocqueville thought that the teachings of Jesus, especially the command to "love thy neighbor," helped curb the pursuit of individual self-interest by emphasizing concern for others. "The main business of religion," Tocqueville wrote, "is to purify, control, and restrain that excessive and exclusive taste for well-being" he found so prevalent among Americans.[5]

In addition to providing a private code of behavior, religion also offers a source of consolation and social support to individuals when they are uncertain and afraid. Because suffering and death are most difficult to explain rationally, much religious activity centers on providing meaning and social support for the individuals concerned. The fears and doubts of the dying person, as well as those of friends and family, are

A Haitian voodoo ceremony invokes magical powers. In contrast to religion, magic seeks immediate results in this world.

---

[5] Alexis de Tocqueville, *Democracy in America,* trans. George Lawrence, ed. J. P. Mayer (New York: Doubleday/Anchor, 1969), p. 292.

An individual's private faith does not become a religion until it is shared by others. The teachings of Buddha eventually became the basis for a great religious institution.

reduced by the religious belief in an afterlife—a belief that is affirmed through such rituals as the last rites of the Catholic Church. By such means religion provides emotional support and reassurance to the dying and the bereaved. Religious ceremonies also mark other critical points in the life cycle, when people are most in need of the comforts of shared beliefs. The universal human experiences of puberty, marriage, and death are celebrated in religious coming-of-age rituals (such as bar mitzvahs), in weddings, and in funerals.

Finally, religion is a means of defining one's own identity. To be a Moslem or a Jew, for example, is to accept certain values and beliefs concerning one's own nature and destiny. Religion thus links us to a distant past and to a promised future, giving us a sense of who we are and where we belong in the greater scheme of human life.[6]

PUBLIC RELIGION

Every society requires a shared set of beliefs and practices to strengthen the bonds among its members. In most societies religion fulfills this function. Religious activities also bring people together to reaffirm the solidarity of the group. A death, for example, threatens the continuity of a community by taking away one of its members. Religious ceremonies surrounding a death are therefore intended to restore equilibrium by celebrating life; this has often been done through ceremonies ranging from feasts to sexual orgies. The traditional Irish wake, with its consumption of great quantities of food and drink, is an affirmation that life goes on and that the community will survive the loss of one of its members.

Religious doctrines also lend spiritual backing to social norms and values. Fair play, honesty, telling the truth under oath, and prohibitions against violence are all part of a moral and legal code that takes its authority from the Bible, the Koran, or other divine sources. Even when people can get away with cheating or dishonesty on a mundane level, they may not do so if they believe that they will be punished by God. This is what the eighteenth-century English historian Edward Gibbon meant when he wrote that the various religions of Rome, in the second century A.D., were all considered "by the people, as equally true; by the philosopher, as equally false; and by the magistrate, as equally useful." [7]

Finally, religion exerts social control by lending legitimacy to other social institutions. The medieval church, for example, endorsed the claims of kings and emperors that they ruled by divine right or by the "grace of God." In Great Britain the Archbishop of Canterbury still confers divine approval symbolically by crowning the king or queen. And in the United States, where there is no official state church, a new president places his hand on the Bible when he swears to uphold the Constitution.

The family is another social institution that is upheld by religion. Religious beliefs tend to guide emotional and sexual life, reproduction, and child care along traditional lines and thus to promote social stability and continuity.

To some observers, the social energies that religion used to release have been dissipated into a vague and passive benevolence. Instead of challenging the assumptions of a self-seeking and materialistic world, religions in modern societies sometimes seem to be in danger of reinforcing that world by becoming merely a source of comfort to its victims.

Yet religion does not always act as a restraining force in society. Religious zeal has spurred many radical social movements, from the medieval Crusades to the Iranian revolution of 1979. In the United States, evangelical Protestantism has spawned an array of political organizations — from the Anti-Saloon League to the Moral Majority — which have had historic political impact. Just what effect religious beliefs have on

---

[6] Thomas F. O'Day, *The Sociology of Religion* (Englewood Cliffs, N.J.: Prentice-Hall, 1966).
[7] Edward Gibbon, *The Decline and Fall of the Roman Empire* (New York: Harcourt Brace Jovanovich, 1960), Chapter 2.

A funeral is a religious ritual that marks a turning point in the life cycle, when people most need the comfort of shared beliefs.

social behavior is usually argued from one of three sociological perspectives: that of Durkheim, Marx, or Weber.

SOCIOLOGICAL APPROACHES TO RELIGION

This chapter has so far emphasized the way private religious beliefs are connected to public life. The unifying functions of religion were identified by Durkheim, who saw religious faith primarily as a means of control over the social order.

SOCIAL COHESION: DURKHEIM

"Religion is an eminently collective thing," Durkheim wrote.[8] The word itself derives from the Latin verb meaning "to bind," and religion to Durkheim was first and foremost

---

[8] Emile Durkheim, *The Elementary Forms of Religious Life* (New York: Free Press, 1954), p. 47.

a binding force. By making such social ideals as brotherly love and loyalty to king and country into sacred duties, religion gives individuals a sense of moral obligation to uphold the community's norms and values. Religious rituals act out and reinforce a group's shared ideas of its character and destiny. In committing themselves to a religious doctrine, the faithful are actually committing themselves to the rules of their society. This view is the rationale for Durkheim's famous statement that religion is society worshiping itself.

American sociologists who have applied Durkheim's theory to their own society agree that religious beliefs do reinforce loyalty to secular authority. W. Lloyd Warner has asserted, for example, that Memorial Day ceremonies have religious functions. In prayers and speeches praising the patriotic sacrifices of the war dead, Americans are reaffirming the collective commitment of the living to the "American way of life." Thanksgiving and the Fourth of July are other occasions when religious and social values converge in national rituals of feasting and parading.[9]

Robert Bellah went one step further by suggesting that the United States has a "civil religion" of beliefs and rituals sanctifying the American way of life.[10] The pledge of allegiance to the flag declares that the United States is one nation "under God," coins and dollar bills proclaim "In God we trust," and American politicians and some court-room witnesses swear to uphold their oath, "so help me God." The American civil religion reveres its patriotic symbols (the eagle, the flag), hymns ("America the Beautiful," "The Star-Spangled Banner"), and saints (the founding fathers, the mar-tyred President Abraham Lincoln).

In the civil religion, according to Bellah, the American Way is favored by God and must be defended against the forces of evil. President Ronald Reagan, for example, urged Americans in a 1983 speech to struggle relentlessly against those who have no "respect for the rule of law under God." America's "crusade for freedom" is sanctioned by the Bible, he said, and "those who live in totalitarian darkness," who do not have "the joy of knowing God, . . . are the focus of evil in the modern world." [11] The notion that Americans are the "chosen ones," charged with a divine mission to redeem the world, has deeply influenced the national culture. On the political right, this sense of mission has justified the country's involvement in Vietnam and Nicaragua; on the political left, it has inspired abolitionism, pacifism, and the civil rights movement.

In a pluralistic society with many different religious traditions the civil religion offers a unifying faith in democracy and the American Way. Its overlapping religious and secular values have brought the United States close to Durkheim's "society wor-shiping itself."

CLASS DOMINATION: MARX

Durkheim saw that religion cements society together, but Marx saw that religion also reinforces the divisions of power and privilege. In Marx's view the principal effect of religion on society is to support the interests of the rich and powerful. Religious beliefs

---

[9] W. Lloyd Warner, *The Family of God* (New Haven, Conn.: Yale University Press, 1961).

[10] Robert N. Bellah, *Beyond Belief* (New York: Harper & Row, 1970).

[11] Quoted in the *Los Angeles Times*, June 21, 1983, Part II, p. 9.

In a society with many different religious traditions, the civil religion offers a unifying faith in democracy and the American way of life. The Vietnam War memorial in Washington, D.C., serves such a religious purpose by celebrating martyrs who died in a patriotic cause.

help distract attention from inequality and injustice in this world by centering attention on the next. Furthermore, Marx found, the consolations of religion contribute to the exploitation of the poor by keeping them resigned to their fate. Class domination is legitimized by religious doctrines teaching that "servants should obey their masters," that "the meek shall inherit the earth," and that humility and submissiveness are virtues. Religion, Marx wrote, is the "opium of the people" — a painkiller that dulls the workers' awareness of their misery and oppression.

In Marx's time many religious doctrines supported the existing economic system. Protestant preachers, for example, justified nineteenth-century capitalism, praising the rich for their success and extolling the virtues of thrift, sobriety, and hard work to the poor. In his classic study of late-nineteenth-century textile mills in North Carolina, Liston Pope showed how the owners and managers went to great pains to support the local churches. The owners' aim was not so much to ensure workers' salvation as to prevent their organizing into unions or otherwise protesting their working conditions.[12]

There are numerous examples of religious beliefs protecting the interests of the ruling class, but the most extreme example is probably the Indian caste system. Since Hindus who fail to perform their caste obligations believe they will be reborn as members of a less privileged caste, the devout are hardly likely to protest their station in life. The persistence of the system over thousands of years makes a strong case for the effectiveness of religious beliefs in preventing social change.

---

[12] Liston Pope, *Millhands and Preachers* (New Haven, Conn.: Yale University Press, 1942), Chapter 2.

In Christian countries the Biblical story of Adam and Eve has been used for centuries to justify male domination. People who believe that the first woman was created out of a man's rib to be his companion, and that she tempted him into the original sin, have often thought they had divine proof that women were physically and morally inferior to men. Clearly, the people at the top of the social ladder have found certain religious beliefs comforting when they justified their own privileged status.

SOCIAL CHANGE: WEBER

Max Weber refused to regard religious ideas as merely reflections of economic interests or as the means of promoting solidarity and stifling dissent. In reply to Marx and Durkheim, Weber proposed that the primary function of religion is to give meaning to human existence. In order to explain the purpose of human life, religions create a world view, or definition of reality. The Christian world view, for example, divides reality into three layers: human life on earth lies between heaven above and hell below. For Christians their behavior on earth determines whether they will spend eternity in the bliss of heaven or in the torments of hell.

The influence of such a world view extends beyond purely religious matters because it affects the way men and women live (see "Islam in World Politics"). A society's norms of conduct — its "design for living" — are adapted to what its members believe the ultimate reality to be. Americans, for example, assume that wanting to get ahead in life is human nature, not realizing that this secular concern is influenced by the Christian striving for heavenly rewards. Hindus are unlikely to make the same assumption; in their religious world view reality is an endless chain of being in which human desires are insignificant.

In his famous work, *The Protestant Ethic and the Spirit of Capitalism*, Weber argued that religious ideas influenced the emergence of capitalism in seventeenth-century Europe (see Chapter 12, "The Economy"). While Catholics traditionally were hostile to business and worldliness, early Protestants regarded hard work as a virtue and sought material success as evidence of divine favor. Protestants, especially Calvinists, valued both hard work and personal frugality in spending the money they earned — an ethic that was tailor-made for the growth of investment capital.

Regarding the influence of religion on society, Weber believed that it worked both ways. He contended that intellectual, psychological, political, and religious forces are separate but influence each other. While he did not believe that ideas are simply tools serving material interests, Weber did see an "elective affinity" between the religious beliefs of Protestant reformers and the economic concerns of European businessmen. The same affinity existed between ancient Greek warriors and their powerful, passionate gods who fought among themselves and could be bribed with sacrificial offerings. In traditional China peasants had an affinity with magic and nature worship, while Mandarin scholars found Confucian ideas of order and tranquility more congenial.

Far from shoring up the status quo, religion has often proved to be the ideology of the oppressed. While it can support social harmony, it can also justify social conflict. Christian beliefs were a major force behind the movement to abolish slavery in the United States; a century later the religious belief in the sanctity of the individual helped bind together the black civil rights movement and legitimate civil disobedience to

ISLAM IN WORLD POLITICS

Recent events have made clear the extraordinary force Islam exerts in world politics. Fundamentalist Muslims now control the governments of Pakistan and Iran; Islamic law guides the national policies of Libya and Saudi Arabia; and religious differences fuel conflicts between Armenians and Azerbaijanis, Arabs and Israelis, Pakistanis and Indians, Iraqis and Iranians, and Turks and Bulgarians. As Daniel Pipes, a Lecturer in History at Harvard University, argues here, Muslim beliefs are such a powerful political force because Islam — alone of all the major religions — prescribes specific laws of behavior in politics, war, economics, and justice. To the extent that Muslims have lived according to these sacred laws, Islam has had a direct influence over political life.

Approaching Islam in politics with the Christian experience in mind is misleading. Because the community of Christians shares almost no political traits, there is a mistaken predisposition to assume that Muslims also do not.

• • •

The answer is that Islam, unlike Christianity, contains a complete program for ordering society. Whereas Christianity provides grand moral instructions but leaves practical details to the discretion of each community, Islam specifies exact goals for all Muslims to follow as well as the rules by which to enforce them. If Christians eager to act on behalf of their faith have no script for political action, Muslims have one so detailed, so nuanced, it requires a lifetime of study to master. Along with faith in Allah comes a sacred law to guide Muslims in all times and places. That law, called the Shari'a, establishes the context for Islam as a political force. However diverse Muslim public life may be, it always takes place in the framework of Shar'i ideals. Adjusting realities to the Shari'a is the key to Islam's role in human relations. . . . [S]acred law [is] the motor force of Islam in politics.

• • •

There are other sources of confusion between religion as a personal faith and as a factor in social relations. . . . Islam [is] a source of laws, affiliations, customs, attitudes, and traditions, . . .

[which] influence . . . behavior in the public sphere. . . . [T]he faith of the individual Muslim . . . usually has little direct bearing on matters of power. Private feelings need not be related to political actions.

Examples may help to demonstrate this point. Muhammad Ali Jinnah, the founder of Pakistan, and most of his strongest supporters were Western-educated and not notably pious Muslims, yet it was they who fought to establish a state defined along religious lines. In contrast, the Islamic leaders opposed the creation of Pakistan and preferred to remain citizens of India. (This parallels the Israeli case: Zionism appealed mostly to assimilated Jews.) By all accounts, Muhammad Anwar el-Sadat was a pious man, yet he strenuously resisted the efforts of Islamic fundamentalists in Egypt, he made the country's family law more European, and he was assassinated by Islamic extremists. In contrast, some of the leaders of the Iranian Revolution, notably Abolhassan Bani-Sadr, were suspected of indifference to the Almighty; this did not prevent them, however, from taking an active part in the most rigorous re-assertion of political Islam in the twentieth century. Throughout the 1970s, as Mu'ammar al-Qadhdhafi developed his own ideology and moved further away from Islam, he placed increased emphasis on Islam as a political bond and identity. In secularizing societies, the notion of a "non-believing Muslim" is widespread; in the Soviet Union, for example, Communists of Muslim origin routinely avow that while they are atheists, they are also Muslims and proud to be so. Perhaps the sharpest distinction comes from Lebanon: a driver, the story goes, was stopped at a checkpoint sometime during the civil war and asked to tell his religion. "Atheist," came the answer. But in the midst of a war fought along religious lines, the guard needed to know the driver's confessional affiliation, not his personal beliefs, so he asked, "Are you a Christian atheist or a Muslim atheist?"

SOURCE: Daniel Pipes, *In the Path of God: Islam and Political Power* (New York: Basic Books, 1983), pp. 10–13.

segregation laws. In Poland, the Catholic Church supported the Solidarity movement's attempts to win concessions from the Soviet-sponsored military regime; in Latin America, Catholic priests preach liberation theology, a radical mixture of Marxist and Christian doctrines calling for political and economic reform.

Again and again, at crucial points in history, religious fervor has proved to be a revolutionary force for good and ill. Although religious differences were not the only reasons for the Moslem Turks' massacre of the Christian Armenians in the 1890s, or for the Indian civil war between Moslems and Hindus in 1948, they certainly contributed to their ferocity. Because religion can confer divine approval on human effort, legitimizing almost any atrocity against the enemies of God, religious wars have been among the most terrible in history.

Religion, then, can justify both keeping the status quo and changing it. We turn now to the question of why some religious groups support the social order while others stand in opposition to it.

THE CHOICE OF FAITH

Religions tend to have a developmental pattern: when newly founded, they stress personal consolation, salvation, and rejection of worldly values. New religions often appeal to the oppressed and underprivileged. As they develop, however, they are more likely to support the values of their society and therefore to appeal to privileged classes with a larger stake in the social order.

Freedom marchers pray beside an Alabama roadside before demonstrating against discriminatory voting laws in 1965. The civil rights movement was sustained by Christian beliefs, particularly Biblical accounts of the struggles of the oppressed.

Ernst Troeltsch distinguished between two different types of Christian religious organization: the sect and the church.[13] The church, in Troeltsch's formulation, is a large organization with a formal structure, an official priesthood, an elaborate theology, and a broad membership of people who were born into it. Because the church is large, it tends to acquire social and political power. To maintain this power, it frequently allies itself with the government and the leading economic interests. The church's religious beliefs harmonize with the values and the institutions of its society and tend to support the status quo. The Church of England and the Catholic Church in South American countries are examples of this.

The sect, in contrast, is a smaller, more loosely organized group of individual believers. An informal priesthood or the members themselves provide leadership. Sects focus on the purity of their members; they are overtly opposed to many of the values and institutions of their societies; and they often represent the interests of the lower classes. Christianity, for example, began as a sect of Jews who believed in the divinity of Jesus. The largest Protestant denominations today have sectarian origins.

The most important distinction between a church and a sect, according to the sociologist Benton Johnson, is the amount of tension that exists between the group and the larger society. A church accepts its social environment, while a sect rejects it.[14]

THE DEVELOPMENT OF RELIGIOUS INSTITUTIONS

Expanding upon Troeltsch's concept, the theologian Reinhold Niebuhr and the sociologist Liston Pope both found that sects become churches through an evolutionary process. In their view, the development of religious institutions proceeds through five stages: from cults and sects to denominations, churches, and ecclesia.[15]

CULTS.   Cults are loosely organized groups whose beliefs and practices are strongly mystical and magical. Their leader usually claims to receive divine revelations and possesses great charisma (personal magnetism or leadership of a mystical sort). This self-appointed leader may predict a cataclysm or a marvelous deliverance; in such cases the cult is said to be *millenarian*. Cults are distinguished by the personal ties of their members to a guru or a group rather than to an institution or a theology.

Cults spring up outside the confines of established religions. Although they may be imported from a culture in which they are highly regarded, they are viewed as unorthodox in their own society.[16] The Hare Krishna movement and the Reverend Sun Myung Moon's Unification Church are two examples of religious cults in the United States.

SECTS.   Most sects originate as groups of reformers who break away in protest from existing churches. Sects are still rather loosely structured, intimate, and informal; their leaders are sometimes self-appointed, but most congregations choose their own preachers.

---

[13] Ernst Troeltsch, *The Social Teaching of the Christian Churches* (1912) (New York: Macmillan, 1931).

[14] Benton Johnson, "On Church and Sect," *American Sociological Review* 28 (1963): 539–49.

[15] H. Reinhold Niebuhr, *The Social Sources of Denominationalism* (New York: Holt, 1929); Liston Pope, *Millhands and Preachers.*

[16] Rodney Stark and William Sims Bainbridge, "Of Churches, Sects, and Cults: Preliminary Concepts for a Theory of Religious Movements," *Journal for the Scientific Study of Religion* 18:2 (1978): 117–33.

Sects are opposed to many of the values of their society, and some are openly rebellious. Seventh Day Adventists and Jehovah's Witnesses, for instance, strongly resist public education and public health laws. The authorities have occasionally viewed certain sects as a threat to social order and sought to exterminate them. Such was the Roman treatment of the Christians and, later, the Christian treatment of the English Quakers and American Mormons.

DENOMINATIONS.   Given time, most sects will change. If they attract members and grow, they generate offices, titles, and a national organization. Beliefs, taught and repeated, become more sophisticated and less emotional. Through repetition the spontaneous behavior of worshipers and their leaders turns into fixed ritual. Religious leaders are trained for their work, so that they act more like priests than prophets; they lose charisma but gain authority through official standing.

The process of institutionalization also causes a shift in membership. Subsequent generations, who have grown up in the faith instead of being converted to it, have a less intense, less self-sacrificing attitude toward their sect.

If sects do not die out or rejoin the parent church, they will develop into **denominations**. These range from the emotional and fundamentalist (Church of Christ, Baptists), which maintain a strong appeal for the working class, to the more formal and rationalist (Unitarians, Congregationalists), which appeal mainly to the middle class.

CHURCHES.   Churches are generally larger than denominations and more accepting of the existing social order. They have a bureaucratic structure and a hierarchical priesthood, a fixed ritual, and a complex, abstract theology. The Lutheran Church and the

Episcopal Church are two examples. They appeal even more strongly to upper- and middle-class people than denominations do.

ECCLESIA.   The largest form of religious organization, the **ecclesia**, is also the most completely identified with other social institutions. As the sociologist Howard Becker has summed up this type, "The fully developed ecclesia attempts to amalgamate itself with the state and the dominant classes, and strives to exercise control over every person in the population." [17] Examples of ecclesiae are the Roman Catholic Church in Italy and the Islamic mosques in Iran.

The movement from "hot" to "cold" religious expression is not necessarily the natural progression of every faith. Nor is any denomination or church in the United States likely to become an ecclesia; the constitutional separation of church and state makes an official religion impossible. Some sects and some denominations remain relatively stable and do not change further. In others the tendency toward institutionalization and conservatism is reversed by innovation from within.

RELIGIOUS PREFERENCE IN THE UNITED STATES

Instead of a state church the United States has long had a profusion of organized religious groups, professing a wide variety of faiths. Many groups represent only a few hundred or a few thousand members. But nearly ninety groups report memberships of over 50,000 each, and twenty-two of these report memberships of over a million. Some are centralized organizations, while others are loose federations of autonomous congregations.

Given this array of possibilities, Americans do not choose their church at random. This fact becomes clear when we break down the membership of each group according to such sociological variables as education, occupation, and income (see Table 15-1). Only one out of ten Baptists finish college, for example, but one out of three Episcopalians do. More than one out of three Jews earn more than $40,000 a year, but fewer than one in five Catholics earn as much. About one out of five Presbyterians, but half of all Baptists, are Democrats. How do people get sorted out in this fashion? As a general principle it appears that relatively new, informal, and evangelical religions appeal to the poor and deprived, while relatively older, highly organized, and conservative churches appeal to people with high social and economic standing. People are also likely to change from one type of religion to the other as they move up the social ladder.[18]

Hervé Varenne analyzed the social patterns of religious preference in "Appleton," a small town in southern Wisconsin. Local residents were quite aware of the cultural style of each congregation, and they tended to rank churches according to the social class of their members. Varenne found that the small fundamentalist sects appealed to the poorest townspeople and that members of the Catholic church had the most varied

---

[17] Howard Becker, *Systemic Sociology* (New York: Wiley, 1932), p. 624.
[18] Galen L. Gockel, "Income and Religious Affiliation: A Regression Analysis," *American Journal of Sociology* 74 (1969): 632–46.

class backgrounds. While the Protestant congregations were actually quite diverse, a rather small group of members gave each a distinctive social character:

> As perceived by many people in Appleton, the Presbyterian church, for example, was supposed to be "intellectual" and "sophisticated"; the Methodist was the church both of older, established small farmers and younger, "up-and-coming" businessmen in the town. Indeed, the Presbyterian church appealed mainly to professionals and high-level civil servants, the Methodist to merchants. The school board was dominated by Presbyterians, the town council by Methodists. There was clearly a feeling of competition between these two churches, the most important ones in Appleton. For the time being, the advantage appeared to lie with the Presbyterian church for the top spot in the ranking system.[19]

The most fundamental choice the individual can make is whether or not to go to church at all—and here there is a clear-cut relationship between social class and religious behavior: middle- and upper-class people attend church more regularly than the lower class. Not only has this finding been widely reported both in Europe and the United States, but it holds true within each faith: while Catholics go to church more regularly than Protestants, middle-class Catholics go to church more regularly than working-class Catholics.[20]

Church attendance, however, is probably not a measure of belief so much as a measure of commitment to the social order. The business or professional person may be more comfortable in church, and find it more important to be seen there every week, than the clerk or factory worker. According to the available evidence members of the working class pray more often, believe more literally and unquestioningly, and have stronger religious feelings than members of other groups.[21]

THE PROTESTANT ETHIC AND SOCIAL CLASS

Social class appears to play a part in religious behavior, but it has been argued that the opposite is true: that people's religion influences their economic behavior and hence their class position. Following Weber's lead, sociologists have investigated whether Protestantism and its work ethic could affect economic and social standing.

Weber's thesis was convincing for the period of emergent capitalism and seems to apply even in the present. Surveys and polls since the 1940s have shown American Protestants ranking well above American Catholics in average income, occupational level, and education.[22] Table 15-1 shows how things stood in 1986. These data do not show that lower-income people "choose" Catholicism, for Catholics are usually born into their religion; rather, they have been interpreted to show that Catholicism interferes with worldly success.

---

[19] Hervé Varenne, *Americans Together: Structural Diversity in a Midwestern Town* (New York: Teachers College Press, 1977), pp. 99–100.

[20] H. Paul Chalfant, R. E. Beckley, and L. E. Palmer, *Religion in Contemporary Society* (Palo Alto, Calif.: Mayfield, 1981).

[21] N. J. Demerath III, *Social Class in American Protestantism* (Chicago: Rand McNally, 1965), pp. 20–25.

[22] Norval D. Glenn and Ruth Hyland, "Religious Preference and Worldly Success," *American Sociological Review* 32 (1967): 73–75.

TABLE 15-1   **PROFILES OF MAJOR FAITHS***

	Roman Catholic	All Baptists	Methodist
	100%	*100%*	*100%*
Sex			
Men	49	48	46
Women	51	52	54
Age			
18–29 years	31	25	21
18–24 years	19	13	12
25–29 years	12	12	9
30–49 years	37	37	31
Total 50 and older	32	38	48
50–64 years	18	21	23
65 and older	14	17	25
Race			
Whites	96	70	91
Blacks	3	29	8
Hispanics	17	1	1
Education			
College graduates	16	10	21
College incomplete	26	18	26
High school graduates	37	35	33
Not high-school graduates	21	37	20
Politics			
Republicans	25	27	38
Democrats	42	50	34
Independents	29	21	27
Income			
$40,000 and over	18	11	18
$25,000–$39,999	26	19	23
$15,000–$24,999	21	22	23
Under $15,000	29	44	30

* Results compiled from a poll taken nationally in 1986.
† Less than one percent.
SOURCE: "Religion in America," *The Gallup Report* 259 (April 1987), pp. 24–25.

In twentieth-century America, however, several factors besides religious attitudes toward work help explain the differences between Protestant and Catholic incomes. Catholics were, by and large, late-arriving immigrants and therefore had to start more recently at the lower levels of employment. These lower-class Catholic immigrants apparently did not teach their children to strive for success as persistently as middle-class Protestant parents did, but this probably resulted more from class attitudes than religious ones. Finally, Catholics tended until recently to have more children, and large families reduce children's chances of having a higher education — the most important

Lutheran	Presbyterian	Episcopalian	Jewish	Other	None
100%	*100%*	*100%*	*100%*	*100%*	*100%*
47	43	49	54	46	60
53	57	51	46	54	40
17	19	19	24	32	42
7	11	12	12	20	25
10	8	7	12	12	17
36	33	40	42	41	42
46	48	41	34	27	16
24	19	18	17	19	9
22	29	23	17	8	7
100	96	92	100	83	86
†	1	4	†	3	11
1	2	4	†	4	6
19	34	34	44	22	21
27	26	35	25	27	28
33	30	22	27	35	28
21	10	9	4	16	22
43	53	44	18	32	26
29	22	26	34	34	31
26	22	29	29	29	37
20	30	31	34	19	18
26	26	20	13	26	22
24	11	20	15	20	21
27	30	20	22	33	34

single factor in upward mobility. In sum, the Protestant ethic seems to have been at best a minor factor in the class differences between American Protestants and Catholics.

RELIGION IN AMERICAN SOCIETY

Many observers have argued that modern life tends to undermine the authority of religious beliefs. Skepticism, materialism, an emphasis on applying rational means to utilitarian ends — these are the intellectual aspects of modern industrial society. Some philosophers have even announced the death of God, calling the late twentieth century a "post-Christian" era in which psychology is replacing religious views of human nature and space-age technology is well on the way to solving all the mysteries of the universe.

In view of the universality and importance of religion in all previous human history, the weakening or denial of religious experience is bound to have cataclysmic effects. Peter Berger finds that the decline of religious authority not only makes human beings more alone in the world, it also makes modern institutions and societies "alone" in the sense of losing the legitimacy provided by sacred symbols and values.[23] Because people find it difficult to be alone in the cosmos either as individuals or as collectivities, he argues, sacredness has been transferred from the supernatural to the profane. Soviet communism, for example, has its saints in Marx and Lenin, its scriptures in the works of Marx, its ritual May Day celebration, and so on. Communism has been called a secular religion because it offers a rational explanation for human history and gives its followers a faith in an ultimate reality — the classless society of the future.

Berger goes on to say that modernization also produces a second kind of result, namely, the resurgence of religious symbolism. For example, Iran and other parts of the Moslem world have lately been the scene of violent reactions against secular values and a strong reaffirmation of the authority of Islam. In American society both the established denominations and the "new" religions, particularly evangelical Christianity, have responded in their own ways to the modern situation.

TRADITIONAL RELIGIONS

By any measure, the United States is one of the most religious societies in the world. Researchers studying such variables as church attendance, professed faith, importance of religion in one's life, and frequency of prayer and devotion all report the same finding: American society attaches greater importance to religion than any other major nation except India and major Islamic nations.[24]

Modern life does not appear to have weakened Americans' religious commitment. A large proportion of Americans continue to go to church regularly: in 1940, 37 percent of American adults said they had attended a church or synagogue in the past week; in 1958 the comparable figure was 49 percent, and in 1972 and 1985 it was 40 percent.[25] Researchers have consistently reported that three-quarters of Americans pray at least once a day and that more than 90 percent say they believe in God.[26] According to the latest survey, 55 percent of American adults say that religion is "very important" in their lives, and another 30 percent say it is "fairly important."[27] Moreover, the percentage of Americans who agree that "religion is increasing its influence on American life"

---

[23] Peter L. Berger, *The Heretical Imperative* (Garden City, N.Y.: Doubleday/Anchor, 1979), p. 55.

[24] "Religion in America, 50 Years: 1935–1985," *The Gallup Report* 236 (May 1985).

[25] Ibid., p. 42.

[26] Kenneth A. Briggs, "Religious Feeling Seen Strong in U.S.," *The New York Times*, December 9, 1984, p. 30.

[27] "Religion in America," *The Gallup Report* 259 (April 1987), p. 16.

INFLUENCE OF RELIGION ON AMERICAN LIFE   FIGURE 15-1

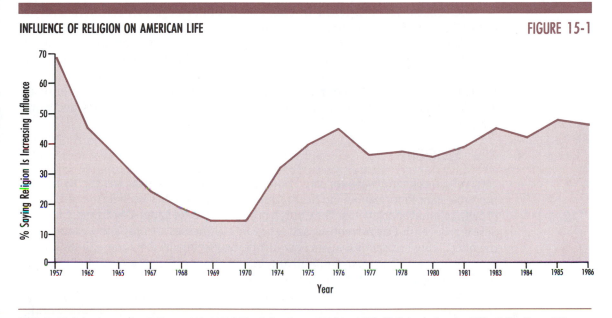

SOURCE: "Religion in America, 50 Years: 1935–1985," *The Gallup Report* 236 (May 1985); "Religion in America," *The Gallup Report* 259 (April 1987).

is at its highest level in three decades, reaching a peak of 48 percent in 1985 (see Figure 15-1).

Whether religion is actually gaining or losing importance is a debatable issue, however. One national survey found that "religion is rapidly becoming a more powerful factor in American life" and that the impact of religious values is being felt in virtually every political and social institution.[28] On the other hand, the Gallup Report's review of American religious life since 1935 concluded that the impact of religion has been remarkably stable. Over the past 50 years, the polls found, the basic religious beliefs and practices of Americans have actually changed very little.[29]

Although the available evidence does not indicate any dramatic change, Americans do seem to be finding new ways to express their religious beliefs. Within the established churches there has been a declining emphasis on miracles and a continuing shift toward a more "liberal" interpretation of the Bible and other dogma. In 1976 only 31 percent of all Catholics in one survey believed that the Bible should be taken as a literal description of actual events.[30] Americans also appear to be turning away from the teachings of organized religion and defining their faith according to their own individual search for meaning.

[28] *The Connecticut Mutual Life Report on American Values in the '80s* (Hartford, Conn.: Connecticut Mutual Life Insurance Co., 1981), p. 6.
[29] *The Gallup Report*, p. 5.
[30] Chalfant, Beckley, and Palmer, *Religion in Contemporary Society*, p. 455.

Sociologists have also noted the emphasis in Christian ethics has shifted from the ideal of personal holiness to a concern for social justice.[31] In 1984, for example, a committee of American Catholic bishops proposed sweeping economic changes to help the poor, including reform of the welfare system, reduction of unemployment, and lower levels of military spending. Moreover, the social movements of the 1960s and 1970s were partly a revival of religious feelings about such social issues as ecology, international peace, opposition to nuclear weapons, the rights of minorities, and world hunger.

NEW RELIGIONS

New religions have always appeared from time to time in American society. Ever since the Protestant Reformation, the North American continent has been fertile soil for the growth of unorthodox faiths. The Church of Jesus Christ of Latter-Day Saints, Christian Science, Seventh-Day Adventists, and Jehovah's Witnesses are only a few examples of the once "new" religions that are now firmly institutionalized.[32] Although the United States has always had many innovative religious groups, it does appear that there are more new cults and sects today than ever before.

Some scholars have explained the growth of "fringe religions" as a response to feelings of anxiety and powerlessness in an increasingly rational and scientific world.[33] Robert Bellah argues, for example, that the traditional denominations are failing to provide spiritual guidance or a "national sense of ethical purpose." [34] Far from being marginal members of society, however, the dropouts from conventional religions are usually highly educated young people from affluent, middle-class families.[35] Dissatisfaction with the mainline churches may well be part of the widespread alienation from traditional institutions in the post-Vietnam, post-Watergate era.

New religious movements have also swept the established churches. Self-styled conservative or liberal groups helped to organize the antiabortion right-to-life movement and the feminist women-church movement. These activist groups are not trying to establish separate religions, but to express the interests of their constituencies, as in the case of the Fellowship of Christian Athletes, or to provide the basis for political action, as in the case of the Moral Majority. According to Robert Wuthnow, this diversity within institutionalized religion is a way for individuals to maintain their religious commitment in an overwhelmingly complex society.[36]

Despite all the ferment, few Americans are turning away from religion entirely. Levels of church membership and church attendance have remained remarkably stable

---

[31] Ibid., p. 451.

[32] Patrick H. McNamara, ed., *Religion: North American Style* (Belmont, Calif.: Wadsworth, 1984).

[33] Anson D. Shupe, Jr., *Six Perspectives on New Religions: A Case Study Approach* (New York: Edwin Mellen Press, 1981).

[34] Robert Bellah, "Religion and Legitimation in the American Republic," in *In Gods We Trust,* ed. by Thomas Robbins and Dick Anthony (New Brunswick: Transaction Books, 1981).

[35] James D. Hunter, *American Evangelicalism: Conservative Religion and the Quandry of Modernity* (New Brunswick: Rutgers University Press, 1984).

[36] Robert Wuthnow, *The Restructuring of American Religion: Society and Faith Since World War II* (Princeton, NJ: Princeton University Press, 1988).

SHIFT IN MEMBERSHIP FROM MAINLINE TO EVANGELICAL RELIGIONS   TABLE 15-2

Evangelical Churches	1973	1983	Change
Southern Baptist Convention	12,295,400	14,185,454	Up 15%
Church of Jesus Christ of Latter-Day Saints	2,569,000	3,593,000	Up 40%
Assemblies of God	1,099,606	1,879,000	Up 71%
Seventh-Day Adventists	464,276	623,563	Up 34%
Church of the Nazarene	417,732	507,574	Up 22%
Mainline Churches	**1973**	**1983**	**Change**
United Methodist Church	10,192,265	9,405,083	Down 8%
Presbyterian Church (U.S.A.)	3,715,301	3,157,372	Down 15%
Lutheran Church in America	3,017,778	2,925,655	Down 3%
Episcopal Church	2,917,165	2,794,139	Down 4%
Christian Church (Disciples of Christ)	1,330,747	1,156,458	Down 13%

SOURCE: "Religion in America, 50 Years: 1935–1985," *The Gallup Report* 236 (May 1985), p. 11.

for at least 50 years. Table 15-2 shows, however, that there has been a significant shift in membership from the mainline churches to conservative, evangelical religions.

EVANGELICAL CHRISTIANITY

Evangelical Protestant groups vary in the substance and style of their beliefs and practices, but they are united by two things: an unquestioning faith in the word-for-word accuracy of the Bible and a militant resistance to any individual, social, or religious deviation from scriptural doctrines. Evangelical Christians also emphasize personal salvation and the experience of being converted, or "born again," and they are committed to bringing all nonbelievers to an acceptance of Jesus Christ. Approximately 20 percent of the American adult population describe themselves as Evangelical Christians by these criteria. Most evangelicals live in the South, about two out of five are members of households with incomes of $15,000 or less, and nearly two out of five have not finished high school.[37]

Evangelical reform movements have appeared throughout the nineteenth and twentieth centuries, especially in times of economic and social dislocation, when uncertainty and insecurity create a need for absolute standards of behavior. It is not surprising, therefore, that the Sun Belt phenomenon of the 1970s and 1980s, which brought new industrial development and social changes to the South and Southwest, coincided with the rise of fundamentalist political movements.[38] Their leaders fre-

[37] Kenneth A. Briggs, "Evangelicals in America." *The Gallup Report*, p. 3–5.
[38] Frances FitzGerald, "Reagan's Band of True Believers." *The New York Times Magazine* (May 10, 1987), p. 39.

quently used televised religious programs to build a constituency and promote their radically conservative views on personal morality, social welfare, and the role of religion in public life. In 1987 one television evangelist, Jimmy Swaggart , was accused of sexual transgressions, and another, Jim Bakker, was found guilty of fraudulent fundraising activities. These scandals caused a loss of public trust that has weakened the evangelical movement as a political force.

The growth of Christian fundamentalism and other kinds of new religious groups should not be read as a sign of religion's decline but as a sign of its persistence in different forms. The Hare Krishna movement, the Unification Church, and the televised Crusades for Christ are new forms of religious expression that are not really "new" at all. They are the mystical, personal, small-group, utopian, often millenarian kind of religion that is reborn whenever the established churches — and the society of which they are a part — fail to provide moral guidance and spiritual meaning, especially to the young.

Reports that "God is dead" have obviously been exaggerated. Modern society has threatened the authority of religion but it has not changed its essential functions. Science has not yet settled the basic questions of the human condition, nor has it been able to provide a sense of community and shared purpose. The rise of Oriental cults and "born again" Christianity are signs that a profane, rational social order is not enough. In the world of the neutron bomb and test-tube baby, the need to find a meaning in human existence appears as desperate as ever.

SUMMARY

1. A religion is an institution of shared beliefs and practices by which people respond to the forces that are regarded as beyond human understanding and that give meaning to life. Every known society has had some religious beliefs and activities.

2. Religion is both a source of private beliefs and a powerful social force. Religious values guide the behavior of individuals, and they also have urgent political implications. Finally, religion is a social institution made up of numerous churches and community organizations.

3. Durkheim identified a concern for the sacred as the central feature of religion. Other characteristics of religion are symbolism, rituals, and shared beliefs and moral values.

4. Malinowski concluded from his research in the South Pacific that magic is practiced to provide a sense of control over uncertainty. While religions do have some magical components, they emphasize the ultimate meaning of life's rewards and frustrations.

5. In addition to providing a private code of behavior, religion offers a source of consolation during times of grief, fear, or uncertainty. Religious beliefs also define one's identity and place in the larger scheme of human life.

6. Religion affects public affairs because it offers a unifying set of beliefs and practices, because it lends spiritual authority to social norms and values, and because it is a means of social control.

7. For Durkheim religion was "society worshiping itself." He described religion as a force that binds society together by reinforcing the community's commitment to its own norms and moral values. Bellah suggested that the United States has a patriotic "civil religion" that sanctifies the American way of life.

8. Marx argued that religion maintains class domination by justifying the status quo. He called religion the "opium of the people," which dulls the lower classes' sense of oppression. Religious beliefs have often served the interests of the dominant

class, but they are also frequently a force for social change.

9. In Weber's view the purpose of religion is to give meaning to human existence. He found an "elective affinity" between a religious world view and a society's cultural, economic, and political characteristics.

10. Over time religions tend to develop in stages, from cults and sects to denominations, churches, and ecclesiae. It appears that relatively new evangelical religions appeal to the poor and deprived, while long-established and conservative religions appeal to the upper and middle classes. Members of the upper class attend church more often than members of lower-ranking groups. While Catho-

lics have tended in the past to have a lower class standing than Protestants, the Protestant ethic itself does not appear to be a decisive factor in American class differences.

11. Many observers have argued that modern life tends to undermine the authority of religious beliefs. By every measure, however, the United States is one of the most religious societies in the world. Americans' religious commitment has remained stable for over 50 years, and there is some evidence of a resurgence of religious feeling. Membership has shifted from mainline churches to conservative, evangelical religions, apparently because traditional religious organizations are failing to provide moral guidance and spiritual meaning, especially to the young.

KEY TERMS

religion 474
sacred 474
profane 474
ritual 475

magic 476
church 486
sect 486
cult 486

charisma 486
denomination 487
ecclesia 488

SUGGESTED READING

Theodore Caplow et al. *All Faithful People: Change and Continuity in Middletown's Religion.* Minneapolis: University of Minnesota Press, 1983.

Marc Galanter. *Cults: Faith, Healing and Coercion.* New York: Oxford University Press, 1989.

Charles Y. Glock. *Religion in Sociological Perspective: Essays in the Empirical Study of Religion.* Belmont, Calif.: Wadsworth, 1973.

* Andrew M. Greeley. *Unsecular Man: The Persistence of Religion.* New York: Schocken, 1985.

John Lofland. *Doomsday Cult: A Study of Conversion, Proselytization and Maintenance of Faith,* enl. ed. New York: Irvington, 1981.

* Thomas F. O'Dea and Janet O. Aviad. *The Sociology of Religion.* Englewood Cliffs, NJ: Prentice-Hall, 1983.

Robert Wuthnow, *The Restructuring of American Religion: Society and Faith Since World War II.* Princeton, NJ: Princeton University Press, 1988.

Milton J. Yinger. *The Scientific Study of Religion.* New York: Macmillan, 1970.

* Available in paperback.

Politics is a
strife of
interests
masquerading
as a contest of
principles.

Ambrose Bierce

CHAPTER 16

POLITICS

President Dwight D. Eisenhower once remarked that his administration tried to stick to Abraham Lincoln's rule that "it is the function of government to do for the people those things they cannot do for themselves and to stay out of . . . places where the people can do things for themselves." [1] Since Lincoln's time, however, the number of things people "cannot do for themselves" has greatly increased. As you can easily see in your own life, the government is everywhere, even in places where people used to "do things for themselves."

- If you were born in a hospital, it was probably built partly with federal money. If you went to a public school, the government paid for your school building, your teachers, your books, and your lunch.

- All your life you have eaten meat that has passed government inspection, food that comes in boxes or cans with descriptive labels required by the government, and vegetables picked by workers living in camps whose sanitary facilities must meet government standards. You have driven on highways that were built with government funds and flown on airplanes that were directed by federal air traffic controllers.

---

[1] Quoted in *The Lost Soul of American Politics* by John P. Diggins (New York: Basic Books, 1984), pp. 335–36.

No matter how often Americans may deplore "big government" and praise "individual initiative," people in complex modern societies expect more help from their government.

■ When you go to work, your salary will not legally be less than a minimum wage set by the government. Your employer will most likely be the beneficiary of government subsidies, government contracts, or government tax incentives. If you lose your job, the state will pay you unemployment compensation while you look for work. If you cannot work at all, you will probably be eligible for government welfare benefits. When you retire, you will receive a pension from Social Security and health services from Medicare. Finally, if you are a veteran, the government will even help pay for your funeral.[2]

From birth to death, there are obviously many fewer places where people find they can "do things for themselves" in a large, complex, highly industrialized society like the United States. Moreover, people in modern societies expect more from their government. No matter how often Americans may deplore "big government" and praise "individual initiative," poll after poll shows that the majority firmly support the government's efforts to reduce unemployment, control environmental pollution, protect consumers, and help the needy.[3]

Politics has been defined as the process of deciding "who gets what, when, and how."[4] It thus involves the clash of *interest groups,* or groups of voters and lobbyists trying to advance or protect the special interests of corporations, unions, consumers, veterans, elderly people, farmers, or the like. Politics, therefore, always involves a struggle for **power**, or the ability to control scarce resources or determine how other

---

[2] Robert Sherrill, *Why They Call It Politics: A Guide to America's Government,* 4th ed. (San Diego: Harcourt Brace Jovanovich, 1984), pp. 357–59.

[3] Ibid., p. 357.

[4] Harold D. Lasswell, *Politics: Who Gets What, When and How* (New York: McGraw-Hill, 1936).

people will behave. The political institution is made up of the norms and organizations by which political power is distributed, society is governed, and the rules of daily life are enforced.

Politics is a necessary ingredient of social life. Even in small, pre-industrial communities, incompatible human needs and desires must be controlled and coordinated if social life is to go on. Any group — a family, a sorority, the crew of a sailboat — would find it inefficient and demoralizing to decide every question by calling all its members together, debating the pros and cons, and voting on the matter. Leaders, either chosen or self-appointed, exercise the power to decide and thus govern the group. Members of the group who are left out of the decision-making process are said to be powerless.

The most familiar form of competition for leadership and power is also the most carefully studied one: the contest among candidates for public office and among opposing parties for the control of federal, state, and local governments. However, politics involves much more than elections to public office. It is a nearly universal social process that appears in all kinds of groups. A power struggle between two factions in a corporation is known as "company politics"; "sexual politics" is a relatively new term for the age-old battle between the sexes; and the decision-making process among parents and children has been called the "politics of the family." [5]

The sociologist's interest in politics differs from that of the political scientist. Sociology emphasizes the relationship of politics to the rest of society — how it is affected by social class, for example, or by the economy or religious beliefs.

The first two sections of this chapter discuss political power — where it comes from and who has it. The third section is an analysis of the American political system, especially the decline of party politics and the growing power of special-interest groups. The last section, "Two Cheers for Democracy," briefly describes nondemocratic systems of government and then assesses the strengths and weaknesses of American democracy.

POLITICS AND POWER

Power in the sociological sense is always a relationship between two or more people. As Max Weber defined it, power is the ability, within a social relationship, to carry out one's own will despite opposition from others. This control over other people involves influence, coercion, or authority.

Influence is the power to persuade. This kind of power can come from personal appeal, prestige, wealth, numbers, or effective organization. Christopher Columbus's personal charm gave him influence over Queen Isabella of Spain. When she financed his voyage to the New World, his power of persuasion changed Western history. Newspaper editors and TV news analysts wield tremendous political power because of their potential ability to persuade millions of voters. The prestige of a Nobel Prize gave the Reverend Martin Luther King, Jr., more political power; wealth gives political campaign contributors influence with the candidate. Sheer numbers give China more

[5] R. D. Laing, *The Politics of the Family* (New York: Vintage, 1972).

Weber described
three types of
authority on which
legitimate power is
based. Prince
Rainier has
traditional power
over his subjects in
Monaco; Nelson
Mandela commands
the loyalty of black
South Africans
because he has
charismatic
authority; and
justices of the
Supreme Court
exercise *rational-
legal* authority in
interpreting the law.

power than Taiwan in international relations; in Washington an effective organization has given the National Rifle Association enough power to outbalance the much larger number of people supporting gun-control legislation.

Coercion is Weber's term for the power that comes from superior force. Ultimately, all governments exert control over a people by using force, although they may use that power only as a last resort. Physical force alone, however, is never enough. Every government seeks **legitimacy**, or the consent of the governed. Legitimate power comes from the belief that the political system is justified by tradition or law. Without legitimacy a government is like a gang of terrorists holding hostages at gunpoint; neither can afford to turn its back or fall asleep for fear of being overwhelmed. A legitimate government is like a commander leading an army into combat; the soldiers may not want to obey orders, but they will do so.

Even the most repressive dictatorship must rely on voluntary support from a large part of the population in order to survive. The 1975 collapse of Nguyen Van Thieu's regime in South Vietnam is an example of the ineffectiveness of illegitimate power. As the war in Vietnam dragged on, most of the South Vietnamese population became indifferent or hostile to the government, which continued to exist only because of American military support. Once the American troops were withdrawn, the South Vietnamese government collapsed and Thieu rapidly fell from power. In the words of the eighteenth-century French philosopher Jean Jacques Rousseau, "The strongest is never strong enough to be always the master, unless he transforms strength into right, and obedience into duty." [6]

Authority is legitimate power, power that is generally considered appropriate and acceptable by those who must obey. The robber's power to take your money is based on

---

[6] Jean Jacques Rousseau, *Contrat Social* (1762), Book I, Chapter 3.

the illegitimate use of force, but the Internal Revenue Service's power to take your money in taxes is recognized as legitimate even if you dislike it. Political contests are struggles to attain such authority — the legitimate power of the judge, the bishop, the chairman of the board, the secretary of defense.

TYPES OF AUTHORITY

Max Weber used the concept of authority to explain why people obey when they are not physically coerced or persuaded to do so. He proposed three types of authority, or three ways of claiming legitimate power — traditional, rational-legal, and charismatic.[7]

TRADITIONAL AUTHORITY.   Weber referred to tradition as the authority of the "eternal yesterday." The sanctity of tradition legitimizes the old ways of doing things and gives power to such leaders as the village chieftain, the aga khan, and the prince of Monaco. **Traditional authority** is received from the past; it is conferred on particular people by birthright or by such higher authority as the College of Cardinals. Those who hold traditional authority have a great deal of leeway in exercising their power. In centuries past, European kings and queens, for example, had relatively unlimited authority over their subjects. Whatever they did, from taking a lover to ordering the execution of a royal minister, was considered "right" because they did it.

RATIONAL-LEGAL AUTHORITY.   In contrast to traditional authority, **rational-legal** authority comes not from the past, but from the office presently held. Power is legitimized by

---

[7] Hans Gerth and C. Wright Mills, eds., *From Max Weber: Essays in Sociology* (New York: Oxford University Press, 1946), pp. 295–99.

law, not by the "way things have always been." Instead of the personal, loosely defined authority of princes, rational-legal authority is restricted by explicit, impersonal rules established by legislation or legal contract. It is the right of a tax auditor to examine an income tax return, the right of a manager to fire an employee, and the right of a judge to impose a fine. Individuals who hold the office, however, have only its specific powers, and only for as long as they hold it. Judges have no authority to audit tax returns, and a retired sales manager no longer has the right to fire the company's employees. Richard Nixon retained all the authority of the presidency even after the Watergate scandal had disgraced him personally. The moment he resigned the office, he lost his presidential powers and became an ordinary citizen again.

CHARISMATIC AUTHORITY.   Extraordinary personal qualities also command loyalty and obedience. Great leaders who lack traditional or rational-legal authority have *charisma* — Weber's term for the unique personal power of exceptional individuals. Charismatic leaders usually appear in disordered or unstable situations when the established rules and traditional rulers have lost authority. Jesus, Joan of Arc, Gandhi, Winston Churchill, and the Ayatollah Khomeini are examples of leaders who seem to have extraordinary abilities, and who provided **charismatic authority** in times of crisis. Such figures derive their power from their followers' belief in their mission, whether it is to save the country, to save souls, or to bring power to some deprived group. Weber stressed that charismatic authority is always a relationship between leaders and followers and not a characteristic of the leader alone.

Charismatic authority is accepted as legitimate even when it is illegal or untraditional. When Napoleon returned to France from Elba, for example, he was only an escaped prisoner, with no formal authority. Nevertheless, many of his former soldiers rallied to his side, called him "emperor," and accepted his right to lead them into battle at Waterloo.

Once charismatic leaders are dead, their charisma may gradually become "routinized" as traditional or rational-legal authority. The extraordinary authority which Charlemagne possessed as the first Holy Roman emperor became traditional as it passed to the heirs to his title; Lenin's charismatic appeal became routinized as the rational-legal authority of the modern Soviet leadership.

In his description of the three kinds of authority, Weber was referring to ideal types; he realized that legitimacy usually has more than one source. Hitler, for instance, had charismatic appeal, and his National Socialist party had a legal basis as well as a foundation in German traditions.

THE RISE OF THE STATE

According to Weber's definition, a **state** is the institution that "claims the monopoly of the use of force within a given territory." [8] The state is a comparatively recent historical development. Political institutions apparently did not exist in early hunting and gather-

---

[8] Ibid., p. 78.

ing societies, where decisions were made by consensus in kinship groups and communities. The empires of the ancient world were actually rather shaky federations of separate territories; emperors could hardly claim a monopoly of authority over such far-flung and disparate peoples. The Catholic Church was the dominant political institution of medieval Europe, exerting its control over kings and commoners alike. The nation-state emerged only after the church lost authority at the end of the Middle Ages, when another central governing institution was required to organize an increasingly complex social and economic life. In the modern era the state became the sole political custodian of the social order, taking over many of the rights of the medieval guilds, the landed aristocracy, and the church. Politics in the modern state was also transformed. In contrast to traditional societies, modern political systems developed a centralized government, rational-legal authority, and mass political participation.

A CENTRALIZED GOVERNMENT.   In ancient and medieval times political power over a large territory was fragmented among many military rulers, aristocrats, and churchmen. As its authority spread, however, the state took over some of the functions of other institutions. From religion and the family the state took responsibility for enforcing the norms of moral behavior. Instead of being informally punished by the injured party, wrongdoers are now fined or imprisoned according to the laws of the state. The education of the young and the care of the aged are now more the duty of the state than the family or religious institutions. From the economic institution the state took over the authority to develop trade and business; it also assumed the nobility's right to make war and to form alliances with foreign governments. Furthermore, the scope of the state's activities has widened enormously. While traditional rulers tried mainly to increase their own wealth and personal power, most modern heads of state attempt to increase the wealth and well-being of the nation. The state now sponsors such diverse

"I agree he's a homicidal maniac, but I'm saluting the office, not the man.

Drawing by Lorenz; © 1980 The New Yorker Magazine, Inc.

enterprises as agriculture, business investment, scientific research, recreation, public transportation, unemployment compensation, racial integration, and so on into most areas of social life. In short, the sole authority to maintain and protect the social order became entrusted to a centralized *government,* or the complex of institutions that exercises the power of the state.

RATIONAL-LEGAL AUTHORITY.   Citizens of modern states obey the law rather than the commands of a traditional ruler. Although heads of state retain some of the authority of historical tradition, their power is rarely as personal as it is rational-legal in origin. Even such dictators as Ferdinand Marcos and Jean-Claude Duvalier claimed to rule according to law.

MASS POLITICAL PARTICIPATION.   In traditional societies political power is closely held by a small aristocracy. With the breakdown of the European feudal system the urban middle class acquired the political resources of wealth and social prestige. These newly rich bankers and businessmen were able to bargain for political influence as well, and they eventually came to dominate the modern state. During the last century or so, when poor people and women gained the right to vote, political power became spread over a much wider social spectrum. The expansion of the vote led to the development of mass political parties, which diminished the power of hereditary rulers in favor of leaders chosen by the party and the people themselves. In repressive dictatorships voting is often compulsory because it legitimizes the rulers' power. Mass political participation has become a characteristic of the modern state, democracy and dictatorship alike.

The widening authority of the state, combined with a highly centralized and bureaucratic government, carries with it a tremendous potential for both good and evil. On the one hand, a powerful central government can be mobilized to solve problems beyond the ability of any smaller organization. But the enlarged authority of the modern state also can be used to restrict its citizens' individual freedoms and support dictatorship.

THE POLITICS OF MODERN STATES

In democracies the concentrated power of the state is restrained by the political participation of interest groups and active, concerned citizens. Their effect on modern politics continues to be the subject of much sociological controversy.

THE ELITIST VIEW OF POWER

In Western democracies such as the United States power is ideally shared equally by every voter. "Government of the people, by the people, and for the people" is supposed to have eliminated the domination of a ruling class and given every citizen an equal say in the decision-making process. However, the fact is that some people are still "more equal than others" and that even in mass democracies power is concentrated in a privileged group of leaders, or *elite.*

Some theorists have argued that elitist rule is inevitable. According to Robert Michels's *Iron Law of Oligarchy,* no large organization can function without creating a hierarchy of positions. Special powers must be delegated to a few people who have the time, energy, and ability to run the organization effectively. Even in voluntary organizations, which are intended to promote the interests of their rank and file, Michels believed that people at the top of the hierarchy would begin to think and act like an elite. His Iron Law states that any large organization will inevitably become an oligarchy in which the ruling elite defends its own interests against the interests of the larger membership.[9]

A similar view was expressed by Vilfredo Pareto, who believed that every social group is dominated by an elite. Because some people are always going to be more talented and ambitious than others, Pareto predicted, the superior few will always rule the many.[10]

In *The Power Elite* (1956), C. Wright Mills applied the elitist perspective to the United States. He found that about 500 men held the highest decision-making positions in the organizations that dominate American society: the government, the large corporations, and the military. Members of this power elite had similar social backgrounds, attitudes, and interests. Most of them were white urban Protestants who had attended the same prestigious universities and who belonged to the same clubs, corporate boards of directors, and government commissions. Since the federal government, the defense contracting companies, and the armed forces worked closely together, their leaders often knew and understood each other. They also had interlocking interests: government officials and legislators approved billions of dollars in military appropriations, which created jobs, provided business for large corporations, and supported defense installations in their districts. Corporations, in turn, hired former military personnel and donated campaign money to politicians. In addition, Mills found, these men moved back and forth among the three groups.[11] Between 1940 and 1967, ninety-one individuals served as secretaries or undersecretaries of state or defense, or as heads of the armed services, the CIA, and the Atomic Energy Commission; seventy of the ninety-one had worked for major corporations or for Wall Street investment banks.[12]

At the end of his term in office President Eisenhower popularized Mills's thesis by warning of the power of the "military-industrial complex" in directing foreign policy. A decade later many Americans were convinced that what Mills called "military capitalism" had drawn the nation into a losing war in Indochina. Nearly three decades after Eisenhower's speech, the ties among defense contractors, the Pentagon, and the government appear to be as strong as ever. Alexander Haig, President Reagan's first secretary of state, was himself a one-man military-industrial complex: a former four-star general; former White House chief of staff; former supreme allied commander of NATO forces; and former president of United Technologies, a manufacturer of helicopters and jet engines that receives billions of dollars in Pentagon business every year. In an era of trillion-dollar military budgets, the overlapping interests of professional

---

[9] Robert Michels, *Political Parties* (1911) (New York: Free Press, 1967).

[10] Vilfredo Pareto, *Mind and Society* (New York: Harcourt Brace Jovanovich, 1935).

[11] C. Wright Mills, *The Power Elite* (New York: Oxford University Press, 1956).

[12] Norman Goodman and Gary T. Marx, *Society Today,* 3rd ed. (New York: Random House/CRM, 1978), p. 405.

The Rockefellers represent Mills's power elite concept in an extreme form. David was chairman of Chase Manhattan, and chaired the U.S. Council of Foreign Relations; Winthrop was governor of Arkansas and director of Rockefeller Center, Inc.; John D. III was a leading art collector and headed the Rockefeller Foundation; Nelson was governor of New York and vice-president of the U.S.; Laurence chaired Rockresorts, Inc., and headed the Rockefeller Brothers fund.

soldiers, defense contractors, and government officials will almost certainly continue to influence foreign policy in the next decade.

Mills's theory of the power elite inspired William Domhoff to make systematic studies of the American ruling class. While Mills's power elite was drawn equally from the government, large corporations, and the military, Domhoff's elite represents mainly business interests. He found that the members of the governing class are all millionaires with great social prestige. They are listed in the *Social Register*, they were educated at select private schools and universities, and they belong to exclusive men's clubs. Although this upper-upper crust represents less than one-half of 1 percent of the population, its members control 25 percent of all wealth and about 15 percent of all income in the United States. They also hold most of the high-level positions in business, banking, government, prestigious universities, charitable foundations, and so on. According to Domhoff, the governing class exerts power not only by holding important decision-making positions but also by lending its services and expertise to such policy-making organizations as the Brookings Institution, the Council on Foreign Relations, and the National Planning Association. Finally, Domhoff's governing class influences the political process by making large campaign contributions to candidates with similar views, by lobbying for its own special interests, and by accepting appointments to presidential commissions and political offices.[13]

There is some question, however, about whether this professional and intellectual elite is truly a ruling class. Members of Domhoff's group represent diverse interests, so they are unlikely to try to advance a single cause. Their ability to control the govern-

[13] G. William Domhoff, *Who Rules America Now?* (Englewood Cliffs, N.J.: Prentice-Hall, 1983).

ment also appears limited. While people in high positions do tend to have upper-class pedigrees, there is no evidence that they are purely self-seeking or that they consistently promote business interests over other concerns. Another view of power finds that American society is dominated not by a unified power elite but by a variety of powerful groups.

THE PLURALIST VIEW OF POWER

According to pluralist theory, political power is not concentrated in a few hands; it is dispersed among many competing interest groups. If one group or coalition proves strong enough to dominate others, then theoretically the threatened groups will organize and exert **countervailing power** that will offset or outweigh that of their opponents. The political stalemate over the Equal Rights Amendment was an example of the way one political coalition (conservative, pro-family, anti-abortion groups such as the Moral Majority) can block another (the liberal, gay rights, and pro-abortion groups that grew out of the women's movement) when its values and interests are threatened.

Countervailing power is also exerted within elites, weakening their dominance. Groups with competing business interests, for example, do not act as a cohesive elite but fight for different government policies. Importers try to get tariffs reduced, while manufacturers try to get them raised to keep out foreign competition; southwestern oil producers compete with northern coal companies for energy policies favorable to their interests.[14]

Moreover, the same groups do not wield the same amount of power on every issue. In his famous study of New Haven, Connecticut, Robert Dahl found that only a few people are involved in every decision-making process but that the *same* few do not control every decision. He concluded that an individual or a group with one kind of political resource (numbers, money) is often weak in another kind of resource (organization is sometimes more important than money or numbers). As a result, no one group can reliably dominate the others, and, more important, no group is entirely without some resources. Even powerful groups are often forced to bargain, with each other and with organized opposition to their interests.[15]

Arnold Rose took a similar view of the national distribution of power. He argued that American society has many elites, each with power in a different area. The interests of diverse elites — corporations, unions, universities, environmental associations, churches, the military, and so on — do not coincide in a single ruling class. Rose agreed that many people have no ties to any of these groups and therefore lack political power. He also agreed that foreign policy decisions do appear to be made by a dominant group similar to Mills's power elite. However, he concluded that the majority of the population has enough access to the decision-making process to influence its outcome.[16]

In direct opposition to Mills, David Riesman argued that American society is too pluralistic. He noted that the conflicting interests of several elites tend to cancel each

---

[14] Arnold M. Rose, *The Power Structure* (New York: Oxford University Press, 1967), pp. 108–109; Robert E. Dowse and John A. Hughes, *Political Sociology* (New York: Wiley, 1972), p. 135.

[15] Robert A. Dahl, *Who Governs?* (New Haven, Conn.: Yale University Press, 1961).

[16] Rose, *The Power Structure.*

In 1982 a coalition of conservative groups successfully blocked passage of the Equal Rights Amendment by exerting countervailing power against its supporters. This event supports the pluralist view that political power is dispersed among many competing groups.

other out, making effective national leadership difficult. He referred to organized interest groups as "veto groups" because they protect themselves by denying advantages to others. Coalitions of these groups emerge over specific issues and then break apart, so that no one group dominates society as a ruling elite. Where Mills saw the danger of a unified elite pursuing its own selfish interests, Riesman saw the danger of political stagnation in the conflicting interests of many powerful groups.[17]

THE ELITIST—PLURALIST DEBATE: AN EVALUATION

The elitist–pluralist debate is difficult to resolve with empirical evidence. Political bargaining is an informal process that varies from issue to issue and from group to group, and elites rarely let investigators study their decision-making style. Although the wealthy have much in common, there is little evidence that people in key positions will see things the same way just because they come from similar class backgrounds or happen to know each other socially. There is still no doubt that some players in the political game are stronger than others and that the corporate rich exert enormous political power through campaign contributions, lobbying organizations, and control of government agencies.

On the other hand, the interests of the governing class are not usually unified as Mills assumed. Pluralists have verified the existence of many contending factions, even within elites. Coalitions of pressure groups have at times had a decisive political influence, outweighing the power of business interests in decisions involving industrial pollution and consumer protection. Pluralist theory, however, underplays the fact

[17] David Riesman, *The Lonely Crowd* (New Haven, Conn.: Yale University Press, 1961).

that much of the population has little access to the political arena. Lack of money, time, and effective organization severely limits the political power of the poor and disadvantaged (see Chapter 17, "Social Movements and Collective Behavior").

In yet another view of the matter, Charles Lindblom claims that the interests of wealthy businessmen are not separate from those of politicians. In all societies, someone has to decide what is produced, who does the work, which technologies are used, the quality of goods and services, and many other aspects of production and distribution. In a private enterprise system, Lindblom argues, these public policy decisions are turned over to businessmen. To remain in office, politicians must maintain a healthy economic climate. The state thus grants business a number of privileges: tax breaks to encourage investment, underwriting of research and development costs, influence over appointments to important regulatory agencies, and even loans and bailouts. These privileges are the result of deference to business leaders, not bribery or lobbying pressure.

> To understand the character of politics in market-oriented systems requires no conspiracy theory of politics, no theory of common social origins uniting government and business officials, no crude allegation of a power elite established by clandestine forces. Business simply needs inducements, hence a privileged position in government and politics, if it is to do its job.[18]

In sum, American society appears to have a pluralist distribution of power, but it is at best an elite pluralism. When the interests of these elites coincide, as they do in the military-industrial complex, then a power elite emerges; when they diverge, as they do on most domestic issues, then the elites often act as veto groups and hinder effective leadership. It is clear, however, that most important political decisions are controlled by elite groups representing the most privileged strata of American society.[19]

THE AMERICAN POLITICAL SYSTEM

In complex modern societies the political process is the means of devising and carrying out policies for solving common problems. Political systems create laws that establish authority, govern disputes among contending groups, distribute essential services (education, health care, defense, transportation), and regulate economic and political relations with other nations. In a few political systems, such as the ancient Greek city-states and colonial New England towns, such policy decisions were made in open meetings in which every citizen had a vote. Once the rights of citizenship were extended to the entire adult population of the nation-state, such a system was obviously unworkable. In modern democracies participation in government has been limited to a relatively few elected representatives who make the decisions for millions of their fellow citizens. The basis of modern democratic politics is thus free elections and representative government.

---

[18] Charles E. Lindblom, *Politics and Markets: The World's Political Economic System* (New York: Basic Books, 1977), p. 175.

[19] William Kornhauser, " 'Power Elite' or 'Veto Groups'?" in *Class, Status, and Power,* 2nd ed., eds. Reinhard Bendix and Seymour Martin Lipset (New York: Free Press, 1966).

Political parties are crucial elements in democracies. *Parties* are broadly defined as collectivities that seek to gain legitimate control of the government through elections. Because the founders believed that party factionalism would undermine the unity of the new republic, political parties are not even mentioned in the U.S. Constitution. Later generations found, however, that parties were necessary in a large, diverse nation with a complex political system. In the past parties have been the means of uniting different interest groups and regions, assigning priorities to legislation, protecting minorities, and defining a policy agenda, or "party platform," for elections. Parties have also been the link between the people and the government. Party leaders influence decisions by transmitting public opinion to government officials, and they also mobilize grass-roots support for decisions after they are made. National parties link otherwise disparate levels (municipal, state, and federal) and branches (executive, legislative, judicial) of government. Finally, parties recruit and field candidates for public office.[20]

THE TWO-PARTY SYSTEM

All democracies have at least two parties, many have several, and some have dozens. Maurice Duverger, a French sociologist, theorized that two-party systems develop only in a particular situation: a political system in which each party has only one candidate for each office and the candidate with the most votes wins the election. Minority parties tend to disappear because they have almost no chance of gaining a plurality in these winner-take-all contests.[21] For this reason American third parties have usually fared badly. On the other hand, minority parties thrive in Israel, Italy, and other proportionately representative systems. A vote for a losing candidate is not wasted because the party still wins representation proportional to the total number of votes it receives: a minority party polling only 5 percent of the vote will still have five seats in a hundred-seat legislature.

According to Duverger, the winner-take-all system has given American political parties their unique character. In most democracies liberal or leftist parties are identified with the working class, and conservative or right-wing parties with the middle and upper classes.[22] The party programs under this system are specific statements reflecting important policy differences. Members are expected to support the party program in public, and they are required to vote with their party on legislation. Those who do not follow the official line can be expelled from the party. There are no primary elections: candidates are selected by a small group of leaders and approved by the party organization. The electorate usually votes for a party on the basis of its policy, not for individual candidates on the basis of their qualifications and personalities. Without party support incumbents cannot win reelection on their own.

The American two-party system is entirely different. Although the working class has traditionally been Democratic and the upper classes Republican, Americans are

---

[20] Dowse and Hughes, *Political Sociology*, pp. 339–41.

[21] Maurice Duverger, *Political Parties*, trans. Barbara North and Robert North (New York: Wiley, 1954).

[22] Seymour Martin Lipset, "Democracy and Working Class Authoritarianism," *American Sociological Review* 24 (1959): 482–501.

For most of American history, political parties controlled the election process. Today many of the party's traditional functions are being eroded by changes in fund-raising and nominating procedures, television campaigning, and the use of sophisticated polling techniques.

much less likely than other nationalities to vote on the basis of class.[23] Both parties have liberal and conservative wings, and it is not unusual to find conservative Democrats voting with Republicans on social welfare and defense issues. The party platforms try to paper over regional and class differences and appeal to the political center. As a result, campaigning politicians tend to discuss vague generalities rather than specific policies. The party organizations are weak; there is no effective way of disciplining a member who fails to support the party platform or even votes in opposition to it. Anyone can seek political office, and candidates can win nomination without party support through primary elections. In this situation people tend to vote for the candidate, not the party. Popular incumbents therefore have a strong advantage in elections.

THE DECLINE OF PARTY POLITICS

For most of American history the major political parties operated as loosely organized coalitions of diverse interests. Nevertheless, the parties won the loyalty of voters and candidates and brought some unity to the political process. The president was the leader of his party, and even unpopular presidents, such as Herbert Hoover in 1932 and Harry Truman in 1948, had little opposition in being renominated. As recently as 1968,

[23] Robert R. Alford, *Party and Society: The Anglo-American Democracies* (Chicago: Rand McNally, 1963).

Democratic party leaders delivered the presidential nomination to Hubert Humphrey, the incumbent vice-president, who had never even entered a primary, bypassing Eugene McCarthy, who had proved his popularity by winning several primary elections. In the 1970s, however, control of the nominating process passed from party loyalists to the state primaries. In the election of 1980, another unpopular incumbent, President Jimmy Carter, had to fight for renomination without the support of most of the Democratic leadership.

Party identification has declined along with party loyalty and discipline. In the last twenty years voters have become more likely to vote outside their party, and people in general are more dissatisfied with the performance of both parties. A few politicians have even advanced their careers by switching parties — a maneuver that would have been unthinkable a few years ago. National polls taken during the 1980s have regularly reported that over a third of the American public now consider themselves independents, members of neither the Republican nor Democratic Party.[24] Among actual voters, one exit poll (taken as the respondents left their polling places) found that 26 percent of the people who voted in the 1984 presidential election called themselves independents.[25]

Two other developments — election reform and the increasing importance of television and polling — have hastened the decline of traditional party politics.

ELECTION REFORM.   During the 1970s the well-publicized corruption of some party bosses led to reform of the ways candidates are nominated and campaign money is raised. Local and state nominations are now decided by direct primaries open to all voters; presidential nominations are by and large determined in some thirty-five state preferential primaries, some of which permit crossover voting between parties. The choices are then formally ratified by delegates to national conventions, where political bosses have little influence. Most public officials, from the county sheriff to the president, run for office with the backing of their own organizations, even though they still wear the labels of Republican or Democrat. Once in office they owe little or nothing to party leaders.

Reform of campaign fund-raising procedures has also weakened political parties. Today campaign money is given to the candidates directly either by the state or federal government or by political action committees (PACs) representing individuals and private interest groups (labor unions, businesses, trade organizations). Individual contributors are legally prohibited from giving more than $1,000 to a federal candidate's campaign, and from giving more than $25,000 to all federal candidates combined. PACs, however, may contribute up to $5,000 to a single candidate and *unlimited* total amounts to all candidates. As television advertisements, political consultants' fees, and polling costs have made political campaigning more and more expensive, PACs have become a more and more important source of campaign funds. In 1976 the average amount the winner of a U.S. Senate race spent was $609,000; in 1986 it was $3.1 million. During the same 10-year period the average cost of a successful campaign for

---

[24] The National Opinion Research Center's *General Social Survey for 1984,* for example.

[25] *The New York Times*/CBS News Poll, reported in *The New York Times,* November 8, 1984, p. A19.

the U.S. House of Representatives increased from about $87,000 to about $355,000.[26] A little over 4,000 PACs spent $133 million in the 1986–1987 federal elections — or between a quarter and a third of all campaign dollars.[27] In such a situation, the party war chest is usually unimportant and often nearly empty.

Election reforms have also contributed to the further decline of urban political machines. Welfare, unemployment insurance, and Social Security benefits have already undermined the power of the party bosses to hand out patronage in return for votes. The unintended result of reducing the power of political machines has been to shift the traditional roles of local party organizations to national poll-takers and professional fundraisers.

Reform of traditional party structures has spread to Washington as well. In the wake of the Vietnam War and the Watergate scandal, members of Congress have become more independent and suspicious of their leadership. The House of Representatives has dispersed power by curbing the seniority system and creating dozens of new subcommittees. Without party discipline a new coalition has to be cemented together for every roll-call vote.[28]

The weakening of party loyalties has further blurred the line between personal candidacy for office and public service. The never-ending campaign for reelection distracts officials from the work they were elected to do, and the fear of offending a particular group of voters makes for cautious and unimaginative legislators. According to long-time Speaker of the House Thomas P. O'Neill, Jr., most members of Congress thirty years ago had served in their state legislature or city council and had been part of a party organization. The majority of the members of the 1982 Congress, however, had never before served in any legislative body, and had won election largely because they were able to get their message across to the voters on television.[29]

TELEVISION AND POLLING.   John Anderson, a third-party candidate for president in 1980, was called the first nominee of the "Television Party." While parties were once the only way to declare a candidacy and win support, Anderson found television a practical alternative. By the time Ronald Reagan was reelected in 1984, television was acknowledged to be the single most important — if not decisive — factor in presidential politics. For Reagan's media advisors, campaigning for national office was no longer a matter of stump speeches and whistlestop tours, but a meticulously planned strategy of advertising "spots," staged "news events," and "photo opportunities" — all skillfully designed to project images based on the techniques of modern marketing.

Today televised political debates, interviews, and advertising have taken over the parties' function of communicating information about candidates to voters. Nearly all the federal subsidy given to the candidates in each party is spent on TV spots, leaving

---

[26] Citizens' Research Foundation figures reported in Randall Rothenberg, "The Boom in Political Consulting," *The New York Times* (May 24, 1987), Section 3, p. 1.

[27] U.S. Bureau of the Census, *Statistical Abstract of the United States* (Washington, D.C.: U.S. Government Printing Office, 1989), Tables 442 and 444.

[28] John Herbers, "The Party's Over for the Political Parties," *The New York Times Magazine*, December 9, 1979, pp. 159, 174–75.

[29] Ron Suskind, "The Power of Political Consultants," *The New York Times Magazine*, August 12, 1984, p. 62.

little money for traditional campaigning. Although political scientists disagree on how much, if any, influence television debates have on the outcome of presidential elections, the fact is that they reach virtually every voter: in 1976, 120 million people — or 89 percent of all registered voters — saw at least part of the first debate between Gerald Ford and Jimmy Carter.[30]

At the same time, political polls have replaced the party's role in communicating public opinion to the candidate. Instead of relying on local politicians to inform them on how the voters feel about the issues, candidates now consult a media adviser and have a computerized poll taken. By pinpointing what voters care about and what they like or dislike about a candidate, polls help political consultants decide which issues to stress and which images to project on television.

The decline of party politics has produced the new no-party hack, or what the historian Arthur Schlesinger, Jr., has called a "political adventurer":

> He was elected to office by having money, or by being a celebrity in his district or by looking good on television. The usual procedure is to hire a political consultant who polls the district, then tells the candidate what to do and say. He enters the primary of one party or the other, follows the advice of his consultant and is likely to be elected. Once in Washington, he knows little of the pull and tug of politics, the compromising and logrolling that is a part of any political process. He is naked to constituent pressure, good and bad, without the insulation that the party provided in the past, and the result is a Congressional body that is both neurotic and timid.[31]

POLITICAL PARTICIPATION

Another symptom of the decline of party politics is the lack of interest in voting. Since 1960 voter turnout has been decreasing almost steadily (see Figure 16-1). A little over half the potential electorate votes in presidential elections, and about one-fifth turns out regularly for other contests. Two out of three eligible voters did not bother to go to the polls in the congressional elections of 1974 and 1978, and Ronald Reagan's landslide victory in 1984 was based on the support of less than one-third of the qualified electorate.[32]

Voting behavior is partly correlated with party partisanship and partly with other factors. In the nineteenth century, when party loyalties were strong, 80 percent of the eligible American voters went to the polls; between 85 percent and 90 percent of the potential voters still regularly vote in Great Britain, Denmark, and West Germany. In the United States only about half of these between 18 and 30 are even registered to vote, and disadvantaged groups show a lower-than-average turnout.

Several explanations of low voter participation have been suggested. The most optimistic interpretation is that the electorate is happy with things as they are, finds no disturbing political conflicts, and sees no reason to vote. The more likely explanation is that nonvoters are dissatisfied but think they cannot change things by voting. Younger, poorer, and less-educated people, the argument goes, are even more likely to feel

---

[30] *The New York Times,* September 14, 1980, p. D20.

[31] *The Wall Street Journal,* May 14, 1979, p. 20.

[32] Norman H. Nie, Sidney Verba, and John R. Petrocik, *The Changing American Voter* (Cambridge, Mass.: Harvard University Press, 1976), p. 74.

APATHY AT THE POLLS: PARTICIPATION IN ELECTIONS FOR PRESIDENT AND U.S. REPRESENTATIVES, 1964–1988*   FIGURE 16-1

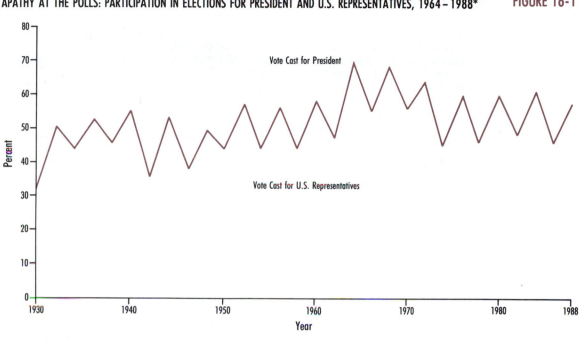

* Percentage of eligible voters reporting they voted.

SOURCE: U.S. Bureau of the Census, *Voting and Registration in the Election of November, 1986* (and of 1988). Current Population Reports, Series P-20, No. 440 and 414, 1989 and 1987.

ignored by the "system." Moreover, the practical necessities of registering to vote and getting to the polls are made more difficult by young people's geographical mobility (moving between college and home or from one city to another) and poor people's ill health and lack of transportation (see "Why Americans Don't Vote").

Political participation of all kinds — voting, campaigning for a particular candidate, making political contributions, running for office — seems to be increased by a sense of **political efficacy**, or the feeling that one can affect the outcome of a political process. This sense of power comes with education, higher social standing, the feeling of being part of a group or community, and a sense of personal competence in coping with life.[33] At any social level those who feel competent are more likely to vote than those who do not. Generally speaking, relatively few young, black, poor, and poorly educated people have this sense of competence, while relatively many older, middle- and upper-class, well-educated white people do. Education and high status are conducive to the feeling of political efficacy and hence to political participation.

Ironically, the recent reforms of primary election and campaign fundraising procedures, which were supposed to strengthen political participation, have actually

---

[33] Kenneth Prewitt, "Political Efficacy," in *International Encyclopedia of the Social Sciences,* Vol. 12 (New York: Macmillan, 1968), pp. 225–28.

WHY AMERICANS DON'T VOTE

American voter turnout is the lowest of any major democracy. Whether or not this low voting rate is a problem is a question that has not been resolved. Some scholars view nonvoting as a tacit acceptance of the status quo: since nonvoters are satisfied with the government they have no reason to try to change it. Others argue that democracy benefits from having large numbers of nonvoters. According to this view, mass political participation tends to overload political parties with the voters' demands — particularly popular economic demands. A lower turnout provides politicians with more latitude and reduces conflict.

In one study, Frances Piven and Richard Cloward explain the low American voting record by focusing on social structural factors. They note, for example, that nonvoters tend to be younger, poorer, and less well-educated than voters. According to a psychological view of this phenomenon, people abstain because their young age, low income, or lack of education limits the motivation, skills, capacities, or sense of civic duty necessary for voting. This psychological profile does not describe the nonvoter in other democracies, however, nor does it explain why political participation has *decreased* in the twentieth century despite higher levels of income and education. If there is no nonvoting "personality," then what accounts for the low turnout in the United States?

Piven and Cloward argue that the structure of the American political system discourages certain segments of the population from voting. In particular, the distinctly American system of voter registration makes it hard to vote. Citizens are often required to appear in person at the registration office to be certified to vote. Election boards usually refuse to deputize campaign volunteers to register people in their homes, but they permit the League of Women Voters and the Moral Majority (but not the NAACP, for example) to register voters. Welfare and unemployment offices, public housing, and family planning centers are sometimes declared off-limits. Finally, bureaucratic rules often limit voter registration to working hours when wage earners are frequently unable to appear.

> *In New York City, the Board of Elections routinely discards forms that are completed in pencil, or signed only on one side, or signed with a middle initial on one side but not the other, or with Mr. or Mrs. on one side only. For the less well educated and the less confident, the application process can be humiliating.[1]*

Local election officials justify these elaborate registration requirements in the name of maintaining the quality of the electorate or preventing fraud. In other democracies, however, citizens are eligible to vote as soon as they reach a certain age and receive identification cards. Government employees in some countries go door to door to register voters before an election. In fact, the United States is the only major democracy where the government does not assume the responsibility for helping its citizens register to vote.

As a result of the restrictions on voter registration, about 40 percent of the American electorate was unregistered in 1980, and two out of three lived in households with less than median incomes. Poor or not, however, once people are registered, they vote. Over 80 percent of the registered voters went to the polls in the 1980 election, and the turnout among those with little education and low incomes was only marginally lower.

Piven and Cloward believe that the major political parties have based their election strategies on an electorate that excludes most of the poor. Barriers to voter registration maintain the socioeconomic skew by discouraging low-income groups

tended to alienate local party members from the process of selecting presidential candidates and financing their campaigns. The unintentional results have been to reduce the voters' sense that they have political efficacy and to weaken their allegiance to particular candidates, thus increasing political apathy.[34]

---

[34] Byron E. Shafer, "Reform and Alienation: The Decline of Intermediation in the Politics of Presidential Selection," *Journal of Law and Politics* 1:1 (Fall 1983): 93–132.

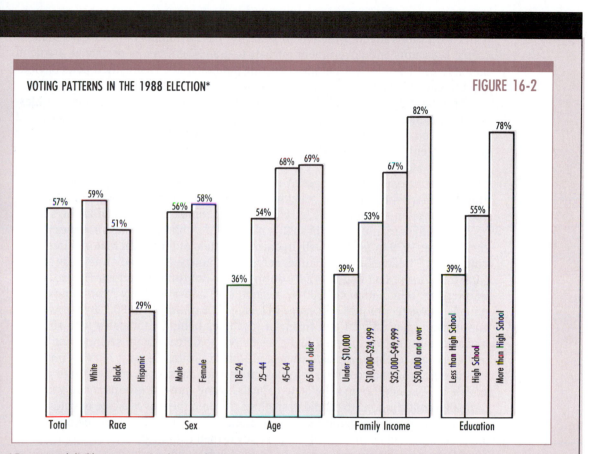

VOTING PATTERNS IN THE 1988 ELECTION*   **FIGURE 16-2**

- Total: 57%
- Race: White 59%, Black 51%, Hispanic 29%
- Sex: Male 56%, Female 58%
- Age: 18-24 36%, 25-44 54%, 45-64 68%, 65 and older 69%
- Family Income: Under $10,000 39%, $10,000–$24,999 53%, $25,000–$49,999 67%, $50,000 and over 82%
- Education: Less than High School 39%, High School 55%, More than High School 78%

* Percentage of eligible voter reporting they voted.

SOURCE: U.S. Bureau of the Census, *Voting and Registration in the Election of November, 1988,* Current Population Reports, Series P-20, No. 440, Tables A, B, and C, 1989.

from registering. As Figure 16-2 shows, the young, the poor, and the less educated are much less likely to register or to vote than the middle-aged, the affluent, and the better-educated. To increase the registration of the nonvoting population would be to risk raising political issues concerning the less well-off—issues that have been given no significant part in recent American national elections.

[1] Frances F. Piven and Richard A. Cloward, *Why Americans Don't Vote* (New York: Pantheon Books, 1988), p. 179.

SOURCE: Frances F. Piven and Richard A. Cloward, *Why Americans Don't Vote* (New York: Pantheon Books, 1988).

THE RISE OF SPECIAL-INTEREST POLITICS

Lower voting rates and decline in party loyalty are usually seen as signs of political apathy. Other signs, however, indicate intense political activity and partisanship. Disillusioned with efforts to achieve their goals through the national parties, new pressure groups have sprung up to advance special interests: banning abortion, supporting farm prices, defeating the Equal Rights Amendment, putting a quota on imported cars, cutting taxes, closing nuclear power plants.

Pressure groups, or interest groups, are organizations that attempt to influence political decisions affecting their members. They have a number of ways to persuade or coerce legislators and government officials to grant them favors or change a vote in their interest. Their tactics include collecting petitions, advertising their point of view, and bringing a lawsuit against the government.

Appeals to the "grass roots" — the concerned public — can be very effective. Masterful use of mass communications has given the New Right a political influence out of all proportion to its membership. This coalition of diverse conservative organizations attempts to enlist evangelical Christians in a political crusade based on fundamentalist values. The Moral Majority, for example, uses a computerized mailing list to send a monthly letter explaining proposed legislation on a certain topic (abortion, school prayer, military spending) and soliciting funds to help support or defeat it. The Moral Majority's leader, the Reverend Jerry Falwell, has increased the organization's membership (and its mailing list) through a number of public relations strategies. In the election year 1979 to 1980 Falwell organized chapters of the Moral Majority in all fifty states, staged "I Love America" rallies across the country, and aired a television special (*America, You're Too Young to Die*) during prime time on 215 stations. He also started a newspaper (circulation 482,000 by election day) and a weekday radio show on 260 stations. These techniques succeeded in raising $3.2 million in 1980.[35] By throwing its impressive organizational and financial resources behind candidates who share its fundamentalist views, the New Right has helped to defeat liberal senators and representatives and to elect President Bush and North Carolina Senator Jesse Helms.

Interest groups also *lobby,* or approach decision makers directly through professionals in Washington and the state capitals. Many interest groups make generous campaign contributions to candidates; others threaten the loss of a bloc of votes in the next election if the legislator does not go along. PACs exist solely for the purpose of influencing candidates by contributing money to their campaigns, and as we have seen, candidates increasingly depend on PACs for fundraising. According to one study of PACs' influence, however, constituents' interests far outweigh the influence of PACs or other special-interest groups.[36]

From one point of view the existence of so many pressure groups serving so many different interests has a beneficial effect on a democracy. Seymour Martin Lipset has argued that the competition among organized groups leads to multiple, crisscrossing loyalties, which prevent the formation of solid blocs with a monopoly on political power.[37] Political ferment is thus viewed as healthy and creative.

On the other hand, powerful interest groups have been able to frustrate the will of the majority on certain issues. Despite the fact that opinion polls showed strong public support for national health insurance, the American Medical Association's intense and persistent lobbying prevented passage of the Medicare program for almost twenty years. Groups that are not organized effectively — consumers, non-union workers,

[35] Jeffery K. Hadden and Charles E. Swann, *Prime Time Preachers: The Rising Power of Televangelism* (Reading, Mass.: Addison-Wesley, 1981).

[36] Larry J. Sabato, *PAC Power* (New York: W.W. Norton, 1985), p. 140.

[37] Seymour Martin Lipset, *Political Man: The Social Bases of Politics* (New York: Doubleday/Anchor, 1963), p. 77.

lower-bracket taxpayers, and the like — have little influence compared to the power of large lobbying organizations.

Because corporations are able to raise a great deal of money for political purposes and because they represent economic interests that the government wishes to protect, business holds unique power in the decision-making process. A recent example of a large corporation's clout was the granting of federal loan guarantees to the Chrysler Corporation. After the energy crisis of 1978 Chrysler's "gas-guzzling" automobiles could no longer compete in the marketplace; by 1979 the company was near bankruptcy and unable to borrow the money necessary to retool for smaller, fuel-efficient cars. After intense lobbying by the company and a massive public relations campaign in the mass media, Congress voted to guarantee Chrysler's bank loans. Rather than put a major manufacturer out of business and eliminate thousands of jobs, the government "saved" Chrysler by risking public money on a private business venture.

Furthermore, without strong national parties to sort out the claims of conflicting interest groups, the government is often stalled and indecisive. In recent years both Republican and Democratic administrations have tried and failed to form a coherent policy on such major issues as environmental protection, welfare reform, arms control, and the escalating foreign trade deficit.

The Reverend Jerry Falwell, head of the Moral Majority, addresses an "I Love America" rally during a presidential campaign. The decline of party politics has increased the power and influence of such special-interest groups.

TWO CHEERS FOR DEMOCRACY

"Democracy is the worst system devised by the wit of man, except for all the others." Winston Churchill's famous statement acknowledges that there are drawbacks as well

Voters in El Salvador jam the polls to cast their ballots in a general election. Authoritarian regimes often seek legitimacy by requiring mass political participation.

as advantages to a democratic system of government. Before assessing the strengths and weaknesses of the American political system, we shall take a brief look at "all the others."

THE AUTHORITARIAN STATE

An **authoritarian government** is based on the rule of a strongman or a small elite. A few authoritarian governments are dictatorships led by an individual who has seized illegitimate power, but most are oligarchies ruled by an aristocratic, bureaucratic, or military elite that has come to power the same way.

Authoritarian governments rule largely through coercion. Since most oligarchies and dictators have seized power in an illegal coup, they cannot plausibly claim legitimacy. Their regimes forbid all opposition by the press or rival political groups, and they suppress dissent ruthlessly. Authoritarian rule is typically corrupt and often short-lived. The late shah of Iran and Idi Amin of Uganda were both repressive dictators; the military juntas of Latin America are examples of oligarchies.

THE TOTALITARIAN STATE

In **totalitarian government** systems the state controls all social institutions. Every aspect of social life must be acceptable to the government: family life, the educational system, the kind of work people do, and the kinds of values and attitudes they have. This total control is justified by an official ideology specifying how everyone should live and promoting a utopian social order. Political power is concentrated in a single party, which is run by a self-appointed leader and an elaborate bureaucracy. While the authoritarian leader wants only obedience, the totalitarian wants the people's hearts and minds as well. The state claims legitimate authority in the name of a higher good:

its utopian end justifies its harsh means. Suppression of individual liberties is more severe in a totalitarian state than under authoritarian rule. Any deviation—in art, religion, economic activity—is subversive because it undermines the goals of the state. Conformity of attitude as well as behavior is enforced through a combination of propaganda and terror.

Nazi Germany probably came closest to the totalitarian "ideal" of total control over all human activities, but the Soviet Union under Stalin and China under Mao were also totalitarian systems.

At the end of the 1980s, the leaders of the Soviet-bloc nations of Eastern Europe and the People's Republic of China became more flexible and receptive to change. Harsh repressive measures, combined with the debilitating effects of a system in which everyone spied on everyone else, had helped cause a decline in motivation and general work effort among their citizens. While relief from totalitarian controls led to more democratic regimes in Eastern Europe, the student reform movement in China was brutally suppressed. However, since industrializing nations like China depend on the loyalty of their technical workers and professional classes, the current period of rigid repression will probably be followed by a period when stringent controls over students and workers will again be somewhat relaxed.

THE DEMOCRATIC STATE

In contrast to authoritarian and totalitarian regimes, a **democratic government** rules by the consent of the governed. Every citizen has the right to participate in politics by running for office, voting, and other political activities. The power of political leaders comes from legal authority rather than the use of force.

Democracies also have representative institutions: legislatures, boards of education, city councils, and so on. Officeholders generally are chosen in free elections; they must win and keep the support of their constituents by representing their interests.

The power of the democratic state is restrained by laws that define the rights of the people. Such civil liberties as the right to assembly, free speech, and equal protection under the law limit the authority of the state.

Democracies are rare among the world's governments and appear almost exclusively in the advanced industrial countries of Western Europe, North America, Australia, New Zealand, and Japan. Lipset has theorized that democratic institutions exist only in developed economies because democracy requires a literate, urban population and a stable, middle-class social order. An educated electorate is more likely to demand political participation in the government, and power in developed economies is less likely to be concentrated in a few hands.[38] The British government, for example, has long practiced a policy of "creaming" or giving outstanding members of the working class high political offices, thus depriving the labor movement of its leaders.

In any case, democracy does not appear able to survive very long in societies with deep internal conflicts. When compromise among opposing interests is impossible, and when there is little tolerance of dissenting political opinions, then democratic

---

[38] Seymour Martin Lipset, "Some Social Prerequisites for Democracy," *American Political Science Review* 53 (1959): 74–86.

institutions are weak or nonexistent. Developing countries, for example, typically have a large, oppressed peasant class and a much smaller ruling elite. The social cleavage between rich and poor as well as the lack of a moderate, educated middle class lead to political instability and authoritarian rule.

THE DEMOCRATIC STALEMATE

In E. M. Forster's essay collection, *Two Cheers for Democracy*, the British writer praised democratic political systems for their tolerance of individual freedom and their capacity for self-criticism. He withheld his last hurrah because he *believed* in elites ("of the sensitive, the considerate, and the plucky") and thought that democracy encourages mediocrity.[39]

The problem of elites is an ancient one for which Americans have not found a solution. Unlike other democracies the United States today lacks a traditional governing class, an "establishment" that represents common values. Robert Nisbet has called this situation a "twilight of power" in which "the loss of confidence in political institutions is matched by the erosion of traditional authority in kinship, locality, culture, language, school, and other elements of the social fabric."[40]

Declining participation in traditional politics is one symptom of the government's loss of authority. According to the polls most Americans now find their political system unresponsive to their needs and their leaders untrustworthy and ineffective. About one-third of the electorate takes no part in politics of any sort.

The erosion of political authority has given rise to special-interest politics. In a pluralistic society interest groups fight for the policies they want; but in a political system dominated by special interests, every group fights *only* for the policies it wants, and no one speaks for the majority. When powerful interests overlap, as they do in the military-industrial complex, they exert far more influence than their unorganized, politically apathetic opposition.[41]

Moreover, without the discipline of national party loyalty, government officials have no responsibility to support a president's policies or a coherent party program. When the two-party system is weak, members of Congress become political "free agents" representing only the particular district and the few special interests that elected them. The most important of these free agents are currently the conservative Senators of the New Right, who have often come to Washington with their own agenda for advancing fundamentalist religious beliefs about such social issues as abortion and school prayer. Some engage in "monkey-wrench politics" — the blocking of a legislative program to achieve their own goals, no matter what the cost to the country or their party. Since every important policy — on farm supports, taxes, defense, Social Security, foreign trade — hurts some interest group, the decline of party politics has made it much more difficult to make and carry out the controversial decisions on which the future welfare of the country depends.

---

[39] E. M. Forster, *Two Cheers for Democracy* (New York: Harcourt Brace Jovanovich/Harvest, 1951), pp. 70–73.

[40] Quoted in William Pfaff, "Reflections: Aristocracies," *The New Yorker*, January 14, 1980, p. 70.

[41] Stanley Lieberson, "An Empirical Study of Military-Industrial Linkages," *American Journal of Sociology* 76 (January 1971): 562–83.

Compared to authoritarian and totalitarian systems, American democracy deserves its two cheers for individual freedom and tolerance of criticism. Like other democracies, however, it can be faulted for its failure to find a satisfactory means of reconciling the special interests of elites with the interests of the less powerful majority.

SUMMARY

1. Politics, the institution for government, determines the distribution of political power. Power is the ability to control scarce resources or determine others' behavior, a social relationship based on influence, coercion, or authority.

2. Authority is a relationship between leaders and followers when the leaders' power is accepted as legitimate. Webers three types of authority are: traditional, rational-legal, and charismatic.

3. The politics of modern states is characterized by the struggle for power among contending interest groups. Unlike traditional societies, modern political systems are based on centralized governments, rational-legal authority, and mass political participation.

4. According to the elitist view of power, ruling elites defend their own interests against the majority. Michels's Iron Law of Oligarchy states that large organizations necessarily create hierarchical elites. Mills claimed that American society is dominated by a power elite with members occupying high positions in the government, the large corporations, and the military. Domhoff found an American governing elite that mainly represents business interests but encompasses other decision-making positions as well.

5. The pluralist view of power finds that political power is dispersed among many competing interest groups and that countervailing power is exerted between and within them. Dahl's study concluded that powerful groups are forced to bargain with each other; Rose argued that the interests of diverse elites do not coincide in a single ruling class. Riesman claimed that American society is threatened with political stagnation because veto groups are able to block effective decision making.

6. American society appears to have a pluralist distribution of power, but a power elite does emerge on some issues. Since the interests of the many different elites do not overlap, they often act as veto groups.

7. Duverger noted that minority parties thrive in proportionately representative systems, but the winner-take-all elections in the United States tend to weaken party organizations. Party identification has recently declined as primary elections and television have become more important in selecting candidates. Reform of fund-raising procedures and the use of opinion polls have taken away other traditional functions of the political party.

8. Partly because of weakening party loyalty, political participation has been declining steadily for twenty years. Turnout is especially low among poorer, less-educated, and younger people. The voters' apathy also seems to result from their lost sense of political efficacy.

9. Other signs indicate renewed political interest and activity. The growth of the New Right is an example of a religious pressure group that is influencing the political process. Powerful lobbies for corporations and other interest groups continue to affect decision making by bringing pressure to bear on elected officials.

10. Authoritarian governments rule largely through coercion. Totalitarian states claim legitimate authority to control all social institutions in the name of a utopian goal, while democratic governments have legal authority and rule by consent of the governed.

11. Democracies are found only in advanced industrial societies, where power is rather widely distributed and where there are no deep internal conflicts that make compromise impossible. In the United States the decline of political parties and the erosion of governmental authority have given rise to special-interest politics.

KEY TERMS

politics 500

power 500

influence 501

coercion 502

legitimacy 502

authority 502

traditional authority 503

rational-legal authority 503

charismatic authority 504

state 504

countervailing power 509

political efficacy 517

authoritarian government 522

totalitarian government 522

democratic government 523

SUGGESTED READING

* G. William Domhoff. *The Powers That Be: Processes of Ruling Class Domination in America.* New York: Random House/Vintage, 1979.

V. O. Key, *Politics, Parties and Pressure Groups,* 5th ed. New York: Crowell, 1964.

Charles E. Lindblom, *Democracy and Market Systems.* New York: Oxford University Press, 1988.

* Seymour M. Lipset. *Political Man: The Social Bases of Politics.* Baltimore, MD: Johns Hopkins University Press, 1981.

Byron E. Shafer. *Quiet Revolution: The Struggle for the Democratic Party and the Shaping of Post-Reform Politics.* New York: Russell Sage Foundation, 1983.

* Robert Sherrill and James D. Barber. *Why They Call It Politics: A Guide to America's Government,* 4th ed. San Diego, CA: Harcourt Brace Jovanovich, 1984.

Hendrick Smith, *The Power Game: How Washington Works.* New York: Random House, 1988.

* Alexis de Tocqueville. *Democracy in America.* Edited and abridged by Richard D. Heffner. New York: New American Library/Mentor, 1956; originally published in 1835 and 1840.

* Available in paperback.

PART 5

CHALLENGES OF CONTEMPORARY SOCIETY

Man is the only
animal that
laughs and
weeps; for he is
the only animal
that is struck
with the
difference
between what
things are, and
what they ought
to be.

William Hazlitt

CHAPTER 17

SOCIAL MOVEMENTS AND COLLECTIVE BEHAVIOR

On May 29, 1985, the final match in the European Cup soccer championships was played at Heysel Stadium in Brussels. An hour before kickoff the terraces, or unreserved standing room areas, were packed with spectators. Fans of Liverpool, the British team, were assigned to section Y, which was separated by a high wire fence from section Z, where supporters of Juventus, the rival Italian team, had bought tickets. The British and Italian fans began to chant insults at each other through the mesh fence, then threw cans and beer bottles. Suddenly hundreds of Liverpool fans stormed over the fence, brandishing broken bottles and swinging flag sticks. The Italians pulled back in panic, scrambling over each other to reach the exit ramp. Hundreds quickly found themselves cornered between a chain-link fence and a concrete wall, as more and more terrified people crushed in behind them. Three minutes later, the fence and wall collapsed under their weight, pitching the crowd on top of each other and burying hundreds under the rubble and the bodies of other fans. Even as rescue workers dug out the victims, the Liverpool fans continued their attack, fighting the Belgian police in full view of reporters and prime-time television cameras. When order was finally restored, the soccer riot had left 38 dead and 437 injured.

At the time commentators offered two different explanations for the Brussels disaster. The first was that the soccer riot was an emotional outburst brought on by the frustrations of poverty and unemployment. Soccer in Britain is traditionally a working-man's sport, and most of the troublemakers came from the rough neighborhoods of Liverpool, a city with an unemployment rate of nearly 25 percent. A British social psychologist claimed that the rowdy fans were "products of Thatcher's Britain" and that "this is what happens when a group is subjected to deprivation, denied hope and a future."

The fatal Brussels soccer riot was widely interpreted either as an emotional outburst by deprived working-class youths or as a drunken brawl among "mindless hooligans." Sociological theories of collective behavior offer other — and perhaps more plausible — explanations for the crowd's brutality.

The second, more popular explanation blamed the personalities of the rioters. Many observers referred to the British soccer fans as "animals" and "mindless hooligans." The Pope expressed horror at "such ferocious and irrational behavior," and the Italian press accused the rioters of "fanaticism," "blind rage and madness," and "bestiality." Some thought that the anonymity of the crowd allowed the Liverpool fans to lose the inhibitions that would otherwise have restrained them from attacking the hated "Eye-ties." Still others mentioned the day-long drinking bouts that took place before the game. *The Guardian,* the liberal British newspaper, described the Liverpool mob as so many "boozed-up cretins." Most people, in other words, looked for psychological reasons for the riot. They emphasized the Liverpool fans' state of mind and their motivations.

But psychological explanations cannot account for some of the most puzzling aspects of crowd behavior. Being in a crowd does not always trigger irrational acts. For example, in the spring of 1989 more than a million Chinese took to the streets of Beijing in a peaceful appeal for democratic reforms. The self-controlled behavior of the huge crowd in Tiananmen Square provides a marked contrast to the violence in Brussels. Furthermore, not all crowds behave the same way even under similar circumstances. For 21 years before the soccer riot, Liverpool fans had been known for their good behavior. In fact, Everton, the city's other professional team, had just finished five uneventful matches on the Continent, including a final championship match in Rotterdam two weeks before.

This chapter is about both **collective behavior**, the relatively unorganized and spontaneous behavior of people in crowds and masses, and **social movements**, which are highly organized and relatively long term collective efforts to bring about or prevent social change. Although the two terms appear from their definitions to represent opposite sorts of behavior, social movements and collective behavior share some outward characteristics. The same actions that "just happen" in episodes of collective behavior are often made to happen by the leaders of social movements. A rowdy street demonstration or a bloody popular uprising might be the senseless emotional outburst it looks like on the surface, but it might also be a calculated political protest.

The first part of the chapter evaluates the major theories explaining why people in crowds sometimes behave in strange and unexpected ways. The rest of the chapter discusses social movements — why they start, how they develop into organized political efforts, what strategies and tactics their leaders use to win support, and the way they affect general social attitudes.

COLLECTIVE BEHAVIOR

The term "collective behavior" usually refers to the activities of people in crowds. A **crowd** consists of a number of people whose physical proximity to one another influences their behavior. The definition of collective behavior also covers *mass behavior,* or the actions of people who never meet face to face but influence each other indirectly through television, movies, and advertising.

Collective behavior has two distinctive features. First, it appears to be improvised on the spot; crowds lack the enduring structure and predictability of established groups. Shoppers on a busy street, for example, seem to come and go haphazardly. A disorderly crowd at a football game might get so carried away that it rushes onto the playing field and tears down the goal posts.

Second, collective behavior often looks strange or unusual. Because people generally behave more or less as they are expected to, it is surprising when a crowd suddenly begins to act in peculiar and unexpected ways. Puzzling episodes of collective madness have been common throughout history. In the seventeenth century, for example, a national obsession with tulips swept over Holland. This "tulip mania" caused such wild speculations on the market that fortunes were made and lost on the price of a single bulb. More recently, the Procter & Gamble Company was forced to drop its 100-year-old trademark because of the persistent, bizarre rumor that the moon-and-stars design was a sign of satanism and devil worship. According to other mysterious rumors, McDonald's put worms in its hamburgers and Life Savers' Bubble Yum contained spider eggs. Over the centuries men and women have eagerly embraced such unlikely fashions as whale-bone corsets, powdered wigs, stiff collars, and spike-heeled shoes, in spite of the pain and discomfort they caused. Fads and crazes — skateboarding, health foods, Nintendo, break dancing — are suddenly "in" and just as suddenly "out." The varieties of collective behavior range in seriousness from passing

Fashionable ladies in eighteenth-century France willingly endured painfully tight corsets, heavy headdresses, unwieldy hoopskirts, and uncomfortably small shoes. Much collective behavior is puzzling because it seems to be entirely irrational.

fads and fashions to epidemics of mass hysteria such as the Salem witch hunts, financial panics such as the 1987 stock market crash, and frenzies of mob violence leading to lynchings and massacres. The irrational and unexpected element in all of these activities distinguishes much collective behavior.

Not all collective behavior, however, is entirely spontaneous and unregulated. In busy street crowds most people walk on the sidewalk, stay to the right, and cross at the corner. A crowd of football fans may appear emotionally out of control, but shouting insults and tearing down goal posts are conventional, even ritual, activities. Much crowd behavior, in fact, is somewhat predictable. Herbert Blumer distinguished among four types of crowds[1]:

1. The *casual crowd* is made up of people who have not gathered for any common purpose and have little to do with each other. Shoppers in a mall make up a casual crowd.

2. The *conventional crowd* is more structured and follows certain established norms. The cheering fans at a wrestling match are conforming to the convention of making noise; the audience at a concert is conventionally quiet.

3. The *expressive crowd* gathers in order to have its emotions aroused by a particular event or activity. Its members want to be "carried away" by their feelings. Rock concerts and political rallies have expressive crowds.

---

[1] Herbert Blumer, "Collective Behavior," in *New Outline of the Principles of Sociology*, ed. Alfred McLung Lee (New York: Barnes & Noble, 1951), pp. 165–220.

4. The *acting crowd* takes concerted, often violent action in panics, riots, and massacres. Casual, conventional, and expressive crowds can all be transformed into acting crowds. A fire may cause a casual crowd in a department store to panic and run for the exits; the conventional crowd at a World Series baseball game may riot when the local team wins; and the expressive crowd at a rock concert may "go wild" and mob the musicians. How can we account for such a sudden change? What causes the usual social restraints to break down in a crowd? Why do people in crowds sometimes show such uniformity of behavior, heightened emotion, and violence?

CROWD BEHAVIOR AS ABNORMAL BEHAVIOR

The earliest, and for a long time the most influential, answers to these questions were found in Gustave Le Bon's *The Crowd* (1895). A journalist with aristocratic sympathies, Le Bon was deeply disturbed by the popular political upheavals that were threatening the French Third Republic in the 1870s and 1880s. He was frightened by the rapid social changes that accompanied the industrialization of France — particularly by the growing wealth and power of what he believed to be the "uncivilized masses." To Le Bon the crowd was an irrational, uncontrolled, and destructive mob. Alone, he believed, people are ordinarily quite reasonable and well-behaved, but immersed in a crowd they lose self-control and become susceptible to emotional and violent impulses. No matter how different individuals might be in personality and intelligence, Le Bon thought that in a crowd they would begin to think and act like the "lowest common denominator." Today people who use the phrases "herd instinct" and "mob psychology" are agreeing with Le Bon that mere membership in a crowd results in abnormal, even subhuman, behavior.

CONTAGION THEORY.   Le Bon's observations are the basis for the theory of contagion. According to this theory behavior is "contagious": the actions of one person in a crowd tend to be imitated by the next person, who is imitated by the next, and so on. If a few people jump up and scream at a ninth-inning home run, for example, then others nearby will do the same, and soon everyone in the ballpark will be standing up and cheering. In what Blumer referred to as a "circular reaction," each person's feelings become intensified when they are reflected by others in the crowd. In this heightened emotional state baseball fans have been known to overrun the playing field, tear up the bases, and mob the players.

CONVERGENCE THEORY.   Contagion theory emphasizes how being in a crowd can affect the behavior of its individual members. From another point of view, the crowd's individual members can also affect its behavior. In convergence theory, only those people who are likely to engage in a certain kind of behavior will "converge" to form a crowd in the first place. A lynch mob consists of hostile, angry people who are prone to violence; a revival meeting attracts only religious believers. Applied to riots and civil disorders, convergence theory is sometimes called the "riffraff" theory of collective behavior. Le Bon and many of his contemporaries, for example, believed that the mobs of the French Revolution were made up of dangerous criminals, vagrants, and social misfits.

The first ticker tape parade may have been an irrational, spontaneous outburst of enthusiasm, but they are now urban rituals. Sociological theories assume that collective behavior is the rather predictable response of ordinary people in extraordinary situations.

LIMITATIONS OF PSYCHOLOGICAL THEORIES. Contagion and convergence theories focus on individual psychology to account for the character of the crowd. Either people are driven to abnormal behavior by crowd situations, or else abnormal people get together in crowds to act upon their impulses. These psychological interpretations have several drawbacks.

Contagion theory fails to take into account the fact that not all members of a crowd share the same emotions or act alike. Jerry M. Lewis's study of the Kent State incident described below shows that individuals in an emotionally aroused crowd have different sorts of feelings and inclinations.

In May 1970 two violent demonstrations at Kent State University protested the American invasion of Cambodia during the Vietnam War. The governor of Ohio called on the National Guard to keep order by breaking up any assembly of students on campus. The day after the Guard arrived, a crowd gathered on the Commons, a central meeting place, and were dispersed with tear gas. A few minutes later Guardsmen actually fired on the students, killing four undergraduates and wounding nine others.

This tragic event might not have taken place had the soldiers seen the crowd for what it was — a mixed collection of hecklers and by-standers, not a unified, dangerous mob. In fact, Lewis identified three separate groups of students according to their behavior: the "active core" taunted and threw rocks and dirt at the Guardsmen; the "cheerleaders" shouted encouragement to the activists; and the "spectators," who were in the majority, simply watched what was going on. After the tear-gassing began, some of the students went back to their dorms, while others moved off in different directions toward a football field and a parking lot. Only the students in the parking lot, most of whom were spectators, were fired upon.[2] Studies such as this show that the uniformity of crowds is an illusion.

Empirical research has also undermined the premise of convergence theory that only abnormal people become involved in collective behavior. George Rudé's studies found that so-called criminal riffraff had little to do with the Paris riots preceding the French Revolution. All 662 people killed in the mob that stormed the Bastille prison, for example, had regular occupations and places of residence.[3] In the 1960s, a U.S. presidential commission investigating urban ghetto riots also found that the typical rioter did not fit the riffraff stereotype. The typical rioter was a young, black, unmarried man with a menial or unskilled job. Far from being alienated, antisocial criminals, the rioters on the whole were better informed about political issues and more likely to be involved in civil rights activities than other urban blacks.[4]

CROWD BEHAVIOR AS NORMAL BEHAVIOR

Psychological explanations consider collective behavior to be the extraordinary and unpredictable responses of unusual individuals. Sociological theories assume the opposite: that collective behavior is the predictable response of ordinary, rational people who find themselves in extraordinary situations.

EMERGENT NORM THEORY.   Have you ever noticed that students who meet regularly in a classroom nearly always sit where they have sat before? In their research on small groups, Ralph Turner and Lewis Killian noticed that people in groups gradually establish certain standards of behavior, or **emergent norms**. Once a particular norm emerges — such as the seating pattern of the class — members of the group feel social pressure to comply with it. If someone breaks one of these informal rules, everyone is a little surprised.

According to Turner and Killian, people in crowds tend to act alike because they are reluctant to violate an emergent norm.[5] From this point of view the "cheerleaders" in the Kent State incident were going along with the practice of taunting the Guardsmen, which the "activists" had established. The "spectators," who were only curious bystanders, felt the social pressure not to violate this norm of behavior. As a result, no

---

[2] Jerry M. Lewis, "A Study of the Kent State Incident," *Sociological Inquiry* 42 (1972): 87–96.

[3] George Rudé, *The Crowd in the French Revolution.* (Oxford, Eng.: Oxford University Press, 1959), p. 200.

[4] U.S. Riot Commission, *Report of the National Advisory Commission on Civil Disorders* (New York: Bantam, 1968).

[5] Ralph H. Turner, "Collective Behavior," in *Handbook of Sociology,* ed. R. E. L. Faris (Chicago: Rand McNally, 1964), pp. 382–425; Ralph H. Turner and Lewis M. Killian, *Collective Behavior,* 2nd ed. (Englewood Cliffs, N.J.: Prentice-Hall, 1972).

one interfered with the activists, and the illusion of a completely hostile mob was unfortunately created.

Emergent norm theory offers a persuasive explanation for some of the other puzzling aspects of collective behavior. In a new or threatening situation, when the usual norms are no longer applicable, other norms develop. Individuals in crowds act alike not because they are infected with a contagious emotion or because they have converged with like-minded people but because certain kinds of behavior seem appropriate. If a fire breaks out in a theater, for example, the prevailing norm quickly changes from sitting quietly to running for the exits.

Emergent norm theory has the virtue of explaining everyday crowd behavior as well as the extreme forms of collective behavior. If two people who are talking and laughing together immediately fall silent when they enter a church, it is not because they are suddenly "infected" by the reverent mood of the congregation (contagion theory) but because they recognize that chattering noisily is not the appropriate way to behave. The orderly lines that form outside a box office can be seen as the result of emergent norms regulating butting-in and saving places. Fashions in food and dress represent emergent norms that have adherents and neutral bystanders. Fads and crazes can be interpreted as attempts to be "in," that is, to conform to the new norms of one's group.

GAME THEORY. Emergent norm theory emphasizes the normal social processes involved in even the strangest episodes of collective behavior. **Game theory** emphasizes that crowd behavior often has rational and logical elements. Game theorists such as Richard Berk assume that every individual, even in a crowd, makes rational decisions

Panic looks like a purely emotional response to a threatening situation, but it is not entirely irrational. After poisonous fumes from a chemical plant killed 2,000 people in Bhopal, India, in 1984, the logical thing for the survivors to do was to leave the affected area as quickly as possible.

about how he or she will behave. In any situation, Berk claims, people weigh the probable costs and rewards of different courses of action and then try to choose the one that will bring the highest net reward.[6] The gathering of a crowd is an opportunity for individuals to gain certain rewards at a lower cost. Some of the British soccer fans, for example, obviously went to Brussels looking for a fight. Soccer matches have often been the setting for the ritualized aggression known as "aggro" (short for aggravation), which is enacted by young men wearing distinctive dress and sometimes carrying hidden knives and razor blades. The crowd provides these "football thugs" with the opportunity to get into a brawl with much less risk of being arrested. For bored, lower-class youths, the rewards of aggro are excitement, a sense of power, and a feeling of solidarity with a winning team. "In the mob," a self-styled soccer rowdy wrote in *The Guardian,* "I got something that I never had before — respect."[7] While the emergent norm approach would view the soccer riot as conformity to a new norm (charging the Italian fans), game theory sees it as members of a crowd cooperating to get what they want (excitement, aggro posturing, victory over their Italian rivals) from the situation.

Game theory offers a safety-in-numbers explanation for why people are willing to do things in a crowd that they would never do alone. It also explains why not all norms break down in a crowd situation. During the 1965 riot in Watts, a poor black section of Los Angeles, observers noted that looters driving away with stolen goods in their cars continued to stop for red lights and crosswalks.

Though rioters may not act in a way that everyone would call rational, emergent norm and game theories draw attention to the normal and logical aspects of their behavior. From an emergent norm theorist's point of view, panic appears to be a rational response to a threatening situation. The logical thing to do about a falling stock market, for example, is to sell out as soon as you can. To a game theorist a riot looks less like an emotional outburst than a realistic attempt to make the most of an unusual situation. On closer observation, collective behavior looks more like ordinary behavior after all.

The opposite point could also be made: human behavior that is accepted as normal has some irrational and unpredictable elements as well. From a purely objective point of view, many social conventions look a little crazy. Why is it that American women may wear pants but American men may not wear skirts? Is it more sensible for a factory worker to be paid by the hour instead of by the work accomplished? In the acutely overpopulated countries of Asia, is it reasonable that a large family is a source of social prestige? Perhaps the motivations behind what we call "normal" behavior are not entirely rational either.

Episodes of collective behavior turn out to be variations on such familiar social processes as the development of norms, conformity, decision making, and leadership. These familiar processes, in turn, often have some of the transitory and unexpected qualities associated with collective behavior. The study of collective behavior reminds us that the social structures we think of as "permanent" — the institutions, roles, and norms of proper conduct that endure over long periods of time — are actually changing

---

[6] Richard A. Berk, "A Gaming Approach to Crowd Behavior," *American Journal of Sociology* 79 (June 1974): 355–73.

[7] Daniel Goleman, "Brutal Sports and Brutal Fans," *The New York Times,* August 13, 1985, pp. C1, C3; Jo Thomas, "British Soccer Fan: Why So Warlike?" *The New York Times,* May 31, 1985, p. A10.

and that a spontaneous and therefore unpredictable element exists in all social interaction. We turn now to social movements, the deliberate and organized attempts to change social structures.

SOCIAL MOVEMENTS

Some years ago, the telephone company in California announced a new all-digit dialing system. Thousands of telephone subscribers, indignant at the prospect of losing the names of their exchanges to automation, started a protest organization — the Anti-Digit Dialing League. Their attempt to force the telephone company to retreat from its new policy was unsuccessful, and the league soon disappeared along with the old exchanges. The goal of this particular social movement was trivial, and its efforts were rather short-lived. Other social movements have sought profound and long-lasting social change, and some of them have been spectacularly successful. The rise of Islam and the Chinese Communist Revolution, for example, ultimately changed the behavior of millions of people and affected the course of history.

All social movements have three characteristics in common:

1. *Social movements seek specific goals.* Neil Smelser has distinguished between **norm-oriented social movements**, which attempt to protect or change social norms, and **value-oriented social movements**, which seek to protect or change social values.[8] The labor union movement, for example, was norm-oriented: it sought to change the norms affecting workers by advocating such reforms as higher wage scales and better working conditions. The value-oriented abolitionist movement, on the other hand, was largely a moral and religious crusade against slavery.

   A third type of social movement, the *revolutionary* movement, is discussed in Chapter 18, "Social Change and Social Conflict." Revolutionary movements seek to bring about fundamental changes in an entire social structure. Successful revolutions, such as the Protestant Reformation and the French Revolution, transformed existing institutions and ushered in new eras in social relationships.

2. *Social movements are cohesive organizations.* Participants in social movements share a sense of purpose that helps the organization survive for a relatively long time. It is this feeling of commitment to long-term goals that distinguishes social movements from collective behavior.[9]

3. *Social movements have a unifying ideology.* All social movements have a set of ideas, or an ideology, that justifies protest and change. The members may not all have exactly the same beliefs, but they share basic values and convictions.[10]

---

[8] Neil J. Smelser, *Theory of Collective Behavior* (New York: Free Press, 1962).

[9] Mark Traugott, "Reconceiving Social Movements," *Social Problems* 26:1 (October 1978): 43.

[10] Stanley Milgram and Hans Toch, "Collective Behavior: Crowds and Social Movements," in *The Handbook of Social Psychology*, 2nd ed., eds. Gardner Lindzey and Elliot Aronson, (Reading, Mass.: Addison-Wesley, 1969), Vol 4, p. 602.

HOW DO SOCIAL MOVEMENTS START?

Social movements often have unlikely beginnings. Hardly anyone could have guessed, for example, that a few followers of a Jewish heretic in a remote corner of the Roman Empire would start a religious movement that would eventually convert the entire Western world. Nor was there any way of knowing that a handful of Russian conspirators, inspired by the ideas of an obscure German economist, would become the vanguard for political revolutions all over the globe. However, several theories explain the reasons social movements such as Christianity and communism get started, how they attract followers, and why they eventually succeed or fail.

The Chicago school of sociology, led by Robert E. Park and his students, developed a natural history, or "stages," approach to the study of social movements. According to this classical model, social movements arise out of three conditions: (1) deep and widespread discontent, (2) a generalized belief in some cause of or solution to the problem, and (3) grass-roots support for a collective effort to do something about it. Popular grievances may be due to either *absolute deprivation,* such as poverty or oppression, or *relative deprivation,* the sense of being poor or oppressed in comparison to other times or other people (see Chapter 18, "Social Change and Social Conflict"). Fluctuations in the level of popular discontent are thought to affect the rise and fall of social movements.

An application of this model to McCarthyism, a social movement of the early 1950s, shows its weaknesses. Joseph McCarthy, the junior Republican senator from Wisconsin, became nationally famous for exposing what he claimed was a communist conspiracy against the United States. Using his Senate subcommittee as a forum, McCarthy publicly harassed and humiliated accused communist sympathizers on the basis of little or no evidence. McCarthyism reached its peak in 1951 and 1952, when thousands of alleged subversives were discredited and blacklisted from employment in government and business. McCarthy suddenly lost public favor in 1953, however, and the movement shrank to a small radical right group and eventually disappeared. The "stages" explanation of the rise and fall of McCarthyism emphasizes widespread discontent in the post–World War II period and the relative deprivations of the groups who suffered from the economic and social changes of the 1950s. In fact, support for McCarthy did appear to come mainly from two groups: older people with fixed incomes who were unhappy about postwar inflation, and political conservatives who resented the social legislation of the New Deal. This discontent (the first stage) gave rise to a second stage, the generalized belief that communists were subverting the country. McCarthyism, as a movement, thus represented grass-roots support (the third stage) for McCarthy's campaign to drive subversives from the government. According to the classical model, McCarthyism declined when Cold War antagonism toward communists subsided after the Korean War.

Although popular discontent is obviously an important stimulus to the growth of social movements, it cannot alone explain why McCarthy gained and lost public favor so suddenly. Most of the economic and political developments that are supposed to account for the movement were evident well before and long after McCarthyism reached its height. Other studies have concluded that McCarthy's success was actually due to his support by a powerful elite in the Republican party. Turner and Killian have pointed out that a freshman senator such as McCarthy could not have held a subcommittee chairmanship or received national publicity without his party's support. While many Republican politicians may have found McCarthy's tactics objectionable, most were willing to benefit from his attacks on the Democratic establishment's patriotism. When Dwight D. Eisenhower became president in 1953, and McCarthy began to abuse the Republican administration, the party soon withdrew its support. Within a few months the Republican leaders stripped him of the privileges and resources that had enabled him to attract a mass following. "In short," Turner and Killian concluded, "the movement prospered when it served the purposes of the Republican party and quickly declined when it no longer did so." [11]

The best empirical evidence indicates that social movements do not derive from the vague discontents of frustrated groups.[12] The rise of McCarthyism, for example, appears to have been the result of conventional party politics.[13] There is also little support for the assumption that people join social movements for purely ideological reasons. Robert Stallings's study of the environmental movement found that its members disagreed on the fundamental issues of who is responsible for environmental problems and what should be done about them.[14] Not only do rank-and-file members hold diverse opinions, but often they differ with the movement's leaders on crucial questions.

Although discontent and ideology are motivating factors, they clearly do not fully explain the existence of social movements. Other theorists have focused on what kinds of people join social movements and what kinds of societies produce them.

WHO JOINS SOCIAL MOVEMENTS?

When Le Bon described the submersion of the individual personality in the crowd, he began a tradition of social criticism that emphasizes the harmful effects of modern **mass society**. Instead of the close primary-group ties of traditional societies, the mass society is dominated by anonymous secondary-group relationships. According to this view people in industrial societies are uprooted from community life and isolated from each other in impersonal bureaucracies. Their loneliness and sense of alienation makes them susceptible to the appeal of social movements that promise to reintegrate them into a meaningful community.[15] This theory appeared to be borne out in the 1930s and 1940s, when fascism was sweeping Germany and Italy. Mass movements then seemed to be symptoms of a sick society, an expression of irrational fears and hatreds released by a rent in the social fabric.

The theory of mass society offers two testable propositions: (1) extremist movements will appear in societies where few people participate in civic and religious groups; and (2) large numbers of alienated people who do not belong to such groups

---

[11] Turner and Killian, *Collective Behavior*, p. 251.

[12] John D. McCarthy and Mayer N. Zald, "Resource Mobilization and Social Movements: A Partial Theory," *American Journal of Sociology* 82:6 (May 1977): 1214–15.

[13] Michael Rogin, *The Intellectuals and McCarthy* (Cambridge, Mass.: MIT Press, 1967), pp. 232–39.

[14] Robert A. Stallings, "Patterns of Belief in Social Movements," *Sociological Quarterly* 14 (Autumn 1973): 465–80.

[15] Philip Selznick, "Institutional Vulnerability in Mass Society," in *Protest, Reform, and Revolt*, ed. Joseph R. Gusfield (New York: Wiley, 1970), pp. 263–70.

In the 1930s fascism appeared to be a symptom of a shattered, alienated, "sick" society. The fact is, however, that Hitler was legally elected by ordinary farmers and small-town residents, whose interests he claimed to represent.

will join extremist movements. Neither of these predictions has passed the empirical test. Even studies of Nazism, the very movement that the theory sought to explain, have failed to support its hypotheses. The Germans were not uprooted and atomized; on the contrary, they showed a high level of participation in voluntary associations, unions, and political parties. Furthermore, Nazi support came not from the urban masses but from farmers and people in small towns who were already politically active and highly organized. This rural class was dissatisfied with the existing party programs and felt ignored in national politics. When the Nazis promised to serve their interests, farmers joined the movement in large numbers precisely because they were already organized and ready to do so.[16]

It is strange but true that even movements that represent deprived and alienated groups are not joined primarily by the people for whom they speak. When Fidel Castro started the movement that led to a communist revolution in Cuba, for example, his original followers were mainly young, well-educated, middle-class professionals and intellectuals.[17] An analysis of the women's movement showed similar results: discontented housewives were *least* likely to join a feminist group.[18]

The answer to the question "Who joins social movements?" is clear. Activists and "joiners" join social movements. Moreover, as the Nazi example indicated, people who are already organized are more easily mobilized for collective action than others. Some of the reasons for these phenomena are explored in the next section.

---

[16] Anthony Oberschall, *Social Conflict and Social Movements* (Englewood Cliffs, N.J.: Prentice-Hall, 1973), pp. 108–11.

[17] Theodore Draper, *Castro's Revolution: Myths and Realities* (New York: Praeger, 1962), pp. 42–43.

[18] Jo Freeman, "The Origins of the Women's Liberation Movement," *American Journal of Sociology* 78:4 (1973): 803.

SOCIAL MOVEMENTS AS POLITICAL ORGANIZATIONS

As we have seen, neither ideology nor the stresses of modern mass society can fully account for the rise of social movements. Theories that find the causes of social movements in the motivations of their participants, Herbert Blumer claims, "overlook the fact that a movement has to be constructed and has to carve out a career in what is practically always an opposed, resistant or at least indifferent world."[19] Blumer and other scholars in recent years have stressed the political processes involved in social action. Some have developed the theory of **resource management**, which argues that social movements are rational political organizations that seek specific goals, mobilize resources (for example, money and members), and invent strategies and tactics to win support. According to this theory social movements occur not merely because there is widespread discontent but because organizations channel that discontent in concerted action.

RECRUITING MEMBERS.   Why do people join a social movement? The obvious answer is that they get together in order to pursue a collective good. The union movement, for example, is generally thought to be made up of workers who are acting together to obtain benefits for all. Mancur Olson, however, finds this assumption flawed. He points out that rational, self-interested individuals usually will *not* act together to achieve a common goal.[20] Although all the members of a collectivity may have a common interest in obtaining a certain benefit, they have no interest individually in paying the cost of providing it. A truly rational, purely self-interested person will ask this question: If workers who don't join the union movement will benefit just as much as workers who do, why should I waste my time? If I stand to get the same raise as everyone else, why should I take the risk of going on strike? Olson's theory of rational self-interest argues that the logical thing for individuals to do is to ignore group goals, look out for themselves, and take a free ride.[21]

In order to succeed, a social movement has to overcome this free-rider problem by offering private inducements to members. Unions frequently offer life insurance plans; feminist groups provide child-care services. The inducements can also be negative. Nonstriking workers who cross picket lines today are likely to be harassed or threatened with violent reprisals.

On balance, Olson's theory probably underestimates the importance of loyalty to a cause as a motivating factor in social movements. Furthermore, although rank-and-file members of a successful movement get only the same benefits as nonparticipants, Olson overlooks the fact that its leaders have the additional incentives of social prestige and political office.[22] Nevertheless, he has provided a plausible explanation of why movements appealing only to loyalty or solidarity are generally less successful than those that offer additional incentives.[23] He is also correct in noting that common

[19] Herbert Blumer, "Collective Behavior," in *Review of Sociology: Analysis of a Decade,* ed. Joseph B. Gittler (New York: Wiley, 1957), p. 147.

[20] Mancur Olson, Jr., *The Logic of Collective Action,* rev. ed. (Cambridge, Mass.: Harvard University Press, 1971), p. 2.

[21] Ibid., pp. 105–106.

[22] Oberschall, *Social Conflict and Social Movements,* p. 116.

[23] William A. Gamson, *The Strategy of Social Protest* (Homewood, Ill.: Dorsey Press, 1975), pp. 68–70.

interests cannot fully explain participation in a social movement. Many large collectivities with shared grievances — income taxpayers, white-collar workers, and the urban poor, for example — have been unable to organize successful protest movements. "The groups that have no lobbies and exert no pressure," Olson writes, "are among the largest groups in the nation and they have some of the most vital common interests." [24] Why have these groups failed to organize? It is precisely this question that the theory of resource management attempts to answer.

MOBILIZING RESOURCES.   According to the theory of resource management, as developed by Charles Tilly and Anthony Oberschall, the political arena of any society is dominated by a few powerful interest groups. In the United States these groups include business, labor unions, and the military. Other social groups are always left out of the political game. Until the 1960s, they included racial and ethnic minorities, students, and women. The outsiders must wait until they can mobilize enough resources to attempt to enter the arena, while the insiders marshal their resources in order to keep them out. **Mobilization** refers to the process by which an opposition group assembles resources for the pursuit of its goals; **social control** refers to the processes by which the incumbents try to protect their vested interests.[25] The contending groups frequently compete for some of the same resources as each tries to win over uncommitted third parties and obtain unallocated resources for its own side. **Demobilization** refers to the loss of resources that were formerly committed to one side of the conflict. During the Iranian

---

[24] Olson, *The Logic of Collective Action,* p. 165.
[25] Oberschall, *Social Conflict and Social Movements,* p. 28.

The women's movement was able to mobilize several crucial resources: time, numbers, sympathetic third parties, ideology, and experienced leaders.

Revolution in 1979, for example, the shah was an incumbent whose major resource was the military; then the army withdrew its support, and the shah's regime was unable to survive the demobilization of this key resource.

The crucial issue, then, is what resources a social movement can mobilize. Several of the most important are discussed below.

TIME.   Participating in a social movement takes time. For this reason movements are typically made up of people who are — as Max Weber put it — "dispensable." Office workers, for example, are dispensable: they can leave their routine work to subordinates when they are away on movement business or marching in protest demonstrations. Small farmers and the poor, on the other hand, are not dispensable: they must spend all their available time tending their farms or earning an hourly wage. In general, the higher a group is on the social ladder, the greater its dispensability. This helps explain the curious fact that lower-class movements are usually led by those who have the most to lose, members of the middle and upper classes.[26] A profile of the fifty-two founders of the Chinese Communist party shows, for example, that 69 percent of their fathers belonged to the landlord-gentry class, 10 percent were officials, 10 percent were teachers, and only 6 percent (or three leaders) came from the peasant class.[27]

University students are often in the vanguard of social movements partly because they have the free time to devote to them. Students contribute other valuable resources as well: youthful energy and enthusiasm, idealism and faith in the future, and lack of family or job obligations.

NUMBERS.   A large potential membership is obviously a useful resource for a mass movement. Some collectivities, however, are more difficult to organize than others. A problem for the gay rights movement, for example, is that relatively few homosexuals are willing to "come out of the closet" and participate in public demonstrations. As we have seen in the case of the Nazis, social movements are more easily built on an existing organizational base. Oberschall suggests, therefore, that the more organizations there are in a collectivity, and the higher the rate of participation of its members in this organizational network, the more rapidly it can be mobilized into a conflict group.[28]

The birth of the student protest movement at the University of California at Berkeley bears out Oberschall's hypothesis. When the university administration banned political campaigning during the 1964 national elections, the Free Speech Movement (FSM) seemed to spring up virtually overnight. Berkeley students were easily mobilized because they were already highly organized into several groups that were threatened by the ban on politicking. These groups quickly mounted mass demonstrations that made national news for weeks, making the FSM the forerunner of the nationwide student protest movement of the 1960s.[29]

---

[26] Ibid., p. 152.

[27] Ming T. Lee, "The Founders of the Chinese Communist Party," *Civilisations* 18 (1968): 115, 118.

[28] Oberschall, *Social Conflict and Social Movements*, p. 125.

[29] Seymour M. Lipset and Sheldon Wolin, *The Berkeley Student Revolt* (New York: Doubleday/Anchor, 1965).

Oberschall's second hypothesis is that individuals and groups are more likely to participate in a social movement if the risks of protest are low and the rewards of success high.[30] It is not surprising, therefore, that lawyers, writers, professors, and physicians frequently have taken the lead in opposition movements. Aside from their organizational and intellectual skills, these professionals have independent economic resources and a following among their clients and colleagues that allow them to be relatively free of economic reprisals. Groups with high ratios of risks to rewards, on the other hand, are rarely able to support a protest movement by themselves. Exploited peasants in tsarist Russia, for example, engaged in brief riots and rebellions but were never able to sustain an effective protest movement. The same has been true of urban slum dwellers — a deprived collectivity vulnerable to reprisals by employers and police officers and thus unlikely to organize for the common good.

MONEY. Money, the "mother's milk of politics," also nourishes social movements. Economic resources lower the risk-to-reward ratio and underwrite the cost of protest activities. Social movements generally need a sizable income just for printing newsletters, renting offices, and paying legal fees. For this reason they are more likely to thrive in prosperous times than in hard times, when the public has less disposable income to invest in a cause. The severe economic recession of the early 1980s, for example, is partly responsible for cooling interest in the environmental movement.

POWERFUL THIRD PARTIES. In order to launch a successful movement, powerless groups need strong outside support. The mass media (television, newspapers, and newsmagazines) often provide the link between protesting groups and sympathetic third parties that can contribute money and political influence.

The story of César Chavez's United Farm Workers (UFW) shows what a difference external resources can make. At the time the UFW began, California's farm labor force had never been successfully organized. Immigration from Mexico had caused an oversupply of farm laborers ever since the 1940s, and most were seasonal migrant workers who never stayed in one place long enough to form a stable group. Whenever Chavez called a wage strike, the growers refused to bargain with the union, and enough nonunion workers crossed the picket lines to prevent a serious loss of the harvest. Because Chavez's union obviously was not strong enough to overcome the growers' resistance on its own, he had to mobilize outside support. He did so through a series of protest demonstrations designed to get sympathetic public attention and dramatize the justice of his cause. After the marches, arrests, and public speeches were publicized on television, the wife of Senator Robert F. Kennedy and other wealthy Easterners became interested in *La Causa.* Local organizations across the country started a boycott of grapes, and friendly unions went out on strike against grocery chains that sold "scab" produce. Within a year the UFW had achieved most of its goals. Over one hundred contracts had been signed with the growers, wages had been raised by almost one-third, and the union was operating in every major agricultural area of California. The success of Chavez's movement had little to do with the resources of the farm workers

---

[30] Oberschall, *Social Conflict and Social Movements,* pp. 164–68.

themselves. Massive third-party support had forced the growers to the bargaining table.[31]

IDEOLOGY.   Ideas are a vital ingredient in social movements (see "The Women's Movement, 1848–1990"). In fact, movements are often started by people with a social philosophy that identifies a problem and offers solutions. Because ideology mobilizes third parties who would not immediately benefit, it is also an important resource of social movements. During the American Revolution the idea that there should be "no taxation without representation" brought many more groups into the struggle against the British government than the few merchants who stood to benefit from tax relief.

LEADERSHIP.   Skilled leaders are another important resource for social movements. As activists and agitators, movement leaders recruit followers, devise a program, and inspire the rank and file with their example.

Of course, leaders can attract a large following only if their ideas appeal to an aggrieved group. Ralph Nader alone could not have created the consumer movement, and Betty Friedan was not solely responsible for the rebirth of feminism in the 1960s. But once the stage is set for social action, the actors make the play begin. Before union organizers arrived on the scene, migrant workers in California were poor, unskilled, and totally dependent on the growers for their livelihood. It is unlikely that their discontent would have led to a union movement without the skilled leadership of an activist such as Chavez.

A COMMUNICATIONS SYSTEM.   Ease of communication facilitates the growth of social movements. In the nineteenth century Marx wrote that French peasants were unable to start a successful social movement because they were separated from each other in remote rural areas. They could only be thrown together like "potatoes in a sack." Workers, on the other hand, could be organized readily because they were concentrated in factories. As Marx might have predicted, the student protest movement of the 1960s began at huge urban universities, where thousands of students lived on a single campus. Moreover, the radical New Left's underground press, circulating among these campuses, provided a communications system that reached millions of potential members of the antiwar and civil rights movements.[32] The mass media, in general, frequently have served as sources of information and publicity for movement activities.

THE CIVIL RIGHTS MOVEMENT: AN EXAMPLE OF RESOURCE MOBILIZATION[33]

On February 1, 1960, four black North Carolina A & T College students sat down at a "whites only" lunch counter in a Woolworth's store in downtown Greensboro, North Carolina. Although they were refused service and were continually insulted, they

---

[31] J. Craig Jenkins and Charles Perrow, "Insurgency of the Powerless: Farm Worker Movements (1946–72)," *American Sociological Review* 42 (April 1977): 249–68.

[32] Gary T. Marx and James L. Wood, "Strands of Theory and Research in Collective Behavior," *Annual Review of Sociology* 1 (1975): 387–88.

[33] Much of the following analysis is based on Oberschall, *Social Conflict and Social Mobility*, Chapter 6.

remained there until the manager closed the lunch counter an hour later. The next day they came back and, again, "sat in" until closing time.

When the first sit-in demonstrations began, black citizens had no legal right, either in federal or local law, to use the services of any public place in the South. Nearly every public facility, from drinking fountains to hospitals, was racially segregated. Throughout the southern and border states blacks were kept from voting by the use of force and such legal strategems as poll taxes and literacy tests. In the North discrimination against blacks was also widespread in housing, employment, and public accommodations. There were hardly any black politicians or reporters or corporate executives. After hundreds of dramatic protests and demonstrations, the civil rights movement succeeded in breaking this hundred-year-old pattern of racial injustice. The movement achieved its most important goal in June 1964, when Congress passed the Civil Rights Act. New federal laws protected the right to vote, outlawed discrimination in public places and federally funded programs, and established the Equal Employment Opportunity Commission to investigate instances of job discrimination.

The civil rights movement succeeded because it had more resources, and made more effective use of them, than earlier black protests had. These resources turned out to be greater in the South, where segregation was firmly entrenched, than in the North, where resistance to integration was not as strong.

OUTSIDE INTERVENTION.   The 1954 Supreme Court decision banning school segregation had a tremendous psychological impact on both blacks and whites in the South. It raised black expectations of equal treatment, but it also intensified white determination to resist change. At best, the southern whites' resistance movement meant only token compliance with the law; at worst, it led to outright repression, violence, and even death for blacks. When the attempt to bring social change through legal and institutional channels failed because of white intransigence, the stage was set for mass action and confrontation.

Ironically, the very success of the southern white resistance movement served to increase outside support for the black cause. The public was outraged at national press reports of the acquittal of known white murderers of blacks by all-white juries, the bombings of black churches, and the refusal of southern governors to enforce integration in schools and colleges. The Eisenhower administration was reluctantly drawn into enforcing court decisions, supporting civil rights laws, and otherwise attempting to check the white resistance movement.

Shocked by the ferocity of southern resistance, sympathetic northern whites poured money and workers into the civil rights cause. The Legal Defense Fund of the National Association for the Advancement of Colored People (NAACP), which paid the costs of civil rights litigation, raised most of its funds from white individuals and organizations. Half the members of the Congress of Racial Equality (CORE) in 1961 were white, and many of them were students at northern colleges.

Resource mobilization theory contends that oppressed minorities are unlikely to start a social protest movement entirely on their own. Especially in the early stages, outside support and the impact of outside events are key factors in loosening social controls, thus permitting the mobilization of a group's resources. Without the Supreme

THE WOMEN'S MOVEMENT, 1848 – 1990

Helman: Before all else, you are a wife
and mother.
Nora: That I no longer believe. I believe
that before all else, I am a human
being, just as much as you are—
or at least that I should try to be-
come one.

Henrik Ibsen, *A Doll's House* (1879)

Feminism is not new. In fact, the American struggle for sexual equality officially began as long ago as 1848, when 300 women and men convened in Seneca Falls, New York, to protest the oppression of women. This first phase of the women's movement grew out of the social reform movements of the 1830s and 1840s; many of the first feminist leaders had been active abolitionists. The experience had given female reformers training in organizational skills and firsthand experience with sexist discrimination in public affairs. When women activists were refused the right to make a public speech against slavery, or when they were denounced from the pulpit as "unnatural," their outrage fueled the feminist movement.

In the mid-nineteenth century, however, feminism had little to do with most women's lives. The United States at that time was largely a rural society of farmers and townspeople. In the typically large family of the period, women were kept busy with children and household chores. Except for domestic servants and schoolteachers, women had few job opportunities outside the home. Moreover, most people at the time subscribed to the Victorian cultural ideal of feminine purity and helplessness. In such a setting only a few middle-class women could pursue a professional or business career, or cultivate a "masculine" interest in politics. Since its ideology and program could not appeal to a large constituency, the women's movement generated little support at first and shortly faded from view.

A second phase began in another reform-minded period, the Progressive era of the early 1900s. This time feminist ideas found a much larger response. Almost 7.5 million women held jobs in 1910, many of them in the factories and offices of the newly industrial economy. More women were going to college; consequently, more women were dissatisfied with the limitations of their traditional roles. Furthermore, industrialization had enlarged the middle class. More people had time to devote to social reform movements, especially Temperance and female suffrage.

Female suffrage had become a more respectable issue since the Seneca Falls convention. Male Progressives supported it in the hope of gaining women's votes for social welfare legislation; feminists supported it as the way to end sex discrimination in general. Feminist leaders of this era, however, made a serious strategic error. In making the vote their primary goal, the suffragettes overestimated the power of the franchise to bring about changes in the workplace, the university, religion, and the family. As it turned out, women got the vote but it made little difference in their lives.

The revival of feminism in the 1960s had far greater consequences. Like its predecessors, this women's movement was born during a period of social reform, when the climate of ideas favored an attack on injustice and discrimination. Feminists in the 1960s and 1970s had learned their leadership skills in the civil rights, antiwar, and student protest movements. Like the abolitionists before them, many of these young women had been infuriated by the sexist attitudes of their male co-workers, perhaps best expressed in black leader Stokely Carmichael's infamous statement, "The position of women in our movement should be prone." This time, however, the feminist movement appealed to a much larger constituency and drew upon a much deeper level of discontent with traditional female roles. For one thing, the social norm that "woman's place is in the home" was harder to maintain in a world where half the female population was in the labor force. The more liberal sexual attitudes of the 1960s, together with a trend toward smaller families and an increase in the number of college-educated women, also contributed to the acceptance of feminist ideas. When these wider opportunities for women were blocked by sexist discrimination, the stage was set for a significant protest movement.

The extent of female discontent in the United States was shown by the enthusiastic response to Betty Friedan's 1963 best seller, *The Feminine Mystique,* which became the ideological basis for the contemporary women's movement. American women, Friedan claimed, were victims of a cultural image of women as dependent wives and self-sacrificing mothers. Women were probably not suffering more from the feminine mystique in 1963 than they had been in 1848 or 1910, but at this moment in history Friedan's book caused millions to reexamine their lives from a new point of view.

In the early 1960s, then, most of the elements of a successful protest movement came together: a large potential middle-class and student membership, experienced leaders, a loosening of social controls enforcing traditional norms, and an ideology that focused a widespread sense of grievance. All that was needed was the organization. This was provided by the 1961 President's Commission on the Status of Women, which did much to document women's oppression in American society. An unanticipated consequence of the commission (and fifty similar state commissions) was the establishment of a communications system among knowledgeable, politically active women. Out of that network came the National Organization for Women (NOW), still the chief organization in the older, reform-oriented wing of the women's movement. In general, this wing seeks to end legal and economic discrimination against women, particularly working women. Its tactics are likely to depend on conventional pressure-group lobbying on such issues as abortion rights and government-sponsored day care for children.

If NOW's wing of the movement is the norm-oriented, "women's rights" side, then the value-oriented, more radical wing could be called the "women's liberation" side. Women's inferior position in society, in their view, is due to institutionalized male supremacy in the family and other social structures. Only a revolution in values ending male domination, they say—not, as the moderate wing would have it, the integration of women into a man's world—will change this sexist system.

Though it has rallied considerable support for women's rights, the movement still faces serious obstacles. A countermovement has succeeded in preventing passage of a constitutional amendment guaranteeing women's rights. Nevertheless, contemporary feminism has won public acceptance and attained new economic and legal advantages for women. By bringing women's grievances to national attention, the movement has made even its opponents realize that American society is still in many respects a man's world. It seems likely that feminist ideas will continue to influence the social issues that concern us, as well as what young people study in school, what kinds of jobs are available to women and men, and how our children are raised.

SOURCE: Based on William H. Chafe, *Women and Equality* (New York: Oxford University Press, 1977), pp. 117–42; and *The American Woman* (New York: Oxford, 1972), pp. 226–39; Jo Freeman, "The Origins of the Women's Liberation Movement," *American Journal of Sociology* 78:4 (1973): 792–811; Sara Evans, *Personal Politics: The Roots of Women's Liberation in the Civil Rights Movement and the New Left* (New York: Knopf, 1979), pp. 3–23, 212–32.

Female suffrage supporters celebrate their victory in 1920. Winning the right to vote actually did little to change women's traditional sex roles.

The civil rights movement succeeded because it made effective use of its available resources. Under the charismatic leadership of the Reverend Martin Luther King, Jr., activist ministers mobilized the black middle class, raised money, and sought the help of the national media and the federal government.

King's nonviolent strategy was designed to win public support for his cause. In 1963, when the television news showed police dogs attacking helpless student demonstrators in Birmingham, national opinion swung over to his side.

Court decision, which undermined the legal basis of segregation, and without the intervention of such powerful third parties as the federal government and the northern liberal organizations, the civil rights movement probably would not have begun where and when it did.

THE RESOURCE BASE.   In addition to mobilizing white support, the black community had a number of resources of its own. One of these was a group of young, activist ministers from urban churches—the one area of black social life that was both independent of white control and highly organized. Because their jobs depended only on their congregations, these clergymen ran a lower risk of white economic reprisals than other blacks and could aspire to the rewards of social prestige and power. The most outstanding of these new leaders was the Reverend Martin Luther King, Jr.

The black church organizations also shared a Christian ideology that contributed to their sense of solidarity and dedication to the cause. Members of the movement drew their moral guidelines from the Bible, especially Old Testament passages describing the struggles of the oppressed.

From the resource mobilization perspective, southern blacks in the early 1960s had most of the resources necessary for a successful social movement: a large potential following with a low risk-to-reward ratio (the substantial urban middle-class and student population), money (from northern whites as well as southern blacks), skilled leaders (especially the charismatic Dr. King), a sustaining ideology, and the help of powerful third parties in the national media and the federal government. All that was necessary was the means of mobilizing them.

MOBILIZATION.   In the South the black churches provided the vehicle for mobilization. Along with such northern-based organizations as the NAACP and CORE, they became the support base upon which a mass movement was built. The southern churches played another crucial role by bringing Martin Luther King into national prominence. King's genius lay in his tactics of passive resistance, which confronted superior physical force with moral courage. Instead of staging an open revolt, which would have been easily suppressed and might not have won much sympathy, King used the strategy of nonviolence and persuasion to combat injustice. His moral stand appealed to common values: the public perceived him to be a soft-spoken, middle-class preacher who was seeking only the "liberty and justice for all" promised to every American. By presenting a national protest movement in the language and moral framework of Christian brotherhood, King reassured fearful whites and inspired other blacks to follow his lead.[34]

After 1964 the civil rights movement lost momentum and split into rival factions. Advocates of black power rejected integration with whites and tried, without success, to organize the urban lower class into a black nationalist movement.

Under King's direction sit-in demonstrators and protest marchers offered no resistance to harassment and arrest. The turning point of this nonviolent campaign came in Birmingham, Alabama, in the spring of 1963, when the police dispersed a student march with fire hoses and police dogs. When television news broadcasts showed the snapping dogs and the high-pressure streams of water knocking down helpless human beings, the entire country was shocked. Hundreds of sympathizers sent letters of support to King "in care of the Birmingham jail." King's strategy had worked: his moral

[34] Lerone Bennett, Jr., *Confrontation: Black and White* (Baltimore: Penguin, 1966), p. 194.

stand against brutal police tactics not only brought him a sympathetic public opinion but sparked similar nonviolent protests in both northern and southern cities.

Resource mobilization theory suggests why the civil rights movement began in the South. Although they were not denied the vote as southern blacks were, northern blacks were equally victimized by discrimination and de facto segregation. In the North, however, the social division between middle- and lower-class blacks was too great to be easily bridged by opposition to a common foe. Moreover, there was no network of churches and associations that could have supported a mass movement. The problems of the northern city ghettos were linked to unemployment: a largely young, poorly educated population was unable to get work because of lack of skills, discrimination in craft unions, and automation in urban industries. Short of massive federal programs to provide jobs and training, a civil rights movement could accomplish little for the urban poor. As a result the more intractable problems of the northern ghetto were relatively neglected.

FRAGMENTATION. By the time the Civil Rights Act was passed in 1964, the civil rights movement had made substantial progress in the northern border states and the cities. It ran aground, however, in the rural Deep South, where most of the black population was concentrated. In the closed social system of the "Black Belt," it proved impossible for an exploited, subordinate group to defy a powerful elite of judges, police, employers, and officials. The risks involved in protest were too high, and the rewards were relatively low. In the summer of 1964, when four civil rights workers were murdered in Mississippi, movement leaders in the Black Belt began to lose heart. (Passage of the Voting Rights Act in 1965 eventually did bring changes in the rural South, but at the time the situation seemed hopeless.)

Another blow came when a dissident group of black delegates was refused recognition at the 1964 Democratic convention. This double failure split the civil rights movement into rival factions. Led by Stokely Carmichael, the black power faction responded to failure by rejecting integration and white support. Carmichael adopted revolutionary aims and rhetoric, and sought to organize the urban ghettos for the cause of black nationalism. That fall, the movement's white student members returned to college disillusioned and frustrated. Many of them turned from civil rights to the growing antiwar movement.

As it turned out, Carmichael's black nationalists were never able to organize lower-class blacks into an effective movement. This failure of organized protest, added to increased economic hardship and disappointment with President Johnson's antipoverty programs, contributed to the violent confrontations between ghetto blacks and white authorities in the urban riots of the late 1960s.

Resource mobilization theory predicts that fragmentation of a social movement will occur when outside resources are progressively withdrawn and social controls are again tightened. At that point some groups will leave the movement, and the remaining activists will compete for the scarcer resources that are left. The Vietnam War drained two outside resources from the civil rights movement: white students, who joined the antiwar movement instead; and the federal government, which had to devote more time and money to pursuing the war and less to programs concerning civil rights and urban black problems. The movement lost another resource when white liberals, put off by radical threats and ghetto violence, stopped contributing to black causes. When King was assassinated in 1968, the movement lost a unifying leader who has never been effectively replaced. Finally, much of the black middle class has also left the civil rights movement. Resource mobilization theory also predicts that the gains a social movement has made will be unevenly divided, and that those members who have benefited most — as the black middle class did from better jobs, education, and housing — will take their gains and then withdraw from active participation.

Today the civil rights movement is largely institutionalized in various pressure groups. The NAACP and CORE have shifted from direct action to political lobbying, and black power is likely to mean the ability to swing a bloc of votes in an election. These developments do not necessarily mean that the civil rights movement has ended, only that its energies are now devoted less to mass protest from outside the system than to routine politicking within it.

STRATEGIES AND TACTICS

Insurgent groups have certain strategic problems. Because they lack political influence, they must rely on mass support to bring about social change. Or, if their own numbers are insufficient, they must find ways to get help from outsiders.

Robin Williams suggests these rules for low-power minorities:[35]

1. If you can persuade, do. If you think the authorities will favor your interests once they know what they are, the best and cheapest strategy is *persuasion*. Exclusive reliance on this strategy, however, means that you cannot press too hard for immediate changes or you will spoil your friendly relationship with the powers that be. For this reason American church groups have generally failed in their attempts to correct racial injustices by making purely moral appeals to their congregations.[36]

2. If you cannot persuade, try *inducement*. If you think the authorities are basically neutral, use whatever resources you have to induce them to join your side. The ability to swing blocs of votes, for example, can be a positive or negative inducement to politicians at election time.

3. If neither persuasion nor inducement brings results, consider the available means of *constraint*. If the authorities are generally opposed to your interests, then try nonviolent direct action. A strike or a boycott may force your opponents to negotiate. If negotiations fail, then you must decide whether more drastic means are justified.

Because powerless groups typically have very limited means of persuasion and inducement, they frequently rely on a strategy of nonviolent or violent constraint.

---

[35] Robin M. Williams, Jr., *Mutual Accommodation: Ethnic Conflict and Cooperation* (Minneapolis: University of Minnesota Press, 1977), p. 255.

[36] J. K. Hadden and C. F. Longino, Jr., *Gideon's Gang: A Case Study of the Church in Social Action* (Philadelphia: Pilgrim Press, 1974); H. E. Quinley, *The Prophetic Clergy: Social Activism among Protestant Ministers* (New York: Wiley, 1974).

NONVIOLENT DIRECT ACTION

Civil disobedience and nonviolent direct action are among the strategies available to opposition movements. Marches, petitions, sit-ins, boycotts, slowdowns, strikes, refusal to pay taxes, draft resistance, and other protest demonstrations are the tactics of the powerless. What excluded groups lack in individual resources they can sometimes make up in large numbers and disciplined organization.

Nonviolent tactics are intended to show that the movement has widespread support and is thus a force to be reckoned with. By offering evidence of popular discontent, mass demonstrations shake the public's confidence in the government and threaten political leaders with the prospect of open rebellion. The limitations of a nonviolent strategy are that (1) it depends on mass participation and (2) the protesters, with fewer resources to fall back on, are often hurt more than their antagonists.[37]

To be effective, nonviolent tactics must mobilize the support of third parties. Mahatma Gandhi's campaign of passive resistance to British rule in India succeeded when British public opinion swung over to his side. A nonviolent strategy will not work so well, however, if both sides are not eager to resolve the conflict or if both sides do not share at least some of the same moral values legitimizing a protest movement. For example, nonviolence tragically failed to prevent the Nazi slaughter of European Jews. Humanitarian appeals were an effective tactic when Gandhi used them, but they proved useless against the Nazi government.[38]

VIOLENCE

Violence is often thought to be self-defeating. Any use of physical force risks scaring off potential supporters and antagonizing the public. When used by the authorities, violence can backfire by arousing sympathy for the victim. Nevertheless, violence is frequently a successful tactic for both insurgent and incumbent groups.

After studying fifty-three protest groups in American history, William Gamson decided that the "meek don't make it."[39] He found that "unruly groups" — those that used force of one sort or another — had a higher-than-average rate of success. Of the twenty-one groups using constraints, two-thirds won concessions from their antagonists. The ten groups that had been victims of violence through arrests or reprisals, on the other hand, were completely unsuccessful in winning new advantages. Gamson concluded that violence is not so ineffective after all.[40]

A key factor in the success of both violent and nonviolent strategies is whether the movement's activities appear to the public to be legitimate protest or illegal disruption.[41] The public tends to think that any use of force by the authorities is legitimate, but violent protest is usually defined as lawless and destructive.[42]

---

[37] Oberschall, *Social Conflict and Social Movements,* pp. 307–308, 322.

[38] Williams, *Mutual Accommodation,* p. 226.

[39] William A. Gamson, "Violence and Political Power: The Meek Don't Make It," *Psychology Today* 8:2 (July 1974): 35–41.

[40] Gamson, *The Strategy of Social Protest,* p. 87.

[41] R. H. Turner, "The Public Perception of Protest," *American Sociological Review* 34 (December 1969): 827.

[42] Williams, *Mutual Accommodation,* p. 229.

A terrorist bomb caused the crash of this Pan Am air-liner in Locherbie, Scotland in 1988. Such terrorist acts are the tactics of groups with few resources to lose and no other means of bargaining with their opponents.

In any case, violence is usually a second-best or fallback strategy. Conflicts generally become violent only after nonviolent means of redressing grievances have failed. Violence is also likely to occur when a movement lacks mass support for nonviolent action. Terrorism, kidnappings, and assassinations are the tactics of weak groups that have no resources to lose by violence and no other means of bargaining with their opponents.

TERRORISM

Terrorism, or the use of covert violence by a group for political ends, is usually directed against a government, but it can also be used against specific ethnic groups, classes, or parties.[43] Terrorists try to cause political, social, or economic disruption by deliberate, often indiscriminate attacks on the innocent. The terrorist strategy is to gain these objectives not through the violent acts themselves, but through the fear that violence causes in an audience much larger than the immediate victims. Political assassins murder government officials responsible for the policies they oppose, but terrorists choose their targets at random to frighten the government into changing its policies to meet their demands. Most terrorists are thus in the paradoxical position of killing and maiming people they have no particular desire to hurt.

Oppression of ethnic minorities and social injustice are usually cited as the main factors in the spread of terrorist incidents in the twentieth century. Terrorism, however, is an insurrectional strategy that can be used by groups of many different political convictions.[44] Since killing a relatively small number of innocent bystanders is a horribly ineffective means of bringing about political change, terrorist campaigns nearly always turn out to be an unsuccessful strategy for social movements.

---

[43] Walter Laqueur, *The Age of Terrorism* (Boston: Little, Brown and Company, 1987), p. 72.
[44] *The Age of Terrorism*, p. 4.

SOCIAL MOVEMENTS AND SOCIAL CHANGE

Social movements have an impact beyond their stated goals. That is because, as Joseph Gusfield put it, social movements "have audiences as well as adherents." [45] While many women might deny any association with feminist ideas, there is no doubt that the women's movement has changed the way they look at their families, their jobs, and themselves. "I'm not a women's libber," they say, "but I believe women ought to be equal." Although most American women do not belong to women's rights organizations, survey after survey shows their support for such feminist goals as day-care centers, abortion services, and greater career opportunities for women.

The most lasting effect of a social movement, then, may not be the laws passed or the reforms made but the new attitudes of people who are not directly involved — the "audience." The gay rights movement has given homosexuality a different social meaning than it had ten years ago. The civil rights movement has made being white and living next door to a black family a different experience than it was in 1960. Social movements bring social change not only through specific reforms but also by transforming a society's ideas of what is normal, right, and possible.

---

[45] Joseph Gusfield, "The Modernity of Social Movements," (Paper presented at the American Sociological Association Meeting, San Francisco, September 4, 1978).

SUMMARY

1. Collective behavior is the relatively unorganized and spontaneous behavior of crowds and masses; social movements are highly organized and relatively long-term collective efforts to bring about or prevent social change.

2. Collective behavior often appears strange and unpredictable, but people in casual crowds, conventional crowds, and expressive crowds generally behave in expected ways. Theories of collective behavior focus on the unrestrained behavior of acting crowds.

3. Contagion theory, which derives from Le Bon's *The Crowd*, contends that heightened emotions are contagious and that the crowd situation leads individuals to act in irrational and similar ways. Convergence theory finds that people who are likely to engage in certain kinds of behavior converge to form crowds. The empirical evidence, however, disputes both the notion that people in crowds act alike and that only criminal riffraff or other abnormal kinds of people engage in collective behavior.

4. Sociologists argue that collective behavior is the predictable response of normal people in abnormal situations. Turner and Killian found that people in crowds tend to act alike because they are conforming to an emergent norm. Game theorists note the rational aspects of crowd behavior. The study of collective behavior reminds us that even "normal" behavior can be quite puzzling and that there is a spontaneous and transitory element in all social interaction.

5. Social movements have three characteristics: (1) they seek specific goals either through reforms (norm-oriented movements) or changes in social values (value-oriented movements); (2) unlike episodes of collective behavior, they are cohesive organizations; and (3) they have a unifying ideology justifying protest or change.

6. According to the classical, or "stages," approach, social movements arise out of deep and widespread discontent, a generalized belief in some cause or solution to the problem, and grass-roots support. The best empirical evidence shows, how-

ever, that social movements do not derive from the discontents of frustrated groups, nor do people join movements for purely ideological reasons.

7. Others have argued that the loneliness and alienation of modern mass society give rise to social movements that offer a sense of purpose and community. Studies of Nazism, which seemed at the time to be a symptom of a "sick" society, fail to support this idea. In fact, deprived and alienated people are less likely to join protest movements than activists and members of other kinds of organizations.

8. The theory of resource management views social movements as political organizations that seek specific goals, mobilize resources, and devise strategies and tactics to win support. Olson argued that, to attract members, social movements have to overcome the free-rider problem by offering positive or negative inducements to join.

9. Social movements can mobilize the following resources: time, numbers (particularly groups that are already organized and people for whom the risk-to-reward ratio is low), money, third parties

with political influence, ideology, leadership, and a communications system. The civil rights movement is an example of how such resources were mobilized and later demobilized as the movement became largely institutionalized as a pressure group.

10. Social movement strategies include persuasion, inducement, and constraint. Powerless groups frequently have to rely on nonviolent or violent constraint. Nonviolent tactics must mobilize powerful third parties to be effective. Violence is usually used as a last resort. It can be a successful tactic, especially when a movement is viewed as a legitimate protest. Terrorist campaigns, the strategy of groups who have no resources for bargaining with their opponents, are nearly always unsuccessful.

11. Social movements have audiences as well as adherents, and their impact often goes beyond the attainment of specific goals. The women's movement, for example, not only brought about legal reforms but changed social attitudes.

KEY TERMS

collective behavior 531
social movement 531
crowd 531
contagion 533
convergence 533
emergent norm 535

game theory 536
norm-oriented social
  movements 538
value-oriented social
  movements 538
mass society 540

resource management 542
mobilization 543
social control 543
demobilization 543
terrorism 555

SUGGESTED READING

Robert R. Evans, ed. *Readings in Collective Behavior.* Chicago: Rand McNally, 1975.

Jo Freeman, ed. *Social Movements of the Sixties and Seventies.* New York: Longman, 1983.

* Joseph R. Gusfield. *Symbolic Crusade: Status Politics and the American Temperance Movement,* 2nd ed. Urbana: University of Illinois Press, 1986.

* Walter Laqueur. *The Age of Terrorism.* Boston: Little, Brown and Company, 1988.

* Charles Mackay. *Extraordinary Popular Delusions and the Madness of Crowds.* New York: Crown, 1980.

* Charles Tilly. *From Mobilization to Revolution.* New York: McGraw-Hill, 1978.

* Malcolm X. *Autobiography of Malcolm X.* New York: Grove, 1966.

Mayer N. Zald and John D. McCarthy, eds. *The Dynamics of Social Movements: Resource Mobilization, Social Control, and Tactics.* Lanham, MD: University Press of America, 1988.

* Available in paperback.

The lion and the calf shall lie down together but the calf won't get much sleep.

Woody Allen

CHAPTER 18

SOCIAL CHANGE AND SOCIAL CONFLICT

There is an ancient Chinese curse that sounds like a blessing: "May you live in interesting times." We do live in interesting times, and they are both a curse and a blessing. On the one hand, the curse: terrorist bombings, religious persecutions, bloody wars, and brutal dictatorships; on the other hand, the blessing: material abundance, technological breakthroughs and medical miracles, civil rights and women's rights, victories over poverty, ignorance, and disease. We are both the victims and the beneficiaries of social change and conflict more "interesting" than the ancient Chinese could have imagined.

To a sociologist **social change** means any significant alteration in a social structure. This definition also includes any new norms, values, and cultural products of a material or symbolic kind, but not minor changes such as fads and fashions. Although the distinction is often made between continuity and change, no society can be completely static. All societies, even those we might consider stable and "uninteresting," are constantly changing and adapting in response to new circumstances.

Conflict is also a perennial feature of social life. **Social conflict** refers to the antagonism of social groups with opposing interests or values. Such conflict is often intense but not necessarily violent. Most special-interest groups oppose each other peacefully through the use of economic and political power. Much conflict is unregulated, but some conflicts are institutionalized. The American legal system provides a formal structure for resolving disputes in the courtroom; today labor and management conflicts are institutionalized in noisy but bloodless bargaining sessions.

Social change hardly ever takes place without some social conflict, and most social conflict eventually produces change. Groups left behind by social changes, such as manual workers who are replaced by machines, have often turned to violent protest or organized strikes. Groups that wish to bring about social change, such as advocates of women's rights, come into conflict with other interest groups. Because of the frequent interdependence of social change and social conflict, this chapter considers them together. We begin with a discussion of how and why societies change and then consider the forces accounting for social continuity and resistance to change. The next section examines the social effects of internal and external conflict. The final part takes up the special case of revolution, a situation in which violent social conflict is combined with fundamental social change.

THE PROCESS OF SOCIAL CHANGE

At one time the United States was quite a different society than it is today. Nearly half the population lived outside cities, towns, and suburbs. One out of three homes had no toilet, and one out of four was without running water. The average wage in manufacturing was 63 cents an hour, or about $24 for an average week, and the average farm family's annual income was around $1,000. Still, you could buy lunch in a good restaurant for 65 cents, a summer suit for $8, a new Ford sedan for $685, and a colonial-style house in the suburbs for under $20,000. The average annual income of doctors and lawyers was about $4,300, but those who were married and had two children paid an income tax of only about $25. The average industrial worker paid no income tax at all.

The rate of population growth in this society was the lowest in history, and experts were predicting a depopulated country for the distant future. The average American had only an elementary-school education. Schools in southern New Jersey, as well as in the Deep South, were racially segregated, and blacks were discriminated against nearly everywhere they sought jobs — in factories, state and local government, and even federal projects. No law had been passed to correct racial inequality in the sixty years since Reconstruction.

Does this society seem backward and far away? It was the United States in 1939 — the society your parents probably grew up in. It was a time when nearly half of today's population was alive — a period, in other words, well within the life span and the memory of millions of Americans.[1]

Obviously American society has changed dramatically since the 1940s. What makes today's society so different from the one that preceded it? First, it is about 50 percent larger and consequently more crowded. The Bureau of the Census now classi-

---

[1] John Brooks, *The Great Leap: The Past Twenty-five Years in America* (New York: Harper & Row, 1966), pp. 9–33.

One of the dramatic changes in American society in the last forty years was a population shift from rural areas to the cities and suburbs.

fies three quarters of the population as urban, compared with a little over half in 1940. The farm population has dropped accordingly, making the United States a society of city dwellers and suburbanites. Second, Americans are obviously richer. In terms of real buying power in current dollars, the industrial worker's wage has doubled; the median family income in 1987 was $31,135. Americans are also better educated now. The average citizen is a high-school graduate, and about half of all 18- and 19-year olds are attending college. Racial barriers in education and employment have been lowered. Integration is now the law of the land at school, on the job, and in all public facilities. Nearly everyone today has a bathtub, an automobile, a television set, two days a week off from work, and a paid vacation.

Still, not everything has changed. American society in the 1990s remains recognizably American. The political system has changed very little, even though the government has mushroomed in size and importance. The economic system continues to be industrial capitalism. A democratic faith in the rule of law, in public education, and in equal opportunity has been threatened from many quarters but not shaken. In fact, if a radical reform group had set out to rebuild society in 1940, it would have long since despaired at the slow pace of the changes that have taken place.

The last fifty or so years, then, were a period of gradual rather than revolutionary change. That is, there have been changes or readjustments within a basic structure rather than a change of the structure itself. The fact that more black children now go to school with white children represents a major social change, but not a revolutionary one: they still go to Public School 49, not Communal Educational Center 49 or Regional Youth Group Section 49.

Looking at the differences between the two American societies, we might wonder why the society of 1939 changed at all. What changed it? Why did it change the way it did? Why did Americans enthusiastically welcome such innovations as the high-speed freeway and chemically flavored foods, and only grudgingly accept such novelties as automobile safety devices and women in public office?

Many sociologists have tried to explain how and why society changes. Some theorists have focused on the introduction of new ideas, while others have emphasized the importance of population, technology, or economic changes. In addition to considering different elements of social change, various theorists have found different reasons why it occurs. This section will first discuss what kinds of changes take place and then examine what causes them.

TECHNOLOGICAL CHANGE

Technology is the socially accumulated knowledge of how to make use of nature. Technological invention has been an agent of social change in every period of history. The invention of the horse collar in the Middle Ages was a tremendous technological advance for agriculture; the mariner's compass so improved navigation in the fifteenth century that it ushered in the age of exploration; and the steam engine was an essential factor in the industrialization of Europe in the nineteenth century.

The rapid growth of Houston and other cities in the Sun Belt occurred in large part because of a single invention — air conditioning.

We live in the age of technology. The jet plane, air conditioning, the computer, and the photo copier are so much a part of our daily lives that it is hard to believe that not one of these inventions was in widespread use thirty years ago. Countless social changes have come, directly or indirectly, from these new technologies.

Industrialization—the process of shifting from hand tools to power machinery—led to a number of specific social changes. Its long-range result is a shift from a manual to a nonmanual labor force and an increase in white-collar jobs. An industrial economy requires specialized factory workers and trained managers to supervise them; hence, the required level of education tends to increase. Per capita income also rises. The growth of a more affluent and educated middle class tends to reduce inequalities by distributing income more widely.

Technological development brings the benefits of a generally higher standard of living, but it also creates new social problems. Manual workers often find themselves out of work, and traditional values are frequently disrupted in the industrialization process. These effects of industrial development are the same no matter where it occurs—in a social democratic society such as Sweden, a communist system such as the Soviet Union, or a capitalist democracy such as the United States.

Because each invention makes more inventions possible, the rate of technological development tends to accelerate. Benjamin Franklin experimented with electricity in the eighteenth century, but it was a hundred years before Thomas Edison moved from theory and experiment to practical application. In the hundred years since Edison invented the light bulb, the discovery of electricity has spawned tens of thousands of inventions, from the internal-combustion engine (which led to the automobile and the airplane) to the computer (which made space exploration possible). What to do about this proliferation of inventions and how to control the social changes they produce pose some of the greatest challenges of our time.

CULTURAL CHANGE

One of the most obvious transformations in American society since the 1940s has been a change in ideas. It is commonly said, for example, that a sexual revolution and a civil rights revolution have taken place. The idea of equality between men and women and between blacks and whites—though certainly not new—has seemed suddenly to have caught on. This shift in our cultural values and attitudes has already led to a number of specific changes in society and will probably lead to many more.

In *The Protestant Ethic and the Spirit of Capitalism*, Max Weber argued that ideas can be a compelling force for social change. According to his analysis, certain Western European religious values—specifically the Protestant ethic of industriousness and thrift—favored the development of the modern capitalist economy (see Chapter 12, "The Economy"). The Calvinist idea that worldly success was a sign of salvation, combined with the idea that worldly pleasures were sinful, created an attitude toward life that Weber called the peculiar "spirit of capitalism." These ideas encouraged continuous hard work and personal frugality, which in turn produced profits that were saved instead of spent. According to Weber, the inevitable practical result of the Protestant ethic was the accumulation of more and more capital for reinvestment, and hence the development of modern capitalism.[2]

CULTURAL BORROWING.   Societies usually change at least as much from contact and exchange with other peoples as from independent development and invention. In fact,

---

[2] Max Weber, *The Protestant Ethic and the Spirit of Capitalism* (New York: Scribner's, 1958), p. 172.

human societies left in isolation, such as the Australian aborigines, tend to stagnate.

Many of the ideas and objects we think of as native to this country are really borrowed from other cultures. About 50 years ago the anthropologist Ralph Linton estimated that 90 percent of our cultural elements — the things we wear, eat, and use every day — originated somewhere else.[3] Today the percentage is undoubtedly even higher. In an age of jet travel and satellite communication nearly every country is in contact with others, and all are able to exchange inventions, ideas, and beliefs. The modernization of the developing world is part of this process of cultural diffusion; modern values and technology are being introduced into completely different cultures, creating disruptions as well as improvements.

CULTURAL LAG.   Writing in the early 1920s, the sociologist William F. Ogburn noted that different parts of a culture do not change at the same rate.[4] Changes in material culture, or man-made objects, eventually bring about changes in adaptive culture, or ideas, customs, and beliefs. Because adaptive changes take time to develop after material changes occur, there is a culture lag between them. Today, for example, scientists have developed the machinery and laboratory techniques for genetic engineering, or creating new forms of life. Modern culture, however, has not yet devised new values and norms to cope with its potential uses.

STRUCTURAL CHANGE

Of course, ideas must be accepted before they can be influential. The idea of human equality, for instance, is at least as old as the New Testament and has been proposed many times since. Why was it suddenly more acceptable in American society in the 1970s?

Since only an "idea whose time has come" will be accepted, the impact of a new idea depends largely on the social structure in which it appears. For many sociologists, the real question is not how ideas have changed but how the structure of society has changed.

The first answers to this question came from a group of nineteenth-century philosophers who were impressed with the theory of biological evolution. If animals could evolve from one species to another, they thought, then human society could have developed in a similar way. Herbert Spencer (1820–1903) was the foremost theorist of the evolutionary point of view. He proposed that human societies, like animal species, developed from the simple to the complex, and from the homogeneous to the heterogeneous. Primitive hunting and gathering societies, over time, evolved into highly developed, highly differentiated industrial societies. Just as a human being could develop from a jellyfish, so the advanced civilization of Spencer's Victorian England could develop from a few Anglo-Saxon tribes.[5]

Evolutionary theories such as Spencer's were discredited when archaeologists and anthropologists found that they rested on a shaky foundation. It turned out that socie-

---

[3] Ralph Linton, *The Study of Man* (Englewood Cliffs, N.J.: Prentice-Hall, 1936), pp. 326–27.
[4] William F. Ogburn, *On Culture and Social Change* (Chicago: University of Chicago Press, 1964).
[5] Lewis A. Coser, *Masters of Sociological Thought*, 2nd ed. (New York: Harcourt Brace Jovanovich, 1977), pp. 90–97.

According to Ogburn, changes in material culture eventually bring about changes in ideas, customs, and beliefs. The popularity of the automobile was at least partly responsible for the new independence and sexual freedom of American youth during the "Roaring Twenties."

ties with simple and complex structures had developed simultaneously in different parts of the world. Spencer had used so-called evolutionary steps to link cultures that in fact had no historical connections to each other.

The evolutionary approach is still considered valid, however, for explaining the development of individual societies. Gerhard Lenski, a "new" evolutionary theorist, points to some clear long-term trends in European history: population growth, especially in cities; increasing specialization of labor; growth of trade and commerce; increased production of goods and services; the shift in employment away from agriculture and toward white-collar work; and the increasing power of the state.[6]

For Émile Durkheim a fundamental social change is the shift from a society based on mechanical solidarity, or similarity of values and beliefs, to one based on organic solidarity, or the interdependency of a complex division of labor (see Chapter 1, "The Sociological Perspective"). Durkheim called population density "material density" and the intensity of communication among individuals he called "moral density." When populations grow, both material density and moral density increase. The result is greater social differentiation and a larger number of social relationships, or organic solidarity. Mechanical solidarity unites simple societies based on the relationships of similar individuals who are competitive with each other; organic solidarity unites complex societies based on the relationships of disparate individuals who are dependent on each other.[7] The change from one social structure to another occurs as a

[6] Gerhard Lenski, "History and Social Change," *American Journal of Sociology* 82:3 (November 1976): 548–64.

[7] Raymond Avon, *Main Currents in Sociological Thought II* (Garden City, N.Y.: Doubleday, 1970), p. 23.

population becomes larger and more diverse. The next section discusses the effects of other changes in the structure of a population.

POPULATION CHANGES

The passage of time causes the most obvious social change of all — the change from youth to age and from generation to generation. Your date of birth, the year you came of age, and your age at any moment in history give you a common experience with your generation that is different from those older or younger — thus the "Lost Generation" of the 1920s and the "Silent Generation" of the 1950s. A **cohort** is the sociological term for a group of people born and raised in the same period. Coming of age during the Great Depression of the 1930s, for example, meant not being able to get a good job and thus delaying marriage and children. Coming of age during the Vietnam War meant post-poning college or graduate-school education for military service. These events were formative experiences for the cohorts involved, and they changed both behavior and attitudes toward government and society.[8]

Karl Mannheim (1893–1947) based a generational theory of social change on this concept: the natural transition from one generation to another permits change to occur and is therefore a basic factor in social development. The continuous introduction of new age groups into the cultural process means that there is always a fresh contact with the cultural heritage and the possibility of forming new attitudes; the continuous withdrawal of the former members of a culture enables the new members to forget the old ways of doing things and to look at the same problems in a new light. According to this view, young adults' relative lack of commitment to the past makes them more receptive to innovation and more likely to support major social change.[9]

Since 1960 the population of the United States has "aged" dramatically.[10] Between 1960 and 1982 the number of children under 15 declined by seven percent, largely because of the drop in the birth rate following the post–World War II "baby boom." In about the same period (1960 to 1980) a sharp decline in the death rate among the elderly caused the number of people over 65 to grow by a remarkable *54 percent*. The change in the relative size of the two groups might have been expected to help the young and hurt the old, since fewer children should mean less competition for social services (education, welfare) and more older people should increase the pressure on such public resources as hospitals and social security benefits. In fact, the opposite has happened. Many social programs for children (especially Aid to Families with Dependent Children) have been cut back, while government benefits for the elderly (Social Security and Medicare) have been increased. In 1983 people over 65 received $217 billion in federal benefits (or about $7,700 per person) and federal spending on child-oriented programs (AFDC, Head Start, food stamps, child health, child nutrition, and aid to education) was about $36 billion. On a per capita basis, the average child received less than a tenth as much as the average elderly person.

---

[8] Norman B. Ryder, "The Cohort as a Concept in the Study of Social Change," *American Sociological Review* 30:6 (December 1965): 843–61.

[9] Karl Mannheim, *Essays on the Sociology of Knowledge* (London: Routledge & Kegan Paul, 1952), pp. 276–322.

[10] Samuel H. Preston, "Children and the Elderly in the U.S." *Scientific American* 251:6 (December 1984): 44–49.

Between 1960 and 1980 the U.S. population "aged" dramatically. While the number of children declined by 7 percent, the number of people over 65 grew by 54 percent. This change in the relative size of the two age groups has given the elderly greater political influence and thus a larger share of social resources.

Of course the relative size of the young and old populations is not the only factor in these figures. In American society, for instance, the government assumes a large share of responsibility for the care of the elderly, while the family is the chief source of support for children. Nevertheless, the increasing size of the over-65 population has obviously worked to its advantage, giving the elderly greater political influence and thus a larger share of social resources.

ACCIDENTS OF GEOGRAPHY AND HISTORY

Climate and natural resources are important factors in social change. Warm weather permits a longer growing season and thus the production of enough food to support a large population. Abundant deposits of coal in Great Britain and Germany fueled the furnaces and factories of the Industrial Revolution, while countries that had to buy coal were handicapped in their economic development. Geographic location on trading routes promoted the growth of such cities as Alexandria, Constantinople, and Venice; when the routes changed, they declined in power and influence.

Natural disasters disrupt and even destroy societies. Earthquakes, floods, and plagues have had obvious immediate effects but also secondary ones. The short-term effect of the Black Death (bubonic plague) was a drastic drop in the population of

Europe during the fourteenth century. The long-term effect was economic: loss of population caused a labor shortage and higher wage rates.

Critics of the evolutionary theory of change argue that social change is not continuous but sudden and intermittent. History, according to Robert Nisbet, is not a gradual evolution but "only one emergency following upon another," the unique "play of the contingent and the unforeseen."[11] Indeed, much social change does seem to depend on historical accidents. If William the Conqueror had lost the Battle of Hastings, if Napoleon had considered himself Italian instead of French, if the South had won the Civil War, if President Kennedy had not been assassinated—if a few accidents had not happened—then perhaps everything might have been different (see "The Hero in History").

EXPLAINING SOCIAL CHANGE

During the 1970s major social changes took place in American society. Newspapers reported them, statisticians analyzed them, and scholars have tried to explain them ever since. Here is one account:

More Children Have Mothers Who Work

Washington, Feb. 28 (AP)—Forty-six percent of American children under 18 had mothers who worked outside the home last year, according to new Labor Department figures.

The percentage of working mothers has risen seven percentage points since 1970 and probably reflects a growing divorce rate and a trend toward increased female participation in the work force, the department said.[12]

The increasing number of working mothers in our society is an example of an important social phenomenon that has not just one but several explanations. (By the mid-1980s more than half the mothers of infants were in the labor force.) The first is a shift in cultural values: the idea of equality between men and women caused a corresponding change in occupational and family roles. Most people no longer believe that men's work lies exclusively outside the home and women's work lies exclusively within it. According to a recent poll, women now find their work outside the home as satisfying as their family life.[13] This change in attitudes and values is reflected in the increased number of working women, the higher divorce rate, and the larger proportion of working mothers.

How would the new evolutionist explain the change in women's roles? One long-term trend in the economy has been the shift in employment away from the production of goods and toward the production of services. The result has been an increased demand for white-collar workers, many of whom have traditionally been women. The new service industries—nursing homes, data-processing services, fast-food restau-

---

[11] Robert Nisbet, *Social Change and History* (New York: Oxford University Press, 1969), p. 284.

[12] *The New York Times*, March 1, 1977, p. 1.

[13] *The New York Times* Poll, conducted in November 1983. Reported in *The New York Times*, December 4, 1983, pp. 1, 66.

THE HERO IN HISTORY

Do men and women make history? If Alexander, Mohammed, Charlemagne, Joan of Arc, Napoleon, or Mao Tse-tung had never been born, would world history have been different? Did they cause the historical events we associate with them, or did historical events make them heroes by necessity?

Sociologists argue that men and women do make history, but they have to make it under certain conditions. Theories of social change try to account for the great historical events that seem, on the one hand, to be the inevitable results of social processes and, on the other, to be the accidental outcomes of the right people being in the right time and place.

The role of the great man or woman in history is an endlessly fascinating issue. At one extreme there are those who argue that individuals play the decisive role. At a moment of great danger or great opportunity, it often appears that the fate of millions depends on what a single person decides. When Neville Chamberlain, the British prime minister, returned home after signing the Munich pact with Hitler in 1938, he told the House of Commons that the question of whether there would be war or not had depended on him alone and that by his action he had kept the peace.

Chamberlain's claim that he and he alone had prevented war with Germany was very shortly shown to be pathetically untrue. With the benefit of historical hindsight we now know that World War II resulted from the political and social conditions that gave birth to fascism and that a hundred peace-loving prime ministers could not have prevented it. Chamberlain thus represents the human being as victim of historical forces that seem entirely beyond individual control.

It is also hard to argue the opposite view that great men and women are made only by historical necessity. Social conditions cannot entirely determine the effect of the unique personality who ruled the country, led the army, or otherwise seized the initiative at the critical moment. The historian Sidney Hook maintains that Lenin provides at least one example of a single person who changed the course of history. In *The Hero in History* Hook advances the thesis that without Lenin's leadership the Russian Revolution of October 1917 would certainly have failed and world history would have been different. He points out that nearly everyone expected the first, or February Revolution, which destroyed the czarist regime and introduced a kind of Western democracy to Russia. But no one, including the Bolsheviks, expected the second, or October Revolution, which created a minority party dictatorship. Lenin alone devised the policy, strategy, and daily tactics for taking power. If he had not returned from exile to lead the Bolsheviks, there would have been no October Revolution. And, if Russia had become a parliamentary democracy, the history of the twentieth century would have been profoundly different.

Hook concludes:

There are situations in the world no hero can master. . . . {Social catastrophes can} burst on society with the elemental force of natural phenomena and overwhelm alike the just and the unjust, the wise and the foolish.

But there are other situations in which a gifted man of good or evil genius can so profoundly affect men and events that he becomes an event-making man. . . . There has been at least one event-making man in our time who has redetermined the course of history and, in so doing, has influenced the life of the great majority of men, women, and children on the face of the globe.[1]

---

[1] Sidney Hook, *The Hero in History: A Study in Limitation and Possibility* (Boston: Beacon Press, 1943), pp. 174–75.

rants — rely largely on female employees. It seems that just when women were ready to go to work, the jobs were there for them. From a structural point of view the occupational structure had to change first in order to make room for more women in the labor force.

World War II was an accident of history that contributed to the change in sex roles. When millions of men went to war, women took up their jobs at home. "Rosie the Riveter" and the women she represented changed the popular idea that women were physically incapable and emotionally unsuited for demanding, heavy labor. After the

World War II brought millions of American women into the paid labor force for the first time. One result was a change in the popular idea that women were incapable of doing a "man's job."

war most women did return to their former occupations, but they were never completely replaced by men. They had found they could do "men's work," and many of them continued to do it.

Technological development also helps explain the greater number of women in the labor force. Many jobs now involve sitting at computer terminals, and automation has made modern factory work less demanding of sheer muscle power. A comparatively simple invention — the baby bottle — was important because it provided new mothers with an alternative to breast feeding and made infant day care possible for working women.

The birth-control pill is another technological invention affecting family roles. Effective birth control and legal abortions have almost certainly contributed to a lower birth rate. The average American mother now has her last child while still in her twenties. The prospect of living thirty productive years without young children tends to make women reluctant to give up jobs to which they may later want to return.

All these factors probably contribute to the increase in the proportion of working mothers who have young children. In sum, major social changes are complex events that require more than one explanation. A change in the relationship between men and women represents both a change in social attitudes and a change in the structure of the family and the economy. The sources of these changes are technological, economic, ideological, and even accidental. But there is still another factor. If social change is to occur, people have to be willing to change. Much change is not inevitable and can be successfully resisted. The next section considers the reasons why some changes are welcomed enthusiastically and others are found to be socially unacceptable.

RESISTANCE TO CHANGE

In 1976 the all-male tradition at American military academies was abolished by federal law. For the first time female cadets entered West Point, Annapolis, and the Air Force Academy (whose motto, "Bring Me Men," at once became quaint). Daily routines, habits of thought and behavior, the rituals of military life — all the mores and structures of a masculine society appeared threatened by this sharp break with tradition and custom. The reaction of some senior officers bore out Nisbet's point that human beings will constantly think up new ways to justify continuing behavior that is no longer appropriate. It was "silly" to permit women to enroll at West Point, said General William C. Westmoreland. "They're asking women to do impossible things. I don't believe women can carry a pack, live in a foxhole or go a week without taking a bath." [14]

Writing from the perspective of the early twentieth century, the political economist Thorstein Veblen (1857 – 1929) emphasized the role of technological invention in bringing about social change.[15] He thought that a new invention does not automatically lead to new social behavior and attitudes but instead provokes resistance by challenging traditional morality and old institutions. Those who have what Veblen called a **vested interest** in the old order — or a strong commitment to a social arrangement that benefits them — will resist change even if the institutions they support are out of tune with technological developments. In the end, Veblen thought, the new technology will erode old ideas, overcome vested interests, and reshape institutions in response to its own needs. In the meantime there might be a considerable time lag, and society might suffer from the clash between new technology and old institutions or be weakened by the discrepancy between them.

Innovations that run counter to moral values are likely to be strongly resisted; witness the controversy over abortion. In nineteenth-century Great Britain the use of anesthesia in childbirth was considered immoral because labor pains were the female sex's punishment for Eve's role in committing the original sin. The prohibition was eventually weakened partly because Queen Victoria insisted upon anesthesia during the births of her nine children. Today the Amish, a strict religious sect, still refuse to use electric lights, motorized transportation, and zippers because they believe that any contact with modern technology undermines their special way of life.

Vested interests may also oppose an invention. An industry with a large capital investment in an old product will naturally try to prevent the development of a new one. The automobile industry lobbied vigorously against legislation requiring antipollution devices on every car; the oil and coal industries opposed government programs to develop solar energy.

Fear of change is understandable, for most changes are costly to someone. The invention of the automobile did not just add a new form of transportation but replaced the horsedrawn vehicle. Its widespread use caused the trolley car and the short-line

---

[14] *The New York Times*, May 31, 1976, p. 5.
[15] Coser, *Masters of Sociological Thought*, pp. 272 – 74.

Social changes that run counter to moral values are likely to be strongly resisted. Members of the Amish community refuse to use electric lights or automobiles in order to protect their special way of life.

railroad to disappear as well. The legendary buggy whip manufacturer went out of business. Today American society has an enormous vested interest in the automobile. Most people depend on automobile transportation to get them to places where they live, work, shop, and go to school. Many of the largest industrial corporations either manufacture cars and parts or produce the oil and gas that keep them running. Millions of people are employed, directly or indirectly, by automobile-related companies — in motels, shopping centers, resorts, drive-ins, and gas stations. Americans are now beginning to realize that they may no longer be able to afford the environmental cost of dependence on the automobile. They have begun to be concerned about auto safety, air pollution, the depletion of energy resources, the loss of the American countryside to concrete and urban sprawl, and the shameful inefficiency of the automobile as a means of getting from one place to another.[16]

What would happen though, if the United States decided to change to another form of transportation? What if a public monorail system made the family car obsolete? The social cost of such a change is nearly unimaginable and would be strongly resisted. As Veblen pointed out, a society without such a huge investment in an obsolescent technology would be much better off. It could develop an alternative system of transportation without having to overcome its tremendous vested interest in the automobile and in the economic and social institutions that depend on it.

ACCEPTANCE OF CHANGE

When archeologists excavated the remote Peruvian city of Machu Picchu, they unearthed wheeled vehicles. Their discovery proved that the ancient Incas had invented the wheel long before European explorers could have introduced it to them. However, in the mountainous terrain in which they lived, the Incas had no practical use for their discovery. The vehicles they made were small toys, apparently used only to amuse children. Similarly, Leonardo da Vinci's drawings show that he "invented" the helicopter and the submarine in the sixteenth century, but they were solutions for which there were as yet no problems.

The mother of invention is not simply necessity but *conscious social need:* necessity plus the accumulated cultural knowledge to meet it. Native American tribes needed heat as much as the European settlers, but they never thought of digging for coal to burn; they did not have the cultural background for inventing the coal furnace. A cure for cancer is a "necessity" for every society, but only modern societies have the essential technology for cancer research. Once both an adequate cultural basis and a focused social need exist, an invention appears inevitable. The automobile, atomic fission, and the space satellite, for example, were all created independently in different countries at about the same time.

ADOPTION AND DIFFUSION.   Some inventions are adopted quickly, some slowly, and some never catch on at all. Whether people will accept an innovation or not seems to depend on both the nature of the invention and the character of the society. If a new product is superior to the one it replaces, if it is cheaper, or if it has some other comparative advantage, then it is more readily adopted. Quartz watches—which are inexpensive, tell time precisely, and do not have to be wound—have advantages over other timepieces and, consequently, have largely replaced them. To be readily accepted, an innovation must also be compatible with cultural values. Birth-control techniques, no

---

[16] Each year cars and trucks burn 40 percent of all the petroleum used in the United States, or one-eighth of all the petroleum used in the world, in a manner that can only be called wasteful. Eighty-two percent of American commuters drive to work, and two-thirds of them go alone. In spite of their reliance on automobile transportation, Americans have so many cars that the average one is parked twenty-two hours a day. See Emma Rothschild, *Paradise Lost: The Decline of the Auto-Industrial Age* (New York: Random House, 1973), pp. 246–49.

"I'm absolutely against total war, but then I'm not for total peace, either."

Drawing by Joseph Farris; © 1984 The New Yorker Magazine, Inc.

matter how relatively advantageous in poor countries, often conflict with cultural values that favor large numbers of children.[17]

In studying the process of cultural diffusion, researchers have found that new social patterns are accepted more readily if they satisfy a need that was not previously met, and they are resisted most strongly if they compete with an old pattern that is still satisfying. Thus, modern medicine will be accepted in Southeast Asia but Christianity will not; new medical techniques have little competition, but Buddhism already fulfills the functions of the religious institution.

PLANNED CHANGE AND UNPLANNED CONSEQUENCES

Much social change today is planned change. In addition to attempting to anticipate and control new developments in the economy and society, governments try to foster social change for the greater good of the community. Many government programs — Social Security, unemployment compensation, welfare, and health insurance — benefit nearly every U.S. citizen. By investing in education and scientific research, government policy makers hope to bring about a better future for society.

It is usually easy to assess the effects of changes in the material culture. It is more difficult to weigh the advantages and drawbacks of the adaptive changes they bring about. The conveniences and dangers of applying nuclear fission to produce electricity were fairly evident. But the effects of birth-control technology, which alters the fertility patterns of families, are not so easy to evaluate. Over and over we have discovered how

---

[17] Francis R. Allen, *Socio-Cultural Dynamics: An Introduction to Social Change* (New York: Macmillan, 1971), pp. 292–93.

difficult it is to predict the consequences of any social action affecting millions of people. Supposedly beneficial programs have sometimes turned out to be mixed blessings.

SOCIAL CONFLICT

Change, as we have seen, breeds strain and conflict. The opposite is also true: conflict between social groups can bring about changes in the larger society. The preeminent theory of social change through social conflict was devised by Karl Marx. In addition to its profound influence on political events that followed it, Marx's analysis has provided the basis for the sociology of social conflict and revolutionary change.

THE MARXIST MODEL

To Marx the "normal" condition of a society is not stability and order but continual change and conflict. He saw history as a succession of class struggles in which power

To these New Hebrides tribesmen, a helicopter is just a curiosity. Only modern societies have the cultural basis for putting this invention to practical use.

shifted from one ruling group to another. Social change, in Marx's view, was impossible without conflict.

Marx's theory of history rests on his concept of an economic class system. As societies emerged from undifferentiated hordes of primitive peoples, he argued, they develop a division of labor and a social organization for producing a means of subsistence. This social order leads to a class system based on the relationship of each class to the means of production: those who own the means of producing the society's subsistence have power and property, those who do not own the means of production are dominated and exploited by the ruling class (see Chapter 7, "Social Inequality"). Free men and slaves in ancient times, barons and serfs in the feudal period, and the bourgeoisie and the proletariat in the modern capitalist era — each pair constitutes the two basic antagonistic classes of owners and workers. Human history is a continuous process of change from one mode of production to another and from one ruling class to another.

Marx predicted that the capitalist era would end in social revolution. At a critical historical moment, when the weakness of capitalism forced a breakdown of the economic and political system, then an aroused, well-organized proletariat would seize the means of production and overthrow their corrupt bourgeois oppressors. The ultimate stage would be a Marxist utopia: a classless society without private ownership of property and without class conflict.[18]

Critics of the Marxist model have pointed out that much of what Marx expected to happen in capitalist economies has actually happened in agrarian or underdeveloped societies. Communist revolutions did not take place in the industrialized nations of Great Britain or Germany but in the agrarian nations of Russia, China, and Cuba. Modern industrial societies have not polarized into oppressors and oppressed, or capitalists and proletarians. Workers today are not equally poor and exploited, a large middle class (neither owners nor workers) has come into existence, and a high standard of living has blurred economic class distinctions in industrialized countries. Unemployment insurance, welfare, public health care, and a progressive tax system are among the ways in which the ruling class has given up some of its profits for the benefit of the ruled.[19]

Despite its shortcomings Marx's analysis of class conflict continues to stimulate sociological thought. He saw the potential for social conflict inherent in every stratified society, and he showed how economic conditions affect power relationships. Much of the following discussion of the nature of social change and conflict derives from Marx's ideas.

HOW CONFLICT CAUSES CHANGE

Pressure to change society is expressed in social conflict. During periods of social change new groups and classes rise to power and influence, and other groups decline or fall. If the social system is flexible enough to adjust to the new situation, then social

---

[18] Coser, *Masters of Sociological Thought*, pp. 55–57.

[19] Richard P. Appelbaum, *Theories of Social Change* (Chicago: Markham, 1970), pp. 92–93; Ralf Dahrendorf, *Class and Class Conflict in Industrial Society* (Palo Alto, Calif.: Stanford University Press, 1959), p. 63.

conflict has led to a change *within* the system. If, on the other hand, the social system is not able to adjust — if the strain and frustration are allowed to accumulate, and, as a result, the system breaks down and is replaced by another social order — then conflict has brought about a change *of* system. A change of system can come peacefully, over a long period of time, as the social structure transforms itself by continual small adjustments to conflict within. It can also come rapidly, violently, as the result of pent-up resentment over deep, unresolved divisions in society.

CHANGE WITHIN THE SYSTEM.   Conflict, by its very nature, prevents a society from stagnating. Conflict within and between social groups disturbs habits of thought and behavior and creates pressure for innovation and creativity. The clash of values and interests, the tension between what is and what some people think ought to be, the conflict between vested interests and new contenders for power — these forces can produce vitality and release creative energy.

Though few social conflicts have entirely positive consequences, many bring unanticipated long-term benefits. "Conflict," the philosopher John Dewey wrote, "is the gadfly of thought. It stirs us to observation and memory. It instigates to invention. It shocks us out of sheep-like passivity, and sets us at noting and contriving. . . . Conflict is a *sine qua non* of reflection and ingenuity." [20] As Orson Welles, playing the villian in the film *The Third Man,* said in a famous bit of dialogue: "Look at Italy under the Borgias. Only warfare, terror, bloodshed, and Michelangelo. In Switzerland they had brotherly love and five hundred years of peace. What did that produce? The cuckoo clock."

CHANGING THE SYSTEM ITSELF.   The distinction between changes *within* the system and a change *of* system is sometimes rather arbitrary. There is always some continuity between the past and the present, between the old social system and the new one. Societies do not have precise dates of birth and death, although they may be assigned one. Americans celebrate the Fourth of July as the birthday of a new way of life, but it took years of gradual political and social change before the United States became much different from thirteen British colonies. A change of system may be said to have occurred when all major social relations, basic institutions, and values have been drastically altered. The Chinese Communist Revolution changed a whole social system rather abruptly, for example. A change of system may also be the cumulative result of changes within the system. The American Revolution did not immediately result in fundamental social changes, and for this reason it may not deserve to be called a "revolution" at all. At what point, then, did the American Revolution — in the sense of a change of social system — occur? When the Constitution established a republic that would protect the rights of the people? When the Civil War ended slavery? When the Nineteenth Amendment gave women the right to vote? Certainly, American society is now fundamentally different from those thirteen British colonies. A change of system has occurred. But the point at which the shift was large enough to be called the turning point, the moment of revolution, is hard to determine.

---

[20] Quoted in Lewis A. Coser, *Continuities in the Study of Social Conflict* (New York: Free Press, 1967), p. 25.

Whether conflict will lead to readjustment within a system or to breakdown and the formation of a new system seems to depend on the behavior of dominant groups. If powerful interests resist change and suppress dissent, they tend to intensify the conflict. If the pressure for change continues to be frustrated by the dominant groups, then society divides into "us" against "them," and violent confrontations are more likely to occur. A flexible social system, however, will permit open airing of grievances and adjust itself to changes in the internal balance of power. Such a system is less likely to be divided into hostile camps, and contending groups are more likely to resolve their conflicts peacefully.

If we take the American Revolution again as an example, the American colonies rebelled because their protests against "taxation without representation" were resented or ignored. The British government, for its part, thought the colonists were being disloyal subjects and sent troops to force them back into line. The redcoats became "them" — an occupying army sent by a tyrannical king — and the colonists were "us" — legitimate defenders of the rights to property and freedom. The rigid colonial system was unable to adjust to the new situation, frustrations on both sides mounted, violence erupted at Lexington and Concord, and the rest is history.

THE FUNCTIONS OF CONFLICT

Social conflict is not always destructive. In open, flexible societies, internal conflict can resolve tension and restore stability. Some specific benefits of internal conflict are maintenance of group unity, readjustment of group norms, and rearrangement of the balance of power.

MAINTENANCE OF GROUP UNITY.   In flexible social structures each individual participates in many different groups. He or she belongs to a family group, a religious group, an ethnic group, a social class, an occupational group, an age group, and so on. Several of these groups may be naturally antagonistic toward each other, and the individual may be involved in conflicts between them. Middle-aged, white members of the Construction Workers Union, for example, may be opposed to giving young, black, nonunion workers construction jobs. They may go on strike, picket the construction site, and prevent nonunion workers from doing their jobs. However, both the middle-aged, white, union member and the young, black, nonunion member belong to other groups in which they are natural allies. Both are members of the working class, both vote Democratic, and both, of course, are construction workers. In a struggle with the construction company's management over wages, they would be on the same side.

In open, pluralistic societies these multiple small conflicts crisscross and prevent the society from being split down the middle. Affiliation with many groups that are sometimes allies and sometimes enemies is a stabilizing factor in social relationships. Multiple conflicts may thus be said to sew society together.

In contrast, rigid societies that repress conflict are more likely to divide into hostile camps. When members of rival groups finally do act out their long-suppressed antagonisms toward each other, the resulting conflict is likely to be intense and emotional. For these reasons civil wars are usually far more cruel and bloody than international conflicts.

THE ARGUMENT OF NATIONALITY.

This late nineteenth-century cartoon expresses nativist hostility to job competition from Chinese immigrants. Conflict with outsiders tends to increase a group's cohesion, define its values and interests, and suppress internal dissent.

When there are no multiple, crisscrossing associations among its members, a society may divide in half along a single axis. Such is the case in Northern Ireland, where the members of the conflicting groups have few common bonds. The social system of Northern Ireland has broken down into two opposing camps: in one, the Irish Catholic working class seek a larger share of power; in the other, the Scotch-Irish, property-owning Protestants control the government and the economy. The membership of the two groups does not overlap on any major basis. The Irish conflict is particularly intense and bitter because each side has tended to keep to itself and resent the presence of the other. For years open hostility has been suppressed, often by force. In such a rigid, closed society there is little basis for compromise, and the conflict is likely to continue.

READJUSTMENT OF GROUP NORMS. Conflict continually creates new norms and modifies old ones. In bringing about new situations to which the usual rules do not apply, conflict stimulates the establishment of appropriate guides to action.

Even wars, which are considered the most "lawless" conflicts, take place within certain limits and are defined by rules of behavior that are understood by both sides. There is general agreement, for example, on what constitutes a provocation serious enough to cause a war. The Japanese attack on Pearl Harbor drew the United States into war, but the American bombing of Colonel Qaddafi's headquarters in Libya did not.

When a Korean Airlines passenger plane was shot down over the Soviet Union in 1984, a disturbing feature of the incident was that no one knew what norms applied to it. Was the unauthorized appearance of a commercial aircraft in Soviet airspace an act of war or not? Was shooting down an unarmed civilian plane a violation of an international agreement or was it justified under the circumstances? Apparently there were no rules that covered the situation, and new guidelines had to be devised.

REARRANGEMENT OF THE BALANCE OF POWER.   Because conflicts with some groups produce alliances with others, conflict maintains or revises the balance of power among antagonists. When conflict breaks out, the former accommodation between the parties involved is rejected, the relative power of each group is tested, and a new social relationship can be established.

The shifting coalitions that control European parliamentary governments provide examples of continual rearrangements of power within an institution. At every election — which is, of course, an institutionalized social conflict — the number of representatives from each political party increases or decreases according to the vote, the balance of power among the parties is readjusted in parliament, and a new coalition is formed to run the government.

Such rearrangements in the balance of power prevent any one group from dominating and exploiting the rest. As long as their power is continually challenged, members of the ruling group will be blocked from exclusive control of the social system.

THE EFFECTS OF EXTERNAL CONFLICT

Conflict with other groups also affects internal group structure. Some of the effects of external conflict follow.

1. *Definition of in-groups and out-groups.* Differences in values, interests, and goals are identified in periodic social conflict between insiders and outsiders, between "us" and "them."

2. *Increase in group cohesion.* The threat of attack, preparation for war, or any hostile challenge from outside can strengthen a group's solidarity and cohesiveness. "We must all hang together, or assuredly we shall all hang separately," Benjamin Franklin warned at the signing of the Declaration of Independence. Heeding his advice, groups tend to "pull themselves together" when they face a common enemy.

3. *Suppression of dissent.* Groups engaged in a continuing struggle with outsiders must mobilize all the energies of their members to support the cause. When internal conflict arises, such groups either suppress it or force the dissenters to leave the group. During the Vietnam War, bumper stickers expressed this attempt to bolster morale and repress dissent: "America: Love It or Leave It."

As long as the social system is stable and group values still hold, external conflict will strengthen group ties. Suppressed internal conflicts may build up hostilities and resentments, but they will not hinder concerted action against what everyone perceives as a common threat. For this reason black Americans, despite their underprivileged status, showed no interest in Japanese war propaganda calling for "solidarity between the dark and yellow races." External conflict, in this case, had a unifying effect. In contrast, unstable social systems that lack consensus are likely to disintegrate in the face of attack from outside. During World War II the weakened and divided French society fell apart after the Nazi invasion, while the British system pulled together its various political and social factions and closed ranks against the German attack.

REVOLUTION

"It was the best of times, it was the worst of times," Charles Dickens said of the French Revolution. It was the best of times, he thought, because a heartless and foolish regime had been overthrown and basic human rights declared. It was also the worst of times because it unleashed the destructive forces of hatred and anger that led to the guillotine and the Reign of Terror. These are two of the many aspects of revolution that fascinate social historians. The causes of revolution are often debated: Why do people rebel? At what point do formerly peaceful citizens stop putting up with a corrupt or inefficient system? Or, to reverse the question, why don't people rebel more often? Considering all the cases of tyranny and injustice in the history of the world, why are revolutions so rare?

Revolutions can be partly explained by the mechanisms of social change and social conflict that were just discussed. In many ways, however, revolutions are unique.

THE SPECIAL CASE OF REVOLUTION

Revolutions are special cases of fundamental social change combined with violent social conflict. The word "revolution" is often used loosely to describe any far-reaching change in social patterns, as in the Industrial Revolution or the sexual revolution. To the sociologist, a true revolution must be a basic change *of* system. Revolutions with a capital R—the French, Russian, and Chinese Revolutions, for example—are great upheavals that tear societies apart and rebuild them on a new basis.

By this definition, a **revolution** is "a sweeping, fundamental change in political organization, social structure, economic property control and the predominant myth of a social order, thus indicating a major break in the continuity of development."[21] Although they may have underlying causes that date back for centuries, revolutions take place rather suddenly. They are also characterized by the use of violence—both by the revolutionaries to force change and by the ruling elite to prevent it.

Human history has known a great many coups, rebellions, and uprisings, but true revolutions are modern social phenomena. Human suffering and discontent seem to take revolutionary forms only in centralized, bureaucratized states in which power is concentrated in a ruling elite. In times and places where power was dispersed, such as the Middle Ages in Europe, rebellions tended to peter out in sporadic, spontaneous outbursts of rage and frustration.

Revolutions, then, are special cases of both social change and social conflict. There are a number of special theories to explain them.

---

[21] Sigmund Neumann, "The International Civil War," in *Why Revolution?* eds. Clifford T. Paynton and Robert Blackey (Cambridge, Mass.: Schenkman, 1971), p. 122.

PSYCHOLOGICAL THEORIES

Psychological theories of revolution hold that political stability or instability depends on the generalized mental state of a society. "It is the dissatisfied state of mind rather than the tangible provision of 'adequate' or 'inadequate' supplies of food, equality, or liberty which produces the revolution."[22] According to this view revolutions are most likely to occur when there has been a long period of economic growth and social progress followed by a short period of reversal. The experience of hard times when people expect more good times causes frustration, anger, and a burning desire to change the system.

In order to feel this dissatisfaction, people have to think that they lack more of the good things of life than other people. They have to feel deprived in comparison to what they had in the past or in comparison to what others have. Sociologists call this discrepancy **relative deprivation**. For this reason peasants living in abject poverty in isolated areas of the world are not likely to revolt. They have no way of knowing what is obtainable and little means of comparing their lot with that of others. A social group that is better off by absolute standards is more likely to revolt if its members are able to see how much more others have or if they remember the better life they once had.[23]

These ideas were the main thesis of Alexis de Tocqueville's study of the French Revolution. He noted that the eighteenth century in France was a period of dynamic economic and social growth, which resulted in less absolute deprivation. He concluded: "The regime which is destroyed by a revolution is almost always an improvement on its immediate predecessor. . . . Evils which are patiently endured when they seem inevitable become intolerable when once the idea of escape from them is suggested."[24]

In contrast to Tocqueville's interpretation, Marx believed that worsening economic and social conditions would finally cause the working class to revolt. While Tocqueville claimed that revolution is caused by increasing prosperity, Marx claimed that it is caused by increasing misery. But Marx also described the social unrest that would result from any improvement in the workers' economic condition:

> A noticeable increase in wages presupposes a rapid growth of productive capital. The rapid growth of productive capital brings about an equally rapid growth of wealth, luxury, social wants, social enjoyments. Thus, although the enjoyments of the workers have risen, the social satisfaction that they give has fallen in comparison with the increased enjoyments of the capitalist, which are inaccessible to the worker. . . . Our desires and pleasures spring from society; we measure them, therefore, by society and not by the objects which serve for their satisfaction. Because they are of a social nature, they are of a relative nature.[25]

Once again, it is how a situation is defined, rather than its objective features, that is important. Misery and social injustice are endured as long as they appear inevitable, but as soon as things improve, then people expect further progress. The Russian serfs, for example, generally accepted their seemingly intolerable condition for centuries

---

[22] James C. Davies, "Toward a Theory of Revolution," in *Why Revolution?* p. 179.

[23] Ted Robert Gurr, *Why Men Rebel* (Princeton, N.J.: Princeton University Press, 1970), pp. 22–58.

[24] Quoted in Davies, "Toward a Theory of Revolution," p. 178.

[25] Quoted in Davies, "Toward a Theory of Revolution," p. 177.

before the revolution. They revolted after social reforms during the nineteenth century had already freed them from bondage.

Revolution also comes when a period of concessions and reforms is followed by a period of withdrawal of privileges and repression. When formerly liberal rulers think they have gone too far and try to crack down, as George III did with the American colonies, then their subjects are sure to feel deprived of their rights. Since people are usually much more angry if they lose what they already have than if they lose hope of getting something they do not have, violence is a likely result.

POLITICAL CONFLICT THEORY

Conflict theorists do not deny that discontent and unrest lead to rebellion and disorder, but they argue that the motivation for violence is not enough to start a revolution. To them, revolutions are not simply explosions of anger and frustration but long, complex struggles among different groups with different motives, ending in new political and social arrangements.

According to Theda Skocpol's model[26] there are two necessary and sufficient conditions for a social revolution: the breakdown of a partially bureaucratic state and widespread peasant insurrections. The breakdown of the state can be caused by overwhelming military pressure (as in the case of the Russian state during World War I) or the presence of a politically entrenched and landed upper class that prevents reform (as in the case of France on the eve of revolution). In both Russia and France the breakdown of the state permitted peasant rebellions that the ruling group could not effectively suppress.

James Rule and Charles Tilly have proposed the theory that revolution results from the breakdown of a political system into separate power centers. "A revolution begins," they contend, "when previously acquiescent citizens faced with strictly incompatible demands from the government and an alternative authority obey the alternative authority. It continues until only one central authority remains." [27]

In Rule and Tilly's model the revolution unfolds in stages. First, the emergence of two authorities tests everyone's loyalty and forces a choice between them. There are likely to be violent confrontations between the contending groups. Second, the two authorities win over large sections of the population, and the conflict becomes polarized between "us" and "them." Third, the successful revolutionary coalition seizes the government, tries to reestablish control over the country, and meets resistance. Finally, the original coalition is likely to fall apart, leaving a few contenders exceptionally powerful. The combination of these fairly independent processes is rare, but then so are revolutions.

This model fits the historical sequence of events in the French Revolution. In the early stages the revolutionaries were a coalition of discontented groups with different objectives. Some were middle class, some were intellectuals, and some were workers and small shopkeepers. All wanted a greater share of power for themselves and were

[26] Theda Skocpol, *States and Social Revolutions* (Cambridge, Eng.: Cambridge University Press, 1979).
[27] James Rule and Charles Tilly, "1830 and the Unnatural History of Revolution," *Journal of Social Issues* 28 (1972): 54.

In December 1989, Rumanians demonstrated angrily against declining living standards, severe rationing of food and energy, and oppression of ethnic Hungarians. After the massacre of thousands of protesters was reported in Timisoara, the uprising spread, causing President Nicolae Ceausescu to lose the support of the army and eventually his own security police.

According to system dysfunction theory, revolutions are caused by the failure of a social order to adjust to severe, multiplying problems. If Ceausescu had reacted to popular discontents in a less rigid and despotic fashion, he might never have been overthrown.

willing to work together to get it. Finally, one of the groups, the Jacobins, became supreme, took over the leadership of the revolution, and claimed everyone else's allegiance in fighting its cause. This group then seized the central government in the capital and tried to extend its control over the countryside. More violence broke out as local officials resisted the revolutionaries. Finally, there was a purge of the revolutionary coalition that left a small ruling elite in command until it too was overthrown by a revolt of the moderates.

Of course, governments and revolutionaries rarely contend for power on an equal basis. If the government is strong enough to suppress conflict, the revolution will never take place. The democracy movement that swept China in 1989 was swiftly suppressed because, like many other rebellions, it lacked the resources of organization, weapons, and outside support. Moreover, a stable social system is able to change in response to conflict and keep the allegiance of its discontented members. Mikhail Gorbachev's reforms, for example, are an attempt to satisfy Soviet citizens' demands for greater economic and political freedom. For these reasons true revolutions are rare.

THE IRANIAN REVOLUTION

The Islamic revolution of 1979 in Iran was a true revolution in the sociological sense, a mass movement which resulted in a new political, economic, and ideological order. The Iranian Revolution thus offers a unique recent example of how revolutions occur.

During the 1960s and 1970s, the shah's programs for land reform and modernization brought him into conflict with the landholding religious establishment and the merchants who benefited from the status quo. Many other Iranians resented the intrusion of Western ideas and customs, the corruption and cruelty of the government, and the shah's flouting of traditional Islamic beliefs. By ruthlessly persecuting his opponents, the shah was able to suppress the mullahs and other dissenters. As system dysfunction theory predicts, his rigidity intensified opposition to his regime.

In 1978, under pressure from U.S. President Jimmy Carter and other foreign heads of government, the shah began to pursue more liberal policies. The revolution began at this critical moment of rising expectations. Followers of the exiled religious leader, the Ayatollah Khomeini, mounted a series of strikes and marches against the shah that ended in destructive riots.

As political conflict theory explains, the struggle for power between the mullahs and the government divided the political system into separate centers of authority. By November the shah had only the support of his large, well-equipped army. His downfall came when the military refused to fire on their own people. The shah fled the country, a box of Iranian soil in his pocket. A new order was established when Khomeini returned from exile and formed a reactionary government based on traditional religious principles.

The philosophical basis for the French Revolution was the eighteenth-century Enlightenment, and its revolutionary ideology was expressed as "liberty, equality, fraternity." The Russian Revolution's background was nineteenth-century socialism, and its revolutionary ideal was a classless proletarian state. The Iranian Revolution's ideology was Islam, and its revolutionaries were religious leaders who saw themselves engaged in a life-and-death struggle with the satanic forces of paganism, oppression, and imperialism.[1]

"The parallel," according to one scholar, "is . . . very close between what happened in the Islamic world in our day and what happened in Europe and beyond following the Russian and French Revolutions—the same upsurge of emotion, the same uplifting of hearts, the same boundless hopes, the same willingness to excuse and condone all kinds of horrors, and the same questions. Where next?"[2]

[1] Bernard Lewis, "Islamic Revolution," *The New York Review* (January 21, 1988), p. 46.   [2] Ibid, p. 50.

SYSTEM DYSFUNCTION THEORY

System dysfunction theory relates the causes of revolution to the causes of social change. From this perspective society is a functionally integrated system of interrelated parts. If one of its components is not operating as it should to maintain equilibrium, it can throw the whole system off balance. Social changes result from attempts to restore order by altering the social structure. If there are many serious problems that go uncorrected, there may be a breakdown and a revolution. In some cases the system fails to adjust because the ruling group resists any change in the status quo. If the elite is less intransigent, reform rather than revolution generally occurs.

A system may also fail to adjust because severe dysfunctions cannot be corrected in time to prevent a breakdown. There may be an "accelerator" that acts to multiply and intensify the system's dysfunctions to a revolutionary level. The loss of a war, for example, often precedes a revolution. If the armed forces are crippled by a crushing defeat or lose faith in the government, they will not function in support of the system.

All three theories of revolution — psychological, political conflict, and system dysfunction theories — help explain the 1979 Iranian Revolution.

Because the elite cannot depend on an incapacitated army to fight the revolutionaries, the loss of a war is a double accelerator in a revolutionary situation.[28] If Imperial Russia had not entered World War I, for example, there might not have been a Russian Revolution.

The trouble with system dysfunction theory is that it fails to identify the point at which imbalance is severe enough to lead to a revolution. Nearly every system has structural defects that are not corrected, and perhaps cannot be corrected, by the action of the ruling elite. Sometimes measures that are taken to restore order themselves

---

[28] Chalmers Johnson, "Revolution and the Social System," in *Why Revolution?* pp. 199–213.

precipitate change. Half-hearted reforms by the French king and the Russian czar to regain stability provoked actions that led to revolutions. The resistance of the elite to change, however, may be effective in preventing a revolution. The history of Latin America has proved again and again that ruthless, efficient repression can crush a revolutionary movement entirely.[29]

The three theories of revolution are not mutually exclusive; each one provides part of the story (see "The Iranian Revolution"). The long-run, underlying causes of a revolution may be found in the period of social change that precedes it. If the changes are rapid and profound, the old order may break down because it cannot adjust quickly enough. The system dysfunction theory would cover such situations. The psychological consequences of rapid social change may be feelings of deprivation, alienation, and resentment in a variety of groups — feelings that may lead to the outbreaks of violence explained by the theory of relative deprivation. Conflict between the ruling elite and the revolutionaries polarizes society, and a struggle for power begins along the lines of the political conflict model.

Revolutions are extreme cases of social change and social conflict, and they seem to be caused by some of the same forces. The reasons that revolutions happen so infrequently are the same reasons that major social change does not come easily. Vested interests, an entrenched elite, and a conservative population often present effective resistance. And, like other sweeping social changes, the effects of revolutions are often difficult to evaluate.

---

[29] Lawrence Stone, "Theories of Revolution," in *Why Revolution?* pp. 263–79.

SUMMARY

1. A social change is any significant alteration in a social structure, including new norms, values, and material and symbolic cultural products. Social conflict refers to the antagonism of groups with opposing interests or values. Conflict is not necessarily violent, and much of it is institutionalized. Social change hardly ever takes place without social conflict; most social conflict eventually produces social change.

2. Major social changes are complex events that require more than one explanation. Technological development has produced countless social changes, and industrialization has transformed modern society. In *The Protestant Ethic and the Spirit of Capitalism* Weber emphasized that ideas can also produce social and economic changes. Ogburn noted that there is a culture lag between changes in the material culture and the adaptive culture.

3. Spencer proposed that human societies evolve like animal species, from the simple to the complex. While not all social structures have developed in this manner, Lenski has applied the evolutionary theory to changes in individual societies.

4. According to Mannheim's theory of generational change, the continuous introduction of new age cohorts into the cultural process permits social change to occur. Changes in the age structure of a population, such as the "aging" of the U.S. population, also have social effects.

5. Geography, climate, natural resources, and natural disasters influence how societies develop; historical accidents are also factors in social change.

6. Veblen believed that major technological inventions eventually bring about social change, but he pointed out that people with vested interests will resist changing social arrangements that benefit

them. Fear of change is understandable, for most innovations are costly to someone. Changes in moral values and cultural patterns are often strongly resisted.

7. Changes are likely to be accepted when there is an adequate cultural basis and when they meet a conscious social need. Planned change frequently has unexpected consequences that are difficult to evaluate.

8. Marx devised the classical model of social change through social conflict. He predicted that the conflicts of the capitalist era would bring about a social revolution. Capitalist societies have not developed along the lines that Marx expected, however, and much of what he thought would happen in capitalist industrial systems has occurred in agrarian societies instead.

9. Conflict can cause change within a system as well as a change of the system itself. Although change is usually gradual, a change of system is said to have taken place when all the basic institutions and values of a society have been fundamentally altered. Whether conflict leads to readjustment or breakdown of the system seems to depend on the responses of dominant groups.

10. Internal conflict can restore group unity in open societies with multiple associations among members. Conflicts are likely to continue in rigid societies, where few common bonds and little basis for compromise exist. Conflict also tends to readjust group norms and realign the balance of power among various groups.

11. Conflict with outside groups has the following effects: definition of in-groups and out-groups, an increase in group cohesion, and suppression of dissent.

12. Revolutions combine fundamental social change with violent social conflict. Psychological theories find the cause of revolutions in feelings of relative deprivation.

13. Political conflict theory emphasizes that revolutions are complex struggles among different groups that end in new political and social arrangements. Skocpol traces their causes to the breakdown of the state and to peasant rebellions; Rule and Tilly maintain that revolution results from the fragmentation of a political system into separate centers of power.

14. According to system dysfunction theory a breakdown in the system occurs when there are many serious uncorrected problems. If the system adjusts, social change occurs; if it does not, there may be a revolution.

15. All three theories of revolution are useful in explaining the underlying causes of social change and social conflict.

KEY TERMS

social change 559	cultural diffusion 564	cohort 566
social conflict 559	material culture 564	vested interest 571
technology 562	adaptive culture 564	revolution 581
industrialization 563	culture lag 564	relative deprivation 582

SUGGESTED READING

* Shaul Bakhash. *The Reign of the Ayatollahs: Iran and the Islamic Revolution.* New York: Basic Books, 1986.

Lewis A. Coser. *Continuities in the Study of Social Conflict.* New York: Free Press, 1967.

* Amitai Etzioni and Eva Etzioni-Halevy, eds. *Social Change: Sources, Patterns, and Consequences,* 2nd ed. New York: Basic Books, 1974.

* Paul Kennedy. *The Rise and Fall of the Great Powers: Economic Change and Military Con-*

flict from 1500 to 2000. New York: Random House, 1989.

Michael Mann. *The Sources of Social Power.* New York: Cambridge University Press, 1986.

* William G. Rosenberg and Marilyn B. Young. *Transforming Russia and China: Revolutionary*

Struggle in the Twentieth Century. New York: Oxford University Press, 1982.

* Theda Skocpol. *States and Social Revolutions,* New York: Cambridge University Press, 1979.

* Available in paperback.

If all the year
were playing
holidays,
To sport would
be as tedious as
to work.

*William
Shakespeare*

CHAPTER 19

WORK AND LEISURE

From the art historian's perspective, the French Impressionist painters of the late nineteenth century mark the end of the dominance of the Old Masters and the beginning of modern art. From the sociologist's perspective, the Impressionists coincide with another modern development, the growth of urban, industrialized society. Manet, Monet, Renoir, and their followers lived in an extraordinary time, when the conditions of most people's daily lives were changing more rapidly than ever before. The familiar scenes they painted — the shimmering afternoons in Parisian parks and cafés, the family picnics in the countryside, the boating parties on the Seine — represent both a new kind of art and a vastly different way of life.

As we have seen in earlier chapters, industrialization brings about basic changes in the structure of a society (see especially Chapter 12, "The Economy"). Most of these changes were apparent in the 1860s and 1870s, when the Impressionists began to exhibit their works, and these new social arrangements are reflected in the subjects of their paintings.

One fundamental change is that most people in industrial societies are now employees rather than self-employed farmers and craftsmen. Because industrial workers are concentrated in workshops and factories, the home and the workplace are separated. Economic production is no longer a part of ordinary family life; now there are "working hours," when wages are earned and nonworking hours, or unpaid **free time**. Because the factory system makes each worker much more productive, a second feature of industrial societies is a generally higher standard of living. During the nineteenth century the rise in per capita income accelerated the growth of an affluent middle class and ushered in a new era of mass consumption of goods and services. A third effect of industrialization is urbanization, or a shift in population from the countryside to the cities. Seen from the sociological perspective, the Impressionists' paintings of parks and restaurants and sailing parties are pictures of a new, distinctly modern way of life. For the first time, an urban middle class had the time and the money to spend on recreation — on excursions to the seaside, on cafés and music halls, on ballets and horse races and other public entertainments.

By reorganizing the way most people spent their time, industrialization changed the meaning of work and leisure. **Work** became defined as paid employment, or what we do to make a living. In industrial societies, where and when we work is thus limited to certain times and a certain place. But if work, by Mark Twain's larger definition, is "whatever a body is obliged to do," [1] then most of us also have a great deal of unpaid work to do in our spare time. Only part of our free time is thus available for **leisure**, or time occupied by freely chosen activities that are enjoyable or self-fulfilling in themselves.

This chapter examines the relationships among free time, work, and leisure. The first section considers how industrialization radically changed the meaning of work and how loss of work affects the worker. Next we discuss the alienating nature of the modern workplace, as well as some attempts to improve the way people work. The fourth part analyzes the way work affects leisure, the meaning of leisure activities, and what Americans do with their leisure. The final section suggests some problems raised by the possibility that automation will bring about a new age of leisure.

THE MEANING OF WORK

Work is central to our sense of self. Ask the proverbial man on the street who he is and he'll say, "I'm a bank teller" or "I'm a truck driver," not "I'm a father" or "I'm a music lover." Work affects our lives in other ways as well. Our occupation usually determines our income and life style, and, as we have already seen in Chapter 7, it also influences what other people think of us. Since what we do is so important to what we are, changes in the nature of work have deeply affected the way people think about themselves and the world in which they live.

THE AMERICAN WORK ETHIC

Every year since 1972 a national sample of American adults has been asked this question: "If you had enough money to live as comfortably as you like for the rest of your life, would you stop working?" Every year seven out of ten people have said they would continue to work.[2] Clearly, most Americans want to work or believe they *should* work even if they do not need the money.

---

[1] Mark Twain, *The Adventures of Tom Sawyer* (London: Octopus, 1978), p. 21.
[2] National Opinion Research Center, *The General Social Surveys: 1972–1983* (Storrs, Conn.: Roper Public Center for Opinion Research, 1988).

Like other Impressionist paintings, Renoir's *Boating Party* pictures a new, distinctly modern way of life. During the late nineteenth century the process of industrialization created, for the first time in history, a large urban middle class with the time and the money to spend on this sort of recreation.

The Phillips Collection, Washington.

The view that work is more than an unpleasant necessity is a modern, and in some ways a particularly American, idea. From Benjamin Franklin's Poor Richard, who taught that "a penny saved is a penny earned," to Ralph Waldo Emerson's "Self-Reliance," to Dale Carnegie's advice on how to succeed in business, generations of Americans have been exhorted to be industrious and thrifty in order to get ahead. This American tradition is linked to the Protestant Ethic, the belief that work is a virtue and a duty. To the early Calvinist reformers, work was a "calling." They strove to succeed because worldly success was a sign that they were predestined to be among God's elect, but they did not spend their wealth because idleness and self-indulgence were sinful and only frugality and sobriety pleased God. Max Weber called this Protestant tradition "the spirit of capitalism" because it provided the moral basis for the accumulation of investment capital (the detailed discussions of Weber's classic work, *The Protestant Ethic and the Spirit of Capitalism*, are in Chapters 12 and 18).

Along with the Protestant idea that work is a moral duty, the American experience led to the related notion that work is the basis of individual accomplishment and self-worth. Given the vast resources the continent offered to those who were willing to exploit them, it is not surprising that Americans came to associate work with achievement and financial success. The American liberal tradition of equality and opportunity also contributed to the idea that everyone can and should "make something of yourself," "get ahead," and "be somebody." To this day, most Americans believe that everyone (or at least every man) should work for a living, and they admire "self-made men" and disapprove of "bums" and "good-for-nothings."

According to the pollster Daniel Yankelovich, the American work ethic is derived from four traditional values:

- Americans tend to equate masculinity with being a good provider. Men are the traditional breadwinners, and a "real man" is able to take care of his family.
- Americans believe in "standing on your own two feet." A paying job means freedom and independence; having to depend on others for financial help makes most adults uncomfortable.
- Americans admire material success: a prestigious job, a high income, expensive possessions, the achievements of their children.
- Americans believe in "doing a good job." Work is a source of self-respect: people who work hard and do their jobs well tend to have greater self-esteem than those who do not or cannot work.[3]

Many studies show that people value work not only because it is socially approved, but because it provides opportunities for relationships with co-workers. Getting up every morning to go to work also gives daily life purpose, structure, and content. Finally, "a job tells the worker day in and day out that he [or she] has something to offer. Not to have a job is not to have something that is valued by one's fellow human beings."[4]

LOSS OF WORK

Because work means so much more than just earning a living, Americans who cannot work are troubled by more than loss of income. Men who cannot support their families feel especially humiliated and worthless, but losing a job or failing to find one has a devastating effect on nearly every worker.

THE UNEMPLOYED.   The U.S. government counts among the unemployed only people who can work, are not working, and have tried to find a job during the previous four weeks. This definition includes laid-off workers who are waiting to be recalled to their jobs and workers who are reporting to a new job within 30 days. It excludes so-called "discouraged workers" who have given up trying to find employment. Since the government's definition of unemployment covers only people who are actively looking for work (or waiting to start work), the official unemployment rate underestimates the number of people who want to work but cannot find a job.

The officially unemployed are concentrated in certain groups (see Table 19-1). Blacks generally have much higher rates of unemployment than whites; widowed, divorced, or separated people have higher rates than those who are married; manual workers have higher rates than other workers; and young people have higher rates than the middle-aged. Since these groups are also likely to have the highest proportion of discouraged workers, their true unemployment rates are probably even higher than the official figures indicate.

---

[3] Daniel Yankelovich, "The Meaning of Work," in J. M. Rosow, ed., *The Worker and the Job* (Englewood Cliffs, N.J.: Prentice-Hall, 1974).

[4] U.S. Department of Health, Education, and Welfare, *Work in America: Report of a Special Task Force to the Secretary of Health, Education, and Welfare* (Cambridge, Mass.: MIT Press, 1973), p. 14.

UNEMPLOYMENT RATES, PERSONS SIXTEEN AND OLDER, OCTOBER 1988   TABLE 19–1

	Males	Females
White—Total	4.3	4.5
Married, spouse present	2.6	3.5
Widowed – divorced – separated	5.4	4.8
Never married	7.8	6.5
Black—Total	10.7	10.8
Married, spouse present	5.5	5.4
Widowed – divorced – separated	9.8	9.5
Never married	17.9	17.5
Occupation—All Races		
Managers and professionals	1.5	2.5
Sales workers	3.4	5.8
Clerical workers	4.6	3.4
Service occupations	6.6	8.1
Operatives and laborers	6.3	7.1
Age—All Races		
16 – 19	16.9	12.8
20 – 24	9.5	7.7
25 – 54	4.1	4.5
55 and older	3.0	2.4

SOURCE: U.S. Bureau of Labor Statistics, *Employment and Earnings* (Washington, D.C.: U.S. Government Printing Office, November 1988), Tables A-11, A-12, and A-38.

EFFECTS OF UNEMPLOYMENT.   In the relatively prosperous 1960s the official U.S. unemployment rate hovered around 6 percent, which meant that at least 6 million people could not find a job. During the recessions of the 1970s, the unemployment rate rose to 8 percent; in the recession of 1981 – 1983, it reached a post-war peak of nearly 11 percent. In 1988 and 1989 unemployment stabilized at between 5 and 6 percent, a rate that is becoming accepted as the norm for the American economy.

According to M. Harvey Brenner, a sociologist at The Johns Hopkins University, increasingly higher levels of unemployment can cause lasting physical, mental, and social damage. His research finds that a rise of one percentage point in the unemployment rate, if sustained over 6 years, is associated with a 4.1 percent increase in suicide, a 5.7 percent increase in homicide, and an increase in first-time admission to state mental hospitals of 4.3 percent for men and 2.3 percent for women.[5] These figures do not show, of course, whether unemployed individuals are actually causing the rise in suicides and homicides. Moreover, many variables affect physical and mental health, and it is usually impossible to say whether mental illness is a cause or effect of unemployment. Nevertheless, Brenner's findings have been supported by studies of unemployed individuals.

[5] M. Harvey Brenner, "The Social Costs of Unemployment," Testimony offered to the Joint Economic Committee of Congress, 96th Congress of the United States, October 31, 1979 (Washington, D.C.: U.S. Government Printing Office, 1980).

One work and unemployment project, based on interviews with blue- and white-collar workers' families, found that laid-off husbands were more likely to have symptoms of mental illness than those who were still at work. As time went on, wives with unemployed husbands became significantly more anxious and depressed than other wives; after their husbands were reemployed these symptoms tended to disappear.[6]

A ten-year study of aircraft workers in Hartford, Connecticut, found that periods of unemployment in this cyclical industry lead to serious physical and emotional strain as well as financial hardship for most workers who are laid off. High blood pressure, alcoholism, increased cigarette smoking, insomnia, neurasthenia, and anxiety were among the commonly reported symptoms of strain.[7]

Some behavioral scientists believe that jobless workers today are psychologically worse off than they were in the Great Depression of the 1930s, when the unemployment rate is estimated to have been 25 percent. The unemployed in the Depression had no welfare system, Social Security, food stamps, or unemployment benefits to fall back on, but they saw their misfortune as part of a temporary disaster that was affecting the entire country. Today when people cannot find a job they are less likely than workers in the 1930s to see their situation as part of a larger social problem (the failure of the economy to provide jobs for all who want them) and more likely to blame themselves for not having the necessary skills or abilities.[8]

Moreover, many people who have lost their jobs today are victims of *structural unemployment,* or unemployment that results from a restructuring of the economy (see Chapter 12, "The Economy"). When previously well-paid workers find that their jobs have permanently disappeared, making their skills and seniority worthless, they do not define their situation as a temporary setback. Finally, compared to the large-scale efforts to get people back to work during the Great Depression, the rest of the country does not appear to be much concerned with the plight of people who do not have work. As a result, some psychologists believe that today's unemployed are more despairing and thus more likely to suffer from depression and other kinds of mental illness.[9]

THE EXPERIENCE OF WORK

The transformation of the economic institution over the last two centuries has been reflected in the changing nature of work in modern societies. The automated world in which most Americans earn their livings is drastically different from the world their

[6] Ramsay Liem and Joan Liem, "Social Support and Stress: Some General Issues and their Application to the Problem of Unemployment," in L. Ferman and J. Gordus, eds., *Mental Health and the Economy* (Kalamazoo, Mich.: UpJohn Institute, 1979).

[7] Paula Rayman and Barry Bluestone, *The Private and Social Response to Job Loss: A Metropolitan Study.* Final report of research sponsored by the Center for Work and Mental Health, National Institute of Mental Health, 1982.

[8] Stanley Parker, *Leisure and Work* (London: Allen and Unwin, 1983), p. 66.

[9] Ramsay Liem and Paula Rayman, "Health and Social Costs of Unemployment: Research and Policy Considerations," *American Psychologist* 37 (October 1982): 116–23.

colonial ancestors knew, where men worked the fields with horsedrawn plows and women made clothing and candles at home. This section describes how industrialization has changed the character and experience of work in the United States and how it has affected both the labor force as a whole and the individual worker.

WORK IN THE UNITED STATES

In a **pre-industrial society** most people extract their living from the land, primarily through agriculture. Until about a century and a half ago, the United States was such a society, a nation of farmers, fishermen, and trappers. As the economy industrialized, however, farmhands began to be replaced by such machines as the cotton gin and the mechanical reaper. Large numbers of workers left the farm to take the new jobs that were opening in offices and factories. By the end of the nineteenth century, most of the work force was engaged in manufacturing and service occupations (banking, clerical work) instead of agriculture. The United States had become an **industrial society**, or a society that produces more fabricated goods, such as steel and textiles, than raw materials. Another change in the American economy began in the 1950s. During that decade more workers became employed in providing services than in manufacturing or agriculture (see Figure 19-1). Largely because of the growth of service occupations —especially health care, education, retail trade, and government—white-collar workers now make up a majority of the work force.[10] The shift to a **post-industrial**, or service-based, **society** is rapidly changing the nature and meaning of work.

THE SERVICE REVOLUTION.   The kinds of work people do on farms, in factories, and in offices are obviously very different from each other. Work in a pre-industrial economy is what Daniel Bell calls "a game against nature." [11] Farmers and ranchers must deal with the uncertainties of weather and other natural forces. Only about 3 percent of the American labor force still work this way.

In industrial societies most work is a game against *things*. Workers in manufacturing occupations must contend with the predictable forces of the machine. Work is regulated by such artificial devices as time clocks and eight-hour shifts. The pace of work is mechanical and routine. The proportion of goods-producing workers has steadily declined to less than one-fifth of the American labor force. Automation has replaced many of these workers with machines.

Work in post-industrial societies is a game between *persons*. Most workers are not up against the forces of nature or the demands of machinery; they must contend primarily with the uncertainties of human relationships. The place of work changes to offices, classrooms, and sales counters. The product of this work is not goods but information, recreation, or assistance. In 1990, seven out of ten American workers held jobs in service industries. About one in six workers held a clerical job, which often involved electronic data processing and other computerized operations.[12]

---

[10] U.S. Bureau of the Census, *Statistical Abstract of the United States* (Washington, D.C.: U.S. Government Printing Office, 1985).

[11] Daniel Bell, *The Coming of Post-Industrial Society* (New York: Basic Books, 1973), p. 126.

[12] U.S. Department of Labor *Employment and Earnings* (Washington, D.C.: U.S. Government Printing Office, March 1988), Table A-22.

FIGURE 19-1 THE SHIFT FROM GOODS TO SERVICES, 1870–2000

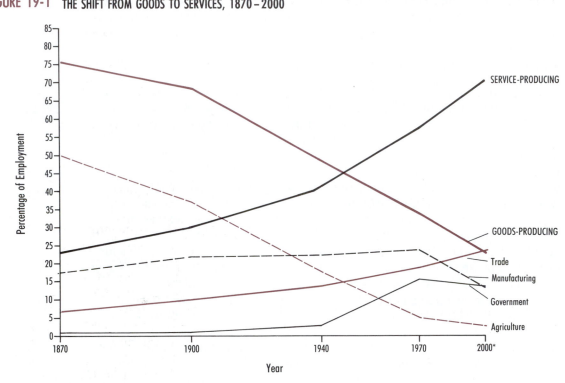

*2000 estimates are based on the assumption of moderate growth.

SOURCE: U.S. Bureau of the Census, *Historical Statistics of the United States: Colonial Times to 1957* (Washington, D.C.: U.S. Government Printing Office, 1960): U.S. Bureau of Labor Statistics, *The U.S. Economy in 1980* Washington, D.C.: U.S. Government Printing Office, 1980); U.S. Bureau of the Census, *Statistical Abstract of the United States (*Washington, D.C.: U.S. Government Printing Office, 1989), Table 646.

The *service revolution* became evident during the 1970s, when employment in the United States grew at a truly remarkable rate. Of the nearly 31 million new nonagricultural jobs created between 1970 and 1989, 70 percent were in services and retail trade.[13] Many of these new occupations—in fast-food restaurants, nursing homes, and data-processing centers—are part of the secondary labor market of low-paying, relatively unskilled, dead-end jobs (see Chapter 7, "Social Inequality").

The post-industrial economy clearly represents a revolution in how and where Americans work. It is less clear, however, whether the quality of most people's working lives has greatly changed.

INDUSTRIAL VERSUS POST-INDUSTRIAL WORK. In an early analysis of the modern economy, *The Coming of Post-Industrial Society* (1973), Bell argued that the shift from produc-

---

[13] Ibid., Tables B-1, B-2.

ing goods to providing services marked the decline of industrial society. Industrial economies, he wrote, have three distinguishing characteristics: (1) the large corporation is the predominant kind of organization; (2) machine technology controls the work process; and (3) social relations are shaped by the conflict between employers and workers. All three features are significantly altered in the post-industrial society.

First, Bell found that most service businesses employ fewer than 1,000 people. While giant corporations do exist in such service industries as banking, utilities, and transportation, most nongovernment services are provided by such relatively small enterprises as hospitals and retail stores.

Second, Bell noted that service occupations usually involve communication with other people:

> From the irritation of a customer at an airline ticket office to the sympathetic or harassed response of teacher to student . . . the fact that individuals now talk to other individuals, rather than interact with a machine, is the fundamental fact about work in the post-industrial society.[14]

Finally, Bell contends that the antagonism between worker and boss no longer dominates social relationships in the post-industrial economy. Disputes over wages and working conditions are settled in negotiations between labor and management, which represent more or less equal parties. All in all, Bell concluded, the post-industrial society has helped solve the "old" industrial problems — the dehumanizing effects of highly mechanized factory work and the uneven struggle between capital and labor.

In another influential work, *Labor and Monopoly Capital* (1974), Harry Braverman denied that the service economy has improved the workers' situation. He argued that rational control of the work process is as crucial to profit making in service industries as it is in manufacturing. The more efficiently workers do their jobs, the more productive and profitable they are — no matter whether the product to be sold is a bar of steel or a long-distance telephone call. At an airline ticket office as well as on the automobile assembly line, controlling the work process for maximum efficiency leads to further division of labor, a high degree of automation, and close supervision of individual workers. According to Braverman, computers and other automated machinery have downgraded most clerical work until it is just as monotonous and mindless as old-fashioned factory work.

Capitalist employers, Braverman noted, treat all forms of labor the same way on the balance sheet. Like blue-collar operators, white-collar typists and keypunchers are paid not to think but to run machines as quickly and skillfully as possible. Clerks as well as factory workers can be exploited to achieve the greatest possible return at the least possible cost. The demand for efficiency, combined with technological change, has led to **deskilling**, or downgrading the skills of both craftsmen and office workers. Just as computerized typesetting has downgraded the printer's job, electronic word processors have in many cases reduced the secretary's varied skills to filling a certain quota of typed materials. In Braverman's view the post-industrial economy has not eliminated what Adam Smith identified as the stupefying effects of dull, repetitious work.[15]

---

[14] Bell, *The Coming of Post-Industrial Society,* p. 163.
[15] Harry Braverman, *Labor and Monopoly Capital* (New York: Monthly Review Press, 1974).

According to Daniel Bell, work in a pre-industrial society is a game against nature. In the Middle Ages most players were peasant farmers. Work in an industrial society is a game against things. Workers in this 1895 cotton mill had to contend with the predictable routines of the machine.

THE DESKILLING DEBATE.   Increasing automation has clearly been accompanied by a decline in both the skills required of the worker and the physical hardships involved in work. It is equally clear, however, that some computer-based technologies require workers to develop new skills and to reintegrate a fragmented work process. Clerical workers who use central data bases, for example, can handle all the transactions for a client's account: taking orders, filing information, making adjustments, and answering inquiries.[16] While automation often replaces skilled workers with unskilled ones, new information technologies also offer more demanding and rewarding work for comparatively unskilled white-collar workers.

In a recent analysis of the transformation of the workplace by "smart machines," Shoshana Zuboff finds that the liberating possibilities of information technology are frequently opposed by entrenched bureaucratic interests. When computers are used only to "automate," or achieve speed and consistency, workers are robbed of their skills and their sense of control over their work. However, computer-based technology can also raise work to the abstract level of information, so that the necessary skills have to do with the manipulation of symbols and knowledge. In this case, computers "informate," or give workers an unprecedented understanding of the production process, enabling them to collaborate with managers in decision making. If old assumptions about the bureaucratic hierarchy and managerial authority interfere — if those in

---

[16] Heidi Hartmann, Robert Kraut, and Louise Tilly, *Computer Chips and Paper Clips: Technology and Women's Employment* (Washington, D.C.: National Academy Press, 1987), p. 63.

Work in a
post-industrial
society is a game
among persons. The
typical workplace is
an office, and the
product of work
is technical
information,
professional
assistance, or some
other service.

charge of the organization choose to "automate" rather than "informate" — Zuboff argues that the advantages of a more knowledgeable and egalitarian work force will be lost.[17]

How much has work really changed in the United States? Obviously, work in the post-industrial society is generally safer and more pleasant. Compared to workers in the early industrial era, workers today have many more legal rights and more effective union protection. On balance, it does not seem that computer-based technologies have either greatly improved or greatly downgraded the level of skill required of American workers. Finally, as Bell suggested, the trend toward working with people instead of things has often made work more fulfilling and enjoyable.

On the other hand, many white-collar service workers have jobs that are just as dreary and monotonous as blue-collar operations. *Work in America*, a 1972 report to the Secretary of Health, Education, and Welfare, described the "white-collar woes" as not much different from the "blue-collar blues": "Dull, repetitive, seemingly meaningless tasks, offering little challenge or autonomy, are causing discontent among workers at all occupational levels. . . . Many workers . . . feel locked in, their mobility blocked, the opportunity to grow lacking in their jobs, challenge missing from their tasks." [18] It is to American workers' shared circumstances and experiences that we will now turn.

---

[17] Shoshana Zuboff, *In the Age of the Smart Machine: The Future of Work and Power* (New York: Basic Books, 1988).

[18] U.S. Department of Health, Education, and Welfare, *Work in America*, pp. xv, xvii.

ALIENATION

The Industrial Revolution, which transformed the kind of work people do, also changed its meaning and purpose for the worker. The Calvinist doctrine of predestination is now forgotten, but we still feel its effect. "The Puritan," Weber wrote,

> wanted to work in a calling; we are forced to do so. . . . The modern economic order . . . is now bounded to the technical and economic conditions of machine production which today determine the lives of all the individuals who are born into {it}. . . . In Baxter's[19] view the care for external goods should only lie on the shoulders of the "saint like a light cloak, which can be thrown aside at any moment." But fate decreed that the cloak should become an iron cage.[20]

Karl Marx developed the concept of **alienation** to describe the loss of human control over the forces of industrial society. Alienation is a condition of all modern institutions, Marx concluded, but it is especially important in the workplace, where men and women are separated from the finished products of their work, from the mechanical process of production, from other workers, and from their own feelings and inclinations. Work is not a realization of the worker's own creativity or aspirations but a contribution to some other goal. "Work is external to the worker," Marx wrote. "It is not a part of his nature; consequently he does not fulfill himself in his work but denies himself. . . . In work {the worker} does not belong to himself but to another person."[21]

The industrial methods that Adam Smith described in the pin factory have fragmented the work process and changed the nature of modern work (see Chapter 12, "The Economy"). Instead of artisans capable of doing a variety of tasks needed to produce a complete product (cabinetmakers, shoemakers, dressmakers, and so on), most modern workers specialize in only a single, repetitive task and contribute to only part of a product. Unlike the shoemaker who could say "I make shoes," no modern industrial worker can say "I make shoes" because no one person does make shoes.

In the factory, workers must keep pace with a work process that is determined by mechanized production and rational planning. No shoe factory worker sets his or her own schedule of work; workers coordinate their efforts with a machine that is geared to a certain production goal. Like the factory worker most people in modern societies are not able to exercise much personal control over their work. In the United States only 9 percent of all workers are self-employed; the rest work for someone else.[22] That "someone else" is often a large organization. Even professionals, whom we think of as independent individuals, are usually part of a bureaucracy (large law firms, universities, medical research laboratories). When people have little control over how they do their jobs, they are more likely to feel overwhelmed, unnecessary, and alienated from their work (see "White-Collar Woes and Blue-Collar Blues").

In a classic study, *Alienation and Freedom*, Robert Blauner described the psychological effects of the industrial worker's job.[23] Feelings of alienation have four dimensions:

---

[19] Richard Baxter, an English Puritan minister and author.

[20] Weber, *The Protestant Ethic,* p. 181.

[21] Karl Marx: *Early Writings,* trans. and ed. T. B. Bottomore (New York: McGraw-Hill, 1964), pp. 124–25.

[22] U.S. Bureau of the Census, *Statistical Abstract of the United States,* 1989.

[23] Robert Blauner, *Alienation and Freedom* (Chicago: University of Chicago Press, 1964).

1. *Powerlessness,* or the inability to control the pace of work, the work setting, or other aspects of the workplace.

2. *Meaninglessness,* or lack of a sense of purpose in work. Typists in a large insurance company, for example, might find little connection between the forms they type and the goals of the organization.

3. *Isolation,* or the worker's feeling that he or she does not belong to a meaningful social group. A worker may be physically isolated or may be unable to communicate for other reasons.

4. *Self-estrangement,* or detachment from work. People who are not personally committed to doing a good job find working to be only a way of earning money and not a worthwhile end in itself.

In the post-industrial economy, service workers' separation from the product of their labor is almost complete. Accountants and lawyers make no product at all in the Marxist sense, nor do workers who monitor such automated equipment as computers and data processors. In modern bureaucracies a highly specialized division of labor might give some office workers a sense of mastery over their very small part of the work process, but it also isolates these workers from the larger tasks of the organization. Clerks who enter tax return figures into the Internal Revenue Service's central data bank, for example, are hardly likely to feel they are contributing to a final "product" as nebulous and remote as the collection of federal income taxes. Finally, automation and computerization of the workplace make the individual worker's decisions and instructions less and less important.

Feelings of alienation are one result of the great change from the rural world of the self-employed farmer and merchant to the urban society of the salaried employee. In almost any modern job employees sell some of their independence, as well as their time, energy, and skills. The act of labor becomes a means to an end, not an end in itself. The end may be money, material comfort, or production; but the means to that end is often regarded as a tiresome necessity.

In his 1985 presidential address to the American Sociological Association, Kai Erikson made the provocative argument that alienation in the workplace "spills over" into other spheres of life. "The moods of the workplace," he said,

> are carried across the threshold into the household, and, of course, the moods of the household are carried back. . . . We have every reason in the world to think, for example, that taking drugs and drinking too much and sinking into a kind of numbed depression are correlated with alienating working conditions." [24]

We shall return to the "spillover" hypothesis later in this chapter, when we discuss the relationship between work and leisure. Meanwhile, the next section will consider some other social effects of alienating working conditions.

THE AFFLUENT WORKER

Many observers have suggested that monotonous, unfulfilling work is the price that people in industrial societies must pay for their high standard of living. According to

---

[24] Kai Erikson, "On Work and Alienation," *American Sociological Review* 51 (February 1986): 7.

WHITE-COLLAR WOES AND BLUE-COLLAR BLUES

In these excerpts from Studs Terkel's interviews, white-collar and blue-collar workers talk about their responses to the alienating conditions of their jobs.

The White-Collar Woes

A woman who worked as an airline reservation clerk for twelve years:

> *My job as a reservationist was very routine, computerized. I hated it with a passion. Getting sick in the morning, going to work feeling, Oh, my God! I've got to go to work.*
>
> ■ ■ ■
>
> *You were allowed no more than three minutes on the telephone. You had twenty seconds . . . to put the information into Sabre (the computer). Then you had to be available for another phone call. . . . We adjusted to the machine.*
> *They monitored you and listened to your conversations. If you were a minute late for work, it went into your file. I had a horrible attendance record—ten letters in my file for lateness, a total of ten minutes. You took thirty minutes for your lunch, not thirty-one. If you got a break, you took ten minutes, not eleven.*
>
> ■ ■ ■
>
> *I remember when I went to work for the airlines, they said, "You will eat, sleep, and drink airlines. There's no time in your life for ballet, theater, music, anything. . . . When you get*

airline people together, they'll talk about planes. That is all they talk about.*

An auditor in a large public accounting firm:

> *The company I work for doesn't make a product. We provide a service. Our service is auditing. . . . We will certify whether a company's financial statement is correct.*
>
> ■ ■ ■
>
> *Many people in our firm don't plan on sticking around. The pressure. The constant rush to get things done. Since I've been here, two people have had nervous breakdowns. . . .*
> *Our firm has a philosophy of progress, up or out. I started three years ago. If that second year I didn't move from SA-3, staff assistant, to SA-4, I'd be out. . . . By the time I'm thirty-four or so, I'm a partner or I'm out.*
>
> ■ ■ ■
>
> *Is my job important? It's a question I ask myself. . . . Whether it's important to society. (A long pause.) No, not too important. It's necessary in this economy, based on big business.*
> *I have a couple of friends there. We get together and talk once in a while. At first you're afraid to say anything 'cause you think the guy really loves it. You don't want to say, "I hate it." But then you hear the guy say, "Boy! If it weren't for the money I'd quit right now."*

this view, increasing productivity and a rising GNP depend on machine technology, bureaucratic supervision, and a highly specialized division of labor. Life in the industrial society thus involves a trade-off between degrading jobs and the benefits of increased leisure and mass consumption.

Two British sociologists, J. Goldthorpe and D. Lockwood, have found evidence for this view in studies of "the **affluent worker**."[25] They discovered through their research that most industrial workers bitterly dislike many aspects of their jobs—the

---

[25] J. H. Goldthorpe, D. Lockwood, et al., *The Affluent Worker: Industrial Attitudes and Behavior* (Cambridge: Cambridge University Press, 1968).

The Blue-Collar Blues

A utility man on the assembly line at the Ford Motor Company:

> I refused to do a job one time and I was fired. . . . They took me up and said, "We don't need you any more." They say, "You're fired." Make you feel like you're through. . . . Then they said, "We're gonna give you another chance." They tear a man down and threaten 'im and then they're gonna give him another chance. I guess they just want to make you feel bad.

■ ■ ■

> My day goes pretty good on the average. . . . It's the same routine. But I can rotate mine just a little bit, just enough to break the monotony. But when it catches up with ya and all of a sudden it's real quiet, nobody says nothing—that makes the day go real long. . . . You would look at your watch and it would be nine twenty. And you look at your watch again and it's twenty-five minutes of ten. It seems like you worked forever. And it's been only roughly fifteen minutes. You want quittin' time so bad.

A long distance telephone operator at Illinois Bell:

> It's a strange atmosphere. You're in a room about the size of a gymnasium, talking to people thousands of miles away. . . . They don't know you, they never will. . . . You feel like they put a coin in the machine and they've got you. You're there to perform your service and go. You're kind of detached.

■ ■ ■

> A big thing is not to talk with a customer. . . . If you get caught talking with a customer, that's one mark against you. You can't help but want to talk to them if they're in trouble or if they're just feeling bad or something. For me it's a great temptation to say, "Gee, what's the matter?" You don't feel like you're really that much helping people.

■ ■ ■

> This company is the kind who watches you all the time. The supervisor does listen to you a lot. She can push a button on this special console. Just to see if I'm pleasant enough, if I talk too much to the customers, if I'm charging the right amount, if I make a personal call. Ma Bell is listening. And you don't know.

■ ■ ■

> It's something to run into somebody who says, "It's a nice day out, operator. How's your day, busy? Has it been a rough day?" You're so thankful for these people. You say, "Oh yes, it's been an awful day. Thank you for asking."

SOURCE: Studs Terkel, *Working* (New York: Avon, 1975), pp. 82–83, 352–55, 236–37, 65–69.

monotony, the fragmentation of the work process, the stifling of individual initiative, and so on. By Blauner's definition, the British workers they studied were alienated in every way. The researchers were surprised to find, however, that most of the same men were also very committed to their work and had made few efforts to find other jobs. Goldthorpe and Lockwood explain this paradox by looking beyond the conditions of industrial work to the attitudes and values the men brought to their jobs. They argue that the workers valued their work as a means of earning the money necessary for the kind of life they wanted. They tolerated demeaning jobs for the extrinsic reward of good wages, and they did not expect their work to be intrinsically satisfying and fulfilling. This instrumental orientation toward employment is a predictable consequence of the alienating nature of the modern workplace.

Owning a yacht was once the exclusive privilege of the very rich; today many thousands of "affluent workers" are able to afford one. Some observers argue that life in the industrial society involves a trade-off between unfulfilling work and the enjoyment of increased leisure and material possessions.

American sociologists have also noted that work is losing its central meaning in people's lives. As we saw in Chapter 3, "Culture," the traditional American work ethic appears to be giving way to an emphasis on self-fulfillment in leisure or other private activities. Only 13 percent of Americans questioned in a 1978 poll said that "work is the center of my life," compared to 34 percent only eight years before.[26] In *The Cultural Contradictions of Capitalism* (1976) Daniel Bell argued that mass production and mass consumption have undermined the Protestant Ethic — the very "spirit of capitalism" itself — by encouraging spending and self-indulgence.[27] In this view, hard work is no longer valued as a "calling" but as a means to the private enjoyment of leisure and material possessions.

At the same time as attitudes toward work were changing, both the total American labor force and the proportion of the population at work were growing by leaps and bounds. Between 1977 and 1987 the labor force increased by over 21 million, or 21 percent; by the end of the decade more than half (56 percent) of all American women were working outside the home.[28]

Moreover, as we have seen, the American work ethic still strongly influences how people feel about work. A 1983 poll reported, for example, that a majority (58 percent) of American working women would rather work than stay home; so would 31 percent

[26] Daniel Yankelovich, *New Rules: Searching for Self-Fulfillment in a World Turned Upside Down* (New York: Random House, 1981), p. 11.

[27] Daniel Bell, *The Cultural Contradictions of Capitalism* (New York: Basic Books, 1976).

[28] U.S. Bureau of the Census, *Statistical Abstract of the United States* (Washington, D.C.: United States Government Printing Office, 1989), Tables 620, 621.

of women who do not have a job outside the home.[29] About 26 percent of the women surveyed also said that having a job is one of the "most enjoyable things about being a woman today." For whatever reasons, most Americans clearly *like* to work.

George J. W. Goodman, an authority on the stock market, is also a shrewd observer of social behavior. Writing under the pseudonym "Adam Smith," he summed up the situation this way:

> I suspect . . . that two things are true in this country. One is that there are certainly a lot of jobs . . . that are boring, not built to the human spirit or the human body, or not fulfilling in some other way, and that most of American industry is only beginning to pay attention to this. The second is that people like to work, as opposed to not working or hanging around the house. They like to work, or at least they like to go to the place where work is, because they see their friends, they have a beer afterward or a coffee break during, and it gets them into motion, and anyway we have not developed the tradition of playing the lute and counting that as a good afternoon. Given any degree of pleasantness, encouragement and satisfaction, they would go to work even without the exhortations of the {Protestant} Ethic. . . . How hard, or with what care, people work is something else.[30]

We will now turn to the problem of this "something else."

CHANGING WORK

During the prosperous 1950s and 1960s the traditional economic motivations for doing tedious or dangerous work lost some of their force. Many more workers in the "affluent society"[31] could take for granted a good job with economic security, relatively high wages, and a chance for promotion. Many also found industrial work to be distasteful and dehumanizing. Managers discovered that the threat of unemployment was not enough to motivate workers to do their jobs well. Strikes, high turnover, absenteeism, and poor workmanship were common. In 1966, for example, when the demand for labor was especially high, Saab (the Swedish automobile company) had to replace *100 percent* of its assembly line workers every year. In 1972 Volvo, Saab's competitor, admitted that it was holding one-seventh of its work force in reserve to fill in for workers who didn't show up.[32]

In 1973 *Work in America* reported a startling amount of job dissatisfaction. When researchers asked "Would you pick the same job over again?" fewer than half the white-collar workers and only about one quarter of the blue-collar workers said they would choose the same kind of job again (see Table 19-2).[33] Professors and scientists were the most satisfied workers, and unskilled factory hands the least. Many surveys have shown that people who do highly complex and difficult work are much happier than everyone else.[34]

---

[29] New York Times poll reported in *The New York Times,* December 4, 1983, pp. 1, 66.

[30] 'Adam Smith,' *Supermoney* (New York: Random House, 1972), pp. 277–78.

[31] See John Kenneth Galbraith's *The Affluent Society* (Boston: Houghton-Mifflin, 1958).

[32] Paul Dickson, *The Future of the Workplace* (New York: Weybright and Talley, 1975), pp. 30–32.

[33] U.S. Department of Health, Education, and Welfare, *Work in America*, p. 16.

[34] Robert L. Kahn, "The Work Module: A Tonic for Lunchpail Lassitude," *Psychology Today* 6:9 (February 1973): 35–39; U.S. Department of Health, Education, and Welfare, *Work in America*, p. 13.

TABLE 19 – 2   PERCENT OF PEOPLE IN OCCUPATIONAL GROUPS WHO WOULD CHOOSE SIMILAR WORK AGAIN

Professional and Lower White-Collar Occupations		Working-Class Occupations	
Urban university professors	93	Skilled printers	52
Mathematicians	91	Paper workers	42
Physicists	89	Skilled autoworkers	41
Biologists	89	Skilled steelworkers	41
Chemists	86	Textile workers	31
Firm lawyers	85	BLUE-COLLAR WORKERS, CROSS SECTION	24
Lawyers	83	Unskilled steelworkers	21
Journalists (Washington correspondents)	82	Unskilled autoworkers	16
Church university professors	77		
Solo lawyers	75		
WHITE-COLLAR WORKERS, CROSS SECTION	43		

SOURCE: U.S. Department of Health, Education, and Welfare, *Work in America; Report of a Special Task Force to the Secretary of Health, Education, and Welfare* (Cambridge, Mass.: MIT Press, 1973), p. 16.

As a general rule, workers are least likely to be alienated when they are given personal recognition and meaningful work to do. Although a good income and the chance for promotion are serious considerations, workers at all levels say the most important feature of the ideal job is the ability to decide how and when the work will be done. Given these findings, it is not hard to see why professors and mathematicians are so much happier with their jobs than assembly-line workers. Most people, it seems, want to do a good job, and they are frustrated and unhappy when their working conditions do not permit them to use their abilities to do so.

So far, the implications of this research have not done much to change the world of work. Early efforts to improve the workers' lot were centered on wages and physical working conditions, and unions traditionally still seek better pay, pensions, and insurance benefits for their members. Although unions enroll only a minority of the work force, their members are generally the best paid and best protected workers.

On the management side the human relations movement has done much to improve working conditions since the 1930s. After studies apparently showed that productivity could be improved by treating workers as people instead of machines, some company executives thought up such amenities as sales awards, newsletters, background music, and employee cafeterias. Neither the union movement nor the human relations movement, however, has ever dealt with the basic issue of control: most workers still have to do just what others decide is most efficient and productive.

WORKPLACE DEMOCRACY

Bored and apathetic workers are not only unhappy with their jobs, they are less efficient and productive. Since satisfied workers have lower absentee rates and do better work, making work more interesting and rewarding might make it more profitable as well. Recent experiments in improving work have attacked the basic cause of alienation by giving employees more control over the work process. Instead of concentrating on the company's concern for efficiency, corporate planners have now begun to analyze their operations in light of workers' concern for self-esteem, autonomy, and a sense of accomplishment.

Between one-third and one-half of America's *Fortune 500* companies have instituted worker-participation programs, or **workplace democracy**. These programs give rank-and-file workers more direct involvement in decision making, more variety in the tasks they perform, more control over the organization of the work, and more opportunities to learn.[35]

In the Shell Canada chemical plant in Sarnia, Ontario, for example, eighteen-member teams of workers are responsible for the entire production process. Rotating tasks on a day-to-day basis, each team completes the lab work, shipping, warehousing, administration, and janitorial and maintenance work. Grade levels are based on skill, which is measured by exams and performance tests. More specialized jobs are available, but there are no quotas on how many workers will be promoted, and everyone is expected to reach the top level eventually.[36]

Workplace democracy is designed to prevent the deskilling which often accompanies automation. When their jobs become little more than monitoring machines, workers' morale benefits from rotating tasks and having some control over the work process. Today's generation of workers is better educated than ever before, and most of them expect to have jobs that are interesting and meaningful and for which they will be respected.

For the manager, workplace democracy is one way of blocking unionization. When the tasks of workers and supervisors overlap, there is less inherent conflict, less need for collective bargaining, and greater satisfaction for the worker.

Given the larger economic structure, it may not be possible to make most occupations in an industrial society more challenging and rewarding. Work teams cannot do highly specialized technical tasks, nor can they make intrinsically boring jobs more interesting. Making the industrial world run often requires workers to be disciplined and dependable, not independent and innovative.

ROBOTS AND COMPUTERS

One way to improve work is to eliminate boring and unpleasant jobs. Some experts believe that computerized "smart" robots could soon replace three-quarters of the factory work force. Several lines of automobiles are already manufactured almost entirely by robots. Nearly all of the more than 3,000 welds on the body of a Ford Taurus, for example, are made by computer-controlled mechanical arms.

In 1985 there were about 16,000 industrial robots in the United States. About half were used in the automobile industry, where most of these "steel-collar" workers perform such uncomfortable and dangerous tasks as die casting, spot welding, and spray painting. Robots are also widely used in electronics assembly plants. About 90 percent of Apple's Macintosh computer, for example, is assembled automatically.

[35] William Schwartz, "Toward a Theory of Worker Participation," *Sociological Inquiry* 53 (Winter 1983), pp. 61–78.

[36] Carmen Sirianni, "Worker Participation in the Late Twentieth Century: Some Critical Issues," in *Worker Participation and the Politics of Reform,* Carmen Sirianni, ed. (Philadelphia: Temple University Press, 1987), pp. 10–12.

Automation is one of the reasons why Japanese production techniques are so efficient: some Japanese manufacturers say they have automated one half to three quarters of their assembly operations.[37]

Like the steam engine and the discovery of electricity, *robotics,* or the science of self-moving machines, seems destined to be part of a technological revolution. A few companies are already implementing computer-integrated manufacturing, a computerized process that fuses design, manufacture, and marketing into a single flow of information. To the corporate executive, the advantages of robots are obvious. Robots

> didn't get bored, take vacations, qualify for pensions, or leave soft-drink cans rattling around inside the assembled products. They "cheerfully" worked around the clock and would accept heat, radioactivity, poisonous fumes, or loud noise, all without filing a grievance. They were at their best in dangerous jobs like handling irradiated parts of a nuclear reactor, and in stupefying jobs like auto welding or painting—both of which are best done at temperatures hotter than a human could stand. They revolutionized the auto industry.[38]

Although robots are far more productive than human beings in some jobs, they are too expensive and exotic for most purposes. The first generation of industrial robots cost $40,000 to $100,000 each, and an average of $6 an hour to operate—hardly less than a human worker. Ironically, the attempt to eliminate dependence on workers who operate machines sometimes leads to greater dependence on workers who repair the equipment.[39] Moreover, less sophisticated kinds of computerized operations are often as efficient as computer-integrated manufacturing techniques. Nevertheless, robots will soon be capable of manufacturing and assembling nearly all important industrial products; the only uncertainties about their uses concern the economic question of whether they are more expensive to operate than human beings.

While the future of industrial robots is still unknown, the impact of automation on the work force is rather predictable. Researchers in Michigan estimated that the United States will have lost between 100,000 and 200,000 manufacturing jobs to robots by 1990, mainly in the automobile industry. In fact, experts expect that most of this kind of blue-collar industrial work will disappear over the next generation.[40]

Other experts are predicting that employment in service industries will also decline because of automation. Central data-processing systems, word processors, and electronic scanners already handle much of the routine typing and filing that clerical workers used to do. The fast-food industry is on the eve of a technological revolution that will put robots in the kitchen as well as in the factory. Computer-controlled machines are expected to flip hamburgers, bag french fries, stuff burritos, spread pizza dough, and deliver orders to drive-up customers in about half the time and at half the cost of human workers.[41] The social changes caused by the dawning of this new industrial revolution pose an urgent challenge to the sociological imagination.

[37] Roger Draper, "The Golden Arm," *The New York Review of Books.* October 24, 1985, pp. 48–52.
[38] T. A. Heppenheimer, "Man Makes Man," in *Robotics,* ed. Marvin Minsky (Garden City, N.Y.: Anchor/Doubleday, 1985), p. 62.
[39] Harley Shaiken, *Work Transformed: Automation and Labor in the Computer Age* (New York: Holt, Rinehart, and Winston, 1984), p. 5.
[40] Draper, "The Golden Arm," p. 50.
[41] Calvin Sims, "Robots to Make Fast Food Chains Still Faster," *The New York Times* (August 24, 1988), p. D5.

When the Industrial Revolution separated the workplace from the home, some social activities began to be defined as "nonwork," or recreation. New York's Central Park, shown here about 1860, offered a larger urban population opportunities for outdoor entertainment and recreation.

LEISURE

In a faraway land, an old American folk song claims, the trees are full of fruit and the hens lay soft-boiled eggs, there's a lake of stew and whiskey, too, and "you can paddle all around them in a big canoe." It's place to stay, where you sleep all day, and they hanged "the jerk that invented work." It's called the Big Rock Candy Mountain, and it represents what most people, for most of human history, called leisure — a life of ease, abundance, and complete idleness.

THE HISTORY OF LEISURE

Before the Industrial Revolution leisure for most people meant rest from work. Leisure activities were not a matter of individual choice but part of the regular pattern of social life.[42] County fairs, quilting bees, and sheep shearings were social gatherings that combined work and play. These pleasures were justified as a reward for work, or as a means of restoring oneself for more work.[43] As the workplace became separated from the home, such social activities began to be defined as "nonwork," or recreation. During the first half of the nineteenth century, new forms of commercial entertainment became available to people in all social classes. Variety shows and minstrel shows transformed the theater; travelling circuses reached even out-of-the-way small towns; horse races, boxing matches, and foot races became popular. In the cities more people

---

[42] Parker, *Leisure and Work*, p. 17.
[43] Richard Kraus, *Recreation and Leisure in Modern Society* (Pacific Palisades, Calif.: Goodyear, 1971), p. 163.

had more money to spend at amusement parks, public dance halls, and beer gardens. In short, the leisure industry was born.[44]

In response to a larger urban population's demand for open-air recreation, local governments created public parks and playgrounds. New York's Central Park was opened in 1857, Philadelphia's Fairmount Park in 1867, and Boston's Franklin Park in 1883. Believing that "Satan finds mischief for idle hands to do," worried city dwellers encouraged public schools and other agencies to provide "wholesome" pastimes during the nonworking hours. Libraries and public recreational centers were built as noncommercial alternatives to the pool halls, burlesque theaters, and saloons that social reformers saw as breeding grounds for vice.

In *The Threat of Leisure* (1926) George Barton Cutten, the president of Colgate University, expressed the popular view that increasing leisure might be a menace to society. For some people, he wrote, "freedom from labor means liberty for the indulgence of low tastes, . . . and most vice and crime take place in spare time."[45] At the time Cutten was writing, English farm workers were describing the ideal life as

> Eight hours' work and eight hours' play;
> Eight hours' sleep and eight shillin's a day.[46]

Cutten thought that most of us could be trusted with the work and the sleep, but what would future generations do with all that money and free time?

TIME, WORK, AND LEISURE

Leisure is usually measured in free time, or the opposite of paid work. As Figure 19-2 shows, a gradual decrease in working hours over the past century has reduced the average work week by about 25 hours since the 1890s. This dramatic increase in free time has actually been somewhat overrated, since it is measured against the exceptionally long working hours that prevailed during the early stages of capitalism. A hundred years ago steelworkers worked a 12-hour shift, seven days a week, and 14-hour days were common for factory workers.[47] Seen in longer historical perspective, the amount of free time we have today seems less like a remarkable modern achievement and more like a return to normal. In pre-industrial England, for example, the length of the working day was about 11 or 12 hours in the fifteenth century and 10 hours in the seventeenth.[48] Workers in other historical periods also enjoyed more holidays. The medieval calendar generally observed 115 holidays a year, which, when added to 52 Sundays, made 167 days of rest—or an average work week of less than four days.[49]

A better way to measure leisure is to separate it from free time. If time spent on the job totals about 40 hours a week, and a week is 168 hours long, how much free time is available for leisure—128 hours? No, of course not. First, there are sleeping and

---

[44] Foster R. Dulles, *A History of Recreation: America Learns to Play* (New York: Appleton-Century-Crofts, 1965).

[45] George Barton Cutten, *The Threat of Leisure* (New Haven, Conn.: Yale University Press, 1926), p. 92.

[46] Ibid., p. 44.

[47] Sebastian de Grazia, *Of Time, Work, and Leisure* (New York: The Twentieth Century Fund, 1962), pp. 87–88.

[48] Hannah Arendt, *The Human Condition* (Chicago: University of Chicago Press, 1958), p. 132.

[49] de Grazia, *Of Time, Work, and Leisure,* p. 89.

AVERAGE HOURS WORKED WEEKLY SINCE 1890   **FIGURE 19-2**

SOURCE: U.S. Bureau of the Census, *Historical Statistics of the United States: Colonial Times to 1970* (Washington, D.C.: U.S. Government Printing Office, 1975): U.S. Bureau of the Census, *Statistical Abstract of the United States* (Washington, D.C.: U.S. Government Printing Office, 1989).

eating — which account for over half our free time — and then there are all the essential chores, or unpaid work that everyone has to do — bathing, dressing, shopping, travelling to and from work, cleaning, cooking, making household repairs, and so on. Americans actually have, on average, only about 39 hours a week left to spend on what they define as leisure.[50]

Some people have a great deal of free time but relatively little leisure. One sophisticated analysis of data from a large national sample of households concluded that the average American woman spends about four hours a day doing housework and about three and one-half hours caring for children (making a seven and one-half hour day and a 54-hour week).[51] The working hours for a modern housewife are not much different from the number of hours an affluent wife spent on housework in 1912, when domestic servants were members of all well-to-do households, or from the number of hours that rural and urban housewives spent on such chores in 1935. Roughly speaking, American wives who are not gainfully employed spend 50 hours a week on housework; wives with outside jobs spend 35 hours on work in and for their homes.[52]

Housework today is more productive (because more services are performed and more goods produced for every hour of work) and less laborious than it was at the turn

[50] U.S. Bureau of the Census, *Social Indicators III* (Washington, D.C.: United States Government Printing Office, 1980), Table 11/13.

[51] John P. Robinson, *How Americans Use Time: A Social-Psychological Analysis of Everyday Behavior* (New York: Praeger, 1977), pp. 61–78.

[52] Ruth Schwartz Cowan, *More Work for Mother: The Ironies of Household Technology from the Open Hearth to the Microwave* (New York: Basic Books, 1983), pp. 199–201.

of the century, yet most women find it just as time-consuming and demanding (see "Why Women's Work Is Still Never Done"). For working wives with full-time jobs, a 75-hour week of paid and unpaid work leaves precious little time for leisure.

Compared to 50 or 100 years ago, Americans today seem to have more free time but not proportionately more leisure. The next section considers the question of how they spend it.

THE USES OF LEISURE

Sociological theories of leisure contend that the kind of work we do is reflected in the activities we choose for our hours of leisure. According to the *spillover hypothesis*, for example, alienation from work carries over into the rest of life and the drudgery we do on the job has a mentally stultifying effect. In Harold Wilensky's caricature, this hypothetical worker

> goes quietly home, collapses on the couch, eats and drinks alone, belongs to nothing, reads nothing, knows nothing, votes for no one, hangs around the home and street, watches . . . the TV programmes shade into one another, too tired to lift himself off the couch for the act of selection, too bored to switch the dials.

The *compensatory leisure hypothesis*, on the other hand, suggests that leisure activities can provide an outlet for the frustrations built up by unsatisfying work. Wilensky's caricature pictures an automobile assembly line worker who,

> for eight hours gripped bodily to the main line, doing repetitive, low-skilled, machine-paced work which is wholly ungratifying, comes rushing out of the plant gate helling down the super-highway at eighty miles an hour in a second-hand Cadillac Eldorado, stops off for a beer and starts a bar-room brawl, {and} goes home and beats his wife.[53]

The British sociologist Stanley Parker theorizes that there are three kinds of relationships between work and leisure.[54] The first is the **extension pattern**, in which at least some work and leisure activities are similar and daily life is not clearly divided between the two. This pattern, which corresponds to the spillover hypothesis, is typical of social workers, high-level business executives, physicians, teachers, and other professionals who enjoy many of the same kinds of activities with many of the same people both at home and at work. As Wilensky has suggested, people in these positions are often so overwhelmingly committed to working that they have little time left over for leisure.[55] The popular image of the workaholic fits the extension pattern.

The second type of relationship between work and leisure is the **opposition pattern**, in which leisure activities are intentionally very different from experiences at work and "business and pleasure" are never mixed. People with physically tough jobs, like miners and waitresses, find relief in leisure; others hate their work so much that they don't want to be reminded of it off the job. This pattern corresponds to the compensatory leisure hypothesis.

---

[53] Harold L. Wilensky, "Work, Careers and Social Integration," *International Social Science Journal* 12 (1960): 545.

[54] Parker, *Leisure and Work.*

[55] Harold L. Wilensky, *Family Life Cycle, Work, and the Quality of Life* (Berkeley: University of California Institute of Industrial Relations, 1981).

WHY WOMEN'S WORK IS STILL NEVER DONE

Economists do not consider housework to be "productive work," partly because they cannot measure it. No time clocks record how much time is spent preparing a family's dinner, and no dollar value is placed on a nutritious meal. Nevertheless, in spite of all the advertising claims to the contrary, it still takes time to launder clothes, clean floors, and scrub the stains out of the kitchen sink. Although housewives are not called workers and are not officially employed, everyone knows that housework is work.

Ruth Schwartz Cowan's history of household technology explains why modern appliances and a higher standard of living have not meant less work for mother.

The {postwar} move to the suburbs carried with it the assumption that someone (surely mother) would be at home to do the requisite work that made it possible for someone else (surely father) to leave early in the morning and return late at night, without worrying either about the welfare of his family or the maintenance of his domicile. Having made the move and purchased the house and invested in the cars and the appliances without which the suburban way of life simply was not possible, people discovered that the technological systems in which they had invested (not only so much money, but also so much emotion) simply would not function unless someone stayed home to operate them.

When this "someone" had, however, decided that, for whatever reason, staying at home was no longer her cup of tea, neither the house nor the cars nor the appliances nor the way of life that they all implied could simply be thrown into the dust-bin, nor did anyone wish to throw them there. All of these were long-term investments (consumer *durables*); and the technological systems of which they were a part (houses, roads, telephone lines, gas mains) were built to last for more than one lifetime. The transition to the two-income family (or to the female-headed household) did not occur without taking a toll — a toll measured in the hours that employed housewives had to work in order to perform adequately first as employees and then as housewives. A thirty-five-hour week (housework) added to a forty-hour week (paid employment) adds up to a working week that even sweatshops cannot match. With all her appliances and amenities, the status of being a "working mother" in the United States today is, as three eminent experts have suggested, virtually a guarantee of being overworked and perpetually exhausted.

The technological and social systems for doing housework had been constructed with the expectation that the people engaged in them would be full-time housewives. When the full-time housewives began to disappear, those systems could not adjust quickly. Not even the most efficient working wife in the world can prepare, serve, and clean up from a meal in four minutes flat; and even the best organized working mother still cannot feed breakfast to a toddler in thirty seconds. Homes cannot automatically be moved close to a job or even close to public transportation, so someone still has to be available to drive the man of the family to the train or a child to the soccer field or to a party; and day-care centers cannot quickly be built where they have not existed before, so someone still has to leave a career behind for a while when babies are born — or find a helpful grandmother.

Indeed, given the sacred feelings that most Americans seem to attach to meals, infants, private homes, and clean laundry — and given the vast investment individuals, corporations, and municipalities have made in the technological systems that already exist — our household technologies may never evolve so as to make life easier for the working wife and mother. In the generations to come, housework is not likely to disappear.

SOURCE: Ruth Schwartz Cowan, *More Work for Mother: The Ironies of Household Technology from the Open Hearth to the Microwave* (New York: Basic Books, 1983), pp. 212–13.

The third type of relationship is **neutrality**. Although leisure and work do not overlap, work and play are not deliberately segregated. This pattern is typical of people in "gray" jobs, such as routine clerical or semi-skilled manual workers, who find their jobs boring but not oppressive. They define leisure as relaxation.[56]

[56] P. Berger, *The Human Shape of Work* (London: Macmillan, 1964).

TELEVISION AND SPORTS

Parker's hypothesis suggests that the way we feel about our work influences how we use our leisure. Time-use studies find that most Americans choose to relax in rather passive recreation. Favorite leisure activities, in order of preference, are

Watching TV
Reading
Staying home with family
Going to movies or theater
Visiting friends
Playing games
Listening to radio and records[57]

Of these activities, watching television and reading newspapers are by far the most popular. The average American adult watches TV more than 15 hours a week (out of the 39 hours that are available on average for leisure). One national telephone survey reported that 72 percent of the respondents watched television every day or almost every day, and 70 percent read newspapers as often. As we saw in Chapter 11, "The Family," Americans also find family life a haven from work. A large majority (79 percent) of those polled said that spending time with their families was the most satisfying aspect of their leisure hours.[58] Eight of the ten most popular leisure activities are also typically done at home.

Sports are such a pervasive aspect of American culture that it is rather surprising that they do not take up more leisure hours. According to the Miller Lite Report, seven out of ten Americans exercise at least once a week, but far fewer participate in organized sports (see Table 19-3). However, the same study found that nearly three out of four Americans say they watch sports on television every week.[59]

Sports and television are so closely linked that only old-timers can remember a day when the World Series always took place in the afternoon, when tennis matches had no tie-breakers to prevent prolonged deuce games, or when football was never played on Monday nights — traditions that were all changed to accommodate the preferences of prime-time television viewers.

In many respects, professional sports *are* television. Few professional sports franchises could exist without TV revenues, and fewer still would be worth $5 to $20 million a year.[60] The Super Bowl, the championship football game that has always been television's most profitable sporting event, generated $17 million in revenues in 1986 and attracted an audience of 115 million people. At $550,000 for a 30-second commercial during the game, the NBC television network sold about $32 million worth of advertising for the six-hour program.[61]

---

[57] U.S. Bureau of the Census, *Social Indicators III* (Washington, D.C.: U.S. Government Printing Office, 1980), Table 11/8.

[58] "Where Does the Time Go? The United Media Enterprises Report on Leisure in America" (New York: Research and Forecasts, 1982).

[59] Miller Lite Report, *American Attitudes Toward Sports* (Milwaukee, Wis.: Miller Brewing Co., 1983).

[60] George H. Sage, "Sport in American Society: Its Pervasiveness and Its Study," in *Sport and American Society,* 3rd ed., George H. Sage, ed. (Reading, Mass.: Addison-Wesley, 1980), p. 6.

[61] Michael Goodwin, "TV Sports Money Machine Falters," *The New York Times Magazine,* January 26, 1986, pp. 26–27.

Television and professional sports are inseparably linked. TV revenues make most professional sports possible, and professional sports account for a large share of prime-time television programs.

In other respects, television *is* professional sports. Professional games fill up to 25 hours of TV programming every week, and it is not unusual to have six or eight hours of sports programs on a single day.[61] On an average fall Sunday, about 22 million households are watching a professional football game on TV.[63]

[62] Sage, "Sport in American Society," p. 5.

[63] Eldon E. Snyder and Elmer A. Spreitzer, *Social Aspects of Sport,* 2nd ed. (Englewood Cliffs, N.J.: Prentice-Hall, 1983), p. 221.

TABLE 19-3   AMERICAN PARTICIPATION IN SPORTS, EXERCISE, AND LEISURE ACTIVITIES (IN PERCENTAGE OF POPULATION WHO PARTICIPATED AT LEAST ONCE IN THE PREVIOUS 12 MONTHS)

Swimming	41	Softball	19
Bicycling	31	Jogging, Running	17
Fishing	30	Visit museums	22
Bowling	23	Read novel/story/poetry/play	56
Hiking	22	Attend classical music performances	13
Camping	21	Attend plays	12
Weight training	20	Attend jazz performances	10
Pool/Billiards	19		

SOURCE: U.S. Bureau of the Census, *Statistical Abstract of the United States* (Washington, D.C.: U.S. Government Printing Office, 1989), Tables 389, 396.

As we have already noted in Chapter 3, "Culture," sports reflect and reinforce many American values. Sports heroes are often seen as living proof that individuals who try their best will succeed, that competition brings out the best in people, and that every player has an equal opportunity to win the game. These cultural myths are probably one reason why professional sports are so popular; another reason is that Americans love "winners" and every sports event guarantees one. Coaches who win games are assumed to have coached their teams well; coaches who lose games usually lose their jobs too. American colloquial speech is sprinkled with sports terms: "drop the ball," "strike out," "jump the gun," "touch base," "game plan," "teamwork," "ballpark figure."

All in all, the evidence is that most Americans are consumers of sports rather than active participants. The great appeal of sports is symbolic: they are the means of acting out such values as individualism and cooperation, activity and work, competition and success. Although millions of Americans engage in active sports on weekends and vacations, the majority of sports enthusiasts spend many more leisure hours reading the sports pages[64] and watching sporting events on television.

A NEW AGE OF LEISURE?

In *The Theory of the Leisure Class* (1899) the political economist Thorstein Veblen argued that the upper classes cultivate a way of life that deliberately demonstrates their superior social position (see Chapter 7, "Social Inequality"). **Conspicuous leisure**— or what Veblen defined as obvious, nonproductive consumption of time—was the way the wealthy showed the world that they had no need to work for a living.[65] In other words, the rich spend their free time in activities that are not defined as work: sports, games, social gatherings, and such hobbies as breeding dogs and racehorses. As the history of fashion proves, upper-class clothing has often proclaimed that the wearer

---

[64] By one estimate, 30 percent of the people who buy daily newspapers are primarily interested in the sports section. See Harry Edwards, *Sociology of Sport* (Homewood, Ill.: Dorsey Press, 1973), p. 4.

[65] Thorstein Veblen, *The Theory of the Leisure Class* (New York: Macmillan, 1899), p. 43.

"Mind if I put on the game?"

Drawing by Mankoff; © 1986 The New Yorker Magazine, Inc.

never performed any useful activity. In Veblen's time, for example, women laced themselves so tightly into their corsets that it was impossible to bend over and wore dresses that forced them to drag long trains of heavy fabric behind them. Evening clothes for men meant stiffly starched shirt fronts and pointed collars that made it difficult for them to turn their heads or look at anything below waist level.[66]

These conspicuously "leisurely" styles are no longer in fashion, and the way of life they represent has almost disappeared. Recreation and leisure have become more widely available in all social classes, and prestige today is more likely to come from one's occupation than from one's use of leisure. As we have already seen, the "idle rich" have never been much admired in American culture. Estée Lauder, Ross Perot, Donald Trump, and most other very rich Americans continue to work — they just don't work for a living. In other industrial societies, even queens and princes are likely to think of their roles as jobs that must be done for the good of their countries.

Even at the top of the social ladder, the enjoyment of leisure largely depends on having work to justify it. The loss of opportunities to work through automation and technological change is therefore a frightening prospect. Much as we might think we would like to have robots do all our work for us, nearly all of us would find a life of perpetual idleness intolerable.

About 30 years ago, when scientific progress seemed about to produce a new age of leisure, Hannah Arendt wrote that the ancient wish to be liberated from labor's "toil and trouble" was about to be granted.

The modern age has carried with it a theoretical glorification of labor and has resulted in a factual transformation of the whole of society into a laboring society. The fulfillment of the wish, therefore, like the fulfillment of wishes in fairy tales, comes at a

---

[66] Alison Lurie, *The Language of Clothes* (New York: Random House/Vintage, 1981), p. 139.

moment when it can only be self-defeating. . . . What we are confronted with is the prospect of a society of laborers without labor, that is, without the only activity left to them. Surely, nothing could be worse.[67]

---

[67] Arendt, *The Human Condition*, pp. 4–5.

SUMMARY

1. Industrialization and technological change altered the character and meaning of work in modern societies. As industrial workers were concentrated in workshops and factories, the workplace became separated from the home. Work is now defined as paid employment, and working hours are distinguished from unpaid free time.

2. The American work ethic is based on the traditional values associated with masculinity, independence, hard work, and material success. Because work is an important source of identity and self-esteem, loss of work is a devastating blow. Brenner's research indicates that higher rates of unemployment are correlated with higher rates of suicide, homicide, and mental illness.

3. Industrialization also changed the experience of work. According to Bell, work in the pre-industrial society was a game against nature; in the industrial society it was a game against things; and in the current post-industrial, or service-based, society it is a game between persons. While most jobs are safer and generally more pleasant than they were in the early industrial era, the shift to white-collar occupations has not ended the exploitation of labor for profit, nor has it eliminated dull and demeaning jobs.

4. In some cases, increasing automation has tended to downgrade the skills required of the worker; in other cases, computerized information systems require the development of new skills and offer new opportunities for autonomy. On balance, de-skilling does not appear to have affected much of the American labor force.

5. Marx used the term "alienation" to describe the human loss of control over the forces of industrial society. Alienation from work arises from fragmentation of the work process, the requirements of machine production, and impersonal bureau-

cratic supervision. Blauner described the psychological aspects of alienation as feelings of powerlessness, meaninglessness, isolation, and self-estrangement.

6. Some sociologists argue that the industrial society involves a trade-off between degrading jobs and the benefits of increased leisure and mass consumption. Affluent workers have an instrumental orientation toward employment: they tolerate unsatisfying work for its good wages and other extrinsic rewards.

7. During the 1970s, at the same time as work appeared to be losing its central meaning, the labor force was growing rapidly. A higher proportion of Americans than ever before are now working.

8. Most Americans are strongly committed to working, but many are unhappy with the jobs they have. People are more likely to be satisfied with their jobs when they are given personal recognition and meaningful work to do. Workplace democracy attempts to relieve alienation by giving workers more control over the work process.

9. The most significant changes in the workplace in the near future will probably come from technological innovation. Computerized robots and electronic data processors are expected to do much of the monotonous, routine work that is now done by assembly-line workers and clerical employees. Employment in these jobs is already declining because of automation.

10. Before the Industrial Revolution leisure activities were less a matter of individual choice than part of the regular pattern of social life. Urbanization and industrialization created the leisure industry of paid entertainment and commercial recreation.

11. The decrease in working hours during the twentieth century has resulted in more free time but

not proportionately more leisure. Unpaid work, especially for housewives, leaves an average of 39 hours a week available for leisure activities.

12. Parker's theory contends that the kind of work we do affects the kind of leisure we choose. He suggests three relationships between work and leisure: the extension pattern, corresponding to the spillover hypothesis, in which work and leisure activities are similar and relatively undifferentiated; the opposition pattern, corresponding to the compensatory leisure hypothesis, in which leisure activities are intentionally very different from work experiences; and the neutrality pattern, in which work and leisure unintentionally do not overlap and leisure is generally viewed as relaxation.

13. Time-use studies find that watching television and reading are by far the most popular American lei-

sure activities. Few Americans participate in organized sports, but many read the sports pages and watch sports on television. In many respects, professional sports and television are inseparable.

14. Sports are a pervasive part of American culture, probably because they symbolize the values of individualism and cooperation, activity and work, competition and success.

15. Nearly a century ago Veblen proposed that the upper-class way of life was characterized by conspicuous leisure. Today prestige more often comes from one's occupation, and even the very rich usually engage in productive work. Because the enjoyment of leisure is justified by work, a future age of leisure through automation is a disturbing prospect.

KEY TERMS

free time 591
work 592
leisure 592
pre-industrial society 597
industrial society 597

post-industrial society 597
deskilling 599
alienation 602
affluent worker 604
workplace democracy 609

extension (pattern of leisure) 614
opposition (pattern of leisure) 614
neutrality (pattern of leisure) 615
conspicuous leisure 618

SUGGESTED READING

Daniel Bell. "Work and Its Discontents," in *The End of Ideology*. Glencoe, Ill.: Free Press, 1960.

* D. Stanley Eitzen, ed. *Sport in Contemporary Society: An Anthology*, 3rd ed. New York: St. Martin's Press, 1988.

* Barbara Garson. *All the Livelong Day: The Meaning and Demeaning of Routine Work*. New York: Penguin Books, 1977.

* Harley Shaiken. *Work Transformed: Automation and Labor in the Computer Age*. Lexington, MA: Lexington Books, 1986.

* Neil J. Smelser. *The Sociology of Economic Life*, 2nd ed. Englewood Cliffs, N.J.: Prentice-Hall, 1976.

* Shoshana Zuboff, *In the Age of the Smart Machine: The Future of Work and Power*. New York: Basic Books, 1989.

* Available in paperback.

For progress
there is no cure.

*John von
Neumann*

CHAPTER 20

POPULATION, ECOLOGY, AND URBANIZATION

On July 7, 1986, the population clock at the World Population Institute in Washington, D.C., registered 5,000,000,000. The estimated population of the world had just reached five billion. If the population clock had been operating in 1850, a few generations ago, it would have recorded only one billion human beings. Your grandparents were part of a population that had doubled to about 2 billion by 1930; you can expect to share the planet with *four times* that number — or over 8 billion people — by the year 2020.[1]

In a way, rapid population growth is part of the human success story. Human beings have been able to multiply faster than any other species because of their unique ability to surmount the limitations of their natural environment. Through technology they have overcome many of the famines and diseases that still check the growth of other animal populations. Yet this great success story is threatened with a tragic ending. Sooner or later, a continually growing population will eventually outstrip its food supply. Some societies already do not have enough food to go around: according to the World Bank, nearly one-quarter of the world's population today is starving or undernourished.

---

[1] "1988 World Population Data Sheet" (Washington, D.C.: Population Reference Bureau, April 1988).

Scientists debate whether the earth is reaching the limits of its *carrying capacity,* the ability of an area to maintain a population of any species without a reduction in the natural resources available for the next generation. The developed nations of the world are already painfully aware of the depleted resources of fossil fuels (oil, coal, and gas) and the destructive effects of industrial pollution on the supply of clean air and water. Just as every day the population clock registers more mouths to be fed, every day in industrializing countries brings more machines to be supplied with energy and raw materials. Every new day thus accelerates the depletion of natural resources and the deterioration of the global environment.

Perhaps the most noticeable effect of the multiplying human population is the spectacular growth of cities. Not only have urban populations themselves grown, but the migration of surplus workers from the countryside has swelled the number of city dwellers to the point where whole societies can be said to be "urban."

One way or another, the world's population growth will have to stop. Will it stop because millions of people are slaughtered in warfare or die in catastrophic famines? Or will it stop because fewer babies are born? These are ultimate questions for the future of society. Once again the answers depend on how well human beings are able to control their environment. This time, however, the environmental forces to be overcome are not largely natural, but social and cultural. A lower birth rate depends on changing the feelings of hundreds of millions of married couples about having a third child—and their decision depends, in complex ways, on their religious beliefs, their income, the role of women in their society, and a host of other sociological variables. The alternative answer is a higher death rate, and this too would have human causes: a nuclear war, a severe and prolonged economic depression, a decline in maternal and infant health care, or a disruption of world trade and food distribution.

The challenge of the future lies in dealing with the expanding human population and its profound consequences for society. It will be met in a world that men and women are now devising—the mechanized, urbanized society of tomorrow. How safely and how comfortably the inhabitants of this world will live is a question only human beings can answer.

This chapter discusses population growth and its implications for the future. It covers three areas of population study: **demography**, the analysis of the size, composition, and distribution of human populations; **human ecology**, the science that deals with the relationship between human beings and their natural environment; and **urban sociology**, the study of city life. The first section explains the causes of the world population explosion; the second assesses how such population growth is depleting the earth's supply of critical resources. The next section discusses the population crisis of developing countries and the social incentives that would reduce their disastrously high birth rates. The fourth part summarizes the effects of worldwide **urbanization**, or the increase in the proportion of a population living in cities. The chapter ends with the suggestion that the challenge of the future lies in applying our knowledge of human behavior to improving an increasingly human-made world.

THE POPULATION EXPLOSION

A French riddle for children illustrates the principle of population growth. It goes like this:

Suppose you have a pond on which a water lily is growing. Each day the number of leaves floating on the pond doubles — the plant has two leaves on the second day, four on the third, eight on the fourth, and so on. If allowed to grow at this rate, the lily plant will completely cover the pond in 30 days, choking off all other forms of life in the water. For a long time the lily seems small, so you don't worry about cutting it back until it covers half the surface. On what day will that be? On the 29th day, of course. You have one day to save your pond.[2]

The children are always amazed that the final disastrous surge in growth happens so *fast*.

When most people think of growth, they think of **linear growth**, the process of adding a constant amount in a given time period. If you stash away $10 a year under your mattress, for example, your money will grow linearly; in ten years you will have $100. The amount of increase each year is not affected by the amount of money already under the mattress. However, if you take the $100 and put it in a savings account at 7 percent interest, so that the total amount accumulated increases by 7 percent each year, your money will grow exponentially: it will double every ten years. In ten years you will have $200, in twenty years $400, in thirty years $800, and so on.[3]

Population growth is also **exponential growth**: each increase occurring in a given time period becomes part of the basis to which the growth rate is applied for the next time period. Let us say, for example, that a town with 10,000 residents is growing at an annual rate of 5 percent. After one year its population will have increased by 500 people (10,000 × .05); the next year it will have increased by 525 (10,500 × .05). Even at relatively slow rates of growth, the **doubling time** — the number of years required to double the original population — is remarkably short. A population growing at the rate of 1 percent a year, for instance, doubles in two generations, or seventy years. With higher growth rates the doubling time of the world's population is getting shorter and shorter. In the year A.D. 1 only about 250 million people inhabited the planet, and that population did not double until around 1650. The second doubling took 200 years, the third 80 years, and the fourth 45 years. At the current annual growth rate of 1.7 percent, it will take just 40 years for the world's population to double again, adding about 5 billion people to the earth by 2030. Figure 20-1 shows how the population of the world has grown since 8000 B.C. If the horizontal axis were shown uninterrupted all the way back to the earliest evidence of human life around 280,000 B.C., it would be an invisibly thin line stretching almost 25 feet to the left. No wonder some observers have spoken of an exploding "population bomb" in recent times. Like the owner of the lily pond, the human race does not have much time left to prevent disaster.

THE CAUSES OF ACCELERATED GROWTH

For most of its history, the growth of the human species was severely restricted by limited food supplies. The estimated doubling time of the early hunting and gathering populations was 60,000 years. Around 8000 B.C., however, a food-producing revolution speeded up the growth rate enormously. Larger populations were maintained by the

---

[2] Donella H. Meadows et al., *The Limits to Growth* (New American Library/Signet, 1972), p. 37.
[3] Ibid., pp. 33–37.

FIGURE 20-1   **WORLD POPULATION GROWTH, 8000 BC TO THE PRESENT**

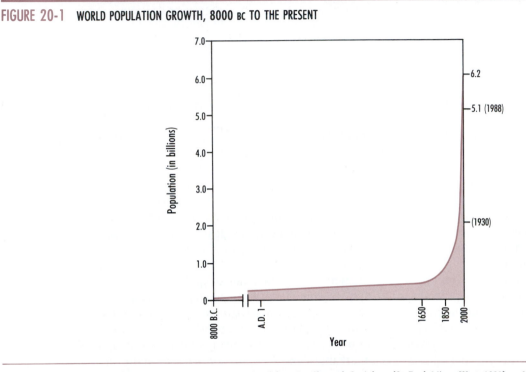

SOURCE: Population Reference Bureau, Washington, D.C. Reprinted from Jon Shepard, *Sociology* (St. Paul, Minn.: West, 1981), p. 371; "1988 World Population Data Sheet" (Washington, D.C.: Population Reference Bureau, April 1988).

invention of agriculture, the domestication of animals, and the development of permanent urban settlements. After this period the growth rate leveled off until about 1750, when the social effects of the Industrial Revolution caused it to take another upward jump. Again, technological progress brought more abundant food supplies, which supported both larger and denser human populations. After World War II, when modern medical technology and health care were diffused through much of the less developed world, the population growth rate rose again, to approximately its current level. Of the three population explosions, however, the present one is by far the greatest. After 1750 the industrial nations of northwestern Europe multiplied more rapidly than other peoples; their proportion of the world's total population doubled from about 18 percent in 1650 to about 35 percent in 1920. Since World War II, however, non-European peoples have grown about twice as fast as the industrialized nations. The less developed regions of the world account for two-thirds of its inhabitants, so it is their accelerating growth rate that has caused the population explosion.[4]

According to Eric Breindel and Nick Eberstadt, the less developed countries are growing so rapidly "not because their peoples have suddenly started breeding like

---

[4] Kingsley Davis, "The World's Population Crisis," In *Contemporary Social Problems*. 4th ed., eds. Robert K. Merton and Robert Nisbet (New York: Harcourt Brace Jovanovich, 1976), pp. 268–70.

rabbits, but rather because they have finally stopped dying like flies." [5] Improvements in public health that took a century to develop in Europe are now being transferred directly to the rest of the world. The effect on the population growth of poorer nations has been spectacular. In just one generation life expectancy in the developing world has gone from 40 years to almost 60, infant mortality has been reduced by two-thirds, the incidence of crippling diseases has gone down sharply, and more people are better fed than ever before.[6] In demographic terms the world's population has grown because of a drop in the death rate, not a rise in the birth rate. In fact, the long-run trend of the birth rate has been downward, but it has not fallen nearly as fast or as consistently as the death rate. This situation has brought the world to the brink of a nightmare envisioned by an eighteenth-century parson, the Reverend Thomas Robert Malthus.

THE MALTHUSIAN NIGHTMARE

The population problem of our times is simply stated: it is the pressure exerted by rapidly growing numbers of people on the limited resources available to support them. The problem was first described in 1798 by Malthus, an economist who is often called the father of demography. In *An Essay on the Principle of Population* Malthus argued that the multiplying tendencies of the human race would inevitably cause it to increase beyond its food supply. While populations grow exponentially, he argued, the amount of farmland can only grow linearly. Assuming that every couple had four surviving children, Malthus estimated that the human population would double almost every generation.[7] (In an era of large families and declining mortality, his assumption was not

---

[5] Eric M. Breindel and Nick Eberstadt, "Paradoxes of Population," *Commentary* 70:2 (August 8, 1980): 42.
[6] Ibid.
[7] The same prediction is made in the old Chinese proverb "Two in the first generation means a thousand in ten generations." The exponential progression is 2, 4, 8, 16, 32, 64, 128, 256, 512, 1024.

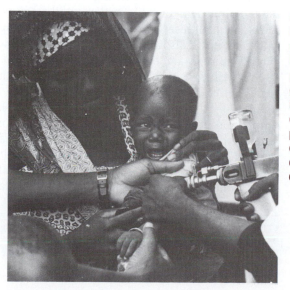

An African child is inoculated against cholera. Improvements in public health have greatly reduced infant mortality and caused a population explosion in developing countries.

implausible.) But farms, unlike people, do not breed: more cultivated land can be added only very slowly, acre by acre. No conceivable increase in food production, he thought, could ever keep up with the number of new mouths to be fed. To Malthus the result was inescapable: without enough food to go around, most of the human race would be forced to live miserably in a state of poverty and malnutrition.

Malthus believed that population growth could be checked either by decreasing **fertility** (the average number of children each woman has) or by increasing **mortality** (the death rate). Decreasing fertility would come from the **preventative check** of "moral restraint," which to Malthus meant that people would postpone marriage until they could support a family. He disapproved of other preventative checks, such as birth control or homosexuality, as "vice." But Malthus was not optimistic about the effectiveness of moral restraint. "Towards the extinction of the passion between the sexes," he wrote, "no progress whatever has hitherto been made." [8]

If fertility does not decline, then population growth can only be stabilized by the **positive check** of "misery" — wars, disease, infanticide, and eventual starvation:

> The power of population is so superior to the power in the earth to provide subsistence . . . that premature death must in some shape or other visit the human race. The vices of mankind are active and able ministers of depopulation. . . . But should they fail in this war of extermination, sickly seasons, epidemics, pestilence, and plague advance in terrific array, and sweep off their thousands and ten thousands. Should success be still incomplete, gigantic inevitable famine stalks in the rear, and with one mighty blow, levels the population with the food of the world. [9]

This dreadful prediction inspired the historian Thomas Carlyle to name economics the "dismal science."

There is an even more pessimistic aspect of Malthus's theory, which the economist Kenneth Boulding has termed the "Dismal Theorem": if the only ultimate check on population growth is "misery," then the population of the world will grow until it is miserable enough to stop growing. Worse still is the "Utterly Dismal Theorem," which states that any temporary improvement in the situation will in the end only increase the sum of human misery. Technological process might raise the standard of living for a while, but it will also allow the population to grow and thus condemn more people to living in misery than ever before. [10]

Yet Malthus himself did not despair of a solution to the dilemma he described. His analysis, like Adam Smith's concept of the free market, proposed a self-regulating social system (see Chapter 12, "The Economy"). The invisible hand that balanced supply and demand in Smith's system is at work in Malthus's system to balance population and resources. In both systems each participant pursues only selfish interests, yet collectively they produce unanticipated consequences for society. Malthus believed that population and food supplies could be brought into equilibrium by strengthening preventative checks. The lowest classes, he noticed, had the most chil-

---

[8] Thomas Robert Malthus, *Population: The First Essay* (Ann Arbor: University of Michigan Press, 1959), p. 5.

[9] Ibid., p. 49. To satisfy the curious: Malthus himself married late and had three children, only one of whom lived to maturity.

[10] Kenneth E. Boulding, "Foreword" to Malthus, *Population: The First Essay*, p. vii.

Almost 200 years ago Malthus predicted that the human race would inevitably grow beyond the limits of its food supply. Today rapid population growth has brought the world to the brink of the Malthusian nightmare of misery and mass starvation.

dren. Since the poor seemed to him to lack moral restraint — the self-control and industriousness that come with more money and education — then the answer lay in providing them with more money and education. People who earned middle-class incomes would naturally, he thought, aspire to a middle-class life style, which typically included a smaller number of children.[11] We shall have more to say about this solution later in the chapter.

---

[11] William Petersen, *Population,* 3rd ed. (New York: Macmillan, 1975), p. 155.

The weakest part of Malthus's argument was his contention that food supplies can increase only by linear progression. As the demographer Kingsley Davis has pointed out, it is logically impossible for a population to outrun its means of subsistence: "The very fact that numbers are increasing indicates that the means to support them is increasing too. Otherwise mortality would have risen and the population would never have grown to its present size." [12] Even if fertility does not decline through preventative checks, the Malthusian equilibrium may be restored by increasing food supplies fast enough to keep up with population growth. According to some scholars the population of England doubled between 1800 and 1850 largely because of the "miracle" vegetable, the potato.[13] Mechanized agriculture and improved transportation have also made food production and distribution far more efficient. The "Green Revolution," a new agricultural technology based on chemical fertilizers and high-yielding wheat and "miracle rice," has doubled the world's production of grain and cereals since 1960. For the moment, at least, world food supplies are still outrunning world population growth.

Technology has thus postponed the Malthusian nightmare, but it may not have refuted its logic. In fact, the specter of overpopulation has caused a revival of the Dismal Theorem. Neo-Malthusian ecologists are forecasting not only mass starvation but also a disastrous depletion of natural resources and the ultimate destruction of the world ecosystem. They repeat Malthus's prediction that a constantly expanding population must inevitably come up against the absolute limits of a finite planet.

PEOPLE AND RESOURCES: THE LIMITS TO GROWTH

On the Malthusian assumption that population growth will automatically stop at a certain point, a group of researchers at the Massachusetts Institute of Technology (MIT) devised computerized models to predict how and when this point will be reached. With the backing of the Club of Rome, an international organization founded out of concern for the world's future, the researchers projected current trends in population growth, use of resources, food production, industrial output, and pollution levels. Their results, as published in *The Limits to Growth* (1972), were gloomy indeed.

If twentieth-century rates of population growth and industrialization continue, the MIT group found, the drain on nonrenewable resources would cause "overshoot and collapse" of the world economy within a century. At that point mass starvation would cause population growth to stop. What if technology could double the recoverable resources and energy supplies were unlimited? Population growth in this case would still stop—in fact, world population would begin to decline about ten years earlier. Without any scarcities of resources and energy, the growth of population and industry would be so great that mortality would rise from environmental pollution. What if pollution could be reduced through technology? According to this computer model population would still decline because of food shortages. Loss of farmland from soil

---

[12] Kingsley Davis, *Human Society* (New York: Macmillan, 1949), p. 612.
[13] Thomas McKeown, *The Modern Rise of Population* (New York: Academic Press, 1977).

erosion and industrial use would eventually reduce per capita food production. In sum, if population and industrialization continue to grow at the same rate, what the authors call the "predicament of mankind" is a choice between starving and being poisoned to death. All the computer models showed that the world's population would temporarily rise above some limit (set by food production, pollution levels, or resources) and then collapse. The only way to prevent this disaster is to stop population growth *and* industrial development before their natural limits are reached.

The key question, as Davis has commented, is not whether the MIT group's basically Malthusian logic is correct but whether their assumed limits and assumed causes and effects will come to pass.[14] There is no way of proving that the development of a miracle vegetable could not raise soil productivity twenty times or that the food of the future will not be manufactured instead of grown. No one can predict which resources will be needed in the technology of the future or what effect pollution controls will have. Most important of all, computer models cannot predict how human beings will act to change the course of their own future. Population growth could stop very quickly if there were a nuclear war or even a sharp drop in the birth rate. A simple projection of past trends into the future does not take into account such unforeseeable social changes. As an English reviewer of *The Limits to Growth* remarked, "In 1872 any scientist could have proved that a city the size of London was impossible, because where were Londoners going to stable all the horses and how could they avoid being asphyxiated by the manure?"[15]

Nevertheless, the MIT group's warning that there are limits to growth cannot safely be ignored. The real question is how quickly and irrevocably the combination of population growth *and* industrial development is depleting the earth's resources.

MINERALS

Such minerals as iron, copper, and bauxite are the basis of modern industry. Since 1950 human beings have used more minerals than were mined in all previous history; by the year 2000 they will use even more, about three or four times more minerals than have ever been used before.[16] In spite of this ferocious mining and utilization, deposits of most important industrial minerals appear almost inexhaustible, and the deepest mines have so far only scratched the surface. In addition, although minerals are not renewable resources, their use can be extended through improved processing and recycling; much new steel production, for example, uses scrap iron and steel. For industrial societies the short-term problem is uneven distribution: Japan, for example, imports over 90 percent of its iron, copper, and tin, and all of its bauxite and nickel, from other countries.[17]

Current reserves of some minerals, however, are in short supply. If industrial production continues to grow at the same rate, a 1977 study estimated that the world's known sources of bauxite ore would run out in thirty-three years, iron in forty years,

---

[14] Davis, "The World's Population Crisis," p. 287.
[15] *The Economist,* March 11, 1972, p. 69.
[16] Wassily Leontief et al., *The Future of the World Economy* (New York: Oxford University Press, 1977), p. 5.
[17] Richard J. Barnet, *The Lean Years* (New York: Simon and Schuster, 1980), p. 116.

mercury in nineteen years, and zinc in fifteen years.[18] Unforeseen shifts in the use of metals make such long-term predictions difficult. For example, modern ceramics have replaced metals as heat conductors, and, because of a miners' strike in Zaire, manganese is now used instead of cobalt in the manufacture of paints.[19]

FOSSIL FUELS

As everyone knows, oil provides most of the energy on which modern industrial life depends. Between 1973 and 1980 the world suffered a series of "oil shocks" from interrupted supplies and price increases. If recovery of the world's vast oil reserves becomes technically and economically feasible, the known oil deposits represent enough potential fuel for hundreds of years of consumption.[20] Nevertheless, the dependence of nearly every industrialized nation on imported oil as well as the accelerating depletion of world oil reserves have increased demand for coal, gas, and nuclear power.

Although western Europe and the United states have abundant coal reserves, mining coal is difficult, physically dangerous, and ecologically destructive, and burning it pollutes the air with toxic chemicals. Furthermore, the burning of wood and fossil fuels releases carbon dioxide into the atmosphere, risking a "greenhouse effect." [21] For various reasons, the production of natural gas is not expected to increase beyond current levels, and nuclear power is still a very limited and controversial source of energy.

The energy crisis is certainly one of the world's most difficult problems ecologically, politically, economically, and socially. Its short-term remedies probably lie in conservation, or using less energy more efficiently to achieve the same results. The shift from "gas guzzlers" to fuel-efficient automobiles during the 1970s is an example of how quickly social attitudes can change with the right incentives. The long-term prospect is not so encouraging. In spite of the American public's faith that a technological miracle will arrive just in time to save the day, not much is being done to find a practical means of harnessing sunlight, wind currents, and other renewable sources of energy.

AIR AND WATER

The world's supplies of fresh air and water are "free," but they are not inexhaustible. The oxygen we breathe is supplied by trees and other plants, most of them in the great equatorial green belt of rain forests and woodlands that reaches from the Amazon to Malaysia. These "lungs of the earth" [22] are being lost at a faster rate than they can be

---

[18] John Tilton, *The Future of the Nonfuels Minerals* (Washington, D.C.: Brookings Institution, 1977).

[19] Robert Repetto, "Population, Resources, Environment: An Uncertain Future," *Population Bulletin* 42 (Washington, D.C.: Population Reference Bureau, 1987), p. 33.

[20] Ibid., p. 31.

[21] Since carbon dioxide absorbs some of the heat that would otherwise be reflected off the earth, significantly increasing it would raise the atmospheric temperature, with possibly disastrous effects. A 2° rise in average temperatures, for example, would melt enough polar ice to raise sea levels over 20 feet. Heat waves, droughts, and food shortages have also been predicted. See Harold W. Bernard, Jr., *The Greenhouse Effect* (Cambridge, Mass.: Ballinger, 1980).

[22] Barnet's phrase, in *The Lean Years*, p. 75.

A brown cloud of air pollution, largely from automobile emissions, blankets Denver. By overburdening the earth's capacity to absorb such wastes, industrialization has caused almost incalculable damage to the environment.

replaced. Between 1 and 2 percent, or 25 to 50 million acres a year, are cut down for firewood (still the principal fuel for three quarters of humanity), for logging purposes, and to clear land for farming and grazing. More than one-third of the tropical forests in Central America and nearly one-quarter of Africa's have been lost since 1960.[23]

Population growth, which is largely responsible for the deforestation of the world, has also put heavy demands on water resources. Over the last two centuries from one-quarter to one-half of the world's wetlands have been drained for farming.[24] In the United States the use of water doubled between 1950 and 1980, permanently lowering future supplies in the underground water table. Nearly 90 percent of this water is used for irrigation, but modern plumbing and industrial cooling devices have also increased demand.

Pollution can be considered another form of consumption because it reduces the quality of air and water. Pollution of lakes and rivers from toxic wastes is one of the familiar consequences of rapid industrial growth. The dangers of air pollution from automobile exhaust and industrial processes are not as well understood. There is convincing evidence, however, that *acid rain*—the combination of water vapor with sulfuric emissions from coal-burning power plants and factories — is causing the slow death of the great forests of Europe and North America, as well as damaging crops and endangering animal life. By overburdening the earth's capacity to absorb such wastes, unregulated industrialization involves far-reaching, almost incalculable costs.

LAND AND FOOD

Food supplies were the basis of Malthus's calculations, and the world's potential food production is still used to mark the absolute limit of population growth. The earth now

---

[23] Peter Hendry, "Food and Population: Beyond Five Billion," *Population Bulletin* 43 (Washington, D.C.: Population Reference Bureau, 1988), p. 21.

[24] Robert Repetto, "Population, Resources, Environment," p. 21.

The earth still produces enough grain to provide an adequate diet for its population — if this food were distributed equally to everyone. But industrial societies, which have the most productive farming methods, grow more food than they can eat, while agricultural societies constantly go hungry.

produces enough grain to provide a basic diet of 3000 calories a day to every man, woman, and child — if it could be distributed evenly around the world. But food supplies are not evenly distributed. Industrial nations such as the United States, where farmers make up less than 3 percent of the labor force, produce more food than they can eat, while agricultural nations such as India and Egypt are perpetually undernourished. This paradox occurs because food production has become part of the industrial process: the most productive farming methods require enormous amounts of mechanical energy to irrigate the fields, to run tractors and reapers, to manufacture fertilizer and pesticides, to process and package foods, and to transport produce to market.

In his 1977 study for the United Nations, Leontief estimated that hunger could be eliminated by a 5 percent increase in food production in the developing regions of the globe.[25] It is physically possible, he argued, to increase the land under cultivation by 30 percent through irrigation and land reclamation, and to triple crop yields by expanding the Green Revolution. Expansion of the Green Revolution will not be easy, however. The "miracle rice" of Asia does not thrive in Africa, for example. Furthermore, the high cost of pesticides, fertilizers, and fuel for tractors and irrigation pumps is more than most small farmers can afford.[26] Feeding the world's future population will apparently depend less on developing new agricultural technologies than on overcoming the social and institutional barriers to the sweeping land reforms and huge economic investments that are required.

As the economist Julian Simon has argued, famines and crop failures often have more to do with politics than population growth.[27] In 1984 at least half a million people

[25] Leontief et al., *The Future of the World Economy*, pp. 4–5.
[26] Peter Hendry, "Food and Population: Beyond Five Billion," pp. 9, 24, 25.
[27] Julian Simon, *The Economics of Population Growth* (Princeton, N.J.: Princeton University Press, 1977).

died during the worst famine in African history. Many could have been saved if international aid had not been delayed by ideological conflicts with the Marxist government of Ethiopia, or if mismanagement, corruption, and civil war had not aggravated the effects of drought and land abuse. With every famine relief effort go stories of food and medical supplies arriving too late because of clogged roads and airports or shortages of fuel and vehicles. Agricultural countries like India and Indonesia, which are prone to disastrous famines, export food even though their own peoples cannot afford enough to eat. Once again, feeding the world seems to depend less on using scientific knowledge to control the forces of nature than on using social scientific knowledge to influence how men and women behave.

SUMMARY

The world appears to be fast approaching the absolute limits of its carrying capacity. Furthermore, the depletion time of critical resources is being compressed by accelerating population growth and industrialization in the developing nations. Doubling times are shortening, and human beings today have only a few decades to adjust to the kinds of population changes that their ancestors had millennia to work out. Serious problems are already being caused by local shortages of oil, food, and water. It may be, as Lester Brown has put it, that "humanity is beginning to ask more of the earth than it can give." [28]

Since the absolute limits of the earth's capacity to give have not yet been reached, most of humanity's problems still come from uneven distribution of the available resources. Population problems — now and in the future — occur because most of the world's people live in those places where scarcity is greatest.

POPULATION AND POVERTY

For most of human history, large families and a growing population were the sources of a nation's wealth and power. In the days of kings and tribal chiefs, according to Breindel and Eberstadt, "a ruler could no more have too many subjects than a herder could have too many cattle." [29] A larger population means more mouths to feed, but it also means more workers in the fields, more conscripts for the army, and more taxes in the treasury. After the Industrial Revolution economic and political power no longer depended on strength of numbers. By making each pair of hands much more productive, machine technology enabled Great Britain to dominate an empire ten times the size of its own population. Today West Germany, with one of the highest per capita incomes in the world and a declining population, is so underpopulated that it depends on millions of foreign "guest workers" to supplement its labor force. India, on the other hand, has a huge population, and millions of its people live on the edge of starvation.

[28] Lester R. Brown, *The Twenty-ninth Day* (New York: Norton, 1978), p. 37.
[29] Breindel and Eberstadt, "Paradoxes of Population," 41.

The **optimum population** is the number of people that produces the maximum economic return possible within a given area's natural, cultural, and social environment.[30] "Underpopulated" and "overpopulated" describe situations where there are either too few or too many people to bring the maximum economic return. "Optimum," however, is a relative concept which depends on culture and life style. Poverty in the United States, for example, would be considered prosperity in Bangladesh. But even when this consideration is taken into account, it appears that the populations of developed countries have tended to stabilize below the optimum, while those of less developed countries have grown above the numbers they can adequately support. In other words, fully developed industrial societies tend to be underpopulated, and developing societies tend to be overpopulated. Another world dilemma, therefore, is how to control the size of a population in order to maintain the desired standard of living.

THE THEORY OF DEMOGRAPHIC TRANSITION

"The rich get richer," the old saying goes, "and the poor get children." Throughout history, as Malthus and many other observers have noticed, the upper class in all societies have had fewer children as a rule than the lower classes. Furthermore, the prosperous societies, which could theoretically support more people, have had lower birth rates than poor societies, which cannot afford more children. This phenomenon is explained by the **theory of demographic transition**.

According to this theory the process of industrialization is accompanied by a shift from high rates of births and deaths to low rates of births and deaths. Pre-industrial societies balance high fertility with high mortality so that their populations grow slowly or not at all. As these societies modernize, better nutrition and health care increase longevity while the birth rate is still high. The result is rapid population growth. Many sub-Saharan African countries are in this second stage. Later, the birth rate begins to fall, but the death rate falls even faster, and the population still increases rapidly. Much of Latin America is in this situation. With further industrialization, however, the birth rate drops sharply and population growth begins to level off. Puerto Rico, Taiwan, and South Korea are now entering this fourth stage. Finally, fertility is low enough to balance low mortality, and population growth stops. Only the fully developed societies of western Europe, the United States, and Japan have reached this stage (see Figure 20-2). In fact, some advanced industrial societies in Europe are now showing a long-term population decline.

Industrialization sends the birth rate down for several reasons. In agricultural societies children are economic assets: even 6-year-olds can increase the family income by providing extra labor in the fields. In industrial societies children are liabilities: they do not enter the labor force until they are adults, and they drain the family's economic resources while they go to school and college. In modern societies such as the Soviet Union and Japan, women are not confined to a domestic, childrearing role; many, even most, wives have a paying job outside the home. Finally, higher living standards and better health care reduce infant mortality to such an extent that parents can have fewer children and expect all of them to survive. All in all, the conditions of modern industrial

---

[30] Petersen, *Population,* pp. 165–166.

STAGES OF THE DEMOGRAPHIC TRANSITION

FIGURE 20-2

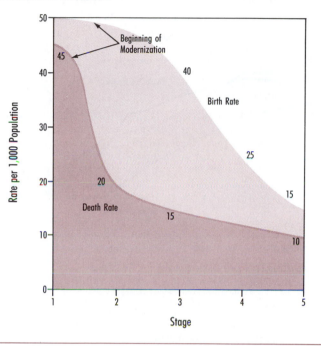

SOURCE: James H. Scheuer, *Growing Awareness of Population and Health Issues in Africa* (Washington, D.C.: U.S. Government Printing Office, 1978).

society provide the incentives to reduce family size. These social patterns are thought to underlie the demographic transition.

The theory of demographic transition is largely a description of what has already taken place in industrial societies. It may not reliably predict the future of less-developed countries which, compared to nineteenth-century Europe, have had a much faster decline in mortality, higher initial fertility, less emigration, and, consequently, far greater population growth.[31] On the other hand, the pace of economic development is faster now than it was in the past, birth control methods are more effective, and both local governments and international agencies are making a conscious, organized effort to control population growth. In the ten years between 1947 and 1957, for instance, the Japanese birth rate plummeted from thirty-four to fourteen births per thousand, astonishing proof that the final low-birth stage can occur virtually overnight.

Since 1965 the birth rate has fallen by 10 percent in the world's two largest populations, China and India, and in other major developing countries as well. The result is a gradual slowing of the developing world's growth rate — from a high of 2.4 percent in 1965 to 2.1 percent today. Even more encouraging is the fact that the rate of

[31] Michael S. Teitelbaum, "Relevance of Demographic Transition Theory for Developing Countries," *Science* 188 (May 1975): 420–25.

FIGURE 20-3 TRENDS IN BIRTH RATES IN DEVELOPED AND DEVELOPING COUNTRIES, 1775–2050

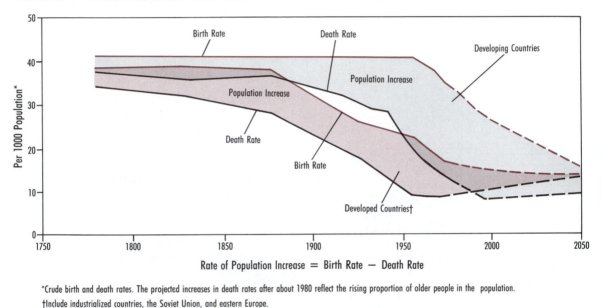

Rate of Population Increase = Birth Rate — Death Rate

*Crude birth and death rates. The projected increases in death rates after about 1980 reflect the rising proportion of older people in the population.
†Include industrialized countries, the Soviet Union, and eastern Europe.

SOURCE: The World Bank, *World Development Report, 1980* (New York: Oxford University Press, 1980), p. 64.

decline in developing countries has been much faster than it was during the nineteenth-century transition; in Indonesia, Colombia, and Chile it has been three times as fast (see Figure 20-3).[32]

The demographic transition, then, is far from automatic. The time lag between the first and last stages has already caused the world's population explosion along with acute problems of poverty and overpopulation in less developed countries. The crucial question is whether birth rates can be brought down before dwindling resources impose Malthus's positive checks. The outcome of this race against time is still very much in doubt. Whether the demographic transition is completed soon enough depends on innumerable individual decisions about how many children to have, and human decisions are never entirely automatic.

THE SOCIAL BASIS OF BIRTH CONTROL

History has shown that people have fewer children when they are willing and able to do so. "Able" is less of a problem than one might think. Every culture seems to have the knowledge necessary to prevent births, and some contraceptive methods are as old as recorded history. Moreover, the modern means of birth control are effective and readily

[32] The World Bank, *World Development Report, 1980* (New York: Oxford University Press, 1980), pp. 64–65.

available in much of the world. Knowledge of birth-control techniques and easy access to contraceptives, however, do not explain why people use them. The Western demographic transition, for instance, did not depend on modern contraceptive technology. In fact, the consistent decline of the western European birth rate between 1870 and 1932 occurred *in spite of* vigorous legal, religious, and medical opposition to birth control. "Willing" is obviously more significant than "able."

Social conditions, not convenient contraception, determine the willingness to practice birth control. Family-planning programs in less developed countries assume that population growth can be slowed by preventing the birth of unwanted babies, but the fact is that most couples in traditional societies want large families. Three years after a national birth-control program went into effect in South Korea in the 1960s, a survey found that it had made no difference in the ideal family size. Almost every woman said she wanted "two or three sons with one or two daughters."[33] If couples want to have fewer children, they will take advantage of government family-planning services. If they do not, then offering them free abortions and contraceptives will have little effect.

Changing traditional roles for women appear to have the greatest effect on contraceptive practices and the shift to smaller families. Increased educational opportunities, in particular, are strongly related to declining fertility rates.[34] The overwhelming evidence is that socially patterned incentives and family-planning services are *both* important in reducing birth rates—and they tend to reinforce each other.[35]

[33] "Korea: Trends in Four National KAP Surveys, 1964–67," *Studies in Family Planning* 43 (June 1969): 7.
[34] Thomas Merrick, "World Population in Transition," *Population Bulletin* 41 (Washington, D.C.: Population Reference Bureau, 1986), p. 32.
[35] Davis, "The World's Population Crisis," p. 295; The World Bank, *World Development Report, 1980*, p. 64.

An Indian doctor explains how to use an intrauterine device. Willingness to practice birth control, however, is determined by social conditions, not convenient contraception.

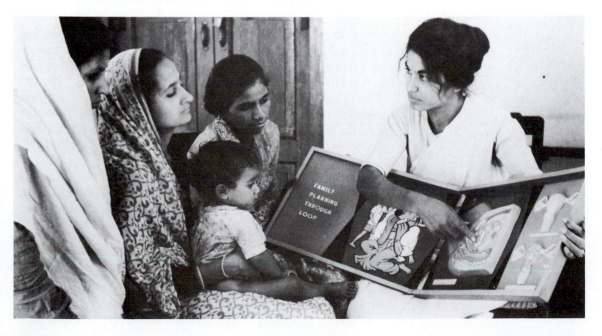

CHINA'S BABY BOOM

In a matter of only a few years, China's stringent birth control campaign has succeeded in reducing its population growth rate to about 1.2 percent, the range of most developed countries. Nevertheless, the relentless effects of population momentum are causing a new baby boom in the world's most populous country. And, in spite of powerful inducements to have only one child, Chinese peasants continue to find several children an economic necessity.

Liu Chunshan, an illiterate peasant from Shandong Province, had a problem: a four-year old daughter and a wife who was pregnant in violation of the state's one-child-per-family policy. After a soothsayer told him the new baby would be a son, Liu threw his daughter down a well. He watched while she drowned, ignoring her tearful pleas of "Papa, Papa." "Without a son, the generations cannot be passed on and we remain childless," he said later. Caught and convicted, he was sentenced to 15 years in prison. And his wife gave birth to a second daughter.

One after another such horror stories make the papers in China. Despite efforts to stop female infanticide, the practice has become an ugly side effect of the country's efforts to control a runaway population. Family-planning officials are up against relentless demographic pressure: more than half of China's 1 billion people were born since 1949, and a vast "baby boom" generation is now reaching childbearing age.

■ ■ ■

To meet China's goal of limiting the population to 1.2 billion by the year 2000, Chinese officials are taking harsher measures to enforce the one-child-per-family rule. The 1982 constitution makes practicing birth control a civic duty, and the state has launched vigorous abortion and sterilization campaigns.

. . . Couples who pledge to have one child are granted monthly bonuses, priority in school enrollments, jobs and housing; those who have more than one are subject to stiff fines, have their paychecks docked and lose benefits and raises. The plan has worked fairly well in urban areas, {but} . . . in the countryside new agricultural policies allowing peasants to keep much of what they produce have made large families profitable —and many peasants wealthy enough to pay the fines.

■ ■ ■

In industrial societies, where social conditions favor small families, it is interesting to note that efforts to *increase* fertility are also likely to be ineffective. East Germany's problem is population decline: a steady drop in the birth rate since the 1950s (plus emigration to the West) created a critical shortage of youthful workers. In 1974 eight out of ten women of working age had a job, legal abortions and free contraceptive services were available, and the birth rate was at an all-time low. In the 1970s the government began a costly program of financial incentives to increase the national population. Young couples were given a grant of $500 for each child and interest-free loans for baby clothes and furniture. The birth of a second child in eight years reduced this debt; a third child eliminated it. Day care nurseries were expanded and working mothers were given paid leaves and other elaborate benefits to stay home and bear children. In addition to these economic incentives, government propaganda increased the pressure on young women to fulfill their social responsibility by marrying and having children.

The initial results of the East German program were called "spectacular" in the West: the birth rate rose from 10.8 per thousand in 1975 to 13.3 in 1977. In the longer run, however, the government's efforts are likely to fail. The East German baby boom probably reflects a temporary inclination to marry and have children at a younger age, not a permanent commitment to having more children. Moreover, two unrelated

The most sensitive issue is where birth control leaves off and human-rights violations begin. There have been reports of pregnant women forced to undergo abortions as late as the eighth month of pregnancy. Last year even women expecting their first child without permission were pressured to take "remedial measures." Sterilization is increasingly common as well; 10 million such operations were performed between January and August last year. Officials in Peking deny the practice is obligatory, which would violate United Nations guidelines and jeopardize China's request for additional U.N. family-planning aid. But officials in some provinces have proclaimed that compulsory sterilization for at least one parent of two-child families is indeed part of China's official family-planning policy.

Prime Minister Zhao Ziyang publicly condemned female infanticide in 1982. No one knows how widespread the practice has become since then; but Chinese newspapers report that in some rural areas the ratio of male to female children is as high as 5 to 1. The problem is rooted in economic reality: lacking a nationwide retirement system, Chinese peasants rely on their children to support them in later years. Sons represent old-age insurance, while daughters traditionally support their husbands' families.

. . . The practice is likely to persist until China establishes a pension system — or relaxes its one-child-per-family rule, something authorities say will not be possible until the baby-boom generation passes out of childbearing years. In the meantime, some women are illegally removing birth-control devices; some families are sending children to live with grandparents in distant provinces. Others have reportedly even murdered meddling family-planning cadres. China "could achieve the numerical population goal by the year 2000 — but it would be at tremendous social cost," says University of Chicago sociologist William Parish. The alternative is also bleak. As Chinese couples are constantly reminded, unchecked population growth will mean shortages of jobs, food, clothing, housing and services for them and, for China, a future no brighter than the present.

SOURCE: Melinda Beck with Larry Rohter and Carolyn Friday, "An Unwanted Baby Boom," *Newsweek*, April 30, 1984, p. 47.

factors probably contributed to the rise in the birth rate: an improvement in the standard of living for young families and a temporary increase in the number of women of childbearing age.[36] Economic incentives and propaganda might encourage a few parents to have an "extra" child, but the social patterns favoring small families have not been changed significantly.[37]

Lower birth rates do not appear to be the result of development per se; they seem to be caused by the increased social equality that accompanies industrialization. When people have access to the basics of life — enough food, shelter, clothing, health care, education (especially for women), and an opportunity to get ahead — they are more inclined to limit the size of their families. Efforts to control population growth in traditional societies will not be effective until the mores and institutions that favor large families are changed. As long as women are secluded at home and denied educational and professional opportunities, as long as early marriages are arranged between children, and as long as large families are the chief source of income and security in old age, developing countries will not have the positive social incentives necessary to lower the birth rate (see "China's Baby Boom"). Advanced industrial societies, on the contrary,

[36] Dirk J. van de Kaa, "Europe's Second Demographic Transition," *Population Bulletin* 42 (Washington, D.C.: Population Reference Bureau, 1987), p. 20.

[37] Breindel and Eberstadt, "Paradoxes of Population," 46–47.

The economic development of poor countries has been hindered by lack of capital. Their growing populations literally eat up the money that would otherwise be available for investment.

offer inducements to small families and alternatives to the services children tradition-ally provide: wage labor, social security, opportunities for education and upward mobility. The change from one social structure to the other is the essence of the industrialization process.

THE POPULATION CRISIS IN DEVELOPING COUNTRIES

Population growth is a global problem, but in the less developed regions of Asia, Africa, and Latin America it has become a crisis. From an economic viewpoint these poor countries are literally eating up capital: their multiplying numbers are slowing and even halting economic development by taking money away from investment to finance consumption. In a stable population 3 to 5 percent of national income must be invested to produce a 1 percent increase in per capita income; in a population growing by 3 percent a year, 12 to 20 percent of national income must go to capital investments in order to produce the same increase in living standards. Because poor countries usually cannot invest more than 10 percent of their incomes, and because their population growth rate is between 2 and 3.5 percent, economic development in these countries is extremely slow and difficult.[38]

The recent history of Egypt illustrates many of the problems of population growth in developing countries. In 1949 there were about 2100 Egyptians for every square mile

---

[38] Davis, "The World's Population Crisis," p. 273.

of arable land in this desert country. To relieve their extreme poverty, the high dam at Aswan was built on the Nile River; it provided irrigation for a million acres of desert, increasing Egypt's arable land by 12 percent by 1971. During the same period, however, Egypt's population increased *71 percent,* largely because of a rapid drop in mortality. There were now about 3200 people for every square mile of cultivated land. The rising demand for food forced the government to reduce the acreage devoted to cotton, the farmers' most profitable crop. Huge numbers of the destitute migrated to cities looking for work, an estimated twenty-seven of them for every industrial job available. Just to keep its citizens alive, the Egyptian government started expensive make-work projects and expropriated all income above a modest amount. It also began a national birth-control program. Today, Egypt is still one of the poorest countries in the world: it had a per capita annual income of $760 in 1986. Technological improvements such as the Aswan Dam had borne out the Utterly Dismal Theorem: more people are now living miserably than ever before.[39]

When mortality drops rapidly with little decrease in fertility, as it did in Egypt, the result is a bulge in the **population pyramid**, or distribution of age groups in a society. Because most of the lives saved by better nutrition and health practices are those of infants and children, the next generation of youths is unusually large. In industrial societies such as Sweden about 25 percent of the population is less than 15 years old, but in developing countries such as Mexico, children make up roughly 45 percent of the population (see Figure 20-4). As this younger generation grows up, it drains the national income for its education and support. As it enters the labor market, the economy must expand fast enough to accommodate millions of new workers. If the economy cannot absorb them, then large numbers of young adults will be homeless, poor, and politically restless. Some will migrate to cities, but some will emigrate, legally or illegally, to look for work in the developed countries. Finally, as these more numerous young people start families of their own, they will prolong the population explosion by generating more births than the relatively small numbers of older people will generate deaths. As a result of this **population momentum**, a population that has disproportionately more young people than old people will continue to grow even if the fertility rate does not (see Figure 20-5). If there were a birth-control miracle, and world fertility suddenly fell to replacement level (only one birth for every person), population momentum would still cause a rise in births and a time lag of two-thirds of a century before growth would actually stop.[40] Even with the most sincere efforts to reduce the birth rate, the world population is still expected to grow beyond 6 billion by the end of the twentieth century and to reach between 8 and 14 billion by the twenty-second.[41]

SOCIAL EFFECTS OF SLOWER POPULATION GROWTH

The disparity between a rising world population and the earth's limited resources is clearly going to be a critical problem for the foreseeable future. Some economists

---

[39] Ibid., p. 274.; "1988 World Population Data Sheet," Population Reference Bureau.
[40] Otis Dudley Duncan, "Observations on Population," *The New Physician* 20 (April 1971): 243.
[41] "1988 World Population Data Sheet," Population Reference Bureau.

FIGURE 20-4 POPULATION AGE PYRAMIDS, 1985 AND 2025: LESS AND MORE DEVELOPED COUNTRIES

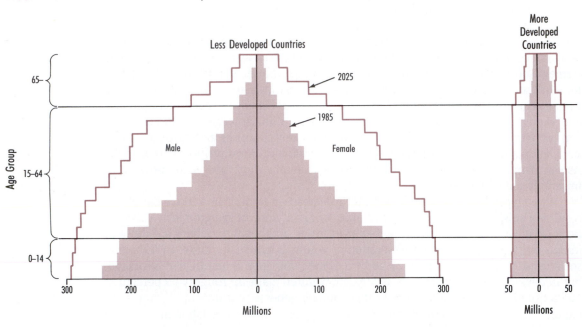

SOURCE: Population Reference Bureau, "1988 World Population Data Sheet" (Washington, DC: Population Reference Bureau, April 1988).

consider population growth a spur to economic progress, but most demographers agree that reducing birth rates is necessary to improve the standard of living in developing countries.[42] By increasing per capita income and productivity and by protecting environmental resources, slower population growth is thought to contribute to economic development.

We have already seen that poverty, not overpopulation, is the most important cause of malnutrition and famine. The world produces enough food to feed its population, but distributes it so unevenly that poor countries go hungry because they cannot afford to feed themselves. Since poverty also encourages a high birth rate, economic development precedes the demographic transition to lower birth rates. Slowing population growth, then, is an economic and political problem to be solved by economic development and political change.

The implications of the population problem are not limited to the Malthusian nightmare of famine and pestilence. The pressures of population on resources are also a factor in international politics. Most wars are fought to protect the vital interests of competing nations — and vital interests usually mean natural resources (oil, land, strategic minerals). Poverty and exploitation can also lead to war. The hostility and

---

[42] Julian Simon and Herman Kahn, eds., *The Resourceful Earth: A Response to Global 2000* (New York: Basil Blackwell, 1984); *Population Growth and Economic Development: Policy Questions*, National Research Council of the National Academy of Sciences, 1986.

resentment between the peoples of the southern and northern hemispheres, or between the poor, less developed countries and the rich, industrial areas of the globe, pose a constant threat to world peace.[43]

Population pressures cause problems within as well as between nations. As the birth rate falls in Europe, a smaller proportion of working taxpayers will have to pay for pensions and medical care for a larger proportion of elderly retirees. Different growth rates among ethnic groups can also be a factor in democratic politics. In Lebanon, for example, the average Moslem family has over six children and the average Christian family has three. For thirty years the Christian-dominated government would not take a census for fear of losing seats in parliament. In 1976 the Moslems rebelled, and the outnumbered Christians found themselves a minority in a Moslem-controlled state.[44] (In the United States the population shift to the Sun Belt of the South and West would not be so important if it did not bring about a shift in political power as well.)

---

[43] *North-South: A Program for Survival.* The Report of the Independent Commission on International Development Issues under the Chairmanship of Willy Brandt (Cambridge, Mass.: MIT Press, 1980).
[44] Breindel and Eberstadt, "Paradoxes of Population," p. 44.

POPULATION DOUBLING TIMES IN WORLD SOCIETIES   FIGURE 20-5

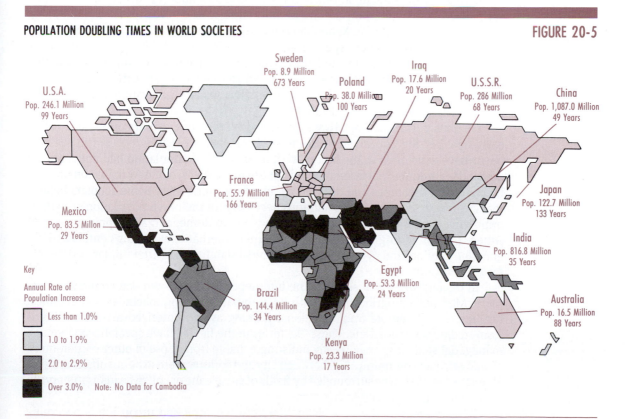

Sweden
Pop. 8.9 Million
673 Years

Iraq
Pop. 17.6 Million
20 Years

Poland
Pop. 38.0 Million
100 Years

U.S.S.R.
Pop. 286 Million
68 Years

U.S.A.
Pop. 246.1 Million
99 Years

China
Pop. 1,087.0 Million
49 Years

France
Pop. 55.9 Million
166 Years

Japan
Pop. 122.7 Million
133 Years

Mexico
Pop. 83.5 Millon
29 Years

India
Pop. 816.8 Million
35 Years

Egypt
Pop. 53.3 Million
24 Years

Brazil
Pop. 144.4 Million
34 Years

Australia
Pop. 16.5 Million
88 Years

Kenya
Pop. 23.3 Million
17 Years

Key

Annual Rate of
Population Increase

Less than 1.0%

1.0 to 1.9%

2.0 to 2.9%

Over 3.0%   Note: No Data for Cambodia

SOURCE: Population Reference Bureau "1988 World Population Data Sheet" (Washington, DC: Population Reference Bureau, April 1988).

Many of the challenges of the future reflect such questions of population and resources. One other consequence of the population explosion, however, is so important that it deserves more extensive treatment — urbanization and the growth of cities.

THE GROWTH OF CITIES

Civilization began with cities. The first urban settlements were built about 3500 B.C. in the fertile valleys of Mesopotamia, and more appeared later along the banks of the Nile in Egypt, the Indus in India, and the Yellow River in China. Cities developed rather late in human history because their growth depended on a sizable surplus of food. People could give up farming only when agriculture was producing more food than the population needed to survive. Once better techniques of ploughing and stock raising created abundant food supplies in these irrigated areas of the earth, then human beings were no longer restricted to hunting and gathering but were free to engage in diverse occupations as merchants, artisans, priests, and soldiers.

A **city**, then, consists of a large number of people who are densely concentrated in a small area and dependent on others for food. Concentration makes possible a highly specialized division of labor, and size permits large-scale enterprises to be undertaken. And, as the Greek historian Xenophon remarked in the fourth century B.C., "Of necessity he who pursues a very specialized task will do it best." The urban areas of the ancient world became centers of culture where writing and accounting were invented and where new forms of religion, science, and commerce began. Cities are thus associated with the great rise in intellectual activity, social organization, and economic productivity that we call "civilization."

Obviously, the city has always depended on the agricultural countryside for its existence, but the countryside also depends on the city. Large food surpluses may never have developed in the first place if a nonfarming population had not created a demand for produce that farmers could not use themselves, or if new irrigation projects had not been organized and directed by an urban ruling elite. Some scholars believe that city dwellers created the conditions necessary for their own population growth by improving the distribution of food (all roads led to Rome, and all shipping routes to Athens), by providing banking services in such international trading centers as Florence and London, and by creating more political stability and better military protection for the peasantry.

In modern industrial societies the interdependence of town and country is complete. Mechanized agribusiness, with its automatic milking machines and chemical fertilizers, is as remote from traditional farming as computerized manufacturing is from traditional handicrafts. These "factories in the fields" have specialized labor and managerial staffs that are virtually indistinguishable from those of other corporations. Moreover, if all communication between city and country were to be cut off, it would be almost as easy to starve surrounded by fields of sugar cane or coffee beans as to starve in a city where nothing edible is grown.

In most respects the very distinction between rural and urban life is becoming blurred in modern societies. The goods Americans use — vegetables from California,

The huge size of Tokyo provides an example of the worldwide urban explosion caused by population growth and industrial development.

automobiles from Michigan, meat from Kansas, furniture from North Carolina, heating oil from Texas—are the same in the city and the country, and cultural values and attitudes are influenced by the same nationally distributed magazines, films, and television programs. Much as Americans might want to cling to their small-town heritage, their rural traditions are being submerged in an increasingly urban culture and social structure.

Rather than a separate and unique development, the rise of cities is part of the social changes that accompanied the historic transformation of agrarian societies after the Industrial Revolution. This shift from rural to urban life—from small, intimate communities tied together by bonds of kinship and shared concerns to complex, more impersonal societies based on competing or complementary interests—is a central theme in the works of such classical sociologists as Ferdinand Tönnies, Émile Durkheim, Max Weber, and Karl Marx.

THE URBANIZED SOCIETY

However important the ancient cities may have been, they were "islands in an overwhelmingly rural sea."[45] The urban population was small in two senses: only a tiny proportion of people lived in cities, and most cities were not large by modern standards. The great Babylonian city of Ur had only about 25,000 residents, and Rome, the largest city of the ancient world, had just 650,000 residents in 100 A.D.[46] As recently as 1900 the population of the world was still 85 percent rural.

---

[45] J. John Palen, *The Urban World*, 3rd ed. (New York: McGraw-Hill, 1987), p. 3.
[46] Ivan Light, *Cities in World Perspective* (New York: Macmillan, 1983), Table 1-1.

A new housing complex and the makeshift shacks of the poor exist side by side on the outskirts of Bombay. All over the developing world, millions of displaced peasants are moving to the cities in search of jobs.

Today this picture has changed dramatically. About 40 percent of the world's population are now city dwellers, and before the century ends the world for the first time will be more urban than rural.[47] This rapid urbanization is as significant for the future as the more familiar population explosion.

The urban explosion is partly a result of the growth of the population as a whole and partly the result of industrial development. In agricultural economies workers are scattered in small villages or on isolated farms. Industrial enterprises, in contrast, are concentrated in cities where proximity to labor, materials, and transportation makes production more efficient. As modern technology reduces the demand for farmhands, surplus workers migrate to cities and enter industrial occupations. This "pull" of jobs in the city and "push" off the farm have set the pattern of urban growth and rural depopulation in the United States over the last century.

OVERURBANIZATION.   Developing countries today, however, are not simply repeating the typical history of advanced industrial nations. In the past cities grew primarily from migration. Their own populations were so reduced by disease that they could not reproduce themselves. Improved sanitation and health services have largely eliminated the epidemics that decimated other urban populations, and city dwellers now have high rates of internal population growth. At the same time, rural populations are growing three or four times as fast as before. Millions of destitute peasants still move to cities, but they are more difficult to absorb. They are forced to settle in shantytowns or

---

[47] "1988 World Population Data Sheet" (Washington, D.C.: Population Reference Bureau, 1988).

sleep on the streets. Nearly every large city in developing regions is ringed by these squatter settlements, and in Latin American cities the homeless make up 40 to 60 percent of the population.[48]

Mexico City is a textbook example of such **overurbanization**, the excessively large and rapidly growing urban populations found in developing countries.[49] Mexico City's stunning growth rate of 4.4 percent — or over one million people a year — is due to the lack of rural development that would keep Mexico's large youthful population in the countryside. The concentration of people and industrial activity in the capital has caused appalling urban problems: huge, overcrowded slums and shantytowns, many of them without water, sewers, or electricity; an acute shortage of public transport; paralyzing traffic jams; and, on most days, a sky darkened by air pollution from automobile emissions, factory smokestacks, and burning garbage. The urban crisis in Mexico and other developing countries is the result of a vicious circle: rural areas are underdeveloped because capital is being pumped into the cities to provide roads, housing, and other public services; lack of rural development brings millions of poor, unskilled people to the cities; the rapid growth of the cities puts a further strain on the scarce resources needed for development.[50]

Urban problems are clearly not confined to cities but have roots in the larger society. The poverty of urban slums is not caused by living in cities; it is caused by the inability of the economy to employ millions of surplus workers. The *barriada* in Lima, the streets of Calcutta, and the ghetto of South-side Chicago are places where people go *because* they are poor; they are refugee camps for the victims of rural poverty.

PATTERNS OF URBAN GROWTH. However rapidly cities have grown, they have not grown at random. The form of the city also reflects larger economic and social processes. Sociologists have devised three theoretical models of urban growth.

Concentric zone theory describes cities in terms of circular zones spreading out from a downtown center. The heart of the city is the central business district, where the major stores, theaters, office buildings, and so on are located. As the city grows, the business district spreads outward into old residential sections. This "zone in transition" contains deteriorating housing, warehouses, and light manufacturing businesses. The outer rings of the city are residential areas. The third zone from the center is a working-class district, the next contains middle-class housing; and the outer ring consists of upper-class suburbs.

The concentric zone theory was developed by Ernest Burgess, a member of the Chicago school of sociology, in 1924.[51] Taking the growth of Chicago as his chief example, Burgess proposed that urban land-use patterns reflect the competition for space among different social groups. The most valuable land — which is usually the

---

[48] Thomas Merrick, "World Population in Transition," *Population Bulletin* 41 (Washington, D.C.: Population Reference Bureau, 1986), p. 599.

[49] Michael Timberlake and Jeffrey Kentor, "Economic Dependence, Overurbanization, and Economic Growth: A Study of Less Developed Countries," *The Sociological Quarterly* 24 (Autumn 1983): 489–507.

[50] Mexico City (current population: over 18 million) may be the world's largest city by the year 2000, with a projected population of 31.6 million (Palen, *The Urban World*, p. 338).

[51] Ernest W. Burgess, "The Growth of the City," *Publications of the American Sociological Society* 18 (1924): 85–97.

most centrally located — goes to those who can pay the costs: large department stores, banks, and other businesses dependent on downtown locations. Any inner-city housing must make intensive use of land to be profitable. As a result, there are two types of centrally located housing: luxury high-rise apartment buildings, where the number of rooms and the rent per acre are high; and slum tenements, where the rooms are small and crowded together, so that the rent per acre is also high. Land in the outer zones is less valuable, so it is used less intensively. Two-family houses on small plots are typical in working-class neighborhoods, single-family houses in middle-income communities, and a property of two acres or more at the edge of the city in upper-class suburbs. The concentric zone pattern best describes such cities as New York and Philadelphia, whose growth during the nineteenth century relied on steam railroads for commuting from the suburbs to downtown.

Sector theory identifies another spatial pattern for urban growth. On the basis of a study he did for the Federal Housing Administration, Homer Hoyt concluded that land use is more strongly influenced by transportation routes than by distance from the central business district.[52] The industrial, commercial, and residential sectors, he found, are not circular but wedge-shaped. Residential areas tend to push out from the center of the city along existing routes — a railroad, for example, or a new expressway. Factories and businesses dominate other sectors because of their proximity to water-front docks or highways.

The sector pattern is characteristic of cities that developed at the turn of the century, when horse-drawn trolley cars provided transportation to work. Houses were built a short distance from the rail lines, leaving undeveloped land in between which extended out from the center of the city in a star-shaped pattern. Minneapolis and Washington provide examples of sector development.

Multiple nuclei theory, in contrast to the other theories, suggests that there is no common pattern of urban development, but only local economic or social reasons why cities grow the way they do. Chauncey Harris and Edward Ullman argue that certain economic activities require special facilities: retail stores have to be where their customers are and manufacturing plants need large spaces and transportation services. People want peace and quiet, so residential housing will not be in the same part of town as heavy industry. Historical tradition and geography also affect where people live and work.[53] The multiple nuclei form applies best to cities that grew most rapidly during the heyday of the automobile. Los Angeles, of course, is the prime example of the type.[54]

Each of these theories tries to explain how social factors have shaped the growth of cities, but none can predict the pattern that every city will follow. Many pre-industrial cities have reverse concentric zones: the upper classes occupy the central core, and the poor live in the outlying districts. In Paris the outer ring of the city is known as the "red

---

[52] Homer Hoyt. *The Structure and Growth of Residential Neighborhoods in American Cities* (Washington, D.C.: U.S. Government Printing Office, 1939).

[53] Chauncey Harris and Edward Ullman, "The Nature of Cities," *Annals of the American Academy of Political and Social Science* 252 (1945): 7–17.

[54] Zane Miller and Patricia Melvin, *The Urbanization of Modern America*, 2nd ed. (San Diego: Harcourt Brace Jovanovich, 1987), p. 51.

MEGALOPOLISES IN THE UNITED STATES

FIGURE 20-6

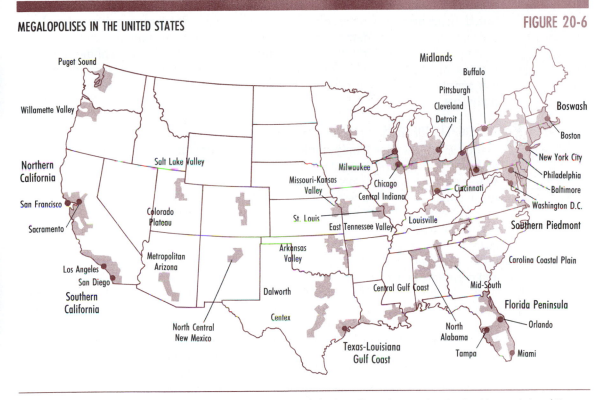

SOURCE: From *Social Problems* copyright © 1982 by Michael S. Bassis, Richard J. Gelles, and Ann Levine. Reprinted by permission of Harcourt Brace Jovanovich, Inc.

belt" because it is the home of politically left-wing industrial workers; in Mexico City the "suburbs" are miserable shantytowns.

SUBURBANIZATION.   In the United States, the most visible urban development is **suburbanization**, or the increased proportion of the population living on the outskirts of central cities. Since 1960 the percentage of Americans living in large cities has been decreasing while the percentage living in "urban fringe" areas has been growing rapidly. As a result, nearly three out of four Americans are now defined as urban residents. As suburbanization and "urban sprawl" continue, cities merge into a single, huge metropolitan region, or **megalopolis**. By 2000 a continuous city of 35 million is expected to stretch from Boston to Washington, D.C. On the West Coast a similar megalopolis is developing between San Francisco and San Diego. Other large metropolitan areas appear in Florida and along the Great Lakes (see Figure 20-6).

Suburbanization is the result of the same social factors that have shaped other patterns of urban growth. As concentric zone theory predicted, the affluence of the 1950s and 1960s caused a movement toward the outer rim of the city, creating a suburban expansion. The zone in transition, or decaying inner-city neighborhoods, remained the place where the poor and the newly arrived immigrants were concentrated. In accordance with sector theory, suburban development has proceeded along transportation routes: new towns spring up near commuter railroads and highways leading into the city. Multiple nuclei theory best explains the growth of metropolitan regions, in which residential suburbs are separate from industrial areas, and commercial activities are concentrated in shopping centers and the "neon strips" of major highways.

THE PLIGHT OF THE CITIES.   The American white middle class began to move to the suburbs in the 1930s, when the family automobile made it possible to escape the noise and dirt of the inner city for what was defined as a more pleasant life in the country. After World War II government-sponsored mortgages underwrote the cost of a suburban house for the average family. As a result, the white working class began to move in the 1950s, leaving behind only those who could not or would not leave the city: the poor; minorities who would have suffered housing and job discrimination in the suburbs; and the cosmopolitan, professional classes. The suburban middle class was soon joined by retail stores and other service businesses. Suburbs also attracted manufacturing plants and corporate headquarters looking for lower rents and taxes. The white exodus was thus followed by a shift of jobs and business away from the inner city. At the same time, the central cities continued to attract poor migrants looking for work, especially unskilled immigrants from the developing countries.

The financial plight of the cities comes from the loss of their commercial and middle-class tax base, combined with the increasing cost of providing public services (schools, police, sanitation, transportation) and welfare benefits to the poor and unemployed. Raising taxes drives more taxpayers away, but allowing housing and services to deteriorate also makes the suburbs more attractive to city residents. This urban crisis is particularly severe in the older cities of the Northeast. There the loss of jobs has been accelerated by the decline of the steel industry and the shift of manufacturing businesses to the Sun Belt, where taxes and wage rates have so far been lower. Once again, urban problems are not unique to cities. They are the result of much larger economic and social processes.

URBAN REVIVAL.   During the 1970s the mass media reported a "back to the city" movement among middle-class suburbanites. One result is **gentrification**, the settlement and renovation of rundown inner-city neighborhoods by affluent newcomers. However, it turned out that the "gentry" are generally not middle-class suburbanites but young, white, highly educated professionals who are already residents of the city.[55] In most cases the renovators are replacing poor (often black) tenants for whom rising property values mean higher rents and prices. The gentrification of central cities is probably caused by several factors: the maturing of the postwar baby boom generation, a shortage of urban housing, the higher cost of suburban houses, the inconvenience of commuting, and a new appreciation of historic neighborhoods and the advantages of city life.[56]

---

[55] Shirley B. Laska and Daphne Spain, *Back to the City: Issues in Neighborhood Renovation* (Elmsford, N.Y.: Pergamon Press, 1980).

[56] Claude S. Fischer, *The Urban Experience*, 2nd ed. (San Diego: Harcourt Brace Jovanovich, 1984), p. 249.

After a period of rural growth in the 1970s, the size of metropolitan areas began to expand more rapidly in the 1980s. Although many manufacturing and service jobs have moved to the countryside in the last few years, high unemployment rates, especially in the oil and mining industries, have hurt the rural economy. With poverty rates in rural areas now as high as those in the central cities (18 percent in 1986), younger and better educated workers are once again leaving the country for the city.[57]

In the last few years a rundown section of the Boston waterfront has been transformed into a fashionable residential district. Gentrification of central cities is one aspect of the urban revival.

THE URBAN WAY OF LIFE

For centuries, many enterprising people have left farms and small towns to seek a new way of life in the city. Aristotle said, "The people come to the city to live; they remain to live the good life." Just how good this life is, and what effects it has on the people who lead it, has been a subject of popular and scholarly debate ever since Aristotle's day. On the one hand, cities have always been celebrated as oases of cultural diversity, intellectual stimulation, and personal freedom. To most Americans, on the other hand, urban life is not "good" at all: cities are often thought of as corrupt, wicked, filthy, and callous places. One Gallup poll found that four out of five of the city dwellers themselves would rather live somewhere else, preferably a suburb or small town.[58] Antiurban themes also pervade Western culture, from the Bible's sinful Sodom and Gomorrah to Thoreau's escape to Walden Pond. Nevertheless, cities all over the world are growing mainly because people move to them for economic reasons, in the hope of the "good life." More and more, the future appears to belong to the city and to the social arrangements it fosters.

---

[57] William P. O'Hare, "The Rise of Poverty in Rural America" (Washington, D.C.: Population Reference Bureau, 1988).
[58] *Gallup Opinion Index*, 1973, p. 31.

Sociological approaches to **urbanism**, or the culture of cities, take three major directions: *determinist theory*, which agrees that cities are lonely places that bring on personal and social problems; *compositional theory*, which denies that cities have such harmful effects and finds their demographic composition a more important influence on behavior; and *subcultural theory*, which combines the first two approaches to analyze the distinctive consequences, both positive and negative, of city life.

DETERMINIST THEORY.   The determinist view of urbanism was developed by Louis Wirth, a member of the Chicago school of sociology, to explain what seemed to him to be peculiarly urban phenomena: emotional stress; social isolation; and *anomie,* the weakening of social controls over behavior.

Cities are characterized by their size, density, and diversity. They are crowded, busy places where hundreds of strangers encounter each other every day, never to meet again. The urban environment, Wirth maintained, affects both individual personalities and the social structure of cities. The onslaught of sensory stimuli — the roar of traffic and machinery, the neon signs and newspaper headlines, the weirdly dressed and oddly behaving people — causes what was later called "psychic overload." [59] To protect themselves from urban stress, city dwellers "turn off": they resist some of the claims being made on them by becoming blasé, aloof, "always in a hurry." Their social ties to others weaken, leading to the loneliness and deviant behavior that are associated with city life.

Wirth also believed that these same conditions caused the urban social structure to break down. The diversity of city activities, he thought, divided time and attention among many different and unconnected groups. Family life, work, recreation, shopping, meetings with friends — all might take place in different areas of the city and among people with different interests and backgrounds. So many different life styles make moral consensus difficult. Because people disagree about the rules of acceptable behavior, they are likely to engage in unconventional and criminal activities. [60]

On the other hand, Wirth also believed that people who are exposed to a variety of beliefs and life-styles will be more tolerant of differences. A recent national survey supported Wirth's hypothesis: urban Americans were found to be less racially prejudiced than rural Americans. [61]

Nevertheless, determinist theorists argue that the impersonality and diversity of city life undermines the sense of affiliation and community.

COMPOSITIONAL THEORY.   Wirth's theory has been criticized on several grounds, especially by other writers in the Chicago tradition. Quoting Robert Ezra Park's famous description of the city as a "mosaic of social worlds which touch but do not interpenetrate," compositionalists argue that these private social worlds survive even in the supposedly hostile urban environment.

---

[59] Stanley Milgram, "The Experience of Living in Cities," *Science* 167 (March 1970): 1461–68.

[60] Louis Wirth, "Urbanism as a Way of Life," *American Journal of Sociology* 44 (July 1938): 3–24: Fischer, *The Urban Experience,* pp. 32–35.

[61] Steven Tuch, "Urbanism, Region, and Tolerance Revisited: The Case of Racial Prejudice," *American Sociological Review* 52 (August 1987), 504–510.

For many people large cities such as Paris represent the "good life."

Herbert Gans, a leading compositional theorist, asserts that cities do not destroy intimate relationships or a sense of common purpose. City dwellers congregate in homogeneous neighborhoods; they live in Little Italies and Chinatowns, and they work in such occupational districts as Wall Street and the Loop. The common social and ethnic characteristics of local neighborhoods shelter their residents from the negative effects of the big city's diversity. Although some people are trapped in the city, unable to move because of age or poverty, many others have chosen to live there because they like urban convenience, cultural attractions, or ethnic community ties.

Compositionalists do find differences between urban and rural residents, but they account for them by citing such demographic factors as differing distributions of age, class, education, ethnic background, and marital status. But, they say, the size or density of a population has no *direct* effects on the personal traits and social experiences of its members.[62]

SUBCULTURAL THEORY. Claude Fischer has recently proposed a third theory of urbanism. He notes that the sheer size of city populations promotes the development of an amazing variety of subcultures, which does have an effect on social life. Like compositional theory, the subcultural approach finds that close personal relationships do persist in cities; like determinist theory, it maintains that the urban environment does have direct effects on city dwellers because they are able to join distinctive political, religious, ethnic, or other subcultural groups.[63]

Fischer explains that a large city population, with its cultural diversity and occupational variety, permits subcultures to develop. A small town of 5000, for example, might have five people who are intensely interested in vegetarianism. If the five meet, they would probably not do much more than talk about their interest. But in a city of 1 million, there might be 1000 vegetarians, enough to constitute a vegetarian subculture with its own restaurants and food cooperatives.

Thriving subcultures and the conflicts among them are direct effects of urbanism. Subcultures produce the phenomena that the Chicago school saw as evidence of a disintegrating social order but that Fischer maintains is evidence that new communities are being formed. There is more deviant behavior in cities, he claims, because deviance and other kinds of diversity are supported by subcultures. Cities thus encourage not only such nonconforming groups as artists and intellectuals but also deviant subcultures of criminals and drug addicts.[64]

Some sociologists have speculated that the Chicago school would have had a rosier view of urbanism if its members had not happened to live in Chicago in the 1920s and 1930s. Not only was Chicago a notoriously unpleasant place to live during the Prohibition era, but the professors of the Chicago school were from small towns, where people were inclined to be prejudiced against city ways. Many contemporary urban sociologists note instead the advantages of big-city freedom and diversity and the disadvantages of small-town conformity and intolerance.

Whether life in the city is better or worse, whether it has a fundamental or only a superficial effect on personality, the fact remains that urbanism is becoming a way of life for more and more people. The challenge of the future, therefore, will be met in a largely urban environment and in the artificial world that men and women have collectively built.

---

[62] Herbert J. Gans: *The Urban Villagers* (New York: Free Press, 1962) and *The Levittowners* (New York: Vintage, 1967).

[63] Claude S. Fischer, "Toward a Subcultural Theory of Urbanism" *American Journal of Sociology* 80 (May 1975): 1319–41.

[64] Fischer, *The Urban Experience*, pp. 35–39.

THE ARTIFICIAL WORLD OF THE FUTURE

Lester Ward, one of the first American sociologists, made a statement about the future of society that is still relevant nearly a century later. In taking issue with Malthus's belief in the "natural laws" of population growth, Ward wrote: "The fact is that man and society are not, except in a very limited sense, under the influence of the great dynamic laws that control the rest of the animal world. . . . If we call biologic processes natural, we must call social processes artificial." [65] The dominance of the artificial, or the nonnatural and human-made, will be the most significant feature of the society of the future. Human beings have always exerted some control over their natural environment — the first Mesopotamian settlement was no less artificial than the megalopolis — but never before to the extent that they do today and will tomorrow.

From the human point of view the artificial is an improvement over the natural. Social progress has come from increasing control over the forces of nature — damming the Nile's flood, for example, or extracting energy from oil or conquering famine and disease. The population explosion itself is not the result of natural law but of social processes: nature is not bringing more babies into the world; men and women are keeping them alive longer. If Malthus's natural law had not been thwarted, if nature's bounty had not been multiplied by human effort and ingenuity, then the population problem would have been solved by mass starvation. Human history would still be as Malthus saw it, a story of misery, want, and early death. When compared to the "natural" condition of humankind, the risk of overpopulating the world seems less terrifying.

Indeed, most of our social problems seem almost trifling compared to those earlier generations have suffered. Our economic problems are minor compared to the dire poverty that has been the lot of the human race through most of its history; our educational problems are less serious than virtual universal illiteracy; and our health problems seem mainly to be the consequences of living longer and better than any generation before us.

If the human race is no longer the victim of natural forces, it may be the victim of its own social processes. Primitive peoples were helpless to prevent droughts and epidemics, but they also lacked the technological capacity to "smog" themselves to death or to cause a "greenhouse effect" and render much of the planet uninhabitable. Above all, no previous generation has had the seemingly unlimited destructive power of nuclear weapons or the biochemical means of bringing human history to a close. The ultimate challenge of the future, then, is to avoid doing to ourselves what we feared nature might do over the last million years (see "Thinking about the Unthinkable").

To a greater extent than ever before, human beings make their own world. They will also make the opportunities and problems they face in the future. People are more than ever aware that their problems are caused by their own behavior and that this behavior can be changed. To solve the energy crisis, nearly every industrial country is attempting to reduce its use of gasoline and encourage conservation. To solve the

---

[65] Lester Ward, *The Psychic Factors of Civilization* (Boston: Ginn, 1893), pp. 134–35.

THINKING ABOUT THE UNTHINKABLE

The publication of Jonathan Schell's best-selling book, **The Fate of the Earth,** *has undoubtedly contributed to the nuclear disarmament movement. By forcing his readers to think about the "unthinkable" prospect of destroying the earth in a nuclear holocaust, Schell helped reawaken public concern about the logical absurdity and infinite dangers of the arms race. After tracing the strategy of deterrence to the notion of sovereign states, he analyzes here the strategy's inherent contradiction: the world's leaders are ready to exterminate the entire human race to protect their national interests.*

The self-extinction of our species is not an act that anyone describes as sane or sensible; nevertheless, it is an act that, without quite admitting it to ourselves, we plan in certain circumstances to commit. Being impossible as a fully intentional act, unless the perpetrator has lost his mind, it can come about only through a kind of inadvertence — as a "side effect" of some action that we do intend, such as the defense of our nation, or the defense of liberty, or the defense of socialism, or the defense of whatever else we happen to believe in. To that extent, our failure to acknowledge the magnitude and significance of the peril is a necessary condition for doing the deed. We can do it only if we don't quite know what we're doing. . . . What is needed to make extinction possible, therefore, is some way of thinking about it that at least partly deflects our attention from what it is. And this way of thinking is supplied to us, unfortunately, by our political and military traditions, which, with the weight of almost all historical experience behind them, teach us that it is the way of the world for the earth to be divided up into independent, sovereign states, and for these states to employ war as the final arbiter for settling the disputes that arise among them.

■ ■ ■

. . . We are told that it is human fate — perhaps even "a law of human nature" — that, in obedience, perhaps, to some "territorial imperative," or to some dark and ineluctable truth in the bottom of our souls, we must preserve sovereignty and always settle our differences with violence. If this is our fate, then it is our fate to die. But must we embrace nihilism? Must we die? Is self-extermination a law of our nature? Is there nothing we can do? I do not believe so. Indeed, if we admit the reality of the basic terms of the nuclear predicament — that present levels of global armament are great enough to possibly extinguish the species if a holocaust should occur; that in extinction every human purpose would be lost; that because once the species has been extinguished there will be no second chance, and the game will be over for all time; that therefore this possibility must be dealt with morally and politically as though it were a certainty; and that either by accident or by design a holocaust can occur at any second — then, whatever political views we may hold on other matters, we are driven almost inescapably to take action to rid the world of nuclear arms. Just as we have chosen to make nuclear weapons, we can choose to unmake them. Just as we have chosen to live in the system of sovereign states, we can choose to live in some other system. To do so would, of course, be unprecedented, and in many ways frightening, even truly perilous, but it is by no means impossible.

. . . We are indeed fated by our acquisition of the basic knowledge of physics to live for the rest of time with the knowledge of how to destroy ourselves. But we are not for that reason fated to destroy ourselves. We can choose to live.

SOURCE: Jonathan Schell, *The Fate of the Earth* (New York: Knopf, 1982), pp. 186, 218–19.

population crisis, nearly every developing country has government-sponsored birth-control programs. The results are already beginning to show in a worldwide "oil glut" and a declining fertility rate. Today concern for environmental issues is worldwide and every industrial country has legal restraints on pollution of the earth with toxic wastes. So far most of these efforts at sacrificing personal profit and convenience for the common good have been modest and half-hearted at best. Yet our hope for the future lies in realizing the full potential of the uniquely human ability to create artificial situations vastly superior to what nature alone has provided. As Ward wrote a century ago,

Thus far, social progress has in a certain awkward manner taken care of itself, but in the near future it will have to be cared for. To do this, and maintain the dynamic condition against all the hostile forces which thicken with every new advance, is the real problem of Sociology considered as an applied science.[66]

[66] Lester Ward, *Dynamic Sociology 1* (New York: Appleton, 1883), p. 706.

SUMMARY

1. Rapid population growth and industrial development are depleting natural resources and damaging the environment to such an extent that the earth may be reaching the absolute limits of its carrying capacity.

2. Because population growth is an exponential process, the doubling time becomes shorter and shorter. At the current growth rate of 1.8 percent, the world's population will double again in forty years.

3. The population explosion was caused by improvements in public health, which brought a sharp drop in mortality rates in the developing regions of the world.

4. In 1798 Malthus argued that the multiplying tendencies of the human race would inevitably cause it to increase beyond its food supply. He doubted that preventative checks could reduce fertility before positive checks stabilized population at a subsistence level. New technologies have so far increased food production and postponed the Malthusian nightmare.

5. Neo-Malthusian ecologists predict that unchecked population growth will end in disaster because of food shortages, industrial pollution, or depletion of natural resources. A simple projection of past trends into the future, however, does not take into account unforeseeable social and technological changes.

6. Supplies of critical resources—minerals, fossil fuels, air, water, and land—are rapidly being diminished by industrial development and population growth. Since the limits to growth have not yet been reached, most of humanity's problems still come from uneven distribution of the available resources.

7. Modern industrial societies provide many incentives to reduce family size; developed societies tend to be underpopulated and to have lower birth rates than developing societies. According to the theory of demographic transition, the process of industrialization is accompanied by a shift from high rates of births and deaths to low rates of both. Since death rates typically fall faster than birth rates, the population growth of developing countries results from the lag between much lower mortality and much lower fertility.

8. In poor countries the transition to lower birth rates can be slowed by lack of capital for development; in rapidly developing countries it can be speeded up. The developing world's population growth rate has fallen from 2.4 percent in 1965 to 2.1 percent today. These countries have shown a much steeper decline than the one that accompanied the Western demographic transition in the nineteenth century.

9. Social conditions, more than convenient contraception, determine whether or not people are willing to practice birth control. In industrial societies there are many drawbacks to large families, but the mores and institutions of traditional societies favor having many children.

10. Population momentum is causing population growth to reach critical proportions in poor countries and is stalling their industrial development. The pressure of population on resources is often a factor in international and local conflicts.

11. Industrialization and larger populations have led to rapid urbanization all over the world. Overurbanization in developing countries is caused by lack of rural development and by the inability of the industrial economy to absorb large numbers of surplus farm workers.

12. Three major patterns of urban growth have been identified: concentric zones, sectors, and multiple nuclei.

13. In the United States the demographic trend is toward suburbanization and the growth of megalopolises. Gentrification has slowed the decline of some central cities.

14. Wirth and other determinists argued that the impersonality of city life undermines the sense of community; compositional theorists such as Gans maintain that cities have demographic variety but no direct effect on individual personalities;

Fischer's subcultural theory finds that diverse subcultures have positive and negative effects on city life.

15. The future prospects and problems of the human race will be increasingly determined not by the forces of nature but by people themselves. The challenge lies in applying our knowledge of human behavior to the goals of social progress.

KEY TERMS

demography 624
human ecology 624
urban sociology 624
urbanization 624
linear growth 625
exponential growth 625
doubling time 625
fertility 628

mortality 628
preventative check 628
positive check 628
optimum population 636
theory of demographic
   transition 636
population pyramid 643

population momentum 643
city 646
overurbanization 649
suburbanization 651
megalopolis 651
gentrification 652
urbanism 654

SUGGESTED READING

* Richard J. Barnet. *The Lean Years: Politics in the Age of Scarcity.* New York: Simon and Schuster/ Touchstone Books, 1982.
* Lester R. Brown. *The Twenty-ninth Day.* New York: Norton, 1978.
* Rachel Carson. *Silent Spring.* Boston: Houghton-Mifflin, 1987.
Pranay Gupte. *The Crowded Earth: People and the Politics of Population.* New York: Norton, 1984.
Ivan Light, *Cities in World Perspective.* New York: Macmillan, 1983.
* John R. Logan and Harvey L. Molotch. *Urban Fortunes: The Political Economy of Place.* Berkeley: University of California Press, 1988.
* Zane L. Miller and Patricia M. Melvin. *The Urbanization of Modern America,* 2nd ed. San Diego: Harcourt Brace Jovanovich, 1987.

* David Popenoe. *Private Pleasure, Public Plight: American Metropolitan Community Life in Comparative Perspective.* New Brunswick, NJ: Transaction Books, 1988.
J. L. Spates and J. J. Macionis, *The Sociology of Cities,* 2nd ed., Ed. Sheryl Fullerton. Belmont, CA: Wadsworth, 1986.
* Ann W. Spirn. *The Granite Garden: Urban Nature and Human Design.* New York: Basic Books, 1985.
John R. Weeks. *Population: An Introduction to Concepts and Issues,* 3rd ed. Belmont, CA: Wadsworth, 1986.

* Available in paperback.

CAREERS IN SOCIOLOGY

Sociology is the study of social life and the social causes and consequences of human behavior. Sociology's subject matter ranges from the intimate family to the hostile mob, from crime to religion, from the divisions of race and social class to the shared beliefs of a common culture, from the sociology of work to the sociology of sport. In fact, few fields have such broad scope and relevance. Because sociology seems to offer something for everyone, it may seem suprising that its career potential is just beginning to be tapped.

Twenty years ago, there was really only one career in sociology. To be a sociologist was to be a professor, or at least a teacher of some sort. But there are now a number of possible careers for sociologists. Although teaching remains the dominant activity among the more than fifteen thousand professional sociologists today, other forms of employment are growing in both numbers and significance. Not all of these jobs are reserved exclusively for sociologists; in some sectors, sociologists are joined by economists, social workers, psychologists, and others. All of this represents a growing appreciation of sociology's potential contribution.

And yet, career payoffs are not the only reason for studying sociology. Its subject matter holds considerable interest for its own sake. Certainly, sociology offers valuable preparation for other sorts of careers. Sociology is a popular major for students planning futures in such professions as law, business, education, architecture, and even medicine — not to mention social work, politics, and public administration. Sociology provides a rich fund of knowledge directly concerning each of these fields. Sociology also provides many distinctive ways of looking at the world so as to generate new ideas and assess the old. Finally, sociology offers a range of research techniques which can be applied in many specific arenas — whether one's concern is with crime and criminal justice, client satisfaction in a business firm, the provision of medical care, or problems of poverty and welfare.

SOCIOLOGICAL CAREERS: SELECTED VIGNETTES AND BASIC OPTIONS

The following vignettes describe what different types of sociologists actually do. Of couse, these career profiles are oversimplifications, and they represent only a few of the total careers in sociology. Nevertheless, they focus on some of the basic options available. The vignettes are listed in no particular order. The names are all fictitious.

SOCIOLOGIST IN A HEALTH CENTER.
Howard H. has a faculty position in the state-supported Health Science Center which includes Schools of Nursing, Medicine, Dentistry, Public Health and allied health professions. He and six other social scientists form a unit in the Department of Community Health. Howard's responsibilities include teaching students in every one of these schools. He and his colleagues teach future physicians, nurses, and other health workers about sociological aspects of health care and health care organizations. Howard also works with the health services agencies as a sociological consultant providing data about the population groups to be served and about sociological aspects of the distribution of disease and health needs. He and his colleagues are used as resources by the staff of hospitals and clinics who turn to Howard to seek advice about a number of problems which they encounter with patients. Howard serves on the Medical School Admissions Committee, and serves on other committees in various health center schools. He also conducts research and currently is studying how patients with heart disease fare in their family and in their work after release from a hospital. Howard is rather well paid, but works in an environment in which he still has to convince some health professionals about the relevance of sociology to health care.

STAFF MEMBER OF A FEDERAL AGENCY.
Linda L. has only recently joined the staff of the U.S. Department of Justice where she serves as a staff member of a program which administers and monitors grants given to researchers throughout the country. After graduating from a small, predominantly black college in the South, Linda received a fellowship for graduate work at a private university in the North. Following some initial difficulties, she progressed quickly, choosing to specialize in criminology and deviance. While completing her PhD (or "doctoral") dissertation, she had a job with a large regional prison where she participated in evaluating the effects of treatment programs. In her new job, she discusses research plans with applicants for grants. These applications come from many disciplines. Linda has also been assigned a number of current projects which she supervises through communication with the project directors. Linda has been surprised to find many sociologists in federal departments in Washington, D.C. As in her own case, job titles do not always indicate who the sociologists are. In fact, there are many more opportunities for sociologists in government than strict job titles might indicate. Sociologists work as "statisticians," "welfare workers," "economists," and so on. Linda's salary is determined by the U.S. Civil Service scale. It provides her with a good income, even though Washington is a very expensive city in which to live.

MEMBER OF THE PLANNING STAFF IN A STATE DEPARTMENT OF TRANSPORTATION.
Paula P. has worked for five years in the State Department of Transportation and has now risen to the title of Assistant Director in the Office of Long-Range Forecasting. The job involves considerable sociological knowledge and skill, especially in projecting population shifts into and out of the state's major urban areas and suburban spin-offs. Here Paula is asked not only to commission research on her own, but to keep up with a growing research literature published in a wide variety of sources. While Paula does relatively little research herself, her work is particularly important since she keeps informed about relevant studies wherever they may be conducted and prepares frequent reports and analyses based on new findings. She serves as a bridge to outside research experts working on contracts with the department. In addition, Paula has taken on administrative responsibilities for a growing staff working under her supervision. Her PhD in Sociology is a good preparation for many of her functions. However, she was never really trained to work with budgets, make personnel decisions, or allocate staff work assignments. These tasks all have their

own challenges. In addition to making a good living, Paula is contributing to some critical decisions concerning the state's future transportation system. Without the research and professional judgment of such people, decisions concerning the routing of highways through urban areas, environmental conservation sectors, or suburban shopping tracts might be made with little regard for important social factors, that is, either haphazardly or on political gounds alone.

PERSONNEL MANAGER IN A SMALL MANUFACTURING FIRM.   Chris C. is viewed by most of his friends as a business executive rather than a sociologist. Nevertheless, he owes his start in the firm to his background in industrial sociology and social psychology. Starting as a lower-level assistant in the Personnel Department, Chris now has a post with considerable control over the company's personnel policies in general — that is, strategies and programs for hiring, training, supervising, promoting, etc. Ultimately, Chris may be either promoted to a higher executive position within the firm or seek advancement by joining another organization. He received a BA in sociology and did not go on to graduate school. In fact, he has not really kept up with sociological research for the past ten years, and he now thinks of himself more as a practitioner than a scholar. However, he does read specialized publications on organizational behavior and industrial and business practices, and here his sociological training is especially helpful. While the company does not consider his postion as that of a "sociologist," it is one among many firms which is coming to realize that sociological training is worthwhile for administrators and executives.

PROFESSOR IN A UNIVERSITY DEPARTMENT OF SOCIOLOGY.   Shelly S. is Assistant Professor of Sociology in a large university. Her department teaches both undergraduate and graduate students; it offers the MA and the PhD degrees, as well as the BA. Shelly recently received her own PhD from a similar department in a different region of the country. In fact, she began her teaching career there, serving as an Instructor before her PhD dissertation was actually finished. During her first year in her new job, she worked on her doctoral project evenings, weekends, and every other spare moment. Shelly has ample company and stimulation from her new faculty colleagues. After all, the department has twenty-five faculty members in order to handle the department's 400 undergraduate majors and 75 graduate students. Five of these faculty members are also assistant professors. In one sense, they are competing with Shelly for promotion to associate professor and the award of tenure. Shelly teaches five, sometimes six, courses a year, including two advanced seminars for graduate students. As important as teaching is to Shelly, research and writing may be even more important to her career development. In fact, at the graduate level, she teaches largely through her research. She has hired two graduate students as research assistants on a study financed by a grant from a federal research agency located in Washington. Shelly's tenure decision will be made in her sixth year at the university, and her chances will be improved considerably if she is able to publish a number of scholarly articles and perhaps a book before then. But these are the kinds of activities that attracted Shelly into sociology and academic life in the first place. Although her salary does not compete with the financial opportunities in the business world, it is more than adequate, especially when combined with that of her husband who teaches in the Physics Department of the same university. Shelly has avoided summer school teaching supplements to work on a book which could produce some additional income in the form of royalties. But she knows that scholarly books rarely make much money for anyone. In fact, only a few of the basic textbooks sell well in a highly competitive market.

STAFF MEMBER OF A RESEARCH INSTITUTE.   Marion M. is a member of the staff of a private research institute which does sociological studies on specific problems of interest to government agencies, business concerns, and political groups. The institute is located in a large metropolitan center and many of the studies concentrate on the city and the surrounding region. Marion began the job with a BA in sociology. She had focused her studies around courses in research methods and statistics. Since joining the institute she has gone back to graduate school for an MS degree and has had considerable on-the-job training. During her first several years, she was a "research assistant," but she is now an "associate project director" with more responsibility for developing new research projects as well as supervising the actual research process. She has developed a sense of how clients' problems can be met by appropriate research studies. She is learning to write research proposals and then to follow them through discussion and revision to actual funding. Her work schedule is basically 9 to 6. But she sometimes puts in considerable evening and weekend work, especially when she is conducting interviews, supervising an interviewing staff, or doing the statistical analysis and writing necessary for a final report to a client. Her salary is now somewhat above average for those in her graduating class. With success in obtaining contracts and advising clients, her income will probably increase considerably in a short period of time. Marion may stay here or move to another research firm, or consider starting her own agency. Some research agencies are run on a nonprofit basis and are associated with an educational or governmental institution. If Marion were to open a research firm for profit, she would be facing the same substantial risks involved in launching any new business.

STAFF ADMINISTRATOR IN A PUBLIC ASSISTANCE AGENCY.

Throughout his studies, Wally W. was interested in using his knowledge to serve people. Unlike many students who go into sociology to become teachers or researchers, Wally saw sociology as a field which could be used to provide services. He now works for the city's Department of Social Service as a program coordinator. In this position, he draws on his studies in such areas as the family, social stratification, urban communities, and group dynamics. His work includes routine processing of reports and legal forms, but it also involves much contact with agency clients and direct confrontation with the problems of the poor, disabled, aged, and minorities. He also works with other employees, mostly professional social workers who work with individual families and clients. Actually, many people blur the distinction between social workers and sociologists. However, Wally brings a unique perspective and special resources to his job. He has mixed feelings about the possibility of taking on more administrative responsibility, since this would mean less time available to work with families directly. He often serves as a kind of troubleshooter by providing help in the personal crises of his clients. This, in turn, requires him to maintain contacts with various other public and private agencies that affect the lives of the poor. For example, one of his fellow undergraduate majors is now working on the staff of a large community mental health center, and another is involved in supervising rehabilitation for state penitentiary inmates. Like Wally, these two are using their undergraduate sociology as a basis for social service positions. All three receive satisfaction from being able to experience day to day accomplishments in their work. Their salaries are commensurate with the wage scales of public agencies generally. Wally could progress through Civil Service channels to a career of relative security. However, he still thinks about going back to school to earn a graduate degree, which would give him a considerable boost along the way.

TRAVELLING REPRESENTATIVE FOR A PUBLISHER.

Terry T. works for one of the country's leading book publishers. She serves as a regional representative with responsibility for colleges and universities in a three-state area. Her job has two major aspects. She is expected to establish and maintain contact with faculty members who are teaching courses in which the publisher's texts can be adopted — here sales are her principal concern. She is also required to seek out those professors who are likely prospects to write new books for her firm — here she serves as an editor and talent scout. Terry's sociology BA was one reason why she was hired, and it continues to be important to her duties. Although she has responsibility for all of the social sciences, including psychology, anthropology, political science, and economics as well, sociology was a good preparation for her responsibilities. Moreover, Terry may have a future opportunity to specialize in sociology. One avenue of advancement might involve promotion to "sociology editor" in the firm's New York headquarters. Here she would be less involved in sales and more involved in the choice of materials to be published and the form and schedule of publication. Alternatively, Terry could also be promoted within the sales division, and this too could lead to the New York office. Meanwhile, she enjoys the continued contact with campus life and the opportunity to interact with faculty members in community colleges, four-year colleges, and universities. The heavy travel associated with her job has reduced her appetite for restaurant food and is sometimes exhausting; but she realizes that her current duties are a necessary first step in the occupational world of college text publishing. Her salary is competitive with most junior executive trainees in the business world and all expenses are paid. She even enjoys a free book now and then.

So much for a few of the things that sociologists do. It should be especially clear by now that there are various careers available, and the options are increasing. But it is important to underscore what lies beneath all of these vignettes: namely, sociology itself. A sociologist is someone concerned with understanding human behavior and human relationships in various kinds of groups and social settings. Of course, sociologists pursue this concern in different ways. Quite apart from pursuing different career lines, sociologists pursue different specialty subjects within the very broad range of the field as a whole. Thus, sociologists may specialize in the family, the urban community, education, health, old age, occupations, environmental issues, sex roles, sports, the operation of government, the military, law enforcement, and any other area in which human behaviors are organized to pursue social functions.

Apart from such specific specialties, there are other types of specialization which crosscut these interests and apply to them all. For example, that aspect of sociology which focuses primarily on the interaction between individuals and the behavior of small groups is usually referred to as "social psychology." On the other hand, a specialization in "social organization" involves studying characteristics of larger social institutions, agencies, occupations, and associations. "Human ecology" is that branch of sociology which looks at the spatial distribution of social behavior with reference to its environment. "Demographers" are primarily concerned with population processes; they study birth and death rates, migration and mobility, and the changing distribution of age, sex, marital statuses, etc. As a last important example, it is possible to specialize in the methods of sociological research as a subject in its own right. The "methodologist" is generally concerned with designing and assessing new research procedures. This often involves considerable quantitative or statistical know-how, but there are also experts on qualitative research concerned with techniques of depth interviewing, careful observation, and the use of historical documents.

CAREER PREPARATION

Success in most careers depends upon both long-term career preparation and short-term responses to changing circumstances. It is virtually impossible for anyone to fully anticipate what lies five years ahead, much less ten, twenty, or forty. Still, it remains true that some kinds of training are more appropriate than others for a given career. Even within sociology, different career options may require different types of career preparation. But many people put it the other way around and ask what kinds of careers are possible with a given type of preparation.

JOB PROSPECTS FOR THE BA

One of the most frequent questions asked of any sociology teacher is, "What can I do with a sociology BA?" Actually, there are several answers. Certainly a BA in sociology is at least as good as any other BA degree in preparing the student for future graduate work or for general employment. On the other hand, if the question concerns professional employment specifically as a sociologist, the only honest answer continues to be "very little." There are still very few employers who are looking for sociology BAs in the same sense in which they might look for BAs in engineering, nursing, accounting, etc. Sociology BAs will often find themselves competing with other liberal arts students who have majored in English, history, psychology, etc. Here, a strong undergraduate program in sociology can conceivably produce a competitive advantage. For example, students interested in business careers after the BA might emphasize courses in industrial sociology and complex organization; students seeking work with public welfare agencies might concentrate their course work in areas such as stratification, race and ethnic relations, sociology of the family, and urban sociology.

Regardless of one's special interests, many students would do well to emphasize research methods and statistics. It is precisely these courses that are cited as most valuable by persons already employed in non-academic jobs who are asked to reconsider their education with the wisdom of hindsight. Statistics is not as difficult as many students fear and it often provides the most valuable and marketable career skills. This is especially true for the student who plans to stop with the BA.

And yet, even the most thorough BA degree is limited in the kinds of employment for which it prepares the student. Most professional work requires graduate education. Undergraduate sociology majors frequently go on to graduate work in other areas such as social work, education, public health, business administration, and urban planning, not to mention law, medicine, and divinity school. A sociology major offers good training for them all, though many have additional prerequisities. These various degrees take different lengths of time and lead to different types of activities, opportunities, and economic and social rewards. For example, many law schools offer a professional degree after three years of study; a Master of Business Administration will likely take two years, and a Master of Education can be achieved in only one year in some schools. By all means, consult your local campus counselors for further information on such programs.

GRADUATE TRAINING IN SOCIOLOGY

What about graduate work in sociology itself? Certainly this is necessary for a career in academic sociology, at least beyond the secondary school level. It is also important for many non-academic careers — or to put it another way, it is hard to imagine any career for which no graduate training is preferable to some. But how much training, of what sort, and where?

There are two basic graduate degrees available in sociology, the "doctorate" and the "master's degree." The Doctorate in Philosphy (PhD) is typically the highest degree awarded in sociology. The Master's degree may be either an MA (Master of Arts) or an MS (Master of Science), depending upon the educational institution or the preference of either the department or, in some cases, the individual student. The PhD requires at least four or five years of study beyond the BA or BS and signifies competence for original research and scholarship as evidenced by the completion of a book-length research study called a "dissertation." The Master's degree can be either a step toward the PhD or an end in its own right. It generally signifies sophisticated knowledge of the field's perspectives and methods, but does not necessarily indicate that any original research has been conducted. The Master's may take anywhere from one to three years, depending upon the particular department, whether or not a thesis is required, and the speed of the students.

There are some jobs and careers for which a Master's alone is adequate. A sociology MA or MS is sufficient for teaching at the secondary school or two-year college level and for work with public agencies and private businesses. However, there are few stiutations in which a PhD would not be preferable to a Master's degree. A PhD is usually required for teaching and research at the university level and for high-level employment with good promotion prospects in non-academic research institutes, private industry, and government agencies.

Most graduate schools which offer the PhD also offer a Master's degree as part of the program. However, there are a number of schools which offer the Master's only, and a few which are exclusively devoted to the PhD.

A publication of the American Sociological Association, this statement reflects the collaboration of a number of sociologists. The original draft of this publication was prepared by George K. Hesslink, Pomona College. Additional contributions came from Albert E. Gollin, Bureau of Social Science Research; Kiyoshi Ikeda, University of Hawaii; Thomas E. Lasswell, University of Southern California; Raymond W. Mack, Northwestern University; N. J. Demerath III, University of Massachusetts; John W. Riley, Jr., The Equitable Life Assurance Society of the United States; and Matilda White Riley, Bowdoin College. Several students provided contributions and reactions to earlier versions of this manuscript.

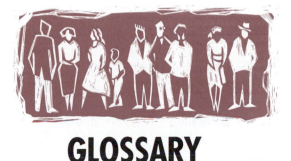

GLOSSARY

Numbers in parentheses indicate the pages on which the terms are discussed.

A

Aberrant behavior. Secret violations of norms chiefly motivated by self-interest, as contrasted with nonconforming behavior. (230)

Achieved status. A status acquired through personal effort or sometimes by chance. (98)

Adaptive culture. Ideas, customs, and beliefs, as opposed to material culture. (564)

Affluent worker. An industrial worker who values an unfulfilling job only because it is a means of earning the money necessary for a comfortable life style. (604)

Aggregate (collectivity). A collection of individuals who do not know each other, do not interact frequently, and do not consider themselves (and are not considered by others to be) members of a particular social group. (104)

Alienation. Marx's term for the condition in the industrial workplace in which people are separated from the finished products of their work, from the mechanical process of production, from other workers, and from their own feelings and inclinations. (602)

Anomie. Durkheim's term for the social and moral disorder that results from loss of the social controls provided by generally accepted norms. (11)

Anomie and opportunity structures (theory of). A theory that attributes deviance to the discrepancy between what people want and what they have the opportunity to achieve in legitimate ways. (235)

Anticipatory socialization. The informal learning of future roles, easing the transition from stage to stage. (144)

Ascribed status. A status assigned without regard for innate differences or individual abilities. (98)

Assimilation. The form of ethnic relations in which one group loses its ethnic identity and blends into another group; according to Hraba, the "process by which diverse ethnic and racial groups come to share a common culture and have equal access to the opportunity structure of a society." (262)

Attitudinal conformity. Personal commitment to the prevailing norms. (136)

Authoritarian government. A government based on the rule of a strongman or a small elite. (522)

Authority. Legitimate power which is considered appropriate and acceptable by those who must obey. (502)

B

Back-to-basics movement. A movement in American education that advocates a return to traditional teaching methods and a renewed emphasis on basic skills. (434)

Behavioral conformity. Outward compliance with the prevailing norms regardless of one's personal beliefs. (136)

Bourgeoisie. In Marx's theory, the owners of the means of production. (192)

Bureaucracy. An organization designed to accomplish the large-scale tasks of complex societies by systematically coordinating the work of many individuals. (158)

C

Capitalism. An economic system in which the means of production are owned by private firms and individuals, and in which the distribution of income is primarily determined by competition in the marketplace. (383)

Case history. A sociological study of an individual's biography. (49)

Caste stratification. A system of stratification in which individuals are permanently assigned a social position purely on the basis of race, religion, or some other ascribed characteristic. (195)

Causal relationship. An association between events, behaviors, persons, or things in which one leads to the occurrence of another. (41)

Charisma. Personal magnetism or leadership of a mystical sort, such as that usually characterizing leaders of religious cults; Weber's term for the unique personal power of exceptional individuals. (486)

Charismatic authority. Authority held by individuals by virtue of exceptional personal magnetism. (504)

Church. A large religious organization with a formal structure, an official priesthood, an elaborate theology, and a broad membership of people who were born into it. (486)

City. A large number of people who are densely concentrated in a small area and dependent on others for the production of food. (646)

Class stratification. A system of stratification based on achievement, especially the economic achievement of individuals. (198)

Coercion. Weber's term for the power that comes from superior physical force. (502)

Coercive power. The ability of some organizations (including prisons and military training camps) to compel their members to cooperate in achieving goals by punishing any failure to perform. (174)

Cohort. A group of people who are born and raised in the same era. (566)

Collective behavior. The relatively unorganized and spontaneous behavior of people in crowds and masses. (531)

Command economy. An economy in which economic activities are centrally controlled by political institutions. (378)

Concepts. Ideas that enable us to organize and interpret our experiences. (44)

Conflict. The antagonism of social groups with opposing interests or values. (559)

Conflict theory. A sociological approach that emphasizes the social processes arising from the struggle to attain wealth, high social position, power, prestige, or whatever else is considered desirable. (19)

Conspicuous leisure. Veblen's term for obvious, nonproductive consumption of time. (618)

Contact hypothesis. Park's argument that personal intimacy between ethnic groups will prove stronger than impersonal competition, and that ethnic relations will always evolve toward accommodation and assimilation. (269)

Contagion. LeBon's theory that the actions of one person in a crowd tend to be imitated by the next, and so on. (533)

Content analysis. A reserach method that uses written documents as a data base. (56)

Convergence theory. Turner's theory of crowds which holds that only people who are likely to engage in a certain kind of behavior will come together to form a crowd in the first place, thus determining the character of the crowd. (533)

Correlation. A measure of the empirical relationship of two or more variables. (42)

Countervailing power. The power exerted by a group or coalition of interests to outbalance a group or coalition that threatens to dominate them. (509)

Crime. A deviant act that is forbidden by law. (241)

Crime rate. The proportion of reported crimes to the total population under consideration. (243)

Crowd. A number of people whose physical proximity to one another influences their behavior. (531)

Cult. A loosely organized religious group whose beliefs and practices are strongly mystical and magical, distinguished by personal ties to a leader or group rather than to an institution or a theology. (486)

Cultural consistency. Myrdal's theory of assimilation that held that the further modernization of American society would eventually overcome white racism, resolve the moral conflict between the creed that all men are created equal and the practice of racial discrimination, and permit blacks to be assimilated into American society. (271)

Cultural diffusion. The spread of technology, beliefs, and ideas to other cultures. (564)

Cultural inconsistency. The existence of contradictory values and norms within a society. (82)

Cultural transmission. The function of education to pass on accumulated knowledge and thus protect cultural standards. (408)

Cultural universals. Types of social behavior that exist in much the same form in every culture; for example, language, music, and terms for kinship. (75)

Culture. A set of shared ideas, or the customs, beliefs, and knowledge that characterize a society's way of life; ideas learned from other people and passed on from generation to generation. (4, 64, 74)

Culture lag. The maladjustment that occurs when one aspect of a culture changes more rapidly than other, related aspects; the lag between changes in material culture and changes in adaptive culture. (84, 564)

Custom economy. An economy in which goods and services are exchanged according to established tradition. (378)

D

De facto discrimination. Discrimination in practice. (264)

De jure discrimination. Discrimination by law. (264)

Demobilization. The loss of resources that were formerly committed to one side of a struggle for power. (543)

Democratic government. A government that rules by the consent of the governed, the power of the leaders coming from legal authority rather than from the use of force. (523)

Demographic transition (theory of). The theory that a shift from high to low rates of birth and death accompanies the industrialization process. (636)

Demography. The analysis of the size, composition, and distribution of human populations. (624)

Denomination. A religious sect that has grown, developed established rituals and a degree of formal leadership, and therefore become somewhat institutionalized. (487)

Dependent variable. In a research study testing a causal relationship, the outcome or effect of the independent variable. (42)

Deskilling. The downgrading of the skills of craftsmen and office workers because of technological change and the demand for efficiency. (599)

Deviance. Any significant departure from social norms. (225)

Differential association theory. A theory of criminal behavior that holds that membership in a deviant group leads people to adopt the norms of that group and to violate those of the larger society. (235)

Discrimination. The unequal treatment of certain people on the basis of race, ethnicity, sex, age, or some other characteristic. (264)

Displacement of goals. A characteristic of bureaucracies by which sticking to the rules becomes an end in itself rather than a means to a larger organizational goal. (168)

Divorce rate. The number of divorced persons for every 1000 married persons. (364)

Doubling time. The number of years required to double the population. (625)

Dysfunctional. Having a negative impact on the system or some parts of it. (16)

E

Ecclesia. The largest form of religious organization, closely identified with other social institutions. The Catholic Church in Italy is an example. (488)

Economy. The social institution that specializes in the production and exchange of goods and services to satisfy the wants and needs of a population. (377)

Education. The deliberate, formal transfer of knowledge, skills, and values from one person or group to another. (406)

Emergent norm. A standard of behavior gradually established by people in groups. (535)

Emergent social reality. A social structure that appears from an arrangement of parts, or in patterns of interaction among members of a society; a relationship that exists independently of the particular individuals who belong to it. (10)

Empirical facts. The phenomena which are observed through the senses and which are considered scientific evidence. (35)

Endogamy. The rule requiring marriage inside a certain group. (348)

Equality of achievement. The democratic ideal of American education adopted after the mid-1960s and based on the assumption that equal schools can provide equally effective education for everyone. (420)

Equality of opportunity. The stated goal of equality in American schools until the mid-1960s. (420)

Estate stratification. A system of stratification based on family membership. (196)

Ethnic group. A number of people sharing a common origin or a separate subculture who are thought of (and who think of themselves) as a distinctive group because of their origins or subculture. (260)

Ethnic stratification. The form of ethnic relations in which groups continue to interact on an unequal basis. (262)

Ethnicity. The distinctive characteristics of an ethnic group. (260)

Ethnocentrism. The belief that one's own culture or group is superior to that of others; according to Sumner, "the view of things in which one's own group is the center of everything." (80)

Ethnomethodology. The study of how people

invent and convey shared meanings in everyday routines. (23)

Exchange theory. As an explanation for divorce, the theory that the divorce rate is affected by the trade-off between the costs and rewards of staying married. (365)

Exclusion. The form of ethnic relations in which one group voluntarily withdraws or is forced to withdraw from further interaction. (262)

Exogamy. The rule requiring marriage outside a certain group. (348)

Experiment. A test of cause and effect under highly controlled conditions. (53)

Exponential growth. Growth (as of a population) in which each increase during a given time period becomes part of the basis to which the growth rate is applied for the next time period. (625)

Extended family. A family group, including relatives outside the nuclear family, that shares the same household and engages in common activities. (340)

Extension (pattern of leisure). Parker's term for a relationship between work and leisure in which at least some work and leisure activities are similar and daily life is not clearly divided between the two. (614)

Extrapolate. In a survey, to estimate the opinions and values of larger populations based on known data about a sample. (47)

F

Family. Two or more persons who are linked by marriage or descent and who engage in common activities. (340)

Femininity. The psychological attributes connected with the roles played by women; personality traits defined by a culture as appropriate only for women. (301)

Fertility. The average number of children born to each woman in a population. (628)

Folkways. Norms that develop spontaneously, as if by common consent. (72)

Formal sanctions. Enforcement of norms and punishment of deviant behavior by legal means. (228)

Free market. An unregulated, competitive economic system. (379)

Free time. Nonworking, unpaid hours. (591)

Functional and structural analysis. Sociological theories that relate one part of society to another part or to the social system as a whole. (16)

Functional illiteracy. The inability to perform basic reading, writing, and mathematical tasks. (432)

Functional rationality. The characteristic of a bureaucracy by which every individual action leads logically and predictably to the achievement of some ultimate aim. (183)

G

Game theory. Applied to crowd behavior, a theory that stresses rational and logical elements. (536)

Gemeinschaft. A community; a closely involved group held together by largely primary bonds. (109)

Gender. The social and psychological characteristics associated with masculinity and femininity. (317)

Generalized other. Mead's concept representing the attitudes of the whole community as they influence the socialization of a child. (127)

Gentrification. The settlement and renovation of rundown inner-city neighborhoods by affluent newcomers. (652)

Gesellschaft. A society; a group characterized by impersonal ties of rational self-interest or secondary relationships. (110)

Gross National Product. A nation's total national production of goods and services, valued at market prices. (383)

H

Health. The absence of illness together with a state of physical and mental well-being. (439)

Hidden curriculum. In education, the transmission of cultural values and attitudes (such as punctuality and obedience) through the school situation, in contrast to the manifest, or formal, curriculum. (416)

Homogamy. The tendency of similar kinds of people to marry each other. (350)

Human ecology. The science that deals with the relationship between human beings and their natural environment. (624)

Hypothesis. A hunch about a possible or probable relationship between variables. (43)

I

Ideal-type. A conceptual model, used by Weber, for analyzing bureaucratic structure. (159)

Identity crisis. A changing definition of the self brought on by a new situation in the life cycle. (133)

Incest taboo. The virtually universal rule prohibiting sexual intercourse between close family members. (341)

Independent variable. In a research study testing a causal relationship, the element that is taken as the given, the starting point in the relationship leading to the dependent variable. (42)

Industrial society. A society that produces more fabricated goods than raw materials. (597)

Industrialization. The process of shifting from hand tools to power machinery, whose long-range social results are a shift from a manual to a non-manual labor force, a rise in per capita income, higher levels of education, a wider distribution of income, a large middle class, and a generally higher standard of living. (563)

Influence. The power to persuade; one source of control over other people. (501)

Informal sanctions. Enforcement of norms and "punishment" of deviant behavior by such means as public ridicule and disapproval. (228)

In-group. A group toward which one feels strong loyalty coupled with hatred and intolerance of outsiders (the out-group). (113)

Institutionalized discrimination. Discrimination against some groups that results simply from adhering to social norms, with no direct connection to race or ethnicity. (281)

Institutionalized sexism. Discrimination on the basis of sex which results from a social structure that assigns different places to men and women and from the cultural values that support these arrangements. (335)

Instrumentalism. Rational, goal-oriented behavior. (419)

Interaction. Directing behavior toward one another. (4)

Interview. A research method consisting of guided conversations between an investigator and research subjects. (49)

Invisible hand. The laws of the free market by which the competing self-interests of all the members of a society combine to promote the public good. (380)

K

Kinship. A social relationship among family members. (351)

L

Labeling theory. A theory of deviance that holds that the prejudices and class biases of those who enforce the law help define who and what is deviant, so that official classification as deviant has less to do with what a person has done than with how he or she is perceived by law enforcers. (239)

Laissez-faire (free market) economy. An economy in which the principles of the competitive market are allowed to work without hindrance by authorities. (379)

Latent functions. Unintended consequences of social actions. (16)

Laws. Norms that are enforced by the formal sanctions of the state. (229)

Legitimacy. The social process of linking a father to every child; the heritage or ascription of social position; the consent of the governed. (324, 502)

Leisure. Time occupied by freely chosen activities that are enjoyable or self-fulfilling in themselves. (592)

Life chances. Weber's term for the likelihood of having a particular standard of living. (193)

Line. Administrators, in an organization. Their job is to manage the actual production of the organization's output. (166)

Linear growth. Growth in which a constant amount is added each time period, such as $10 per year. (625)

Looking-glass self. In Cooley's theory of socialization, our self-image as a reflection of how others see us or what we believe others see us to be. (127)

M

Magic. The practice of rituals and the use of devices believed to exert some control over uncertain forces. (476)

Manifest functions. Intended consequences of social actions. (16)

Masculinity. The psychological attributes connected with the roles played by men; personality traits defined by a culture as appropriate only for men. (301)

Mass society. Modern society, which is dominated by anonymous secondary-group relationships rather than by the close primary-group ties of traditional societies. (540)

Material culture. Man-made objects. (564)

Matriarchy. The family system in which women would exercise the greatest authority, as opposed to patriarchy. No such system has yet been discovered. (352)

Mean difference. The difference between two averages, as for example, the mean difference between the test scores of men and women. (315)

Mechanical solidarity. Durkheim's term for social unity based on a moral consensus among people who have many social similarities. (25)

Median income. A statistical measure used to describe the typical family by placing it at the point at which half the families in the nation earn more and half earn less. In 1987 the U.S. annual median income was $31,135. (201)

Medicalize. To view a physical or emotional condition or event (such as childbirth or depression) as an illness that requires—and ought to have—medical attention. (446)

Medical model (of illness). An explanation of illness in terms of disease. (444)

Medicine. The treatment of illness. (439)

Megalopolis. A huge metropolitan region formed by the spread and eventual merger of cities. (651)

Midlife crisis. A feeling of estrangement from one's children, boredom with married life, and lack of fulfillment in work. An experience in middle age analogous to the adolescent's identity crisis. (149)

Minority group. According to Wirth, "A group of people who, because of their physical or cultural characteristics, are singled out from the others in the society in which they live for differential and unequal treatment, and who therefore regard themselves as objects of collective discrimination." (261)

Mixed economy. An economic system that combines a relatively free market with some government controls. (401)

Mobilization. The processes by which an opposition group assembles resources for the pursuit of its goals. (543)

Mode of production. Marx's term for a society's organization of its productive activities, both the technology and machines that increase the efficiency of human labor and the social arrangements by which the products of this labor are distributed. (192)

Monogamy. Marriage between one man and one woman; the most common form. (347)

Mores. Moral rules; ways of behaving that most members of a society believe are essential to its welfare. (72)

Mortality rate. The number of deaths per 100,000 people; the death rate. (441, 628)

N

Nature/nurture controversy. With regard to sex differences, the disagreement between the evolutionists and biologists who argue that hormones and other physiological factors account for the differences between men and women and the psychologists and sociologists who emphasize the role of social learning in producing the differences between the sexes. (312)

Neutrality (pattern of leisure). Parker's term for the relationship between work and leisure in which work and leisure activities do not overlap but are not deliberately segregated. (615)

Nonconforming behavior. Public violations of norms that risk punishment in order to change those norms. (230)

Normative power. The motivating force in an organization whose members identify with its goals, accepting them voluntarily. (174)

Norm-oriented social movement. A social movement that attempts to protect or change social norms. (538)

Norms. Shared expectations of how people should behave. (72)

Nuclear family. A married couple and their children. (340)

O

Oligopoly. A market dominated by a few firms. (384)

Opposition (pattern of leisure). Parker's term for the relationship between work and leisure in which leisure activities are intentionally very different from experiences at work. (614)

Optimum population. The number of people that produces the maximum economic return possible in an area's natural, cultural, and social environment. (636)

Organic solidarity. Durkheim's term for social unity based on the mutual dependence of people with different backgrounds and beliefs. (25)

Out-group. Outsiders, to members of an in-group. (113)

Overurbanization. The excessively large and rapidly growing urban populations found in developing countries. (649)

P

Participant observation. A type of field study in which the researcher becomes a member of the group being studied. (52)

Particularistic norms. Standards based on faith and love that apply to only one individual, according to which the family, unlike other modern social institutions, is expected to deal with its members. (344)

Particularistic standards. Criteria for making judgments based on each individual case. (165)

Patriarchy. The system of male dominance in which the father or male head exercises the greatest power in the family. (352)

Peer groups. Groups of equals in age, sex, occupational level, and the like. (140)

Pluralism. The form of ethnic relations in which groups continue to interact on an equal basis. (262)

Political efficacy. The feeling that one can affect the outcome of a political process; a sense of power that seems to increase political participation. (517)

Political institution. The norms and organizations by which power is distributed, society is governed, and the rules of daily life are enforced. (500)

Politics. The process of deciding who gets what, when, and how; the efforts of contending groups and individuals to influence the outcome of a decision-making process. (500)

Polygamy. Marriage to more than one partner. (347)

Population. In a social science research study, the group of people being studied. (43)

Population momentum. The phenomenon of a population with disproportionately more young people than old people continuing to grow even though the fertility rate does not rise. (643)

Population pyramid. The distribution of age groups in a society. (643)

Positive check. According to Malthus, the ultimate limitation of uncontrolled population growth by war, disease, and starvation. (628)

Post-industrial society. A society whose economy is based on providing services rather than on manufacturing or agriculture. (597)

Poverty line. An annual income figure used by the federal government to define poverty. In 1987 it was $11,611 for a family of four. (200)

Power. The ability to get what one wants even in the face of opposition; in Weber's theory, one of the three measures of inequality; the ability to control scarce resources or to determine how others will behave. (193, 500)

Pre-industrial society. A society whose economy depends largely on agriculture. (597)

Prejudice. Literally, a "pre-judgment," or an opinion based on insufficient evidence. Racial or ethnic prejudice is a judgment (usually unfavorable) of an individual that is formed solely on the basis of his or her membership in a racial or ethnic category. (278)

Prestige. The favorable opinions of others; in Weber's theory, one of the three measures of inequality. (193)

Preventative check. Malthus's term for a measure, such as birth control, that limits population growth. (628)

Primary deviance. According to the labeling theory of deviance, the original deviant act that can lead to a deviant identity and way of life. (240)

Primary group. A social group characterized by intimate, long-lasting relationships among a small number of people. (106)

Principle of legitimacy. Malinowski's theory that the second function of the family is the orderly placement of new members into society through the kinship system. (342)

Principle of reciprocity. Malinowski's term for the rule of family exchange by which the prohibition against incest ensures that every marriage will unite not just two people but two previously unrelated families, so that everyone is in effect made part of a larger social structure. (341)

Productivity. The condition of getting more goods and services for less effort. (381)

Profane. That which is ordinary, understandable, and inspires no particular respect, in contrast to the sacred. (474)

Proletariat. In Marx's theory, the wage laborers. (193)

Protestant ethic. The belief that hard work is a moral obligation. (387)

R

Race. People sharing genetically inherited characteristics who are thought of as a distinctive group and who think of themselves as such. (260)

Racism. A systematized belief that biological differences cause members of different races to behave in different ways. (262)

Rational-legal authority. Authority that rests not in particular individuals but in the offices they hold. (503)

Reference group. A group whose behavior is used as a model by outsiders. (113)

Relative deprivation. A feeling that one lacks more of the good things in life than other people; deprivation in comparison to what others have or in comparison to what one had oneself in the past. (582)

Religion. An institution of shared beliefs and practices created by human beings as a response to forces which they cannot understand rationally and which they believe give ultimate meaning to their lives. (474)

Remunerative power. The ability of some organizations to buy members' acceptance of goals by rewarding performance with money. (174)

Replication. The technique of repeating a research study with different researchers and different subjects in order to minimize errors. (50)

Resocialization. Learning the requirements and limitations of a new role. (144)

Resource management. A theory that argues that social movements are rational political organizations seeking specific goals, mobilizing such resources as money and members, and using tactics and strategies to win support. (542)

Returns to scale.   Efficiencies of size; the lower unit costs associated with large-scale production. (384)

Revolution.   According to Neumann, "a sweeping, fundamental change in political organization, social structure, economic property control, and the predominant myth of a social order, thus indicating a major break in the continuity of development." (581)

Rites of passage.   Ritual celebrations in which an old identity (child, for example) is put aside and a new one (adult) initiated. (143)

Ritual.   A set of acts required and acts forbidden, especially by a religion. (475)

Ritualism.   The slavish obedience to regulations and obsessive concern with forms and procedures characteristic of some bureaucrats. (168)

Role.   The cluster of norms that go with a certain status; the behavior expected of a person in a particular social position. (97)

Role conflict.   Incompatibility of or competition between different roles. (102)

Role-set.   The array of roles associated with a single status. (102)

Role strain.   Any difficulty in performing a social role. (102)

S

Sacred.   That which is extra-human and mysterious, therefore inspiring awe and respect. (474)

Sample.   In a research study, a portion of a population under study. (43)

Science.   A system of rational inquiry disciplined by empirical testing. (35)

Scientific method.   Observing significant facts and finding the general laws that govern them. (34)

Secondary deviance.   According to the labeling theory of deviance, the deviant identity and way of life that result from earning a reputation for deviance by an original deviant act (primary deviance). (240)

Secondary groups.   Social groups whose members have disparate, rather than common, goals and value the extrinsic political, economic, or other benefits of the relationship rather than the relationship itself. (107)

Sect.   A small, loosely organized religious group of individual converts who are led by an informal priesthood or by the members themselves and who usually oppose many of the values and institutions of their society. (486)

Selection and screening.   A traditional function of education, by which candidates are selected for various occupational roles. (408)

Self.   A personal identity that is shaped in relation to the expectations of others; a conception of one's own identity and personal characteristics largely based on how other people define one's place in society (status) and what behavior (role) they expect of someone in that status. (98)

Self-fulfilling prophecy.   The tendency to produce expected social behavior by closing off opportunities to behave in other ways. (240)

Sex.   The biological fact of maleness or femaleness. (317)

Sexism.   Unfair discrimination on the basis of sex. (300)

Sex roles.   Sets of expectations that define how men and women are supposed to act according to the norms of their society. (301)

Sex-typed.   Considered by a culture to be appropriate for only one sex. (302)

Sick role.   The role adopted by one who is physically or mentally ill and cannot carry out his or her social role. (445)

Significant others.   People, like mothers and fathers, who are influential as models during a child's socialization. (127)

Simple random sample.   A sample in which everyone in a population has an equal chance of being chosen for a research study. (44)

Social categories.   Statistical groupings on the basis of a particular social characteristic, such as age or income. (105)

Social change.   Any significant alteration in a social structure, including new norms, values, and cultural products of a material or symbolic kind. (559)

Social conflict.   The antagonism of social groups with opposing interests or values. (559)

Social control.   The practices all societies adopt to enforce conformity; in resource management theory, the processes by which the groups in power try to protect their vested interests. (226, 543)

Social group.   A number of people who interact frequently according to established and enduring patterns, who define themselves as members of a group and so expect certain behavior from members that they do not expect from outsiders, and who are defined by both other members and nonmembers as belonging to a group on the basis of some shared characteristic. (104)

Social health movement.   A social movement aimed at taking the responsibility for health away from the institution of medicine and giving it back to other social institutions. It emphasizes prevention of disease by changing social behavior. (469)

Social inequalities. Differences among people that are considered important in the society in which they live. (191)

Social institutions. Groups and organizations that together carry out the tasks that are necessary for a society to survive; the family, the economy, education, and the religious, political, and health care institutions. (120)

Socialism. A system of public ownership and management of the means of production and distribution of goods. (399)

Socialization. The interactive process by which individuals acquire some of the values, attitudes, skills and knowledge of the society to which they belong. (124)

Social mobility. A characteristic of industrial societies, in which people are free to move from status to status, both upward and downward; the movement of individuals and groups from one social position to another. (210)

Social model (of illness). An explanation of illness not in terms of the bodies of the individuals who are ill but in terms of the social situation in which disease occurs. (444)

Social movement. A highly organized and relatively long-term collective effort to bring about or prevent social change. (531)

Social sciences. Academic disciplines devoted to the study of human behavior. (23)

Society. A system of patterned interactions among organized groups of human beings; organized groups of people who have distinctive social patterns, occupy a defined territory, and share a sense of common identity. (4)

Social structure. The relatively predictable and continuing patterns of human relationships and interactions; the stable set of relationships among individuals and groups that enables them to function as a society. (4, 96)

Sociology. The scientific study of the patterns of social interaction. (4)

Staff. Specialists of various kinds in an organization who make no direct contribution to the output of the organization but who are necessary to its smooth operation. (166)

State. According to Weber, the institution that "claims the monopoly of the use of force within a given territory." (504)

Status. Any social position that has socially defined rights and obligations. (97)

Status consistency. The tendency, in a society, for people to take on new statuses that are easy to acquire or that cause them little social strain. (99)

Status inconsistency. Incompatible demands and rewards in a status-set. (100)

Status-set. The array of social positions occupied by one person. (98)

Stereotype. A simplified, rigid mental image of what members of a certan group are like. (278)

Stratification. The sociological term for the ranking of members of a society according to the unequal distribution of desirable resources. (190)

Stratified sample. A sample of people under study in which various categories in the population are represented in proportion to their numbers in the total population. (45)

Structural unemployment. The loss of jobs from a restructuring of the economy. (391)

Subculture. Distinctive cultural ideas that people share because they are members of a certain group. (83)

Substantial rationality. The capacity to act intelligently on the basis of one's own interpretation of events and to be aware of the consequences of one's own actions. (183)

Suburbanization. The increased proportion of a population living on the outskirts of central cities. (651)

Survey. A poll of a sample of people whose responses are likely to be representative of the population being studied. (47)

Symbol. Something—a word, an object, a gesture, a drawing—that stands for something else and conveys a shared meaning. (66)

Symbolic interactionism. A social psychological theory that developed from Mead's concept of the self. In sociology, the theory emphasizes how people's behavior is affected by the meanings they attach to social events. (21)

T

Taboos. Deeply held cultural beliefs that absolutely forbid some kinds of behavior (for example, incest). (73)

Technology. The socially accumulated knowledge of how to make use of nature. (562)

Terrorism. Covert violence by a group for political ends. (555)

Theory. A general statement that explains the relationship among facts. (44)

Total institutions. Institutions that extend bureaucratic control to every aspect of human life. (176)

Totalitarian government. A system in which the state controls all social institutions. (522)

Traditional authority. Authority, such as that of the Pope or a king, conferred on particular people by birthright or by higher authority. (503)

Trained incapacity. A characteristic of bureaucracies that makes officials with the same training and skills precise and reliable in dealing with routine problems but also makes them inflexible in dealing with changing or extraordinary situations. (167)

U

Universalistic norms. Objective criteria according to which modern social institutions (with the exception of the family) are expected to treat individuals. (344)

Universalistic standards. Standards applied impartially to everyone, as the criteria by which employees are hired in a bureaucracy. (161)

Urbanism. The culture of cities. (654)

Urbanization. An increase in the proportion of the population living in cities. (624)

Urban sociology. The study of city life. (624)

V

Value. A shared belief about what is morally right and desirable. (70)

Value-oriented social movement. A social movement that seeks to protect or change social values. (538)

Variable. Any measurable characteristic or property that is subject to change. (42)

Verstehen. Weber's term for the interpretive understanding of social behavior that provides an explanation of "its causes, its course, and its effects." (27)

Vested interests. Benefits from the status quo that cause one to resist change in the old order. (571)

Victimless crimes. Offenses against conventional standards of moral behavior, which many argue should not be considered crimes since they typically harm no one except possibly the person who commits them. (247)

W

Wealth. Material possessions and economic opportunities; in Weber's theory, one of the three measures of inequality. (193)

White-collar crime. Theft on the job, typically by respectable employees who finds ways to rationalize and excuse their behavior. (248)

Work. The performance of economic roles; in industrial societies, paid employment, or what one does to make a living. (592)

Workplace democracy. Worker-participation programs which attempt to relieve alienation by giving rank-and-file workers more control over the work process. (609)

World-system theory. Wallerstein's theory that industrialized nations exploit less developed countries and keep them from modernizing. (396)

Y

Youth culture. The subculture of the adolescent peer group; a culture created by the young and characterized by fun-loving, irreverent, and expressive behavior. (145)

COPYRIGHTS AND ACKNOWLEDGMENTS

PHOTO CREDITS

tures; **312,** © Ken Karp; **316, 317,** Ira Bergner, Woodfin Camp and Associates; **321,** Warne Books; **326, 331,** AP/Wide World; **334,** Drawing by Donald Reilly; © 1985 The New Yorker Magazine, Inc.; **337,** © Impact Visuals.

CHAPTER ELEVEN **338,** © Hennings Christopher, Black Star; **344,** Staatsbibliothek, Berlin; **346,** Brown Brothers; **351,** © Friedel/Black Star; **355,** Courtesy of the Essex Institute, Salem, MA; **357,** Warner Books; **362,** National Alliance for Optional Parenthood; **365,** Drawing by Donald Reilly; © 1985 The New Yorker Magazine, Inc.; **370,** © Mary O'Grady, Woodfin Camp and Associates; **372,** © Melchior DiGiacomo, The Image Bank, West.

CHAPTER TWELVE **376,** AP/Wide World; **378,** © Marc and Evelyn Bernheim, Woodfin Camp and Associates; **381,** Spencer Grant, Monkmeyer Press Photo Services; **385,** An Exxon Photo; **392,** Brown Brothers; **395,** Eric Kroll, Taurus Photos; **397,** NYT Pictures; **399,** © G. Henoch, Gamma-Liason.

CHAPTER THIRTEEN **404,** Jeffry W. Myers, Stock, Boston; **406,** The Bettmann Archive; **409,** © Deborah Kahn, Stock, Boston; **413,** Brown Brothers; **418,** © Jim Anderson, Woodfin Camp and Associates; **422,** Courtesy Northfield School/Lionel Delving, Stock, Boston; **424,** Drawing by Robert Weber; © The New Yorker Magazine, Inc.; **426,** Paul Conklin; **428,** Library of Congress; **430,** Mimi Forsyth, Monkmeyer Press Photo Service.

CHAPTER FOURTEEN **438,** © Richard Jarecke, Contact Press Images; **440,** South African Tourist Office; **442,** Left: Mimi Forsyth, Monkmeyer Press Photo Service; **442,** Right: Paul Conklin, Monkmeyer Press Photo Service; **443,** Spencer Grant, Stock, Boston; **449,** The Bettmann Archive; **451,** © 1986 by The Reader's Digest Association, Inc. Art Director: Sal DeVito; copywriter Jamie Seltzer; Chiat/Day Advertising, Inc., New York; **454,** © Tom Ballard/EKM-Nepenthe; **459,** Drawing by Oliphant; © 1979 Universal Press Syndicate; **464,** © M. E. Warren, Photo Researchers; **466,** © Eric Kroll, Taurus Photos; **469,** *Newsweek*-Bernard Gotfryd.

CHAPTER FIFTEEN **472,** AP/Wide World; **475,** © Paul Conklin; **477,** Felber, Monkmeyer Press Photo Service; **478,** Mimi Forsyth, Monkmeyer Press Photo Service; **480,** © Jim Wilson, NYT Pictures; **482,** © Ellis Herwig, The Picture Cube; **485,** AP/Wide World; **487,** Serge Schmemann, NYT Pictures.

CHAPTER SIXTEEN **498,** © Gale Zucker, Stock, Boston; **500,** © John Troha, Black Star; **502,** Left and right: AP/Wide World; **503,** Supreme Court Historical Society; **505,** Drawing by Lee Lorenz; © 1980 The New Yorker Magazine, Inc.; **508,** Bernard Gotfryd/Woodfin Camp and Associates; **510,** © Martin A. Levick, Black Star; **513,** Paul Conklin, Monkmeyer Press Photo Service; **521,** UPI/Bettmann Newsphotos; **522,** UPI/Bettmann Newsphotos; **527,** © Impact Visuals.

CHAPTER SEVENTEEN **528,** AP/Wide World; **530,** © David Cannon/All-Sport; **532,** The Bettmann Archive; **534,** Neal Roenzi, NYT Pictures; **536,** © Alain Nogues, Sygma; **541,** AP/Wide World; **543,** © Eugene Gordon; **549,** UPI/Bettmann Newsphotos; **550,** Left: AP/Wide World; **550,** Right: © Hap Stewart, Jeroboam; **551,** © Leonard Freedman, Magnum; **555,** AP/Wide World.

CHAPTER EIGHTEEN **558,** Bettmann Newsphotos; **561,** © George W. Gardner; **562,** © Russell A. Tompson, Taurus Photos; **565,** State Department of Archives and History, Raleigh, NC; **567,** © Bob North, Picture Group; **570,** AP/Wide World; **572,** Mark Chester, Stock, Boston; **574,** Drawing by Joseph Farris; © 1984 The New Yorker Magazine, Inc.; **575,** © Kal Muller, Woodfin Camp and Associates; **579,** The Bettmann Archive; **585,** Reuters/Bettmann Newsphotos; **586,** AP/Wide World.

CHAPTER NINETEEN **590,** © Jiri Jiru; **593,** The Phillips Collection; **600,** Left: Giraudon/Art Resource; **600,** Right: Brown Brothers; **601,** Impact Visuals, photo by George Cohen; **606,** © Peter Menzel, Stock, Boston; **611,** The Bettmann Archive; **617,** © Ellis Herwig, Stock, Boston; **619,** Drawing by Robert Mankoff; © 1986 The New Yorker Magazine, Inc.

CHAPTER TWENTY **622,** © Anthony Suau, Black Star; **627,** © Alain Nogues, Sygma; **629,** Reuters/Bettmann Newsphotos; **633,** AP/Wide World; **634,** © J. P. Laffont, Sygma; **639,** AP/Wide World; **642,** United Nations; **647,** Nik Wheeler, Sygma; **648,** Nik Wheeler, Sygma; **653,** © Jaye R. Phillips, The Picture Cube; **655,** © J. P. Laffont, Sygma.

AUTHOR INDEX

SUBJECT INDEX